Collected Poems and Short Stories

BY THE SAME AUTHOR

Mount Pleasant	Buchan Observer 1961
Fit Like, Skipper?	Aberdeen Journals 1984
Fisher Blue	Peter Buchan 1988
Buchan Claik (with David Toulmin)	Gordon Wright Publishing 1989

Collected Poems and Short Stories

Peter Buchan

Ye canna say a thing that's new
However hard ye try,
Ye can but tak the thing that's aul
An say't anither wye.

Ecclesiastes 1 v. 9 and 10.

GORDON WRIGHT PUBLISHING
25 MAYFIELD ROAD, EDINBURGH EH9 2NQ
SCOTLAND

British Library Cataloguing in Publication Data

Buchan, Peter
  Collected Poems and Short Stories
  I. Title
  821.914

  ISBN 0-903065-77-0

The publisher acknowledges subsidy from the Scottish Arts Council towards the publication of this volume.

Typeset by Gordon Wright Publishing Ltd., Edinburgh.
Printed and Bound by Butler & Tanner Ltd., Frome, Somerset.

Poems

Short Stories

Acknowledgements

The publisher wishes to thank Mrs Alison Massie, the author's younger daughter, for assisting with the editorial work and picture research necessary to complete this book.

Acknowledgement is also given to the *Buchan Observer* who originally published much of this work and Aberdeen Journals who published many of the short stories.

The James Valentine photographs are from the St Andrews University photo collection.

The Thumb-Mark of St Peter

An Introduction by David Toulmin

The thumb-mark of St Peter, the Big Fisherman of the New Testament. In this book, Peter Buchan says it is to be seen on the haddock, near the gills, 'as bold and clear as a birth-mark'. But Peter, who died 12 December 1991, has left his own water-mark on the North-Sea scrolls of fisher tradition, and he has seen to it that Peterhead, 'The Blue Toon', is well established on the map of social history.

To see that beautiful colour photograph of Peter on the cover of his collection of poems, gutting fish in his smaa boat, surrounded by a flurry of white gulls against the glinting blue of the Harbour of Refuge, you can imagine him on the Sea of Galilee.

I am glad to see this complete collection of Peter's poems and stories in print, thanks to our publisher's enthusiasm for the Scots language. And I am also pleased that Peter had written the best of his poems before he discovered that poetry is the poor man of literature. Not that Peter was an ambitious writer, he wrote poetry for the fun of it, and the fact that other people shared his enjoyment was reward enough.

By the time I met him in 1982, his book of poems *Mount Pleasant* was in its sixth enlarged edition, and it could be said that by then his 'romantic' period was over, which coincided with the discovery that he could also write prose. In fact, Peter didn't compose a stanza of verse in the last four years of his life. To the best of my knowledge his last poem was published in the *Buchan Observer* on 14 September 1985, two years after the last edition of *Mount Pleasant* but the poem also appeared in *Fisher Blue* in 1988. It is a song of Autumn and the comparing of grey hairs with approaching winter. It is also a celebration of the beauties of nature and the matrimonial blessings he enjoyed. 'September' is the title of the poem, and to call it a 'Swan Song' might be disrespectful, which is not intended, yet to my mind, that is exactly what it is, and most befitting in the circumstances.

I say this because it was during this period that the muse deserted our fisherman poet in his fear of the present and his dread of the future; not for his own safety, because he was retired from the sea, but a fear for others. By that time, like farming, the fishing industry was in turmoil. With the advent of computerisation, radar installations and mechanised fishing equipment, Peter didn't like what he saw. And with all this scientific gear in the modern wheel-house, bureaucracy decided that safeguards like fog-horns could be silenced, lighthouses would be automated and their keepers dismissed, and even the coastguard services were faced with redundancy, all of it creating navigational hazards the older seamen would find it difficult to cope with.

The Golden Calf became a statue on the pier and the old ways of fishing with reasonable caution were being irreversibly sacrificed for bigger profits.

Peter appreciated that the modern fisher crews enjoyed greater comfort and better conditions than they ever had in his day; that the catches were bigger and mechanically handled, and the financial returns were far greater, but in aiming for these rewards through investment in technological aids, modern ship design was too top-heavy for stability in a 'lump o watter', and he instanced several vessels that had disappeared without trace. He said skippers now ventured to sea in stormy weather when the older men would have stayed in harbour. Peter chose this dilemma of the modern fisherman as the theme for one of his later poems. It was called 'Reflections' and was written in English, which, in the circumstances, gives greater emotional impact to his message. Two verses will suffice to convey the meaning:

> But the seas still rise to an awesome height
> When the raging gales blow shrill,
> And a faith in things that are made by man
> Is no substitute for skill.

> It would seem alas, as the years roll on,
> And the pages of time unfold —
> That the thirst for power is a terrible twin
> To the terrible thirst for gold.

I think Peter felt that the thumb-mark of St Peter, the walking on the waters and the calming of the storm were symbols being cast overboard in the interests of financial gain.

When I met him he was still basking in the radiance of his poetical achievements and I was awaiting the appearance of his latest poem. I had to wait three years for the 'September' poem already mentioned.

By that time, Peter's daughter Alison had been persuading her father to turn his hand to prose to relate his experiences on sea and shore. Now I am almost convinced that our meeting gave the decisive tilt to his windmill in that direction. He confided in me that he wasn't sure of himself in prose and had never tried other than verbally, to construct a story, and that an article in print would be even worse.

After our interview I gave Peter a write-up in the *Aberdeen Leopard* magazine and the publicity was to his advantage with several people who were interested in his work phoning me for his address. Perhaps this was the encouragement he needed, but then, I discovered he couldn't type. It had all been very pleasant when he was in the mood to pen a poem for the *Buchan Observer* and see it in print the next week, but if Peter was to turn professional in a literary sphere, longhand wasn't good enough for discerning editors. I hadn't the nerve to tell Peter this, but he seemed to sense it. Even so, he had his first stories accepted by the Aberdeen *Evening Express* in longhand, although an editorial meeting was held before they could agree on some of his off-beat phrases, and their editing was severe, much to Peter's displeasure, although he eventually learned to comply with their wishes.

The first time Peter visited us in the city, I showed him a typescript I had prepared for a publisher and he was highly impressed. Addressing Agnes, his wife, he exclaimed, 'Michty, mither, look at iss! Isn't 'at a tidy job! I could nivver dee 'at!' But he did, and very quickly, after he purchased a nearly new electric typewriter. His published stories were highly successful and were later collected to publish his first prose book *Fit Like Skipper?*

As with his poems, the main theme in Peter's stories (I hesitate to call them fiction) is human behaviour. That is what interested him most, and much of that behaviour is described in the Doric language. He excels in the dialogue, which is almost stagecraft, keeping his characters where they belong, never far from boats or fishing-nets or even the coo's tail; and if there is a laugh to be found in the narrative, Peter will find it.

'There's naething sae queer as folk,' he was fond of saying, 'an the aaler they grou, the queerer. Some o them wid kick ye in the belly fin yer back wis turned!'

In his younger days he knew sadness, poverty and hardship and the emotional experiences, though many, are brightened with a smile if possible, like the rainbow in a storm.

Peter puts everything into his work, his heart and soul are at his fingertips and he writes with a bible sincerity and a philosophical wisdom on the intricacies and follies of the human spirit.

In Peter's work the most commonplace becomes important. Take Solo, who chewed tobacco and was a crackshot with his spittle. 'Psssst! His aim was deadly, and I have seen him extinguish a candle at the first shot from a distance of ten feet.' Solo wasn't a kirk-goer but being persuaded to go, he entered the kirk forgetting to remove his chaw. Realising there was nowhere to spit, Solo placed his chaw in his hankie. When the elder came round with the tin tray for the collection, the tin empty and Solo the first subscriber, Solo thought it was a spittoon. 'I'm nae needin that, freen,' he mumbled, 'I'm stoppit spittin noo!'

'Boys' to use Peter's favourite expression, Peter could fairly tell them and here the telling is sometimes more important than the story.

There was a time in his youth when Peter had to pay the gutting quines, and with their hands full and no pockets in their oilskin overalls, it was sometimes a problem where to deposit the envelope. There was the Busty Bombshell who indicated her cleavage, saying, 'Pit the packetie doon there, my loon!' Three weeks later, Peter was on the job again but Busty wouldn't allow him to repeat the deposit. 'Foo nae?' Peter enquired. 'Cos I had tae tirr (undress) afore I could get my pey yon day! Ye're nae near sic a gweed-faced, innocent loon as I thocht ye wis, ye coorse vratch!'

The stories abound with these snatches of wit and humour, like Lugs for instance, who thought it was important that his hame port, Finechty (Findochty) the Holy City, had 'oor ain stroop wallie an oor ain kirk hallie.'

Then there is the Blue Toon fisherman in Yarmouth looking for a present to take home for his little daughter who is learning to play her granny's organ. 'Fit is't ye're lookin for onywye?' Peter asks. 'Is't a Bach Fugue or a Mendelssohn Sonata? Ye're jist a fashious brute!'

'Oh no,' says the lad. 'It's nae naething lik 'at! I'm lookin for yon kin o stuff that the darkies sings! Somethin aboot a Sweet Chariot, ye ken.'

'That'll be the Negro Spirituals that ye're needin,' says Peter.

'Oh gweed help's, is 'at fit ye caa't? I've been seekin spooky music!'

The great baa-heidit oof!

There is also a wealth of serious social history recorded in Peter's work, especially concerning Peterhead and its environs. He mentions old and new buildings that have changed the appearance of the town, with special reference to the old spa which was called 'The Wine Waal' and the commodious Inn across the street for the visiting gentry, latterly known as 'The Hallelujah Lobby', a residence for waifs and strays, since demolished and replaced by a block of council flats. He also mentions the old branch railway from the station to the harbour, which crossed two main streets on the way.

I like Peter's association with the motor car and travel...'After years of aiming for it, I got myself a car, a birch-grey Morris 1000, and suddenly a whole new world opened up. Places which heretofore had been names on a map became realities within easy reach. Deeside and Tomintoul, the Moray Firth Ports and West Coast villages became part of life, and what a transformation that was! After a week of looking at the sea, I could go and feast my gaze on beauty.'

But there had to be a story in it for Peter, and if you read 'The Fite Rubbit', you will find it ends rather ruefully: 'Next time I see a quinie at the roadside greetin for her fite rubbitie, she can bloomin-well greet!'

It has been said that a writer's life is a lonely existence, and I will agree to the extent of saying that our co-authorship of the book *Buchan Claik*, a compendium of words and phrases from the North-East of Scotland, was one of the most pleasant experiences in my long career. On several occasions we met to compare notes or got in touch by phone, and I can still hear Peter laughing at the other end of the line, especially when I asked if he could smell our kippers frying. One day he told me he was 'biggit oot wi tatties' and it went right into the book. Another time he said, 'It's that caal the day I've pitten on an extra pair o galluses!'

Expletives were flying between us in our search for the exact Doric word or phrase. Peter was adroit in his choice and always had the ball at his foot. But he was no push-over, and if he decided on a certain word or expression he stuck to it and our publisher had to intervene as referee in sorting things out, usually printing both versions as a compromise. Yet I can't think of anyone with a firmer grip on the dialect, and it gives me great satisfaction to have completed this book with such a forthright and worthy compatriot and lexicographer.

Peter and I joined the Buchan Heritage Society on the very first evening of its inception at Aden Park Theatre in March 1984. Here we met the founder and President, Mr James M Duncan of Oldmeldrum. Although Peter and I both acted as judges for the poetry competitions organised by the society, Peter eventually became much more deeply involved with the activities of the committee, while I was content with the role of a 'trustee'. When failing health forced Mr Duncan to resign, Peter became President and editor of the society's magazine *Heirskip*, a service he conducted with the utmost proficiency for five outstanding years until his illness forced his resignation, much to the regret of all the members.

14

Peter had a life-long association with the Congregational Church in Peterhead from the age of three. He became a member at sixteen and was later married in the church. He was secretary for twenty-four years; he was chief deacon; he sang in the choir and also sang solo with his fine baritone voice. He also took the service in the minister's absence and carried out all these duties until failing health interfered with his devotion, though he was attending church until a few weeks before his death.

Peter is a wiser man than the rest of us now that he is gone. He has the answers to all the questions concerning the great hereafter that so many of us would like to know. It was a subject that Peter was greatly concerned about and his faith in the great almighty and the promise of eternal life never faltered.

A church filled to capacity for his funeral service acknowledged the deepest respect and gratitude of a sorrowing community for a lost brother and poet.

In the hours of his greatest suffering, no matter though his face was pale and weathered, his eyes still shone clearly as if an inner light brightened his soul. Peter's smile in adversity made cowards of the rest of us. He was a survivor of the deep. A lighthouse beam on the stormy waters of life.

David Toulmin
April 1992

To my wife Agnes
and my daughters
Anne and Alison

Poems

Nae the Same

I spoke til a freen at the shore the day,
Man, he wis unco-like an grey,
Dytin aboot like a half-shut knife
An vooin oot at the ills o life.
'Things is nae the same,' says he,
'Nae the same as they eesed t' be.'

Girnin sair at the wintry blast,
Mindin on Paradise lang, lang past —
Saat fish dryin on sunny braes,
The bleachin greens an the spotless claes.
'The wither's nae the same,' says he,
'Nae sae fine as it eesed t' be.'

'Look at the fearsome price o coal —
It's mair than the pension's fit to thole,
An, Lord, I near gid throwe the reef
Fin I heard the price o a pun o beef.
Things is nae the same,' says he,
'Nae sae chaip as they eesed t' be.'

'An fit div ye get fae the doctor chiels?
A line for a pucklie o fancy peels!
Yalla eens if ye canna sleep,
Pink if yer sark tail cracks like a wheep.
Medicine's nae the same,' says he,
'A mixter's a thing ye nivver see!'

He rantit on til my heid wis sair,
I steed til I couldna thole nae mair.
'Ye're awaa?' says he. 'I'm awaa!' says I,
'But I'll tell ye this in the passin by —
Wi a hantle mair ye're jist like me,
Nae sae young as ye eesed t' be.'

Mount Pleasant

There is a place my eager feet
    Were wont to seek when I was young:
Mount Pleasant! Is there name as sweet
    In any tongue?

Frail primroses, with timid eyes,
    Remembering the vanished snow,
Peeped forth, to view with sweet surprise
    The stream below.

There April sun and April rain,
    Fair sisters of the singing breeze,
Wrought hand in hand, to clothe again
    The leafless trees.

And Oh! the joy on golden days,
    When summer reigned in robes of green,
To see, a-shimmer in the haze,
    The lovely scene.

The quilted fields, the gardens bright
    With many tinted summer flowers;
O happy place of pure delight
    And sunny hours.

The old grey bridge, the lazy stream,
    The ivy-covered castle wall;
The lark's clear, lilting joyous theme
    Above it all.

But Autumn wore the fairest gown
    And bore, thro fields of tawny sheaves,
Her vivid shades of red and brown
    To stain the leaves.

Alas, her stay was all too brief,
    This maiden with the auburn hair;
Her passing left the world in grief
    And grey despair.

The child is gone who watched so well
   The fleeting seasons come and go.
His shadow cannot catch the spell
   Of long ago.

Pan Loff

There are among us those who fain
Wid treat wi scorn an great disdain
And, gien the slightest chance, wid hain
   The Doric phrase.
To hear them spik, ye'd think that they
Were born five hunner miles away,
Instead o 'tween Burnhaven Bay
   And Ugie's braes.

They think it impolite to say,
Fin freen meets freen, 'Fit like the day?'
Oh no, that's not the proper way!
   It's 'How d'ye do?'
At phrases sic as oors they scoff;
They toss their heids an spik 'Pan loff'.
They dinna hoast, Oh no, they cough!
   Their bleed is blue.

But drap a haimmer on their feet,
Or stick a needle in their seat,
Ye'll get the Doric pure an sweet,
   Aye! Rich an rare!
If they were richt, they'd need nae shock
To gar them spik like Buchan folk;
They widna be the lauchin-stock
   That noo they are.

The Buchan Clan

I've read aboot the gallant clans that shine in Scotland's name —
McFlannels an a lot o ither Macs o equal fame,
But it surely is a peety that we nivver see a jot
Aboot the famous Buchan clan, the foremaist o the lot.

Altho they are a weel-kent tribe, their origins are dark.
An yet 'tis said THE Buchan wis the mate on Noah's Ark.
He fechtit sair wi Noah till he got a weekly wage,
Syne fechtit mair for stoker an put Noah in a rage.
He girned aboot the grub bill an the affa price o coal
Till Noah shivved him ower the side, for mair he couldna thole.

He swam aboot for fourteen days until the sea gid doon,
A fortnicht! Aye, a fortnicht, he wis ower coorse tae droon!
He landed sair forfochen at a place caa'd Almanythie,
Far he wed a bonnie lassie fae the Mains o Kittlie-hythie,
An plantit there a faimly tree 'at grew at sic a speed,
That verra seen they built a toon an caa'd it Peterheid.

In coorse o time, like ither folk, the aal man met 'is daith,
Some say it wis the mirrles, but I think 'twis want o braith.
Wi broken herts they beerit him aside the aal 'Oo Mull',
Syne hurried hame to fecht aboot the wordin o the wull.
There wis a fearsome stashie an the faimly splut in three —
I'll tell ye aa aboot them if ye'll only lat me be.

The main branch, 'at's the Pirates, sattl'd doon at Rottra Heid
Far they made a canny livin in a wye that wisna gweed,
For they plunder't ivvery wreck that cam to grief aroon 'at coast,
An wisn't it a funny thing that ilka crew wis lost?

But the biggin o the Lichthoose fairly spiled their bonny game,
An the hale jing-bang o blackgairds hid to flit an leave their hame.
They cam to Buchanhaven, far the Ugie meets the sea,
Tho some socht Burnhaven, far there wis a breweree.

Ye'll meet their wild descendants fae North Rona to the Well,
Fae Barra to the Bergen and fae Flogie to the Bell.
Fin herrin seek the Knowle gruns, they're like to hae a birst,
An the war-cry on their fivvered lips is 'Men wi gear first!'

The second branch wis tinkies, an they gid aboot wi packs,
An they made a bonny profit aff o safety preens an tacks,
Till competition drove them fae the country to the toon
Far ye'll see the Tinkie Buchans yet, if only ye'll look roon.

They hiv their representatives in aa the different trades
An ye'll ken them by the packmark in atween their shooder blades.
Ye winna recognise them if ye dinna see the mark,
But they tell me that they dinna shift their claes unless it's dark.

The third branch wis the Royals, an they're few an far atween,
An the world wid be a better place supposin there wis neen;
For they're the folk that like to think they're better than the lave,
An they cairry that opinion fae the cradle to the grave.

They say, 'My goodness gracious' far the lave say, 'Govey Dicks',
An they say they're chopping firewood fin they're only brakkin sticks.
But still-an-on for aa their fauts, 'twid be a cryin shame,
To brand them waur than ither folk that hae a different name.

Altho yer name's nae Buchan, if ye come fae Peterheid,
It's surely mair gin likely ye've a drap o Buchan bleed,
For the Buchans, thro the centuries, for better or for waur,
Hae mairrit into ither tribes till gweed kens fit ye are.
Ye're a Pirate, or a Tinkie, or a Royal in yer pride —
Or ye're come o aal man Noah, that shivved Buchan ower the side.

23

The Ootlin

Geordie MacPhee had a humph on his back,
A wart on his nose an a cast in ae ee.
The set o his beens made him shooder-the-win,
An his legs gid a bittie agley at the knee.
Aye! Geordie wis ill-shooken-up an slack tied;
He hirpled aboot like a bird wi ae wing.
Tho beauty an fortin had baith passed him by,
Yet Geordie had this — man, he fairly could sing.

He sang like a lintie 'The Rose o Tralee',
Or 'Drink to me Only' or 'Bonny Strathyre';
He'd sing the 'Messiah' an sing't fae the hert,
Tho deil the sowl socht him to sing in the choir.
The aal sangs o Zion cam sweet fae his lips,
An him wi a body sae twisted an bent.
He sang o the pangs o 'The Aal Rugged Cross',
An some that were listenin thocht surely HE kent.

The soles o his sheen aye gid flappity-flap;
His stockins, aye marless, had seldom a heel;
At oxter an elbow he nott a bit string,
An his briks could ha deen wi an owergaan as weel.
The mitherless ootlin had nivver a lass —
The quines leuch at Geordie, peer orra-like thing;
But spite o them aa he'd a star in his sky:
The bairns likit Geordie for Geordie could sing.

He sang o yon Bairn that wis born hine awaa:
The Bairn that had naething, like Geordie himsel.
He sang aboot shepherds an wise men forbye,
An angels that cam the sweet story to tell.
He sang hoo the Bairn, at the end o his days,
Wis a chiel that had nails in his hans an his feet.
He sang o the day fin we'll aa be made hale,
An fit could a buddy dee ither than greet?

Fin Geordie gid up to yon gates made o pearl,
Aal Peter said, 'Geordie man, come awaa ben!
Yer hoosie's aa ready — we've watched ye this fyle;
Ye've heen a sair trauchle doon there amon men.

An noo that it's feenished ye'll just sattle in,
For aa that ye're needin ye'll get fae the King;
Syne efter ye're restit, I'll gie ye a job,
A job to yer likin! Aye Geordie, ye'll sing!'

If ever ye traivel the pavement up there,
Ye'll get a begick, man, for there at yer feet,
The gold that men worship, an fecht for, an steal,
Is coonted fine stuffie for sortin the street.
Ye'll tramp aboot gapin at mansion an haa,
An siccan a hantle o ferlies ye'll see!
But mak for the Square fin ye hear the choir sing,
An there he'll be tapster. Faa? Geordie McPhee!

Best-o-the-Bunch

Best-o-the-Bunch has a curly heid
   An rosy cheeks an a lauch in her ee;
An sweet are the lips sae bonny reid
   Fin they're held up wi a kiss to me.

I canna tell if she misses me
   On days fin my work taks me awaa;
But I ken that it's fine to come hame fae the sea
   An hear my Best-o-the-Bunch say, 'Da!'

Since she wis born it seems like a day;
   Noo Best-o-the-Bunch'll seen be three
Wi a gift that only a queen should hae —
   The power to command a slave — that's me.

Buchanhaven Shorie

There's a canny leethe fae the sou-wast win
   At the fitt o the middle street,
In the neuk at the back o the gairden dyke,
   Far a lang, low widden seat
Looks oot ower the pier an the half-sunk rocks
   Wi their skirts o dark-broon weed,
To the bonny sweep o yalla san
   An the licht at Rattra Heid.

It's a canny leethe, an it's there ye'll see
   At the close o a simmer's day,
When the tang o the sun-dried waur on the beach
   Comes stealin up the brae,
The aal men gaitherin roon aboot
   For a smoke, an a yarn forbye,
As they watch the ships fade oot o sicht
   Ower the hazy line o sky.

There's mair than een wi their carpets on,
   An there micht be a staff or twaa;
Tho the fuskered race, wi the cheese-cutter caips
   Are maistly worn awaa.
There's twaa-three mair wi their hans weel-dug
   In the taps o their hair-back briks,
An the antrin een that wants the pipe
   Has a chow in his 'lastic chiks.

An there, while the sun shines through the nets
   That hing fae the dryin poles,
They yarn as they sit on their corner seat
   Or lean on the drawn-up yoles.
An fit's aa the topic? Jist stan tee,
   For they'll seen forget ye're there,
An ye'll hear the tale o a poachin ploy
   For a reid-fish or a hare.

Aal Donald fills his mishaachled pipe
   Wi the silver knob on its doup,
An spins a yarn o the happy days
   When the flukes in Scotston Houp

Were spear deep, an the haddocks cam
   To the verra watter mou;
Syne ends his tale wi a shak o's heid —
   'It's a different story noo!'

Ye'll hear hoo the weemen lang lang seen
   Could cairry the heavy creel;
An ilka een in the but an ben
   Had to redd or bait or sheel;
Hoo the young quines gaed to the mussel scaup
   On a bitin winter's morn,
An gaithered bait fae the frozen lochs
   Till their dirlin hans were torn.

Ye'll hear aboot distant sailboat days
   Fin they gaed to Baltasoun
In the zulu boats wi their pinted starns,
   An the scaphs so blunt an roon.
Hoo the drifters cam wi their pooer an speed
   An ruled the sea supreme.
Till the motor boats, tho poor at first
   Wrote an end to the days o steam.

An names crop up that ye hear nae mair
   Tho bonny names they are —
Sweet Promise, Hope an *Star of Faith.*
   Bydand, an *Guiding Star*.
An so, in the oor or twaa ye've stood
   On the Buchanhaven Shorie
Ye've covered sixty 'ear an mair
   In the aal men's grippin story.

An man, tho ye've nivver said a word,
   They'll say they've enjoyed yer crack;
An syne fin ye leave to warstle hame —
   'Gweed nicht an hist ye back!'

The Happy Man

It's an airish kind o mornin, wi the sky jist growin grey,
   An there's twaa-three black-like shooers up t' norrit.
I'm skipper for the meenit for the mannie's at his tay,
   An he's nivver in a hurry comin forrit.
We're nae lang deen a-haulin, an I'm happy as a lark,
   An I widna change my place wi ony man.
It's Setterday, sweet Setterday, it's nae this week we 'bark',
   An we're set awaa for hame wi ninety cran.

The boys are in the cabin, crackin jokes an tellin lees,
   An the air'll be as thick as brose wi rick;
There's naethin like a joog o tay, a sheave o loaf an cheese,
   For makkin weary men buck up an spik.
They'll hae to start directly for we got an awkward haul,
   An we had to haul them in abeen the han.
The reddin up's the warst o't if yer hans are deid wi caal,
   An it taks a fylie's time wi ninety cran.

Accordin to the wireless news they're spotty-kind the day,
   An mair than half the fleet has neen avaa.
Still, that'll pit the price up. 'That's a selfish thocht,' ye'll say,
   But that's the herrin fishin efter aa.
There's some that wid condemn my joy wi chapter, verse an line,
   An preach aboot the sinfu greed o man;
But, still-an-on, fin herrin's scarce it thrills this hert o mine
   To strick a bonny shot like ninety cran.

There's some that's nae contintit till she winna hud nae mair —
   They maun be made o stuff that's affa teuch.
I've hauled an rived 'is mornin till my shooder heids are sair,
   An I think that ninety ony day's eneuch.
My face is thick wi spawn an scales, my lips are stiff wi saat,
   An I feel as if my een wis full o san.
There's ragnails on my fingers, but they dinna hae a faut,
   For we're makin for the shore wi ninety cran.

Noo here's the skipper comin so I'll dodge awaa doon aift,
   An I only hope the tay's been keepit het.
I winna feel sae cheery if there's nae a drappie left,
   Tho it's seldom that the Cookie dis forget.

I'm tired, an weet, an hungry, but I'm happy as the lark,
   An I widna change my place wi ony man.
It's Setterday, sweet Setterday, we dinna need to 'bark',
   An she's gaan full butt for hame wi ninety cran.

Leebie

I couldna spell, I couldna coont past twinty,
Nor could I read unless the words were smaa.
I couldna name the highest hill in England,
For maps were things for hingin on the waa.
I couldna mind a date nor place a battle,
And so I was 'The girl who was no use
For any earthly purpose whatsoever!'
So said yon primpit craitur, young Miss Bruce.

The years hae flown, the aaler aye the faster,
The kings an queens, the battles are forgot,
I've kent this fyle the highest hill in England,
Tho learnin-wise I hinna gained a lot.
But I've my man an fower bonny bairnies,
A happy hame far some folk has a Hoose;
An sometimes, fin I think hoo I've been guided,
I greet for yon peer craitur, aal Miss Bruce.

Div Ye Mind?

Ye mind yon times fin we were bairns?
  The happy careless days?
We'd traivel up the water-side
  An clim the Pinkie Braes.
As cheery an as hardy as a caravan o tinkies,
  Contented if we got a bunch o bonny yalla pinkies.
For us the vexin things in life
  Were things like whin-bush prickles,
An dogs that barkit ower lood,
  An coos — an jobby nickles.

Ye mind the bonny simmer nichts
  Fin aa the loons gid dookin —
An nae a stitch o claes upon's
  Nae maitter faa wis lookin?
We shivered as we drew oor briks up ower oor hardy knees,
  An stowed awaa the linners that were flappin in the breeze.
Syne aff we'd rin across the rocks
  An mak for some wee shoppie
To buy a luckie tattie
  Or a maikst o treacle toffee.

Ye mind the simmer holidays,
  The bonny sunny wither?
The tar cam up atween oor taes
  An stuck them close thegither.
We played aboot the curin yards amon the roosin tubs,
  An splashed through lochs o pickle bree an seas o sappy dubs.
We likit aye the reckless thing
  Cos mithers widna hear o't,
An only ran an eerin
  If we couldna weel get clear o't.

An even in the winter days,
  Fin wild north winds were blaain,
Altho oor knees were blue wi caal,
  We'd wish that it wis snaain,
We'd showd upon the battens if the timmer boat wis in,
  An licht oor stave-built hoosie wi a cannle in a tin.
An there the bigger loons amon's
  Wid mak a wily plan
To fecht the Queenie Arabs
  Or some ither war-like clan.

Ye mind yon day, ye witless breet,
    Ye stole yon quinie's baa?
An thinkin ye wid mak her greet,
    Ye took her lames an aa?
She wisna muckle aaler fin she twined ye roon her cranny,
    An if she gied ye half a smile, ye thocht ye wis 'the mannie'.
Her game o playin lairies
    Wi a huskle lost its joy,
An verra seen she had yer hert
    To play wi like a toy.

An noo the happy, careless days
    Are oot o sicht astarn;
But still-an-on ye'll hae yer thochts —
    Aye! mony-a-time aswarn.
The feet that eence were free an bare hae come a weary road,
    The shooders that oor schoolbags kent hae borne a heavy load.
The future may seem drear an dark,
    The present soor an wauch;
We dinna ken fit lies ahead,
    So lat's look back — an lauch.

Summer Dawn

Cool, clear air with the wind from the west
    Breathing a hint of rain,
Ruffling the cornfield's golden tresses
    And smoothing them out again.

Quiet gleam of the sleeping bay;
    Furrows on firm wet sand;
Clean fresh tang of the brown wrack mingling
    With the soft sweet breath of the land.

Lapping of water round the old stone pier
    And the sound of simple things;
The plaintive cry of a lonely gull,
    And the beat of questing wings.

Genesis

Lo! the Ark wis nearly ready an the water risin fast
    Fin Noah caa'd a meetin o his clan;
'Listen, Shem an Ham an Japheth, ye're a young an willin squad,
    But I'm thinkin that we need anither man!

We're a crew o country billies, an altho we've built a ship,
    Ye'll agree that nae a soul has been afloat,
So we need a fishin skipper that's been steepit lang in saat,
    Aye! a chiel that kens his wye aboot a boat.

Ye'll be busy wi the beasties in the darkness doon below,
    An it's nae a twa-three heid o Heilan kye,
For there's elephants an camels, an there's kangaroos an goats
    Raivelt up wi yaks an polar bears forbye.

Noo, as lang's the shippie's steady ye'll aye manage to keep tee,
    But if storms arise an seas come ower the starn,
She'll be showdin up an doon an roun an if ye miss yer fit
    Ye'll ging skitin ben the pass amang the sharn.

So we need a heid that's steady, an we need a fit that's sure,
    An a hert that winna greet for sicht o lan;
A prodeegious navigator wi a compass in his heid
    An my lads I think I ken the verra man.

Ging ye ben the shore for Buchan; Ham, ye ken far Buchan bides.
    He'll be sittin buskin fishies in his cave!
Wi his taes amang the shunners an his hunkers on a kist,
    Watchin Maggie-Annie scrubbin like a slave.

Noo ye'd better tak a cannle for his lobby's affa dark,
    If ye dinna watch ye'll tummle doon the hole
Far he keeps his luggit-bonnet an his rippers an his beets,
    Hingin up abeen the saat-fish an the coal.

Fin ye reach the inner chaumer ye'll tak aff yer greasy caip,
    For he's royal an he likes to get his place;
So ye'll stan as stracht's a ramrod an say, "Mister Buchan, sir!"
    An ye'll see the gleam o pride licht up his face.

32

He'll say, "Hoo's yer father deein? Is yer mither keepin weel?
   Is't the case yer peer aal grunnie's growin blin?
Is yer deydie fartin firmer since he drank yon clort o stuff
   That he got fae Doctor Hanok for the win?"

Then ye'll gie him a ceevil answer, state yer business, lat him think —
   If he's suppered he'll be riftin like a Turk —
It's an officer we're needin, a commander, mak it clear,
   For there's ae thing loon, ye darna mention "work".

Oh! he'll hum-an-hae a fylie, but ye'll sense that he's fine pleased
   Tho he winna gie ye answer aiven oot;
Na, he'll hae to tell ye something o his history, jist to prove
   He's the leader we require withoot a doot.

So ye'll hear hoo Sherpa Tensing, yon intrepid mountaineer,
   Wi Sir Hilary hard sloggin in his track,
Wis but fifty feet fae glory fin he got a fearsome fricht,
   He cam face to face wi Buchan comin back!

Buchan crossed the tropic ocean on a pair o bakin boards,
   An he slew the great sea-serpent wi a spike;
He wis frozen in for fourteen 'ear on Greenland's icy coast,
   Noo the Yakkies there greet strangers wi, "Fit like?"

He'll discourse on ony subject, for he's read a book or twaa,
   An he'll tear the present government to bits;
Aye! ye'll learn a lot fae Buchan but the fastest thing ye'll learn
   Is to jouk aside a bittie fin he spits.

But we need his canny coonsel an his knowledge vast an wide,
   For, my loons, I dinna ken aboot the sea;
Ye can offer him tobacca and an antrim tot o rum
   If he'll only pass his word to sail wi me.'

'Wyte!' says Japheth, 'Da, caa canny, it wid be a cryin shame
   To pit Ham alang the shore in aa this rain,
Fit's the eese o gaan for Buchan? 'twid be just a waste o time,
   For the sinner has a boatie o his ain.'

Noo then, Japheth, for his impudence, wis sent along the shore,
   Shem and Ham were kept at hame the work to dee;
Late that nicht came Buchan's answer, in a Ministerial note,
   'I'll be doon the back o Sunday. Yours, P.B.'

Where There's Life

'Fit like are ee the day?' says I,
Til a freen I've kent since days gone by.

'Weel noo!' says he, an he draws his breath,
'I've been this fyle at the door o death!
Ye'll mind last 'ear I took the flu?
Weel, I'm only gettin the back o't noo;
But it's teen a gey sair pick, ye'll see,
For I'm lantered noo wi a cockle ee.
There's inflammation in my jints,
So I canna boo doon to tie my pints,
An if I try, my bubbly nose
Begins to skite like a gairden hose,
An afore I get pooer to gie't a dicht,
It jist rins dry an it bungs up ticht.
Syne that affects my peer aal heid,
An it lies on my shooders like a lump o leid,
So ye'll see my loon (an he stoppit for breath),
Jist fit it's like at the door o death!
I'm bothered fyles wi my watter tee,
An its twinty times a day, ye see.
It's nae neen handy tho it's nae ower sair,
But ye ken oor bathroom's up the stair.
My bowels hisna meeved for a fyle,
So I doot it's back to the castor ile,
An that itsel's nae fine, ye ken,
For ye canna get peace for a meenit on en.
Like the atom boom it works on the dot,
So I'm up the stairs like a mountain goat!
Ye speir at me "Fit like?" That's feel!
Ye can surely see that I'm nae neen weel!'

'There's nae muckle wrang wi yer sicht!' says I,
As he eyed a deem that wis passin by.

The Skipper's Wife

Jock, neist door, has a score o cran,
    But yer father hisna neen.
They say there's a hantle o herrin tee,
    So faar can the gowk hae been?
He'll seen be hame wi's fool black face,
    An he'll look for mait, 'at's mair.
An he'll fidge an pech an he'll grunt an blaa
    Like a bear fin its belly's sair.
He'll hae to be deein wi pottit heid
    Tho its nae jist ower sair jeeled.
'Anither tattie or twaa', did ye say?
    'Na, we'll just chap the thing 'at's peeled';
It's a gey sair fecht, an it's true aneuch,
    The wordle's ill-pairtit for some o's;
It's time he wis gettin a shottie noo
    Or it's gweed kens fit'll come o's.

Jock, neist door, has a cran or twaa,
    But yer father's a hunner an twinty!
Hing in noo quine! Rin for fillet steak,
    An be sure m'dear ye get plinty,
An ye'll sort it richt wi a fine fresh egg
    An a bonny hame-made chip;
An ye'd better cry-tee for a curran daad
    For he disna get that in the ship.
Is there plinty o watter het noo quine?
    He'll be yirdit wi scales an saat.
If he starts t' sing like the Rattra Horn,
    Jist dinna say it's a faat.
He's a richt smairt man yer father, quine,
    There's fyowe on the coast to beat 'im.
I think I'll pit on my Sunday hat
    An ging doon on the pier to meet 'im.

Hairy Tatties

Bring me a ling fae the Viking Bank,
A tusk fae the Patch or the Reef,
Or catch me a cod on the Buchan coast
An I'll greet nae mair for beef.
Steep her in saat for a three-fower days
Then dry her slow in the sun
In the month o Mey, fin the safter win's
Bring the green growth up thro the grun.

Bring me a bile o the finest Pinks
Fae a craft on Mormon Braes,
At the tail o the hairst, fin the first fite frost
Tells a tale o winter days.
Peel them an bile in a fine big pot
Wi my bonny fish in anither;
Bree them baith when ye think they're richt,
Syne ye'll chap them baith thegither.

A knottie o butter an a glaiss o milk —
Ye've a feast that's weel worth a Grace;
Then waste nae a meenit as ye fill yer speen
An stap it into yer face.
Bring me a tusk fae the Patch or the Reef,
Fae the Viking Bank, a ling;
Or catch me a cod on the Buchan coast
Then I ken I'll dine like a king.

Shift o Win
(Conversation Piece)

Watch:	'Hey Jock! Watch oh!
	'S twal o'clock!'
Reply:	'Right oh!
	Hoo's 'e win?'
Watch:	'Nor-wast
	Mak ee tay — ee're last!'

Watch:	'Hey, Skipper!'
Skipper:	'Fit noo?'
Watch:	'Sky's as black's a wolf's mou!'
Skipper:	'Hoo's 'e win?'
Watch:	'Sooth-east.'
Skipper:	'Govey-dick; fit neist?'

Skipper:	'Ho-ro lads, turn oot
	Seems 'e win's geen roon aboot!
	Gless's teen an affa faa.
	Think we'd better haul awaa!'

Cook:	'Gaan to sea's nae eese;
	Sure as daith there's nae peace;
	This is jist a job for feels,
	We'd be better twistin dreels.'

Note: Cleveland Twist Drill opened a factory in Peterhead in 1956.

St Luke 3, Verse 11

'Had ee twaa richt gran hooses, Dod,
Wi carpets waa to waa,
Wi double glazin, central heat
An curtains fite as snaa,
Wi fancy lichties at the door
An gairdens green an fine —
Ye widna see me bidin
In a place jist fit for swine?'

'Had I twaa richt gran hooses, Tam,
An ee had neen avaa,
Wi richt gweed-wull I'd lat ye pick
The better o the twaa.
An there ye'd sit rent free for life,
At my expense ye'd dine,
Nae thocht o want wid furr yer broo,
Yer cares wid aa be mine.'

'Had ee twaa richt fine motors, Dod,
Wi automatic gears,
Wi fartin horns an flashin lichts
An seats like easy cheers,
Wi polished wid an silver knobs —
Ye nivver saw the like —
Ye widna see me lantered
Wi an aal deen roosty bike?'

'Had I twaa richt fine motors, Tam,
An ee had neen avaa,
Wi richt gweed wull I'd gar ye tak
The better o the twaa.
Syne faa like hiz, in aa the toon?
Fine motors, fancy biggins!
I'd help ye tak yer roosty bike
An dump it ower the diggins.'

'Had ee twaa richt fine rippers, Dod,
Weel buskit, clean an bricht,
The thing to tak a codlin's ee
At th' income o daylicht,

Ye widna see me fishless
For the want o heuks an leed,
An me wi fourteen bairnies
An a nae-weel wife to feed?'

'O I hae twaa fine rippers, Tam,
An forty mair forbye,
An ripper strings an ither things
That ee're nae fit to buy.
But this religion's gaan ower far;
Ye've geen clean gyte the day.
Ye're nae supposed to seek a share
O something that I hae!'

'Aa richt noo, Dod, I'll lat ye be
Wi aa the gear ye hae.
Hing in noo, tak the gweed o't aa,
But mind there comes a day,
Fin up the Toon-hoose stairs ye'll clim —
Fit gars ye think ye winna?
To hear the Maister seek the fruits
O something that ye hinna.'

The Choice

Were I but young an feel again —
    An that can hardly be,
I'd like to mak a change or twaa;
    I widna seek the sea.
Could I but pick an chyse again
    I'd tramp anither road,
An keep my fit weel plantit
    On the firm dry sod.

Could I but pick an chyse again,
    I'd like a wiser heid,
Then in the ups an doons o life
    I micht come mair speed;
But were I at the start again
    An tellt ae choice wis mine,
It's land or sea I'd taikle —
    Wi the same aal quine.

Ye Widna be Sellt!
(For a Special Day)

Were I a poet, lass o mine,
   I'd snare the crescent moon
An set it in a bonny line
   To ryhme wi rose in June.
The proper bard pits flooers an birds
   In sangs o love, that's true;
But lass, I dinna hae the words
   To say sic things to you!

Were I to whisper 'Precious heart!'
   Ye'd think I wisna weel!
Or, did I mention Cupid's dart,
   Ye'd say, 'Ye great aal feel!'
A fancy card I micht ha bocht —
   'Twid been an easier plan —
But lass, ye're worth a sweeter thocht
   Than verse that's second-han.

For mony a year, for mony a mile
   We've sodjered on thegither.
Could words that made oor bairnies smile
   Nae still delight their mither?
Then harken close, my sonsie lass —
   Fit better could I tell ye?
'Tho moons an June awaa may pass,
   Ye ken I widna sell ye!'

Note: 'Ye widna be sellt for a thoosan powen!' An endearment normally reserved for the bairns.

40

Craigewan

Pace-aiggs bricht on the yalla san
  In the pale clear sun o Spring.
Young heids bent in a kysie search
  'Mong the rocks far limpets cling.
Lang fine days wi their happy ploys,
  An bare feet rinnin free;
The lilt o win throu wavin girss,
  An the strong clear call o the sea.

Lad-'n-lass traivlin airm-in-airm,
  Ower the bents on a simmer's nicht,
Sweir t' ging hame, like aa their kind,
  Tho the sun's lang oot o sicht.
The cry o a whaup at the watter-mou,
  An the smell o the tangle-bree;
The whisper o win throu quiverin girss,
  An the low saft sang o the sea.

Oot-win, caal wi the threat o rain,
  Or it micht be wi grey sea fog.
An faa's on the bare grey bents the day
  But an aal grey man wi's dog,
Traivlin the aal paths, hearin soun's
  O the days that eesed t' be
In the sough o win throu shiverin girss,
  An the dreary dirge o the sea.

41

Buchan Beauty

Have you seen the mighty flail
Of the roaring north-east gale
Drive the billows to destruction
On the rocks at Buchan Ness?
Have you seen the sunlit waters
'Tween the Geddle and the Outers
With the wavelets dancing brightly
To the off-shore wind's caress?

Have you seen the peaceful sight,
On a windless summer night,
Of Dutch boats snug at anchor,
All a-mirrored in the bay —
While their crews, with their quaint patches,
Long cheroots, and bright-hued matches,
Joined the Lewismen on Broad street
Just to hear the 'Army' play?

Have you seen the silver gleam
Of the Ugie's placid stream
In the gloamin, by the Collieburn,
Where bright-eyed lovers go?
Do you know each pool and stone
From Craigewan to the Roan,
Each rock, each nook and cranny,
From the Peel to Craig-na-bo?

Have you seen the rich ripe corn
On a clear September morn,
Near the Howe o Buchan, ready
For the binding of the sheaves?
Aye! and Richmond's golden broom,
Inverugie's hawthorn bloom,
And Ravenscraig's bright rowans
'Mid the rustling dark green leaves.

If to you these scenes are dear,
If your memory holds them clear
As a photograph before you,
Tho parted far from home;

If this rugged, wind-swept part
Of Aal Scotia grips your heart,
Yours and mine are kindred spirits
No matter where we roam.

The Peel

Twa-three heukies in his ganjey;
  In his pooch a penny line,
Or, could he nae raise a penny,
  It micht be some barkit twine.

Ower the Queenie Brig, this loonie
  Watched a chance to scran his bait,
Far the gutters teemed their coggies,
  Jist inside some curer's gate.

Syne across the rocks he'd warstle;
  Loons were there fae far an near,
Shyvin oot their hame-made linies,
  Aften raivelt, seldom clear.

O, the happy oors he'd spend there,
  Blithe an cheery, young an feel;
Jist a barfit, careless craitur,
  Catchin podlies in the Peel.

Dinna speir at me, 'Faa wis he?'
  That's a thing I couldna tell.
Steek yer een an think a fylie —
  Could he nae ha been yersel?

Brotherly Love

Ye ken the kind o some folk —
   They like to get their place,
Content wi verra little
   If their neeper man has less.
An tho they had a fortin,
   It wid hurt them affa sair
To think some ither body
   Micht hae jist a bittie mair.

Ye ken the kind o some folk —
   Ye'll meet them ilka day.
Their ivvery thocht's clean conter
   To fit ye hear them say.
Their words are sweet as honey
   But their herts are black as coal;
To see their neeper gettin on —
   That's mair than they can thole.

Ye ken the kind o some folk —
   They'd like to claim the sea.
Their share o loving kindness
   Widna full a budgie's ee.
The love of cod constraineth them
   To work wi craft an guile
To chase their neeper aff the sea
   An pit 'im in the jile.

We canna aa be perfect;
   I'm nae ower gweed masel;
But Aal Nick has for some folk
   A special place in Hell,
An says, as on their firie
   He piles anither log —
'The mair I see o some folk
   The better I like my dog.'

44

Herrin Fivver

Had we but steered oot east-by-north
  Instead o east-nord-east,
We michta heen the biggest shot
  Instead o haein least.

Had we but geen the thirty mile
  Instead o thirty-twaa,
We michta gotten twinty cran
  Instead o neen avaa.

It widna rankle jist sae bad
  Could we get neeper's fare,
But seein ither folk wi shots
  Fair maks yer belly sair.

I'm thinkin that we've met the cat;
  She's surely been a bummer!
At scalders, dogs an bare black yarn
  We've teen a proper scunner.

There's cure for ills that smit the hert,
  The kidneys or the liver;
But doctors canna help ye if
  Ye tak the herrin fivver.

It brings nae pain, this strange disease,
  But man, it's hard to thole.
A cran-the-net's the only cure —
  Or else a sax-fit hole.

The Humble Door

Lord, I've been readin in the Beuk
Aboot yon bonny place —
The gates o pearl, the paths a-shine
Wi gold as clear as glaiss.
The crystal river flowin close
Alang the bonny street,
Far trees o healin cast their leaves
Aboot a buddy's feet.
I hope it's jist a picter, Lord,
For yon's nae place for me,
A chiel that's spent his mortal days
Close-oxtered wi the sea.
I canna see mysel in fite;
The harp I canna play;
I'd mak a shape at singin
But I couldna sing aa day!
I'd need to leave the likes o that
To better folk than me —
The multitude that ging aboot
Wi naething else to dee
But ficher wi their harps o gold
An tune their vocal cords
For singin in the heavenly choir
'The Glory is the Lord's.'
I doot that mine, in sic a throng
Wid be an ootlin's face —
A daisy on a perfect green,
A megrim among plaice.
The palaces an mansions
Wid be ower gran for me,
I'd rather hae a quaet neuk,
A hoosie near the sea
Wi five-an-twinty ripper codlins
Dryin at the door;
A clinker-biggit Fifie yoll
Drawn up along the shore.
Then, maybe, some fine quaet nicht
Fin, deeved wi aa the soun,
Ye're lookin for a meenit's peace,
Ye'll tak a turnie doon,
An there we'll sit afore the door
The pair o's, You an me,

46

An ait a roasen fishie
As Ye did in Galilee.
We'll sit a fyle an news a fyle
As evenin wears awaa,
Syne, could it be I'll unnerstan
Fit wye I'm there avaa?

An — should Ye hae a meenit spare
To grace my butt-an-ben,
Grant that I'll hear Ye welcomed there
By somebody I ken.

The Difference

He's nae kirk-greedy —
He can hardly pass a pub,
It's nae a pint he's fond o,
It's a suppie in a tub.
He likes to back a horsie
An I ken he taks a lass,
An some wid shak their heids to see
That Jock's at sic a pass.

He's nae neen bigsy
An he'll help ye if he can,
He'd rather dee in poverty
Than swick his fellow-man.
I ken he wastes gweed siller,
But there's aye a bob or twaa
To spare for folk that's stairvin,
Be they here or hine awaa.

I'm nae lang-heidit
But I'm thinkin that I see
The unimportant difference
Atween aal Jock an me.
It's surely this — fan we ging oot
To meet the Judge Divine,
The sins that Jock'll answer for
Are nae the same as mine.

Kirsty

Her mither wis a guttin quine
That vrocht wi Sandy Wid.
Her father wis a canny sowl,
An aa he ivver did
Wis scutter oot an in at hame
Wi twaa-three string o line;
An gey sair made they were at times
To please their only quine.

'Twis Kirsty this an Kirsty that
An Kirsty's needin sheen!
An Kirsty's darlin sheenikies
Maun come fae Aiberdeen.
The verra sark upon her back
Wis sent for, hine awaa;
For common dab fae Peterheid
Jist widna dee avaa!

Her brithers could rin barfit
As they plowtered doon the braes,
But Kirsty aye nott fancy gear
To hap her ten'er taes.
The loons, like aa the ither loons
Had patches on their docks,
But nivver smaad nor patch wis seen
On Kirsty's bonny frocks.

In coorse o time they aa grew up;
The loons they socht the sea.
But Kirsty, she did naething,
Like a deem o high degree.
A silly gypit craitur
Needin aathing on a plate —
The siller that wis spent on her
Wis sairer nott for mait!

She widna gut a herrin
An a mask she couldna shue
For Kirsty wis a lady
An she thocht her bleed wis blue.

Her satin hans were ower fine
To blaad wi nets or fish,
But jist the verra dunt
For pittin dahlias in a dish.

She mairried, twa-three simmers back,
A quaet, decent chiel.
He's nivver aff the watter
An I hear he's deein weel.
He'll need to keep the shippie gaan
To ply his Kirsty quine
Wi her sets o Doulton idols
In their gran formica shrine.

She's socht ye to yer supper?
Weel! I'm sure ye'll get a feed!
Ye'll spend a pleasant evenin, lass,
But dinna loss the heid
An mention in the bye gaan —
'Twid be naisty if ye did —
That her mither wis a guttin quine
That vrocht wi Sandy Wid.

Shiftin the Clock

The clock's geen back an it's early dark
So I'd better look oot my flannen sark,
An then, wi the first o the winter haars
I'll hae a rake for my worsit draars.

Lord! fin ye thocht t' fashion me
Could ye nae hae changed the recipe
So that, like craiturs o a lower state,
I micht hae been able to hibernate?

49

Siller

O siller's like a fairy wand,
It smoothes a steenie road,
It opens doors that ticht were shut
An lifts a weary load.
Aye! siller's sic a pleasant thing
We're maistly seekin mair o't,
An few there be that widna tak
A bigger, fairer share o't.

But siller's like the saaty sea —
It slakes the drouth at first,
But aye as deeper dips the speen
The stronger grows the thirst.

O siller's sic a precious thing,
In time o stress we flee till't,
An some, for want o better gods,
Wid bow the verra knee till't.
For siller Judas sellt his Lord —
Wis ivver bargain poorer?
The ready cash in greedy niv
Made retribution surer.

O siller's like the saaty sea,
Far boats an men are lost,
For aye as deeper dips the speen
The steeper grows the cost.

O siller's like a sinkin san
For aa the bonny glint o't.
The honest man's sair made to stan
Fin eence he gets the scint o't.
'If siller be the loaf o life
Lat's hae a muckle sheave o't,
An be it mair than we can chaw
The mair we'll hae to leave o't.'

But siller's like the saaty sea
Faar tide spins magic web,
For nivver wis there yet a flood
Withoot there cam an ebb.

A Time to Get

They tell me, loon, ye've left the school;
    Ye'd like to try the sea.
Yer mither's sent ye doon the road
    To seek advice fae me?
She micht ha socht some better chiel
    To keep her loonie richt —
But sit ye doon; I'll dee my best
    To shed a bittie licht
On paths that dark afore ye lie
    If fishin be yer aim;
Syne, if some day ye rue the start
    Ye'll hae yersel to blame.

Ye'll lowse the rope, a cocky chiel,
    Gran notions in yer heid.
Afore ye're oot o sicht o lan
    Ye'll wish that ye wis deid,
For sickness disna pick an chyse;
    It lays the mighty low.
Ye'll lie an shiver on the deck
    Nae fit to ging below.
'If only she wid bide at peace!'
    But that can nivver be —
Ye've left the steady lan astarn
    An noo ye're on the sea.

But that'll wear awaa come time;
    Ye'll learn to keep yer feet.
Ye'll walk the deck as deil-may-care
    As if it were the street.
Till some coorse day she'll tak a lump
    An then ye'll get a scare!
Ye'll sweel aboot the scuppers
    An ye'll learn the lesson there
That nae sometimes, but aa the time
    Ye need a wary ee.
Ye've left the steady lan astarn
    An noo ye're on the sea.

A growin loon, a workin loon,
   Ye'll aye cry oot for mait,
An then ye'll learn the secret knack
   O keepin't in yer plate.
The table's showdin up an doon,
   It's reelin back an fore,
An tattie soup taks queer-like tigs
   It nivver took ashore.
High broadside motion nivver moved
   Yer mither's kitchen fleer —
But that wis in the steady world
   Ye've left upon the pier.

Ye'll learn to tyauve along wi men,
   Ye'll work the clock aroon.
Ye'll rise afore the simmer sun,
   Ye'll see him beddit doon.
Come winter an ye'll get a taste
   O lang nichts black wi sleet.
The bitter, bitin, cruel caal
   Wid gar a buddy greet.
The time'll come ye'd sell yer sowl
   For twaa sweet oors o sleep.
The lowsin times for folk ashore
   Are eeseless on the deep.

As time wears on ye'll see the sichts
   Ye'd nivver see on lan.
There's beauty in the wilderness
   An wisdom in the plan
O calm an storm, o flood an ebb;
   For aathing there's a reason.
The ocean, like the fruitful earth,
   Has everything in season.
'A time to plant and a time to reap'
   Suits fairmin to the letter;
'A time to get and a time to lose'
   Would fit the fishin better.

A year or twaa, my bonny loon,
   An then ye'll be a man,
Weel worth a place in ony crew,
   An fit to turn your han
To ony job yer trade requires
   Wi needle or wi knife;

As gweed, ye'll think, as plenty that's
　　Been at it aa their life.
In time o want — an come it will,
　　Ye'll think the skipper's feel;
Ye'd mak a better job yersel
　　Could ee but get the wheel.

Gin ee be spared an weel, my loon,
　　Ye'll get the chance anaa.
In your domain ye'll be the king —
　　Ye'll hae the thocht o't aa!
Is't north or sooth, is't aff or on?
　　Is't line or drift or seine?
Ye'll hum an hae an claw yer pow
　　But answer maun be gien.
An gin ye're aftener richt than wrang
　　Ye'll be a lucky man,
But richt or wrang aye keep in mind
　　Ye've men's lives in yer han.

Ye ken yersel sun moon an star
　　Are seldom seen thegither.
An so it is wi shots o fish,
　　Gweed prices, bonny wither.
There's aye a somethin wantin, loon,
　　Ye'll seldom get the three,
An mony a time ye'll tell yersel
　　That een o them wid dee.
'A time to plant and a time to reap'
　　Suits fairmin to the letter;
'A time to get and a time to lose'
　　Would fit the fishin better.

Ye're young an strong, ye're quick an keen;
　　Nae doot ye'll tak yer share.
I dinna think ye'll be a feel
　　That wither disna scare.
'Gainst wind an wave, the biggest boat's
　　A verra smaa defence.
A lot that looks like iron nerves
　　Is jist the want o sense.
But common sense wi patience mixed
　　Will help ye guide the wheel.
I think, come time ye'll learn them baith,
　　Gweed-nicht. I wish ye weel.

Gale Warning

Hear the oft repeated tale —
  'Fresh-to-strong soon reaching gale,
Wintry showers of sleet and hail
  Spreading from the west.'
Ragged clouds of sombre grey,
  Mourners of the dying day,
Ride the winds that tear the spray
  From each snarling crest.

Darkness falls, the wild sky clears,
  Crystal bright each star appears,
While the Merry Dancers' spears
  Cleave the bitter north.
Now the banshee sea-wind raves
  O'er her host of maddened slaves;
She, the mistress of the waves,
  Drives her minions forth.

See, from out the eerie night,
  Roaring demons plumed in white
Hurl their weight with cruel spite,
  O'er the weather rail,
Seeking in their wrath to deal
  Blows that make our stout bark reel,
Tortured sore from truck to keel
  'Neath their awful flail.

While the slow hours onward creep,
  Weary eyes their vigil keep.
Aching limbs that long for sleep,
  Peace nor respite find.
Hearts that fear can seldom move
  Hope, with breaking day, to prove —
'Even tho the earth remove
  Providence is kind.'

The Back o Sunday

Cold and clear the starlight,
  Bitter keen the breeze,
Chasing midnight shadows
  On the shrouded quays.
Silently the fishers
  Come from far and near,
Murmured words of greeting,
  Orders low yet clear.

Click of wheel-house switches,
  See the side-lights glow,
Ruby-red and emerald
  On the frosted snow.
Splash of ropes in water,
  Stamp of snow-soled feet,
Swirling of propellers,
  Diesel's steady beat.

Mast-head lights a-gleaming;
  Single line ahead;
Spreading out a little
  Once they clear the Head.
Deep and dark the silence,
  Now that they are gone.
Eastward on the waters —
  Eastward to the dawn.

Stormy Bank

I'm tired an weary, lookin
At the coiler-spoots gaan roon,
Fae brak o sky till gloamin brings release.
The water's smaa, the tide's aa richt,
The sun's jist beatin doon,
An yet I canna get a meenit's peace.

As seen as it comes denner time,
An there's a chance, at last,
To satisfy the hungry inner man,
As sure as daith the cry gets up
'Ho-ro now lads, she's fast!'
So it's up on deck again as quick's ye can.

It's been the same for twaa-three days
Baith in the deep an shaul;
A satchel full o dogs at ilka drag.
An should we miss the dogs an huds,
An get a clear haul,
It's ten to one we'd get a lockit bag.

There's shoutin on the wireless
That wid deeve yer verra heid,
Fae them that canna get their nets to come.
There's plenty information gien
Fin folk's nae comin speed,
But them that's gettin on are singin dumb.

I hear the drifters sayin
That there's herrin in the Minch,
An heavy shots in Kyle an Stornowaa.
But still, afore we got oor nets
An altered aa the winch
I'm certain sure the brutes wid be awaa.

It's fine to hae the skipper's job
If luck signs on as mate,
For then ye're caa'd an eident, clivver chiel.
But should 'at mate desert ye, weel,
The job's nae jist sae great,
For then ye're caa'd an eident eeseless feel.

56

Hech aye! I'll hae to stick it
Wi the greet within my throat;
They say the road's gey lang that disna bend.
It's time there wis a turnin,
But there's nae appearance o't,
An I wish this weary trip wis at an end.

To a 'Burnie'

There's a bit o the 'Burnie' aboot ye,
A something I canna weel name,
  It's nae verra gweed,
  But it rins in yer bleed;
So I'm thinkin ye're hardly to blame.

Ye're jist like the lave in appearance,
Tho that's nae a terrible faat.
  But the things that ye've seen
  Maun get hose, aye! an sheen;
An yer yarns needs a grainie o saat.

It seems to the truth ye're a stranger —
I'm gyaan b' the binders ye tell;
  But it's aa richt wi me,
  Tho ye come wi a lee,
For I'm mair than half-Burnie masel.

Note: 'Burnies' were the natives of Burnhaven who had a great reputation for spinning yarns, a talent which has seemingly been inherited by their descendants.

Drifting

Grey October,
  Motion rinnin high;
Full moon bleezin,
  Thro a raggit sky;
Nord-east win —
  An plinty o't at that —
Drifters seekin Yarmooth
  Thro the Cockle Gat;
Cargie-load for Yarmooth
  Thro the Cockle Gat.

Sou-wast stiffener
  Fusslin doon the Minch;
Drifters punchin,
  Fechtin ivvery inch;
Caal bleak winter,
  Mountains fite wi snaa;
Wheelhoose windas broken,
  Mizzens blaan awaa;
Drifters seekin shelter
  In canny Stornowaa.

Springtime, line time,
  Trees in bonny leaf;
Smoke trails on the Viking,
  Drifters on the Reef.
East side, wast side,
  Seekin sair for bait;
Haulin, tyauvin,
  Halibut an skate.
'Market's teen a drap,
  Ye're jist a day ower late.'

Lang days, fine days,
  Herrin time awyte,
Time for the farlin
  The futtle an the cwite.
Drifters seekin,
  Fog, or rain, or shine.
Surface veins
  O th' oceans' silver mine.
Drifters seekin herrin
  Fae the Shetlan's to the Tyne.

Still grey gloamin
    Thocht o days lang seen;
Weel kent picters
    Clear on memory's screen.
Lean times, gweed times,
    Coorse an bonny days;
Noo the final chapter
    Opens to the gaze.
Drifters lyin broken
    On the silent braes.

Kirsty's Dother

I'm scunnert sair at jewelry an fancy figurines —
The things that were in vogue yestreen are oot o date the day.
I've presses full o bonny sheets an kists o silver speens,
But oh, to hae a something that my neeper disna hae!

My pearls are growin dirty so I'll dabble them in wine,
Wi aa my bonny trinketies, my diamond rings anaa;
There's naething like a vintage port to gar the thingies shine
But my neeper, bein better aff, can jist throw hers awaa.

I hear she's changed her car again; the glaiss wis growin dull,
The colour o the velvet seats jist didna match her sheen.
It's time we had a change oorsels, I see the ashtray's full
An the cover on the driver's seat! It's nae jist ower clean!

It disna maitter fit I dee, she keeps a step aheid;
I gain a fitt, she steals a yard, 'twid gar a buddy greet,
The gear I hae's as gweed as hers; Aye! ivvery bit as gweed —
But fit's the eese o bonny gear faar ithers canna see't?

I'll buy a silver dirler an pit rubies roon the brim,
Syne stick it on the gate post — Aye! I'll dee't this verra day!
I ken my man'll hae a fit, but och! to pot wi him,
For I maun hae a something that my neeper disna hae!

The Fifty-Footer's Prayer

Lord, fin the gales o winter blaa
    An sough across the grumlie sea,
There's fyles I gie my pow a claa
    An winner fit's to come o me.
The glaiss is doon at sudden daith,
    The sky's fair hingin doon wi drift,
An tho I'm sweir to leave my hame
    It seems I'll hae to mak a shift.

I ken there's fish at ninety mile,
    But Lord, that's ower far awaa.
They're little eese to me oot there;
    Ye ken my boatie's ower smaa.
Lord, shift them to the Buchan Deep
    Or nearer, if it suit Your will,
An should they reach the Castle Hard,
    Lord, that wid be far better still.

I ken an antrin codlin wags
    Its tail along Belhelvie Beach,
But since by law I shouldna poach
    Ye've sent them jist beyond my reach.
They're that far in, the fairmer folk
    Could catch them wi a horse an gig.
They're little eese to me in there;
    Ye ken my boatie's ower big.

O shift them aff a bittie, Lord,
    But keep them far the boddim's saft,
An then I'll get a box or twaa
    In waters that'll suit my craft.
But dinna send them ower thick —
    It widna dee to hae them chaip —
As lang's Ye keep the water smaa
    I'll be content wi jist a scrape.

Ye ken I'm nae yon kind o chiel
    That likes things aa his ain wye;
I'm only thinkin oot a plan
    That You may aa my need supply.

An fit aboot the sattle-up?
   I think we'll pairt like ither men:
For You a bittie o the praise,
   For me the shinin cash! Amen.

Medicinal Purposes

'Daavit! Faar's yon bonny bottlie
That we bocht in Peterheid
Jist in case some caal coorse mornin
Een o's took a sair heid?

Mind ye said ye'd keep it siccar
Neth yer pilla oot o sicht,
Jist for fear some drunken decky
Took a swig o't thro the nicht?

Daavit man, wi caal I'm shakkin,
Yet I'm in a bog o swyte!
Want o foosion in my legs
Wid gar me fear I'll seen faa clyte!

Daavit! Hear my belly rummlin;
Sure as daith I'm richt nae-weel.
Could I only sniff the cork
A hantle better I wid feel!

Daavit! Dinna lie there sleepin;
Rise an gie's a drappie noo
For I see the Longstone flashin
Clear upon the starboard boo.'

'Jock! I dinna like to tell ye!
Jock, my loon, the bottlie's teem,
For I took a fearsome hoast
Fin Buchan Ness wis close abeam!'

Note: Peterhead to Longstone Light — 113 miles. Peterhead to Buchan Ness — 1½ miles.

The Incomer

Sandy Todd wis the biggest chiel
  That ivver trod this earth;
He wis come o a rovin tinkie tribe
  Fae the foreign side o Perth.
He wis broad in the beam like a garage door,
  An I'm sure he wis nine fit three
The day he cam North for a job at the ile
  An to bide neist door to me.

Sandy Todd wis the strongest man
  I'd ivver seen in my life
An the things he could dee wi's great muckle hans
  Fair mesmerised the wife.
He could fire a steen as far as the meen,
  He could haaver a tree in twaa,
An to cairry coal a ton at a time
  Wis jist nae bother avaa.
He could lift a faddom o railway line
  An bend it ower his knee;
Noo the wife thinks she wis thrown awaa
  Fin she mairried a dreep like me.

Sandy Todd wis the finest cook
  That ever steered a pot.
He could taikle a ten course jamboree
  An master-mind the lot.
His beef-steak pies won a special prize
  This year at the Turra Show,
Fin a certain firm sent a spy to steal
  The secrets o his dough.
But he widna stoop to tattie soup
  Or stovers or potted heid,
For that wis grub ye could get in a pub
  Wi folk o a lesser breed.
His damson tart wis a work o art
  That thoosans cam to see;
Noo the wife thinks she's been thrown awaa
  On an eesless lump like me.

Sandy Todd wis the smairtest chiel
    That ever yet drew braith;
He could ficher wi ony mortal thing
    Fae marzipan to claith.
He could sort a slate, or hing a gate,
    Or alter a slidin door;
He carved a statue o Robbie Burns
    Fae wid washen up on the shore.
There wisna a job in aa this earth
    That Sandy couldna dee;
Noo the wife thinks she's been thrown awaa
    On a warriedrag like me.

Sandy Todd wis the best kent chiel
    This toon has ivver seen;
He wis fine acquaint wi the Prince o Wales,
    An 'Liz' wis his name for the Queen.
He expressed the hope he would meet the Pope
    Again, when he went to Rome,
An he tellt me his country residence
    Wis as big as the Parish Home.
He collieshangied wi Arab sheiks
    An ithers o high degree;
Noo the wife jist disna ken fit wye
    She bides wi the likes o me.

But there's been a change this day or twaa;
    A change, I think, for the better.
I'm expectin the bobbies doon the nicht
    Wi a special kind o letter.
For noo it's ME that's the smairtest chiel
    That ivver yet wis born:
I stuck a knife in Sandy Todd
    An he's beeryin the morn.

Note: Sandy Todd's real name will be divulged when his next-of-kin have been informed.

The Kistie o Gold

The year that Cripple Kirsty deet
There cam a fearsome breeze —
South-east, near han a month it blew;
Ye nivver saw sic seas.
The heid o Buchanhaven pier
Wis oot o sicht for days,
An froth lay foamin five fit deep
Along the Geddle Braes.
The sheep in Johnny Mattha's parks
Wis maistly smored wi snaa;
Syne on the fourteenth day o Mairch,
The wither eased awaa.

Neist mornin, twaa fine strappin chiels
Set oot alang the san,
To see fit micht be lyin there
Fae Providence's han;
For Famine's braith wis on the peen
An Want wis at the door,
Aye chappin lood — Aye! looder
Than he'd ivver deen afore.
They wydit ower the water-mou
Syne strode along the san;
The bits o broken timmer there
The only sign o man.
Like Crusoe in a byegone day
They viewed a desert beach,
Wi tangle piled on tangle heap
As far as sicht could reach.
Abeen their heids the taariks skirled,
Their ilka note a greet,
An aa the time the surly sea
Wis sweelin roon their feet.
They rypit ilka hole an bore
Aboot Craigewan's braes,
Faar bairnies gaither kysies
On the bonny simmer days;
But naething there save orra stuff
Amang the washen steens —
A box or twaa, a broken oar
An twaa-three bits o beens
That had been in some distant day

The timmers o a whale;
A figure-heid, a shivered spar,
A strip o tattered sail.

So north a bit, an further,
An along by Jenny's Burn,
An ilka heap o raivelt waar
Got aye an overturn
For, twaa-three days afore, a ship
Had struck on Scotston Heid,
A mile or twaa or fully mair
Richt north fae Peterheid.
Her crew, a puckle foreigners
Fae sooth o Aiberdeen,
Had perished in the fearfu gale
For neen wis ivver seen.
But there on Scotston's rocky shore
An Kirkton's bonny sans
Lay spread the bounty fae the wreck.
Twaa pair o willin hans
Began to pick an chyse an lay
Aside the best o't aa —
The legs o ham, the casks o rum,
An linen fite as snaa;
A fortin, aye a fortin scattered
There amon the rocks,
An then, half happit wi the waar,
They spied a bonny box!
A half a faddom lang it wis
An made o foreign wid,
Wi lock an hinges made o brass
An carvin on the lid.

They left the ham, they left the rum.
(On ae cask had they yokit.)
They took the bonny widden kist
An wi a steen they broke it.
Then twaa fine chiels, sair teen aback,
Stood petrified wi shock,
For there afore their verra een,
Their poverty to mock,
A proper pirate's moggan lay
To human view laid bare:
A mint o bonny sovereigns,
Twaa hunner-wecht an mair.

65

Says Daavit, fin his braith cam back,
'We'd better leave the ham,
An surely ae gweed cask wid dee
To gie's an antrin dram.
But this gryte heap o siller's
In a kist athoot a name,
So we'll haaver't throwe the middle
Could we eence but get it hame!'
Says Jock, 'To cairry't ower the san
Wid rax a buddy's hairt.
We'd better tak it to the road
An pit it on a cairt.
Still, Mains is sure to winner
If we cairry't throwe his park
So, it micht be best to plunk it
An come back for't fin it's dark!'

'Na, na!' says Daavit, 'nivver een!
At dark I'll nae be here,
For darkness brings the ghosties oot
Wi ither things that's queer!
On nichts as dark's yer oxter pooch
They roam the bents an howes.
I've heard the fearsome skirls they gie,
An Jock! they're jist nae mowse!
We'll tak the kistie up the brae
An beery't oot o sicht,
Syne come for't wi John Baird's cairt
As seen as it grows licht!'

They ruggit it an tuggit it
An got it up the brae;
They happit it an clappit it
An there the kistie lay
Wi twaa-three faal o knotted girss
To mark the secret spot,
An twaa fine hams gid hame instead
To fill the hungry pot.
At brak o sky they yokit,
An altho they rakit sair
The nestie had been hairried
An the kistie wisna there.
'Twis efter dark o'clock afore
Their weemin heard them come,
The cairtie load wi wobs o claith,

An hams, an casks o rum.
The pairtin took a fylie, syne
The baith o them gid hame,
But efter that their freenliness
Wis nivver jist the same.

Noo tell me this, if tell ye can —
Tho tell ye maybe winna —
Fit wye has Daavit's folk been blest
Fin Jock's peer folk jist hinna?
Ye ken that Daavit's wife wis cleyed
In silks an bonny tartans
Fin Jock's peer lass wis wearin rags
An dinin high on partans.
As time gid bye, to Daavit cam
Baith boats an gear an aa,
Tho Jock, peer sowl, wis gled to tak
A job to shuffle snaa.
An so its been doon throwe the years —
Atween the generations
There grows a gulf aye wider, like
The difference in their stations.
The Scriptur says, 'To him that hath
It shall again be given.'
Faa got the kist? Ye'd like to ken?
Ye micht be tellt in Heaven!

Fisher Blue

Jock an Daavit bocht a shippie,
Changed her name to *Mary Jane*;
Spent a heap o hard-won siller
Jist to rig her oot again.
Jimmy Anderson the tinsmith
Sowdered ivvery broken licht,
Keithie Hutton shued the mizzen,
Sidney made the compass richt.
Alan Cardno, supervisor
Wi the firm o Milne and Robb,
Trotted up an doon the jetty
Like a scout on bob-a-job.

Souter Davidson did the pintin,
Ilka deck-board fisher blue;
Geordie Cruickshank did the caulkin,
Swore that he could see richt through.
Kysie sorted up the caipsan,
Sticker lined the plummer-block;
Geordie Grant cleaned oot the biler,
Saat an scale as hard as rock!

'Noo!' says Daavit, 'I'll be skipper!
I'm the man wi aa the thocht.'
'Fine!' says Jock, 'Then I'll be driver
On this gallant craft we've bocht.'
Sic a fancy celebration
Fin the trial trip wis made;
Bobby Taitie sent a hurley
Load wi pies an lemonade.

Fourteen wiks athoot a docket,
Onward sailed the *Mary Jane* —
Daavit took the herrin fivver,
Jock jist swore an swore again —
'Daavit man ye're waar than eeseless!
Can ye nae dee naething richt?
Ither folk can mak a livin,
Yet in debt we're oot o sicht!
Ticket nivver made a skipper,
Sookin bairn could furl a wheel,
Pit her in amon the herrin
Daavit, or we'll aa ging feel!'

68

'Richt,' says Daavit, 'you that's clivver
Come an tak a spell up here.
Brains I dinna hae for skipper?
Weel, I'll dee for engineer,
Ficherin wi a five-eight spanner,
Dichtin wi a greasy cloot;
Ony feel could fire a biler,
Shovel't on an rake it oot!
Sweat-rag nivver made a driver,
Skill ye need to save the coal,
So my lad we'll jist change places,
I've heen mair than I can thole!'

See her swingin roon the jetty,
Ilka deck-board fisher blue,
Jock aye tittin at the fussle,
Tootin like a tooteroo:
Daavit peepin thro the skylicht;
Aa the weemin folk wis doon,
Bonny dressed, to see the heroes
Settin oot for Yarmooth toon.

Fylie efter, Daavit's skirlin,
'Canna see a thing for steam!
Biler's burstit! Launch the smaa-boat!
Jock, ye ken I canna sweem!'

Thro the clouds o steam an sorra
Comes the sad reply fae Jock —
'Daavit, nivver mind the smaa-boat!
Jump! we're on the Skerry Rock!'

The Philosopher

He wis aye at the Lazy Dyke,
An he kent ilka sowl in the toon.
Abreist o the lamp-post he stood,
An the grun at his feet wis aye broon
Wi the bree that he scattered abroad
Fae the chaw that he likit sae weel.
Some say he wis idle an feel.

Feel? Na! nae feel.

'A berth?' he wid say, 'Man, I'd ging,
But the wife's teen a dose o the flu.
It's aye been the dream o my life
To sail wi a skipper like you.
But skipper, ye ken hoo it is —
Fin the wife's feelin nae verra weel
Ye're tied like a slave til a wheel.
So skipper, I canna weel ging.
Nae eyvnoo!'

Feel? Na! Nae feel.

He wis aye at the Lazy Dyke —
To strangers the saat o the sea,
Wi the sang o the win on his tongue
An the glint o the wave in his ee.
An mony's the dram that he got
In the leethe o the lees he could shiel.

Feel? Na! nae feel.

'A cook?' he wid say, 'Man, I'd ging,
But the bairn's teen the kink-hoast eyvnoo.
It's aye been the dream o my life
To cook for a skipper like you.
But skipper, ye ken hoo it is —
Fin a bairn has her braith at her mou
Ye're tied like a horse til a ploo.
So skipper, I canna weel ging.
Nae eyvnoo!

Feel? Na! nae feel.

70

I hear that he's worn awaa
An we'll see him nae mair at the shore.
Ye can think fit ye like o the chiel
But ye miss an aal creel fae the door!
An faa div we hae for his place
At the dyke that he likit sae weel?

A feel? Na! nae a feel.

'A Mate?' he wid say, 'Man, I'd ging,
But I've nae need o siller eyvnoo.
The last that I got's hardly deen,
An to sail wi a skipper like you
Wid mean I'd hae mair than I need.
An skipper, ye ken hoo it is —
Fin a buddy has mair than they need
It's likely to ging to their heid.
So skipper, I canna weel ging.
Nae eyvnoo!'

Faa said he wis feel?

Potential

Fain would I be a tower of strength,
A spreading oak, a friend in need.
And oh, when life is at its length,
To gain the prize — 'Well done indeed!'
Fain would I leave a shining scroll
The Lord might with some pleasure scan,
That men might read from pole to pole
And say, 'Behold! there was a Man!'

But wishing will not make it so
If, while a traveller in Time,
Content with dross, with sights too low,
I see the Mount and will not climb.
And, should I miss the Promised Land,
'Twould never be excuse enough
To say, 'Alas! the Potter's hand
Was working with poor shoddy stuff!'

71

Reflections

Mahogany and cedar
Are stuff of a bye-gone day.
With the paraffin lamp and the mizzen sail
They have gently passed away.
Now laminates and plastics reign
In the fisher's cabin home,
And the cold white gleam from the deck-head light
Meets the cold clear glint of chrome.

But the picture of wild white horses
That's framed in the galley door
On a surly winter morning
Is the same as it was of yore.

Technology and science
Have claimed the bridge for their own.
Now the auto-pilot takes command
Where the helmsman ruled alone;
Where the paper scrolls and the flashing lights
In the instruments on view
Bewilder a seaman of former years
Like a scene from Doctor Who.

But the seas still rise to an awesome height
When the ranging gales blow shrill,
And a faith in things that were made by men
Can ne'er take the place of skill.

The iron steeds in their stable
Have tripled their mighty power,
And the raging thirst in their white-hot throats
Would an ocean of oil devour.
It would seem, alas, as the years roll on
And the pages of time unfold,
That the thirst for power is a terrible twin
To the terrible thirst for gold.

But the power of the sea is a matchless power
That throttle nor bridle can tame,
And it laughs at the iron horses' breath
As the torrent laughs at a flame.

72

'Ye are old,' cries youth in anger,
'Ye know not the present time!
Your days are now in the yellow leaf
And will soon be white with rime!
But we have our years before us,
We play on a better pitch.
The tools and the will to win are ours,
In the strength of our youth we are rich!'

We are old! Who knows it better?
But let this at least be said:
That once we were young, and strong, and poor,
And 'twas seldom we counted our dead.

Hielan Briggie

It's a briggie ower a ditch, an that's jist aa.
A shortcut fae the pier to the hotel.
There's a railin on baith sides, for fear ye faa,
But I'm thinkin some kind wizard's cast a spell,
For it's nae a timmer briggie, it's a coach for Fairyland,
A larry, load wi Jaffa Cakes, a ship to Samarkand.
It's a shoppie, it's a hoosie that has aathing but a fridge;
A special run to Scourie or the bus to Bonar Bridge.
It's a van like Postman Pat's, wi sweet Fancy for its load.
Man, I leave things to the driver, for she fairly kens the road!

'Ye wis born ower seen!' they tell me, 'Mair than fifty ear ower seen.
Had ye come a lifetime later — Man, faa kens fit micht ha been?'
But it's deil the word I'm hearin — I'm at Cinderella's Ball,
On a shakkin Hielan Briggie — wi my fower-ear-aal.

Not to the Swift

Jock an Daavit played thegither
  On the rocky Buchan braes;
Focht an greed wi een anither
  Aa their happy childhood days.
Shared their humble bits o treasures
  Chance aboot, for friendship's sake;
Shared their simple hamely pleasures,
  Pleased to see an antrin maik.

Schooldays cam wi books an learnin;
  Readin, spellin, three times three;
Jock an Daavit chafin, yearnin
  Fae their prison to be free.
Scoltit for their careless writin,
  Keepit in for bein late;
Spent the weary time o wytin
  Drawin shippies on a slate.

Schooldays deen, they left thegither;
  Sang like linties to be free,
Left ae prison for anither,
  Noo their jiler wis the sea.
'Work aa nicht, my willin nippers!
  Sleep the time o steamin aff,
Dream o days fan ye'll be skippers;
  Royal dreams on beds o caff!'

O the joy o distant places,
  Ports they'd nivver seen afore.
Like the desert's green oasis
  Sweet the antrin nicht ashore.
Yarmooth lichts shone clearer, rarer,
  Wi the glamour o the name,
An the stranger lass seemed fairer
  Than the fisher quine at hame.

Lily waters, ragglish wither,
　　Wintry blast or simmer haze,
Jock an Daavit vrocht thegither,
　　Shipmates, aa their decky days.
Till the path they trod divided
　　Into twaa, as paths aye will,
An maturer years decided
　　Each should clim his ain hill.

Pairted? Aye, but nivver striven;
　　Skippers wi a boat apiece.
Jock wis pleased to get a livin;
　　Daavit socht the golden fleece
Where the distant fields loomed greener
　　Wi the glamour o the name.
Jock, peer, canny sowl wid seener
　　Puddle oot an in at hame.

Nivver aff the sea wis Daavit,
　　Gross the aim an fame the goad,
Sleepin wore his boots an graavit,
　　Sabbath days were in his road.
Jock could steal an oor for leesure
　　On the sunny bowlin-green.
Or to walk in sweetest pleesure
　　Up the waterside wi Jean.

On the scroll o fishin glory
　　Daavit's name's abeen them aa.
Seldom in the hale lang story
　　Will ye hear o Jock avaa.
Thus 'twid seem that aa thegither
　　Daavit cam the better speed.
Yet this ae thing gars me swither —
　　Jock's aye livin, Daavit's deid.

Bird of Passage

I met the perfect peach in Peel
The year that first I sailed the sea;
My glaikit hairt was licht an feel
But still the lassie likit me.
She whispered in her stranger tongue,
She twined her fingers in my hair,
An yet, fin simmer's sang wis sung,
I said fareweel — an didna care.

I kent a bonny Irish lass
When I was young an runnin free,
In County Down, in old Ardglass;
An strange to tell, she likit me.
Her lauch wis like a silver chime,
Her brogue wis soft as simmer air,
Yet, come the tail o herrin time,
I said fareweel — an didna care.

I kent a lass in Pittenweem
Wi starshine glancin in her ee;
I've yet to meet a fairer deem
An strange to tell, she likit me.
'Twis sweet to dally on the braes,
Oor braith like smoke in frosty air,
Yet, come the spring wi safter days,
I said fareweel — an didna care.

I kent a lass in Stornoway
An strange to tell, she likit me.
Her Gaelic lilt wis like a lay
That nymphs micht sing in Arcady.
She wis a princess ivvery inch,
This caileag wi the copper hair;
Yet, fin the scattan left the Minch,
I said fareweel — an didna care.

I met a fisher quine at hame,
A lass I'd kent since she was three;
But faith, she wisna jist the same
For scarcely would she look at me!

Noo that's aa bye — we've spliced richt weel
An coorted thirty year an mair,
But should she ever say fareweel,
Wi clippit wing I'd greet — an care.

The Win in 'is Face

Some folk get the win in their face
    Aa their mortal days,
Fine div they ken the desert place
    Wi its dreich an craggy braes.
Theirs is the world o trauchlin thro;
    Theirs is a dour grey sky,
For the sunny spell an the gentle dew
    Seem aye to pass them by.

Some folk get the win at their backs;
    Theirs is a lichtsome birn,
Wi nivver a flaw in the fine-spun flax
    They draw fae the birlin pirn.
Theirs is the world o fill-an-fess-ben,
    Theirs is a bricht blue sky,
For the caal roch shooer that weets ither men
    Seems aye to leave them dry.

Some can smile in their weary lot
    Altho the fecht be sair;
Some hae aye the greet in their throat
    Tho they've neither cark nor care.
Keep ee the chiel fae the sheltered place
    Wi's hert as caal as a steen;
I'll tak the lad wi the win in 'is face
    An I'll hae a better freen.

The Pairtin

Faa'll get the hoose noo
    Fin Baabie's worn awaa?
It may be gweed an bonny
    But it canna pairt in three.
The aalest quine's a quaet lass,
    She'll mak nae sough avaa,
But th' ither twaa's baith tartars,
    An I'm sure they winna gree.

An fit aboot the siller?
    Wid there be a puckly yet?
D'ye think that Baabie kept it
    In a moggan oot o sicht?
Yon poun or twaa that Dodie made
    Fin he wis on 'is fit,
The aal folk fairly hained it
    But the quines'll gie't the dicht.

An fit aboot the organ
    She thocht sae muckle o?
A source o joy an pleesure yon
    For mony a year an day.
Ye may be sure the bleed an hair
    'll flee like caff; altho
The three o them has room for't
    There's jist twaa o them can play.

An faa'll get the furnitur
    An aa yon bonny gear?
The finery an grandeur
    That wid rig a dizzen queens?
Yon quines'll greet an cairry on,
    An hud a sair maneer
Till peer aal Baabie's happit; syne
    They'll pairt her verra speens.

Noo fit aboot the youngest quine?
    She's nivver teen a man;
That's hardly to be winnert at
    For plainer couldna be.

But she wis aye the favourite,
   Her share wid keep me gaan,
So I'll jist hing on a fylie
   An I'll see if she'll tak me.

Hame Comfort

A wife that I ken has a bonny Room,
   Wi a fleer like polished glaiss.
An the sun, peepin in thro the spotless screens,
   Gets blint wi the bleeze o braiss.

There's this an there's that o the latest style,
   An the dearest o fancy suites.
An could ye but tramp on the basses there,
   I'm sure ye wid sink to the queets.

There's nivver a mark o stue in the place,
   For it's ower weel cleaned an dichtit.
An the grate! Aswarn it wid heat a kirk —
   If the fire wis ivver lichtit.

Her man has a seat that's as hard's a steen
   In the barfit kitchen en.
He kens there's a far better cheer in the Room,
   But he kens he daarna ging ben.

So he sits in the draucht wi a dreep at 'is nose,
   An a hackin hoast at 'is breist,
An he growls as he glowers at the skimpit fire —
   'It's a fittit carpet neist!'

But he shouldna girn, for he ocht to ken,
   If he'd ony sense in his heid,
That he'll get a chance o the Room some day —
   Fin he's caal an stiff an deid.

Note: I'm led to believe there is quite a lot of this kind of Home Comfort in the country places too.

Dan's Dream

Ae nicht we shot a fleet o lines
  Across the Buchan Deep,
Syne set the watch an turned in
  To hae a fylie's sleep.

Oor skipper's name wis Rascal Dan —
  He weel deserved the name;
But, noo I come to think upon't,
  The crew wis aa the same.

At three o'clock we turned oot
  An took a mou'fa tay,
Says Rascal Dan: 'I've dreamt a dream,
  Ye'll get a shot the day!'

We didna tak 'im on avaa;
  Ye'll maybe think that queer,
But Dan, as far as we could tell,
  Wis this world's biggest leear.

We started haulin early on,
  But nae a fish wis gotten.
Says Dan: 'B'jings that's affa queer,
  The bait wis surely rotten.'

Aff-takin words were flung at Dan;
  He didna care a bit,
But said: 'Fit's aa the noise aboot?
  The lines are nae hauled yet.'

The hinmist line wis nearly hauled,
  We wis gey near the dhan,
Fin aa at eence the cry got up —
  'Boys, come an gie's a han!'

We ran wi clips an lowrie hooks,
  To see fit wis adee:
It wis the biggest roker skate
  That ivver swam the sea.

'Twis dark o'clock afore we got
  Her snoot in ower the rail,
An tho we had a searchlicht, boys,
  We couldna see her tail.

Cries Rascal Dan: 'Boys, tak a turn!
  Ye'll dee nae mair the nicht.'
We gied her half a coil o rope
  An turned in till daylicht.

At brak o sky we tried again
  But this time wi the winch.
We got her snoot half up the mast
  But not anither inch.

We workit hard, but aa in vain,
  Till we wis fair bate,
But Dan jist widna pack it in
  For ony dirty skate.

Ye'd scarce believe that sic a fish
  Wis ivver seen by man:
Her tail, tho sixty fathoms doon,
  Wis steerin up the san.

We got the tow-rope roon her snoot
  An gied the shippie jip;
The skate cam trailin close astarn
  As big's a battleship.

We couldna mak much speed, ye ken,
  The strain wis something cruel;
We took 'at lang to come ashore
  We burnt near aa wir fuel.

She wis a bonny fish, nae doot,
  The biggest seen for years —
Man, fin we tried to rin the Bey,
  She stuck atween the piers.

The tow-rope broke, an doon she gid,
  Oor labour wis in vain;
So peer aal Rascal Dan'll hae
  To dream a dream again.

81

Song for a Winter's Night

'Tylie Tylie Tartan
Gid up the lum fartin.
Twinty needles in his dock
An couldna shue a garten.'

Thus we sang in a golden age
When school was a treat in store;
When the world wis the size o a chingle beach
In the hert o a granite shore.
Faar mussel shaals an herrin corks
Cast up by the bounteous sea
Were a magic carpet of pure delight
For barfit bairns like me.

'Ten o'clock the gas goes out.
I can stay no longer,
For if I do Mama will say,
"You've been playing with the boys out yonder".'

Thus sang the quines in a golden age
When school was a joy indeed;
When the world had raxed fae the water-mou
Richt sooth to Sautusheid —
A langer shore wi a richer store
O ferlies fresh fae the sea;
Flotsam an jetsam fae Treasure Isle
For barfit bairns like me.

'There wis a ship gid roon the coast
An ilka sowl on her wis lost
Barrin the monkey climmt the most
An the Boddamers hangit the monkey-o.'

Thus we sang in the golden age
When school was a dreary chore;
When we'd traivel half a dizzen mile
To see a ship ashore.
A trawler, a steamer, a sailin-ship —
Fair game for the fog-bound sea,
An their names were blazoned for evermore
In the minds o loons like me.

'Tiptoe from your pillow
To the shadow of a willow tree
Come tiptoe thro the tulips with me.'

Thus sang the quines in the herrin yards
Fae Lerwick to Yarmooth's Denes;
Sangs o the sweet exotic love
O the Technicolor screens.
But their desert sheiks wore hair-back briks
An ganjies o navy blue —
Their dashing beaus an their Romeos
The lads in a drifter's crew.

'Somewhere the sun is shining,
Somewhere the songbirds dwell.
Cease then thy sad repining,
God lives and all is well.'

Thus we sang as we scoured the deep
Like our fathers did afore;
Our life-mates mended the broken nets
An our bairnies played on the shore.
It wis haul-an-shak wi a willin back —
Rare life for the strong an free;
Yet we spent our years as a tale that is told,
Bond-slaves to the hertless sea.

They tell me this is the golden age
Fin we've neither cark nor care,
For the welfare state'll fill our plate
Wi a mealick or twaa to spare.
But we canna sing aboot ony thing
Save the days that eesed to be,
For we're flotsam an jetsam wi silver hair
Left high an dry by the sea.

If it's fit to be oot we step aboot
Wi the speed o a cripple partan,
Yet oor herts would fain be singin again
On the beach — wi Tylie Tartan.

Lines from a Poacher to an Informer

They tell me, freen, ye've priced a steen
    Wi a bonny marble border;
Ye've trailed yon hidden stockin oot
    An plunkit doon yer order
Wi strict instructions thus to write
    The epitaph sae fine:
'Here lies a simple, trustin chiel
    Who crossed the three-mile line.'

The name ye'd carve across the base
    In letters clear an deep
Belangs t' a chiel I ken richt weel,
    A hairmless, wandering sheep.
He crossed a line an broke the law.
    But micht I be as bold
As say he has a bigger faut:
    He's fae a different fold.

I ken ye'd like to hae yer steen
    Firm plantit ower his heid;
But still he'd like ye — if ye can —
    To wyte until he's deid.
He canna sleep, he canna ait,
    Wi thocht his hert's gey weichty
Aboot the interest that ye'll loss
    Gin he should live till eichty.

I ken he'd like some future day
    To meet ye up in heaven;
To find the thing he did below
    Forgotten an forgiven;
To see ye busy at yer job
    In the leethe o a pearly gable,
There giein ilka man his place
    An ilka cod a label.

Aspiration

Let not the prospect of reward
  My sole incentive be,
When, at the urging of Thy call,
I leave the sheltered harbour wall
  To venture on Life's sea.

Let not the blinding mists of self
  The way ahead obscure.
Help me to play a manly part;
Illumine Thou for me the chart,
  And keep my motives pure.

But let my sense of duty be
  A constant star to guide;
To keep me, Lord, come weal or woe,
Still mindful of the debt I owe
  To Thee the Crucified.

And, should the adverse storms of fate
  Assail with furious force,
Help me, dear Lord, to brave the gale,
To trim faith's torn and tattered sail
  And set anew my course.

Then if, with favouring breezes blest,
  Swift on that course I press,
Forbid, O Lord, that I should fly
Thy colours, heedless of the cry
  Of others in distress.

Till Heaven's peaks are clearly framed
  Against the setting sun,
Help me to toil with heart sincere
That I may worthy be to hear
  Thy precious words 'Well Done!'

The Sea is Yours

I have gazed too long on this barren scene,
  And my restless heart grows weary;
For I find the sea's broad heaving breast
  And its wide horizons dreary.
I would forfeit much to feel the touch
  Of moss on my burning cheek;
Could I lie at ease where the golden bees
  Their scented treasures seek.

I have felt the unbroken noontide heat
  From the blazing cloudless skies,
And the golden glare on the dappled sea
  Has tried my sleepless eyes.
Give me the shade of a leafy wood
  Where the ferns and bracken mingle,
And the quiet gleam of a clear trout stream
  In a bed of rich brown shingle.

I have watched the fulmar wheel and soar
  On tireless wing and strong;
But the birds that dwell mid the ocean swell
  Have never a note of song.
Give me a friend on a winding road,
  With a purple moor before us;
The flaming bloom of the golden broom
  And the song-bird's evening chorus.

I have seen the flaring North Sea dawn,
  And the glow of the splendid west
Like a stained glass window in the sky
  When the sleepy sun seeks rest.
Give me the softer, milder light
  Of a still September gloaming;
Thro a misted glen, 'neath a rugged ben
  I fain would go a-roaming.

I have felt the lash of the stinging spray
    And its bitter taste on my lips,
For my lot is cast with the vast array
    Who go down to the sea in ships;
But my heart would be where it might be free
    From the ocean's vaunted lures;
Give me the trees, the birds and bees —
    And all the sea is yours!

Generation Gap

My loon, I dinna ken yer name
But faith, I think I ken the face!
Ye've the swipe o a chiel I eesed to ken
When the world wis a finer, sweeter place.

Ye needna say faa yer father is,
Or whether or no he gings t' sea.
An tho I wis tellt faa yer mither wis,
'Twid mak nae odds to the likes o me!

Jist say, if ye can yer Grunny's name
Afore she ivver wis a bride;
An then, my loon I'll rype ye up,
For memory's door'll open wide.

The Rickin Lum

Jock cam oot til 'is gavle en
  An he leaned against the waa;
He liftit the snoot o's aal deen caip
  An he gied 'is pow a claa.
He lichtit 'is pipe wi a sook an a smack
  Ere he traivelt back an fore
The same aal wye that he'd deen for 'ears,
  Fae the hoose to the sheddie door.
The watch-keeper stars were bricht an clear
  Abeen in the frosty dark,
An the win's caal nose wisna slow to learn
  That Jock had a gey thin sark.
It wis five steps east, it wis five steps wast
  Wi a thocht aboot this an that,
An nivver a craitur to look near han
  But a meowlin, prowlin cat;
An nivver a soun but the sough o win
  An the girn o the wintry sea,
For the bairns that had played in the street aa nicht
  Were far sleepy bairns should be.

It wis five steps east, it wis five steps wast
  Wi a thocht aboot this an that,
Fin up fae the shore cam a weel-kent fit;
  'Twis 'is crony, aal Dod Watt,
A lang, thin chiel wi's neck weel rowed
  In a graavit sax fit lang,
An throwe the stumps o's broken teeth
  He wis fusslin an aal Scotch sang;
A tune that wis aal as the Heilan hulls
  Tho he couldna gie't a name.
He wis gey sair made at the twirly bits
  But he fusselt them jist the same.

'Sirss!' says he, fin he saw oor Jock
  At 'is traivlin up an doon,
'Ye're the only driftin sowl that I've seen
  This nicht in aa the toon!
Hiv ye nae a hame? Are ye short o coal
  That ye're bird alone oot here?
Ye'd be jist as warm if ye steed a fyle
  At the pint o the convick pier.'

'Man,' says Jock, 'I wis sittin fine
   In the cosy ingle-neuk,
Readin a bit, an singin a bit,
   An beatin an antrin heuk;
The dog wis streetched on the fender-steel
   Wi's sleepy heid on my feet,
An I thocht that life wi its ups an doons
   Could fyles be unco sweet;
Fin doon the lum cam a muckle flan,
   An it fullt the hoose wi rick,
An I hoastit sair, an I cowkit mair
   Like a first-ear loon that's sick.

My een wis waterin thick an fast
   An my nose wis full o sitt,
So I've jist come oot for a breath eyvnoo
   For the air in there's nae fit.'
'Sirss!' says Dod, 'that's a peety noo.'
   An he fell in step wi Jock,
But nivver a word did he believe
   For Jock's wis leein folk.
Since ivver they sailed the stormy sea
   Their cod had aye fower heids,
An the hens o them that wis fairmer folk
   Laid eggs wi twaa big reids.
It wis five steps east, it wis five steps wast
   Wi a word aboot this an that;
Jock wi the rick fleein ower 'is heid
   While Dod jist chowed an spat.

An ilka drag wis a double lift,
   An on ivvery heuk a skate,
An herrin ran doon the th'artship lids
   Like a hielan burn in spate.
So they shot an hauled, an they dodged an ran
   Thro fair an conter seas,
An aye as the dark oor later grew
   Aye bigger grew the lees.
Till oot o the nicht a fearsome yowl
   Cam dirlin wild an clear —
It stilled their speech, an it steyed their step,
   An it froze their herts wi fear.

'Twis Isie oot at the kitchen door
  On the hunt for her gweed man Jock,
An she cyardit 'im up an she cyardit 'im doon
  Baith him an aa 'is folk.
An lood, aye looder grew her note
  An heicher grew her skirl;
It made the cat tak sheet wi fricht
  An it gart the windas dirl.

He wis this, he wis that, he wis naething gweed;
  He wis idle to the bone,
An the only thing that brocht a smile
  Wis the sicht o the southerly cone.
He wis nivver oot, he wis nivver in;
  He wis jist an orra drouth;
Fine did she ken fit wye he wis aye
  Sae keen on a berth for Sooth.

An aye her tongue gid clatter clap
  Like the starn o a cripple deuk;
An the names that she caa'd her man that nicht
  Wis nivver seen in the Beuk.

'Gweed-nicht!' says Dod, til 'is leein freen.
  'I see the rick that's to blame.
But it's time that I wisna here mysel —
  I've a rickin lum at hame!'

Faar Are They Noo?

Faar's aa the happy loons that played aboot Raemoss,
Or smokit secret tabbies oot o sicht in Doctor's Closs?
The loons that made a rocky-on to try an beat the tide,
Or played yon kind o fitba far there's twenty-five aside?
The loons that ran the billy fin the herrin fleet wis sooth,
An for the sake o tuppence aye could magnify the truth?
Faar are they noo? Aye! faar are they the day?
The Queenie loons that rode their sledges doon the Wally Brae,
The Sooth Bey loons that didna care tho mithers gied them jip
For reestin stolen speldins in aneth the Lifeboat Slip.
The wild an gey ill-trickit loons that bade in the Roanheids,
An Buchaners, on the warpath, swingin tangles roon their heids;
The fisher squad that had, at times, a rowdy wye o playin,
An toonser lads that had, nae doot, some capers o their ain
Like rinnin wi their sheen on close ahin the water-cairt,
An comin wi a story that wid brak a mither's hert.
Faar are they noo? They've surely flown like birds,
An teen their peeries wi them an their stumperts an their girds.
An faar's aa the lauchin quines that plowtered doon the braes,
An gaithered dally's-cleysies on the bonny simmer days?
The bonny quines, the plain quines, reid-heidit, dark or fair
That skirlt 'At's tellt ee teacher!' if ye tried to rug their hair.
The quines that chalkit beddies at the tap o ilka street,
An skuffled at the steenie till the sheen wis aff their feet.
The quines that sang like linties as they played their merry games
Wi jumpin-ropes, an wyin weichts, or bonny coloured lames.
At nicht aneth the lamp-post, they'd be singin wi a will —
'Ten o'clock the Gas Goes Out' or 'The Lass o Richmondhill'.
Faar are they noo? The place is nae the same
Athoot them an their 'Fairmer's Dog', an 'Jumbo Wis His Name'.
Faar are they noo? There's some that's hyne awaa,
An some that's nivver even thocht on leavin hame avaa.
But whether they be ower the sea, or still a-tyauvin here,
Let's wish for them an aa their bairns, a happy gweed New 'Ear.

Ripperitis
(For the mosquito fleet)

The tide's as dull as a tide could be,
For she's fillin nine an she's ebbin three,
But I canna see the piers for sea,
So it's nae a chance for the ripper-o.
It may be the breeze'll sattle quick,
An a box o codlins would tak a trick,
But, faar div ye ging fin the water's thick,
In a cockle shaal wi a ripper-o?

On a bakin-board ye could sail the sea,
But the tide's as het as a tide could be,
For she's ebbin nine an she's fillin three,
So that's nae eese for the ripper-o.
The big stream tide'll sattle quick,
An a box o codlins would tak a trick,
But ye may be sure it'll come smore thick,
An that'll connach the ripper-o.

The big-boat man has an easy task —
His kite's as big as a brandy cask,
But a sharger like me wid slide thro a mask
For I'm chief an I'm cook an I'm skipper-o.
There's aye a something to cowp the cairt,
There's aye a sorra to brak the hairt,
But, still-an-on I wid nivver pairt,
Wi my cockle-shaal an my ripper-o.

The ripper mannie's a hardy breed!
There's naething but codlins in his heid,
His wife voos oot he'll be gotten deid,
In his cockle-shaal wi his ripper-o.
Weel, some fine day in the happy land,
She'll see him there on the golden strand,
Still fartin aboot like a one-man band,
Wi his flask, an his piece, an his ripper-o.

Note: The ripper is a primitive yet effective way of catching cod without bait. It has been aptly described as 'A lump o leed at ae en' an a feel at the ither.'

92

Home Thoughts at the Haisboro

November's moon has waned; the sea is dreary,
   December's greyness fills the lowering sky;
But we are homeward bound, our hearts are cheery
   For far astern the Ridge and Cockle lie.

For one sweet year no more we'll dread the Scroby;
   No more we'll fear the Hammond's broken swell,
Nor shall we toil and strive in dirty weather,
   Upon the tide-swept shallows of the Well.

The silver harvest of the Knoll's been gathered;
   The teeming millions from their haunts have flown;
From Ship to South-Ower buoy the sea's deserted,
   And we have reaped whereof we had not sown.

When snow lies deep, in cosy loft amending
   Our nets, the times of danger we'll recall,
The days of joy, the nights of disappointment,
   Each silver shimmer and each weary haul.

And children, sitting chin-in-hand, will listen —
   Forsaking for the moment, every toy;
For there's a deep and wondrous fascination
   In sea-tales, for the heart of every boy.

And we, all wise, forbidding them the sea-life,
   Will see them smile when we have had our say,
Full well we know th' extent of their obedience,
   For are we not the boys of yesterday?

Three hundred weary miles ahead are waiting
   The joys of home, the hand-shake of a friend,
And Buchan Ness will flash her silent welcome —
   'Here now my children is your journey's end.'

The Pharisee
(Luke 18 v. 11)

I'll nivver shot a net again,
    I'll nivver redd a line,
Nae mair I'll steer a compass course
    Nor face a rising gale;
I'll lead nae dark patrols again,
    Nor sweep a German mine,
There's only ae thing left for me —
    The feenish o the tale.

For mair than fifty 'ear, my loons,
    I sailed the saaty sea,
In simmer an in winter baith,
    I seldom missed a day;
Ye ken yersels there's nae a port
    That you can name to me,
But fit the folkies there'll ken
    The bonny *Mandalay*.

In Shetland voes an Orkney firths,
    An Hielan lochs as weel,
I've met a puckle decent men,
    An look on them as freens;
Fae Duncansby to Yarmooth,
    An fae Stornoway to Peel,
I've met some bonny lassies that
    In aa but rank were queens.

But noo-an-than, my loons, I'd meet
    A middlin kind o chiel.
Ye're sure to meet his marra,
    Or ye winna live ower lang;
I'd tak him for an honest man,
    He'd think I wis a feel,
I wisna lang o learnin,
    That the baith o's wis clean wrang!

Afore my braith gings oot, my loons,
  There's ae thing ye maun dee!
Jist bring to me the salesman,
  An a buyer if ye can;
Ye'll sit them doon aside me,
  But in case they canna gree,
Jist split them up an lat them tak
  My port an starboard han.

At sic a time in sic a place,
  They'll wear their Sunday claes,
They'll maybe nae be willin,
  But, my loons, jist gar them bide;
Then like the Lord I've tried to serve
  An follow aa my days,
I'll leave this port for glory,
  Wi a thief on ilka side.

NOTE: This story varies slightly from village to village but it has been a standing joke among fisher folk for generations. The original arch-villains were the herring curers but with the demise of the salt herring industry the curer's mantle had to fall on someone else's shoulders. The choice is left to the story-teller but the fisherman must be portrayed as a paragon of virtue.

Firelicht

I sat at the fire on a winter's nicht
  When the grun wis fite wi snaa,
An I watched the lowes wi their flickerin licht
  Drawin picters on the waa;
Then deep in the hert o the fire sae reid
  I saw the face o a freen —
A barfit loon, wi a curly heid
  An a pair o lauchin een;
Then the win in the lum changed its dreary tune
  An it hummed a lilt to the lauchin loon:

    Div ye see the PD. drifters
    Div ye see them yet avaa?
    Div ye see the PD. drifters,
    Comin hame fae Stornowaa?

A swirl o rick at the back o the grate,
  An the loon gied place till a quine,
Wi her hair in a bonny ribboned plait,
  An her buttoned boots a-shine.
She sat at the fit o an aal steen stair
  Wi a raggit hame-made dall,
An she sang a lang forgotten air
  As she rowed her bairn in a shawl;
Then the win in the lum ceased its weary whine
  An it sang that air wi the happy quine:

    Wee Jockie-birdie, toll-oll-oll,
    Laid an egg on the windi-soll;
    The windi-soll began to crack
    An wee Jockie-birdie roared an grat.

The quine wis awaa ere the sang wis deen,
  So I turned my heid awaa
To see yet anither byegone scene
  Clear-cut on the kitchen waa.
An aal wife bent wi the heavy creel,
  Her cwites jist clear o the grun,
An a squad o bairnies, young an feel,
  Jist trailin ahin for fun.
Then the win in the lum cleared its rummlin throat
  An it sang wi the bairns on a jaunty note:

Tinkie-tinkie tarry-hat, yer hat's nae yer ain,
Ye stole't fae a fisher-wifie, comin fae the train.

The aal wife faded as the fire sank low,
   An the bairns were left their leen;
They seemed to be weary-like, they gaed that slow,
   Crawlin hame when their play wis deen;
But the hailsteens rattled on the windi-peen.
   Like the dirl o a kettle-drum,
An the win cried, 'Bairnies, far hiv ye been?
   Hing in noo! Hame ye come!'
Then the lazy lowes sprang to bricht new life
   Wi the bairns, as they sang in their playfu strife:

   Sling yer gun across yer shooder
   A bag o leid an a saiddler's pooder,
   We're awaa to fecht e Germans
   Ower the hills o Mormon.

I sat till the aise turned grey on the bars
   An the lowes wid play nae mair,
Then I lookit oot at the frosty stars
   Jist afore I climmed the stair:
The same aal stars that eesed to shine
   On oor wind-swept fisher toon,
But they didna see the happy quine
   Nor the lauchin barfit loon.
Said the win in the lum as I fell asleep —
   'Youth's jist like yer dreams — it winna keep.'

Days Gone By

Did ye ivver spend a simmer evenin playin ower the backs,
Watchin lest the Queenie Arabs got upon yer tracks,
Kennin it wis bedtime fin ye saw the evenin star,
An crawlin hame sae happy wi a bandy in a jar?

Did ye ever look for partans at low water 'mong the waur,
Carin little tho yer claes wis clartit thick wi glaar?
Did ye ever tummle in a loch an ruin aa yer claes,
Syne tell yer mither somebody pushed ye in doon the braes?

Did ye ever licht a firie fin the nichts were drawin in
An bile a curny wulks in an aal seerup tin,
Happy tho the bitin smoke wis nippen aa yer een,
Howkin oot the wulks wi an aal hairpreen?

Did ye ivver dirl the windas wi an aal widden pirn,
Syne kill yersel wi lauchin fin ye hard the wifies girn?
Did ye nivver watch a chancie fin it wis growin dark
To steal a puckly peys oot o Johnny Mattha's park?

Did ye nivver scoff yer hamework an dreid the maister's froon,
An wish wi aa yer hert that the school wis burned doon?
Did ye nivver tie the door-knobs across a nerra street,
Syne cut the tow an lat the doors caa the wifies aff their feet?

Did ivver ye rin barfit aboot the Bogie Hole,
An if ye got the chance did ye ever steal a yole
An scoor the Bey a-lookin till the win wis growin caal
For 'Merchant Street wide open an the big clock's hans at twal?'

Lang syne fin we were loonies we had naething bit oor health,
A penny wis a fortin an a saxpence untold wealth!
An noo they're scattered far an wide that ran the braes wi me,
Here's health an happiness to them — farivver they may be!

Name in Brackets

Ye're awaa fae the braes noo, barfit loon,
Awaa fae the sea an the shinin san,
Fae the slippery steens an the raivelt waar,
Far ye'd catch a puller wi practised han.
Ye're awaa fae the pier wi the cairts an the saat,
An the steam an the tar an the herrin smell,
Awaa wi the souns on the mornin air,
The clatter o hooves an the herrin bell.

I've seen yer face in an antrin dream,
Ower the fifty 'ear since I saw ye last,
An I've heard yer word at my gable-en,
Fin a happy bairn gid singin past.
But I didna ken that yours wis the name,
That I've read in the paperie here the day,
Till there, in the brackets, clear I spied,
The name that ye got fae yer chums at play.

It took my ee on the printed page,
It loupit oot an it seemed to shine;
I'd clean forgotten ye'd a proper name,
An I'm winnerin noo did ee ken mine?
Ye're awaa fae the braes noo, barfit loon —
Ye're safe in a better port, aswarn.
Weel! Tell ee the Berthin-maister there,
That the rest o the fleet's nae far astarn.

Note: It is the fisher custom to include the deceased's nickname in the funeral intimations. Since there is such a proliferation of commonly shared Christian names and surnames this is the only method in which the community can identify with certainty which of their number has passed on. A nickname bestowed in childhood becomes the only name by which a man is known for the rest of his life.

The Mennin Laft

It's cosy up here in the laftie at nicht,
  Tho dreary nord-easters may girn roon the lum,
The fire's blinkin bonny, the licht burnin bricht,
  The caal winter's comin? Weel jist lat it come.

The win throws a hanfae o rain on the peen;
  The verra reef shaks wi the wecht o the flans,
But here in the laft, till the winter be deen,
  There's warmth an there's comfort — an work for aa hans.

The wife's sittin mennin, wi Mary oor quine,
  An aal Yarmooth net clickit up at the waa,
A net that's gey picky an greedy for twine,
  An they're nae gettin nearer the gavle avaa.

They're snippin an clippin; they sing as they men',
  Tho theirs is the slowest an dreichest o tasks.
There's nivver a girn, tho they're oors upon en',
  Aye stooin an shooin at three-leggit masks.

An fit aboot me in the corner masel?
  I'm sortin a torn een that's haavert in twaa.
She wis foul o the rope at the back o the Well,
  An it seems there's a skelp o the yarn clean awaa.

I think I'll condemn 'er an leave 'er aleen;
  The weemin'll say I'm a dear if I div;
She'd be gey ill to men', for she's jist fair deen,
  An there's knots on the selvidge as big as my niv.

They're hamely the souns in the laftie at nicht:
  A scrape an a dunt as the wife shifts 'er cheer,
The risp o the twine as she hanks the knots ticht,
  An the clump o the corks on the bare widden fleer.

Noo Mary starts singin a bonny Psalm tune —
  Her mither, fine pleased, as I see by her face,
Jines in noo-an-than as the verses come roon,
  While I sit contented jist bummin the baiss.

A fit on the stair-heid, an in comes a freen,
  To borry a patch an to speir for my hoast.
We crack aboot gear, an the times that we've seen
  Fin the sappers cam hame tho the reid eens wis loast.

He speirs for the folk that are hine ower the sea,
  An hoo they're aa farin, an fan they'll be hame.
We're poor hans at writin — I'm sure ye'll agree
  That writin an spikkin wis nivver the same.

An so the lang evenin wears on till its close —
  The fire's gettin low noo — we'll caa it a day.
We're nae like the fairmers wi bowlies o brose,
  But surely ye'll bide for a shallie o tay?

Kirkyard Rain

I'm thinkin back on Davy —
  He'd aye his ain luck!
Wi canny speed he'd forge aheid,
  Tho ither folk were stuck.
Fin better men than Davy
  Could get nae fish avaa,
The cod wid steer for Davy's gear,
  An gie themsels awaa!

But lat's be fair to Davy —
  It wisna Davy's blame
That tempest wild lay meek an mild
  Till Davy had won hame.
An tho ye'll 'gree that Davy
  Had better luck than maist,
Ye'd surely say this very day,
  'We kent it couldna laist!'

Weel! here to beery Davy
  There's mair than half the fleet.
A teemin sky — still Davy's dry,
  But we're aa dreepin weet!

The Dunderheid

Oh, he wis thick! Man, he couldna coont
The product o three times three.
But that wis a gift that the Lord had kept
For his favoured sons like me.
He sat at the fitt o the snicherin class
Wi his battered bag at his feet,
An the dytit wye that he thocht an spoke
Wid ha gart an angel greet.

Oh boys, he wis thick!

Oh, he wis thick! Man, he couldna tell
A snatchie o verse fae prose.
But that wis a gift that the Lord had kept
For those an such as those.
He sat at the fitt o the snicherin class
An man, ye wid scarce believe
That to clean his slate he spat in its face
Syne gied it a rub wi his sleeve.

Oh boys, he wis thick!

Oh, he wis thick! Man, he couldna see
That the verb wis the predicate.
But that wis a gift that the Lord had kept
Fae the loon that wis short o mait.
He sat at the fitt o the snicherin class
In his orra-like sheen an hose,
An he seemed to think that the back o his han
Wis for dichtin his bubbly nose.

Oh boys, he wis thick!

I've jist been readin the *Daily News*
An there, in the centre spot,
He's sellt some ships to finance a Hame
For bairns that the world forgot.
He's miles aheid o the snicherin class
An I've learned wi shame on my face,
That it's nae for me nor my class to decide
The gift, nor the time, nor the place.

Oh Lord, I've been thick!

Dreams o Heaven

Jock an Daavit bocht a boatie —
Pleesure for their sunset days;
Struck a heavy spot o codlins
Nae far aff the Geddle Braes;
Back an fore aa day they fleeted,
Solid fish at ilka rip!
Daavit, pleased eneuch, yet vexed
He didna hae a bigger ship.

Back an fore aa day they rippit
Till the boatie sappy grew.
Up t' his doup in warrie codlins
Jock cries, 'That's a plenty noo!
Water's lippin ower the gunnel!
Muckle mair she canna thole.
Dinna jump aboot noo, Daavit,
Bide at peace or ye'll sink the yole!'

'Weel!' says Daavit, sweir t' leave them,
'We'll ging hame as lang's it's fleed.
Jock! 'twid be a richt fine thing
If aabody else in the world wis deid;
Then, my loon, we'd mak a fortin,
Powen notes wid flee like spells!
Faa like hiz? Nae competition!
Aa the ocean t' wirsels.'

Jock, gweed sowl, began t' habber,
'Daavit, dinna be sae feel!
Faa div ye think wid buy yer fish
If this gran dream o yours wis real?
Fine ye ken ye'd need a market,
Folk kens that fae here to the Sloch!'
'Dinna fash yersel', says Daavit.
'That's thocht oot! There's aye the Broch!'

The Aal Cannon

Fin I wis jist a toddlin bairn, the aal men eesed to gaither
Upon the Cannon simmer seats an sit aa nicht an blether.
I likit fine to hear their crack o lang forgotten ploys,
Their proticks an their capers fin they themsels were boys.

An if my barfit, scartit legs grew weary, tired o stannin,
I'd climb up ower the roosty wheel an sit astride the Cannon.
The aal men they wid lauch at me, but neen o them wid froon,
An some o them wid clap my knee an speir 'Faa echts ye, Loon?'

For aal clay pipe an box o spunks in pooches deep they'd howk;
The rick fae their black Bogie Roll gey nearly gart me cowk.
Syne, bairn-like, I'd worry them wi question an back-speirin,
An lookin back I canna say I ivver heard them sweerin.

The fearsome tales they spun to me on earth had ne'er an equal;
If they're in Aal Nick's hans the day there's sure to be a sequel.
There wis ae big grey-bearded man; it wis his joy an glory
To lift me aff the Cannon an recite a ghostie story.

Syne fin his eerie tale wis deen my wee scared heid he clappit,
But fin I cuddled doon that nicht that heid wis gey weel happit.
Wi tales o warlocks fierce an wild he nearly jeeled my bleed;
I'm sure my scared een wis big as bowls o potted heid.

But fyles their tales were full o fun to rid my hert o fear,
An ilka ane wid try to see faa wis the biggest leear;
That their great binders wis the truth I nivver had a doot —
The biggest lees ye ivver heard, they stood an shieled them oot.

Fin I look back I hae a lauch at some o their best lees —
To think a man could rin sae far as wear his feet till's knees;
The giant fluke that ae man catched an fed the toon upon it,
Its een as big as bunker lids, its spots as big's yer bonnet.

But noo the times have changed, ye ken, the Cannon's teen awaa,
And thereaboots there's nae a craitur to be seen avaa;
But still I hope fin I grow aal I'll get my ain turn
To clap a loonie on the heid an spin as big a yarn.

September

The simmer's wearin on, lass,
   The rodden's bonny reid
Comes lowein thro the greenery
   Abeen the quaet burn.
Yon reeshlin barley's ripe, lass,
   It's fite, wi hingin heid.
Were I the fairmer here, lass,
   I'd tak it in the morn.

It's surely nae a twalmont,
   Since last we dauchled here?
It canna be a year, lass,
   Wis't nae jist late yestreen?
Ye seem t' think I'm wrang? Weel,
   I canna help but speir,
If that's the time that's flown awaa,
   Then far's the sizzons geen?

It winna be that lang noo,
   Afore the trees'll stan,
In goons o reid an gold, lass,
   The wye they've deen afore,
Till rivin win's come snarlin,
   Oot ower the shorn lan,
T' spread the bonny leaves like
   A bass at Winter's door.

A bittie like the barley,
   We're frail, wi fitened heid;
A bittie like the trees, lass,
   Oor time for beauty's gone.
But lat's aye mind jist fit wis said
   Aboot the bruisèd reed,
An nivver dreid the Winter,
   Tho the simmer's wearin on.

Short Stories

Tall Tales of the Old Salts

In the halcyon days of my youth an old Russian cannon from the Crimean War stood in Harbour Street, with its great muzzle pointing towards the Skerry.

The underside of the massive barrel was pitted by the salty atmosphere, but its top was as smooth as glass, polished by the doups of generations of bairns who had sat astride it. The old relic was removed to help the war effort in the 1940s, but the seats are still there. These old seats were the recognised meeting place for the old salts and ancient mariners of the locality, for in those days there was neither radio nor T.V. to while away the hours of retirement.

Consequently a proper 'Parliament' foregathered around the seats in the afternoons and evenings if the weather was good and many a wonderful tale was told: tales of whaling days, tales of the hellish life in the trenches of Flanders (the old boys were not all fishermen), tales of the mine-sweepers and the Dover Patrol, and tales of every imaginable sort.

One thing is for sure — these old codgers caught far more herring and fish around the seats than they ever did at sea!

For a long time I had the impression that the fishing boats of their day had been very big boats to carry such shots of fish, until I realised that among these ancients there were several practised liars, whose mendacity even I have never managed to equal — and that's saying something!

I soon learned that any member of that illustrious gathering who was without a nickname was bound to be an incomer.

I must have been a proper nuisance to Simon McLeod, a cooper who hailed from Tobermory, and John Skinner, from Balintore, for every time I met them I would speir 'Faar div ee come fae?' simply for the joy of hearing the Highland lilt as they pronounced the names of their birth-places.

Then there was 'Wansie', a local cooper with a huge moustache, from which protruded a beautiful amber cigarette-holder presented to him by Lord Kitchener after the battle of Tel-el-Kebir.

Apparently Kitchener had planned to surprise the enemy by making an overnight forced march across the desert sands, but in the course of this manoeuvre he had got himself hopelessly lost. In despair he brought his army to a halt, with one hand, just as John Wayne does on the screen.

It was a moment for split second decision so he barked the order, 'Go and find Wansie!'

Wansie was immediately brought from the rear of the column, where he had been peelin tatties, to the forefront, where, steering by the stars he led the British Army to glorious victory.

His medal for this stupendous feat had perished in the desert heat, but the cigarette holder had survived. What a man! Very few could peel tatties and march at the same time!

When at a later date I was asked to name, in order of importance, the three greatest navigators of all time, I wrote — Wansie, Nancy's Peter and Beetlies

Daavit, whereupon I was banished from the classroom in disgrace.

This only served to prove that certain school-teachers can be very ignorant indeed!

One of my favourite friends was Jimmy Buchan, known to all the community as 'Trappin'. A little wee mannie, always spick and span, he lived in Hay's Close where a rickle of old tenements served to accommodate an unbelievable number of folk.

When I asked him one day, 'Foo mony folk bides in that close, Jimmy?' he replied, 'Och! A gey lot, my loon! We jist bide mix-max an pairt the bairns at the New 'Ear!'

It would have been most improper of me to ask him how he got his by-name, so I had to inquire elsewhere and it was thus-wise — the old time fishermen wore a fantastic amount of clothing. To begin with, every one had a pair of hand-knitted drawers, which could vary in colour from shocking pink to emerald green.

The upper part of the body was clad in a flannel shirt or 'linner', surmounted by a 'wincey' sark which in turn was covered by a 'frock', a long jersey which reached below the hips and was always of five-ply navy blue Seafield worsit. The galluses which supported the heavy trousers were worn above the frock, whose lower part was always out of sight beneath the breeks. These same galluses would have made an adequate mooring for the *QE2*. If it was an airish mornin, they would don an ordinary ganjie forbye!

But now I must let you in on an awful secret! Between their drawers and their breeks they wore 'drawer covers' which were nothing more or less than a pair of thin white cotton pants which were fastened round the wearer's ankles with lengths of tape. It was mandatory that this tape be tied in a neat little bow or 'doss'.

Jimmy, in his own thrawn manner, refused to accept the modern word 'tape' and insisted on the old term 'trapping'. So for the remainder of his days he was 'Trappin'.

Trappin was one of the remarkable breed who go to sea alone in small boats. Foolhardy? A wee bittie, maybe. Fearless? Aye! Surely!

He would leave port at dawn in his 18ft. sail boatie, his provisions being fourpence worth of buttery cookies and a cutter o fuskie, and his range was wide, indeed, if he could get a seine-netter to tow him 'as far as Cruden Skares or the Slains Buss.'

I'm thinking now of one lovely summer morning during my first year at sea when we found old Trappin in his boatie at Rattray Head. He was fast asleep in the bottom of the boat, snugly wrapped in the sail, and when I boarded his vessel and woke him up he wisna neen suited. But a shallie o tay from our taypot mollified him and he went on his way rejoicing. He had been at sea for twenty-six hours.

One particularly coorse day he was caught in the fearsome tide rip which makes the North Head at Peterhead such a terrifying place. He was battling with wind and tide to bring his boatie to harbour when disaster struck.

The spar which carries the sail (i.e. the yard) broke, so Trappin was helpless. Anxious watchers on shore alerted the lifeboat, which was quickly on the scene to find him trying his utmost to mend the broken yard. The gallant lifeboat coxswain manoeuvred his craft alongside the casualty, ready to snatch the luckless sailor from a watery grave, only to be roundly berated by the irate Trappin with the question, 'Fit on earth are ye deein oot here on a day like this? Ye should hae mair sense, man!'

Thus the worthies who were such an important feature of my impressionable boyhood. As I have already said, the seats remain to this day, but the old men have passed on.

Friendship from a Pain in the Neck

The words 'Shipmate' and 'Friend' are not necessarily synonymous. I have often seen shipmates who just managed to tolerate each other and I have seen shipmates who simply hated each other's guts for no apparent reason.

And then there are shipmates between whom there appears to be a natural bond of sincere friendship which lasts for many years, but having said that, let's not forget the friendships which can blossom between the most 'unsuitable' partners, folk who have absolutely nothing in common.

Once upon a time I had such a friendship with a shipmate whom I shall call John — not his real name.

I was young enough to run rings round him — of this he was daily reminded — and still we were friends. He was the most contermashious divvle I have ever sailed with, having an inordinate passion for the truth and nothing but the truth!

To him a spade was a spade, and in no way would he accept my suggestion that it could be classed as a 'thing for howkin holes'. When I put forward the idea that the truth is not always required, I was a heretic, a man without principle, without solid foundation, to be classed with those who patch their drawers wi velvet! And still, man, still we were friends.

I think it all started when John developed, on the back of his neck, a plook like a half egg, a hideous mass of corruption wi a gut as thick as a pencil. The poor man couldn't see the thing at all and when he tried to ficher wi the plook on his own he simply aggravated it.

So I offered to assist, having suffered greatly myself with a like affliction. With Lysol and hot water for the outside, and a vile mixture of Epsom salts and Cream o Tartar for the inside, coupled with a heap o patience for both sides, the mountain was reduced to a plain and all was well.

From that time onward we became the best of pals. On the rare occasions when he threatened to become a wee bittie obstreperous, I simply had to hint that in future he would 'squeeze his ain plooks', then he would be as meek as a lamb.

In appearance John was naething forbye. He was short and stout, so much so that when he donned his oilskin frock he resembled a herrin barrel wi little feeties on't. His bonnet was always dead flat on his head and my gentle hint that a five-degree tilt might enhance his appearance brought the sharp retort that he had no time for the Nelson touch. If that had been in his mind he 'would ha bocht a bonnet wi the snoot at the side!'

John's normal voice was softer and gentler than any woman's, but when he sang he could gar yer taes curl! He had a glorious bass voice which reverberated like a teem cask, a gift which drew many an admiring glance in the Deneside Chapel in Yarmouth where the locals 'couldn't get a seat for Scotties' unless they were half-an-hour early. Ye'll mind, the Kirk wi the picter-hoose seats?

Such was John, a mixter of soft voice and ill naitur, a blend of coorseness and kindliness, a man whose strongest expletive was 'Ooh me! Ooh me!'

He had started his working life as a cooper, but after a few years at his trade he had forsaken it for the sea, to serve for several years as a trawler cook. The fact that he had been cook in the same vessel under the same skipper for seven years was a great testimonial, for good cooks are worth their weight in gold. John, according to John, was worth at least that, for wasn't he the finest cook that ever steered a pot?

His skipper was one of the top-notchers, a hard man in a hard world. The shippie was a common five eight Aiberdeen trawler and as such she had no shelter decks whatsoever. The crew had to tak their shak on an open deck whatever the weather.

I have never forgotten John's account of one wild stormy day away to the east of the Shetlands. Several trawlers had been fishing in close company, but one-by-one they had knocked off because of the atrocious weather.

John's skipper, as usual, was last to give in and when he did finally give the order to heave up, the crew of seasoned veterans had grave doubts whether or not this could be done without loss of life, but the net, with a bumper haul, was brought safely aboard. The deckies were not too pleased at seeing the 'ponds' brimming with fish, because they wouldn't get off the deck till the fish were gutted and it really wasn't a day for men to be on deck at all.

The skipper asked John to go forrard and lend a hand and this he did willingly, only to be told by the Mate, 'Look here cookie! When ye're on deck ye'll dee fit I tell ye, so fin the skipper's nae lookin, ye'll shovel fish ower the side.

'We want to get below afore dark, but watch that the mannie disna see fit ye're deein!' So John busied himself with a shovel.

Now on such a day a drifter would have had her great mizzen sail set, the wheel lashed in the mid-ships position and with the engine at slow ahead she would have lain head to wind more or less looking after herself. But it was the custom in trawlers to let the ship lie broadside on to wind and sea until the weather abated. Great green seas would come crashing on board filling the decks waist deep in a torrent.

I have never been in a trawler but I can well imagine that to work fish on an open deck in such conditions must have been sheer Hell!

The skipper in his lofty eyrie in the wheel-house kept a sharp look-out to windward and when he saw a particularly nasty 'lump o water' coming he would yell, 'Hud on lads, hud on!' whereupon every man would grab for some immovable fixture and hang on for dear life until the worst was past.

If bad language could have quelled the seas there would have been a flat calm, but the sea is stone deaf to epithets.

Roughly half of the fish had been gutted when a most peculiar incident took place. The deckie nearest to John suddenly 'gid wrang in 'is mind'. Something in the poor chap's brain snapped and casting his knife into the sea, he seized the rigging of the foremast and hoisted himself onto the top-rail, i.e. the top of the bulwark. There he stood erect before setting out on a sort of tight-rope walk along the rail right into the stern of the ship where he squatted for a few moments with his back to the crutch of the mizzen boom, looking steadfastly into the eye of the wind.

Then, erect again, he retraced his steps along the same impossible path, back to the fore-mast where his awestruck shipmates seized him and hustled him below. There he remained under supervision until the proper authorities took charge of him in his home port.

No sooner had his shipmates got him below when one almighty sea came sweeping aboard. It lifted every moveable thing in its path — fish, baskets, pond-boards, the lot, and tossed them contemptuously over the lee side. Had the crew been there, their chances of survival would have been slim indeed.

When John had finished his story he was very close to tears. 'Tell me this,' he said, 'fit wye wis't that nae wan drap o water came in ower the rail as lang as he wis on't?' Alas! I could not answer.

That finished the trip, for the skipper immediately set course for home. It was also the finish for John as far as trawling was concerned. He had witnessed the impossible and he didna like it. In fact he had seen the Supernatural and he was scared stiff.

It's almost thirty years now since John passed on. It's at least forty years since he told me the tale and I think the incident took place some ten or twelve years before that. Say fifty-odd years ago.

Never once have I doubted his word but I have yet to come up with an answer to his question — 'Fit wye?'

Chasing Herring in Stornoway

During the summer of 1934 I was a young lad on our family boat *Sparkling Star*, a 40-footer, built by John Stephen of Macduff.

At that time there was quite a fleet of similar boats, mostly in the Moray Firth, built for skippers who had been obliged to get rid of their uneconomical steam drifters. Most of these skippers had been herring fishermen all their days and had retained their herring nets for use in their new craft, so that particular summer

113

there were several such craft fishing from Stornoway.

And why Stornoway? Simply because the herring shoals at Stornoway are usually near the coast, very handy for such small boats. And why 40ft.? Because the law decreed that on certain parts of the Scottish coast boats of under 40ft. were allowed to use the seine net inside the three mile limit.

So these skippers were actually trying to make dual-purpose vessels out of boats which were too small for that. They were never meant to be herring boats and gradually they forsook the herring fishing to concentrate on the seine-net. But during the summer which concerns our story, Stornoway was full of them, BCK. and BF. We were the only PD.

Boys! That was a disastrous summer! Scarcely a herrin could be found anywhere. It was the same all around the coast, a proper famine. Had there been herrin elsewhere we would have shifted but there was no inducement to move so we stuck it out for several weeks for absolutely nothing.

As a young feel loon I was quite happy with my ten bob (50p) on Saturday. With that I could get all the fags and ice-cream I wanted, Player's being only a shilling (5p) for twenty, but had I been a married man wi bairns, the situation would have been grim indeed.

I have a vivid memory of one particular Monday morning. The harbour at Bayhead was crammed with small craft, their crews all busy making the nets ready for sea. There was an air of bustle and good humour about the place with old veterans telling the loons, 'Watch ee yer wark an I'll watch the pier. If a quine worth lookin at comes along, I'll tell ye!'

Paraffin men were busy with their deliveries and all kinds of message boys were crossing and recrossing the boats when suddenly all activity ceased and there fell on the scene a fearsome hush.

A Post Office boy had appeared on the quay with a bright coloured envelope in his hand. Telegram for somebody! Certain disaster!

It was obvious that the boy was looking for a certain boat, for he scanned every tier closely as he moved slowly along the quay, glancing now and then at the envelope. Countless eyes followed his path and many a man heaved a sigh of relief when the boy passed him by.

The tension was almost unbearable, for telegrams were usually bearers of calamitous tidings. Sure as death it had to be the very last boat that he boarded, with every eye fixed on him. The recipient opened the envelope with trembling fingers then threw his bonnet in the air yelling, 'Twins, twaa quines, b' Goad!' And suddenly aabody wis happy! Oh! what a beautiful mornin.

Later that week we were amazed to see on the quay ten men, in identical new suits and bonnets, led by a mannie in a paddy hat. They too were scanning the fleet for a certain boat and great was our surprise when the boat turned out to be ours.

Paddy-Hat explained that these men were the crew of the *Ocean Princess*, an Aberdeen 'liner' which had grounded during the night near the little village of Ness. The crew had rowed ashore, to be transported to Stornoway where the British Sailors' Society had looked after them and kitted them out. Hence the new suits.

Now they were desirous of returning to the wreck to see if she could be salvaged. Since they were Aiberdeen men they would like a Peterhead boatie to act as ferry-boat. If we undertook to do the job we would be handsomely paid. Indeed we would get 'saxteen powen'. Nae bother! For that kind of money we would take them to the Flannen Isles!

It transpired that the *Ocean Princess* had been heading for Stornoway to procure herring bait before proceeding to distant fishing grounds such as St Kilda or Rockall or Faroe where she would work her long-lines for about a fortnight before returning to her home port. This was common practice with the Aberdeen line boats.

On the way to the wreck, some twenty miles distant, it was chance aboot for tay because our little fo'c'sle was designed for six and we now had sixteen on board. But that was to be a short-lived inconvenience for we'd soon be putting these chaps back aboard their own vessel.

Imagine then our astonishment when we found the *Ocean Princess* afloat with another Aberdeen liner, the *Craigcoilleach*, standing by to render assistance. The casualty had been taken over by two villagers from Ness and in no way would they allow any member of the crew to step aboard. In this they were within their legal rights. Laws of salvage, you see.

It had so happened that the two 'Hielanmen' had boarded the wreck to investigate the situation. Of course, there were some charitable people who said: 'Oh aye! We've heard that before!' The ship had been provisioned in Aberdeen the day before with stores for ten or twelve men for three weeks, plus a fine big locker packed with bond (tobacco and spirits). She was certainly worth investigating. Jealousy is to be found everywhere.

I heard later that the two chaps had just gone below to see if there was water in the ship when there came a fearsome rummle, like an earthquake! In terror they rushed back on deck to find that the ship had slid off the rock and was now afloat and in no immediate danger of sinking. The heroes had enough 'mither wit' to realise that the prize was theirs.

In the off-shore wind the *Ocean Princess* drifted away clear of the land and she was lying fine and handy when the *Craigcoilleach* came along. The prize crew engaged this new arrival to tow them to Stornoway. I doubt if our little boat could have done the job.

We could see that the casualty's rudder was jammed hard to starboard but our offer to act as a rudder during the tow was refused. So all we could do was to take our passengers back to Stornoway.

Next morning the tow arrived in Stornoway where she was successfully beached and repaired.

The two locals were very handsomely rewarded by the courts which settle salvage questions. The amount of the award I have forgotten but I can well remember that, for those times, it was a colossal sum.

It may surprise you to know that only one of these lucky lads was a local. The other was a Peterhead man who had made his home there. Strange how Bluemogganers put in an appearance when there's 'something to be gotten!'

Fog at High Water was Always a Break

'One gun for the Apparatus, two guns for the Lifeboat!' That was a code which I learned at a very tender age, for I was born and brought up about 100yds. from the Lifeboat Shed.

Of course they weren't really guns, but rockets or 'maroons', yet to this day it's aye the 'Lifeboat guns'. These guns were heard a great deal oftener in my youth than they are today, not so much because of ships in difficulty through stress of weather, but because of ships in fog. 'A ship ashore!'

Over the past thirty years fog has lost a lot of its terror. Sophisticated electronic devices — echo-sounders, Decca Navigators and radar — have proved invaluable to fishermen who can now tell at a glance their exact position, the depth of water below the keel, and the presence, if any, of other ships in the vicinity, not forgetting the precise distance of land. No surprise then that so few craft are stranded because of fog.

But when I was a young fisherman, there were no such devices and going to sea in foggy weather could be a great strain on the nerves. Fog can play havoc with one's sense of judgment. There are times when a gull, sitting on the sea, can assume the proportions of a destroyer, and there are times when a streak of soot or the wake from a passing ship can be easily mistaken for rocks.

A few days of seeking the shore in smore thick conditions and your 'een'll be like pipe-lids! Your lugs will be on the alert listenin for the foghorn or the horns of other vessels and afore the week's oot, ye'll be like a rag!'

Now here's a strange thing. Fog has an uncanny habit of lifting at high-water. The reason why is beyond me but nevertheless it is a fact. Those exalted beings who study depressions and fronts (cold or warm) along with swirls of cloud and satellite pictures will naturally pooh-pooh this statement, but jist like ither folk they dinna ken aathing!

For fifty years I've watched this phenomenon, if that be the proper word, and I can say, along with countless others of my generation that, 'if the fog disna lift at high water, ye may as weel ging hame!'

Of course it doesn't always happen, but it happens a great deal oftener than not. Far too often for coincidence, but then a race which has been born into the age of electronics will probably never notice such a thing.

I'm thinking now of a particularly foggy morning in the Thirties. The crews of the inshore boaties were pacing back and fore in the old fishmarket at Peterhead waiting to see if the fog would lift. The 'Boddam Coo' (Buchan Ness Horn) had been roarin the hale nicht and was still roarin. To go to sea in such a fog was unthinkable so we would hing on till high-water and, if it didna clear, we would ging hame. High-water came but there was no change in the weather so the bourachie of fishers dispersed.

On the way home I was accompanied by a friend called Philip Cowe who bade in Merchant Street. 'This is the holiday,' says he, 'an my twaa quines is for Aiberdeen on the first bus. What a price to pey for a fare! Three an ninepence return! It's nae mowse! I'll be in fine time to mak their tay afore they rise.'

Now 'Cowie' is a Moray Firth name, awaa up aboot Buckie somewye, but 'Cowe' is a name fae the Broch to Rattra Heid. It canna hae onything t'dee wi cattle or the name wid ha been 'Coo'. According to Hamewith, 'Cowe' means, 'the branch or twig of a wayside shrub'. Still, that is by the way.

Philip had jist got the kettle bilin when he heard the milk cairt at the door. Like coontless ithers in the toon, he had 'folk bidin up the stair' so he wid hae t' watch that he didna tak the wrang milk!

When Philip got to the door the milkman, a stand-in for the usual man, was in the act of putting two separate lots of milk on the step, so, pointing to the right-hand lot Philip says cheerfully, 'Zat Cowe's milk?'

The stooping milkman slowly raised himself an dichtit the dreep fae 'is nose, then he launched into a proper tirade.

'No! It's nae cow's milk, ye great dytit fisher feel! I'm jist this meenit hame fae the Sahara. I've been up aa nicht milkin camels! I'll gie ye cow's milk! Some o you fisher chiels disna ken dirt fae chappit dates!'

Philip grabbed a bottle an bolted into the hoose.

Next time that fog forced us to call off our day's fishing he says, 'Peter, I'm nae gaan hame till the milkman's by!'

Now, for those who insist that there's nothing in a name, let me resurrect a tale from the distant days of my youth. It would appear that a Moray Firth fisherman with a Moray Firth name gave up the sea to start a sweetie shoppie.

Proud of his new premises, he painted in bold letters above the door his name, R. Slater, then spent the rest of his days wondering how and why he had acquired the nickname 'Heid First'!

Suntie Claas Couldna Beat This Present!

It was the last week in November and the East Anglian fishing was in its final stages.

The herring shoals had left their normal haunts among the tide-swept sand banks off the Norfolk coast and had moved elsewhere. This surprised nobody, because this was an occurrence which had varied very little for many generations, if not for centuries.

The end of November was the time when the Scots in their thousands would leave for home; indeed quite a few boats had already sailed and most of the remaining skippers were 'on the pirr'.

Of course, some of the real die-hards would stick it out for a while and try the notoriously coorse fishing grounds at Sandettie, off the French coast, but none of them would outlast Christmas Charlie from Cairnbulg, who for many years had made it his rule never to leave Yarmouth before Christmas, hence his nickname.

117

His boat was a relic of the days of sail and although she had been fitted with a diesel engine, only a stout heart would have gone to Yarmouth in her at all, let alone stay till Christmas!

Well now, 'twas Saturday and most skippers were advising their crews, 'I dinna think we'll be here anither weekend. We'll try't the first o the wik, an if there's nae herrin we'll just leave fae the sea, so ye'd better buy yer presents the day. Ye'll get a sub if ye need it!' Maist o the lads nott a sub.

Some lucky crews who had been fortunate enough to run to Ijmuiden in Holland with a big shot would have had their presents bought long ago — a bonny tray wi win'mills on't for the wife, or a pair o widden clogs for the bairn. But most of the fishers would have to do their shopping in Yarmouth, and since there were several thousands of them, to say nothing of the guttin quines and the coopers, the local shops did very well indeed and the rock factory had to work overtime.

There was a certain mystique about the Yarmooth present. An identical gift from Aberdeen could not possibly be half as good, and a 'stalk' (not a 'stick') of Yarmouth Rock could far surpass anything in the candy shoppies at hame.

Boys, how the fisher bairns smelt of peppermint in December!

And wasn't it wonderful when Da sent hame a 'boxie' maybe halfway through the season? A boxie wi some rock, twa-three aipples an pomegranates! I'm sure the trees in Eden never bore sweeter fruit!

This reminds me of the true story of the Sunday School class whose earnest teacher asked that every pupil who wished to go to Heaven should raise a hand. Every hand save one shot up.

The startled teacher, gazing kindly at the young heretic, asked in a whisper, 'Fit's adee, my loon? Fit wye div ee nae want t' ging t' Heaven?'

'Cos I hinna gotten my Yarmooth present yet!' was the reply.

Peer loon! Some years later, just shortly after his wedding, he was lost with all his shipmates when the *Quiet Waters* disappeared in a storm in 1954.

Aye, the Yarmooth Present was a highly prized gift but it was seldom expensive. How could it be? Apart from the immediate straitened financial situation, it had to be borne in mind that in a very few weeks 'Suntie Claas' would be expected to come doon the lum on Hogmanay Nicht (not Christmas Eve).

So thus the balance between 'fisher bairns' and 'toonser bairns' was redressed. While the fisher bairns were the envy of their classmates at Yarmooth time, 'Suntie' in due season was remarkably mean towards them. Ye canna get it twice!

But let's get back to Yarmouth River where the fleet was more or less ready to call at Seaham or Shields on the way home. There they would pick up several tons of coal, not for bunkers but 'for the hoose'.

The fish hold would be half filled with the best household coal at nineteen shillings a ton! Now, there was a 'richt Yarmooth present'! Less than a pound per ton. Shades of Scargill and MacGregor!

Each member of the crew could have a share of the coal according to the capacity of his coal-sheddie. This was common practice for many years, until there was some dibber-dabber aboot 'usin fishin boats for cargo boats' and finally the practice ceased. No doubt the local coal merchants had kickit up a stink.

Well now, here was I on that Saturday night on the hunt for suitable presents. That didn't take me very long — gloves for the wife and a toy tea-set for the bairn, but my companion, a shipmate, seemed very difficult to please.

'Ye see, Peter,' says he, 'my quine's gettin her grunny's organ fin she kicks the bucket an seein that the wifie's gey aal noo, it's time the quine wis learnin! I'm lookin for special music til 'er.'

I stood at the door of every music shop in Yarmooth in turn until I wis fair scunnert. On his exit, empty handed, from the umpteenth shop I demanded in exasperation, 'Fit is't ye're lookin for onywye? Is't a Bach Fugue or a Mendelssohn Sonata? Ye're jist a fashious brute!'

'Oh no!' says he, 'It's nae naethin lik 'at! I'm lookin for yon kin o stuff that the darkies sings! Somethin aboot a Sweet Chariot, ye ken!'

'That'll be Negro Spirituals that ye're needin,' says I.

'O gweed help's! Is 'at fit ye caa't? I've been seekin spooky music!'

The great baa-heidit oof!

Crafty Conquistador
fae St Catharine's Dub

The Don was a tall strappin chiel whose dark good looks might well have been envied by the stars of the silent film.

His swarthy handsomeness was accentuated by the white of his teeth when he smiled and by the tiny gold earrings which he wore, not for ornamentation, but in the sincere belief that earrings improved the eyesight.

This strange belief was common among seafarers of his generation, some of whom maintained stoutly that having the ear pierced was sufficient in itself, but I'm sure that this defence of half-measures was simply an attempt to conceal the fact that the price of the earrings was beyond them.

Some folk said there was gipsy blood in the Don. Others, less charitable, said it was 'tinkie bleed', for his deydie (grandad) had been a roving tinker selling pots and pans and his grunny had been a kitchie-deem at Balmoral.

Both rumours were utterly wrong, for the Don was, in all probability, a real Don, descendant of the sole survivor of the Spanish galleon which lies in St Catharine's Dub, near Collieston harbour. *Santa Catarina* was the galleon's name.

Balmoral? Never! A Spanish castle? Aye, surely! I'm thinkin that for many generations the Don's forebears had wrested a precarious living from the sea along the Buchan coast.

From tiny settlements like Collieston and the Old Castle at Slains, they had plied their trade in small boats, catching herring in season, but relying mainly on

119

smaa-lines with mussel bait for haddock, whiting and codling, not forgetting the 'plashies' (plaice) which were plentiful along the shore.

Their source of bait, the Ythan estuary, could hardly have been handier.

Since there were no fish-markets then, the fishers had to dispose of their own catches, so we find the women-folk 'traivlin' far up-country with their creels of fish on their backs, bartering their fish for farm-produce, butter, eggs or an antrin hen. Seldom indeed were there any cash deals, for the country folkies had nae siller. Still, the practice flourished for centuries, but it must have presented problems if a body wis needin a pair o boots or a sark.

Foo mony huddicks for a pair o briks? Foo muckle hard fish for a linner? (flannel shirt).

Speakin aboot hard fish, have ye ever tasted a speldin? No? Then ye dinna ken fit ye're missin!

Speldins were whitings split and cleaned then liberally salted prior to drying in the summer sun. These dried whitings were very tasty indeed and for many a long year Collieston speldins were renowned.

From far and near folk came to the village for the dazzling white fishies which were spread all over the place to dry. I'm tellin ye, the Ritz couldna offer ye onything to beat a speldin roassen (roasted) on a branner abeen an open fire. Serve with home-made 'breid' (oatcake) and country butter. Wow! I ken for a fact that mony a youngster took the speldin by the tail and scoffed the lot, bone an aa, leaving only the lug-been.

Sadly, Collieston speldins are now only memories. You see, the men who caught the whitings and the wives who processed them have long since departed and have never been replaced.

Now then, the need for bigger boats and better harbours drove the Don's forebears to seek pastures new. A bourachie o them settled in Boddam where they are reputed to have hang't the monkey.

Jist watch the Boddamers! Once in a generation (or it micht be twaa — the interval grows wider as time goes by) ye'll see a tall dark Adonis wi flashin een. He should really hae a pointed beard, a helmet, a horse, a lance an a sword! Ten to one his name is Stephen or Philip. Ye'll see the same thing aboot the Broch. Fancy? Weel, if the Buchans came oot o the Ark, the chances are that the Stephens an Philips cam oot o a galleon. Maybe they are entitled to royalties on sherry!

But the Don that I kent wis a Peterheid chiel, a fisherman an a good hand at that. Strictly inshore, of course. Not for him the wide open ocean wastes like the Viking or Bergen Banks. He clung doggedly to the old methods, smaa-lines, cod nets (they are not a modern innovation) and the ripper. Then, with the advent of the motor engine, he branched into trawling for flukes (flat fish).

The Don was also a harbour pilot. For a few bob per annum, he obtained from the Harbour Trustees a licence which permitted him to display on the bows of his boatie a large 'P' (official pilot). Since there were about a dozen such craft in the port, there was great rivalry between their skippers, for first aboard the steamer got the job of piloting her into port.

In those days, Peterhead had a thriving trade in timber, salt and coal, along with the export of vast quantities of cured herrings in barrels.

Mostly illiterate, these pilots knew their own coast and its tides like the backs of their hands and they were first-rate men at their job.

Strange as it may seem, all rivalry disappeared when the sound of the 'Lifeboat guns' was heard, for these same lads were always the lifeboat crew. Then the only rivalry was to see who could be first aboard.

Now, I did mention trawling, and here lay the Don's great weakness, for he was an inveterate poacher. Fancy that now! Oh aye. He was convinced that a box of fish from forbidden waters had a value far in excess of anything caught legally. He was not, and never will be alone in the belief.

Came the day when he was 'catched' with his boat full o fish and her propellor full o rope. Summoned to appear before the Sheriff in Aberdeen a week later, he spurned the local train and made the trip in his ain boatie.

Of course, he trawled all the way there, paid his substantial fine in court, then trawled all the way home, beating all the existing records for one day's fishing. A proper conquistador!

The Don's favourite stamping ground lay between Rattray Head and the Broch. From Rattray Head to the Cairnbulg Beacon you are in a bay called the Cample, and there the flukes are the world's best, as long as a fish-box and almost as broad, with spots as big as half-croons. Eight or maybe ten to the box!

It was risky to lift such a fish with one hand cos she could brak yer thoom if she twisted her tail. How do I know? Let that flee stick to the waa!

From the Beacon northwards you are in the Broch Bay and there the flukes are not quite so big. Ye'll get fifteen o them into a box.

It was the Don's custom to nip into the Broch just before the chip shops closed, then he sent one of his two crew members for a sixpenny supper, which would normally contain two fish, but since the shop was about to close he never failed to get an extra haddock and a double dose o chips.

Enough to give the three musketeers a good meal. A fly bird, the crow! Then the night's trawling would be resumed.

'An faar wis the Brochers aa this time?' ye may say.

At Barra Heid or the Butt o Lewis or shelterin for their lives in some Hielan loch.

Now, to the hardy breed of men who sail the stormy seas with the letters FR on their boats, let me give this earnest warning.

Jist watch this move that's on the cards eyvnoo t' lat the Spaniards intil the Common Market, cos if they're onything like the Don they winna be contintit wi yer fish.

They'll be needin yer chips anaa!

To Catch a Herrin, First Throw a Concrete Block

In the late 1940s, there was a sudden boom in the building of kippering kilns throughout the north-east. The long-suffering British public were now to be provided with the luscious kippers which had been denied them for several years.

However, when it came to the crunch, the public had got themselves acclimatised to spam and powdered egg so the demand for kippers was unexpectedly poor.

The kippering kilns were built with concrete blocks which had suddenly appeared on the scene as acceptable building material, but most people looked on the cement as pure rubbish, which 'wid faa doon an kill aabody!' Still, these same kilns are in use today as net factories, tyre depots etc. and they hinna faan doon yet!

At that time we were seine-netting in a 75 ft. MFV which was a fine craft. We realised she would be even better if we put in extra ballast to offset the weight of the great muckle deck-hoose, so with this in mind, we acquired a lorry load of the cement blockies and stowed them beneath the floor of the fish room. This greatly improved the boat's stability and we soon forgot they were there.

There was a persistent rumour for a while that a certain eminent building firm had gone bust cos somebody had stolen aa their blockies. Jist a rumour! As one of our crew remarked to the baffled police searchers, 'Ye canna leave naething nooadays! They wid tak the een oot o yer heid an come back for the holes!'

Winter wore into summer and soon it was time to switch to herring fishing. But altho it was herrin time, there was, alas, nae herrin, at least not on the local grounds.

Several skippers decided to try 'the boxin'. This meant going to far-away places such as the Patch or the Reef or even further. Any herring caught would be iced into boxes and stowed below so that a second night's fishing could be carried out.

Of course, a bumper haul would mean an immediate return to port, but it was deemed prudent to be prepared for at least two nights at sea, for it was simply not possible to make the round trip in a day.

About half a score of boats, mostly steam drifters, left Peterhead at the back o Sunday and steamed to the eastward until the evening, when it was time to shoot the nets.

Next morning proved that all had drawn a blank except our own good selves. We had fourteen cran, which did not justify a return trip, so into the boxes they went, before being iced and covered with sheets of grease-proof paper. Then they had to be stowed oot o the road in the side-lockers or 'wings' o the hold. Fit a job!

You see, the wings of the hold, owing to the shape of the boat, are very narrow at the bottom but wide at the top, so stowing these boxes was like building a pyramid upside down. Eventually we got them secured, but not without a few jammed fingers and several bad words.

All that day we dodged further to the east, for apparently we had not got far enough the first night.

There was ample time in the afternoon to sleep or to read whatever was at hand. That afternoon I had been reading an article in a very posh publication, concerning the remarkable prowess of certain ring-net fishermen in the Firth of Clyde.

According to the article, the herring was an unpredictable beastie which clung to the seabed all day and rose to the surface at night. I knew this to be true, just as I knew that they didn't always rise far enough.

These fishermen had discovered a method of bringing the herring up to a point where their net could reach them. The secret was to have on deck a few bags of sand. The skipper, having located the herring shoal on the seabed, would order his crew to sprinkle handfuls of sand into the sea, while he steered the boat zig-zag across the shoal. The sand would sink to the bottom, where it would kittle the herrin's backs and gar them rise!

'Weel, weel,' says I, 'I've heard a lot, but this beats aa!'

That night, when we had shot our nets, it was decided that the concrete blockies were now surplus to requirements and should therefore be dumped overboard.

During this, I expressed the humble opinion that 'if herrin wid rise, ower the heids o a suppie o san, they wid ging berserk if we drappit cement blocks on their heids!' We would be fortunate indeed to see a net in the morning. We would 'loss the lot'!

Brother John merely shook his head and said:

'Niver mind 'im. He's only makkin that up!'

Well now, when we started to haul at 1 a.m., we could do nothing at all with the first net. She was absolutely ram-stam full o herrin, and five crews couldn't have hauled her.

Before our eyes, the net tore to ribbons with the strain, and we managed to save only a few fragments. This was disaster indeed, for we had eighty nets to haul.

The second net, however, was not nearly so heavily fished, having only some three cran in her, which was more than plenty. Thereafter the nets were in no danger and we finished up with 170 cran. Then it was full butt for Peterhead. One of my mates remarked: 'It's funny that the overloaded net wis nearest to the spot far we dumped the blocks! It's a good job we didna steam along the fleet o nets, drappin blocks aa the wye!'

When I made no reply he asked: 'Did ee ken that the herrin wid rise like yon?'

'Certainly!' said I, 'Didn't I warn ye aforehand?'

Neither to him, nor to anyone else, would I confess that I hadn't believed one word of the article.

The Drawbacks of Rubber Boots

For the magnificent weekly wage of thirty-four shillings and tenpence, Jeemsie was cook on the drifter *Meadowsweet*.

In today's decimal coinage his pay would be £1.74. For that amount of cash he had to cook every meal for ten men and keep the cabin and the galley clean.

He had to haul the nets like any deckie and assist in the discharging of the catch and, while he was not obliged to keep a watch at the wheel, he was duty bound to relieve the skipper at meal times.

He was not required to keep a watch at the nets and, should the shippie be away from home, as she often was for weeks at a time, he was not obliged to make the supper on Sunday. What a concession!

Peer Jeemsie, like the rest o's, didna ken ony better!

Behold now our hero in the shippie's cabin at 1 a.m., that witching hour when fishermen keep their tryst with the silver darlings. The crew have just had their tay and Jeemsie is donning a brand new pair of rubber boots.

'Ye surely dinna hae big feet, my loon?' says the Turk.

'No, skipper, they're nae big. Six an a half.'

'Man!' says the Turk, 'Fin I wis your age I had the bonniest feeties on the East coast. The quines fairly likit t' dunce wi me, I wis sic a bonny duncer. The Hielan deems jist gid wild fin I took them up for a wultz. I think it wis my little feeties that did it!'

'Fit's come ower yer feeties noo, skipper?' says Duncan the driver, 'Did ye meet in wi a traction engine or something?'

The Turk ignored this sally and addressed Jeemsie thus: 'Ye shouldna wear rubber boots, my loon!'

'Foo nae, skipper?'

'Weel, my loon, there's an affa suction in them. They'll sook yer feet like twaa poultices then ye'll ging blin. Rubber boots is affa sair on young men's een.'

'Faa tellt ye that, skipper?'

'Yon mannie that has the boot shop in the Longate.'

'Aye, aye,' says Jeemsie drily, 'he sells leather boots, I suppose?'

'Dam't,' says Duncan, 'I'll hae to write to my brither at Povertyknap (pronounce the k) an tell 'im aboot this suction ferlie. His wife's an eeseless bizzom an she maks a peer shape at milkin the coo. If she sticks a pair o rubber boots on the coo's udders she winna need to touch the beast avaa! She winna even need a pail — the boots'll kep the milk!'

'Affa clivver!' laughed the Turk, 'But ye canna beat the leather.'

'Weel,' says Jeemsie, 'fit wye div ye hae t' thump an stump like an elephant t' get yours on, an gettin them aff's jist like a horse gettin shaved?'

'Niver mind that! Ho-ro lads, let's get a start!' says the skipper. Then a second later as he heaved his bulk up the trap, 'Good grief, I've torn my briks on a nail! But that'll hae t' wyte.'

The crew trooped forrard to where the deck was brightly lit by the two acetylene lamps on the wheelhouse front. The after half of the vessel remained in darkness.

With a hiss of steam, the captain took the strain on the heavy rope which was pulled into the rope-locker and coiled neatly there by the fireman.

Slowly but surely the vessel moved ahead and soon the first net was being dragged aboard like a great sheet.

The silvery shimmer of herring brought a ripple of excitement, expressed in the tender words of endearment uttered by each and every man. 'Swim up you little dears! Come away now, stick your little heads in! Let this day be spoken about! Just a few more please!'

Duncan never ceased to wonder why his shipmates should unfailingly resort to English when they implored the herring to come to them. They would coax and cajole and wheedle, as if the herring were a reluctant maid. Oh, the feel fishers!

When the net had been hauled, it was immediately slacked away again. 'We'll gie her half-an-hour yet,' says the Turk.

This was common practice. It was simply an effective way of finding out whether the fish were still swimming. The first go at the nets was always called 'Lookin on'.

'Half a cran in her: that's a good markin!' says the skipper. 'Jeemsie, my loon, I wid shue this hole in my briks but it wid mean takin my boots aff an ye ken fit that is!'

'Fine div I ken that.' was the reply. 'But we'll try't athoot the boots an briks comin aff.'

So down to the engine room went the Turk for repairs. Duncan had difficulty threading the needle so he passed it to Jeemsie whose deft fingers made a very neat job of stitching on the stooping Turk's starboard hip.

'Dinna ging ower deep wi the needle,' says Duncan. 'It widna dee t' job the mannie! Gweed folk's scarce ye ken!'

The repair completed, it was time to haul in earnest. Almost a basket of herring had meshed in the clean net so, at the skipper's 'Haul awaa, lads' the crew buckled to, with a will.

It was warm, hard work, teamwork par excellence, a skill gained from long years at the job, with never a man putting a finger through a mesh. Only greenhorns did that.

Duncan the chief was on the side-deck beside the wheel-house working a scum-net which was really a gigantic butterfly net with a heavy pole. With this he was retrieving some of the herring which had fallen loose from the nets; these were usually the cream of the crop and were the perks for the chief, the fireman and the cook. 'Scum' they were called (the herrin, I mean).

The nets were about 'half hauled' when the skipper, who was at the cork-raip, summoned Duncan, 'Tak a hud o this raip a meenit, Duncan. I'll hae t' run!' And with that he disappeared into the shadows near the stem.

'Ho-ho!' chuckled Jeemsie, 'So the skipper wants to be alone. Well it's his ain blame — he winna bide awaa fae pey soup.'

His laughter was cut short by an unearthly yell from the darkness. 'Come wi a knife Duncan! Hing in man, hing in! Come wi a knife!'

125

Duncan ran immediately but he was back in less than a minute, folding his pocket knife before slipping it into his pocket. With a warning shake of the head he gazed at Jeemsie.

'Jeemsie, my freen, ye'll hear the riot act read the day! Ye'll get "Who broke the hurley!" I telt ye nae t' ging ower deep wi the needle but ye didna listen. Ye great goat, ye shewed the mannie's briks til 'is sark so he couldna get a start. I wis jist in time!'

The returning skipper said nothing, but the glower he gave the cook spoke volumes.

About six o'clock in the morning the shippie was under way, with the delighted skipper in a forgiving mood. Well, he had a bonny shot, hadn't he? Eighty or ninety cran was a great night's work.

In fear and trembling the cook came to take the wheel so that the Turk could go aft for his tay. But the expected storm did not materialise. Instead, the skipper gave the youngster a playful punch on the shoulder.

'I believe ye did yon deliberate, ye coorse skate! Ye're an affa lad!'

'Na, na, skip, nae me!' says Jeemsie, 'I wisna seein richt fin I wis using the needle. Maybe it wis the rubber boots sookin my feet!'

The Ghost in the Fite Seemit

Skipper Bob McTurk, 'The Turk' had suffered a major defeat at the hands of his better half.

For years she had begged him to change into lighter clothing when the bonny days came round, but her pleas had fallen on deaf ears.

Now, her patience finally exhausted, she sailed in with all guns blazing.

'Ye great greasy clort that ye are! Ilkie time I wash yer shift the claes-tow braks wi the wecht.'

'Ye should ging up to Jimmy Reid's an get a horse, then get a soord an a battle axe fae the museum. I'll gie ye my ain coal-pail for a helmet but ye winna need armour! Nae wi a shift like that! Then ye can flee the hills like Sir Lancelot!'

Under such an onslaught, the poor Turk wilted. But on one point he was adamant: he would on no account wear shorts.

'They micht dee for liftin a het kettle but they wid nivver hap me!'

Neither would he visit a shop. So, in view of his enormous girth, nothing would suffice but to get a sicht o drawers an seemits fae the shop so that he could wale among them at his leisure.

But still there was one great problem. Any drawers that fitted his middle would need a fathom cut from the legs; if they fitted his legs they would need a yard of elastic at the top! No seemit would fit him athoot a great muckle gushet shued into the front.

126

Fit a maneer! Claes aa ower the place, like a stallie on the Broadgate!

It took a long time to reach a happy compromise but at last the mannie wis riggit oot and the unwanted garments were baled in readiness for their return to the shop.

On the Monday morning our gallant hero left the house to go to the harbour.

Oh boys this wis fine! Pure fresh air wis circulating where fresh air had seldom been afore.

This wis life, this wis freedom as if a door had been opened!

Then in one blinding second panic filled his breast.

There couldna possibly be such a free flow of air unless there wis a doorie open!

Good grief! Had he forgotten to fasten certain vital buttons?

A quick downward glance would reassure him, but his washin-hoose biler o a belly decreed that this wis impossible.

He could hardly ficher wi buttons in the street so he would turn back.

Turn back on a Monday? Never! All the bad luck in Scotland would be his if he did that.

He could stop a passing boy with a question, 'Hey my loon! Is my shoppie door open?' but he didna like.

Were he to venture up a close for a quick check, some wifie would be sure to doubt his intentions and would chase him wi a broom bidding him, 'Ging an dee that at yer ain gate en'!'

The situation was critical but not entirely out of hand.

The Turk's mither wit led him to the nearest shop window where his own reflection assured him that all was well.

So the gentle breezes were part and parcel of his new found freedom? Great!

Thus, in a happier mood, he reached the pier where his own darling *Meadowsweet* awaited him.

Oh, fit a steer! Horses an cairts by the score.

At least a hunner crews busy at their nets.

Coal-heavers walking the precarious planks with ten stone bags of coal on their backs, just like black ballet dancers on a heaving stage, dropping their load with unerring aim into the pit of the drifter's bunker.

Message boys with their baskets and watermen with their hoses; it was all go, for the armada was preparing to sail in the afternoon.

Fit a bonny day it wis! Half the toon wis on the pier to see the shippies gaan oot.

Since it wis Monday, the guttin quines half day, scores of them were doon to wave cheerio to their lads and husbands.

Even Mrs McTurk wis there, wi twaa bairns at her tail an twaa in the coach (pram).

As the *Meadowsweet* rounded the jetty, the Turk stuck his arm out of the wheelhouse window to wave to his excited offspring and in so doing he got a welcome blast of fresh air aneth his oxter.

Late that evening the *Meadowsweet* lay at her nets some forty miles east-by-north off Peterhead. She lay head to wind at the leeward end of a mile of nets which hung like a great curtain two fathoms below the surface. The shippie was tethered by a thick tarry rope which ran the whole length of the nets and on this rope she would be heaved ahead in the morning when the process of hauling would begin.

It was a lovely evening with the sun sinking behind a low bank of dark cloud, a sure sign of westerly wind to come.

Close astern a great white carpet of birds had settled on the calm waters to await their breakfast from the nets. Now and then the silence was gently broken by the soft 'Whoo-oof' of a herring whale.

Monday night meant that there was no back-log of sleep to catch up on so the crew were rather slower than usual to turn in. They sat for a while behind the wheelhouse discussing the past weekend and vying with each other in identifying the vessels nearest to them.

As far as the eye could see, there were ships on the same errand as themselves. Each one had her mizzen sail set and her two paraffin dig lights becoming more readily visible in the gathering dark.

Then, as if by common consent, all hands went below to turn in, leaving one man to keep watch.

There would be three one-hour watches and the last man would mak e tay at 1 a.m.

In the cabin there was a shocked silence as the skipper removed his briks afore turning in.

'This is something new, boys! Here's a man gaan in ower athoot 'is briks!'

'The days o miracles is surely nae past efter aa! An fit's this he's wearin?'

'Surely nae fite drawers an a fite seemit? Ye never saw the like afore, did ye?'

'Nivver! It's a mercy we're aa spared!'

Of course Jeemsie the cook started to snicker and when he whispered 'Moby Dick, the great white whale!' the dam burst and the crew laughed themselves silly.

'Folk'll nivver believe this!' But the amusement faded rapidly when the Turk disappeared into his bunk, treating his men with silent contempt.

The man on watch in the wheelhouse knew nothing of this. Nor was he aware that about eleven o'clock the Turk had come on deck in his new outfit to hae a look at the nicht an to listen intently for the quiet 'plop' o herrin loupin.

The watchman came aft at his appointed time to call his relief. Then suddenly his hair stood on end for there on the starboard quarter stood a ghostly figure, 'clothed in white samite; mystic, wonderful'.

The poor deckie gave one piercing yell of terror and bolted!

'Od, there maun be something wrang wi that loon!' says the Turk and he ambled forrard in the wake of the terror stricken youth, whose yell had brought three of his mates on deck in a state of alarm.

But when these fellas got on deck, the sound of running feet was away in the fore part of the vessel, so they set off to investigate.

At the end of the first lap, the thunder of feet brought the rest of the crew on deck in a hurry and they too joined in the hunt.

Towards the end of the fourth lap, the Turk tripped on a pond board and fell clyte on his belly.

His crew promptly fell on top of him and there was a great stramash.

The sole survivor had scooted down to the cabin and into his bunk like a frightened rabbit.

It was a gey sheepish and tired crew who silently took their tay at 1 a.m. The skipper, for all his bulk, was the fittest of the lot.

'Now, lads,' says he, 'if ye're gaan t' run a marathon ye're better t' weir the richt gear for't. Ye'll nivver see the winnin post wi hairback briks an worsit drawers on!'

'That's fit I had on,' says the watchman, 'an I bate the hale lot o ye!'

Leebie's Solid Sheelters

The eastern sky was pink with the first hazy rays of the rising sun when Leebie, sick again, rose from her bed. As she knelt on the floor and retched miserably into a pail — there was no sink — she reflected rather bitterly, 'This'll be the fifth een an the aalest een's nae at the school yet! It's just nae richt o oor John Willie t' dee this t' me!'

John Willie, the man of the house, had left for the sea some two hours earlier, with his beautiful baited haddock line in a huge wicker scull balanced on his hip. Not till dinner time would he return, with his appetite whetted by the sea and several hours' work. Fish or no fish, he would be hungry.

Od, he wis aye hungry, the bairns were aye hungry, and it was cook an scrub an wash an bait fae brak o sky till lang efter dark. There wis aye a something!

Leebie pulled hersel thegither then dichtit her face wi the flannel clootie afore she lookit oot at the door towards the foreshore less than fifty yards distant. The tide wis perfect for gaitherin mussels.

It wis time she wis at the scaap — she could see some there already — so drawing a thick tartan shawl roon her shooders she hastened to the shore, mussel basket in hand. In the basket there wis a crude iron tool for her to tear the mussels frae the rocks.

Long experience had taught Leebie that to gather bait with bare hands was to invite lacerated fingers. Slacken the mussels first, then gather them into the basket.

A few months earlier a hale cairt-load o mussels hid arrived in the village from the Ythan estuary. The load hid been shared oot by guesswork amon the different families, and each family carried its own 'heap' to the rocky shore far the mussels were spread in a position far the tide could reach them daily, thus keepin them alive.

Each faimly mussel-patch wis caad 'the scaap' an wis separated fae its neepers by little dykies o steens. The mussels seen clung to the rocks and could be obtained by the women (always the women) fan the tide permitted. Honesty wis seldom questioned but fan Job wrote yon versie, 'Some remove the landmarks',

I'm sure he wis writin aboot the mussel scaaps.

Leebie kent her bairns wid sleep a lang time yet so she took the opportunity for a news wi her neepers while they gaithered their bait. Janet, one o the senior members o the group raised a bit o a laach fin she remarked, on seeing Leebie's pale face, 'Aye, Aye my quine, ye're jist like the lave o hiz fishermen's wives! Ye're expected t' be a horse aa day an a meer aa nicht!' Naebody contradicted her but there were a few blushes on the cheeks of the younger women.

Her basket filled, Leebie carried it to the hoose far she hid a quick peep at her sleeping bairns afore returning to the scaap for mair mussels. Then it wis time to start on the daily household chores, for her brood wid seen be clamouring for their porridge.

Although every drop o water had to be carried fae the waal in the street, and although there wis no sanitation, Leebie's hoosie wis spotless, as were her bairns. Certainly, there were fool faces and hands at times but ye ken bairns that are fool temporarily fae bairns that are forivver yirdit!

The hoosie, like sae mony ithers, comprised a butt an a ben wi a little closetie in the middle, and had been hame to several generations of John Willie's folk.

The said John Willie duly arrived for his denner wi his line in its scull, but now the line required to be redd. This would be his work in the efterneen, unravelling the long line and replacing any missing hooks (wants). When he had finished, the line would be ready for baiting again.

While he was engrossed in this task Leebie would sheel (shell) the mussels using a futtle (gutting knife) to slit the shells open and with a deft flick of the wrist skite the juicy mussel into a clean pail. This was an art, a skill gained over years of practice. Meanwhile, the aalest quine would rock her little sister in the cradle while the twaa loons played aboot the door.

The bairns seen learned to keep clear o the line wi its barbed hooks. A skelp or twaa fairly helped their learning.

Fan the mussels had been sheeled, Leebie took the empty 'shaals' and dumped them on the shore. The pail o juicy bait wis laid aside until later; she wid bait the line fan the bairns were beddit, for then she wid get peace an quaet.

The baiting wid tak her aboot twaa oors an she wid need aa the mussels in the clean pail to bait the 450 hooks. John Willie wid hae the line aa ready for her, neatly coiled in a basket wi ivvery hook 'stuck', i.e. the horse-hair tippin was twined lightly round the hook so that when Leebie drew the line through her hand the points of the hooks were pointed away from her. Thus the hooks didn't get entangled in the line itself, and it also saved the baiter's fingers.

Leebie would coil the line neatly into the great wicker scull, baiting each hook skilfully, laying the baited hooks in rows across the mouth of the scull and separating the rows with layers of fresh grass. Everything had to be done with care so that the line would run clear in the dark o the mornin.

Aye, Leebie had few spare meenits aa her mairried life! She bore her trials and tribulations wi a cheerfu hert but one thing really got her riled, an this wis the theft o her sheeled mussels by the loons o the village. These rascals could have got plenty o mussels on the shore to bait the bits o line that they amused themselves wi, but why ficher wi mussels in their shells when they could pinch a few fae Leebie's pail?

Ye see, Leebie had the habit o puttin her pail o sheeled mussels ootside the door in the evening, to prevent the pail being cowpit in the steer as she washed and beddit the bairns. The loons kent far Leebie's pail wis left an they kent that if they were stealthy and swift at the same time, they could get 'solid sheelters' (plenty of shelled mussels).

It grieved Leebie that the fruits of her labours were being pilfered, leaving her occasionally short of bait for her own line.

In vain she cyardit the loons — they just leuch and ran.

'Ee'll sup sorra wi the speen o grief, gin I catch ye!' she would yell at them, to no avail, for fine did they ken that wi their fleetness they were safe.

But this particular night there came to Leebie a brilliant idea whose simplicity and certain dire effect made her chuckle in anticipation.

Among all the pails that Leebie required, one of the most important was the 'orra pail', the slop-bucket which was teemed at least twice daily where the cleansing tide would remove all traces. Now, with fower bairns in a hoosie that lacked sanitation, that bucket could fyles contain some gey ferlies!

So, in the gathering dark Leebie substituted the orra pail for the mussel pail and waited inside the door for results. Soon she heard the stealthy approach, the short pause as two cupped hands scooped their loot from the brimming bucket, then the head-long flight of the juvenile marauder.

In a few seconds she heard his jubilant cry to his pals, 'Solid sheelters, boys! Solid sheelters!' then, 'Oh gyaad! Oh gyaad!'

Then Leebie doubled up wi laughter, kennin that nivver again wid the rascals raid her mussel pail. But as she enjoyed her unaccustomed mirth, a sudden stab o pain brought her up sharp an she muttered to hersel, 'Oh Lord, it's jist nae richt o oor John Willie t' dee this t' me!'

There's aye a something, Leebie!

An Underwater Treasure Trove

I am convinced that, at some time in his career, every fishing skipper has had a wonderful dream in which he discovers an underwater hidden valley, whose bottom is as smooth as a bowling green.

Of course, this hidden valley is surrounded by peaks and ridges of jagged rock where no net could possibly survive, but which, by the same token, form a perfect refuge for millions of fish of every kind.

The floor of the valley is literally spear-deep with prime flatfish; lemon soles and plaice will scarcely be able to find a parking space between the tiers of giant halibut, and immediately above this priceless treasure, cod and haddock of divine proportions gambol to and fro like great flocks of sheep.

Only at great cost has this skipper managed to locate the valley, as masses of torn netting and broken ropes festooning the surrounding precipices will testify, but now that he has the key to this priceless treasure, he keeps the dark secret to himself.

Only when there are no other vessels in sight will he venture to drag his net across the valley floor and only when the diamond market is sky-high will he dip into this boundless treasure store.

Ah well! There's nothing to stop a fella from dreaming, I suppose. But such places, if they ever existed, have long since been accurately charted and relentlessly fished bare, for modern fishing gear and high powered diesels allied to unbelievable electronics have, alas, left no refuge whatever for the denizens of the deep.

Conservation means a lot in the dictionary but it doesn't mean a thing on the sea where every skipper except oneself is just a blasted pirate!

There is, however, an alternative dream to the aforementioned idyll and that is to find a wreck which nobody else knows about. Preferably, this wreck should be a ship which died peacefully and not as the result of some cataclysmic explosion which has scattered great masses of debris over a wide area.

No, she is much better if she is a 'clean' wreck, for then you can get your net close to the sunken ship which, as a rule, has a great attraction for fish. Such wrecks do exist.

I well remember going from Peterhead to Sheerness in a drifter early in 1940. We called at Hartlepool for coal and from there southward it was impossible to steer a straight course because of the masts and funnels of mined ships which littered the fairway.

There must have been many more which had disappeared completely. The seabed for many miles in all directions from the Tyne entrance is strewn thickly with wrecks.

In the 1950s, with the advent of the Decca Navigator, it was possible to pinpoint these wrecks and plot them on an accurate chart so that one could fish between them. At first this was highly profitable but, since there was no rich area of jagged peaks nearby to replenish the valley floor, the fish were gradually fished up, especially when more skippers got to know the exact location of every ship. So it was a case of 'Find your own wreck'.

This we managed to do, quite by accident. Away on our own, seeking pastures new, we unwittingly encircled a bobby-dazzler of a ship in our seine net gear and were promptly brought to a sudden halt. But with great patience and not a little skill, gained in the hard school of experience, we managed to retrieve our gear without serious loss.

Then we steamed slowly to and fro above the sunken Goliath, marking her outline on the echo sounder and plotting her exact length and beam on our home-made chart. For quite a while we managed to keep her location secret, and we did very well off that ship.

Although the fish were seldom plentiful around her, the quality was always supreme. But, like most secrets, her location finally leaked out and she became known, as she still is known, as 'Peter's Wreck'. I suppose few if any of those skippers who fish around her now know who Peter is. I'm sure they don't care!

One lovely November day we were fishing in that area, some eighteen miles east-south-east of the Tyne, when a cargo vessel stopped beside us, waiting for our net to break surface. Flying the Dutch flag, she was from Montrose for the Mediterranean with a cargo of seed tatties which would probably come back to Montrose in the summer as choice Cyprus spuds.

When we hauled the net we went right alongside with the fry her skipper had requested. 'Two baskets of haddocks please.' On seeing my surprised glance he explained that he had on board a big chest freezer which was crying out for fresh fish, so two baskets it was. And the price? Two cartons of Lucky Strike fags and the biggest bottle of booze I have ever seen, freely offered and willingly accepted. The plunder was placed in my bunk while we carried on fishing.

Late that night, in Shields Gut, the great share-out took place. It was Saturday night and, since we did not fish on Sundays, there was no hurry to turn in, so we sat for a while reading our mail over a leisurely joog o tay.

'I've been thinkin aboot the swag,' says the cook. 'There's five o's aathegither; we aa smoke but only twaa o's taks a drink, gie hiz twaa the bottle an pairt the fags amon the three o ye.'

Everybody agreed, so the two rascals mittened the bottle, a great muckle square thing that held about half a gallon. The print on the label was foreign and the contents were crystal clear. The delighted pair put a drappie in their tay and judging by the smack of their lips and the sparkle in their eyes, it was first class. And so to bed.

I was rudely awakened at 1 a.m. by the sound of our two heroes practically fighting each other for the toilet. 'Hing in, min! Come oot o that an lat me in!'

All day on Sunday it continued thus. In fact the two of them never donned their trousers at all.

'Coorse stuff yon!' says the cook, 'It comes through ye like bilin leed!'
'Bilin leed?' exclaimed his pal, 'Pirn threed's mair like it!'

But I was Blinded by the Sun!

In the modern fishing boat, practically everything is controlled from the wheelhouse. It would be no problem for an experienced man to take a boat to sea by himself, provided he knows how to start the engine.

But in the steam drifters this was not the case. The drifters' wheelhouse equipment comprised a steering wheel, a telegraph and a voice-pipe to the engine room, and an overhead compass. There had to be somebody in the engine room to work the engine controls and fire the boiler. These duties were carried out by the 'black squad', the chief and the fireman who, along with the cook received a weekly wage.

The chief's wages were forty-five shillings; the fireman and the cook got thirty-five shillings per week, but they got no share of the catch. From their wages the chief, fireman and cook had to leave ten shillings weekly to pay for their food.

During the hauling of the nets the cook had to haul with the deckies, the fireman had to coil the tarry messenger rope and the chief had to be handy in case a few turns of the propeller were required from time to time. Since this was not often the case, the chief was free to wield a great muckle thing like a butterfly net on the end of a stout pole to retrieve any herrings which had fallen back into the sea from the nets.

This instrument was called a 'scummer' and on a good night the chief could catch a basket, maybe even two baskets of 'scum'. The proceeds from the sale of such herrings he shared with the fireman. If at the end of a week they had ten shillings apiece for 'scum' they would have thought they were doing well.

Many of the chiefs or 'drivers', as they were called, 'drove' the same shippies for several years, so much so that they became synonymous with the ships they sailed in. A good driver was a treasure — he was efficient and economical. He could save a bob or two here and there and in those days a bob or two counted for a great deal.

Such a man was Joe Tait. To me he was an aal aal mannie, who had been a drifter driver for many years. Since I was only eighteen or so, I thought that Joe must be positively 'hairy moulded' with age though he was still going to sea. When the time came for Joe to quit the sea, he got himself a ripper boatie which was a great deal older than he was himself.

She was clinker-built (planks overlapping) and she rejoiced in the name *Star of Fame*. Her length? Say 18ft. Sail or oars but no engine of any kind. So now that you have been introduced to Joe and his boat, I'll get on with my tale.

'Twas the month of December, 1935. I had just finished decarbonising the engine of our family boat which at that time was a 40-footer with a 36 h.p. Kelvin paraffin engine. In fact I had the engine running and was about to take the boat into the bay for a trial run, when down came a regular crewman asking: 'Fit aboot a go at the ripper? I hear the cod's jist solid at Boddam Heid!'

'I'm willin,' says I, 'but we've nae rippers.'

'Och! that's nae bother,' was the reply, 'I'll pinch my father's gear!' And that's exactly what he did, so, fully equipped, we set out for the ripper grounds just north of Buchan Ness. We would fill the boat with prime cod. So we thought.

It was a lovely winter morning with the sun like a ball of golden fire. The glare reflected from the sea was positively blinding and since we were steering into the sun the effect was doubled. I have experienced the same dazzle while driving a car on a wet road on a winter morning. As soon as you drive into the sun you are blinded.

And so it happened that in the glittering brilliance, we failed to see the *Star of Fame* dead ahead of us. At the very last moment I spotted the boatie and spun the wheel hard to starboard but alas, it was too late. Our stem struck the boatie about two feet from her stern post, thus swinging her hard against our port side as we steamed past. Joe's shipmate, Alex Findlay, managed to get one arm and one leg across our bulwark and held on like grim death until we came to his assistance.

Poor old Joe was not so agile and he was left standing in his rapidly-sinking boat. With the helm hard to starboard our vessel executed a tight circle and within a few seconds I had her back alongside the casualty, from whence we dragged the old man by the scruff of his neck backwards on to our deck.

By that time, he was thigh-deep in water and apparently unable to move. His boatie sank immediately we had a grip of him. We salvaged the mast and the oars, but the *Star of Fame* had been extinguished forever.

Of course I had to go and face the music at home. I need not trouble you with the details of that distressing episode, except that it was made perfectly clear to me that had either Joe or his pal been lost we would have been in deep trouble, since we had no insurance cover whatsoever! Meanwhile, I would have to see about replacing the lost boat.

In the afternoon I went in fear and trembling to the Custom House which at that time was in the building now occupied by the British Legion. There I made a full report to the Registrar of Shipping, Mr Cardno, who searched his records diligently but without success for any trace of the *Star of Fame*. He must have seen that I was quite distressed, for he tried his best to reassure me.

'Look here!' says he. 'That boat is not in my books so she must be about a hundred years old! Since nobody has been drowned and there have been no injuries there will be no need for any court proceedings. Settle the affair between yourselves but watch that Joe doesn't demand a ransom for his boatie!'

At an informal afternoon meeting in Irvin's office, Aal Joe was quite adamant that, for the loss of his boat and gear, he wis needin sax powen! There was no dibberdabber, sax powen it was and the salesman paid Joe on the spot. Salesmen can be very useful at times. Of course, he would have to be repaid later. At that time I didna hae sax shillins.

A few weeks later I met Joe at the Cross Keys corner. Rather hesitantly I asked him, 'Fit like, Joe?' 'My loon!' says he, 'Ye did me a richt gweed turn yon day! I took the bus to Port Errol an there I bocht a boatie fae yon nae-weel mannie. I got a larry fae Jimmy Sutherland to tak her to Peterheid, an Reuben's putten an engine oot o a Baby Austin intil her. She gings like an evil speerit an I nivver need to touch an oar noo! The best that ivver cam doon!'

'My govies,' says I, 'that must hae cost ye a fortin afore ye got her to sea!'
'It did that,' says Joe. 'About sax powen!'

He was simply delighted with his 'new' craft. Her present-day equivalent? Say £850!

The Puff Adder and the Eskimo

If ye're lookin for a worthy exponent of the Noble Art of Girnin, ye could try a Buchan fairmer that has blight amon his tatties an canker amon his neeps.

On the ither han, ye could try a Gaimrick that's lost a nicht's fishin at the 'heerin' (nae 'herrin').

The twaa o them wid mak a pair!

But if it's superlative performance ye're efter, ye should hae a news wi a native dyed-in-the-wool Boddamer. I'll guarantee that in less than five meenits ye'll hae a lump in yer throat an the tears'll be trippin ye!

Even tho the chiel's into his second million, ye'll come awaa wi the impression that 'The Lord's better t' strangers than He is til's ain!' It's a gift, man, a gift!

In the Loquacity League, only goal-difference separates the Buckie Blaaver fae the Brocher that's hame fae Yarmooth wi a gweed fishin, while in the Friendly Furlongs, the Lossie man runs neck an neck wi the Duffer, eence they've been half an hour in 'The Gallon Can'.

Now, if by ony extraorinar chance ye're seekin sheer brazen impidence, dinna ging by the Blue Toon! 'Twid be a waste o time.

Here in my native town, the gifts of Effrontery and Mendacity have been so liberally bestowed that no other Scot can possibly hud a cannle to the Bluemogganers.

Div ye want proof?

Weel noo, some fifty-odd year ago, a gang o hiz loons wis playin on the spendin beach that faces ye as ye come into Peterheid Fishery Harbour. This beach is actually on the Queenie.

In those days, Peterhead had two entrances and it was not unusual for great shoals of mackerel to enter the port via the North Harbour and make their exit via the South Harbour.

Strange as it may seem, nobody wanted mackerel then, apart from the gulls and the delighted seals who gorged themselves on the silver bounty. The fish were at times literally in millions.

So it came to pass that on the aforementioned beach we managed to separate a baby seal fae its mither. We didna want to bad-use the beastie; we jist wanted a bittie o fun oxterin an clappin the craitur chance aboot. Och, the beast wis apparently haein a lot o fun tee, fin faa comes on the scene but a chiel caa'd English Harry.

Our intention o returning the pup to its mither wis dashed fin Harry confiscated our prize and made aff wi it. Half an hour later we saw him in earnest consultation with his pal 'Duff', a local whose nickname had been gained in a most unusual fashion.

Apparently Duff had been on a battleship during the Great War and like so many fisher lads he was in constant hot water for not saluting his superiors.

One Christmas Day he was detailed to fetch from the main galley the duff for his mess, and while he was carrying the steaming monster on a great muckle tray

136

he met Admiral Jellicoe to whom he made the earnest request: 'Will ye hud this duff till I salute ye?'

In shocked amazement the admiral took the proffered tray while Duff gave him a really smart salute before resuming his way with his precious load.

Weel noo, the day after Harry took the seal, a strange apparition was seen at Aikey Fair.

In a little broon tintie made oot o a drifter's hatch cover, there wis a drifter's barkin-tank. The tank was about five feet long, three feet wide and four feet deep. Most drifters had such a tank for barking the herring nets. This process entailed the periodic dipping of the nets in a boiling solution of cutch or bark which came from a Burmese tree and was reckoned to be a good preservative. A steam hose from the drifter's boiler kept the water piping hot. Barking the nets was a hot, laborious task which the fishermen didn't like, but without bark, cotton nets soon rotted.

So here was the tintie and here was the tank, filled to the brim with Ugie water, and in the water was our baby seal which had overnight become 'The Strange Monster from the Arctic'.

Beside the tank on one of Irvin's fish-boxes sat Chief Yokiedoke from Greenland, clad in an astrakhan coat and a fur hat that had both seen better days. On his lower legs he wore a pair of Russian boots that his wife couldna pit on cos her legs wis ower fat.

This was the world's leading authority on Arctic wildlife and he bore an uncanny likeness to Duff fae Peterheid. He spoke no English, apparently.

At the door of the tent stood the cashier-cum interpreter, who was to translate into English any answers that Yokiedoke might give to certain questions.

Admission cost three maiks, bairns one maik, and the hardy sons of rustic toil, who had parked their Raleigh bikes in the park across the road, rolled up in goodly numbers.

The seal soon realised she was the centre of attraction and played a real star role, sending great skirps o watter in all directions, much to the relief of Yokiedoke who was swytin far the sheepie swytes. It was the month of July, ye ken.

The favourite question, 'Fit dis she get for her brakfist?' was relayed to Yokiedoke whose standard reply was, 'Easka mala doosh!'

This, being interpreted by Harry, meant, 'She fairly likes a kipper.'

'Wid she ait neeps?' brought a series of queer grunts fae the Eskimo, meaning that there were no neeps inside the Arctic Circle.

The audience were suitably impressed and the siller wis comin in like sklate steens until, about five o'clock, disaster in the shape o a clivver loon fae Byth threatened the entire project.

'Hey, mannie!' says Byth to Harry, 'At's nae a monster ataa! It's jist a common ilka-day seal! I'm seekin ma maik back!'

In consternation, Harry glanced at Yokiedoke, wondering what kind of grunt he would have to translate to pacify the now restive onlookers. Lesser mortals might have given up in despair, but the Bluemogganer streak in Yokiedoke rose nobly to his aid.

Rising majestically to his feet, like Davy Crockett, he addressed the loon, not in Eskimo but in the loon's ain tongue.

'She's nae a common ilka-day seal ataa! Onybody wi a cork ee could see that! She's a guaranteed genuine real-life Arctic Puff Adder, nivver seen afore sooth o the Great Ice Barrier Reef!'

Byth proved to be a thrawn kin o chiel.

'An fit maks a common seal a puff adder?'says he.

'Cos she farts in the tunk an coonts the bubbles! That's fit maks her a puff adder!' was the reply. 'An onywye the shop's shut noo!'

There's the Bluemogganer for ye!

The pair o rascals grabbed the seal, the tin wi the maiks an bolted, leaving the tent and the tank astarn.

Gross takings — three powen half-a-croon. Gross outlay — nil. They nivver peyed for naething!

On the Monday, we got our seal back and promptly restored it to its mither that had been patrolling the harbour entrance for twaa hale days. Great was the joy in that reunion.

Later, when I described to Duff-Yokiedoke the expression on the mither's face, I said it was 'Rapturous! Beatific!'

'There's a better word for that, my loon,' says he.

'It's Easka mala doosh.'

An he clinkit the maiks in 'is pooch.

When Four Walls Equalled Paradise

The floor of the room was 13 ft. square. Since it was an upstairs room the side walls were perpendicular for about 4 ft. and thereafter they followed the line of the roof rafters so that the ceiling measured 13 ft. x 4 ft.

The door was of tongue-and-groove boards on three cross-bars and it was so close to the side wall that the top right-hand corner had been cut off to follow the slope of the roof.

In local parlance this was 'a room wi slopit waa's'. The door which opened on to a narrow landing had an old fashioned 'sneck' (latch).

The staircase from the landing to the ground floor had a twist of one hundred and eighty degrees, so at one side the treads were very broad while at the other side they were almost non-existent. In the dark the stairs were a veritable death trap.

In the end wall of the room, directly opposite the door, there was a recess about 1 ft. deep and 6 ft. high. This recess which served as a press (cupboard) had a few shelves but no door, and on its floor there was a gas meter which took pennies in its slot.

In the centre of the same wall there was an ancient, coal-burning black grate surrounded by a wooden 'Chumla' (mantelpiece). The grate had 'twaa binks' (hobs) and an oven, and on the hearth there was a gas ring.

Near the right-hand end of the mantel-shelf a gas bracket with its fragile mantle adorned the wall. This was for lighting the place.

From the single window, nothing was visible but the slates of the house opposite, and a narrow strip of sky.

Close to the walls the floorboards were as new but most of the floor area was distinctly uneven as a result of the constant punishment it had received from a few generations of feet on its bare surface.

Only the knots in the boards retained anything like their original level. On the walls, the single thickness of paper had been varnished in the good old fisher style and the ceiling had at least a quarter inch of whitewash. The room was perfectly dry.

The nearest water tap was in the washin hoose at the back o the hoose and this would mean a trip downstairs, along the front of the house and round to the back. The toilet was close to the washin hoose, in the back-close.

Now it came to pass in the late thirties that James Forman Buchan (Jeemsie) and Elizabeth Reekie Buchan (Lisbeth) decided they would get spliced if they could get a hoose. The hoose they got has just been described. Lisbeth's mither wis a Fifer, hence her middle name.

When they went to see the minister he ushered the couple into his cosy sitting room and began to ask the necessary questions. 'Ah!' says the good man, 'I know that Buchan is the most common name in this town but this is the first time that I've met both prospective partners with the same surname! Any relationship?'

'Och aye!' says Lisbeth, 'Eence in Yarmooth an twice at hame!'

Apparently the minister didn't understand.

Well now, the happy pair set about preparing their nestie. It was a fine big room, and once it was papered it would look fine. Jeemsie got the len o a cooper's eetch (adze) and attacked the worst of the knots in the floor, knots which would destroy the new fleer o canvas (lino).

According to fisher custom 'He' was obliged to provide the bride's claes, and a frock for the bridesmaid alang wi a fite sark for the best man. 'He' would be responsible for all expenses of the wedding and 'He' would be obliged to provide all kitchen or living-room furniture.

'She' would provide all the linen and the bedroom furniture. The linen or 'bottom drawer' was always called her 'providin'.

For a young fisherman of his day Jeemsie was financially well-heeled, for in the Commercial Bank he had £130. Thus he could lash out on a top quality dining-room suite which cost all of £33.

'Affa gran.'

Lisbeth managed to provide a decent bedroom suite (£26) then she was completely skint. There was very little to be made in a guttin yard!

Jeemsie chipped in to help her with one or two items, for her widowed mother couldn't afford to assist and when the two turtle doves finally moved in they had behind them a healthy balance of £65. Quite comfortable! Many a young couple didn't have the half of that!

Every stick of furniture the newlyweds possessed was arranged in the one room, with the exception of Lisbeth's china cabinet. This had been a present from an aunt who agreed to store it till Lisbeth got mair room. She actually stored it for fourteen years!

You could say the room was a wee bittie congested, but this was commonplace in those days. Very few indeed had two rooms.

So, in the one room, Jeemsie and Lisbeth cooked, ate, slept and washed. Every drop of fresh water had to be carried in and every drop of slops had to be carried out. Ditto with the coal and the ashes. Every call of nature meant a round trip to the close, often in appalling weather.

Then, when the bairn arrived, her crib was set in front of the window — it could go nowhere else, and the pram had to bide in the washin hoose!

There was no lack of problems. With strong north winds the lum would spew great clouds o rick into the room an the gas licht would blink, blink for hours. To stop the rick meant opening the door or the window, then they were frozen!

Visitors usually called at awkward times when Jeemsie was snatching a few hours' sleep. Privacy was an unknown quantity.

Still, in some ways they were fortunate, for hundreds of other couples had two or three flights of stairs to contend wi.

Came the war years when the crib had to be shifted every night so that the black-out — a sheet of stout grey paper on a close-fitting wooden frame — could be positioned in the window frame. It certainly made the place warm but it was oh, so depressing.

Then came the fearsome night (one of the many) when Jerry bombed the toon. Jeemsie, hame on leave, wis fast asleep fin a bomb landed less than a hundred yards away. The black-out flew richt across the room an the hale winda cam in in a spleeter o broken gless. Nae a soun fae the bairn!

In a flash Jeemsie was at the crib, his hert full o dreid, feart to licht his torch, but when his shaky fingers finally switched it on he found the bairn still soun asleep on the pink silk cushion she had for a pilla.

Aa roon the craitur's heid great slivers o gless had been driven richt throwe the cushion, but on the bairn hersel, nae a mark!

Jeemsie an Lisbeth baith said 'Thank You' that nicht!

The crib wis nivver at the winda again.

Wis there nivver a lauch avaa? Jist wyte a meenit noo!

There wis ae nicht that Jeemsie an Lisbeth got unexpected visitors, an that meant tay. The folk had jist left fin in comes mair folk, an that meant mair tay! Ye ken the wye o't. The second lot left for hame in a storm o win an rain, then Jeemsie gied Lisbeth a han wi the dishes an by that time it wis time to turn in for the nicht.

Noo Jeemsie should ha geen roon the back close t' the closet but it wis jist hale watter an he wis in sark sleeves an carpets.

'Och!' says he til himsel, 'I've a fine ticht biler so I should be aa richt till mornin!' So he lay doon an happit his heid.

But at twaa o'clock in the mornin his biler tellt him that, if he didna dee something quick, it wid burst! So oot-ower he scrambled, bare feet on the caal canvas an it wis still hale watter!

'Och!' says he again, 'I canna ging oot amon that! I'll tak the pail, an if I keep it quaet she'll nivver ken! She's soun an roon onywye!'

So in the black dark he fichered aboot for the pail which he lifted before makin a start.

Od! He near lowpit oot o's sark fin she spoke til im oot o the darkness.

'Fan are ye gaan t' stop? Ye'll hae that thing rinnin ower yet!'

Sheer guilt gart him answer a thochtie sharper than usual: 'Jist ee lie doon an be quaet, quine! There's naething t' get excited aboot! It's nae up t' my thoom yet!'

I spoke to Jeemsie yesterday at the shore. After telling me about the pail he said, 'I wis up at my dother's last nicht. Man, ye nivver saw a hoose like it! It's nae canvas noo, but carpets aa wye. An the bathroom! Ye wid be feart t' ging intil't. Ye maybe winna believe me, but there's a thing ye can sit on an scoot het watter at yer ain starn!'

Then as we parted company he remarked: 'Peter, my freen, they dinna ken they're livin!'

The Day Nelson Got Bitten
in a Short Circus

'Foreigners is aa the same!' says the Turk. 'Ye dinna hae t' be coorse t' them, but ye hiv t' be firm wi them!'

The pearl of wisdom was delivered on a bitterly cold morning in February just prior to the Hitler war, as the *Meadowsweet* lay at anchor, close to the east side of the May Island in the Firth of Forth.

The previous evening the *Meadowsweet* had shot her fleet of nets about a mile to the south of 'the Mey' in the quest for herring which were, in those days, quite plentiful when the spirit moved them.

On exactly the same errand, a Dyker drifter (from Cellardyke) had executed the same operation three-quarters of a mile further south. Thus both vessels had a good wide berth, but during the night a freak set of the tide had brought the two fleets of nets together in a tangled mess.

The process of separating the fleets was carried out in silence, apart from a few uncomplimentary exchanges between the skippers, as and when they came within earshot of each other. Since each fleet of nets had 'blinded' the other, there were very few herring and it was exasperation rather than anger which fuelled the heated remarks.

As the nets were finally separated, the Turk fired his first salvo — 'Ye great baa-heidit oof that ye are! Jist ee wyte till ye come t' Scotlan! Syne we'll sort ye!'

The startling reply shook the Turk to the core, for at last he had met a vocabulary even more descriptive than his own.

A hardy breed, the Dykers. For them this inshore herring lark was just a stopgap. With the first hint of spring they would be off to distant waters with their great-lines. The Patch, the Reef and the Viking would be their stamping ground. Aye, and even the Faroes.

Well, now, since there were no herring to land, the Turk had elected to drop anchor for the day and the crew were impatient for breakfast, herring fried as they should be fried.

Here's the recipe: (1) Remove the scales by scraping the fish from tail to head. (2) Remove the head and tail. (3) Split the belly open and remove all contents with the thumb. (4) Wash thoroughly. (5) On each side of the body cut three or four gashes from the back towards the belly taking care not to sever the bone. (6) Dip in oatmeal and fry. On no account should the bone be removed.

Herring fried in this fashion will give you several juicy 'chunks' from each side, chunks jist the richt size for the fingers! Forks and knives to herrin? Nivver! That wid be like sacrilege!

But dinna dee fit the Turk did, for aye fin he wis aitin herrin he keepit dichtin his fingers aneth his oxters so that ae washin-day his wife wis heard to say, 'My man's that fat he swytes grease!'

As a rule the Turk said Grace before meals in his own peculiar way. With his head propped on one hand he would utter a few weird grunts then spit in the stove. The resultant sizzle was the signal for all hands to muck in, but when it was a herring breakfast he made an expansive gesture and said, 'We dinna gie thanks for this, boys. This is oor ain!'

'I've seen better herrin mony a time!' says Jeemsie.

'Weel, my loon,' says the skipper, 'they're winter herrin, nae fat, nae ile, nae naething! Jist like tangles! An forbyes, there's a lot o affluence fae the factories comes doon this river, an there's aa the coal-stew fae the mines, so the herrin couldna be richt!' This, from a man who was on his fourth herring, made the cook blink!

There was a sudden hush at table when Nelson lifted the tin of Ideal milk and shook it over his plate.

'Dalmichty!' cries Duncan. 'Fit are ye deein, mannie?'

'Oh!' says Nelson, 'I thocht it wis the saat! My een's geen aa queer!'

'Control yersel, Duncan,' says the Turk. 'There's nae need for sweerin!'

'Faa's sweerin?' says Duncan. 'Dalmichty's nae a bad word! It's a place atween Dalmally an Dalwhinnie!'

Since the Turk was ignorant on rural things he let the matter drop, but later he consulted Dumplins, the mate, aboot Nelson.

'He's surely as blin as a bat in his aal age!' says the Turk.

'Nivver een!' says Dumplins. 'He's due t' retire this 'ear an he's efter the Lascar Pension. That's aboot seven an six the quarter but if he can produce a physical defect he'll maybe get one an six extra! He's workin the oracle wi's sicht.'

The Turk could hardly believe his ears. 'For one an six? Fancy!'

In his teens the mate had once been confronted with the picture of a Victorian lady in the low-cut dress of that period. In amazement he had exclaimed, 'Jingers! I winner if this quine kens her dumplins is bilin ower!' See now how he got the nickname?

Two nights later a sudden south-east gale sent the whole fleet running for shelter. It was impossible to enter any of the small fishing ports because it was low water, a fact which brought headaches to men accustomed to deep-water ports.

'Aye aye!' says the Turk, 'In oor pairt o the country men gets bothered wi their watter, but doon here they're bothered wi the want o't!'

The nearest deep-water port was Methil, whose multitude of lights of all colours, coupled with heavy snow showers, made it very difficult for the Turk's crew to spot the pier-head light. As you might expect it was Nelson who saw it first.

'Aye aye!' says the Turk again, 'Blin as a bat, is he? But bats could aye see in the dark!'

Daylight found the big dock at Methil well-filled with fishing boats. Cadgers had soon bought up the few herring available and now the only sign of life was butchers' runners canvassing for orders. Their price for top quality fresh meat was 'a shillin the pun, owerheid.' As Jeemsie said, 'It wis fine chaip roast but gey dear for sassidges!'

A good cook could feed his crew like fighting cocks on ten bob per man per week. What price now?

In the evening, both wind and snow had abated somewhat, and several little groups of fishermen could be seen making their way townwards between the lines of coal trucks. A motley, unshaven throng.

'Hid there been a horse or twaa,' says Jeemsie, 'it wid be like yon picter o Napoleon's retreat fae Moscow'! Aa for the sake o a braith o air, a streetch o the laigs an maybe a baggie o chips!

'Hud on a meentie, lads,' says Nelson, 'I winna be lang!' Then he disappeared into the bowels of one of those ancient, green-painted, cast-iron monstrosities which passed as public toilets. Open to the sky, they were usually sited where a lamp-post could shine into them.

By jingers, Nelson wisna lang! Five seconds flat an he wis oot again, howlin pen-an-ink, an his ae ee flashin like Buchan Ness!

'Fit's adee, Nelson? Hiv ye seen a ghost?' says the Turk.

'No, no!' says Nelson. 'I'd hardly gotten a start fin there wis a great blue flash an somethin took a bite o me!'

'Dalmichty!' says Duncan. 'Nae sweerin!' says the Turk. 'I'd better get a bobby,' says Jeemsie, and he ran off.

Nelson's mates carried him back to the *Meadowsweet* and laid him in his bunk. A few minutes later a dock policeman arrived, accompanied by a doctor who examined the patient in the privacy of the cabin, while the rest of the crew remained on deck. Soon the Turk was summoned to receive the doctor's report which he later repeated to his crew in his own impeccable style.

143

'Now, boys, Nelson's nae in a gweed wye! He his t' bide in his bed for a day. It seems that lettric wis gettin fae the lamp-post into the iron water-closet, an seein that water conducts lettric, peer Nelson's gotten a lettric shock. I'm thinkin his fingers is burnt anaa! The doctor says if he hidna been wearin rubber boots he could ha been deid!'

'Dalmichty!' says Duncan. 'Nae sweerin!' says the Turk.

'Ho-ho-ho!' says Jeemsie. 'I'll bet ye Nelson'll get a bittie extra on is pension noo!'

An hour or so later Duncan and Jeemsie 'gid up for chips' and as they made their way back their conversation was largely on electrical matters on which they were both ignorant.

'Hey Duncan! The bobby said they wid need t' investigate fit wye there wis a short circus atween the lamp-post an the urinal. Fit's a short circus, Duncan, an fit on earth's a urinal?'

'I canna tell ye that my loon! I'm nae a Catholic!'

Tales of the Bad Landings

Am Balg is the Gaelic name for a rocky islet which lies a scant mile from the coast some half-dozen miles south of Cape Wrath.

The east coast name for the same isle is Bulgie (with a hard 'g') and this name has come to embrace the rich fishing grounds a few miles to the west.

On these grounds the herring shoals were at times so dense, that to put a drift net in the water at all was simply to court disaster. Many an east-coaster, in the drifter days, met his Waterloo at Bulgie for only the fortunate few could thole the loss of an entire fleet of nets.

Putting only half the nets in the water was one way of reducing the risk; double bowse (floats) was another method.

Some skippers favoured putting a stopper round the middle of each net as it was run out, thus reducing, by at least half, the fishing area of the net.

And still nets were lost through sheer overweight of fish.

The only guarantee of safety was to keep all the nets in the ship — and starve!

And yet one could shoot a whole fleet of nets at Bulgie every night for weeks and catch precisely nothing!

Today's fisher has no such problem. His wonderful electronic devices can tell him whether or not the fish are there.

He can measure the dimensions of a shoal and its rate of movement; its distance from the bottom and from the surface can be accurately plotted and indeed a practised skipper can, at times, encircle just enough and no more of a shoal for his boat and his crew to handle. Guesswork is largely a thing of the past.

But let's get back to Bulgie in the drifter days.

144

The *Meadowsweet* (skipper Bob McTurk) had hauled 160 cran and had made for Stornoway on the Isle of Lewis. Eight nets had been completely lost and many more were severely damaged but these wounds, though serious, were not mortal.

Three of the Turk's less-fortunate fellow skippers had lost the lot and had rounded Cape Wrath on their way home with holds completely empty.

So the Turk considered himself rather lucky.

On arrival at Stornoway, however, his heart dropped into his boots, for he found himself at the tail end of a considerable queue of boats waiting to discharge.

There were a few klondykers in Stornoway Loch but they were simply German trawlers and could not cope with huge amounts of herring.

It was already afternoon and there was no prospect of an early discharge. The ruling price in Stornoway that day was fifteen shillings a cran and there was a distinct possibility that late arrivals would find no market for their catches.

Then out of the blue the Turk received a message from his salesman to the effect that: 'A curer mannie in Loch Clash could take 160 cran and would pay seventeen and six a cran. He had waited all day but not a single boat had entered the loch. Would the Turk accept the offer?'

Of course he would accept! One hundred and sixty extra half crowns was £20 and that was a lot o siller! So the *Meadowsweet* cast off and headed back across the Minch to Loch Clash only ten miles from where her shot had been netted. What a boon radio would have been!

But misfortune stepped in. As soon as the *Meadowsweet* had cleared Stornoway Loch she was swallowed up in a blinding snowstorm. All the way across the Minch, the swirling flakes reduced the visibility to less than a hundred yards and the Turk knew that under such conditions, and in the approaching dark, it would be suicidal to enter Loch Clash.

So there was no alternative but to dodge, and keep a sharp look-out.

During the night the blinding snow gave way to more showery conditions and the great flashing light on the Cape was intermittently visible, but not until first light could the Turk find his desired haven.

Now, Loch Clash is not much of a loch at all, but it is the first available shelter for the mariner who has rounded Cape Wrath from the east, and many a drifter man has been thankful for it.

It is more or less a little bay at the entrance to its big sister Loch Inchard and it had, as it still has, a little jetty at whose head there was a curing station.

Across the end of this jetty the *Meadowsweet* was finally moored and the long hard slog of discharging began.

There was no transport available, so the herring had to be carried basket by basket up the jetty to the yard, then teemed into the farlin, where the guttin quines were waiting for them.

Not a great distance, but if you're clad in boots and oilskins against the weather and if the snow is more than ankle deep, forty yards is far enough, bearing in mind that 160 cran equals 32 tons!

As a concession to the wintry elements, some of the quines had donned hooded oilskin jackets, but some of the younger ones deeming that such attire would simply impede their progress, had pulled on their moggans (home-knitted removable sleeves which covered their arms from elbow to wrist).

Only in very cold weather were moggans worn.

Peterheid quines aye wore blue moggans, hence the term 'Bluemogganers'.

But every one of the quines on Clash Pier was as Highland as a peat! All day long they stood there, heads bowed to the snow showers, and their tireless arms never slacking for a moment except for a short tea-break.

Just before dark, the herrings which were as yet ungutted were 'roosed' — very heavily salted into huge wooden vats — to await the daylight of the following day when they too would be gutted and packed in barrels.

By this time the wind had shifted to the north-west and was freshening rapidly, so the *Meadowsweet* left the pier and turned sharp to port into Loch Inchard.

About three quarters of a mile up that loch she turned sharply to port again and entered that haven of havens Loch Safety, a natural harbour if ever there was one.

The name Loch Safety was the name given to Loch Bervie by east-coasters of a byegone day and it would be difficult to make a happier choice of name.

But Loch Safety had one great drawback — it had no pier, so it was anchor drill for the *Meadowsweet*'s crew.

Loch Bervie is now a busy fishing port whose fleet is fast outgrowing the landing facilities. The pier and market space is hopelessly inadequate and it is quite common to see the boats moored 'twelve off' at the weekend, altho this is to be drastically improved very shortly. The crews commute to their homes in mini buses, each boat having its own vehicle. These men are mostly from the Moray Firth ports and they never use the name Loch Safety or Loch Bervie; they simply call it 'Clash'. Every year, in the spring, they have a real 'posh do' in the Banff Springs Hotel, a 'do' which rejoices in the name 'The Clash Ball'.

But in the drifter days, crews were banished to the Minch for several weeks on end. To go home overland was unknown and the distance by sea was prohibitive.

I once heard of a Moray Firth ship that came home from the Minch after ten weeks away. When they came to their home port (I daren't say what place) it was low water so they couldn't get in!

'Ach!' says the skipper, 'If this is the set o't we'd better jist ging awaa back throwe the Firth!'

'Oh faither,' says the loon, 'wid we nae be better to get a clean shift first?'

'Ach, my loon,' says the skipper again, 'gie yer linner a gweed flap ower the rail an she'll dee for anither month!'

All that night, the *Meadowsweet* lay snug at anchor while the gale raged among the craggy hills and her tired crew slept like logs.

In the morning, as they gazed on the snow-clad mountains, Jeemsie the cook was heard to remark: 'Good grief skipper, this is surely a foreign land!'

'I'm nae sure if it's foreign or no,' says the Turk, 'but I ken the folkies here has their ain National Anthem! They sing Psalm 121 instead o *God Save the King*!'

'Psalm 121? Fit dis that say skipper?'

'I to the hills will lift mine eyes.' says the Turk. 'The Lord Himsel kens there's naething else here t' lift them til!'

Face Down Waiting for the 'Jumpahs'!

I have seen many queer things in my time, and I aye see the queerest things fin I dinna hae my gun!

But I nearly took a dwam early one morning in Shields fin I saw a mannie in a little boatie shovin a great muckle iron bolt doon a salmon's throat!

'Oho!' says I to mysel, 'I'd better get some help, for we hiv a nut-case here, an if he's ootrageous, we'll maybe need the bobby!'

So, accompanied by a deckie I boarded the boatie, making all sorts of soothing sounds to calm the poor wretch.

'Come into my treacly oxter an get a black-sugar kiss! Naebody's gaan t' hurt ye !' I babbled, whereon he lifted his head and looked at me in alarm.

'Mawnin, Peetah, hae we bin taken propah poorly the day?' he asked, laying his hand on the haft of a wicked looking knife, whose glint brought me up sharp.

So it turned out that he wasn't a nut-case; he was simply trying to preserve his reputation for being the man who caught the heaviest salmon on the Tyne!

Apparently he derived a great deal of pleasure from hearing the fishwives on the quay as they cleaned their fish —- 'Oooh, Jessie, come an see what this one's swallowed!' 'Eee! fancy that now, Ruby! It's only washers that's in my one's belly!'

The fact that he was swickin the wifies didn't seem to trouble him in the least, and he came aboard our boat for a joog o tay, and to see if we had any surplus lead sinkers. It might allay suspicion if he varied the salmon's diet!

I had a lang news with this old codger and learned that from time immemorial it had been the legal right of Northumberland fishermen to catch salmon with drift nets. There was of course a close season when the use of nets was forbidden, but even then some enterprising lads just let their boaties drift aimlessly with the tide.

Apparently they lay flat in the bottom of the open boat keeping dead quiet and the chances were that a 'jumpah' would land in the boat. They might be like that a whole night and nivver see a face, but it was quite possible to get four or five bonny fish for a night's work.

The best place for this caper was close outside the breakers along the beach, if you had the nerve to let a boat drift there.

It was policy to lie face down in the boat because a 25 lb salmon dropping from a height of six feet could gie ye a gey sair face. Since the 'jumpahs' had 'lowpit in ower' uninvited, the fishers could not be prosecuted!

My boundless admiration for this old fellow was tinged with not a little envy for at last I had met a bigger and better liar than myself! But when I checked and rechecked the old tale I discovered that it was the truth.

Thereafter I made careful enquiries to see if it was permissible for Scotch (not Scots) fishermen to catch salmon with drift nets, and discovered to my amazement that there was no law against it.

Fancy that now! Generations of fishermen had been brought up to believe that to utter the word 'salmon' was to incur all sorts of misfortune. And to actually handle a salmon was to invite an affliction called the 'Fite Swallin' which would affect our bowels to such an extent that we would have to wear kilts, for in no way would there be time to take trousers down!

Aye willin to try something new, we bought some salmon drift nets and launched into a venture which brought limited success. We found the salmon to be as elusive as the herring; we also learned that a calm night would be a fruitless night and that the real truth was 'the more wind, the more fish!'

When we got home to Peterhead with our new nets, we caused a sensation. We would get the jile, that was sure! But nobody said 'Boo' and we just carried on.

That was how the salmon fishing (drift net) came to the north-east. Others were quick to copy and soon there were salmon nets all over the place, but still salmon were a scarce crap.

The truth is that the salmon drift nets killed more birds than fish! Yon black-and-white birdies that the loons used to call 'marrots' (Gulliemots?) were trapped in the nets when they made their shallow dive and it gave us sair herts to see so many of them drowned.

But nobody was interested in the birdies. They could be slaughtered by the million, so long as the salmon were not molested!

Now let me tell you a story.

'Twas the kind of night that one doesn't easily forget. A few boats had left Peterhead to punch their way round Buchan Ness towards the comparatively calmer waters nearer Girdleness, but one by one they had given up and gone home, leaving one solitary craft to brave the gale.

It was not our usual to be 'the only boat on the sea' but it was so that night.

About two miles off the Ythan estuary, we shot our nets and dodged at them for several hours. There was no sleep for anyone, so chaotic was the 'raivelt' motion, but eventually we got the nets aboard and made for home with a score of lovely fish.

When we reached harbour, we hauled the whole fleet of nets on to the pier, because they resembled a rope with corks on it rather than nets.

These salmon nets had an unhappy knack of rowin themselves up so that the yarn got all twisted up with the cork rope, and that in a thousand different ways. The job of taking the twists out so that the net could be freed from the rope, required infinite patience and a lot of time. It could not be done by mittened hands.

The wind had veered northerly with flurries of snow and it was bitterly cold.

Daylight was just breaking when a beautiful Bentley drew up on the pier beside us. Therein sat a little wee mannie wi a gamekeeper's hat, festooned with trout flies.

The chauffeur sat like a statue while the mannikie opened a window to ask: 'Have you been at sea, chaps?'

Oh aye! We had been at sea!

'Have you caught any salmon chaps?'

Oh aye! We had some!

'Which one of you is skipper, chaps?'

'It's me,' says I. 'Are ye lost, or something, that ye're doon here at this time o the mornin? Respectable folk's still in their beds, ye ken!'

He agreed readily, then he told me a strange tale.

The previous evening, before dark, he had been at Arbroath seeking a salmon, but no boats were at sea.

He had been about to return home when a fisherman told him that Peter o the *Twinklin Star* was at sea; he had heard him on the wireless.

And where would he find this Peter?

Up in Peterheid, of course.

So the great Bentley drove northward, calling at every village on the way in a fruitless search for a salmon. Not even Port Errol and Boddam had been overlooked, but now he had some hopes of success.

Could he see our fish?

Certainly! But he would need to come out of the car!

He stood agape at the sight of the beauties which glistened like silver on the deck. In a mere whisper he asked: 'Can I have one? Please!'

'Aye, surely,' says I, 'but ye'll hae to pey for't. Naebody gets a fry o salmon!'

He was more than willing to pay. And when he had picked the biggest fish, I said: 'That'll be ten bob the pun an she's aboot twinty pun!'

No trouble at all to an exceedingly well-filled wallet. With great reverence he laid the fish in the boot of the car. The chauffeur was not allowed to touch it!

Then, hesitantly, he asked: 'Could I have another, please?'

'Aye! Surely. Ye can tak the lot as lang's ye've siller!'

Just then 'Willicks' appeared on the scene. He was for several years in the Caley shop and was always needlessly early on the job.

'Hey!' says I to the mannie, 'We can wye the fish if ye like! I widna sleep if I'd cheated ye!'

So the two beauties were duly weighed, 21 lbs. and 19 lbs. apiece. Forty pun at ten bob — £20.

Oh, he wis pleased! While he wis washing his hands, I asked the chauffeur to tell me fa the mannie wis.

This he refused to do, but he would tell me why the need for the salmon was so urgent.

The mannie had two sons who went fishing for trout with their dad. They had been at it off and on for a year, and the peer sowl hadna catched a fish yet!

The boys, however, had baith a little trootie or twa to their credit and they jist made a feel o their father.

But this mornin he wid let them see the wye! He wid march up the drive to the mansion wi a great muckle fish in ilka han! That wid shut them up!

No Job for a Volunteer

At the tender age of fourteen Kitty was in the curing yard gutting herring. With two of her former classmates she had taken up the traditional occupation of the fisher quine, and now the trio formed a 'crew o learners'.

There were always three to a crew, two gutters and a packer, and their uniform comprised an oilskin skirt and a bib and a pair o toppers (rubber boots).

Their headgear was a cotton muffler and on the upper parts of their bodies they wore a fisherman's jersey with sleeves only to the elbow, or even an old cotton blouse. As protection against the coorse saat with which the herrings were liberally clarted, the quines' fingers were rowed in 'clooties', strips of cloth wrapped tightly round each finger and secured with cotton thread.

The gutter's tool was a 'futtle', a short, stubby gutting knife with a fixed blade; the packer's tool was a shallow circular metal scoop polished like silver by the abrasive saat.

In a curing yard there could be anything from four to ten crews of women, depending on the status of the curer.

Immediately prior to the start of the herring season the curer would give each crew member her 'arles', sometimes as much as £1, and this was an unwritten, seldom broken contract. For the whole of that season, the recipient would gut herring for that curer as and when required, rain or shine.

The rate of pay would be 'a shillin the barrel' per crew, so for each barrel of herring which any crew gutted, each quine got fourpence! Work that out at an average of 750 herring to a barrel! How much per herring?

The ages of the quines varied from fourteen to sixty-five. Fancy bein a 'quine' at pension age! The packer had to be good, for she had to keep pace with two women's gutting, and without fail the packer was the crew's cashier or treasurer. Kitty was a packer.

Now, the salting of the herring actually began at the quayside. Not until the late 1940s did the herring drifters carry boxes . . . and even then the number of boxes carried was strictly limited. The catch was always in bulk and was swung ashore one basket at a time.

Two deckies would grasp the swinging basket and empty the contents into a 'kit', a container provided by the curer for the transport of the catch to the curing yard. A kit held one basket, or seven stone of herring and it must be clearly understood that the kit was not a barrel, although it was made by local coopers.

The kit had the same shape as a glass tumbler and empty kits could be stowed just like tumblers, one inside the other.

While the herring poured like quicksilver from the basket to the kit, a cooper would dose them liberally with salt from a barrel, using the same metal scoop that the packers used, then he would tilt the kit and 'rowe' it aside, only to replace it with an empty one ready for the next basket. The salt took the slipperiness from the fish, making them much more easy to handle when the quines got them.

Four baskets or four kits made one cran. The salt itself was of Spanish, Italian or Sardinian origin and was like coarse gravel. It was also of a dazzling whiteness.

On motor lorries, or on long flat carts, the kits of herring were taken to the curing yard.

On the stage, which had to be of great strength, the kits of herring were stowed, ready to fill the 'farlin', a wooden trough whose bottom sloped downwards towards the front. The farlin was as long as the stage and along its front stood the row of guttin quines in their oilskin cwites (skirts).

When the farlin had been filled with herring the gaffer would give the signal to start gutting. Since the quines were all on piece-work 'startin afore yer neeper' was strictly forbidden.

In front of her and a wee bittie to the side, each gutter had a small wooden tub or 'coggie' to receive the herring guts, and behind her she would have at least three shallow wooden tubs to catch the gutted fish in three selections, full, matt-full and small. The tubs had iron carrying-handles and were extremely heavy.

To see a practised gutter at her task was to see skill of the very highest order. Two swift jabs of the futtle removed the gills and the gut, a flick of the wrist sent the offal into the coggie and a deft movement of the left hand sent the gutted fish into its appropriate tub. There was no looking behind them, yet very few fish missed their appointed tub. The very speed of the quines' hands was amazing.

As soon as a few tubs were filled, the three quines carried them outside and emptied them into a 'roosin box', a wooden container about four feet square and eighteen inches deep, which stood on four legs. In this container the packer turned the herrin ower wi her scoop and gave them an extra dustin o saat as required before starting to pack them in a barrel, heads outward, bellies up.

Using both hands, she would lift several herring from the box and pack them neatly in the bottom of the barrel. When the first tier or 'boddim' had been laid she would yell for the gaffer to come and inspect it. Not until he was satisfied was she allowed to carry on packing, then her fingers would fly.

Tier after tier of herring, scoop after scoop of salt. It was hot, hard work leaning into the very bottom of the barrel, but naturally things got easier as the barrel filled up. Not that the job was ever easy.

For a summer or twaa I wis 'the loon' in a curing yard.

It was hard, healthy work which I really enjoyed, especially since the stage and the farlin were in the open air. This was quite common. Sometimes when the quines were working late, I would light paraffin flares or bubblies, which were the only illumination.

It was all something of an adventure to a loon, but the quines must have been ready to drop. 'Ramona' and 'South of the Border' were favourite songs with the young women, but oh, when the Hielan deems sang their mournful Gaelic airs aathing seemed so eerie it gart me shiver.

Een o my jobbies as orra loon wis t' gie the quines their pey. If there wis nae herrin on pey-day, I took the pey packet t' the packer's hoose. If the yard wis busy, the packer got her envelopie at her wark.

It wis daft. Fit wis the peer quine supposed t' dee wi a pey packet an her wearin a cwite athoot pooches, her fingers rowed in cloots an hersel clartit wi gour?

151

The first time I gied Kitty her packet she grat like a bairn, cos the amount pencilled on the ootside wis jist pathetic. I left her greetin an passed t' the next quine. Belle wis busy in the boddim o the barrel so I could see her form fae the waist doon only, but fin I gied her sonsie hip a clap she cam oot o the barrel like a jake-in-the-box. Then she wis worth seein!

My private name for her wis 'The Busty Bombshell' an I'm sure I wis in love wi her at that time, tho she widna look at a loon like me, cos she was eichteen an I wis twaa 'ear younger.

'Hey Belle!' says I, lookin at her in silent worship, 'Here's yer pey packet.'

'Ooh, that's fine! But far am I supposed t' keep it?'

'That's up to you,' says I, preparin t' move t' the neist packer.

'Wyte a meenit!' says Belle, an stoopin a wee bittie in my direction she fluttered her bonny lashes towards her copious cleavage (I think that's the richt word). 'Pit the packetie doon there, my loon!'

'Me? Doon there? Nae fear! That wid be rude! My mither wid be reid mad!'

'Nivver mind yer mither, ye gowk; she winna ken. An forbyes ye're jist a gweed-faced innocent loon yet! Go on!'

So I stuck the packetie in the bonny letter-box.

'That's nae eese!' she says, 'Shiv the thing hine doon or I'll loss't in the boddim o the barrel, an that widna dee!'

Oh boys-o-boys! Oh my govies! Spik aboot clootie dumplins? I'll sweer she didna loss yon packetie in the barrel!

Three wiks later I was on the same job again. Kitty didna greet this time — the young quines wis learnin fast!

Then I came to Belle. 'Aye aye, Belle! Will I pit yer pey far I pit it last time?'

'Awyte, no!' says she, wi her cheeks like fire. 'Ye'll dee nae sic thing!'

'Foo nae?' says I.

'Cos I had t' tirr (undress) afore I could get my pey yon day! Ye're nae near sic a gweed-faced innocent loon as I thocht, ye coorse vratch!'

Fancy her sayin a thing like that fin I was jist thinkin that a volunteer wid dee the job far better than ony pressed man!

Working on a Fool, Watery Brute!

Towards the end of World War I, the Government saw fit to order a fleet of drifters for use as 'sweepers, tenders, etc. These shippies were to be of a standard design and the building of them was farmed out to several yards all over the country.

But although the design was standard, it was quite easy for an expert to spot superficial differences which betrayed their yard of origin, and by an 'expert' I mean a fisher loon who could tell you a shippie's name when all that was visible in the distance was the smoke from the funnel!

The iron 'standard boats' were grand craft when punching into a head wind, but otherwise they were 'fool, watery brutes'. The wooden members of the species were good all-rounders.

During World War II, the Government saw fit to build a fleet of motor boats (MFVs), again of standard design, and again it was easy to spot a Geordie Forbes from a Herd and McKenzie or an Irvin. These boats came in three sizes — 50ft., 65ft. and 75ft., powered by 66 h.p. Kelvins, 88 h.p. Kelvins and 150 h.p. Lister Blackstone engines respectively.

There was also a bigger, 90ft. version which was built for fire fighting but they were not popular with fishermen after the war. The most popular as far as fishermen were concerned were the 65ft. and 75ft. vessels which proved very adaptable as dual-purpose craft, i.e. for herring or white fish.

I was in a 75-footer for a few years and found her to be quite a good boat apart from one or two glaring faults.

She, like all the others, had been built for the Navy, so there had to be accommodation for officers. Consequently she had a deck house like a block of flats surmounted by a dirty great funnel.

The Navy always thinks that there's plenty o room up the wye!

When lying head to wind at the herring nets, she wouldn't lie like a Christian at all, but did her best to roll our guts out! Conversely she was a marvel broadside on!

But all these boats had a most annoying fault. The propeller made a terrific racket fit to scare the verra flechs aff ye! The noise in the cabin was like steens on a corrugated roof and although several 'cures' were attempted none proved effective.

I was 'driver' of a 150 h.p. Blackstone for a few years and thus came to know every nut and bolt in the fool, stinkin beast and again, thereby hangs a tale.

It came to pass, in the fullness of time (i.e. when I had managed to rake a few pounds thegither) that I decided it was time we had a bathroom in the house.

At that time I was bidin in the aal fisher district, the Roanheads, where bathrooms were almost unknown — as was the case in most of the town!

I was getting rather tired of having to leave a warm fireside to go and sit in an outside toilet which, in winter, could have passed as a fridge.

'What will the robin do then, poor thing?' was a childhood phrase which seemed to come to mind rather too often. So I ups and goes through the official channels

153

for permission which was readily given, but I didna get a 'grunt' (the Peterhead word for 'grant').

The only grunt I got wis fae the wife, because I started to demolish the inside of the house on a Saturday afternoon. The good woman should have been christened Charity, for charity suffereth long and is kind!

In the course of this demolition I discovered some little holies in one or two jeests so I consulted a friend of long standing. After expert examination he announced 'Och! that's widworm! But it's nae bad! I ken widworm fin I see't. Ye see, I've been thirty 'ear wi the Cooncil!'

My observation that that wis a lang time to be idle didn't seem to ruffle him at all. His advice was to get a suppie diesel ile an pit it on the timmer. It wid stink for a fylie but it wid certainly kill the beasties!

Now, to get a suppie diesel was no problem. All I had to do was to take a tin down to the boat where I could fill it from the tank. So next afternoon I set off gaily with a gallon tin to procure the needful but I had only got a third of the diesel when it started to rain very heavily, forcing me to seek shelter.

The nearest refuge was the open galley door of a fishing boat near the slipway, a stranger who had come to Peterhead for a refit. This was nothing new because in my youth the drifters from Cellardyke came all the way to Peterhead for a new funnel. I had just got into the galley when I collided with two fitters who had just come up from the engine room.

'Hi, Peter,' says one of them, 'if ye're bidin here a whilie, will ye keep an eye on our spanners? We're awaa for wir tay an there's an affa lot o thiefs aboot the place!

'We've left the engine runnin — she's ready to go. If the crew comes for the boat just gar them wyte till we come back!'

I immediately made for the engine-room which was identical to the one I'd had years before. This was a 75 ft. MFV and the newly overhauled Blackstone was tickin ower like a clockie.

For a few minutes I revelled in nostalgia, the old familiar sounds and smell. I revved and slowed the engine, fichered wi this and that and then I spotted the fuel service tank above my head. Boys, here was diesel a-plenty, ready to hand! I could fill my tinnie here and nobody would ever know.

Conscience began to chirp in my lug, but I couldna hear for the dirl o the engine. And besides, it wis only a wee suppie and it wis hale watter and my ain boatie wis hine awaa and I wis guardin ither folk's spanners fae thiefs and it wis force ten increasing to force twelve and if I didna tak it noo I needna bother!

So up went the tin and down came the drain-cock valve and diesel began to flow. The tin was about a quarter full when I spied on the ladder a pair of highly-polished shoes, then a pair of beautifully-tailored trousers followed by an immaculate suede jacket. Finally I saw the whole man, a chiel wi clear blue een, and a fine smell o Brut.

'Hi, skipper!' says I, 'Fit like?'

'Nae bad, nae bad,' says he, eyeing my tin. 'Are ee an engineer? Nivver saw you afore!'

'Och aye, an engineer since I left the school!' which in a sense was strictly true.

'Fit are ye deein wi that tin?'

'I'm jist checkin to see that there's nae water in yer tank. It widna dee to hae ye lyin stoppit ootside wi water in yer fuel.'

'Nivver saw that deen afore,' says he. 'Ye maun be affa parteeclar!'

'Na, na,' says I, 'ye're better to dee the job richt! I aye dee this!'

It was standard practice to drain off a drappie regularly. No doubt his own chief did so, although the skipper hadn't seen him at it. Skippers are out of their element in the engine-room, as a rule.

He asked a few more questions then looking at the donkey pump (i.e. the pump for the hose) he said: 'I hope ye've sorted that pump! I could pee faster than that thing!'

Since that wasn't a question it required no answer but I did ask him civilly whether he was complaining about the pump or bragging about himself. That made him laugh and as he made to climb the ladder he said: 'Ye're an affa lad! My crew's in the Mission for a fly-cup; I'm awaa to the office an fin I come back I'll see that ye get something t' yersel for mindin on that tank!'

Halfway up the trap he paused and said: 'Fit wye did ee ken I wis the skipper?'

'Man,' says I, 'there's something aboot ye that canna be misteen! Ye fairly look the pairt. Ye jist radiate confidence and assurance! Something a buddy could lippen till!'

'Ye could be richt, freen,' says he, nodding his head sagely. 'I'm nae feel, tho I fart in the Kirk!'

I didn't have the nerve to tell him that he wis far ower fat to be a deckie, far ower clean to be a chief an far ower bonny dressed to be a cook.

To the fitters, returned from their tay, I reported that I hidna seen nae thiefs but I had seen the skipper who was to bring something to mysel, a something the fitters could share between them, for I was going home.

When I learned later that the 'something' had not materialised, I reflected sadly as I splashed the mannie's diesel on my timmer that 'the Jews is nae aa in Jerusalem!'

A Lesson in True Kindliness

I derive a great deal of pleasure from the fact that, as I grow steadily older, my boyhood years, my special years, become ever more vividly clear in my memory. Important dates and events of the intervening years may at times be shrouded in a soft haze, yet the most distant days of all still retain the beauty and the freshness of a dream.

The characters who flitted across the stage of my earliest years were mostly old people, but then, to a little boy the greater part of the world's population is old.

Of course I had a veritable host of playmates whom I remember with affection, in spite of the fact that some of them were downright coorse.

But it was the old folk, the real old timers that I remember most fondly, for there was a something about them which I can only describe as kindness; not that these folks had anything to give. On the contrary, they had very, very little.

But then kindness, or kindliness, the bonniest word in the English language, is not necessarily involved with actual giving unless it be the giving of oneself. No, it is a far deeper word than that.

But enough of sermonising. Let me tell you about Cephas, one of my really favourite people.

Cephas was a gentleman, and by that I mean he really was a gentle man. That he was old I had no doubt.

That he was well read I was perfectly sure, for when Cephas used the English language, of which he was very fond, there were no double negatives, no split infinitives, no misrelated participles.

When Cephas 'talked' (i.e. spoke in English) he was a joy to listen to.

He could discourse quite freely on several subjects, and on the Scriptures in particular, not in any dogmatic, Hell-fire-and-damnation manner, but in a sweet persuasiveness that portrayed the love of God as being broader than the measure of man's mind. His theology did not suit everybody, but I loved it, young as I was.

Cephas could be very pleasant company indeed, but oh boys he wis fool! He wis jist fair yirdit. His acquaintance with soap and water could only be described as the nodding variety.

Some of my elder companions took great pleasure in relating the story of how poor Cephas had once been stricken by a sudden and serious malady which decreed that he should be rushed awaa t' Aiberdeen!

There, the ward sister, a proper stickler fae the Garmond was adamant that no such person could be beddit athoot a bath.

The upshot was that they gied Cephas three waters, then they got 'is sark! Ye ken, I never really believed that story!

Cephas was not, and apparently never had been, a man of action. All his days he had loved to stray into bypath meadow from whence he would watch the world go by.

He had a little boat which had no engine and in this frail craft he purported to be a fisherman, never more than half a mile from shore and not even there unless it was flat calm.

Cephas always addressed my father as 'Cousin', a relationship which my father would vigorously deny.

For my father, Cephas had the greatest respect, and while my father certainly admired the intelligence of his professed 'Cousin' he had no time for the old man's way of life. The two were as different as chalk and cheese.

I remember particularly well one day when my Da had just arrived home from Yarmouth. The nets had been taken ashore and hung on fences to dry. Each member of the crew had his whole barrel or 'halfie' of salt herring delivered to his home and now that it was dark, each man was at hame for his supper wi his wife an bairns.

156

In our house, that meant that father and one son had returned from the sea, while three others, a son and two daughters, would be home in a few days from the shore side of the herring trade. The three remaining members of the family, not old enough to leave school, had gotten our Yarmooth presents and we were awaiting our tea. But surely Ma wis on the slow side the nicht?

Then I remembered. This was the night that Cephas would call. And, sure enough, he announced his arrival by knocking gently on the door, which I opened to admit the old man.

Immediately on entering, he removed his battered bowler hat (not a cheese-cutter) and greeted my father warmly.

'Eh, Cousin, it's fine t' see ye safe hame. Oh — it's supper time wi ye? Weel, I'd better awaa hame an come back some ither time. It's nae richt o me. I should ha kent better. Weel, seein that ye insist, I'll tak a bite wi ye, but jist a bite noo, jist a bite!'

And he took his place at table, a place which had been set for him some time ago.

Strange how the old man's visits always coincided with my father's arrival from Yarmouth.

Once we were all seated, my mother served us liberal helpings of skirly, a great favourite with us. The smell of oatmeal an ingins sizzling in the pan — sheer delight!

At once Cephas propped his head on his left hand and launched into a Grace which would have taken high honours in the Dimbleby Lecture programme.

Beginning with Moses in the bulrushes, he accompanied the children of Israel on their escape from Egypt. Then, as soon as the Israelites had crossed the Red Sea my mother reached for Cephas' untouched plate and set it on the bink (hob) to keep it warm.

Sensing, rather than hearing this movement, I opened my eyes to see my father quietly getting on with his supper. On catching my questioning gaze he indicated that we should all follow suit, but as quietly as possible, which we did, in dead silence. It wis like a 'dummy's meetin'.

The old man didna think muckle o David tho, mind ye, Solomon wis a hantle waur, wi aa yon weemin!

Hop step and jump we were led through the Old Testament until, in Ezekiel's valley of dry bones, Cephas faltered a bittie.

Thereupon my mother, using the corner of her spotless apron lifted the sizzling plate from the bink and set it aneth Cephas' nose. This brought a rather abrupt 'Amen!' and the old boy set to with a will.

Then, having cleared his plate in splendid fashion, sink me if he didna set oot on anither Grace fit t' beat the first een!

This time he began in the Acts of the Apostles an wydit thro the Epistles until he seemed to get bogged down in the Predestination portion of Ephesians.

Then my father, who had been leisurely filling his pipe, laid his open tobacco pouch in front of Cephas who drew to a close with 'odours of Edom and incense Divine'. It was actually 'Digger Flake'.

Boys! Yon finger fairly kent the wye to teem a pooch an fill a pipe! I saw my father's een widen in mock alarm at the capacity of Cephas' old briar.

Then, between puffs, the old boy declared that Providence had led him here the nicht. Oh aye! He wid fairly tak a bile o saat herrin, but the barrel widna be open yet surely?

It wis? Gran! Oh, aye! He had something t' tak them hame in, a puddin dish. Faar wis't? Jist ootside the door. Providence again. Boys, yon wis nivver a puddin dish — ye could hae batht a bairn in't!

When Cephas finally departed my father says, 'Is't a hale 'ear since he was here last?'

'Oh aye, Andra, it's a hale 'ear, but it seems like yestreen.'

'He wis on a different text the nicht, lass! A clivver mannie yon.'

'Fit ither could he be? He's a cousin o yours, isn't he?' says my mither. She fairly kent the wye t' torment my Da!

'Aye!' says she, 'Providence led Cephas here the nicht an Providence'll guide him t' some ither 'Cousin' the morn, an the day efter. Cephas has a lot o cousins.'

During my last conversation with Cephas he produced a gem which lingers in my memory yet. 'Peter, my loon,' says he, 'I hiv a lot o freens, an freens is jist like fiddle strings — ye darna screw them ower ticht.'

Finally brethren (I learned that fae Cephas), what was Cephas' name when he 'bedd' in your village?

I'm sure ye kent the peer aal sowl when there was no Welfare State, dependent to a marked degree on the kindliness of 'cousins'.

Wis he a cousin o yours? Wis ee ivver a cousin t' him? And div ye nae think, as I think, that 'kindliness' is the bonniest word in ony language?

Once Upon a Time at a Mendin

There was a period in my life when the magic words, 'Once upon a time' were a sure-fire guarantee that the story which followed would be a really good one.

In fancy I would be borne along paths of mystery and wonder, through a land of light and song, where no-one wept except the willow, and where in the end everybody lived happily ever after.

I was finally convinced that the Land of Once Upon a Time had no stable foundation, by a rather salutary experience.

You see, I had read in a bookie about a loon that got a thripenny-bit fae an aal wifie in the street just cos his cheery smile had brightened her day.

'Oho!' says I to mysel, 'It's me for the thripenny-bits! Nae bother avaa!'

So I positioned myself at the door of Lipton's shop on the Broadgate (now Ronnie Gordon's furniture shop) and there I bestowed on the world in general, and on aal wifies in particular, the most dazzling smile you ever saw.

Great were the multitudes that thronged the street, for streaky bacon was fourpence the quarter, but nobody paid any heed to the threadbare, poverty-stricken loon wi the radiant smile. Not a copper! I'm tellin ye, if ye smile for three solid hours ye'll hae a sair face!

At last there came towards me two vaguely familiar faces so in a last despairing effort I streetched my mou fae ear t' lug but to no avail.

'Good grief! Faa on earth's that?' says wifie number one.

'Oh!' says number two, 'that's een o Jeannie Motherwell's, but he's nae jist affa richt, 'at een!'

Oh boys! I cam doon t' earth wi a richt clyte yon day! This is a richt hard world, an it's a sair fecht! Once upon a time? Tell that to somebody else.

Weel noo, once upon a time (are ye listenin?) I wis a barfit loon makkin for the shore fin I met an aal fisherman, tall an as stracht as a rash. He wore a sleeved weskit abeen his navy blue ganjie an roon his neck a black silk muffler. On his heid a cheese-cutter an on his feet a pair o saft leather ankle-boots. Ye ken him, divn't ye?'

'Hey, ma loon!' says he, 'Faa echts, ye? Faa's yir mither?'

Now I kent better than to say Mrs Buchan, for at that time every second wifie was a Mrs Buchan so I simply said: 'I'm een o Jeannie Motherwell's.'

'Weel noo,' says he, 'ging an tell Jeannie Motherwell that she'll be nott this aifterneen on the Embankment an tell her t' bring her mennin needles.' Then seeing anither wifie across the street he cried: 'Hey, Mary! I'm seekin t' spik t' ye!'

My mither's maiden name wis Motherwell, and it amused her that maist o the fisher folk thocht it wis a bye-name. She wis an incomer. Fit ither could she be wi a name like that?

When I brought the old fisherman's message my mother said, 'There's surely something far wrang the day! Rin doon the shore an see fit news ye get.' The news I got was bad indeed.

At the very peak of the summer herring season, two of the local herring drifters had met with disaster. Every net they had shot the previous evening had been torn to shreds by 'muldoans'.

Some folk said that the proper name for 'muldoan' was Killer Whale. Others said it was a Basking Shark while yet another group said it was a beast as big as a whale with a fin as big as a sail on its back. A sail-fish, they called it.

Well, whatever their proper name might be, the brutes had destroyed two fleets of nets, each fleet a mile long. They had gone in through one net and out through the next one like skiers doing a slalom. Not one single net had they missed and by some weird mischance they had picked upon the gear belonging to those who were least able to sustain such a loss.

Since it was the summer season, only the best nets would be in use. Any spare nets the unfortunate fishermen might have had would be older, harder nets suitable for Yarmouth but useless in the summertime.

As the two crews bundled the shattered nets, there was much head-shaking among the curious bystanders.

'They'd be jist as weel t' tie the boats up noo! Afore they get that lot sorted oot the fishin'll be feenished! That's supposin they get them sorted avaa!'

And they were quite right: it would take months for these men and their wives to repair the awful damage. A long tear in a net was a comparatively simple job as long as the yarn (meshes) was still there but the great monsters had riven great skelps o yarn oot o the nets.

A vast amount of 'patch' would be required and nobody could possibly have that amount, especially since the patch would need to be of the same quality as the nets. So, alas, it was the end of the road.

But Sonnie, wi the sleeved weskit an cheese-cutter caip, had other ideas, so he set out on a recruiting campaign among the fisher folk.

'Come doon an bring your mennin needles. An a hank or twaa o twine wid be a help!' As if by magic the message seemed to precede him and in a very short time the hale toon kent.

Now then, that afternoon on the Embankment a fair-sized crowd of men, women and youngsters could be seen working at a heap of nets.

The men, mostly elderly, would spread out a net for inspection and if the net was simply torn, it would be passed to the women for mending.

But most of the nets required extensive patches so two nets which proved to be beyond repair were cannibalised to provide patches for nets less badly damaged. Patching was for men, mending was for women.

Youngsters could fill needles with twine or they could keep the yarn of a net tight so that a skilled hand could trim a hole to receive a patch. There was work aplenty for all hands.

Some women sent word that they couldn't come because they were gutting, but they would join the fray as soon as they could; others said they 'couldna leave their bairns but if somebody wid tak a torn net up to the hoose, they wid dae't at hame.'

A fine jobbie for a loon wi a barra!

Gnarled old hands which hadn't handled a net for years soon rediscovered their lost skills with needle and knife and the women's fingers, altho unaccustomed to wet yarn, flew like the shuttles of a loom. Sonnie was the gaffer; no dispute about that.

In the evening Sonnie took me and my chum aside: 'Tak that barra an ging ower t' the Ronheids. Ye'll see a puckle folk workin there. Look for a mannie like me b' the name o Buller an tell 'im that I'm rinnin oot o patch. He'll maybe gie ye a net or twaa t' tak back.'

Full of our own importance we set out on our mission, but when we got to the Ronheids we got a shock!

The grassy braes aside the killin hoose (abattoir) wis black wi folk. Nets were spread aa wye an ilka een that could dee onything wi a net wis up t' the een wi wark.

Since the crews who owned the nets lived mostly on the north side of the town, most of the damaged gear had been taken there for repair. Apparently Sonnie had jist gotten a puckly t' sort.

I had never seen anything like this before. It was great fun for loons to be in the thick of such a throng, an yet there wis a something aboot it that wid gar ye greet!

There was no singing, no daffery; there was instead an almost tangible air of dour determination.

No-one called a halt till well after sunset and several were back on the job at the crack o dawn. Women came and went as their other duties required, one taking on where another had left off.

Slowly, slowly the tally of nets 'ready for sea' mounted. Twice did my chum and I go back wi the barra for mair nets to sort, and at the end of the third day the task was completed.

Both fleets of nets were ready, somewhat depleted in numbers of course (it could not be otherwise), but the two ships could carry on fishing.

The impossible had been achieved. I'm relying solely on memory and I'm thinkin that it should have been properly recorded at the time, because such an achievement is worth a place in any book of records.

There have been no herring nets for many years now. The deft fingers which spent so many hours plying the needles are a thing of the past. Fishermen's wives of today do no net-mending.

'Ah!' you may ask, 'But is not the community spirit of former days still alive?'

Well now, in answer to that, I must confess that I'm some like Robbie Burns: 'I guess and fear!'

The Turk Gets a Bite

The good ship *Meadowsweet* had been designed for work on the open sea, and yet, here she was in the calm and tranquil waters of Loch Glendhu, some four miles inland from the ferry at Kylesku!

Richt into the hert o the hills! An fit wid the Turk be seekin here? Surely nae a load o peats?

'Dinna be daft!' says the Turk, 'I'm seekin herrin bait for my gryte-lines, cos lines athoot bait's as muckle eese as guns athoot ammunition! There's nae a herrin to be gotten in the Minch so we maun look for the craiturs some ither wye.

'I've seen the herrin that thick in here that ye could verra near traivel across the loch on them; but I'll be pleased to see a baitin, a basket or twaa!'

Now the gryte-line is completely different from the smaa-line in many ways. It is 'gryte' (big) where its junior is 'smaa'. Its massive hooks and heavy cordage are for big fish such as halibut, skate and cod in deep waters, where a smaa-line could never take the strain, and furthermore the gryte-line was not for baiting in the hoose. No! It had to be baited while it was being 'shot' or run out of its basket while the ship was underway.

The gryte-line basket has approximately twice the capacity of a herring basket. One half of the rim, from handle to handle, is tightly bound with strong hempen cord to give strength and protection to the wicker-work. On the opposite half of the rim, from handle to handle, there is a length of cork about 1 inch wide and 1 inch thick; this also is firmly secured to the basket.

Now, before you coil the line into the basket it is essential that the end is left hanging over the rim. On no account must it be left in the bottom of the basket!

Then you can 'redd' the line neatly into the basket, sticking each hook in turn into the cork and keeping them very close together for you have to stick about 120 hooks into the cork.

It is mandatory that the hooks be 'staggered' in strict rotation, one out and one in, so that when the basket is full of line there will be two rows of hooks in the cork, each hook with its 'tail' inside (never outside) the basket.

Then you'll take the end which is hanging over the rim and hitch it loosely to the other end and lay the big knot or the 'bennins' on top of the line.

As a security measure there should then be a lashing across the top of the heap to keep the line in the basket till required.

Bait for such a line is usually herring cut in halves, or maybe in three, if the herring are scarce.

The actual process of baiting could also be described as hooking the bait. If you are baiting a 'head-half', the hook must go in through the back of the head and out through the back of the neck; a tail-half requires the hook in and out through the bone so that the bait will stay on the hook. See?

Now, let's get a start to shoot the lines. The basket is placed close to the bulwark with the 'bare' rim toward the sea and facing somewhat aft.

Two of you will be seated on fishboxes with a box of cut bait between you, and as the ship steams ahead and the line goes zipping over the side, you'll take it in turn to bait and throw the hooks clear of the line.

Immediately on the aft side of you a man will be 'running the back', checking that the line runs clear and in one hand he'll have a razor-sharp knife in case of accidents.

The bottom end of the line is 'bent' (never 'tied') to the top end of the next line so that the basket, when empty, can be whisked away and a full basket set in its place without a moment's slacking of the pace.

If you want a fag, someone else will have to give you a lighted one, because you 'canna tak yer ee aff yer wark!'

You must not dither, yet you must not be rash and on no account must you let a hook drop into the basket among the line. That would be a disaster. Great-line hooks are lethal and must be handled with care.

Basket after basket, mile after mile of line, several thousand hooks, in conditions which are always bitterly cold and often very wet indeed; then ye'll ken fit caal is!

Well now, let's get back to Loch Glendhu where the Turk has anchored a few nets as close to the shore as it was safe to go with a drifter. Nets on anchors? Aye, surely! There's nae room to drift!

The supper table has been cleared and the lads are having a smoke when the Turk makes a dramatic announcement: 'Jeemsie, I think I've gotten a flech!'

'Nae again, skipper? Flechs seems t' like you! Faar is she this time, back or front?'

'Verra near atween my shooder blades. At least that's far she is eyvnoo!'

'Fine!' says Jeemsie. 'That's jist fine! There's nae near sae mony lurks an faals on yer back as there is on yer belly so we'll hae a better chance o catchin her. Ye mind the job we had catchin the last een cos she wis hidin among the caddis (fluff) in yer belly-button? Lat's hae the tail o yer linner, skip!'

Behold now, the Turk, face down on the cabin table beneath the only light available, the white glare from the naked flame of the acetylene gas jet.

And behold his gallant crew, completely engrossed as they watch Jeemsie rowin up the mannies linner, canny, canny . . .

'Better nor the picters, this!' says Duncan.

'Better nor readin the labels on the jam-jars!' says Lugs, the fireman.

'Gie's a bittie slack, skipper! I canna work athoot slack!' says Jeemsie.

The tension was terrific for a while, till Jeemsie made a lightning pounce before bolting up the trap with his prey.

'I've catched the brute, skipper! I'll throw her ower the side! Jist ee listen for the splash cos she's near as big's a labster!'

Amid the laughter which followed the Turk rearranged his clothing. 'An affa loon that!' says he. 'But he's a great han among the flechs. I'm richt gled it wis a flech an nae a bog. Fin I wis in the Navy we wis affa sair bothered wi bogs!'

'I didna ken there wis bogs at Trafalgar,' says Duncan. 'I thocht that wis on the open sea!'

'I'm nae spikkin aboot weet grun, ye gowk, I mean yon beasties that sooks yer bleed fin ye're sleepin. The Navy ships wis crawlin wi them but ye see they were aa English boats. If we had a Scotch navy we wid flee the Lion Rompin an there widna be a bog t' be seen!'

'Wid they be feart at the lion?' says Duncan.

'Laach if ye like, my freen,' says the Turk. 'But if ye get bogs in the ship ye'll ken aa aboot it. They like t' bide in the seams atween the planks an they breed at twaa thoosan per cent.

'I've seen some lads gaan along the seams wi reid-het pokers an you could hear the beasties crackin like spunks! They sook bleed until they burst an syne the stink wid scumfish ye! They're nae gweed company!'

'Fan are we lookin-on, skipper?' says Dumplin in a hurry.

'The twalt oor!' says the Turk. 'Ye'd better sleep fast!'

On the stroke of midnight the watchman called the sleeping crew by rattling a mug with a spoon and saying sweetly, 'Haway now, Haway! Rise an shine!' His shipmates obeyed immediately and sat down to enjoy their scalding hot tea.

But, alas, the poor Turk was in a parlous state. He sat beside his bunk in fear and trembling, great beads of sweat on his brow.

'Fit's adee, skipper? Are ye nae-weel?' cried Jeemsie.

'If that wis aa, I wid be fine, my loon, but I'm feart that the worst has come hinmaist! There's been something aitin me aa nicht till my back's fair raw an it canna be onything but bogs. Will ye hae a look, Jeemsie?'

'Nae fears!' says the loon. 'A flech's jist a flech but I'm for naething t' dee wi bogs!'

'C'mon, skip! Doon the stoke-hole wi me an we'll hae a look!' says Duncan, and the Turk obeyed meekly.

To a man the crew followed, each and every one with an uneasy itchy feeling atween his shooder blades. From various vantage points they watched in fascination as Duncan seized the skipper's linner an yarkit it up ower his heid.

'Dalmichty! I nivver saw the likes o this afore, skipper. There's great teethmarks aa ower yer back! Dis bogs hae teeth?'

'Nae as far as I ken, Duncan!'

'That's fit I thocht, skipper. An ye'd better stop makkin sic a soun, cos it's time ye wis learnin that a man o your wecht shouldna sleep on his ain false teeth!'

Biggest Lee You Are Ever Likely to Hear

'Aabody's a lot better aff noo, but they're nae near sae happy an contintit as they eesed t' be!'

This is an expression you'll hear every day and usually it is accompanied by a lugubrious shake of the head. By their very nature the words can only be used by an ageing generation and in fact they form the biggest lee you are ever likely to hear!

Nae doot ye'll be sayin — 'We aye kent he wis feel, but he's due for the asylum noo!' But that would be a fatal mistake. Listen!

It was in the early thirties and it was to be my last year at school. But altho I little knew it, my education simply had not begun. In the middle of December, Cousin Jim wis teen awaa t' Aiberdeen wi pendix an his mither, worried about her son's health an also worried at the prospects o Jim loosin his message-boy jobbie, came round to see if I could possibly get off school to keep his jobbie open.

Special dispensation was granted and I joyfully assumed the role of message-boy with John M Thomson (Grocer) in the Longate in Peterhead. At that time the Longate was one unbroken line of all kinds of shops (on both sides) and the maze of lanes and closes which ran from the street towards the harbour gave access to a welter of dingy slums and hovels populated by an unbelievable number of people.

Coal-heavers, stevedores, coopers and kipperers with a scattering of fisher folk were crowded together in appalling conditions and they were all afflicted with one common disease, namely poverty. Their bairns would come to the shop just before it closed at 8 p.m., as all shops did in those days, asking for 'chippit aipples' or 'broken biscuits' which were of course sold at reduced prices, and 'on tick' forbye!

Keepin the chippit aipples aside wis pairt o my job along wi wyin oot half-steens o tatties an fillin jars wi seerip. The customer would bring an empty jam-jar fin she wanted seerip, cos athoot an empty, the seerip wis a maik dearer.

Did ivver ye try fillin jars wi seerip oot o a barrel? Boys, that would further yer education! It fairly furthered mine!

Ae richt caal frosty mornin, I wis at this job in the back shop. The seerip wis stiff stiff wi caal an it wisna ower willin t' come oot o the barrel. It wis tricklin into the jar in slow, lazy fauls when the boss shouted for me to wye tatties, so I jumped to it! But oh, the love o Dod Vricht, I forgot to shut the cockie!

It wis twaa oors afore I got back, an boys, ye nivver saw sic a sotter: the hale back shop wis awash wi seerip, a clorty, sticky sea wi islands here an there. The peer cat wis marooned richt in the middle, on an orange-box reef!

I didna expect the lifeboat wid come for a cat so I just gid in ower the boot-heids an saved the craitur. I didna get a medal. I learned that day that seerip's nae gweed t' shift wi a shovel. Specially if it's mixed wi paper an bitties o cork.

Hogmanay cam roon an I wis nivver aff my bike gaan wi orders. Ten bob the wik plus tips; a proper fortin! I often got a penny fae wifies that could ill spare the tip but nivver a copper did I get at the gran hooses in the select pairt o the toon.

At midnicht on Hogmanay I was sent to Jimmy Reid's to get a horse an cairt to get the orders delivered and I lowsed at half past two on New Year's mornin. And I really enjoyed it.

Noo, listen again! In those days a hale bourachie o folk had their hames on the 'Queenie', ower the brig fae the toon. The Queenie is actually the water you have to cross to get to Keith Inch which was once an island, so anyone 'Gaan ower the Queenie' was doing exactly that, but somehow the name got transposed to the actual island itself whose inhabitants were known as Queenie Arabs.

The mixture as before — fisher folk and tradesmen, decent hard-workin folk sair afflicted wi poverty.

Well, here wis I on the Queenie, gropin my wye up a black, dark close, then up a darker steen stair to the ootside door o the hoose. It wis darker than yer oxter pooch inside the door so it wis a case o feelin my road up a widden stair which my feet tellt me wis completely bare an badly worn.

The door at the stair-heid had nae knob, jist a sneck, an my sharp rap on its face brocht the cry, 'Come in, my loon!' As seen as I opened the door, a great blast o rick cam doon the lum an the gas licht started to blink. Oh boys, fit a place to bide!

I put the basket on a cheer then began to transfer its contents to the table, closely watched by three bairns who sat on a low stool by the fire. Suddenly they jumped to their feet and careered round the table like Red Indians, clappin their hands and chantin, 'Seerip, seerip, seerip!'

'Fit on earth's adee wi the bairns?' says I.

'Ye can surely see,' says the mither, 'Seerip's a special treat for Hogmanay. They're excited wytin for their Da t' come hame fae the trawlin the nicht.'

So there were five in the one attic! And a jar o seerip wis a special treat!

Now listen again! If ye can equate such conditions wi happiness an contentment, I'll gie ye a fiver.

An should ye try to pass this off as an isolated incident ye'd be clean wrang.

I was message boy wi John M Thomson an I ken different.

The Lost Tribe of the Auchies

There is no such thing as 'the fisher tongue', simply because there are as many variations in the fisher tongue as there are fisher communities on the coast. It is quite possible for a keen ear to pinpoint the very village of a fisher-body's origin by noting the inflections and subtle nuances of the speaker's voice.

Boddam is not very far from Peterhead but the difference in the speech is really quite obvious. Buchanhaven, in my youth, was a fisher community completely separate from Peterhead and one could easily recognise a 'Buchaner' by his accent.

Now that Buchanhaven has been for many years engulfed in the big town, the difference in accent has been largely smoothed out, but this applies only to the younger generation. Their elders are quite easily spotted.

Even in the big town itself the Doric has been grossly diluted with excessive doses of John Wayne and the like. When I hear youngsters say, 'It's richt caal, is it?' my ear is deeply offended because such a statement is not merely a grammatical error — it is an abomination. It would appear that this dilution of the Doric is more or less unavoidable, but it is nonetheless regrettable.

Still, one must be thankful that there are still such terms as skurry, myaave and pule, all of them names for the common gull and each one a definite pointer to the native locality of the user. The watering down of local dialect is common along the whole coastline and I'm afraid it is especially evident in the village of Auch (Avoch).

When I was a lad, many 'Auchies' came to Peterhead to find berths in the herring drifters. Indeed many of them married local quines and settled down in the Blue Toon.

On a Sunday morning there would be several pews of Auchies in the Conger Kirk, each one in his navy blue ganjie and black silk muffler.

Their speech was almost incomprehensible and indeed to meet an 'Auchie' with a habber was a severe test of endurance. Their term for ham and eggs was ''am an heygg' and when they meant 'smaa herrin' they said 'smaalairing'.

The Auchies were mostly dark-haired and of medium build. They were, and still are, very hard-working men of a rather quiet disposition. I am not really competent to trace their origins, but I have a suspicion that they are a race apart.

With surnames like Patience and Jack how could they be anything else?

I have heard them described as the Lost Tribe of Israel and I have also heard a whisper that they are descended from a remnant of Cromwell's army which ventured too far north and got themselves surrounded by hordes of war-like Hielanmen.

I think the latter conjecture would be more likely, especially if the term 'Hielanmen' was deleted and 'Hielan Deems' put in its place.

Be this as it may, the Auchies are decent folk and if I consider their speech as comical, no doubt they laugh themselves silly at my uncouth Buchan vernacular.

Avoch is a lovely village in a lovely setting. It stands on the north shore of the

Inverness Firth. (Not the Moray Firth, you silly! Where's your geography?)

To enter the Inverness Firth, you must leave the Moray Firth and take the narrow channel between Fort George and the Chanonry. When you have negotiated this channel you are in the Inverness Firth and away to starboard you'll see Auch with its white-washed houses.

Away in the distance ahead you'll see Inverness and the new Kessock Bridge and should you pass under that lofty span you'll be in the Beauly Firth. See?

The two Firths form a huge, land-locked expanse of calm water which for many years was the scene for a fruitful winter herring fishing. Herring? Aye! The 'smaalairing'!

They were bigger than sprats but much smaller than normal herrings, and there were times when the shoals were very thick indeed.

Fancy shooting a fleet of nets away up in the Beauly Firth at high-water so that you could drift with the ebb through the narrows at the Kessock Ferry! Or drifting from Kilmuir across Munlochy Bay then down past Avoch!

I have heard that the ferryman at Kessock used to set a net at the slipway and when he got a 'good marking' the Auchies got their nets aboard and the season proper would commence.

The nets used for catching the 'garvies' (as the small herrings were often called) were of course narrow in the mesh, very shallow to suit the shallow waters, and made of white cotton. They were never barked or tanned, but were steeped regularly in a boiling solution of alum. The traditional method of weighting the nets was to get stones from the beach— special stones in that they had strong tufts of brown seaweed sprouting from them. By hitching the seaweed to the bottom rope of the nets you could get ballast which would scuff along the seabed without chafffing any tows. A proper Stone Age practice!

When the fleet grew larger, such stones were as scarce as hen's teeth and a substitute had to be found. At last some clever youth came up with the idea of using old metal floats from seine nets. These floats had a metal lug on them and if you punctured the metal sphere so that it could be filled with cement you had a perfect sinker. This was the death knell for the stone weights!

Some of the boaties which prosecuted this particular fishing were not very big at all. Indeed some of them were 'scaphs' or 'scaffies' which were as old as the hills, having been built originally for sails. These scaffies were only 25-30ft. in length, but most of the fleet was composed of first-class craft, 1950s style. Fifty-footers or a bittie bigger.

When the Peterhead inshore fleet decided to horn in on this fine, canny fishing, it was proper pandemonium. There were boats and nets all over the place and we discovered that it wasn't nearly so canny as we had expected.

It was a case of shoot and haul the whole night through because in these restricted waters with their strong tides you could not possibly let her lie all night. On occasion it reminded me of the Dodgems at the shows.

I shall never forget one night in particular. We had drifted down from the Longman with the ebb, but before we finished hauling, the tide had carried us so far that we were away to seaward of the Chanonry lighthouse. For that haul we had twelve cran, so I thought we would steam up the Firth again and repeat the operation.

The narrow channel was choc-a-bloc with boats and nets so the only practical way was to nip past on the east side of the mêlée.

Clever me, until the boat came to a sudden halt! We were well and truly stuck on the sewage pipe which runs down the beach from Fort George.

This pipe is on concrete supports and its top surface would be at least five feet off the bottom. I was black affronted for a while until one of the Auch skippers said very kindly: 'Was that your first time on the pipe, Peter? It winna be your last! It happens so often that we think nothing of it!'

Comfort indeed!

I think the Inverness Firth must be one of the coldest spots in the country. There is a great deal of fresh water around and that is always colder than salt water.

It was quite common to see great sheets of ice coming down from the River Ness and I have seen herring, only a few minutes out of the water, being snapped like twigs — so severe was the frost. I had never believed this possible until I tried it myself.

To work in such conditions is no picnic, especially when one is suffering from lack of sleep.

They say that, 'Ilka cock craws on his ain midden heid!'

Local knowledge is a tremendous asset but it cannot be gained overnight. It may take years to acquire this precious commodity, but to spend years at the 'smaalairing'?

Brrrr! Nothing doing!

Hale Eggs fae the Pearl King!

It was a bitterly cold day with a thin layer of fresh snow when my Deydie (Grandad) and I took the bus to go 'up the country'.

It was 1925 and I was a very small boy whom Deydie addressed as 'littlin' or 'boakie' as his humour dictated. Among all the host of Deydie's grandchildren I was his favourite, his right-hand man, his special envoy, his bosom friend, and many's the time I accompanied him on his rural wanderings.

Sometimes we would go to Neebra (Newburgh) to see about mussel bait; sometimes we would tak a bittie fish to yon mannie at the Moss o Rora. We kent a Longside mannie that made a wooden chain oot o ae bit o timmer and we kent a mannie in Crichie who had 'lost the wife' since he last had seen us. Only the tone of Deydie's voice as he said, 'Eh man! Eh, man!' prevented me from offering to go and look for her. I was as young as that!

Well now, this particular day we were on a special mission; in fact we were on two missions rolled into one. The first was to obtain two horse tails, a black een an a fite een. The best place for such a prize was of course a farm, for in those days tractors were as yet unknown.

We would take the tails home where they would be thoroughly washed and combed, then Deydie would make horse-hair tippins for his haddock lines.

I would give him seven hairs from a tail; he would deftly knot the seven ends into one before drawing the hairs across a leather pad strapped to his leg above the knee while at the same time he rolled the hairs together with his left hand. Then he would finish the job with another neat knot. The end result was a beautiful glossy string of amazing lightness and strength, about eighteen inches long, and onto this tippin he would beat (lash) the hook.

The workmanship was superb and the patience incredible. My job entailed keeping an eye on the tatties which were roasting on the bink (hob) of the grate. Left-overs from dinner-time when they had been boiled in their jackets, they were very good indeed. Champions or Buchan Beauties they were. What was radio? What was TV? Ye must be clean daft!

Our second errand was to find some 'speyngie' or 'spaingie'.

Note that the end of that word is pronounced in the same way as 'springy' or 'thingie' and it means the cane from which baskets are made. Deydie had heard that speyngie was to be obtained at a certain farm and since he was an ardent basket-maker, he was keen to acquire some raw materials. A very versatile mannie was Deydie.

So we left the bus at the first roadie past the Prison and made our way on foot through the snow. When we had covered about half a mile, we met a great muckle deem who ventured to remark that it was 'Helluva caal!'

'Prodeegious caal!' says Deydie, who didna use bad words. Some twenty paces further on he suddenly stopped and turned to survey the receding female, and dashit if she didna do exactly the same. So there the two of them stood glowering speechless at each other. Young as I was I was highly amused.

Deydie was the first to give in, so we resumed our way, with him muttering, 'My govies, littlin, did ye ivver see legs like yon?'

After an interminable walk we arrived at our destination, the farm named Wellbank. 'Noo!' says Deydie, 'This is far the Pearl King bides an his name's Mister Birnie. See that ye behave yersel.' I was glad to get inside to the warmth of the kitchen fire.

The Pearl King, as he was universally known, had made a heap o siller oot East by employing natives to dive for pearls. Naked except for a loin cloth, the divers fastened a big stone to their ankles before plunging overboard from the boat. The purpose of the stone was to get the diver swiftly to the seabed, where he would gather into a bag at his waist as many shellfish as he could, before his breath ran out.

Then he would 'slip his moorings' and return to the surface, where other workers opened the shells in search of pearls. It wis gey sair on the divers, that job, and it is most unlikely that they were well-paid.

'Twaa horse tails?' says the Pearl King, 'I think we wid manage that, but I'm nae sae sure aboot the speyngie. But we'll see!'

169

'Wid ye like to bide for yer supper?' says Mrs Birnie.

'Weel, seein that ye insist, we'll bide!' says Deydie.

Boys! I'll never forget that supper. Biled eggs an oatcakes. What a treat! But what surprised me most was the fact that Mrs Birnie's hens could lay hale eggs! Peterheid hens could only lay halfs apparently. Ye're aye learnin!

'Wid onybody like anither egg?' says Mrs Birnie. 'Aye surely!' says I, 'I could fairly go anither een!'

Deydie gied me a look like a summons. I'm thinkin that wis cos I'd beaten him to the only egg that wis left!

After tea Mr Birnie took us ben the hoose where there was a great muckle roll-top desk. 'Noo, my loon,' says he, 'in this thing there's some secret drawers that I'll let ye see!' Now I had seen a lot o worsit drawers on the claes tows in the Blue Toon; I had often seen the type o wifie's drawers that were called 'open docks', and which must have been very draughty, but I had never seen secret drawers.

But my curiosity was soon satisfied when from a secret drawer Mr Birine drew a little shammy-leather baggie tied with a draw-string. 'Hud oot yer hans,' says he, then into my cupped hands he poured the most beautiful pearls I have ever seen. Even tho I was just a bairn I sensed that they were extra special! Perfection to the nth degree.

'Foo aal are ye?' asked the Pearl King. Then when I had replied he said, 'Supposin ye live till ye're a hunner 'ear aal ye'll nivver earn the price o fit's in yer hans the day!' I ken noo he wis richt.

On the way home, Deydie produced one of his gems when he remarked, 'There's naething like an egg for a soor rift, littlin!' He did ither things besides riftin till I wis near scumfished! But since I was the proud bearer of two lovely horse tails, I said nothing.

Some time later, in April 1925, Mr Alexander Birnie presented to the town of Peterhead the Birnie Bridge which spans the Ugie near its mouth. Prior to the erection of the Brig the only access to the golf course and the beautiful beaches was by means of a flat-bottomed, square-ended coble which was drawn across the river on a wire rope slung from bank to bank.

The opening ceremony for the new Brig wis a great occasion. The hale toon wis there an ivvery bairn got a chocolate egg. I got mine along wi the lave but it could nivver match the egg I got in the Pearl King's hoose.

One mystery remains. For many, many years after the Brig was opened there was a penny fee to get across. Now, it is a stark fact that for most of these years a great many folk in Peterhead simply could not afford the penny. But times changed so that prosperity wis the order o the day, then the charge wis abolished.

It's enough to gie a buddy a soor rift!

A Helpin o Mustard for the Maître d'Hôtel

An observant traveller on the Peterhead-Aberdeen road can scarcely fail to observe that in the not too distant past a railway connected Boddam with Ellon. The rails have long been removed but great lengths of embankment are still plainly visible, as are the great granite supports of several bridges, especially on the outskirts of the village of Cruden Bay. The line ran from Boddam to Cruden Bay to Hatton and thence to Ellon via Pitlurg and Auchmacoy.

The station-master's houses were all built of local granite to a standard pattern and to this day they are sturdy dwelling houses, one of which stands close alongside the main road at Longhaven. Improvements over the past twenty years have ironed out the notoriously dangerous kinks where the road was obliged to cross the railway (and vice-versa) but the younger generation could profitably spend a pleasant afternoon tracing the route of the old line.

I can well remember that the fences which bounded the line were ideal for the drying of fleets of herring nets during the immediate post-war years, when mile after mile of track was filled with decrepit and dilapidated rolling stock. Trucks and wagons of all kinds lay there for years awaiting repair, until bit by bit they were taken south.

There was also the colossal Railway Hotel at Cruden Bay. Comprising 365 bedrooms it stood on the site which is now the Golf Club car park. The big granite building which still stands near the car park was in fact the laundry for the magnificent hotel, which was a welcome source of employment for a veritable army of locals.

Many of the village boys earned a canny wage caddying for the host of wealthy golfers who came from far and near. One of the caddies, Bill Robertson (Weft), was the envy of his pals because he was the regular bag-carrier for Mr Colman, the mustard millionaire, who loved to holiday at Cruden Bay, where everybody knew that Mr Colman's millions came from the mustard which diners left on the edge of their plates.

Now, mustard is a pleasant condiment when it is used wisely. It lifts a humble dish such as hairy tatties to heights which T-bone steaks could never hope to reach. But mustard can be devastating!

In days of old, fisher weddings or 'mairridges' were simple, homely affairs where the wedding ceremony, the 'Feed' and the dance all took place under the same roof, usually a local hall. Indeed my own grandparents, Aal Oxy fae Burnhaven an Meggie Forman fae Buchanhaven each walked halfway, accompanied by their invited guests, to meet at the Ropework (now the Bayview Garage), where they were wed.

The floor had, of course, been cleared before-hand and everybody had a whale of a time, the feed being saat-fish an tatties (hairy tatties) with mustard, a cut abeen the normal tatties an herrin! Of recent years, however, fisher mairridges have graduated to the five-star hotel level, where no expense is spared and where female guests arrive dressed like 'parish models with incendiaries to tone'.

Picture then, such a function in an illustrious establishment: the guests all busy at their caviar, when there appears on the scene an uninvited dog, a mongrel of huge proportions and a very friendly manner. Rather too friendly maybe, because it insists on sniffing at your anatomy where sniffs are definitely not allowed!

At first nobody says 'boo', cos ye see, it's maybe the skipper's dog, but an old shipmate of mine who knows better decides to cure this detestable sniffing habit, so, with the blade of his table knife as a sort of catapult, he skites a great dollop of mustard onto the dog's beauty spot, which is immediately below the root of its tail!

The startled beast decides to investigate by bending itself into a semi-circle first to port, then to starboard without success, so not to be outdone, it contorts its body into a grotesque form so that the nose can sniff the offending substance. There is apparently no smell so it takes one almighty lick, then all hell breaks loose!

The demented beast, with its tongue and belly both on fire goes completely berserk, charging up and down the room like a hairy cannon ball and howling like a banshee, until a quick-thinking flunkey opens a French window and lets the demon escape.

Some sort of order is soon restored to the battlefield and everyone is about to resume operations when the bride's mother, resplendent in shantung silk an fairly dreepin wi jewels, rises groggily to her feet, and gripping the table-edge so hard that her knuckles gleam white, she asks in a strained voice, 'Quine! Faar's 'e watry?'

On receiving specific instructions, she makes for the door with a peculiar gait, apparently desirous of haste and yet not quite able to attain it. She is followed in rapid succession by several other ladies, all suddenly and obviously cripple. Powerful stuff, mustard!

The mustard king, Mr Colman, dearly loved to visit the harbour at Port Errol, a place which is known to fishermen as 'The Ward'. There he had a close friend in Weelum Tait, a local fisherman of forthright speech. Older readers may remember his appearance on TV when he beat the Panel in *What's my Line*, the panel being Gilbert Harding, Anona Wynn and Isobel Barnett.

The millionaire liked nothing better than to sit on the side-deck of Weelum's boatie, the *Posy*, with his bare feet trailing in the sea while the boatie was underway and many a time did he foregather, with a few titled personages, in the kitchen of Weelum's hoosie (directly opposite the Lady's Briggie) to feast on Granny Tait's breid (oatcakes).

One fine morning, desirous of a sail in the boat, he came to the harbour, only to learn that there wis, 'ower muckle motion, ye wid only get weet!' Rather disappointed, he decided that he would gie Weelum a hurl in his Rolls Royce limousine. Weelum required no second bid so, just as he stood, he boarded the great vehicle, sitting in the rear seat with the millionaire while the chauffeur acted as pilot.

Lunch-time found them parked outside the Invercauld Arms at Braemar. Mr Colman had with him a packed lunch which he shared with his chauffeur but there was not sufficient for Weelum who, apart from being very hungry, was also stoney broke, a situation which was promptly remedied with a pound note from the rich

172

man's wallet. 'Go and have a nice meal in the hotel, Weelum!'

So our hero, impervious to the frosty stares of the other diners, seated himself at a window table, tossing his caip onto the window sill. He was immediately informed by a saucy waitress that this was the first-class dining room, no place for any person in fisherman's garb.

'Weel!' says Weelum, 'Ye'll need to unnerstan that I'm a first-class gentleman an I'm needin a first-class denner!'

This merely hastened the arrival of the maître-d'hôtel who was determined to have this fisher lout thrown out until Weelum, pointing to the Rolls outside the window asked, 'Div ye ken faa that is?'

Of course the mannie kent it wis Mr Colman. 'Weel, it wis him that sent me in here for my denner an if I dinna get it he'll see till't that ye dinna get nae mair mustard!'

At that moment the millionaire glanced towards the window and, sensing Weelum's predicament, he gave him a reassuring wave, but simultaneously he raised a very expressive eyebrow at the chief flunkey. So Weelum got his denner!

'Man, Peter,' says he to me, 'yon wis the best feed I ivver saw. If it wis on the menu, I took it, twaa doses o some things until I wis fit to burst. But ye ken the aal sayin — Beter belly-rive than gweed mait spiled! An to feenish aff I had a gless o the finest fuskie! I gied the lassie the powen note an she cam back wi my change in a silver dishie. "Och, quine!" says I, "Keep the change!" Fit wis three half-croons to the likes o me? I felt like a millionaire!' 'A mustard millionaire, Weelum?' says I, with a laugh. 'Ye could say that, Peter! Mustard's powerfu stuff, ye ken!'

Getting to Grips with the Coggie

Prior to the last war, the big Fifie herring boats were a common sight on the east coast of Scotland.

Most of them had been built before the turn of the century, purely and simply as sailing vessels without any kind of machinery whatsoever, apart from a hand-driven winch which was called the Iron Man. This winch was used to haul the heavy messenger rope and was always sited well aft because in those days the boats lay by the stern at their nets.

The invention of the steam capstan was a great step forward. The capstan took the strain off the crew in the hauling of the rope and the handling of the rigging.

Since the practice was still to lie by the stern, the capstan was still sited well aft and the upright boiler was placed in the cabin where the crew ate and slept. Fancy that!

Many years later, another great invention, the internal combustion engine, appeared on the scene, most of the boats opting for the 75 h.p. Gardner paraffin engine.

And where did they put the engine? In the cabin, of course!

It had to be heated with blowlamps before it would start, so you can see that the cabin could be a most unpleasant place. The crew's bedding and clothing stank of paraffin and their food was tainted, although seasoned motor boat men didn't seem to notice.

Sailboats had no wheelhouse. Such a thing was not possible owing to the rig of the sails.

The motor engine changed all that. The entire rig of the boats was changed and it was possible to dispense with the three-ton fore mast and the two-ton mizzen mast and replace them with much lighter spars.

So now we have a wheelhouse which can hold two men and an engine with a reverse gear which is controlled from the deck by means of a key exactly the same as that which plumbers use to shut off the water from your house.

We're gettin on jist fine fin along comes the Board o Trade an says: 'Boys, it's time ye had a smaa boat!' 'Faar are we gaan t' pit it?' says you. 'Pit it faar ye like, but ye hiv t' get it!' says the Board.

I know for a fact that most of these smaa boats were never moved from the day they were installed, being gradually glued to their chocks with countless coats of paint.

For some obscure reason, the old sail or motor boats had no toilet at all. There was a communal 'coggie', a small wooden cask which before use had to be partly filled with water and after use had to be immediately emptied overboard.

'Ye darna wyte a meenit or the thing wid cowp an that wid be a gey job!'

Now, one lovely summer day in 1939, a boat such as I have described was heading east-by-north from Peterhead. She was one of a great fleet seeking the shoals o herrin and, although none of her crew knew it, this would be her last year at the fishing. She would sail no more after the Hitler war.

Except for the helmsman, the crew were in their bunks and all was peace and quiet. Then, about 4 p.m., Hector, a veteran deckie, left his bunk to obey the call of nature.

For a minute or two he sat beside his bunk filling his pipe. From his bunk at the bottom of the ladder, Francie, the young cook, watched Hector go through his normal routine.

Francie knew that Hector would spurn the coggie, and would take up a position on the port quarter, outside the smaa boat, whose gunnel he would grasp as he crouched in a really classic pose, with the North Sea as the coggie that couldna cowp.

Francie also hated the coggie and only lack of nerve kept him from doing as Hector did. What if a foot or a hand should slip?

But today he would hae a lookie to see where Hector placed his feet, so, in his stocking soles the loon crept up the ladder and, without actually leaving the hatch at all, he peeped round the stern o the smaa boat.

What a shock he got! He clean forgot to look at Hector's feet for there, about two feet away, Hector's lily-white stern was in full view along with his badge-of-office.

On a sudden and irresistible impulse the coorse nickum on the ladder reached forth and gave the inoffensive morsel a good hearty 'toot' before vanishing down the ladder and into his bunk.

Poor Hector opened his mouth to yell and immediately lost his pipe overboard. Simultaneously, he sprang to attention like any guardsman while, as part of the same movement, he attempted to vault right across the smaa boat.

But, since his feet had got fanned up wi his breeks, his style was somewhat cramped and he landed, with a fearsome crash, face down amongst the oars and the brooms and the buckets and the jam jars for which the smaa boat made such a handy receptacle.

'Fit on earth's wrang wi ye, Hector?' demanded the skipper.

'A beast o some kind took hud o me. There!' said Hector, pointing a tarry forefinger, but feart to look.

'Weel!' said the mate, who had knelt down to make a close inspection, 'It couldna been a shark or there wid ha been teethmarks!'

'Teethmarks!' cried the skipper, 'If it had been a shark, there widna been naething! Hap yersel, Hector, there's naething wrang wi ye!'

The skipper was no fool! Fit wye had Francie nae come up wi the rest? Like a shot the skipper made for the cabin and tore the blankets off the boy who was lying convulsed with laughter.

At supper, the topic was sharks, Moby Dick and sea monsters.

The unsuspecting Hector asked, as he held out his plate for mair sassidges, 'Francie, my loon, you that's new awaa fae the school, div ee ken fit could ha teen a hud o me the day?'

'Fit wye wid I ken?' wis the reply, 'But gaan b' the noise ye made it could ha been the propellor!'

Hard, Hot Summer Days at the Herrin

There is an old saying that an Orcadian is a crofter with a boat but a Shetlander is a fisherman with a croft. There is quite a difference!

Over the years the Shetland men have prosecuted the fishing far more vigorously than their Orcadian brethren, and during the reign of King Herring, Lerwick was an important centre indeed.

During the summer months the local fleet, crewed by men whose ancient Norse links were still strong and whose language was more or less their own, was augmented by herring drifters from all over the east coast of Scotland.

And, of course, there was the annual arrival of a strong contingent of English boats, mostly from East Anglia. So Lerwick was and always has been a cosmopolitan centre where every fisher accent imaginable could be heard on a Saturday night.

As a rule the herring shoals appeared first in Shetland waters before moving south along the east coast to finish up in the autumn off East Anglia.

The scientist fellas were at great pains to tell the fishermen that these were not the same shoals at all, but different fish altogether, comprising different age groups, etc.

For many years the fishermen paid no heed. 'Faa wid listen til a chiel that said "Veeking Bank" instead o "Viking Bank" an him come o fisher folk himsel?'

Modern fishermen do listen to scientists but in those days they just laughed at them. 'Oh, what know they of harbours who toss not on the sea?' (Radford.) Same sentiments!

During the early part of the Shetland herring season the sea took on a cloudy, brownish hue. This the fishers called the 'growth'. But as the season advanced, the same waters would turn as white as milk. Herring nets which had been used in such waters appeared, on being dried, as if they had been dusted with flour. The fishers didn't like the 'fite watter' simply because the herrings disliked it too.

Herring drifters based in Lerwick called at Lerwick proper with their catches. There the catch was sold but the boat would leave immediately for the buyer's curing station which could be three or four miles away.

These curing stations were scattered up and down the Sound, many of them being on the Isle of Bressay. Each station had its own wharf with its set of rails for the bogies, which carried the herrings from the boat to the yard.

Of course, all the pushing had to be done by the deckies, hard sweaty work on a hot summer day, especially since it was always uphill.

At the curing stations the guttin quines or weemin (never 'girls') would yoke to the gutting of the herring. Three quines to a crew, two gutting and one packing, they had been transported to Shetland at their employers' expense on the deck of the steamer from Aberdeen.

That's richt freen — on the deck. And it's nae aye a summer day tho it's summer time!

The quines dreaded crossing the 'Roost', a particularly nasty stretch of sea which draws its coorseness from the strong tides which sweep between Orkney and Shetland.

In their hundreds the quines 'manned' the curing yards. Drawn from every fishing village from Wick to Peterhead they worked long, hard hours in the open air at what was really slave labour.

Their accommodation consisted of wooden huts furnished with two-tier bunks and precious little else. Cooking facilities were primitive as were also the sanitary arrangements. In these huts the quines had to fend for themselves.

For the coopers, a female cook was employed. There could be other men apart from the coopers for some curers employed a few Irishmen as gutters who could also be utilised as labourers. The cook looked after them, too.

Since most of the curers had stations or yards in the mainland ports, they could follow the herring shoals all the way south to Yarmouth. And since the quines were required there also, there was a continuous migration of fisher folk pursuing the silver darlins, men, women and often bairns forbye.

Ye'll mind on John, my pal wi the great muckle plook on his neck? Then ye'll mind that he was actually a cooper to trade.

When he furhooied the trawling, he returned to his coopering and one particularly hot summer he was gaffer on a curing station on Bressay.

Since there was never any Sunday fishing, there were no herrings to be gutted on Mondays, so Monday forenoon was spent 'filling up' the barrels from the previous week's cure. This meant topping up any barrels whose contents had settled somewhat; additional pickle or brine was poured in via the bunghole and this task kept all hands busy till dinner time. Monday afternoon was the 'half-day'.

Well now, this particular Monday it was the cook's birthday, so she had laid on a super-dooper feed for her 'boys'. The menu could hardly be described as a 'summer' one: Scotch Broth with or without duff, boiled beef an tatties with or without duff, rice and raisins with prunes followed by tay an cheesecakes.

John was a very hard worker with a splendid appetite so he stuffed himself till he was fit to burst, then he stytered oot o the hut to lie face doon in the heather aneth the broiling sun. There he promptly fell asleep.

A few moments later the cook came outside to work at her pots and pans, and on seeing John's vulnerability, a gleam of unholy glee illumined her eye.

With the broth pot in one hand and the pudden dish in the other, she waltzed gaily across the heathery slope to dowp herself doon on John's spine — all sixteen stone of her sonsie Irish frame.

The immediate result was a tremendous explosion in John's innards. Baith his een skited oot; it's a mercy they came back! Peys came doon his nose and cheesecake very nearly choked him.

He never heard the simultaneous eruption at his opposite end because particles of duff were looking for an exit via his lugs; but there was no denying that such an event had taken place!

The hallarackit quine didn't realise that she could have killed poor John. To her, the whole episode was a great joke, altho on this occasion she was obliged to wash his shift for him. Well, somebody had to do it!

What surprised me most, was the fact that through it all, John's strongest words were, 'Ooh me! Ooh me! I dinna like the Irish!'

Dinna Eat Cheese wi Green Bitties!

Not until he was stowing his stores in the cabin locker did Jeemsie discover the little parcel, and by that time the *Meadowsweet* had cleared the breakwater.

'Fitivver this is, it's nae oors, an the smell says it's time it wis ower the side!' And with that he made for the deck.

In the galley he bumped into Duncan, his bosom pal. 'Fit's at ye hiv, Jeemsie?'

'Gweed kens, Duncan! I hinna heen a richt look yet, but I think it's hairy-mouldit cheese, so I'll dump it!'

'Lat's hae a look,' says Duncan, then, 'Ye canna dump that, my loon. It's cheese aa richt, but it's nae hairy-mouldit avaa! That's the kine o't! I dinna mine the richt name o't, but it soun's like Gordon's College an it smells like the skipper's feet!

'I think it micht be richt gweed wi a bittie breid (oatcake). Some peer wifie's gaan t' miss her tasty bite the nicht. Fit aboot a tinkie's maskin for the twaa o's, an we'll try this fancy cheese!'

So the twaa heroes partook of a delectable snack while the rest of the crew, apart from the helmsman, were in the land of Nod. Gorgonzola cheese on a drifter? It'll be blue snaa neist!

Duncan enjoyed the rare treat, but Jeemsie wisna ower happy. 'It's the green bitties that I dinna like, Duncan! I'm sure this stuff'll gar my sark tail crack like a wheep. I'm awaa t' see if I can catch her (have a nap) for an oor afore supper time.'

'Awaa ye go, my loon. I'll sweel oot the twaa joogs,' says his pal.

So in a few minutes Jeemsie was horizontal on his caffsaick, readin *The Coral Island* by his favourite author, R M Ballantyne. But soon the book dropped from his limp fingers and the lad was away in dreamland, on the bonniest beach he had ever seen. The sea was as blue as the een o yon quine in the grocer's shop!

But fit wye wis the *Meadowsweet* stuck oot there on the coral reef wi nivver a sign o life? An fit wis aa this wreckage on the bonny fite san? An faar wis aabody onywye?

'Aabody's lost, Jeemsie! We're the only twaa that's left! We'll jist hae t' mak the best o't!' This from Duncan, who had suddenly appeared on the scene. 'I'm thinkin the sharks got them!'

'Eh! The peer aal Turk, Duncan! Aswarn the shark that taikled him has a gey sair belly noo!'

'Nivver mine the Turk!' says Duncan. 'Ging ee along the san an gaither a puckle sticks t' licht a fire. I see palm trees at the heid o the beach, an far there's palms there's yams. I'll ging up an hae a howk!'

'Fit on earth's yams, Duncan?'

'Things like tatties, but bigger. I see the tattie pot's been washen ashore so we'll manage t' bile the things. We canna live on the win an chaw daylicht!'

'Could ye nae fess back a puckle coconuts, Duncan?'

'First things first, my loon! Get ee the fire goin!'

In a very short time Jeemsie had managed to rake from the wreckage the tattie-pot, twaa packets o fat, half a dizzen loafs that wid seen dry in the sun, an a packet o fardins (butter biscuits).

He had gotten the fire t' licht efter a sair tyauve (cos ye see, the sticks wis weet) fin Duncan cam back wi 'is airms full o bonny big yams.

'We'll bile them wi their jackets on, Jeemsie, usin sea water for the saat.'

'I'd raither hae chips, Duncan! Could we nae hae chips? I'm affa fond o chips! There's plinty o fat!'

'Aa richt, my loon, we'll hae chips, but I'm nae ower fond o chips b' themsel's, so I'll ging into the jungle an see if I can get a bittie o kitchie.

'Chips need kitchie, specially the chips that ee mak. They're like bits o foggy neep. I micht get a turtle or an armadillo or an iguana, ye nivver ken!'

'I'm tellin ye, Duncan, if ye come back wi an elephant ye'll hae t' skin the thing yersel!'

So Duncan disappeared into the dense jungle, leaving Jeemsie to peel and slice the yams and to get the fat boiling hot.

Quarter of an hour later Jeemsie couldna believe his een! Here wis Duncan comin wallopin doon the beach, trailin a little darkie loon b' the hair o the heid!

'Faar did ye get the likes o him, Duncan?'

'In the jungle, ye gowk! There's nae anither livin thing t' be seen. Nae lizards, nae even a cobra. Nae naething!'

'An fit are we gaan t' dee wi 'im, Duncan?'

'Och! We'll roast 'im, my loon! I believe he wid be richt gweed wi chips.'

'Ye'll hae t' kill the craitur first, though, won't ye?'

'Na, na, my loon, that wid be cruel!'

'An fit wye div ye roast a darkie loon, Duncan?'

'Nae bother avaa, my loon. We'll mak a spit wi some o that broken timmer an we'll lash the loon on-till't, an if ye keep turnin 'im slow he'll cook jist gran. The same fire'll dee the chips an the roast at the same time, but if ye turn the spit ower fast he winna cook richt. I canna be deein wi mait that's nae richt teen aboot, so turn 'im slow, slow! I'm awaa back t' the jungle for some fruit. I like a bittie o dessert efter my denner!'

'Mine an fess a coconut, Duncan!'

It wisna lang afore Duncan wis back wi a great muckle bunch o bananas on his shooder, an boys, he fairly got a begick, for Jeemsie wis garrin the spit furl like the verra haimmers!

'Hey! Fit div ye think ye're deein?' cries Duncan. 'He'll nivver cook at that speed! I tellt ye t' furl 'im slow, slow!'

'So ye did!' says Jeemsie. 'I wis furlin 'im fine an canny so that he wid be fine an broon, but ilkie time he cam roon he wis takin a hanfae o chips oot o the pot!'

Nivver again did Jeemsie look at cheese wi green bitties in't!

A Swarm o Locusts Attacked the Wreck!

Fog, to fairmers, is 'mist'. To fishermen it is 'thickness', and according to its density, it can be thick, smore thick, tar thick or as thick as guts, the latter variety being rather opaque.

The Buchan coast is renowned for dense fog and, in the days before echo-sounders and radar were known, many a gallant ship came to grief on this north-east shoulder of Scotland.

One such casualty was the *City of Osaka*, which met her end close to the cliffs jist sooth o the Scaurs o Cruden, in a bicht where Buchan Ness Light is not visible and 'Boddam Coo' seldom heard. As thick as guts? Aye, surely.

The sea was calm and the crew of thirty-two were safely disembarked by the Peterhead lifeboat, leaving the great ship silent and deserted, hopelessly fast on the rocks.

No sooner had the unfortunate mariners been landed than a peculiar fever smote the smaa-boat fraternity in the Blue Toon. Pilots and poachers by profession, and pirates by descent, they had been reared on tales of past wrecks such as the *Union* and the *Princess Mary* whose legendary cargoes had proved to be a heaven-sent windfall for the Buchan fisher folk.

Indeed, every man-jack kent somebody that had an organ or a shewin machine, or great wobs-o-claith-in-aneth-the-bed. In fact ae wifie had a hale tea-set wi floories on't an faar div ye think she got that? An faar did she get the lame (china) chuntie-pot to match? Oot o a wreck! Faar ither could she get sic gran gear?

And so the fever spread until, with a slight lifting of the fog curtain, there came a mass exodus of ripper boats from the port of Peterhead.

Anything from 18-30ft., these clinker biggit boaties had Kelvin paraffin engines and they raced each other for the prize of being first aboard the wreck. Well, after all, didn't the old hymn say 'Where treasure calls, or plunder, be never wanting there!'

Every member of the pirate gang was well versed in the laws of salvage. 'If it's lowse, ye can tak it! If it's fast to the ship ye daurna tak it, cos that's stealin!'

Now this term 'fast to the ship' covered things like engines and bilers, winches an twaa-ton anchors, so there was a vast expanse of territory which was quite legal.

Of course the Receiver of Wrecks and the Police were quite unaware of these loopholes in the law but then they were ignorant folk that didna ken ony better.

Leading the flotilla was the ripper boat *Gem* skippered by the Chemist, a chiel who had in his youth spent a summer wi his mither's folk in Fife. On his return he had spurned the word 'Droggist' which was the north-east term, preferring the title 'Chemist' when he was sent for a Seidlitz pooder. Hence his nickname. His crew were his twaa loons, Dod and Bill.

As they neared the wreck, Dod says, 'Da! Wid there be a pianna aboord there? Ma wid affa like a pianna!'

'Fit on earth wid she dee wi a pianna?' says his Da. 'She has mair need o a tay-pot an a kettle, so mak for the galley at yer hardest! An you, Bill, it's the wheelhoose for you. I could dee fine wi a pair o binoculars!'

The Chemist ran his boatie smartly alongside the rope ladder which the crew had used to board the lifeboat, and the boys swarmed aboard.

Boat after boat arrived a few minutes later and the ship was invaded by a mob of looters who stripped her bare in a matter of minutes.

I'm tellin ye, a bourachie o Bluemogganers could tak a swarm o locusts an learn them a lesson or twaa!

Young Dod had struck it rich in the galley and soon he was lowering into the boatie the biggest copper kettle he had ever seen. This was rapidly followed by several buckets of odds an sods, cutlery, mugs, packets o tay an tins o coffee. 'That's the stuff, my loon! See fit else ye can get noo!' cried his Da.

Suddenly there came a despairing shout from Bill on the bridge. 'Da! There's naething left! I'm thinkin there's been a puckle thiefs here!'

'Thiefs? Faar could they hae come fae? I thocht we wis first here! See if ye can get the steerin wheel aff; 'twid mak a richt fine gatie for the back close!'

'The wheel's awaa an aa Da!'

'Good grief!' says the Chemist. 'Weel, dinna waste time! Try somewye else. Hist ye clivver fast!'

Great sighs of regret arose to the heavens when the pirates, on opening the hatches, discovered some 15 ft. of water in the holds. There was no cargo within reach. What a shame!

Meantime Dod had discovered the paint store whence he had obtained six 5-gallon drums of paint and several brushes.

'I hope the tins wis open fin ye got them!' cried the Chemist anxiously.

'No, Da, they warna. But they're open noo! That maks them legal, disn't it?'

'That's ma boy! Ye're fairly learnin! Lower them doon canny, my loon. It widnae dee t' sink the yole!'

Since the crew, apart from the officers, had all been poor Lascars, their living quarters yielded very little. Indeed every one of them had boarded the lifeboat with a pathetic little bundle aneth his oxter.

But the Chemist did see his next-door neeper wi a hubble-bubble pipe which was to prove 'As sair on tobacco as a drifter is on coal!'

Now Bill, anxious to emulate his brither, had discovered a clothing store and cam to the ship's rail wi a bale o jerseys on his shooder.

The bale landed wi a thump on the boatie's deck. 'I'll be back in a meenit wi some boots, Da!' he cried.

Suddenly a keen-eyed loon in the bows shouted 'A. B. C. R. L.!' (a bobby comin, rin lads) and in a matter of seconds the pirates had abandoned the ship and were off for home with their loot.

'I see the bobby on the tap o the cliff!' says the Chemist. 'It maun be the Collieston bobby, cos there's nae een in Finnyfaul.'

As the *Gem* entered the bay at Peterheid an honest citizen fishing from the breakwater shouted a warning. 'Dinna ging into the hairber, lads! The bobbies is doon like bum-bees searchin ilkie boatie!'

So the Chemist immediately altered course and ran the *Gem* into the Garron, a rocky inlet on the back side o the Queenie. There the treasure was unloaded, carried across the rocks to the pier at Greenhill and dropped into the fo'c'sle of the drifter *Coronet* near the old lifeboat shed.

Of course the *Gem* was searched on entering harbour. Clean bill of health!

After supper the loons widna rest till they got the stuff hame but their father advised caution. 'Better let it lie for a day or twaa.'

'It'll be aa stolen if we wyte ower lang! There's a lot o thiefs on the go, ye ken!' says Bill, near greetin.

So down went the heroes to the *Coronet*'s fo'c'sle where they held a council of war. 'Fit wye div we get it hame?'

'Weel,' says the Chemist, 'the ganjies is gaan hame. The rest o the stuff can wyte!'

Thereupon he donned ganjie efter ganjie till he wis like an advert for Michelin tyres. In fact he couldna get his airms doon t' his sides, there wis that mony fauls aneth his oxters!

'Da!' says Dod, lauchin, 'Ye'll nivver get up the road like that! Ye're like a great muckle penguin. Melodian-hips, the bobby, he'll spot ye a mile awaa!'

'Nivver een!' says the Chemist. 'Leave that to me!'

So, stepping onto the pier, he got a loon on either side and with his arms across their shooders he assumed a very painful limp and trauchled hamewith.

At the Brig 'Melodian-hips' surveyed the trio with concern. 'Fit's happened, skipper? Are ye sair hurtit?'

'Och! I've geen ower my fitt, constable, but wi the twaa loons I'll manage hame. It's gey sair aa the same!'

'I see that,' says the bobby. 'It's fairly garrin ye swyte!'

Thus were the ganjies brought home. The rest of the swag was retrieved in small doses over several days.

It's a lang time noo since the Chemist passed on but the sons are still to the fore. They can be seen ony day at the Lazy Dyke and they are aye dressed in bonny navy ganjies. For mair than fifty 'ear they've been like that!

Now, should you, a stranger, enquire politely of these gentlemen, 'Fit like's the Blue Toon noo wi aa the fish an the coal an the fertiliser an the gas an the ile?' They'll shak their grey heids and tell ye wi the greet in their throats, 'It's nae the same, freen, nae the same! It's an affa place for thiefs noo!'

Sad Tale of the Caley Bannock

There's naething sae queer as folk! In saying such a thing I cannot honestly exclude my ain folk, the fishermen. And why not?

Well now, there's something about fishermen, of whom I am one, that I have never fully understood and it's this — should one of their number forsake the sea to try his hand at some venture on shore, then every eye is upon him.

Should his bold attempt prove to be hopeless failure, it is simply because his innate honesty and lack of guile have proved to be inadequate weaponry in his battle with the sharks who infest the shore.

If, on the other hand, his foray into a foreign clime proves to be a resounding success, then it's 'just what a buddy might have expected, for hadn't he been a droll hare aa his days? Ye ken! Yon kind o lad that wid kick ye in the belly fin yer back wis turned!'

So how can a fella win?

182

One outstanding example of a fisherman quitting the sea to make a real impact on shore was the late Robert Forman, O.B.E., J.P., who finished up a Provost of Peterhead.

In the early thirties he founded a business under the name of Caledonian Fish-selling Co. which was never known as anything else but 'The Caley', just as he himself was never known as anything else but Rob Forman.

The motto was 'Caley for Service' and I'm sure he did his utmost to live up to that motto. Many successful fishermen of the fifties owed their success in great measure to the shrewdness, the encouragement and support of Rob Forman.

The cynic might say, 'Well, in helping others he was helping himself!'

In reply I would say, 'Why not? How many businessmen do you know who are charitable institutions?'

The Caley in its early days was a very small concern, but it grew steadily over the years to become Caley Fisheries Group.

My earliest recollection of Rob Forman is the day he accosted me at the harbour with the query, 'Fit's you smaa-boat men deein this winter?' This would be about 1934. 'Och!' says I, 'We're at the lug lines, sair made to get a livin. Oor bait has to come fae Ardersier, an it disna come here till the late train comes in, an even then there's times it disna turn up. Then we're lowsed!'

'That's lack o organisation,' says Rob. 'Tell aa the smaa-boat men nae to order ony mair lug. I'll see that there's a steady supply, an if ye're needin bait, jist come to the Caley for't.'

So instead of ordering our bait by telegram, we would just go to the Caley store at any time and get our biscuit tin of lug.

Now it came to pass that the Lord sent a mighty south-east wind so that the waters wrought exceedingly. Great seas marched across the bay, like an army of giants, to commit suicide on the foreshore and on Smith's Embankment. The breakwaters were visible only at rare intervals. Every boat was securely moored in the inner harbour and the storm-booms were in position at the Queenie Brig.

For a hale stricken week the gale continued and so did the steady supply of bait. A south-east storm keeps the Buchan fleet in port but it has no effect at Ardersier. So every night at 8.50 p.m., a fresh consignment of biscuit tins arrived by train to be conveyed on a hurley to the Caley store pending the abatement of the storm.

The general welfare of the worms was left in the hands of Jeemsie Bruce who at that time was the Caley's runner-cum-factotum-cum-paraffin man. His boss had given strict orders that under no circumstances could the beasties be allowed to perish because dead worms catch no cod.

Some bright spark advised Jeemsie to spread the worms on a floor then scatter them with the bitties o cork that ye get in grape barrels. This Jeemsie did, but in spite of his efforts the mortality rate was very high and soon he was at his wits' end.

At the height of the storm several fishermen were pacing to-and-fro in the old fishmarket discussing the weather and generally setting the world to rights. They formed an illustrious gathering including Katie Andra and Chielsie Tug (Choice), Nep's Robert (Snowflake), Gordon's Andra (Recruit), Tondin's Jock (Annie

Elizabeth) and Twull's Andrickie (Jeannie). There were also present our late lamented friends the Taylor brothers who were pilots, known world-wide as the 'Wells o Wearie', this being their theme song when they had imbibed rather liberally.

There were others too numerous to mention, and then of course there was myself, a young feel loon whose retentive memory was busy gleaning from the wisdom of these old salts a vast store of knowledge which, in later years, was to prove absolutely worthless!

Suddenly, Jeemsie Bruce appeared, crying in deepest anguish, 'For God's sake boys, come and see this!'

We followed him en masse to the Caley store to witness a scene which I shall never forget. Imagine a bannock of sharn fifteen feet square and four inches deep, then give it a smell ten times worse than the vilest odour you have ever encountered and you will have a faint idea of what we had been called upon to witness.

Forty tins of dead and dying lug worms with their liberal mixture of cork! I was deeply impressed when, in the presence of so much death, each man removed his bonnet, until I realised that the bonnets were being used as gas masks. Then I regretted that I was bare-headed.

With our backs hard to the wall we stood around the room while Jeemsie held aloft an acetylene lamp to illuminate the scene. He reminded me somehow of the Statue of Liberty.

'Fit am I gaan t' dee wi this sotter?' he cried. 'The Boss'll fyle himsel if I lat them dee!'

Silence reigned for a moment then a one-eyed sage remarked: 'The best thing to dee, Jeemsie, would be to mak pies wi them!' Great hilarity as we made our exit!

Late that night the seething mass of corruption was shovelled into the harbour.

Many years later, during one of my many bouts of friendly banter with Provost Forman, I heard him elaborate on the benefits of organisation.

When I asked him, innocently: 'Div ye ken faar I micht get a tin o lug?' he suddenly remembered that he had urgent business elsewhere.

Black Beasties That Bring Golden Reward

The lug worm is not a beautiful sight. It is a fat, black beastie which makes its home in the sandy bottoms of estuaries or sheltered beaches, where it betrays its presence by leaving little heaps of droppings on the sands around low-water mark.

If you dig a hole on the seaward side of these little heaps, you'll find the lug which, despite its appearance, makes a wonderful bait.

Now, to obtain a few lug for an evening's angling is not a major problem, but should you require several hundred to bait a fleet of small lines the problem becomes acute and you'll have to send away for lug in bulk. The best place to get lug is Ardersier, where extensive mudflats make a perfect lug nursery.

So you send a telegram to the mannie at Ardersier. Post-haste he will send you a biscuit tin full of lug which you must collect at Peterhead station where they will arrive on the last train at 8.50 p.m.

The cost will probably stagger you, for, including the telegram and the freight charges, your McVities tin of worms will cost no less than twenty-three shillings! How can you be expected to make a living with bait at such a price?

Well, that's your own problem, so you just have to carry the bait home where the lines are ready for baiting.

But I almost forgot that during the day you've been busy getting a bucket of limpets from the rocks.

The best tool for 'hacking' limpets is an old straight-backed table knife with the handle well bound in flannel to ensure a good grip. This tool you will call a 'sprod' and, like countless others before you were born, you'll make the fatal mistake of holding your sprod like a dagger.

Sure, you'll dislodge the limpet at the first fell swipe but in so doing you'll skin your knuckles on the barnacles, which were invented for the express purpose of drawing blood.

You'll soon get the knack but it will take you a long time to fill a bucket of limpets, especially if several other folks are on the rocks after the same errand.

How to get the beasties out of their shells?

Plot them, you silly! Pour boiling water over them and they'll fairly loup oot! But first you've to carry them home to join the lug.

Baiting the lines is a slow, painstaking job. You'll coil the line neatly into a wooden 'backet', laying the baited hooks in neat rows so that they will run clear during the shooting process. And between the rows you'll put strips of newspaper to keep the hooks apart.

It will take till nearly midnight for you and your mates to bait the six lines, comprising 1,200 hooks. The bait will be lug and limpet alternately, or 'time aboot', and when the job is finished you'll wash your stinking hands with Lysol before having a cup of tea.

Then it's off to sea to shoot the lines in the bitter cold of a winter morning. You'll be in a small boat whose only lights are paraffin lamps or the glare from a 'torch', which is like a kettle with a wide spout from which several strands of twisted wick protrude.

The fuel, of course, is paraffin. You'll have to be very careful because the boatie will do her best to pitch you overboard and there's not a great deal of room. You'll need to watch your fingers, too, because the lines are run out while the boat is forging rapidly ahead and the fresh wind can send the lethal hooks in strange directions.

If all goes well you may be back in harbour at 3 a.m. and you'll be free to sleep till 6 a.m. when you've got to be on your feet again. You see, you've got these lines to haul and so you must be looking for your little flag buoy at the crack of dawn.

Hauling the lines is a slow business at best, but if you're lucky you may be home for dinner, probably a late one, then you'll land your few boxes of fish for the 4 p.m. sale.

That would be your day's work done but the lines have to be redd in preparation for tonight and that'll take you an hour or two. And possibly you've forgotten that you have another bucket of limpets to get, and haven't you to meet the train tonight to collect your lug?

When do you sleep? Mostly on your feet because you and your bed are strangers. If you are to work one hundred hours in a six-day week you can only sleep in snatches, but when codlings are fetching as high as twelve shillings a box you've got to keep going.

Thus the 1930s, when a pound could purchase such a lot — if only you could get the pound.

My most vivid memory of those days is the time when I was landed on the pier in the dark of a winter morning while my shipmates went back to sea to haul the lines.

I had a hook embedded so deeply in my finger that neither my mates nor I could get it out. Most of the hook was out of sight in my flesh so I had to see the doctor.

Not wishing to disturb the good man so early, I waited till daylight before ringing the bell at the surgery in Queen Street.

Dr Taylor, in his dressing gown, admitted me, ushered me into his consulting room, then had a look at my finger.

'I think we'll manage to sort that,' says he, 'but I'll need to get the lassie to hud yer han.'

'Och!'says I, 'I'm nae seekin a quine here avaa!'

But he paid no heed and summoned the maid from the lobby where she was busy with her brush. No hoovers in those days!

He showed the girl how to keep my finger rigid by using her own forefinger and thumb. Of course she could turn her head away if she wanted! Then he set to work with a scalpel and laid my finger open to the bone before he could remove the hook. Oh boys! It was sair!

'Ye can let go noo,' he said to the girl, who bolted like a flash. Then to me he said: 'Ye'd better tak the heuk hame wi ye. It's ower big for my kind o fishin.'

Then the kindly man took me home. That was the first time I had a hurl in a car.

Good old days? Ye must be jokin!

Do it on a Fine Day Next Time

It was early afternoon on Saturday, 4 August, 1962, and I was busy preparing the car for a jaunt wi the wife an the bairn.

It had been blowing a real gale during the night and indeed it was still blowing hard, but I wasn't particularly interested, because I had quit the sea for good.

After several months ashore I was realising that, no matter how much you know about boats and engines and fish, you are on a sticky wicket when it comes to seeking a shore job, particularly when you are forty-five.

But I was determined to give it a real trial, and with such thoughts in mind I was lowering the car bonnet, when I glanced down the street. From the point where I stood, only a narrow strip of sea was visible, but in that same narrow sector I could see two PD boats steering approximately north-east.

'Something funny here,' I thought. 'Awaa t' sea on Setterday efterneen! Some folk winna tak time t' live!'

Within a minute I saw another boat and yet another, then I realised that it wasn't 'something funny' but something wrong that was on the go, so, after shouting to the wife that I would be back shortly, I set out on foot for the harbour.

There I saw boat after boat letting go and putting to sea, but I couldn't find anyone to tell me the reason why until, at the Cross Keys corner, I bumped into Tom Strachan, skipper of the *Silver Hope*.

'Faar are ee makkin for the day?' says he. 'Ye're dressed like a circus horse!'

'Och!' says I, 'I'm for the country places! Fit's aa the maneer aboot, onywye?'

'Nae an affa lot. Jist the *Daisy*'s crew in a life-raft a hunner-an-forty mile aff.'

Only half believing him, I fired back: 'Fit's adee that ee're nae awaa wi the lave?'

'Nae driver!' says Tam. 'I've a muster o a kind, but there's nae a driver to be gotten!'

'I'll be back in five meenits,' says I. 'Ye've a driver noo!'

It transpired that the PD *Daisy*, punching home from Shetland grounds through a southerly gale, had sprung a leak and despite the heroic efforts of the crew, she had finally sunk.

All hands were in a rubber life-raft, but before abandoning ship, skipper Jim Bruce had managed to send out a May Day signal with an approximate position.

Since the *Daisy*'s wireless aerials had been torn away by stress of weather, it was something of a miracle that the May Day was heard at all, but it was picked up by another Peterhead boat only a few miles from her home port, and thus the news was relayed to the shore.

Now Peterhead was full of boats, but since they had been fishing in local waters, they had landed their catches in the morning and the crews had gone home, some to ports as far away as Buckie. Others had gone on picnics as I myself had intended; most had gone beyond immediate recall.

So the boats which left port on their search-and-rescue mission were manned by scratch crews, a motley throng of fishermen, land-lubbers, towrags,

187

warriedrags and swipins o the pier. That afternoon not a single soul could be seen around the harbours.

On the *Silver Hope*, there were five of us: Tam, her skipper, Jim Mair, the singing fisherman; Colin, a school janitor; Neddy, a distillery worker and myself.

Apart from Tam, we were all incomers to the boat. Tam and Jim had been at sea all night so they required some sleep. This meant that for the first few hours I was in charge and boys was I sick!

Sea-sickness is a hellish affliction whose symptoms are as follows: the sense of smell is sharpened to an amazing degree; odours which would normally pass unnoticed assume the power to scunner a buddy; the lips develop a long-lost art of 'spittin saxpences'; then the mouth begins to produce prodigious amounts of saliva.

The entire body is inclined to shiver with cold then the stomach intimates that it wants to rebel against its contents, but somehow the contents do not wish to be evicted and the resultant conflict adversely affects the entire system.

Thus it was with me until I remembered the old-time fisherman's cure. Those interested please note. First approach the skipper gently and ask for eighteen inches of twine. Next, approach the cook, not in your usual manner, but very respectfully and ask for a lump of fat from boiled beef, nice and blubbery.

Attach the twine to the fat, then swallow the fat whole, while keeping a firm grip on the twine. By means of the twine, remove the fat. Repeat process if necessary.

I have never seen the physical process performed. The mental picture suffices to rid the system of unwelcome tenants and thereafter one begins to feel better. Slightly!

We were only a few miles off when we realised that there was no grub aboard. On a Saturday the lockers were empty and would not normally be replenished till Monday. Still, there were two stale loaves and an abundance of tay, so that would have to do. When I informed Colin that he had been elected cook, he lifted his head half an inch off the deck and muttered: 'For God's sake Peter, gwaa an lat me dee in peace!'

When Tam and Jim were called for supper it was a mug of tea and a slice of bread and jam.

Still, we were a lot better off than the boys in the life-raft. Fancy sliding up and down these great watery hills, bracing themselves every time they heard an avalanche of broken sea coming! When I thought of them, I began to feel as if I were on the *Queen Mary*.

When you see a fishing boat coming tearing towards the harbour entrance with a bone in her teeth, you immediately think: 'By jings, she's fairly trampin!' But, believe it or not, she'll not be doing more than 10 knots (say 11 m.p.h.).

So 140 miles was to take us 14 hours and, by that time, the raft could have drifted about 50 miles since she was launched! So that could be another five hours.

In the meantime, the skippers had 'gone into a huddle' on the radio and had elected a search commodore, Jimmy Watt of the *Aurora*. Thus the search would be organised instead of haphazard.

Jimmy had a rare crew: he had jumped aboard his boat and started the engine, then he had 'shanghaied' four fisher loons off the pier before setting sail. A fine baptism the loons got, awyte!

The leading searchers were ordered to slow down to let the stragglers catch up and, at brak o sky on the Sunday, the fleet, acting on instructions, formed a line twenty miles long, the individual boats being about a mile apart and all steering parallel courses.

I can only liken the fleet to the teeth of a giant rake looking for a pebble in a prairie. Each boat's crew would have half-a-mile on each side to scan, apart from a sharp look-out ahead, and everyone was exhorted to be on their toes.

It was not like searching a flat, calm sea with unlimited visibility. Na, na! There were times when the searchers could only see the tops of each other's masts so high was the swell, and it would have been easy to miss the raft without a conscientious look-out — by no means lacking that day!

By this time, the search was international news and a few foreign vessels had joined in. Hour after hour the great 'rake' ploughed on, all twenty miles of it.

Then, towards mid-day, a great muckle Danish boat, which had joined the fleet near the centre and had been keeping pace with the Peterhead men, suddenly forged away ahead with superior speed and ran almost right on top of the raft.

Oh boys! What a sense of joy when we saw this ship rescue the castaways. What did nationality matter? Absolutely nothing at all.

It was 'About ship' and 'Steer for home', and we sang all the way!

In vain did Stonehaven Radio appeal to us to desist! He could go and jump in the dock! Anxious listeners on the distant shore knew, when they heard the singing, that all was well, even when official confirmation had yet to come.

I think it was Alex Buchan (The Deevil) who had a chip shop on Seagate, that gave us a very touching version of 'Remember, Child, Your Mother's Prayer'.

In those days, we had no oil rigs with their helicopters to help — we could do the job in the only way we knew, and, thankfully, we were successful. We all got home early on Monday morning.

Finally, I would request Skipper Bruce, or any other skipper, that should he ever again contemplate taking to the life-raft — 'Please pick a bonny day, dee't a bittie nearer hame an mak sure it's nae a Setterday efterneen! Please!'

Guests for Dinner

Once upon a time when the world was a far sweeter place, I had a classmate whose burning ambition was to earn marks for writing a 'composition'.

Not until we reached a higher plane in our education did we hear the word 'essay'. Without fail, our weekend homework was a composition on a subject of the teacher's choosing and many a weird and wonderful effort was offered up on a Monday morning. When the chosen subject was 'two things for which my home town is famous', Sammy, my pal, wrote that Peterhead was famous for its rain and its agricultural implements. Teacher was not impressed and ordered Sammy to rewrite the whole script.

She would prefer something more sensible, and originality would bring extra marks. In his crest-fallen state, Sammy made a fatal mistake which he never repeated; he came to me for advice.

'Fit gart ye write aboot sic things?' says I.

'Weel, its aye rainin an Simpsons maks cairts aside the Chucknie School!' was the reply.

Thereupon I gave him a lecture on the value of being original and factual at the same time. 'Ach t' pot!' says he. 'The Gut Factory an the Roon hoose an the Prison an the Wine Waal an the Buchanhaven Hotel (a crude open-air toilet on Buchanhaven Pier), that's aa been written aboot! Fit can I write aboot that's original?'

'Try the wifie wi Fog an Dogs Dirt', says I. 'That'll be factual an original tee.' The peer loon should ha kent better. Paraffin Kate gied 'im the strap!

But the same lad shook me next day when he defined 'gravity' as 'a little scarfie'. My govies, he got a penny fae the teacher for the lauch she got! I could be factual and original, but nivver got a penny!

On his fourteenth birthday, Sammy left school for a job in a sawmill which stood on the site of the present telephone exchange. There he spent a 44-hour week 'jointing' staves for herring barrels, his reward being the princely sum of eight shillings and sixpence (42½p).

During Sammy's second year there, his pay rose to ten bob (50p), but he took a proper scunner to the job and left it to join the Noble and Ancient Order of Drifter Cooks, not one of whose illustrious members was normal. Now, before you sue me for libel or dam me for sewages, let me give you a challenge!

Get yourself a steel tank 8ft. 6in. long, 7ft. wide and 6ft. high. In one end of the tank near the right-hand corner cut an arched doorway whose sill must be 10in. high. Now, in the far left-hand corner as you look in at the door, fix a big coal-burning stove and in the near left-hand corner fix a steel bunker 3ft. high to hold two bags of coal.

Between the stove and the bunker, sufficient space must be provided for the oven door to open downwards. Close to your left shoulder, from floor to roof, fix a wooden post about 10in. thick to represent the mizzen mast, and between that and the bunker, rig a little shelf for a seat.

Now at the near end of the stove, cut a hole in the floor (say 2ft. square) to represent the hatchway to the cabin, not forgetting the guard rail to keep you from falling down the hole. The strip of floor in front of you is a passage and must not be otherwise used, so you are left with a floor approximately 5ft. x 3ft., the cook's domain. There is no sink and no running water because the water tank is bolted to the outside wall. The only light is from an acetylene gas jet.

Now, choose any normal man you know, give him a set of pots and pans and a bucket, then put him into the steel tank with strict orders that for the next fortnight he must produce at least three square meals for ten men every day, not counting the fly-cups.

He'll be on his feet twenty hours daily. To make things realistic you'll have to set the tank on a machine which can produce the motions of the cake-walk, helter-skelter and roller-coaster all at the same time and you must flood the place, frequently, ankle-deep in sea water.

At the end of a fortnight of non-stop treatment, have a look at your normal man and, if he is still alive, he'll be a nervous wreck, pleading for mercy.

But not so the drifter cooks. They were not normal men — they were magicians who could teach Paul Daniels a thing or two. We hear aye aboot gallant skippers whose gallantry is usually commensurate with their success. We also hear about heroic deckies toiling on storm-swept decks.

Both skipper and deckie alike may have at home a loving wife who is busy keepin his linner het, while she is lashed to death wi down quilts, but athoot the chiel in the galley the gallantry and heroics would fade and die.

The heart of the ship is the galley, not the wheelhouse.

Noo fit aboot Sammy? Weel, Sammy wis cook in a drifter at Yarmooth far he'd gotten in tow wi a Buckie quine. In a rash moment he had invited her to come doon for her denner on Sunday.

Oh aye, she wid come if her twaa neepers could come an aa. So it was arranged that the three quines would be guests for Sunday lunch. Sammy was no mean cook! His culinary compositions were beyond belief altho his literary compositions had been failures. Roast beef and Yorkshire pudding, followed by a wonderful trifle, then the inevitable cuppa. That was to be the menu.

Sammy saw to it that the cabin was spotless. 'For ony sake redd up that bed o yours, it's like a horse's guts.' This to a young deckie.

But there was one problem — fresh milk. The quines widna like tinned milk in their tay and on board ship there wis nothing else.

'Leave that to me,' says the skipper, who nipped across the pier to a shoppie far he bocht twaa pints o milk and persuaded the good lady to lend him a milk jug with a floral design.

Behold our Sammny then, at the end of a first-class meal when the tea mugs were steaming hot. Behold him at the end of the crowded table wi the bonny joog in his nieve and just listen as he says: 'Sugar yersels noo, quines, and I'll come roon an milk ye!'

Factual? Hardly! Original? Fit sorra idder! I tellt ye he wisna normal!

Scalders and Other Hot Stuff in Beach Pyjamas

When I was a barfit loon, playing along the shore, it was quite common to find the beach thickly strewn with jellyfish of a semi-transparent bluish colour. In diameter they varied from saucer to dinner plate dimensions; in consistency they were fairly firm and every one had four pink rings like eyes. We called them 'slivery doctors' and treated them with contempt. Hairmless breets!

But these were only distant relations of the hellish beasts which are the bane of the fisherman's life. Blue and white or red in colour, with long, trailing tentacles, the fisherman's enemy is a mass of filthy rottenness, a scavenger of the sea. It doesn't rear up and bite you, but if ever you come across one, leave it severely alone.

It thrives in amazing numbers during the warm summer months and it seems to delight in rain and close, smuchty weather. English fishermen call these beasties 'unprintable' jellies; Sooth-kintra Scots call them 'slithers' but the fishers of the north-east call them 'scalders', and a more appropriate name would be hard to find.

They cannot mesh in a net; they would simply disintegrate. But they slide down a herring net when the net is being hauled and they leave particles of filthy slime along the nets' entire length. In the hauling process, which is 'haul-an-shak', to shake the herrings out, drops of water fly all over the place, carrying particles of poisonous jelly which attack any face which may be handy. The effects may or may not be immediate, depending on the texture of the victim's skin, but stand by when you get into the warmth of your bunk! Fire will torment you where the skin is tender, round the eyes, nostrils and mouth, and especially between the fingers. It's like the awful smarting sensation you get when you've put your hand into 'ower het watter', but it doesn't go away!

I have seen men really frantic with the torture. The medical profession may have an antidote in these enlightened days but twenty-odd years ago there was none. It has been known for a crew to refuse duty when the scalders were really thick.

They would leave the nets till daylight in the hope that the beasts would submerge as the sun rose. This didn't always work. One reasonably effective protection was the nylon stocking pulled over the head but it was strange indeed to see a crew of masked thugs hauling herring nets!

Trawlermen and seine-net men do not suffer to the same extent but it is quite common for the tail of a flapping cod to send a splat of jelly into a buddy's face. Some folk swear that the blues are worst, others swear by the reds, most swear at them both.

The biggest scalders I have ever seen were in the Irish Sea, and boys, they were bobby dazzlers! The year? Say 1933? The hit song was '*Auf wiedersehen*' and beach pyjamas had just appeared on the scene. What bold shameless women they were to wear nothing but 'a jacketie an a pair o breekies'. So said some of the letters to the editor!

When we were in any of the Manx ports, bevies of beach-pyjamaed girls thronged the quay to watch the fishing boats. We simply loved it when a shower of rain sent the girls running for shelter. Then it was obvious that there were more jellies on the quay than in the whole Irish Sea! Did I look the other way? That'll be the day!

Our base that summer was Ardglass in County Down. I can remember our surprise at the extreme age of some of the 'girls' who gutted the herrings on the quay. They really were 'aal wifies', who spoke Irish Gaelic.

There we met fishermen from Southern Ireland; quiet, decent men they were, but their boats and gear were no great shakes. Where we had canvas buoys, which we called 'bowse', these Irishmen used the bladders from farm animals.

The mouth of the bladder was lashed tightly round a cotton reel (pirn), so that the float could be inflated by blowing through the hole in the pirn, which could be easily plugged. The inflated bladder was then sheathed in netting which in turn could be tied to the herring net. In Scotland this primitive method had died out fifty years before.

The staple diet of these Irishmen was contained in a great muckle broth pot, wherein a hale ham was boiled with cabbages and peas. Only at weekends did their diet vary and the broth pot was replenished on Mondays.

Doubtless these Irish fishers, like their Scots brothers, have come a long way since those days. The beach pyjama girls would be 'foosty aal fizzers' nowadays and I'm thinkin that the total attire of a modern beach girl would be richt handy for liftin a het broth-pot.

But ye may be sure the scalders are aye the same!

Bounty in the Fog

Visitors to the seaside must be short-sighted indeed if they fail to notice that, at certain times, the sea comes a tremendous distance up the beach, while at other times, it recedes an equally tremendous distance, leaving a great expanse of firm, wet sand exposed to view. 'Aha!' they say, 'The tide's in!' or 'The tide's out!', depending on the amount of beach which is available for use.

Message boys delivering stores to fishing boats like to do the job when they can simply step off the pier on to the boat wi their bags o tatties, etc. If they are obliged to make their deliveries when the tide's out, they find the shippies 'hine doon', so they have to lower their goods on ropes or clamber with them down dirty ladders.

So the tide comes in, then goes out again; it rises and falls. Ah! you knew all this before, did you? Well, it is possible, that you are ignorant of the fact that the tide also flows like a river and a pretty smart river at that!

Without trying to be technical about it, let me inform you that the tide originates away in the belly of the ocean somewhere about the Sargasso Sea or some other God-forsaken place. It is a great surge of water, quite incomprehensible in its magnitude, which makes its way towards the British Isles and many other places besides.

Up the West Coast it comes, round Cape Wrath towards the Orkneys where it roars through the Pentland and Westray Firths like a wild beast, before changing course for Rattray Head.

On the way it fills all the harbours and the lochs, it fills the Moray Firth and its offshoots. In fact, it fills the whole North Sea! That's the flood tide, the tide coming in.

For six hours it runs thus, then it pauses a wee while for breath. That pause is called slack water or 'the slack', then the tide turns and runs all the way back again, only this time it sucks all the water out of the Firths and lochs and bays; that is the ebb tide, the tide going out. That is merely a rough sketch of what is meant by 'tide', and it may help you to understand my tale.

The powers that be make regular studies of the direction and strength of the tidal streams around the British Isles and it is quite simple to obtain a copy of their charts. They may use several methods of measurement, of which I am completely ignorant, but I am well versed in one method which they use, and this is the use of a 'floating body'.

If you drop a floating body into the sea in an accurately plotted position, and recover it later in another accurately plotted position, it should be possible to measure the drift.

Now, about thirty years ago, there appeared in most of the salesmen's offices a notice to the effect that several of these floating bodies were to be released in the North Sea. Any skipper finding one should bring the same to the nearest Fishery Office, the appropriate time and position duly noted. Then he would get five bob! A very generous institution indeed, the Fishery Office.

Picture now the Peterhead fishing fleet, proceeding to sea on a foggy afternoon in search of the silver darlins. It wasn't exactly as thick as guts but still thick enough to necessitate a keen look-out. I should explain here that fishermen usually describe fog as 'thickness'.

Our course was east-by-south, three-quarter speed and we were about ten miles from the shore when one of the deckies yelled: 'Hey, that's een o yon things that's worth five bob!' We had it aboard in a tick then resumed our course after noting the time and the exact position as recorded by the Decca Navigator.

Then a wee while later, we found another and yet another. At five bob a time we were doing quite nicely. It was only when we had half a dozen on board that I noticed that these valuable finds were exactly a mile apart, and certain niggling doubts assailed me, but there was no denying the young deckies who greeted each new find with delight.

The fifteenth body had just been recovered when the fog lifted, and there, dead ahead of us, was a Fishery boat actually planting the things in the sea! All unknown to him we had been following in his wake picking up the bounty.

What to do now? We could hardly claim payment for that which hadn't been five minutes in the water! We could have contacted the Fishery boat and given him back his 'bodies' but to save the good man (and myself) a lot of embarrassment we overtook him at full speed and at such a distance that he couldn't see what we had on our deck. Then, about three miles dead ahead of him we consigned the lot to the deep, where he couldn't fail to find them.

As we sailed away, leaving the little flaggies fluttering gaily in the light breeze, I heard one of the deckies remark: 'I'll bet that'll shak 'is cotton drawers!'

So, if you ever read that the tidal streams in the North Sea gather all floating objects together, to dump them in a heap off Peterhead, you'll know that the information is incorrect.

Hunting in the Dark for Paaps!

From Buchan Ness to Harcla Head, just south of Collieston, the Buchan coast is one long stretch of precipitous cliff, broken only by the beautiful golden beach at Cruden Bay.

The word 'Cruden' is very ancient and means 'the killing of the Danes', so there must have been a great battle in these quarters long ago. But local fishermen never use the term Cruden Bay.

For them it is the Ward Bay; the rocky headland at the north end of the bay is the Ward Head, and the little fishing village of Port Errol is 'the Ward', whose inhabitants are thus 'Wardies'.

The Wardies had a harbour of which they were extremely proud. It was ideal for yawls of up to 25 ft. and the fact that the harbour was practically dry at low-water did not in any way lessen the Wardies' pride. At least they didn't have to draw their boats up on a beach as some folk did! These Wardies were industrious line fishermen but with the advent of the seine net they forsook the haddock line, with its attendant labours, for the new art of seining for 'plashies' (plaice).

Still, the winter months found them back at their lug lines, fishing for codlings as far south as Neebra Water (the Ythan estuary). The entrance to the main basin of the harbour could be sealed off in extreme weather by huge wooden booms which were lowered into slots in the pier by means of a hand-powered crane.

It's not all that long ago, surely, since the Wardies got a set of booms from Peterhead, second-hand, but nonetheless ideal once they were shortened to fit the narrow channel.

Over the last forty years the harbour has silted up to a marked degree, but recent efforts by loyal small-boat enthusiasts have remedied this. The piers, however, are in a sorry state which would be very costly to put right.

The Wardies, before they became extinct, bore names such as Summers, Milne, Robertson, Masson and Tait. Once I asked a Wardie friend whose name was John Robertson (Gorlan's Jock) — 'Is there nae Buchans in this place, Jock?' To which he replied, 'Peter! If the Buchans wis to come here we wid hae t' flit!'

'Faar wid ye ging?' says I.

'We wid ging an bide wi the Cannlies!' says he.

'An faa on earth's the Cannlies?'

'The Faulers! The Finnyfaul men! They hiv cannle lanterns so we caa them the Cannlies.'

'An fit div they use the cannle lanterns for?'

'Oh!' says Jock, 'They ging oot in the dark lookin for paaps!'

'Good grief!' says I, 'I nivver thocht the Faulers wis folk like that! The kitchie deems on the fairms wid need to hae their doors lockit!'

'Ach! Ye ken that's nae fit I mean,' leuch Jock. 'It's bait they're lookin for!'

Fine did I ken fit he meant. The paap (note the long vowel) is a sea creature which clings to the rocks in places where man cannot reach it except at low-water on an extremely big tide. No doubt it has a Latin name as lang as Leith Walk, but fishermen are notoriously poor at Latin.

The paap is about the size of a smaa tattie and has a consistency resembling a stiff jube-jube. It can vary in colour from red to orange and it makes the finest bait you ever saw. Cod find it irresistible.

One really outstanding feature about this beastie is that it can be used over and over again, especially if you sprinkle brown sugar over it. I'm giving away trade secrets now so I'll hae to watch mysel! Dinna say that I tellt ye!

Since low-water with a big ebb is around 8 or 9 p.m. (in this airt), you can see the need for the cannle lanterns.

Whinnyfold or Finnyfaul (hence the name 'Faulers') is a tiny hamlet which sits on top of the cliff at the south end of Cruden Bay. I have a suspicion that the folks who built the houses there had a recipe for some powerful adhesive which stuck the hooses to their foonds, otherwise they would have been blown into the sea.

There is at Finnyfaul no harbour, only an open shore from which the boaties had to be launched daily and whereon they had to be drawn up nightly. The only access to this shore is by means of a precipitous footpath and generations of Finnyfaul women struggled up this path with creels of fish on their backs. Every mortal thing had to be transported via this route and it must have been slave labour indeed. After many weary years of toil, somebody thought of installing a 'Blondin' from the clifftop to the shore. This was a wire cable on which ran a pulley, and goods suspended from this pulley could be pulled up from the beach. It was indeed a great labour-saving device, but it had been in use for only a few years when the fisher population of the hamlet ceased to be.

The shore at Finnyfaul was used by smaa boaties only. It lies just a castie on the south side of that dreaded reef, the Skares. A short distance north of this shore there is another cove called The Breythaven (Broadhaven) and it was here that the Faulers drew up their bigger herrin boats when the season decreed.

Finnyfaul has produced a race of sterling fishermen whose descendants are now mostly in Peterhead. They were Morgans, Formans, Hays and Caies. Once I asked a good friend of mine, Jocky Morgan — 'Is there nae Buchans here, Jock?'

'Peter!' says he, 'if the Buchans wis to come here we wid hae to flit!'

'Faar wid ye ging?' says I.

'Och, we wid ging an bide wi the Hoolits!'

'Faa on earth's the Hoolits?'

'Yon mob that bides in the Ward! They're forivver fartin aboot in the dark athoot a licht. An there's nivver a licht on their boats. They're jist nae mowse! I think they can see in the dark!'

'Wid they ging oot lookin for paaps in the dark, Jock?'

'Aye! I'm sure they wid,' he exclaimed. 'The Hoolits is fit for onything!' Then seeing the twinkle in my eye he gave me a playful cuff on the ear. 'Awaa ye go, ye coorse tink!'

But it is a fact that, one wild morning in the days of sail, the whole Cannlie population stood in awe on the cliff-top watching a boat coming from the southward. The wind was storm-force southerly and the tide was in full flood, creating, at the outer point of the Skares reef, conditions of such awful ferocity that the boat could not possibly survive. Of this the watchers were certain, for they knew the Skares! And still the vessel stood on, heading for disaster.

But her skipper knew the Skares like the back of his hand, so, instead of tackling the maelstrom at the outside, he took his vessel, under full sail, through the narrow, tortuous channel which lies between the inner edge of the reef and the cliff. There the tide had shot its bolt and the sea was much calmer. Many of the cliff-top throng turned their backs as this gallant skipper tackled the impossible.

Only those who know this channel (and there are not many) can judge how daring the feat was. It was seamanship at its highest pinnacle and it succeeded. The boat came safely through.

The skipper was 'Een o yon mob that bides in the Ward' — A Hoolit. An his name wis Milne.

So the Cannlies didn't have a monopoly on seamen.

But, sadly, Fauler or Cannlie, Wardie or Hoolit, they are no longer with us and the world is the poorer for their passing.

Ripping Yarns of the Arctic

Every vessel which enters Peterhead harbour passes a short, stone jetty called the Blubber Box, a name from the days when the whalers landed their blubber there.

At the head of the jetty was the Boil-yard, where the blubber was boiled; the site is now an oil depot. Towards the end of the last century the Blue Toon had such a sizeable fleet of whaling ships that the local *Sentinel* could publish a list of the names of the ships which would sail that particular week.

The fair city of Dundee also had whalers and the Dundee paper used to say:

'Half of the whaling fleet sailed today; the other half will sail next week.' There were only two ships in the Dundee fleet! A touch of professional jealousy maybe.

The actual whaling fleet had disappeared many years before I was born, but I can well remember climbing the rigging of the *Rosie*, an old whaler which had lain dormant in Peterhead for years and I can clearly remember the day she sailed for the Arctic, all decked out with bunting.

Mair than half the toon thronged the quay that day and many a head shook in sheer disbelief that a ship should sail on Sunday. Nae gweed wid come o that!

The Peterhead whalers called the Eskimos 'Yakkies' from the real name 'Yaqui', and I can clearly recall the time when a Yakkie loon spent a holiday in the Blue Toon. The peer loon couldna stan the Peterheid wither avaa! Bugs and germs he had never met before attacked him with gusto, so that he nivver had a weel day. So he was sent home to the Arctic where he recovered completely and lived to a ripe old age.

The last survivors of the whaling race were old, old men when I was a littlin and the few who were still able to work were cooks in the drifters. Decrepit they may have been but boys-a-boys they could fairly spin a yarn!

Every blessed one of them had at least one face-to-face encounter (an 'eyeball') with a Polar Bear! 'It's the best cure for constipation ye ever saw, my loon!' There must have been a Polar Bear behind every ice-hummock.

Life on the whalers must have been very hard indeed. When a whale was sighted, the ship's boats were lowered and their crews would endeavour to row close to the whale so that a marksman in the bow could ram a harpoon into the unsuspecting monster.

Attached to the harpoon there was a line about 200 fathoms in length with a barrel on the end of it. When the wounded whale sounded (dived), the line would go hissing over the boatie's rail until the barrel had to go overboard as well, but since the whale must come to the surface to breathe, the oarsmen could usually keep track of the barrel and having retrieved it, the seamen would 'play their fish'.

Many boats and men were lost in this perilous game, for an enraged whale is not a 25lb. salmon. It was a case of wearing the monster down. 'Gie her line' or 'Take up the slack' were the orders as the occasion required. I widna fancy being towed in an open boat by a thirty ton monster, especially if there were ice floes around!

These rowing cutters, all built in the Blue Toon, were sturdy craft. To this very day the fishermen along the coasts of Baffin Land and Greenland have what they call 'Peterhead boats', faithful replicas of the whalers' boats.

Scarcely a year passed without some ship or another being frozen in among the pack ice. Then the crew would abandon ship and bide in igloos along wi the Yakkies. Since the natives were very hospitable and since there were quite a few females around, ye could get a bidie-in for the winter, nae bother avaa! But the Eskimo belles had a delectable custom of washing their hair in urine to make their tresses glossy and healthy, so the Blue Mogganers didn't have a bed of roses! Oh gyaad! I'm thankfu gled my missus disna dip her heid in the po!

The whalers were not classed as fisher folk altho they lived among the fishers and often married fisher quines. They signed on Articles, and got a fixed wage plus a bonus if the season's catch was good. This was something foreign to fisher folk, who had to accept the maxim, 'No fish — no money', and forbye the whalers had different ranks such as ordinary seamen, A.B., bosun, harpooner, ship's carpenter, etc.

One crack harpooner was a man whom we'll call Robbie. His hoosie was a but-an-ben wi a little closetie in the middle. There was no provision whatsoever for sanitation, not even an outside toilet.

In this respect Robbie's hoosie was no different from the others in the fisher villages. Any boys in the family were expected to seek a secluded spot among the rocks when answering the call of nature; for other members of the household there was a pail which was teemed every morning where the tide would exert its twice-daily purge. This is fact, not fiction. Thousands of houses in Scotland had no toilets until some thirty years ago.

I have very clear memories of living in spotlessly clean two-storey houses on the West Coast and in the Hebrides where the only loo was the byre. Aye, as late as the 1950s, too!

Well now, Robbie was seated at his fireside in the glow of the paraffin lamp along with his better half, Meg. Between them, on the fender-stool, the cat basked in the heat of the open fire.

While Meg busied herself darning Robbie's socks, he gave her an account of the harpooning and eventual despatch of a whale, but Meg was rather green in nautical matters and didn't seem to understand very clearly. So Robbie, in exasperation, decided that an object lesson was required.

'Hud ee this ball o worsit,' says he to Meg as he threaded the end into a darning needle. Then, taking very careful aim he harpooned the cat which took sheet oot the door like an evil speerit while Robbie yelled, 'Gie 'er line, Meg, gie 'er line!'

When the worsit stoppit rinnin oot, the order was 'Tak in the slack noo, Meg: ye've lost the brute!'

Gweed forgie me for thinkin sometimes that the aal whaler that tellt me that story wis jist a born leear!

Foolin the Board o Trade

The gadgetry on a modern fishing boat is something to behold! Electronic devices of all kinds occupy most of the wheelhouse space and since most of the devices are in duplicate the place resembles a power station.

Navigational and fishing aids are largely 'on hire' and several firms have agents in all the major ports to service their products. These agents are on call twenty-four hours a day, seven days a week, so a fishing skipper can call on their services at any time.

The safety devices on the boats are really excellent and rightly so. These are the responsibility of the boat-owners and must be kept up to the mark — the Board of Trade sees to that! I have heard skippers complaining bitterly that first-class gear has been condemned when less than a year old, regardless of the fact that it has been unused and was the best obtainable when purchased. The reason given — 'out of date now!' It can cost a lot of money to keep up to date when inspections are so rigorous.

When I was at sea, however, things were vastly different. There were of course certain requirements which were mandatory, but once the apparatus was there it could lie neglected for years, so that in an emergency it often proved useless. Things were left largely to the conscience of individual owners so in many cases maintenance was poor and supervision lax.

I once heard of an Aberdeen trawler — you know the type — old and battered and more or less devoid of paint. Well now, this shippie was towing her trawl in the North Sea when it fouled an obstruction on the seabed. In fishermen's parlance such an obstruction is 'a fastener'.

The skipper, Rascal Dan, was a man who had through years of bitter experience gained a remarkable degree of skill in the art of recovering gear from fasteners, but apparently this was the daddy of them all. After many hours of fruitless endeavour, with wire ropes twanging like fiddle-strings and bad words fleein like sparks, Dan was almost ready to give up and chop the whole lot away when the mate reported that, 'fitivver this thing is, it seems to be aff the boddim noo!'

This gave Dan fresh heart and, inch by inch, the fastener was brought to the surface where, lo and behold, it turned out to be a trawler, complete in every detail. She had been lost in a storm some fifty years before.

Now to cut a long story short, Dan and his crew boarded their 'find' and scuttled their own ship. As Dan said later, 'It wid hae been a shame t' dee onything else! She wis sic an affa lot better!' True or false? Please yersel!

I recall a certain morning in a chandlery in Peterhead when I picked up a brass object from the counter and started to play idly with it. 'For ony sake lay that thing doon,' said the storekeeper. 'Aabody that comes in fichers wi that, an some lads thumps the coonter wi't fin they're argyin!'

'Aaricht!' says I. 'Fit is't, onywye?'

'It's a spray nozzle for the hose. Accordin t' the Boord o Trade ye're supposed t' hae een o them. Ye'll get it for half-price if ye'll tak it oot o my sicht!'

I took it to the boat and put it in the breist o my bed along wi the ither odds an sods that made my bed so lumpy.

Well, one day that winter we were lying at the pier in Shields with six Duffers (Macduff boats) on our offside. We would all have been at sea had the weather been good.

Suddenly, there appeared on the scene a Boord o Trade mannie on a tour of inspection. Now some of these mannies had a bee in their bonnet about lifebuoys; with others it was lights, or pumps or something else. Well, this mannie started in our fo'c'sle and went through the whole boat. Finally he came to me and said: 'You keep a remarkably tidy boat, skip, but I fail to see your spray nozzle!'

'Och!' says I, 'it's in the breist o my bed. I'll get it!'

'That's a most peculiar place to keep it,' says he. 'It's supposed to be in the hose; for fire-fighting, you know!'

'Fine div I ken that!' says I, 'but ye canna wash fish wi a spray nozzle an to leave it aboot the deck wid be an open invitation to thiefs! It's solid braiss, ye ken!'

He hummed an hawed a fylie then he says, 'O.K. skip, carry on. But without that nozzle you would not have been allowed to sail!'

So this was the bee in this lad's bonnet. Spray nozzles for hoses! After jotting a few notes in his bookie he boarded our next door neighbour, the *Zephyr* of MacDuff and, as before, he started in the fo'c'sle.

'Foo did ee get on Peter?' says Walter, her skipper.

'Aaright!' says I. 'Ye see, we hiv a spray nozzle!'

'A fit did ye say? Nivver heard that een afore! Fit neist?'

'Weel!' says I, 'It's time ye got een or ye winna get t' the sea!'

'Faar can I get sic a thing at this time o day! The mannie's aboord noo. Eh! sirss, sirss!'

'Here!' says I, 'Stick that in the breist o yer bed, Walter!' So Walter got our nozzle on loan with a briefing on how to answer the mannie.

The end result was that seven boats (our tier) were at sea next morning, while the others were delayed, pending the arrival of spray nozzles from Newcastle.

The mannie must have thought that the Scotties were most peculiar folk. 'Every one of them that has a spray nozzle keeps it in his bunk!'

I could hae tellt 'im something queerer than that. Ivvery blessed wan o them got a gweed shot neist day, but deil the sowl said 'Boo' for the len o my nozzle!

I'm tellin ye! The Jews is nae aa in Jerusalem!

Horse of a Different Colour

'Twas late in the summer of 1945 and the sea was like glass, smoked glass gleaming in the light of the half-risen sun. In our 40ft. boatie we were hauling our seine net at the conclusion of our first haul of the day and it was quite obvious that the net was well-filled with fish.

Hordes of screaming gulls were circling the floating bag; some were even standing on it, and solan geese were diving from a great height to catch the small fry which had slipped through the meshes.

Of course we were all pleasantly excited but our pleasure was tinged with alarm, for there was a great muckle ship heading straight towards us. Did he see us? Did he not? If he did see us it was time he was altering course otherwise we would be sliced in two! If we tried to tow the net out of his path we would probably go the wrong way and no doubt we would burst the net.

Ah! Keep the heid lads, he's altering now and apparently he's slowing down.

201

The great bow-wave from the approaching vessel died away and she came to a stop about twenty yards away just as we got the bag aboard.

Oh, what a bonny ship she was! One of the very latest trawlers from Hull, she had been released from naval service and returned to her owners. Even in their wartime camouflage such ships were bonny craft but here was one in her company colours, spick and span from stem to stem, a joy to behold.

'Apologies if I scared the life out of you, lads! I was watching you all the time. Could we have a fry, please?'

Now, fancy a great ocean-going trawler seekin a fry fae a yole! Oh aye! He wid get a fry! Fit wis he seekin?

'A basket of haddock and a basket of sprags (codlings).'

As we passed the fish across we noticed that every one of the crew was clad in new gear. Just home from the Navy. Bound for the White Sea. First trip ever for the ship. Every man sick of the sight of Spam and beans-on-toast and tinned sausages; dying to taste fresh fish! And it would be a few days yet before they caught any of their own, for the White Sea was a long way off!

It was most unusual to see such a ship only three miles from Buchan Ness, but for a long time after the war, vessels bound for distant grounds had to stick to explicit routes until certain minefields had been swept.

Oh aye, he could get a fry and we wanted no payment from fellow fishermen, but he insisted that we accept a bottle of Johnnie Walker and a carton of fags. 'Cheerio boys, all the best! Call again any time!' And he was on his way, no more than twenty-six years of age I'd say. Very young for a skipper of such a ship.

Well, the fags didn't last long, but the bottle lay untouched in a locker for at least a year, then it was stolen. We didna drink it? No! We had not the slightest interest in it!

Most of the fishermen of my generation were teetotal. Of course there were those who imbibed rather freely, but they were in the minority. And then there were those quiet, decent lads whose only vice was a liking for a quiet pint on a Setterday nicht.

Such were two pals from one of the villages which lie between the Broch and Rattray Head. Since these villages had no licensed premises, our heroes had to make a journey of five or six miles to a certain hostelry which stands on the Peterhead-Broch road. Neither of the pair had even heard of a motor car; cars were still a year or two in the future, so they simply followed their normal routine.

Behold then, our two stalwarts hiring a horse and gig to convey them to the inn. Nothing unusual about that in those days, and the horsie would take them safely home should they over-indulge, which was not at all likely. On arrival at their desired haven Jock, the younger of the pair, hitched the horsie to the rail, remarking as he did so that she widna need a starn-rope.

After a very pleasant evening in the company of some country folk, the two mariners set out on the homeward trip. Then in the deep dusk of late summer, just as Fiddler's Green was close on their starboard beam Jock gied Daavit a richt dunt in the ribs.

'Hey, Daavit! We're awaa wi the wrang horse!'

'Dinna be daft, Jock. This is the horse we left hame wi.'

''Tis nott!' says Jock. ''Tis sott!' says Daavit.

'I'm tellin ye, this is nae the horse we left hame wi,' says Jock patiently.

'Weel noo!' replies Daavit, 'Ye may ken aboot boats an gear an fish, but I canna see fit wye the likes o you can possibly ken aboot a horse. Fit gars ye think this is nae oor horsie?'

'Aha!' says Jock, 'This horsie piddles ower the starn; oor horsie piddled amidships!'

An he wis richt!

Jeemsie Lands the Turk in Hot Custard

Duncan Elrick was not quite unique, but he was certainly most unusual, in that he was a country chiel that made his living at the sea.

Born and fessen up on the small holding of Povertyknap (pronounce the 'k'), somewye atween the Prop o Ythsie an the Myre o Bedlam, he had served his time wi the Cooncil amon traction engines and steam wagons, but a desire for adventure had led him to the sea where he had obtained and held for five years the post of chief engineer on the good ship *Meadowsweet*, one of the Peterhead herring drifters.

The *Meadowsweet*'s skipper was Bob McTurk, known all around the coast as 'The Turk', and he had sic a bummer o a belly that, for a while, Jeemsie the cook thocht the skipper had a washin-hoose biler up his ganjie. Mair aboot that later, maybe!

Weel noo, Duncan had been hame for the weekend bidin wi's brither an gweed-sister an their twaa loons. To his young nephews Uncle Dunk was a knight in shining armour! Didn't he have to face mountainous seas and fearsome tempests at Cape Horn to get this bonny fry o herrin for their supper? Weel awyte, that an mair, for he had to keep a constant watch for the cannibals who put out in their dug-out canoes from the Bullers o Buchan to prey upon unsuspecting fishers! In fact, the verra day o the Turra Show, a great muckle sea monster had seized the *Meadowsweet* in its gaping jaws, and only Duncan's presence of mind had saved the day, for he had shovelled red-hot fire from the boiler down the monster's throat!

'Wis she bigger nor a coo, Uncle Dunk?'

'Bigger nor a coo? I'm tellin ye, fin I wis lookin doon her throat I saw three stirks in her stammick!'

'Friesians or Herefords Uncle Dunk?'

'I couldna see them richt for aa the steam!'

Wasn't 'at a shame that their uncle's name was never in the *P & J?* He would get a medal some day. Surely! Little did they ken that while they were fast asleep Duncan wis awaa wi Hilly's kitchie deem.

203

Monday morning saw Duncan step aboard the *Meadowsweet*. There was no real need for Duncan to arrive early for the fireman had everything under control and in any case the ship wouldn't sail till afternoon.

In one hand Duncan had a bag containing twaa dizzen chippit eggs, while in the opposite oxter he carried an enormous bunch o rhubarb, a present fae his gweed-sister who had said: 'If the fishers disna want it, it'll be handy for chokin the neist monster ye meet!'

Jeemsie, the cook, Duncan's bosom pal, eyed the rhubarb with some concern. 'Fit div ye dee wi that, Duncan? My mither nivver learnt me onything aboot rhubarb!'

'Och! ye chap it into bitties and stew't, an it's better if ye hiv a suppie custard along wi't. Hiv ye ony custard in the press?'

'It's nae a press! It's a locker, Duncan, an there's nae custard in't. There's plenty semolina an birdies eenies (sago) but nae custard. Still, we'll seen sort that! I'll get some fae the grocer. Foo muckle will I get?'

'For ten men ye'll need a gweed sup, Jeemsie!'

In the afternoon, as soon as the shippie had cleared the port, most of the crew turned in, leaving a responsible man at the wheel, and Duncan to fire the boiler. As his duties allowed, he would help Jeemsie to prepare an exotic meal for the crew.

'We'll pit the chappit rhubarb in the tattie-pot an let it sooss awaa for an oor or twaa! says he. 'Meantime we'll sort the custard an I think we'll use the broth pot for that.'

'Did yer mither learn ye aboot custard Duncan?' says Jeemsie.

'No, she didna. I dinna ken muckle aboot it.'

'Weel, that maks twaa o's, but we'll hae a go at it!' says the cook.

Soon the custard was ready and pronounced first-class but then our heroes were faced with the problem of over-production.

'Faar are we gaan t' pit the stuff?' says Jeemsie. 'There's nae a pudden dish in Scotland could hud the half o't. We'll aa hae sair airms afore we get this lot suppit!'

Duncan was silent, realising he had miscalculated. Then in a flash of inspiration he cried, 'Fit aboot yon great muckle nammle basin that ye eesed t' hae?'

'The verra dunt!' says Jeemsie. 'I'll get it!'

As a beginner, Jeemsie had not known the golden rule, 'One hand for the ship and the other for yourself', but he had soon learned that a basin required both hands, leaving him helpless when negotiating the cabin ladder. So the basin had been discarded for the superior bucket, but now, in this hour of need, the basin would be invaluable.

'Faar can we pit the thing for safety?' says he, surveying the brimming basin. 'If we pit it ootside it'll be blaadit wi sitt fae the funnel, an it canna bide here in the galley!'

'Och! We'll pit it doon the stair,' says Duncan, again betraying his country origin. 'There's plenty o room doon there!'

So now we find Duncan on his knees on the galley floor, handing the great basin o pudden doon the trap to Jeemsie, who stood in the cabin ready to receive it.

'There's a great sup left in the pot yet!' says the chief. 'Hiv ye nae anither dish, my loon? I suppose a chunty pot wid be better than naething!'

Almost helpless with laughter, Jeemsie laid the basin on the seat locker close to his own bunk where nobody would disturb it, but he forgot that in the upper bunk the ponderous bulk of the Turk lay sleeping.

Well, it had to happen! Some sixth sense had told the Turk that something was afoot so he climbed out of his bunk and promptly sat in the basin of hot custard. His fearsome roar brought to view several startled faces which were immediately assailed by great skirps o fleein pudden! Oh fit a kirn! Siccan a sotter! It wis hingin fae the deck, it wis plaistered ower the clock, it wis aa ower the place!

Nelson, the one-eyed deckie, was heard to remark that, 'Yon wis the biggest splash I've seen since Andra Baird's horse fell into the hairber, an that wis some splash!'

When the dreeps had settled and the furore had died down, our two heroes had to buckle to with buckets and brushes and cloots to clean up the cabin.

As the discomfited pair crouched below the table, Jeemsie whispers to his pal, 'The skipper's reid mad the day, freen.'

'Aye! Fairly that,' says Duncan, 'but ye could easy cheer 'im up, I think!'

'Foo on earth could I dee that, noo?'

'Ging up an speir if he wid like a clean hippen.' was the reply.

Driven Clean Round the Bend!

Visitors to the Moray Firth coast are usually favourably impressed with the spick-and-span appearance of the houses of the fisher folk.

The immaculate paintwork on both wood and stone is positive proof that a great deal of work and not a little money have been lavished on these dwellings, which altho they are not of granite, are nevertheless soundly constructed to endure the rigours of the north-east climate.

There is something about these houses which reflects the nature of their owners, the pride of ownership.

This is not the arrogant pride of bigsiness or conceit but a softer, milder pride in such things as heritage and birthplace.

Where such things are concerned the fisher folk are a proud people indeed, but I must confess that I have never yet met any of them who spent any sleepless nights trying to decide whether they would be born 'fisher' or 'country'.

This same pride can be seen, albeit in a lesser form, in the boats, especially in the boats registered under the letters BCK (Buckie).

Seldom will you see a BCK boat in an orra state. Nae fears! The BCK lads are, on the whole, 'verra parteeclar' with their craft.

The letters BCK embrace that part of the coast which stretches from Portknockie (The Land o Promise) in the east, to Port Gordon in the west, but Buckie is the port of registry.

Peterhead men, in their profound ignorance, are inclined to class all BCK boats as 'Buckiemen', a title which many a skipper would resent.

It is quite common to see a BCK boat with her proper home port's name on the stem e.g. Portknockie, Portessie, Portgordon. There's a flash of the pride of birthplace and a strong hint of independence.

In the heyday of the drifters, the BCKs were a 'speak'. They were renowned for their immaculate appearance. The drifters built by Alex Hall, of Aberdeen, were probably the bonniest shippies afloat and to see one of them with the BCK registration was to see a picture of perfection.

I am thinking now of a particular Saturday afternoon in Yarmouth in 1946, when just under 1,000 thronged the river. Scores of powerful steam-driven donkey pumps were in action as the boats were being washed down for the weekend. Herring scales by the million were dislodged from all deckwork and skited into the river.

I was busily engaged in this task when I noticed the beautiful, spotless state of our next door neightbour, a BCK.

She was like a model, so clean was she! The wheelhouse windows were so clean that they glistened in the autumn sun and a boy who was, to my expert eye, a first-year loon, was busy with the hose meticulously cleaning the decks.

He must have noticed my admiring glances, for he cleared his throat and remarked, 'You Peterheid men's nae verra parteeclar!'

'Fit gars ye think 'at, my loon?' says I, rather taken aback.

'Weel!' says he, 'Ye're leavin a lot o scales on the windaes. Yer skipper winna see through them on Monday!'

I was silent for a moment, then he renewed his attack.

'That ship o yours minds me on a wife wi fool stockens, her masts is nae painted!'

I did my best to wither him with the sort of glance an old man of thirty is entitled to throw at a mere stripling, but it was without effect, so I decided that the best form of defence was attack.

'Peterheid men disna fash themsels ower muckle aboot scales,' says I, 'but they're gey parteeclar aboot hygiene!'

'Fit div ye mean by hygiene?' says the loon.

'Hiv ye washed oot the water closet the day?' I queried.

'Och aye, it's gotten a richt sweel oot wi the hose!'

Now the shippie he was on was an 'iron standard boat' i.e. she had been built by the government during World War I, therefore she had a toilet, something rather uncommon in the fishing boats of those days.

Only 'standard boats' had toilets and the toilet was always on the port side of the galley structure.

It was a little alcove, just through the wall from the galley stove, and consequently it was like an oven and stank like everybody's business.

It had a steel door which opened outwards and was in two halves. The lower half could be closed to keep the sea out and the top half, if closed, would guarantee the suffocation of any occupant.

The actual 'throne' was a monstrous steel funnel or 'filler' shaped contrivance from which a discharge pipe disappeared below deck level to reappear through the side of the ship just on the water-line.

A fousome, primitive affair, to be flushed out with a bucket of sea-water.

'Och aye!' says the loon again, 'It's gotten a gweed wash!'

'Ah, but!' says I, 'the richt wye, the parteeclar wye to dee't is to lean ower the side an pit the hose up the pipe! Then ye'll be sure the pipe's clear!'

'Nivver thocht aboot that! Od! I think I'll try't,' says he.

Behold then, the youngster fechtin with the serpent hose, needing every ounce of his youth and strength to lean over the rail and thrust the hissing nozzle into the pipe. And behold the fearsome aftermath when the toilet door burst violently open and there appeared on deck an apparition which I do not desire to see again.

There stood the loon's ain father with his drawers round his ankles. His sark-tails were in a rosy knot round his neck and his bonnet had been driven forward so that the snoot now covered his nose. The pipe he had been enjoying was now emitting faint wisps of steam, and to crown it all there was, firmly plastered between his shoulder blades, a neat square of paper from last week's *Green Final*.

From the faint watery sounds which were struggling through his clenched teeth, I gathered that he was questioning the legitimacy of his own offspring, who had now abandoned ship and was disappearing rapidly along the quay.

One thing has disappointed me. For the past thirty-seven years yon loon has been convinced that I knew perfectly well that his Da was on the throne when I gave the advice on hygiene.

To think that onybody could be so ill-thochtit!

In Praise of the Fisher's Friend

'The Fisherman's Friend' is the trade-name of a particularly fiery brand of cough lozenge, relished by those whose innards seem to resemble a washin-hoose biler in consistency.

Since such a fraternity must include professional fire-eaters and tough nuts wi hairy teeth, I would ask to be counted out and I would prefer to bestow the title 'Fisherman's Friend' on something of a much more gentle nature, namely corn chaff or 'caff' as it was known to generations of fisher folk.

There was a warmth and natural friendliness about caff that modern mattresses simply cannot hope to match. Foam rubber could never produce the kindly reeshle that a caff bed produced when it was patted, a reeshle all the more endearing if one used the magic words 'Eh, I like ye!'

I'm sure that the good Lord made caff for the comfort and restoration of weary bodies, and for this, countless fishermen have had reason to be grateful.

Caff could be obtained in two ways. You could tak yer caff-saick t' the fairm an get it filled then ye wid hae a gey job takin the thing hame balanced on a bike cos a full caff-saick's near as big as a barrage balloon.

So it wis a common sicht t' see a fisherman walkin along a country road pushin his bike wi its great muckle load, an if he had a loon, the loon wid be on the ither side ready t' steady the monster.

Prood kind o chiels wid seek the milkman t' dee the job but the milkman didna hae a lot o room on his cairt so the carrier sometimes got the jobbie.

Once hame, the caff-saick, which was simply a huge ham (hessian) bag, was clothed in a blue cotton cover then it was ready for service.

The fisherman's blankets were spread on the kitchen floor, one on top of the other, then they were stitched together round the edges, the proper tool being a darning needle, and the materials a ball o 5-ply navy-blue Seafield wòrsit.

Thus the finished 'blanket' could be as thick as individual taste dictated. Coverin the caff-saick an shooin-in the blankets wis a great nicht! For the bairns, at least. A feather pillow completed the fisherman's bedding.

At the start o the herring season, a clean cairt would make the rounds o the crew's homes to collect the beddin and then cam the almighty job o gettin the stuff aboard ship.

To coax the great muckle caff-saicks through the galley door, then doon the ladder into the cabin, and then into the bunks took a lot o coortin an clappin, the unwritten law being that the cotton covers must not be dirtied or torn.

Could you have seen a bunk with its complement of fresh bedding you would have sworn that it was impossible for a human body to enter it, but you would have been wrong!

The first nicht on the caff bed, ye wid be near smored. Ye wid hae t' fecht yer wye in, then lie wi yer nose scrapin the deck, an the caff aneth ye reeshlin an squeakin in the saick that wis fit t' burst.

The second nicht, ye wid hae room t' breathe but efter that the caff began t' sattle, an afore a week wis oot, the 'caffer' wid be into the shape o yersel jist like a nestie.

Oh, what comfort! What bliss! Steep broadside motion could never dislodge ye!

At the end of the year the sea around the Buchan coast bore a liberal coating of caff. Proof positive that a number of deckies were 'seekin a shift' and had duly teemed their caff-saicks ower the side.

I often remember a beautiful spring morning in the early thirties when a certain Peterhead crew were making their way to their ship, every one of them seated on the beddin-cairt, surrounded by rolls of blankets and great saicks o caff.

The cairter wis the kind o chiel that wid gie onybody a shottie o the horse for a Woodbine. In fact, for a packet o Woodbines, ye wid get the horse to keep.

Now, Jeemsie, the young cook had been at the picters on the Setterday nicht to see *Ben Hur*, and now he was regaling his shipmates with vivid accounts of the thrilling chariot scenes in the film.

But Jeemsie's command of descriptive language was rather limited so, sensing that he wasn't getting the message across, he decided to give his pals an object lesson.

'Look!' says he, 'I'll lat ye see the wye that Ben Hur gart 'is horsie go!' Then he passed the mandatory Woodbine to the cairter and seized the reins.

'C'mon ye beast, move!' he yelled. 'Gee-up ye sod, move yer carcass! Yahoo! Yippee! Up the leg o yer draars!' while he laid into the beast's backside wi the bicht o the reins.

He must have touched a tender spot for the startled animal took off, 0-60 in ten seconds flat.

Oh boys! Ye nivver saw naething like yon! Jeemsie didna ken that for twaa hale days the horsie had been stappin her belly wi lush spring grass.

Od! She wis as full o girss as a caff-saick wis full o caff! The sudden acceleration set off some kind of chemical reaction in the intimmers o the horse, so that as she came thundering doon Queen Street, there came from her exhaust a rapid series of short, sharp bursts of warm, moist air in strict tempo with the clatter of the hooves.

There was of course an added bonus in that the unexpected zephyrs were heavily laden with rich green grass particles which were scattered liberally ower everything in the line of fire and this included Jeemsie and his pals.

Now, ony feel can gar a horsie go but it taks a man to stop a Clydesdale, an Jeemsie wis jist a loon! In vain did his shipmates yell, 'Come astarn, for God's sake!' Jeemsie couldna stop her!

Two really brave crew-men abandoned ship in Chapel Street, another was lost overboard on the Broadgate, but the rest survived till the sweating horse came to a stop at the Brig, where Jeemsie received a few bright words from his skipper.

The cairt, the beddin and the crew appeared as if a hunner lawn mowers had been teemed oot ower them!

Everything had to go back for washin or for clean covers and as far as I ken, Jeemsie nivver drove a horse again.

Dod Jist Wisna the Hale Shillin

It was six o'clock on a Saturday night in Yarmouth. Since the month was October, it was pitch dark and although almost a thousand fishing boats were tightly berthed on both sides of the long dark river, there was scarcely a glimmer of light to be seen from any one of them.

The week was finished as far as fishing was concerned and soon the streets of the East Anglian town would be in a turmoil as thousands of Scotties came ashore for Setterday nicht.

On board the steam drifter *Wildfire*, the crew were at their supper in the cabin, which was also the dining-room. Ten hungry men sat around the triangular table of whose surface scarcely an inch was visible so dense was the mass of plates, mugs and jars which covered it. Each man sat in his appointed place, near his bunk; this was standard practice.

The crew had been on the go for eighteen hours. They had hauled a fleet of herring nets containing eighty cran; on the way from the fishing ground to the river they had 'redd up' or cleaned the nets, removing all herring heads and broken fish from the meshes.

The dinner had been a joog o tay and a pie but now that the shot had been livered and the ship washed down, the lads were enjoying a proper meal, a great dish of stewed steak with lashings of rich gravy which could be sopped up with slices of new bread. What a feed! And what a taypot! Of brown enamel it held about two gallons and it was kept continually on the move. Mair tay!

The skipper, in his fifties, was the oldest man aboard. There were three young deckies in their late teens or early twenties and all the others were married men.

Of course the 'young lads' would be off like a shot as soon as their supper wis doon their throats. They would race each other to be first for the communal bucket which was reserved for face-washing. Then, scrubbed, and dressed in their 'go-ashores', they would seek the bright lights and the lasses-o! With ten bob in his pooch a fella could have a rare weekend.

The older men would not be in such a hurry. Some of them might go ashore later for a pint at the White Lion or The Gallon Can; others might drop into the Church of Scotland Bethel to have a cup of tea and a news with old friends.

There they could receive attention to the salt-water boils on their wrists, an affliction which was the bane of their lives. The old-fashioned oilskin frocks chafed a fella's wrists, pulling hairs out by the roots and hey presto, you had a crop of 'plooks'. Very painful they were too! Most fishermen wore bandages of red flannel round their wrists to prevent the chafing. It had to be red flannel!

But sanitary conditions afloat were primitive and usually, if one man got boils, the others would be infected. Penicillin was as yet unknown and home-made cures included 'steepit loaf' or bread poultice. Some lads thought the Scriptures actually said, 'Cast thy bread upon the waters and thou shalt get steepit loaf!'

But no matter where they had spent the evening, they would finish off with a baggie o chips at the open-air stallies where you could buy mussels or shrimps or limpets or winkles. Gyaad-sake! Scotch folk dinna ait sic muck!

There was one deckie, however, who was in no hurry to go ashore. Dod was a year or two younger than the skipper who counted Dod as the best hand in the crew. Experience was something that Dod had in plenty and he was a very shrewd weather forecaster; he was strictly sober and was utterly reliable but alas, the poor man could neither read nor write.

He had left school with the name of 'nae bein the hale shillin' but then his generation had never heard of dyslexia, just as they had never heard of antibiotics or television.

Tonight Dod would sit until everybody had gone ashore, leaving him alone with the skipper. Then Dod would produce the letter he had received that day from his faithful Annie who always posted the letter so that Dod would get it on Saturda,

The letter, unopened, would be handed to the skipper who would ceremoniously open it before reading its contents aloud to the eager listener. Such had been their custom for many seasons.

But this particular evening the skipper laid the open letter on the table and addressed Dod very earnestly:

'Dod! I dinna like this! Here's me readin a letter that's supposed to be private! Man, I hiv to look at it, an I canna help hearin ivvery word that Annie has to say! Fit wye can that be private? The letter's meant for you yersel!'

For a moment Dod sat in silence, then reaching across the table he clappit his twaa hans ower the skipper's lugs and said triumphantly, 'It's private noo, Skipper! Read awaa!'

Nae the hale shillin?

The Three Musketeers

For thirty-six hours, the *Meadowsweet* had lain at the head of the loch while the storm raged among the hills. The surface water of the anchorage seemed to be covered in smoke, as the spray was torn up by the wind and driven, in horizontal sheets, towards the entrance, but there was no swell at all. So, with her great mizzen set, the shippie lay at peace, head to wind.

Long periods of snow had clothed the hills in a deep, white mantle, right to the water's edge. Now and again, a few deer had been sighted but, apart from these, there was no sign of life, although a straggle of low cottages along the shore betrayed the presence of Man.

There was very little the crew could do, apart from keeping anchor watch. There was no radio on board and, since fresh reading material was in short supply, the boys either slept, or sat on the 'fiddley', that cosy space between the wheelhouse and the funnel, where the warmth from the boiler below was so acceptable in this wintry weather.

'It's aye the same!' says Duncan. 'Ye're either gettin ower muckle sleep, or nae half eneuch o't! A peety we canna store the stuff!'

'That mines me,' says Jeemsie. 'It's a peety we didna get mair stores in Lochinver; the beef's feenished. I'm aa richt for loafs, but there's nae beef avaa. If we'd heen a gun, we micht ha shot een o yon deer that I see on the shore!'

'That mines me anaa!' says the Turk. 'Fin I wis a loon, I wis the finest shot in Scotlan. I could dee ony mortal thing wi a gun! I eesed t' ging doon t' the shows wi a copper or twaa, but I aye nott a barra t' hurl hame the prizes that I won at the shottin! There wisna a bairn in aa the toon that didna hae a present fae me, aff o the stallies. It feenished up that the show-mannie gied me a bob or twaa t' bide awaa, or they wid ha been oot at the door! But, mine ye, I didna blaa aboot it!'

'Div ye think ye could shot a deer fae here, skipper?' says Duncan.

211

'Jist wyte or I has a lookie, Duncan,' says the Turk, squinting along the barrel of an imaginary rifle. 'Och, aye! Nae bother avaa! Mebbe nae jist smack atween 'er een, but certainly richt atween 'er lugs!'

'I thocht Buffalo Bill wis the only man that could dee that, skipper,' says Jeemsie.

'Weel, my loon, ye thocht wrang! It wis me that learnt Buffalo Bill t' hannle a gun. That wis fin Bill's father wis cox'n o the Lonmay life-boat. Him an me wis great pals!'

There wis silence for a while, for very few men'll tell their skipper, to his face, that he's jist a born leear.

'Fit's the name o this loch?' says Duncan, to change the subject. 'I've nivver been here afore.'

'This loch,' says the Turk, 'has a name that East-coasters canna pronounce, so I've aye caad it 'Abraham's Bosom'. Didn't I pick a richt name for't?'

'Oh, aye! Ye fairly did that. It's a gran shelter!'

'Och! I've been here hunners o times, Duncan. That little hoosie at the sooth end's the Post-office. It's jist a placie that sells tobacca an pandrops, so we'll get nae beef here, cos there's nae anither shop avaa. A mannie b' the name o Hughie bides in that fite hoose at the ither end. I've kent him for mair than forty 'ear, an I wid fairly like a news wi the aal bodach again. We'll mebbe get ashore shortly, t' send a wire. Oor folk'll be winnerin aboot's, ye ken.'

'For God's sake, skipper!' cries Jeemsie. 'Dinna pit "Safe in Abraham's Bosom" on the wire, or my mither'll tak a dwaam!'

Just after noon on the third day, the wind veered more easterly, so the Turk weighed anchor and brought the shippie alongside the little jetty, where she was securely moored across the end. Then our gallant hero made for the post-office, accompanied by Duncan and Jeemsie. No show without Punch!

A wire? That would be no problem, unless the telegraph wires were down. Beef? Provisions? Now, where do you think such things would come from, with the roads blocked solid for the past week, and likely to remain so for several days yet? Oh, the locals had ways of surviving such conditions, but East-coasters were soft, and wouldn't know where to start.

'We're jist like the three bears,' says the Turk, as the trio made for Hughie's hoosie. 'Did ye ivver hear the richt story o the three bears, Jeemsie?'

'No, skipper. Fit wye dis that ging?'

'Weel, my loon, they were a hairy lot!'

What a welcome they got fae Hughie! In a dolly-mixture of Gaelic and Doric and English, he bade them enter and sit at the glowing peat fire. Jeemsie had never seen a room like this afore. From floor to ceiling, it was lined with tongue-and-groove timber, clear-varnished; the fireplace was white-washed, as white as the snow outside and a great muckle black kettle wis hottrin on the swye abeen the fire. They would take a cup of tea and a home-made scone? 'Aye, Surely. Fit could be better?'

Then the older men began reminiscing on the distant days of Hughie's youth when, with a friend, he had walked all the way to Peterhead to get a berth with the

Turk's father, and had walked all the way home again at the end of the season.

Jeemsie, who would normally have revelled in the old tales, never heard a word. His ee wis rivetted on the gun hingin on the waa.

'Dis that gun work, Hughie?' says he.

'Of course it works, my boy! I clean it regularly. It's an old, old friend.'

'Could ye shot a deer wi't?'

'Certainly! I would be efter a deer myself, but my eyesight's not so good now.'

'Could we get a len o yer gun, Hughie? We're gey short o beef!'

'By all means, take the gun, but I've only three bullets left. It's not easy to get ammunition now, cos that's my old service rifle. I'll have to write to Ramsay MacDonald about it, to be sure!'

'Three bullets is plinty,' says Duncan. 'In fact, ae shot wid dee wi oor skipper. He's the finest shot in Scotlan.'

Hughie gave his old friend a puzzled glance, but the crack shot wis staring at the floor, showing little interest.

'Come awaa, noo, skip! Noo's yer chance! Richt atween 'er lugs!' cries the cook, takin doon the gun.

Eh, wah, wah! The peer Turk! He had t' be badgered afore he wid move! It wis ower caal, he wisna sae young noo! Forty 'ear seen, maybe, but nae the day! But his protests were in vain.

An hour or so later, the three shipmates were leg-weary, wydin amon deep snaa. Fishermen's legs wis nivver made for mountains! Duncan had gotten the first shot at a deer, but it had been a waste o time.

'Ach, Duncan! Ye couldna hit the parish ye wis born in!' says the Turk. The scorn in his voice was sharp and clear. Next to fail wis Jeemsie, and the skipper's verdict, 'A miss is as good as a mile!'

'C'mon, noo, lads, it's time we wisna here! It'll seen be dark, so we'd better get back t' the ship. (Any drifter was aye 'the ship'.) Fin we come t' the tap o this brae, we should be lookin doon on her.'

'There's still a bullet left, skipper!' says Jeemsie. 'An look! There's a bonny beastie at the tap o the brae. Here's the gun, aa ready loaded for ye. Ye ken yer crew's stairvin, so ye can hardly lat them doon. Richt atween 'er lugs, skip, the wye ye eesed t' dee't!'

Eh, the peer aal Turk! Fit wye could he tell them noo, that he had never fired a gun in his life? He jist couldna, so he took the gun, and steadied it on a rock. Then he took his tongue atween his teeth, steekit baith his een, an lat bleeze!

Boys! The deer lowpit sax fitt into the air, an fell stone deid on the wrang side o the hill!

'Dalmichty! I nivver saw the like!' says Duncan.

'Nae sweerin!' says the Turk.

Fin the three musketeers cam pechin t' the tap o the brae, the deer wis rowlin doon the ither side, gaitherin snaa like a snaabaa. An she wis growin bigger, an bigger, an BIGGER! Lang afore she cam t' the boddim, she wis as big as a hoose!

'Good grief!' says Jeemsie. 'If yon thing misses Hughie's hoosie, it'll sink the ship, for sure!' Then the trio set off doon the hill at a run. But, praise be, the only

213

tree for forty mile saved the day, for the snaabaa struck the tree an burst open like a boom! Bowff!

I ken ye winna believe this, but, fin oor heroes arrived on the scene, they found, lyin deid amang the snaa, twaa deer, three hares, an forty-fower rubbits. Wi the one single bullet! Gweed shottin, eh?

Duncan an Jeemsie, fair dumfoonert, called the villagers to come and share in the spoils. Hughie wis the first to congratulate the crackshot.

'How on earth did ye manage that, my freen?' says he.

'Och, that's naething!' says the Turk. 'Here's yer gun back, Hughie. If I'd heen a better gun, I micht ha gotten a twa-three mair! Man, fin I wis a loon . . .'

'I could dee ony mortal thing wi a gun! Maybe nae jist smack atween 'er een, but certainly richt atween 'er lugs!' cries Duncan an Jeemsie in unison!

Uncle Sam

When I was a boy, I had on my father's side no fewer than six uncles. This was entirely due to the prolificacy of the Buchan race; it had nothing to do with me. On my mother's side, I had a couple of uncles whom I saw but seldom, for the simple reason that they came from Stirlingshire and, in those days, that county was 'hine, hine awaa'. So, you see, for uncles I was stuck with the home-grown variety and, as nephews are perfectly entitled to do, I weighed each one carefully in the balance, merely to see which one I liked best.

After a great deal of heart-searching, I decided that, compared to my Uncle Sam, the others were all rather colourless mortals. Uncle Sam was outstandingly different in that he was a most likeable rascal who could actually tell a story in Technicolour, and in 3-D too. When Sam gazed at me from under yon shaggy eyebrows, and launched into a tale, *Jason and the Golden Fleece*, *Scott of the Antarctic*, and *Big Chief Hole-in-the-Ground* faded into obscurity, and I was away in another world. It is verily possible that my rapt attention encouraged him to gild the lily somewhat, yet never did I dream of doubting his word. Fact or fiction? What did that matter? It was good, it was spell-binding, it was magic!

By birth, Sam was 'een o the Oxys', simply because his father was called Oxy, to distinguish him from all the other Andrew Buchans in the town. My own father was Oxy's Andra, and all his brothers were Oxy's So-and-so. Now, that should make me Oxy's Andra's Peter (see how it goes), or, if you like, Jeannie Motherwell's Peter, to distinguish me from all the other Peter Buchans. But, since both of these titles are a bittie unwieldy, I was given a handier name many, many years ago. The Oxy became Oxo, and I became Peter Oxo. Div I care? Fat lot o difference it wid mak, if I did! So, in the Blue Toon, if ye speir, 'Faar dis Peter Oxo bide?' they'll pit ye richt t' my door!

Now, Oxy's Sam was a herring buyer, not a curer, but a 'fresher'. Freshers had

214

little wooden boxes called 'margarines', eight margarines to the cran. These boxies were laid out in a long row on the pier, with a little ice in the bottom; then the fishermen would spread their baskets of herring evenly along the boxes, taking care to leave room for a sprinkling of ice along the top, before the lids were nailed down, when a fresh tier of empties would be laid on top of the first. It was a slow, scuttery job, discharging to a fresher. Ten cran made a 'dykie' of boxes, ten long and eight high, or vice versa. As soon as the boxes were filled, they were whipped off to the station to catch the south-bound train and, all the way south, at practically every stop, cadgers' vans were waiting to uplift their orders. Thus were the fresh herring distributed throughout the country, all the way to Billingsgate in London.

Maist o the freshers wore a white or khaki overall, an cairried a cloot for dichtin their hans; but Sam? Nivver! He jist dichtit 'is hans on's wyskit till he wis jist like a Pearly King fae Cockneyland. I never saw Sam in a hurry, I never saw him in a flurry, an I nivver saw him stuck for an answer.

To one English landlady, who asked if he was related to the Governor-General of Canada, who wrote *The Thirty-nine Steps*, he replied, 'Oh, aye! That's oor John, an affa lad for writin bookies!' And to another's query he replied, 'Haggis? Haggis, my dear, is what we Scots stuff our turkeys with!' Now, I think he tellt a lee that time, cos I'm sure he nivver saw a turkey in his life!

Varying seasons found Sam in diverse ports, following the herring. He was a proper kenspeckle character; he kent aabody, an aabody kent him.

Behold him now, in a certain West-coast port in winter, immediately after the Hitler war. At that time, most of Scotland's whisky was being exported to the States to earn sorely needed dollars; thus customers in all the local hostelries were rationed to one glass, and one glass only, a rule that Sam didna like avaa, for he likit a drappie. Since there were only twaa places in the port, twaa glaisses wis aa that a buddy could get, an that wis jist nae eese avaa t' Sam. So he set himself to devising a scheme whereby the niggardly 'one-glass' ration might be augmented.

There must be (or so he reasoned) many outlying hotels which, due to sheer lack of trade in the winter season, should be sitting on copious stocks of the amber liquid. Aha! He would hie himself thither to sample fresh delights! But, how was he to get there? He had no car, and, even if he managed to borrow one, he couldn't drive. And, to make things even worse, where would he get the petrol in a time of strict rationing? Alas! His castles in the air were crumbling at his feet!

Now, it so happened that the 'Minister of Fuel' in that particular port, had very little to do. (I mean the mannie that wis in charge o the petrol coupons.) There were as yet very few cars on the road, many vehicles having been laid up for years; and even to those who had cars in use, the meagre petrol ration was of little use in such a remote area. Thus, Rory the coupon-mannie had plenty of time for a part-time jobbie on the pier, acting as helper to any fresher who might require his services. And so it transpired that he found himself one day working for Sam.

'Hey, Rory!' says Sam, dichtin his fingers in the usual place. 'Div ye think a man in your position could spare a couponie or twaa for the likes o me?'

Rory was immediately suspicious. 'You know perfectly well, Sam, that I'm in a responsible job, and there are definitely no spare coupons. And, indeed, coupons would be no use to you anyhow! Where would yourself be going, now?'

Rather reluctantly, Sam disclosed his great plan, and, to his amazement, Rory was quite enthusiastic.

'Och, man!' says he, 'If that's what's in your head, I'm sure I could find a coupon or two in a drawer, somewhere. And, if you're needing a driver, I'll do that as well. In fact, we could go this very night, after we've had our one glass!'

So later that evening, we find our warriors in a remote inn, in the winter dark of a Highland glen, only to discover that the same old rule was in force. 'One glass only!' Sam, rather disappointed, was ready to move on, but Rory was apparently in no hurry.

'Ochone, ochone!' cries he. 'It's an aafil world that we're after seeing now! A poor, poor place for those who have a drouth and a motor car, for there's neither whisky nor petrol to be had for love nor money!'

'Indeed to goodness, yes!' was the reply. 'There's not a bottle in the place, else you would be having it! And as for our car, it's been on blocks in the shed for years. We cannot get to Inverness to the pictures, and we've not seen Aunt Jessack in Achiltibuie since the last three years or more. There's no petrol for pleasure motoring at all, at all, and it's weary we are in the winter without a break!'

'Sad indeed!' says Rory. 'No doubt you could use a few petrol coupons then?'

'No doubt whatsoever, but where would they come from, do you think?'

'I've got a few here!' says Rory, producing from his pocket a whole sheet of coupons. 'I'm the Petrol Officer at Portaloo, and these are a few spares I've come across in a drawer. They're yours, if you can find a bottle about the place!'

Goggle-eyed, Sam watched the inn-keeper disappear into the back room with his prize. Then came the excited whispers, 'Portaloo Petrol Officer! Give them another glass, and fetch a bottle! Better make it two, and don't tell a soul!'

Three more times that night did Rory work the Oracle, then, as they rattled their way back to Portaloo, the pair engaged in very earnest conversation on some remarkably deep subjects. Indeed, one confided to the other that it was his dearest wish that, someday, he would present the bairns of his native town with 'a poodlin-pal far they could wyde in watter that wisna full o slivvery doctors' (jelly fish). What a noble thought!

The cold, drizzly dawn found the bleary-eyed pair on the pier, Sam scutterin aboot, levellin oot the herrin an dichtin 'is hans in the usual fashion; Rory scatterin ice an nailin on the liddies.

'Rory, my loon!' says Sam, 'I'm fair affrontit at last nicht, but that winna help a lot, for it's you for the jile, an it's aa my blame! I'm thinkin ye'll get ten 'ear for ilkie couponie!'

Rory ceased his whistling of 'The Drunken Piper' and, gazing earnestly at Sam, he says, 'Not to worry, friend! Not to worry at all, at all! They were all old coupons, out of date and utterly worthless. I meant to burn them long ago!'

Now, if this is nae a true story, I canna help that. It's jist exactly as I heard it, near-han forty 'ear seen!

But I hardly think Sam wid tell me a lee, specially wi him bein an Oxy!

Ferocious Pains

To use his own words, the Turk had, 'the bonniest belly that ever braved the boisterous billow'. This pure, poetic gem was used only when some of his brother skippers teased him about his enormous girth. He had discovered that to reply in jocular terms was the best way to get peace.

'Oh, aye!' he would say, 'My taes is nae the only thing I hinna seen for a fyle!' Then, with a crude laugh, the jesting and teasing would cease. But, secretly, the Turk was 'a wee bittie affrontit' at his corporation, though he made no effort to reduce it. It was common knowledge that the *Meadowsweet* had the biggest grub-bill in the fleet, mainly because of her skipper's insatiable appetite. Sliced bread was as yet several years in the future, and many a time did Jeemsie remark, 'My airms is sair cuttin loaf till 'im.' Indeed, there had been the unforgettable occasion when Jeemsie had made a fly-cup for the skipper, who had just come off watch. Staring goggle-eyed at the two slices of bread left on the plate, the youngster had asked, in an unguarded moment, 'Fit wye did ye nae ait the hale loaf, skipper?', only to hear the good-natured reply, 'There's a mids in aathing, my loon, an I've nae time for greed!'

The Turk's own crew liked and respected him, as was amply borne out by their years of sailing with him. Not one of them would ever think of leaving him to seek another berth and, although they often had a quiet joke at the skipper's expense, the jokes were never malicious.

One day, while Duncan the driver was helping Jeemsie to peel the tatties, the conversation turned to their lord and master.

'I'm thinkin the skipper's nae verra weel 'iss days,' says Jeemsie. 'He's far ower ill-naitered for richtness!'

'Weel,' says his pal, 'Ye can hardly expect a chiel o that size t' be aa weel at ae time!'

'I'm serious, Duncan! I'm sure the mannie's nae weel, an I ken he has a lot o pain at times. Last time I gid up t' the wheelhoose t' lat 'im doon till's denner, he wis fair grippin onto the wheel wi's belly!'

'Fit did ye say, Jeemsie?' Then, with a laugh, 'Oh! I see fit ye mean!'

'It's lefts-an-richts (neeps-an-tatties) the day, Duncan, an he'll scoff half o the pot himsel. I'll tak oot my ain share afore I ging up t' the wheel or there winna be naething left for me, fin I get back!'

As it happened, Jeemsie wis dead right. The skipper wisna weel. For the past few trips, he had been sair bothered wi severe pains in his digestive system, and this had him worried. Many a time had he worried when one of his crew had been ill, but now the worry was for himself.

'The nearest doctor's at least a hunner mile awaa, an that's a dizzen oors o steamin at full speed!' The very idea gart 'im shivver. But finally, the Turk's good lady had read him the Riot Act, insisting that he should see the doctor.

Now, the Turk's vocabulary of nautical terms was very extensive, but when it came to medical words, he wis fair lost.

'What seems to be the trouble, skipper?' says the kindly physician.

'Weel, doctor, it's iss wye. I'm gettin iss ferocious pains in my abomdemen!'

'I trust you mean your abdomen, skipper?'

'No, doctor, I div nutt! The pains is in my abomdemen! Thats the fancy word for yer belly! I thocht ye wid ha kent that, you bein a doctor!'

The good doctor merely smiled, then proceeded to give the patient an extensive examination, questioning him astutely at the same time. After a thorough exploration of the Turk's great hemisphere, the verdict was, 'You're eating far too much, skipper, and you're eating it far too fast. You fishermen are all the same; you simply will not take enough time to your meals. Slow down a bit, or you'll have an ulcer very soon, and I can assure you, you won't like that!'

'Fit did ye say?' cried the Turk in alarm. 'An ulcer? A beelin in my belly?' The fancy word had been forgotten.

'Not at all, skipper. I'll give you some white powder to take after meals, but, unless you follow my advice, you'll be in dire trouble!' This was followed by a short dissertation on the words, 'peptic' and 'duodenal', words which the Turk had never heard in his life.

Oh, doctor!' says he, 'I'm affa gled it's nae a beelin, an I'm mair than thankfu it's nae 'pendix!'

That night, the *Meadowsweet* sailed for northern waters, the intention being to fish with great-lines for cod, ling, skate and halibut between the Orkneys and Cape Wrath. Bad weather was always a problem, and on this trip it was exceptionally coorse. There were no wireless sets on the fishing boats of that period, so the Turk had to be his own forecaster, and he was no mean hand at that trade. Years of experience had taught him to read the tell-tale signs of the clouds and the 'glaiss'.

On the morning of the sixth day at sea, the look of the sky and the state of the barometer convinced the old salt that the best course of action was to seek shelter till the gale was past and where better than in Loch Erribol, that great gash in Scotland's northern coast. It wis a sair battered shippie, and a sair forfochen crew that gained the welcome haven in the early afternoon. As they entered the loch, Jeemsie was summoned to the wheelhouse.

'Noo, my loon,' says the Turk, 'This crew's sair needin mait an sleep, so get the denner ready as fast as ye can! Naething fancy; bully beef an tatties'll dee, syne we'll aa turn in, an jist lat her swing at her anchor.'

So, an hour or so later, we find the shippie safe at anchor in the shelter of the great loch, her crew fed and blissfully 'horizontal'. Jeemsie, having washed the dishes, is about to creep into the cosy darkness of his bunk, when he hears a low moan from the skipper, who has gluffed his denner in his usual fashion.

'Ooh me, ooh me! The ferocious pains is back, my loon! The fite pooder's nae eese avaa, so will ye heat a nammle plate an pit it on the sair bit? They tell me heat's affa gweed for a sair belly!'

So, up the trap goes Jeemsie wi the plate, to heat it on the galley stove. He's back in a meenit or twaa, wi the het plate rowed in a sweat-rag, an lays the thing canny on the sair bit.

'Ooh me, ooh me! That's richt fine!' says the Turk. 'Noo, the time that this plate's cweelin, wid ye nae be better t' heat anither een?'

The faithful cook duly obliges, up an doon, up an doon, but the pain's gey sweir t' shift.

'There's nae gaan t' be nae sleep avaa for me the day!' thinks Jeemsie. Then, a flash of inspiration lichts up his face.

'By jingers!' says he, 'If it's heat that's nott, we'll seen sort that!' So, using the little lever supplied for the job, he lifts the lid o the reid-het stove, an plunks it square on the Turk's equator.

It is impossible to describe the scene which follows. Sufficient to say that, as the curtain falls, the peer Turk is on his back on the table, while Duncan, watched closely by a spell-bound crew, massages the reeking volcano with great dads o margarine.

Jeemsie? Soun asleep on his caff-saick!

The older generation in the area still recall 'the aafil day they heard the monster roaring in the loch. Indeed, it was an eerie sound!'

There wis a day or twaa that the Turk didna speak t' Jeemsie. Wid ye blame him? But, strange as it may seem, he nivver had a ferocious pain aa the rest o his days. In fact, he would advise everybody, whatever the ailment, to 'Hud on the heat!'

Mrs McTurk, however, had certain reservations which were clearly expressed when she met Jeemsie one day in Queen Street.

With a rueful sort of glance at her trinkle o bubbly-nibbit bairns, she sighed, and she said, 'Oh, Jeemsie, Jeemsie! Fit wye did ye nae pit yon reid-het lid a wee bittie further sooth?'

Ping Pongs

If you like fish and chips, the chances are that you have, at some time enjoyed a ping-pong supper. A ping-pong? Aye! That's richt, an it's nae Chinese, for it almost certainly originated in Buckie, or maybe in the Sloch (Portessie). Let me explain.

In the years immediately following the Hitler war, the fishing industry was regulated by the Ministry of Food, a hangover from the war-time. No doubt the same thing applied to farming, but, whereas those appointed to run the fishing industry were invariably farmers, I never heard of a fisherman being appointed to run the farms. Od! They must ha been fairmers, cos they could fairly pit the cairt afore the horse.

Now, there have been regulations regarding the minimum legal sizes for fish ever since I can remember, just as there have been minimum legal sizes for meshes. Every boat should have properly constructed gauges for the measuring of fish. A gauge is very easily made, for it is simply a little board, say 18 x 4 inches, with a stick nailed firmly across it, near to one end. Lines are then scribed across the board at distances varying according to the different species, say ten inches for whiting, and ten inches for haddock. You lay the fishie on the board with her nose against the stick, and her tail must touch or cross the line drawn for that particular species. See? It wasn't possible to measure every single fish, but it's amazing how accurate the human eye can become, with just an occasional check.

Now, then, it came to pass that the Buchan Deep was swarming with haddockies, just a trifle short of the legal size. Mind you, they were bonny fishies, firm and plump, whereas those which were of legal length were thin, thin. Proper shargers. They were also exceedingly scarce! Wouldn't it be sensible to keep the short, plump fishies and discard the long, lean ones?

'This you cannot do! Ye'll get the jile for that!' says the Ministry.

'Aha!' says the Buckie mannie (but not to the Ministry, of course). 'If we clip their blastit tails aff, naebody can mizzer them. Nose to tail's the rule so, if there's nae tail . . . !'

Simple? Surely! Brilliant? Indubitably! Buckie? Ye may be sure! Thus was born a new breed of haddocks known as Ping Pongs, handled by a new breed of fishermen who became amazingly adept with a pair of scissors.

'Aha!' says the Ministry, 'We have seen Manx cats, but this is the first time we have seen Manx haddocks! Are they freaks of nature, in that they have no tails?'

'Na, na!' says the Buckie mannie, 'The peer craiturs is chased t' daith wi sharks, an them that disna sweem fast eneuch losses their tails! It wid gar ye greet, so it wid. We jist tak them aboord t' pit them oot o their misery!'

Weel, weel, boys! It wis good while it lasted.

Now, in those days, there was no open vision (I Samuel 3:1). Many returning servicemen, wishing to become fish-buyers, found all sorts of bureaucratic barriers in their path. Then, when these had been surmounted, there was the personal hostility of certain buyers who had had 'the baa at their fit' for six years and wanted things to remain that way. That took some beating! Mind you, the fishermen wanted more buyers, the more the merrier, and during the awkward period many a box of ping-pongs was hoisted ashore in the dark, to give the newcomers a start.

Behold, now, two of these would-be buyer/merchants in the old fish-market in the Blue Toon. For transport, Bill had a pram, and Fred had a message-bike. It had been a typical March day; gale force winds all day, falling calm after sunset. ('Sun down, wind down!') None of the PD boats had been at sea, so our two heroes were hanging about in the forlorn hope that some stranger might enter the port. And that's precisely what happened. A BCK boatie, which had been fishing near the Broch, came in and tied up in the darkest hole in the place.

'Hey!' says Bill, 'That mannie has ping-pongs, or he wid lie ower here far it's fine an licht!'

'I believe ye're richt!' says Fred. 'We'd better hae a news wi him.'

But the skipper, tho quite friendly, wouldn't listen to their plea.

'It's been a wild day,' says he. 'We jist got the ae drag afore the wither cam doon on's. Half-a-dizzen boxes o ping-pongs on the pier there! I spoke ashore on the wireless, an the wife's breether's comin doon wi a van for the fishes. He's fae Fitehills, an he'll be here shortly!'

Not even the offer of an exceptionally high price would tempt him. In vain did Bill and Fred explain how the half of Buchan was depending on them for fresh fish on the morrow.

'It's the wife's breether, ye see! Nae my breether's wife. He has a chip shop, so he'll be needin the fish. Come doon the caibin, an get a joog o tay the time we're wytin. The van'll seen be here!'

Some twenty minutes later, our heroes, refreshed but still disconsolate, resumed their pacing in the empty fish market. It was on the stroke of midnight, and they were about to call it a day when who should appear on the scene but Arthur, the runner-cum-ship's husband with one of the local salesmen.

Arthur was clad in his usual attire, a double-breasted, belted, military-style raincoat wi strappies on the shooders. Faded till it was nearly white, the coat gave Arthur a rather dashing, distinguished appearance, something like yon chiel that can dee aa mortal thing, 'cos the lady loves Milk Tray'. Rather surprised to see the two pals, he bagan to sing in his rich baritone.

> 'Why weep ye by the tide, you twaa?
> Why weep ye by the tide?
> Ye ken there's jist nae fish avaa,
> So here ye needna bide!'

'It's aa richt for you, Jock o Hazeldene!' says Bill, 'But we're in a hole! Yon mannie ower there in the dark winna sell his ping-pongs t' hiz!' And oot cam the hale sad story.

'If I get the ping-pongs t' ye, is't worth a powen?' says Arthur.

'Oh, aye!' says Fred, 'I wid say it's worth twaa!'

'C'mon, then! We hinna muckle time. Here's the van comin!'

Now then, Arthur stationed himself at the Brig, right underneath a lamp post, while Bill and Fred returned to the scene of their earlier failure, where the fishes were being loaded into the van.

'Ye're back again, lads!' says the skipper. 'Ye're wastin yer time, cos here's the wife's breether for the fish!'

'Oh!' says Bill, 'We're nae seekin the fish noo! We're jist doon t' warn ye that there's a Ministry o Food mannie on the go the nicht, an he sweers that the first een he gets wi ping-pongs'll get sax month in the jile!'

'Dalmichty!' says the van driver, 'I didna see naebody fin I cam doon the pier!'

'Weel!' says Fred, 'Ye'll see 'im noo! Look! Up there aside the lamp-post! Yon mannie wi the fite coatie! "Sax month's jile", he says!'

Boys-o-boys! The boxes wis oot o the van in five seconds, an the driver lowpit inower an pressed the starter.

'Hold on! Nae ower fast' says Bill. 'Drive canny fin ye're passin the mannie, or he'll be suspeecious! Canny, noo!'

So the van crawled up the pier towards the Ministry mannie. When the van was just abreast of him, Arthur lowpit oot an haimmered on the side o't.

'Stop, ye rascal!' cries he. 'It's sax month's jile for you!'

Nivver did a van ging ower the Brig at sic a lick! At least ninety, I'd say. Twenty meenits an the driver wis happin his heid in Fitehills. Nae bad for forty mile. 'If the bobby comes t' the door, I hinna been oot the nicht!' says he.

Helpless with laughter at the van's sudden departure, our two heroes turned to negotiate with the skipper, but lo, the boat was gone! She wis takkin oot atween the piers wi the verra sparks fleein oot o her starn!

'Sax month! Did ye hear yon? There's t' be nae mair ping-pongs aboord here! For God's sake pit oot that licht!' wis the cry.

On the pier, a trio of still laughing pals surveyed the six boxes of fish which had been so hurriedly abandoned.

'We'll need a han wi this lot, Arthur,' says Bill. 'We jist hiv a pram an a message bike. Fit aboot it?'

'I ken far there's a fine big barra!' says Arthur, 'But it'll cost ye three powen noo, seein that ye're gettin the ping-pongs for naething!'

'Three powen for the len o a barra?' cries Fred. 'By jingers, the Jews is nae aa in Jerusalem!'

The B.S.A.

Peter Rennie eatin fish, Alec catchin eels;
Eels catchin Alec's father eatin raw peels.

I'm sure that couplet will jog your memory as to what could be done with the word 'Preface' in a school text book. And, similarly, the 'Contents' could be construed as 'Cows Ought Not To Eat Neeps Till Sunday', although I've never heard that one in reverse order.

When one had acquired the knack of tripping such delectable phrases from the tongue, one had taken a tremendous step upwards on the educational ladder, a step more beneficial than any twelve-times table. Such is the mind of youth!

Today's generation is afflicted with a veritable host of abbreviations, such as TV, VAT, HP (not horse power) and Hi-Fi, to mention but a few of an endless list. On the other hand, my generation had very few abbreviations to handle, but, by golly, we certainly made the most of what we had! Of course we all knew about the English drifter which had been bought by Peterhead owners. Since her name was simply EJM, everybody thought, 'They'll change that, surely!' But everybody was wrong! Her skipper, whose by-name was 'Mumphin', refused to change it, and to anyone who asked what the letters stood for, he replied, 'Everyone's Jealous of Mumphin'.

Then there was the Irish drifter which appeared on the scene bearing the name IFS (Irish Free State). The youngsters around the harbour soon changed that to 'I Feel Her Sinking', but she finally became *Accede* PD.191.

We had a great deal of fun at times with abbreviations. If we knew what the letters meant, we lost interest immediately but, if the meaning was beyond us, we soon coined our own phrases to suit ourselves, the general rule being that, if we could make the meaning vulgar, it was sure to be good. If we could make the meaning unprintable, we had discovered a gem of purest ray serene!

One such gem stared us in the face every day as we left school, for directly across the road was Campbell's bicycle shop, which always displayed an attractive poster with the slogan, 'Lead the way on a B.S.A.'

Little did we know, and less did we care that the letters stood for 'Birmingham Small Arms', one of the finest cycle makers in the land, their trademark being three rifles stacked in a tripod. But it wasn't very long before some brilliant youth, whose name I never knew, produced a really unprintable connotation for the three letters. The new phrase was tested and tried, and finally pronounced good. In language which, I hope, is acceptable, the phrase simply meant, 'A gey sair dock!' Rather innocuous after all, surely.

B.S.A. bikes were British made, and were immensely strong, built to last. By today's standards, they were old-fashioned but, in their day, they were among the very best, although they shared a common fault in that they were rather high. It was quite common to see a boy riding a B.S.A., clinging to the side of the bike, with one leg 'through the bar'. They were as high as that. Only tall men could throw a leg over the saddle with ease. Men of medium stature found the feat rather difficult, and little fat mannies found it impossible.

But lo! A method was devised whereby the impossible might be accomplished, and this was simply by adding to the bike a 'back-step'. The back-step was merely an extension of the rear axle, usually on the left side, and the mounting procedure was as follows: (1) Take the bike by the handlebars in the usual way, then, with the legs, straddle the rear wheel. (2) Raise the left foot and place it firmly on the back-step. (3) With a hopperty-kick motion of the right leg, push the bike forward until it gains a little speed. (4) Using the left leg as a lever, raise the body, just like going up a step. Now all your weight is on your left foot, on the back-step, and this weight must be swiftly shifted to the saddle. You'll know all about it if you miss the seat.

It wasn't everyone who could perform the act gracefully. It was 'better nor the picters' to behold some of the would-be cyclists mounting their steeds from the rear. Quite a few rolled their eyes skyward and gied a richt hairty sweer, if their contact with the saddle was on the heavy side. It was common to hear sundry gasps and grunts, and indeed, some of the more articulate riders announced to the public at large that they were off to Lipton's for cheese. At least, that's what I gathered.

The ladies' version of these sturdy bikes was by no means without its problems. Specially for the young quines! You see, the handlebars were very much higher than the saddle and this made it rather difficult for a lassie to steer with one hand.

With one hand? Aye, surely! They nott the ither han t' hud their hat, or t' keep their skirts doon for fear the loons wid see their bloomers. If only they could ha seem themsels; most ungainly and unlady-like.

The real mistresses of these old bikes were the elderly country ladies who came into town with their black straw hats securely anchored, and with skirts long enough and heavy enough to defy a Force 8 gale. With torso erect on the saddle, with both hands on the handlebars, and with feet all but invisible, these ladies seemed to glide along, like black swans on a placid lake.

One owner of an ancient B.S.A. wis Dod, a 'vricht' fae Rora. In my early days, the country folk spoke of 'the vricht' as a man who could do any mortal thing. And indeed, many of these craftsmen were gifted with exceptional skills.

Such a man wis Dod, a stocky, muscular chiel who had ridden his trusty old bike on more Saturdays than he could remember, to visit his life-long crony Sandy, in the fisher-toon o Buchanhaven. In a boxie strapped to the 'carrier' jist above the rear mudguard, Dod would bring to Sandy a bittie o cheese or country butter, or maybe a dizzen eggs. On his return trip the boxie would contain a fry o herrin, or a bittie o fish, or even a raan (roe) if the season wis richt.

Dod an Sandy wid sit at the fire for an oor or twaa, pittin the world in order, an, seein that this wis a gey sair job, they nott a drap o the Aal Kirk t' help them. Nae a lot, mind ye, jist a drappie. But ae nicht Dod wis richt fine pleased t' hear that Sandy's loon had come hame fae the Navy wi a bottle o Nelson's Blood (Navy rum) till's father. Oh, boys, the twaa o them had a rare nicht.

They nivver haard the twaa fisher loons that took Dod's bike awaa fae the door, nor did they ken that the loons cowpit the bike upside doon an haimmered a hale box o lang, blue tacks, een aifter the ither, throwe the seat! Man, fin the loons put back the bike, the seat wis like a hedgehog.

Noo, than! Jist aifter dark, oot comes Dod t' tak the road hame. He wis steamin a thochtie mair than usual, but och, he wid manage fine. He wid jist tak the bull b' the horns. This he did (fae the back, ye ken), an, wi ae fitt on the back-step, he gid 'Oopie-up' an cam doon wi's usual clyte on the seat!

Oh, boys, oh boys! I dinna think it wid be richt o me t' tell ye ower muckle aboot fit happened neist. I'm sure ye wid greet! But I'm jist as sure that there's nivver been a roar like yon since Hielan Jess put her bust ower near the mangle!

The hale village cam poorin oot t' see the ferlie. 'Fit's adee wi Dod the nicht? He's surely geen baresark! Did ivver ye hear bad words like yon? I'm sure that Tom Mix on his buckin bronco couldna beat that performance!'

Little did they ken that Dod wis on 'is bike an couldna win aff! At last, the peer tormented sowl got hud o a lamp-post an startit t' clim. He had jist gotten a hud o the crossbar at the tap, fin the bike let go an fell t' the grun. Aa clear!

Noo, at that time there wis in the village a resident who had spent several years abroad, doon aboot Norwich or somewye like 'at.

'I think,' says he, 'it would be expedient to fetch a doctor, PDQ!'

'Good idea!' says I. 'An if he speirs, tell 'im it's a mannie wi a B.S.A.'

Noo than, a supergrass tellt Dod faa had meddled wi's bike, but Dod jist bided his time. Then, ae nicht, as he entered Sandy's hoosie, the aal fisherman says,

My paternal great-grandparents on Buchanhaven Shore.

Burnhaven c. 1880. My father's birth-place one mile south of Peterhead. The village was demolished in the 1970s.

Reddin a haddock line in the days of leather sea-boots. The bearded man is holding a tippin, that part of the line to which the hook was attached. The tippins, several hundred to each line, were invariably made from horse-hair twined by the fishermen themselves. The raivelt line is in a wooden backet. Late 1800s.

Pairtin the mussels at St. Combs. Each family had its own private scaap on the rocky fore-shore where the tide kept the bait alive. The mussels are probably from the Ythan Estuary. Late 1800s.

Fisher wives carry their men from the boat to the beach to keep them dry shod. c. 1900.

A Fifie boat. c. 1900. Spot the barfit loon.

The entrance to Peterhead Harbour c. 1900.

Peterhead Harbour c. 1900.

Peterhead Harbour choc-a-bloc, so drifters use Smith's Embankment. Note Cephas on extreme left, bottom. c. 1920.

The steam and the tar and the herrin smell . . . Peterhead 1920s.

The Cannon, at the entrance to Peterhead South Harbour c. 1925. The house I bought in 1973 is in the background. This photograph is from Neish's *Old Peterhead*.

Part of the Peterhead fleet in the mid-1920s. In the background, two famous, vanished landmarks — the Gut-Factory lum and the Black Shed.

Peterhead Harbour c. 1925. *(Photo: James Valentine)*.

Roughly one twentieth of the herring fleet as they enter Yarmouth. Late 1920s.

I have an uncle, three aunts and a sister in this picture. 1930s.

A real family affair! Men, L to R: Skipper, John Hugh Cowe, John Skinner (Balintore), David Cowe (skipper's brother), A. Gowans (St Monance — skipper's brother-in-law), David and Jimmy Cowe, John Cowe and Willie Cowe (skipper's son). Girls: Mary Bruce, Mary Cowe (top) and two Buckie girls. 1930s.

The line skipper, my father, Andrew Buchan, scans the distant horizon. The barrels were for fish livers, perks for the crew. c. 1930.

The Gutting Quine and the Cooper — my sister Madge and elder brother Andrew. Late 1930s.

Livering herring at Yarmouth. My brother John is on the right. 1930s.

The 'Oxies'. Back row: Yours truly, Rob, Madge, Chrissie. Front: Jeannie with wee Sheena and Granma, Jeannie Motherwell. Missing: Andrew and John. 1940s.

Forty-footers for the four o'clock sale at South Harbour, Peterhead. Late 1950s.

The fifty-footer MB *Twinkling Star* PD.137. Now pilot boat at Milford Haven. This was my own command. c. 1960.

Memories are made of this. 11 January 1961, MB *Twinkling Star*, which I skippered. Twelve lines of ninety hooks each. Bait: flusks (ink fish). Grounds: Buchan Deep. Catch: 730 stone of prime cod. Value: £411 (probably a record). Today's value: say £8,000.

On duty in Peterhead Harbour Control Tower. c. 1980.

Codlings drying in the sun and wind of summer 1988. Basic ingredients of hairy tatties in the winter.

Hielan Briggie, Kinlochbervie, 1988, with my grand-daughter, Anna Massie. (*Photo: G. Hamilton*).

Signing copies of *Fit Like Skipper?* in John Miller's shop in Peterhead in 1989. L to R: my grand-daughter Heather, her friend Fiona Kaye, and my elder daughter Anne. *(Photo: Aberdeen Journals).*

Happy among boats. At home in Peterhead, 1989. *(Photo: Gordon Wright).*

With my good friend David Toulmin. A publicity photograph taken in Peterhead just before the publication of *Buchan Claik* which we compiled together, 1989. *(Photo: Gordon Wright).*

With my grand-daughter Anna Massie, who unveiled a portrait of me by the artist Michael Knowles on 17 June 1991. The portrait now hangs in the entrance to the Arbuthnot Museum in St Peter Street, Peterhead. *(Photo reproduced by kind permission of 'The Buchan Observer').*

'There's been a terrible noise oot there this last fyowe meenits! Like somebody gettin murdered, I wid say. Did ye see onything oot o the wye, Dod?'

'Naething forbye, Sandy, naething forbye. I jist met in wi twaa loons, an I've gien the pair o them a B.S.A., so that they'll mine on me lang aifter I'm awaa!'

'Od!' says Sandy, 'Ye're gey gweed-wullie if ye gied them a bike the piece!'

'Na, Sandy, nae a bike! Nae a bike avaa! Jist a gey sair dock!'

An he gied the taes o's tackety beets a close kind o look!

Holiday in the Capital

According to Mrs McTurk, it wis a richt fine day for the fite thingies. The sky wis brilliantly blue, an the few fleecy cumulus clouds were jist as brilliantly white, while a light westerly breeze ruffled the golden grain on the broad fields o Buchan.

Amongst the rich, dark greenery, the roddens were jist a bleeze o reid, an the clean, sweet air wis a joy to breathe.

'Ye'd better tak the gweed o this, lads!' says the Turk to his crew. 'There's nae naething like this on the sea!'

The summer herring season had drawn to a close in the usual way. For a week or ten days, the number of spent (spawned) herring among the catches had gradually increased until finally the total catch was 'clean spent'. Then the shoals had departed to pastures new, and the herring fleet was tied to the pier. It was all over for another summer. Thousands of nets were bundled, to be loaded on carts and lorries which would carry them into the countryside, where the fishers would hang their nets to dry on any available fence.

On this particular day, the *Meadowsweet*'s crew had been obliged to bring their nets five miles inland before they could find a vacant fence. They had actually passed a fence or two but, since they had been of the 'pykit weer' variety, they were not acceptable for the hanging of nets. Now, at last, they had found a suitable stretch of fencing and, as the heavily laden lorry (with solid tyres) drove slowly along the roadside, one man dropped the nets, one by one, along the grassy verge. His shipmates lowsed the bundles and hung the nets on the fence.

'Keep the spaces aiven, noo!' cries the Turk to the man on the lorry, 'An for ony sake, dinna drap the nets amon sharn!' Then, in a quieter tone, he says to Dumplins, the mate, 'Yon chiel that we spoke till said something aboot a fince. I hinna seen nae sign o a fince, but I'm fine pleased we've gotten a palin.'

'Aye, skipper, this is a richt palin, fine smooth weer, an it's nae yon roosty kind either. It's a winner the fairmers disna compleen aboot nets on their palins.'

'Och, they needna bother compleenin,' says the Turk. 'Wallace the Bruce passed a laa that fishermen could hing their nets onywye they likit!' But here the Turk was entirely wrong. The farmers were definitely not obliged to provide the fishers with drying facilities and, many years later, they were to make that fact abundantly clear, and rightly so. Still, isn't it strange that, a few short years after the fishers were told to provide their own fences, there were no herring nets to dry. They were relics of a bygone day. Then the peer fairmers 'couldna get a bittie o net t' hap the wife's strawberries.'

Now the nets that were being hung up on this bonny day would be taken in when thoroughly dry. Each 'man-wi-gear' would take his own nets to his 'laftie' for mending and storing, but these nets would not go, in a week or two, to Yarmouth. No, the older, harder nets would suffice for the stormy shallows off East Anglia, where the risk of loss was so much greater.

As the squad made for the lorry which would take them home, the Turk again exhorted his men to savour the beauty of the scene. 'Tak a gweed look, noo, an maybe ye'll mine on't fin ye're punchin oot o Yarmooth river. There's nae mony days like this in a year!'

'Great holiday weather, skipper! D'ye nivver think on takkin a holiday?' says Fairnie, one of the deckies. Now, with a name like that, Fairnie was sure to be a stranger. Indeed, he was very nearly a foreigner, for, along with his chum Meldrum, he hailed fae Fisherrow, on the south side of the South Firth. Some skippers liked to have a couple of Lewismen in their crew, but the Turk preferred Sooth-kintra men.

'A holiday, Fairnie? A holiday? Holidays is for lawyers, an bankers an doctors, but nae for the likes o hiz! A holiday? That'll be the day!'

'Lots o folk in oor pairt o the world taks holidays,' says Fairnie, 'An they're jist ordinary workin folk; miners an dockers an the like. Mind ye, they get nae pey for their holiday time, but they save up, the hale year, for their annual spree. An they fairly enjoy it!'

'Aye! That's richt!' says Meldrum. 'An I'm shair the day's comin when every man'll get holidays wi pey!'

'Good grief!' says the Turk, 'Holidays wi pey? I've surely gotten twaa idiots this time. Bolsheevicks, maybe!'

'I'll be haein a holiday masel in a week or so,' says Fairnie, 'but I'm gettin mairried first.'

'Mairried?' says the Turk, 'I thocht ye had mair sense! Is she a fisher quine? Will ye be haein a big feed?'

'No, skipper, she's no a fisher lass. She works in a jam factory, makin the seeds for the raspberry jam. Ye ken the kind that sticks alow yer teeth. It's t' be a quiet waddin, jist the twa faimlies, cos I dinna hae verra muckle money, ye see!'

'Peety!' says the Turk. 'Ye should hae a richt fisher mairridge!'

'An what d'ye mean by a richt fisher mairridge, skipper?'

'Oh!' says the Turk, airily, 'Cabs an wine biscuits, an a hurl hame in a hearse! Ho, ho, ho!'

That afternoon, Fairnie and Meldrum left for their homes in the south, on the understanding that the Turk would recall them by telegram in due course. At teatime, our gallant hero mentioned the silly word 'holiday' to his better half, expectin that she wid hae a richt herty lauch, but what a begick he got. She didna lauch! She fell oot on him instead, an she didna miss him an hit the waa.

'Holiday?' she cries, 'Awyte we'll hae a holiday! I've scrubbit fleers an mennit nets since ivver I saw yer face. I'm fochen deen wi bairns an hippens! I'm nivver awaa fae the washin tub! Ower the watter wi a buttery cookie an a bottle o AI (lemonade)! Div ye caa that a holiday? The shippie winna sink, the world winna stop, if ye tak twa-three days aff! Holiday it is, m'lad, an neist wik at that!'

Sufficient to say that 'neist wik', Mr and Mrs could be seen in Scotland's fair capital city, and the Turk hated it, just as his wife loved it. He wanted to see the Castle, and something of Scotland's heritage, but it was, 'Aa richt, noo, but lat's see the shops first.'

Boys! She didna miss a shop, eence she got a start. It wis 'something till my mither, an a thingie till oor Johnnie.' She even got a 'packet o oots-an-ins for oor Meg's hair'. Eh! the peer Turk! He steed at the shop doors like a lost dog, dammert wi the steer an the heat, till, one afternoon a 'smairt-like deemie' spotted him as a stranger and a possible client. So she approached him with a certain proposition.

Noo, the Turk wisna a feel aathegither! He had met this lassie's marra mony a time during the war, an fine did he ken fit she wis aifter.

'Na, na, my quine!' says he, 'Wid ye nae be better t' look for a chiel a bittie younger than me?'

'Ye're no that auld!' says she.

'Mebbe no, lass, mebbe no, but I hiv jist the ae solitary powen in my pooch!'

'Oh, dear, dear!' says she. 'I'm afraid ye'll no get very much for a pound, these days!' And she left him alone in his glory.

Some ten minutes later, the Turk was joined by his good lady, empty handed for once.

'Come awaa noo, darlin' says she, 'We'll ging an see the Castle, an the Royal Mile, an the model shippies in the Museum. Ye've been affa good!'

Happy at last, our hero took his beloved's arm and guided her tenderly through the throng. Scarcely had they gone a hundred yards, when they met the 'smairt-like deemie', busy as usual in her quest.

One single head-to-toe glance at the Turk's companion brought a smile to the city girl's lips and, as she passed the Turk, she whispered in a remarkably accurate Buchan accent, possibly learned from a fairmer at the Hielan Show, 'I tellt ye, Jock! I tellt ye that ye widna get verra muckle for a powen!'

227

Beldie's Maik

It was a glorious summer evening in the late twenties, the third Saturday in July to be precise, and the granite walls of the buildings on the north side of the Broadgate were warm from the unbroken sunshine of the long sultry day. Now the sun's rays were somewhat tempered by the haze of reek from the kippering kilns, a haze which shrouded the whole town in such windless weather. Not an unpleasant odour, that of kipper reek.

'Isn't it close the nicht?' said some.

'Aye! Gey smuchty!' was the reply.

The Salvation Army open-air meeting was in full swing, and an attentive audience of some two hundred listened to the bright music and song from a ring of around forty ardent Salvationists. 'I need no other argument, I have no other plea. It is enough that Jesus died, and that He died for me.' was the theme of their song. Real old-fashioned, blood-and-fire, evangelical stuff.

Very few of the onlookers joined in the singing, mainly because they didn't know the words, and besides, it's not everybody that's at ease singing to the music of tooteroos, and in the street at that.

The congregation formed a most unusual throng of diverse languages and customs, their common bond their fisher calling and their liking for the band. A really astute observer could quite easily have pin-pointed each man's home port from the pattern on his home-knitted jersey. The Hielanmen, who were actually from the Outer Hebrides, had two, or maybe three brightly coloured buttons on the left side of their jersey collars, brilliant red or azure blue the favourite shades. Gaelic was their native tongue, and they used it freely when they were together. East-coasters' buttons were always black, and their speech was a rough-cut mixture of Scots dialects. Practically every village from Avoch to Berwick was represented on the Broadgate that evening and again, a keen ear could have traced a man's origins from the subtle inflections in his voice. The natives of Auch (Avoch) on the Black Isle had indeed a language of their own.

Most of the men were simply passing an hour or so until their wives or lasses would be released from the gutting-yards, for there had been a heavy landing of herring that day and the women were working late. A week-end at home during the herring season was something to be dreamed about; it could never be a reality. Lucky indeed, the local men, who could take their wives and bairns out for strawberries and cream on a Saturday night.

And then there were the Dutchmen, all in black, whereas the Scots wore navy blue. Quiet, decent men, the Dutchmen, broad in the beam and stoutly built like their luggers which lay at anchor in the Bay. These staunch Presbyterians had rowed ashore in their smaa-boats to spend an evening in the town; and how they loved to hear the Army! Among them there were several boys of school age, the envy of the local lads, for here were boys of our own age at sea with their das, in a foreign port, and with wooden shoes forbye. It jist wisna fair. Ye could aye pick oot the Dutchmen by their pleasant smell of scented tobacco and fried herring!

To complete the congregation, a bourachie o local bairns kept bizzin aboot like bum-bees; safe as ye like, for traffic was a thing unknown. Cars! What on earth were cars? Very informal indeed, the Army open-air!

Among the listeners was Beldie, a lass in her early twenties, neat an clean in hersel, but so shabby in her attire that she was verra near orra. Before her, she had an aal battered coach (pram) wherein sat twaa bairns, nae jist ower clean, while a third loon clung to her skirt, sookin 'is thoom. If every picture tells a story, then Beldie's was that of poverty. Fine did she ken far her man wis. In the pub for sure. And he wid come hame at nicht athoot a copper.

Bill had faan oot wi's skipper in the middle o the week an had left his ship, so, that mornin at the office, he had gotten only half a week's wages. This he had keepit till himsel for booze, an he wid come hame sometime, clean skint! Fine did Beldie ken aa that, jist as she kent that there wis naething in the hoose t' gie the bairns. But wid she say a wrang word aboot Bill? Nivver!

Came collection-time, and a few lassies in Army bonnets mingled with the audience, rattling the coins in their tins as they went. One such lassie made as if she would by-pass Beldie, but Beldie widna hear o't. It was, 'Here ye are, my quine!' and into the tin went Beldie's worldly goods, one solitary maik (half-penny).

Daft, think ye? Aye, surely.

A few minutes later, the band struck up a lively tune, and the Army marched briskly up the brae, followed by a motley straggle o raggit bairns. Oh what fun to follow the band!

There wis naething left noo for Beldie but t' ging awaa hame, but first, she wid cry tee an see her father an mither. Fine did her father ken Beldie's sorras. Faa didna? An sair wis 'is hairt.

'Hiv ye onything in the hoose avaa, my quine?'

'Naething avaa, Da, naething avaa!'

'Weel, lass, we canna gie ye ony siller, but at least the bairns'll get a piece here!'

And that was exactly what they got, loaf an seerip, an hungrily they devoured it, afore Beldie left for hame.

Noo than, atween her father's hoose an her ain hame Beldie met her uncle, a weeda man, a droll hare that had nivver been kent t' gie onybody onything aa his days. A quaet man but grippy, grippy. Ye ken the wye o't.

But, this nicht, fin he saw Beldie wi the drawn face, an the bairns trying t' lick the verra hinmist mealicks o loaf aff their fingers, he steed up wi her an said, 'Here's a something t' yersel, lass. Something t' see ye ower the week-end.' Fine did he ken Beldie's sorras. Faa didna?

Nae till her uncle wis hine alang the road did Beldie daar look at the coin thrust into her hand. She could hardly believe fit she saw. A hale half-croon! A complete fortin, an fae him especially!

She wid need milk, so she ran hame for her flagon, for in those days, ye didna get milk in bottles. She wid need her time, for the shops wid shut at eicht o'clock, an she couldna mak muckle speed wi the bairns. But Beldie made it!

At the butcher's she got a bit bilin beef an vegetables for broth, an a puckly sassidges forbye. In the little dairy shoppie she got milk, an sugar, an tay. Twaa plain loafs, an a great muckle pyoke o broken biscuits, an boys, she verra near forgot t' get tatties. Syne, best o't aa, maybe, the bairns got a sweetie!

The hale apothic gid inower the coach, an jist as she cam oot o the dairy, the curfew bells in the Toonhoose began their eicht o'clock chime. Ony langer, an she wid ha been ower late!

It wis a different Beldie that took the road hame. She seemed t' be lifted up. Mait for a day or twaa, fit a blessin! She even managed to hum a tune she had heard the Army playin.

But still, boys, the day wisna deen, for, alang the road a bittie, Beldie met a spinster cousin, a soor, lonely kind o woman whose weekly practice wis t' tak t' the cemetery a little rooser t' water the flooers on her mither's grave. Fine did she ken Beldie's throwe-come. Faa didna? But little did she care! Beldie should ha heen mair sense in the first place! Bill? Wah, wah!

An yet, fin she saw Beldie's smilin face, fin she saw the laden coach wi the bairns clocherin an sneezin at sherbet-dab, she couldna help saying, 'Beldie, my quine, it's a pleesure t' meet ye. Ye're the first happy an contintit face I've seen the nicht. Here's a something t' yersel!' And into Beldie's han she shivved a twaa-shillin bit. Beldie's cup wisna full; it wis rinnin ower!

Noo, maybe ye're thinkin that this is a religious tear-jerker o a story. It wis nivver meant t' be that. Ye see, the truth aye tells twice.

'Weel!' ye micht say, 'I canna see onybody gettin aa that mait for half-a-croon!' In the twenties ye could! Nae bother avaa. Ye see, the powen wis worth something in yon days.

An fit gars ye dibber-dabber aboot the half-croon, onywye? Did she nae get the hale lot for a maik?

Beldie thinks she did!

Hilly's Pension

It took me quite a while to get really close to Hilly, but that was entirely Hilly's blame, for he was forever roarin an bullyin about something or other. Even when he was simply commenting on the weather, he made more noise than I could make with a loud-hailer and, when the weather didn't suit him, his voice was like the trump of doom.

When I first met Hilly, I got the impression that his belligerent tone was the direct result of his taking umbrage that I, a stranger, should have the temerity to trespass on his ground at all. As time went on, however, I perceived that he addressed the world in general in the same blustering fashion, and this made him, in my eyes, an uncouth loudmouth, a bag of wind. Then, quite by accident, I overheard him speaking to his little, orphaned grand-daughter in tones that would have shamed a cushie doo. There was a hidden tenderness about the man, a something completely at odds with his warlike utterances. Was it possible that Hilly was a loving, caring man, afraid that the world might discover that fact?

As was to be expected, Hilly soon discovered that I was from the sea and, from that day, his bark wasn't quite as fierce, his whole attitude a trifle softer. Mind you, it was a slow, slow thaw, but we did eventually become quite friendly. The last of the ice was completely shattered the year that Hilly had his bumper crop of Golden Wonders. Whether or not he had a bigger crop than he was legally entitled to have, I simply don't know. That was none of my business. But he did seem to have an embarrassment of riches, some of which he was anxious to be rid of, without actually throwing them away. And in me he found a friend indeed, for I could dispose of a considerable amount of Goldies among the fisher folk who, as everybody knows, are gey fashious aboot tatties. Mony's the bag o Goldies that I bought at Hilly's; terms strictly cash! And, should I call at the farm in his absence, I was at liberty to help myself from the tattie shed, and 'leave the siller in yon tinnie that's on the easin o the waa.' On no account was I to give the siller to Mrs Hilly. That too, was none of my business, but I did discover that, with this 'kitty' in the tinnie, Hilly bought surprise gifts for the bairn. You see, the tinnie stood on top of a mail-order catalogue whose pages were immaculate, apart from the 'Children's Gift' section. There the pages were filthy, and a few inky crosses opposite certain items betrayed Hilly's secret. I'm sure nobody knew of this side to Hilly, and certainly nobody heard of it from me. Mrs Hilly did once mention to me that, 'He aye winners faa the Hell's this that's aye sennin presents t' oor bairn!' She leuch, quaet kind, then she says, 'He surely thinks I'm a feel, but I jist lat him be.'

Came the day when, over a fly-cup, Hilly asked if I knew anything about sailing-ships. I had to confess that, apart from what I had read, I knew very little indeed, whereupon he took me ben the hoose to a spare room which had been turned into a sort of study. The walls could scarcely be seen for the beautiful paintings and photographs of the China clippers, the wonderfully graceful ships which carried great cargoes of tea from the Far East. *Cutty Sark* and *Thermopylae* were well to the fore, and in a bonny rosewood book-case a profusion of beautifully bound books with gold lettering took the eye. Every one of these volumes had to do with sailing ships and their history. So this was Hilly's secret passion! Strange hobby for a hill farmer who had never been afloat in his life.

Were I to mention a ship's name, Hilly could tell where and when she was built, with details of any subsequent changes in ownership or nationality. From memory, he could give me the precise position of the *Cutty Sark* when she was dismasted in a storm in the Roaring Forties and, along with that, he could name the Captain and the two apprentices who were on watch at the time. Hilly was a walking encyclopaedia on the era of the wind-jammers and, strangely enough, a very quiet-spoken man at the same time.

I managed to tell Hilly how a wind-jammer, on shipping a great sea over the stern, filling the decks level with the tops of the bulwarks, could have up to 1500

231

tons of water on her deck. I also managed to tell him that the wind-jammers were not all ships, for a ship is 'A three-masted sailing vessel, square rigged on all three.' He was simply delighted at receiving this information, which he had apparently missed in his reading. No, I'm not a fountain of knowledge on that or any other subject. The two 'nuggets' which I passed on to Hilly were simply part of the heterogeneous mass of useless facts which clutter my memory. I'm just like you — I could easily be Mastermind if only Magnusson would ask the proper questions.

Despite his vast store of knowledge, Hilly had never heard of the clipper Captain who was a stickler for Divine Service on a Sunday morning. While it wasn't compulsory, most of the crew, as their duties permitted, would gather on the after deck to hear the Captain read a portion of Scripture before engaging in sincere and earnest prayer. This was a pleasant break in the awful monotony of a voyage which could take four months. Now, as long as the weather was warm and kind, the Captain had a substantial and attentive audience but, as the ship reached ever further south toward colder climes, the congregation dwindled steadily, until only one worshipper turned up. That morning, in showers of hail and sleet, the service was unusually brief. Then the Captain invited his lone disciple into his stateroom and gave him a 'hale tumbler o fuskie'. Consternation reigned in the fo'c'sle when the wanderer returned, for the smell of spirits on his breath aroused fierce longings in the hearts of seamen who hadn't savoured such an aroma for months.

Needless to say, on the following Sunday the Service was a packed house, even though icicles hung from the rigging. But there was no welcome stirrup cup to cheer the weary mariners on the way back to their quarters. As the Captain was about to disappear below, an aggrieved voice cried, 'Is there nae gaan t' be a drappie the day, Captain, Sir?'

'No!' says the skipper, 'Nae even the smell o a drappie! An if it's last week that's botherin ye, let me tell ye that last Sunday wis Communion Sunday!'

'Fit wis the ship's name?' says Hilly, mesmerised.

'I canna mine that,' says I, 'but the skipper wis a McKay fae Portsoy, an the chiel that got the drink wis a Coull fae Portgordon.'

'I wid say that proves the truth o the story!' says Hilly, lauchin.

Then cam the day when, in passing, I noticed that somebody had howkit oot a foon for a new hoose on a bit roch grun nae far fae Hilly's hoose, so I called in to see him.

'Are ye gettin folk t' bide aside ye?' says I.

'Na, na!' says he, 'That hoose is for me an the hen!' He nivver said naething aboot the bairn, but I assumed that she was included. 'I'm retirin this year, so I thocht I'd mak some eese o yon grun. It hisna been ony eese for a lang time noo. But man, I'm haein an affa job gettin the Pension. Ye see, I wis born on Boxin Day, but it wis weel into January afore my father could get into the toon t' register my birth, there wis that muckle snaa at the time. Apparently somebody made a mistak wi my birth certificate, for it's a hale year wrang. I'm tellt I've a hale year t' wyte yet. They jist winna listen t' me avaa, unless I can get witnesses t' prove them wrang. Faar's a man o my age gaan t' get witnesses t' prove his date o birth?'

'Ye're nae needin witnesses!' says I. 'A certificate for the 26th o December, if it's made oot in January, maun refer t' the year afore, surely!'

'I've somebody workin on that noo,' says he. 'I'm tellin ye, naething on earth'll stop me fae gettin that pension. I'm nae wytin a hale 'ear for naebody!' Hilly was back to his former roarin self again.

I wished him the best of luck and, a few nights later, he phoned me with the glad tidings that the mistake in the old records had been discovered, and he would, after all, get his pension. 'But it'll tak them a meentie t' sort aathing oot!'

'Fine,' says I, 'Jist gran! I'll be up some day neist wik for a puckle mair tatties. Is the tinnie aye on the go?'

'Oh, aye!' says he, 'Aye on the go. If I'm nae aboot, ye ken fit t' dee. But nivver say boo, nivver say boo!'

When I did get around to calling for my tatties, Hilly wisna t' be seen.

'Och!' says I t' mysel, 'He's likely awaa seein aboot 'is pension.' And I took my tatties as before.

But, boys, there wis nae tin, an there wis nae catalogue. Hilly wis surely nae weel, so I made for the hoose an cried in at the door, 'Faar's the man the day, that he's nae shoutin an roarin? Is he lyin?'

'Oh, aye!' says her ain sel, 'Awyte he's lyin. Lyin ben the hoose in's coffin!'

Boys, oh boys, ye nivver ken!

Me? I put the tatties back in the shed an nivver said boo, nivver said boo.

But I grat a bittie on the road hame.

The Chancer

Solo was a life-long member of that illustrious band of fishermen known as the 'Chancers', or the 'Chance Shot' brigade; a sort of necessary evil in the fisher communities. It is quite possible that their title varied from port to port, but I'm sure that every port had its quota of such characters, the lads who were never very long in the same ship although, at the same time, they were never very long idle. In these fellas, the skippers had a sort of reservoir of casual labour which had its unofficial headquarters at the Lazy Dyke. It would not be uncharitable to call them birds of passage, here today and gone tomorrow, unwilling to be bound by any local customs or usages. (There were no rules and regulations.)

Now, having said that, I should point out that, among the chancers there were some good hands whose only apparent fault was their roving disposition. There were others who were poor hands at their trade, and would never be any better. Then there were those who were just downright lazy, and they, too, would never be any better. I once heard a Fifer describe the latter category as 'one-gallus lads', and I thought the title was rather apt. It also proved the point that the chancer is a ubiquitous species, both ashore and afloat.

Solo, however, belonged to neither category. He was something of a 'one off' job in that he was such a likeable bloke. Any skipper looking for a man to fill a gap in his crew counted himself rather fortunate if he managed to enlist Solo, on the strict understanding that the limit of his stay would be one week. Less than that, maybe, but certainly never longer. You know, the vacancies caused by bereavement, or sickness, or whatever. And, quite often, Solo was better than the man he replaced.

Solo acquired his nickname in the 'thirties, when open-air gambling schools were so common. Groups of unemployed youths would gather in sheltered, secluded spots where look-outs could be posted to warn of any arrival of the police, and all sorts of card games took place. Ditto with bingo (housey-housey) which, at that time, was strictly illegal. Well do I remember the day when three little boys, playing on a raft of planks and oil-drums in the old dry dock, met their fate. The raft had overturned in some three feet of water, and only one of the boys managed to reach the steps. Panic-stricken, the poor lad ran all the way home to tell his mother, unaware that, less than fifty yards away, behind the dyke, some forty men were playing 'housey'. Sad to say, help came much too late. Such, they say, is life.

Elsie Jean, Solo's dear wife, saw to it that he was always clean and tidy, whether he was in or out of a berth. She was, I believe, a native of the Sea-toon o Cullen, where cleanliness is, literally, next to godliness. If there were any niggling doubts about Solo's willingness to work, there were no doubts whatever about Elsie Jean, for she was a proper human dynamo. Scrubbing, cleaning, gutting herring or mending nets, the deemie wis never idle. Although they had no family, the couple were supremely happy, with only one fly in the ointment: there was no way that Elsie Jean, a staunch Christian, could get Solo to the Kirk. He had no time whatsoever for religion, and wasn't slow to advertise the fact.

Some of the many skippers with whom Solo had sailed would have been both willing and able to discuss with him Christ's Sermon on the Mount, or the teaching of the Apostle Paul in any of the Epistles, but Solo simply wasn't interested. He would rather speak to the motion that all boat-owners, skippers, and men-wi-gear were blasted Capitalists, 'sookin the hired men's bleed!' Such an unorthodox dogma convinced most skippers that Solo wis 'jist a Bolsheevick!'

A born philosopher, Solo would not willingly take a temporary berth with a skipper who was doing well, simply because such a man was certain to be due for a 'duff' week. Conversely, a skipper who wasn't doing well at all was considered a safe bet. Under this personal gambling system, Solo had sailed with most of the local skippers and, on the whole, he did quite well, albeit he was 'jist a hired man'.

Like so many others of his generation, Solo chewed Bogie Roll; a filthy habit which Elsie Jean simply wouldn't tolerate in the house. You see, those who chew tobacco have an unbelievable amount of saliva to dispose of, so they are not the best of company in the domestic world. Thus Solo was obliged to pursue his obnoxious habit in the great outdoors, where he could spit to his heart's content. Sorry! I misrepresent the man. Solo never spat; he simply ejected, from between his teeth, a long, needle-thin jet of dark brown fluid. Fsssssssst! His aim was deadly, and I have seen him extinguish a candle at the first shot from ten feet away. Of course, that was no redeeming feature!

I have often heard it said that each one of us has some special talent. It may or may not be dormant, but nevertheless, we've all got a something. Well, Solo's special gift lay in his ability to remove a herring scale from a buddy's eye.

The herring scale can be a terrible irritant to the human eye. It is transparent when wet, so it becomes invisible on the eyeball. Its very nature makes it cling, so it is extremely difficult to remove, but Solo knew how to do the trick! He would go 'Fsssssst', then he would temporarily remove the 'chaa' from his cheek prior to laying the patient flat on his back. Then, all ready for action, Dr Solo would use his sophisticated instruments (fore-finger and thumb), to open wide the afflicted eye which he proceeded to wipe clean with his tongue. Primitive? Well, maybe a wee bittie! Efficacious? In every case! But, oh boys, the tongue felt like a file, an the 'bacca bree stung like fire for a whilie. Still, that was but a slight affliction.

Another chap, whom I know very well, had a similar cure; but, instead of his tongue, he used the well-nibbled end of a match. Nae bother avaa! An him wi fingers like mealy puddens, tee! These are the times when you must have great faith in your fellow slave, whether he chaws tobacca or no!

Came the joyous day in Elsie Jean's life, when she finally managed to get her man to the Kirk, for the first time in his life. Trim and spruce in his best go-ashores, he gid into the seat afore Elsie Jean (nae mainners, ye see), an sat close to the waa, wi's legs hard against the het pipes, an his heid hard against the plaister. But, boys-o-boys, he forgot to tak the chaa oot o's mou. Verra seen he wis needin t' 'Fsssssst', but far could he 'Fsssssst' in the kirk? Doon the back o the pipes, far else?

Kirk or oan kirk, Elsie Jean fell oot on him.

'Ye fool, orra, slivvery, Blue Toon tink! Div ye nae ken ye're in the Lord's Hoose? Try that again, an I'll feenish ye. Ye're nae gaan t' afront me!'

Sensing that this was no idle threat, Solo got the chaa into his hankie, and stowed it in his pooch.

Now, in yon days, in yon Kirk, the offering wis taken up in great muckle open pewter plates, not in velvet baggies, as is the present custom. As it happened, Solo was the very first to have the empty plate offered to him, then, looking the steward straight in the eye, he says, quaet-kind.

'I'm nae needin that, freen! I'm stoppit spittin noo!'

I miss him at the Lazy Dyke! The chancer!

235

West Coast Pirates

From Campbeltown and Carradale and Tarbert on Loch Fyne and from Girvan and The Maidens on the Ayrshire coast they came. Through the Forth-and-Clyde canal they came to raid the Firth of Forth, these pirates from the west. Under the great Forth Bridge they sped on the ebb tide, and like a swarm of locusts they made for that stretch of water which lies between Elie Ness and Fife Ness, a rectangle of sea comprising the waters from half-a-mile to some four miles from the shore; the fringe of gold on the beggar's mantle.

For many, many years prior to the Hitler war, shoals of herring, dense at times, had sought these waters in February, March and April. We called them 'winter herrin' but, before the shoals grew really dense, it was really Spring and, very shortly, the herring would seek shallow water to spawn before disappearing for another year.

This, then, was the treasure sought by the armada from the west. They had every right to be there, those rascals with the peculiar registration letters, CN (Campbeltown), TT (Tarbert) and BA (Ballantrae) on the Ayrshire coast. They were simply Scottish fishermen, seeking a share of Scottish herring but, as soon as they rounded Elie Ness, they met a wave of hostility which is hard to understand. How the St Monans men hated the ring-netters from the west! They would finish the winter herrin; they would sweep the Firth clean, with their murderous nets! They should be completely banned! In fact the ill-will grew so strong that the St Monans men refused to allow the 'ringers' drinking-water, so the West-coasters went to Anstruther, where a more liberal attitude prevailed. Then the St Monans men fell out with the 'Enster' men, just as they had fallen out with the Pittenweem men, for refusing to refuse water and other commodities to the strangers. There were some really ugly scenes, but gradually tempers cooled, although the St Monans men never really lost their ill-will towards the 'pirates'. Indeed they set about collecting a great deal of hard evidence against the West-coasters, very hard evidence indeed, for it consisted mainly of lumps of lead, and reels of piano-wire.

You see, there's a world of difference between drift-net and ring-net fishing. The drift-net boats would shoot their long curtain of nets (about 40 nets) and lie for an hour or two, in the hope that herring would swim into the meshes. Then they would haul in the nets, clean them out and shoot them again somewhere else, if the first haul had been unsuccessful. Indeed, sometimes the nets were hauled three times without success. It was a slow, laborious, haphazard method of fishing, for no matter what happened, the herring HAD to swim into the trap.

The ring-net was a different Muggie Rennie altogether, in that it required a heavy spot, or shoal of fish which it could 'ring' or encircle. Once such a spot had been found and rung, the net was slowly drawn in, until a great seething mass of herring was imprisoned alongside the boat, then the process of 'brailing' began. The brailer was a huge, immensely strong butterfly-net affair on the end of a stout pole which was thrust down into the living mass. Then the great iron ring at the

236

mouth of the brailer was dragged on board and jammed just inside the bulwark, a rope from the winch to the bottom of the bag took the strain, and 'Hey-presto', a cran or two of herring were 'cowpit inower' onto the deck, where they flooded in a ripple of silver into the hold. The process was repeated until the net was empty; then, if necessary, another ring would be made.

Now, how did these highly efficient fishers locate the spots or shoals? Well, every boat (they always worked in pairs) had a 'feeler', a lump of lead roughly pear-shaped, which was towed slowly along, close to the sea-bed on the end of a long reel of piano-wire, usually double. The man who sat in the stern holding the wire could feel the herring strike the wire; he could tell whether the fish were in quantity or not, and if the wire encountered a dense shoal, the wire would be very difficult to hold. In those days, when sonar, echo-sounders and fish-finders were utterly unknown, wire feeler was a simple but effective tool. Now, in such congested waters, with boats from near and far spread all over the place, it was inevitable that some of the lead sinkers would foul the drift-nets, some of which were torn as a result. Now any drift-net man finding a 'feeler' in his nets could have kept it as a feeler for his own use; but no! Most of the offending objects were taken ashore to swell the mountain of lead which was being stored as vital evidence of the havoc wrought by the ringers. Nothing ever came of that lot; the war saw to that.

For ten winters, prior to the war, we fished the Firth in our family forty-footer, *Sparkling Star*. St Monans was our base, not because we liked the harbour (which was terrible), but simply because we had some life-long friends there. Every family had its own erection of spars for the drying of nets, either in the back-yard or up on the 'Mare' which was a veritable forest of old masts. Most families had a barra for taking torn nets up fae the shore an takkin hale nets doon. Indeed, a barra was a most acceptable wedding gift! Torn nets there were in plenty, most of the damage being caused by the great steamers leaving Methil with cargoes of coal. A steamer's propeller can make a fearsome mess of a net, and usually takes away a great part of the sheet. The patch required for the repair was, in St Monans parlance 'net-bit', and was as a rule handled by the women-folk. So expert were they that their men scarcely had to handle a net at all, apart from the shooting and hauling. In fact that was about the only time some of the men saw nets at all. Lucky, lucky chaps awyte!

Now, these grand fellas had a custom whose marra I have never seen anywhere else. Fishermen of my generation (and older) would normally pace to-and-fro, side by side as they conversed on the pier, but on the Middle Pier at St Monans they would form little groups of four, all facing inwards, and step back-and-fore. Thus one walked backwards while his oppo stepped forwards, and the men at each side took a few steps sideways, every man with his hands deep in his pockets. At regular intervals the group would move 'one notch' to the right so that everyone got a change of step. No doubt they were unaware that I, a stranger found the practice completely fascinating and absolutely hilarious! Try it sometime and see.

The old men of the village took a deep, kindly interest in our welfare. We were the strangers within their gates and as such we were accorded the utmost civility and the warmest of hospitality. The spick-and-span appearance of these 'auld yins' proclaimed that loving care was in bountiful supply. Of course, they weren't really strangers at all, for they kent mair o my ain toonsfolk than I did mysel. Hadn't they been gaun t' the 'Drave' (the summer herring fishing) for as long as they could remember? Fine did they ken the ancestry of every one of us, for had they not finished at 'Yermuth' with our fathers? Then they would reminisce how, in the distant past a 'fairmer fae Kingsbarns wid come roond the fishin villages on 'is horse, ringin a bell an shoutin, 'There's herr'n i' the Hakes! There's herr'n i' the Hakes!' Now, the Hakes is a stretch of water just below Kingsbarns so it is actually in the Firth of Tay, and not in the Forth at all. Nevertheless, every year towards the close of the season, the herring came there in unbelievable numbers, and it was the frantic activity of the sea-birds that told the fairmer there was 'Herr'n i' the Hakes'. And they could be jist like a dyke!

I remember vividly one particular night of very dense fog; it must have been thick indeed, for we were the only boat to put gear in the water that night. By making a wide detour to ensure that we were well clear of the North Carr light-ship and dangerous reef which it marked, we literally groped our way into shallow water near Kingsbarns. In those days aids to navigation were unknown, so it was more or less guess-work, or shooting blind. Well, in any case, a bonny clear mornin found us hauling a 'richt heavy strag' from the ten nets we had anchored. It was murderous work for five men (the sixth was in the little wheel-house, steaming the boat ahead as required), but we were young and fit and very hungry for herrin. The very last net was a richt sair fecht, hauling up to the anchor through a strong tide, so we hailed the *Crest* (PD9) which was making empty-handed for port. By golly, the Boddamers didna tak lang t' lift that anchor, then they yokit t' haul the net fae the ither end, so that the twaa boaties lay thegither in the calm, and twaa crews were haulin at the same net. I reckon there wis ten cran in yon net; she wis nivver ony mair eese. Fifty-seven cran we landed that day, oot o ten shallow nets, athoot the fower-an-a-half cran that the *Crest* got. An sic a price we got, tee! Forty-twaa shillins the cran! That's twaa powen ten pence, nooadays. Surely I've made a mistak somewye, 'cos ye'll pey five bob for a kipper noo!

But freen, we've gotten wannert awaa fae the subject, tho that's naething new. Faar's the herrin noo? 'Och,' says you, 'they're awaa in half-cran Klondyke boxes to Altona.' Fine div ee ken that's nae fit I mean! Faar's the herrin noo? Fit wye is't that there hisna been a herrin seen in the Firth nor the Hakes since the middle o the war? Wis't the ring-nets that feenished the Firth?

I jist dinna ken, but I'll tell ye ae thing for sure: the East Neuk o Fife'll nivver be the same athoot the herrin.

A meenit ago, I wis speirin, 'Faar's the herrin?' Noo I'm speirin, 'Faar's the folk?' The herrin didna ging awaa their leen; they took a hale race wi them. 'Fisher villages', did ye say? Weel, faar's the fisher folk?

Mony a time div I ging back t' the East Neuk, through Kingsbarns to Crail syne wast to Cellardyke / Enster an Pittenweem to feenish up in the aal hame, Si Minnins (St Monans). Boys, I likit yon folk!'

I nivver see a fisher face; I nivver hear a fisher word. Oh, I see the fisher hooses still there, but I'm gey feart it's strangers that's in them.

The Fisheries Museum? Aye, surely, at the first o't, but nae noo! It jist gars me greet!

I wid far raither see a fleet o pirates fae the Wast side comin doon ower Elie Ness on a Monday aifterneen!

Nae Dubs Aboot the Door

Great Stuart Street in Peterhead is a narrow, unpretentious cul-de-sac which lies back-to-back with the houses on the south side of Port Henry Road. The street, of whose existence the major part of the town is blissfully unaware, contains nine houses, stoutly built of the local red granite. The houses were built to a standard pattern, with two rooms and a middle closetie downstairs, and two large rooms upstairs. At the rear, each house had a 'back hoosie', brick-built, and back-to-back with that of its next door neighbour. These back-hoosies usually served as washin-hooses, very popular at night with courting couples. Toilets came on the scene many years later, and were always outside, in the back close which afforded barely enough room to swing a cat.

I believe the builder's name was Stuart, and he named the street after himself and also after a famous street in Edinburgh. A private joke, maybe.

But, in any case, apart from official documents, Great Stuart Street has never been accorded its illustrious title. Generations of fisher-folk have called it the Burnie Streetie, simply because its very first occupants were 'Burnies', incomers from the little fishing village of Burnhaven, a straggle of 'butt-an-bens' on the north shore of Invernettie Bay, often called Sandford Bay. In such desperately humble beginnings do so many of today's prosperous fisher-folk have their roots. I use the word 'desperately' quite deliberately, for in Burnhaven poverty was the name of the game, and abject poverty at that. Oh, I know that today's race have a jolly good laugh at some of the tales about the Burnhaven days; they seem to think that such conditions are a figment of older folk's minds but such is not the case, and for this I have as witness the words of my own father, who was born and bred a Burnie.

Take a good look at your eleven-year-old son, if you have one; take a look at any eleven-year-old boy, and tell me how you would rate his chances as cook for eight men on a sail-boat, and away from home, too! That's exactly what my father had to do, as the eldest of a family of nine.

In those days, the fishing boats carried their beef with them, salted into casks, when they went to Shetland. As cook, it was my father's job to take from the cask sufficient beef for the dinner and hang it over-side to steep. The sea water, though salty itself, would still remove most of the salt from the meat. Well, one day in

239

Lerwick, whether by accident or not, the string was cut, with the result that the skipper gave my father a thrashing because there was 'nae beef'.

Well do I remember the story of one of my father's chums who had torn his only pair o breeks so often that there 'wis naething left t' hud the shewin'. As a last resort, his widowed mother shewed a square o claith t' the heid-band o the breeks an jist lat the flap hing lowse! As you might expect, the ither loons wid creep up at his back to lift the flap and cry, 'Peep!' The peer loon wis a sittin target for a byename, so they caaed him the Flapper. A few years later, the same Flapper stowed away to Canada and did very well in the Hudson Bay Company. No doubt his spell with the flap had hardened him off for the Arctic.

Then there was the unforgettable day when a whaling-ship, homeward bound for Dundee, hailed a ripper-boatie off Buchan Ness. Would they take a message ashore? Aye, surely. Then the great ship's Captain handed my father, a loon in the boatie, a sum of money and a written message, with the request that he should go as soon as possible to the Post Office and send a telegram to the owners, to appraise them of the vessel's arrival on the morrow. A hale shillin! And even after paying for the telegram there was a saxpence left! It wis a lang time afore he saw anither een.

Burnhaven had no proper harbour, so the Burnies had to draw their boats up on a stony beach, enlisting all the available women and bairns to help in the laborious task. Finally, however, it became obvious that the days of the small sailing-boats were over. Bigger, heavier boats were required, and you couldn't draw these up on a beach. There was even word of such things as steam-drifters that wouldn't need sails at all. Such craft would require to be kept afloat in a proper harbour, so the exodus to Peterhead began.

There must have been many a tear when it came to leaving the village with its earthen-floored cottages where they had reared their families, cottages whose floors had been regularly spread with clean sand, and just as regularly swept bare, ready for a fresh sanding. Of course, there had been the occasional 'fleer-o-canvas', when the boat had required a new sail and the old one had been taken home to make a fine floor-covering. There, surely, is the origin of the term 'canvas', the fisher (and country) word for linoleum, still a thing of the future. There must have been hairts sair at leaving the little Congregational Chapel where they had worshipped so long; and yet it must have been a great adventure, especially for the youngsters, to whom Peterhead was a 'great muckle toon'.

Like most small fishing communities, Burnhaven had its 'characters', not all of whom lived to see the exodus, but whose profound sayings were handed down by oral tradition for many years, until finally they have been lost. Chief of these old personalities was Deevlick, a mixture of seer-cum-anointed-leear who made some remarkable predictions, some of which came to pass. His son, Deevlick's Willie, was a character in his own right. I knew him quite well when he lived in this town, a little mannie with phenomenal physical strength, and a forthright manner of speech liberally sprinkled with 'Foo? I'll tell ye foo!' He always addressed me as 'Cousin', and boys, he wis a bonny leear!

Now, entirely because of such characters, the Burnie race as a whole has been

240

credited with the gift of mixing truth with fiction so skilfully that a buddy nivver kens far they are wi them. They jist canna help it.

Is this then actually the case? That's a leading question; jist lat's say that some are better at it than ithers.

So, family by family the Burnies sattled in the Blue Toon. Those who came to the Burnie Streetie must have looked on their new homes as palaces. 'Fit? Twaa storey hooses wi widden fleers an nae dubs at the door?'

But the Streetie couldna tak them aa, so they spread far an wide through the toon, finding accommodation where they could. Some took to the Queenie, ithers to the Roanheids, while a goodly number settled in the Sooth Bay area, not very far from the present Life-boat shed.

The Burnies were in at the start of the steam-drifter era; forsaking the old ripper and smaa-line, they became remarkably good herring-and-great-line fishermen. Where a small tarred shed had sufficed for the storage of a few haddock lines, the Burnies now required more spacious accommodation for fleets of herring nets and huge baskets of heavy lines, to say nothing of the coils of tarry rope required by a herring fleet. Such heavy gear was kept in stores near the harbour, but the herring nets themselves were stored at home.

There now appeared on the scene a new breed of fishermen, the 'men wi gear'. In the herring drifters, the 'clear baabees', that which was left after all expenses had been paid, was divided into three roughly equal parts: the boat's share, the nets' share and the crew's share. The boat's share of course went to the owners, of whom there could be quite a number, usually including the skipper. The nets' share went to those who owned the nets, usually the skipper and two or three crew members. Then there were the hired men, who got a share for their labour only. A great many hired men aspired to become men-wi-gear, for as a general rule, a man with a sixth of nets earned two shares, one for his labour and one for his nets. An owner/man-wi-gear could do quite well, depending to a great extent on how big his share of nets was. Complicated? It was actually a sort of caste system, for when a fella became a man-wi-gear he thought he was a cut above the hired man. And so he was, actually, in the pecking order. Hence the mythical tale that a certain life-boat crew, going alongside a drifter in distress, heard a self-important voice say, 'Men-wi-gear first, noo, men-wi-gear first!'

One old custom did the Burnies strictly observe. When a really close relative of the skipper died, the ship's white water-line was painted blue. A not-so-close relative merited only a blue 'mouth-piece' below the white at the fore end. When did you last see a blue water-line?

Noo, fit aboot the female o the species? Weel, fin she got richt waas t' paper, she papered them an varnished the paper. Some o the paper's still on the waas, cos it's near impossible t' shift! Fin she got her new fleer o canvas, she varnished that, an fin she got a fine black grate wi twaa binks an an oven, she black-leaded it, an scoured the clear bits till they shone like silver. She became a first-class herring gutter and a top-notch net-mender, and she nivver had a holiday in her life.

For many years, after the fisher-folk left it, Burnhaven was a community of decent, hard-working country-folk and tradesmen, but gradually these people too moved on, in search of better things. The old fisher houses became roofless, weed-grown ruins, until at the end the remnants of the place were simply a haunt for squatters. Now there is not a single vestige remaining, and I fear it is verily possible that we'll lose even the very name.

Noo, fit aboot the Burnies' descendants? 'Fit? Twaa storey hooses wi widden fleers, an nae dubs aboot the door?' It is perfectly plain that, like the Children of Israel, they have come a long, long way from even that Mount Pisgah of progress.

But I'll tell ye ae thing — they're still the bonniest leears in Buchan, some better at it than ithers!

Can the Ethiopian change his skin, or the leopard his spots? (Jeremiah 13:23.)

The Haddock Rash

It was just last week, the first week of August, 1985, and I was admiring a bonny new boat moored about a hundred yards or so from my own front door. She was new and she was bonny at the same time, a combination somewhat rare in this modern world. To my mind, some of the latest vessels, and in particular a few of timber construction, are positively hideous. They are not merely broad in the beam; they are actually obese. They are not simply high-wooded; they are unnaturally lofty, and the result leaves me with a faint suspicion that somehow these boats were launched minus 25 or 30 feet of their length. Whatever the considerations that prescribed such dimensions, beauty was certainly not one of them; but then, maybe I'm old-fashioned.

But this was a bonny boat and an able boat all in one. A Lossie boat? Aye, surely! A study in black-and-white, all ready for sea.

'Let go!' cried the skipper, and I made for the mooring-rope; but I was forestalled by a swack young chiel on the fo'c'sle-head, or whaleback. Leaping lightly onto the quay, he drew from the hip pocket of his jeans a pair of bright orange plastic gloves which he swiftly donned before lowsin the rope.

'Good grief,' says I to myself, 'I've seen aathing noo.' Then I noticed that every visible crew-man was wearing gloves of various colours, and from that I gathered that this is standard practice, and rightly so. Hands which are doing rough work and handling heavy gear should be protected.

Then my thoughts went back in time to my own days at sea, when the use of gloves was unknown. Now, in the hauling of herring nets gloves were taboo, apart from the hauling of cork-rope, where they were at times permissible. But for the men hauling the 'belly' (the sheet) of the net, bare hands were mandatory. Gloved hands simply tore the net to shreds, as did the unforgiveable practice of sticking one's fingers through the meshes. That simply resulted in lacerated fingers and badly holed nets. The secret was to get as much yarn as possible into your fist, keep the net square, and all haul together. Ragnails were common, but 'richt sair hands' were rare.

242

Seine-net fishing was a different kettle of fish, in more ways than one. Herring did not require to be gutted on board, whereas white fish had to be gutted, washed, and iced as soon as possible, especially if they were not to be landed for a few days; and now we meet the fisherman's deadly enemy, the 'Haddock Rash'. You've never heard of it? I'm not surprised.

You see, at a certain season of the year the haddocks were full of spawn, and in the gutting of these 'spawny haddocks' a mixture of spawn and slime would ooze between a fella's fingers, irritating the tender skin. Liberal dipping of the hands in water served to slow down the process slightly, but the end result was inevitably the 'haddock rash' which wasn't a rash at all, but simply the chafing of the skin between the fingers until the skin was non-existent. Now, THAT'S sair hands for ye. And to work day after day with such fingers was sheer hell. The trawlermen were the chief sufferers; they handled great bags of spawny haddocks, they were longer at sea, and they worked really inhuman hours.

Then there were the times when the haddocks 'took their ballast prior to a storm'. This was a false idea that some fishermen had; nevertheless there were times when the haddocks were full of slimy grit which had the same effect as spawn in that it removed the skin and left the 'prood flesh' atween the fingers. Oh, boys, that can be sair, sair. It's a poor, poor life when you must leave your front buttons undone because your fingers can neither fasten nor undo them.

And isn't it a gey sair fecht when, after three or four hours in your bunk you rise to face another twenty-hour day, only to find that your hands are half-shut as if smitten with arthritis, and will remain so until you have urinated on them? Filthy? Crude? Uncivilised? Maybe so, in the lily-white, sophisticated world of dry land, but the sea has never been and never will be a civilised environment. It has no time for prudery or squeamishness, and drastic pains need drastic remedies. Any trawlerman or seine-net-man of the old school will tell you the same, especially those who never knew what it was to wear gloves.

Now, what about our noble brethren, the line men? How did they fare? Theirs was a completely different trade; no tremendous bags of small fish for them. No! They took their great fish on board one by one, dragging them up from dark depths on strong hard lines so tightly laid that they resembled wire.

Now, although its name means 'heavy line', the great-line is not thick enough to afford the human hand a proper grip, so the strain, terrific at times, really falls where the fingers meet the palm of the hand. Hour after hour, day after day of such unnatural strain is bound to take its toll, and the hands become 'aa grippit', resembling arthritic claws. Same affliction as the trawlermen; same temporary early morning treatment; sair, sair hands. The line man's only protection was 'gags' or 'gyaags', circlets of flannel about two inches wide, worn round the hands to improve the grip when the strain was excessive. Then there were the stobs from the great muckle heuks, usually rusty, and the scratches from the teeth of the great fish as they were 'heukit' (taken off the hook). Septic sores are the bane of the line-man's life. 'Beelins an poultices, sair, sair hands awyte'.

The smaa-line men had their own problems. Since their gear was so much lighter, they had less strain on their hands, but smaa-line heuks are exceedingly sharp, and lug-worm bait is notoriously poisonous. So the smaa-boat lads got their fair share o 'futtlie beelins'.

But smaa lines were not always worked from smaa boats. There was a time when drifters from the East coast went smaa-line fishing around Whiten Head and Loch Eriboll, and also in the Minch. A fine canny jobbie, think ye? It was sheer, murderous slavery. Shoot and haul twenty nets for herring bait; cut the herring into thousands of baits; bait and shoot the lines; sleep for two hours (the two watch-keepers would get only one hour apiece); haul the lines and stow away the gutted catch; redd the lines, making good any 'wants' (missing hooks); shoot and haul the nets again; and so on, and on. I am quite certain that any farmer working his horses in such a fashion would have gone to prison, and rightly so. But alas, there are times when human beings count for less than the beasts of the field.

I have a friend in the Broch who could tell you a harrowing story how, one night when his fingers were literally to the bone, the skipper took pity on him and baited his line for him, not because the bones of the poor lad's fingers were actually visible, but simply because the line was being baited too slowly. The poor sufferer was given a different jobbie instead. Belsen, did ye say? A week at that, and ye'll be like a Zombie!

I've forgotten to tell ye that, shortly after the Hitler war, the fishers tried using cotton industrial gloves, but they were not a success. The seams on the insides of the fingers were themselves a serious irritant, and even when they were 'flypit' the cotton absorbed the irritants from the fish and transmitted them to the fingers so we were back to square one. Then plastic gloves made their appearance, but these were so stiff and unyielding that they were almost useless.

Over the years, however, the boffins have developed plastic gloves which are seamless, waterproof and really pliable, jist the verra dunt.

But have we not overlooked one class of fisher? Fit aboot the ripper men? The ripper is a primitive yet effective method of catching codlings without bait. It has been called 'the poor man's friend' or 'the murderer'. It has also been described as 'a lump o leed at ae end, an a feel at the ither'. I prefer to call it 'the Alpha and Omega', the beginning and the end. How many fishermen have started out as mere boys, 'oot for a go at the ripper in a smaa boatie wi an aal mannie'? And how swiftly do the years come full circle so that, in the end, they themselves are the 'aal mannie'? Alpha and Omega are never far apart.

Now it happens that I'm an aal mannie in a smaa boatie tryin t' catch a puckly codlins t' saat an dry for hard fish t' mak hairy tatties. I've discovered that plastic gloves fairly save a buddy's hands fae the chafe o the ripper string (line). But, boys, they're affa dear! I ken the young fishermen buy them by the bundle, but the likes o me could nivver look at that. Oor tattie man says we'll be lucky t' get mait this winter, an I'm thinkin he's richt. Still, I shouldna compleen ower muckle; ye see, I'm gettin my gloves free noo!

'An far wid ye get that?' says you. 'In the hairber!' says I. 'Fifty or sixty pair ony mornin ye like. Aa sizes an colours, floatin, grisly like wi their fingers to the sky, an nine times oot o ten there's nae a thing wrang wi them. Oh, sic a prodigal, wasteful generation! Fancy aa that siller floatin aboot like caff!'

244

But I'd better nae say ower muckle aboot that, either. Ye see, if the young lads wis t' stop bein careless, I'd hae t' buy gloves, an that jist widna dee avaa.

Keep the glovies comin, lads, keep them comin. Jist mine fit the Lord said, lang, lang ago, 'The poor ye have always with you.'

But, if ye're nae ower happy wi that sayin, ye could aye try, 'The Jews is nae aa in Jerusalem!'

Finally, brethren, let me tell you something else. I'm fine acquant wi a chiel that keeps his boatie aside mine, but he disna pick up ony gloves. No, he picks up lemonade bottles. Fancy that now! Aye, and from the sale of these bottles several charities have in turn benefitted to the tune of several hundreds of pounds. Now, that's MAGIC!

Black and White

On any steam drifter the capstan was an indispensible unit of power. Always sited on the fore-deck, slightly to starboard of midships, it was driven by a sturdy little steam engine (twin-cylinder) on its top storey. A system of cog-and-pinion gearing drove the great vertical barrel which took the heavy, tarred bush-rope during the hauling process. Simply by removing a small cog-wheel, one could dispense with the big barrel and drive instead a small horizontal pulley which was used for hoisting out the catch. If ever there was a boon to fishermen, it was the steam capstan, so rugged and reliable that it was often neglected.

Behold now, Duncan, the Turk's driver, busy at the *Meadowsweet*'s capstan as she lay tied to the quay in her home port. Duncan, conscientious sowl, was checking and lubricating the intimmers o the machine, while close-by the Turk and his deck squad were seated on fish-boxes, busily mending holes in the nets, holes which had been 'laid ower' for attention. It was really amazing how such seemingly clumsy fingers could be so adroit with a mending needle.

The proximity of sailing-time was evident from the steadily thickening pall of smoke from the countless funnels, a pall sometimes dense enough to shut out the very sunlight itself.

'I can hear somebody singin hymns somewye,' says Duncan. 'Faa on earth can that be, at this time o day?'

'Faith Mission Pilgrims fae Ireland, I wid think,' says the Turk. 'They come here ilkie summer. I like t' hear them singin.'

'Ye're a queer lot, you fisher folk,' says Duncan, wi a lauch. 'Ye hiv aboot five-an-twinty different sects in the toon aaready, an still ye're nae pleased. Ye surely dinna need a puckle Irishmen t' come here an preach!'

'Ye're richt aboot the sects, Duncan, but the Irish come here o their ain free will, nae because we need them. Mysel, I wid hae aabody aneth ae reef, but them that's aneth ae reef aaready, dinna aye sowder ower weel, so I'm thinkin that t' pit

245

the hale jing-bang thegither wid be jist like a hawker's rebellion. There's mair than ae sect aboord here, freen, so ye'd better lat that flee stick t' the waa.'

'Hiz country folk's nae bothered wi that cairry-on avaa. Ye see, skipper, we hiv jist the wan Kirk, an that dis fine wi aabody.'

'Gran!' says the Turk, 'Jist gran. Noo, if there's jist the ae Kirk, she'll be rale full on a Sunday mornin. Ye wid need t' be awaa early t' get a seat?'

Duncan had no answer to such a body blow.

'Aye-aye, Duncan, fan wis ye last in the kirk?'

'Christmas, skipper.'

'An fan are ye gaan back, Duncan?'

'Christmas, skipper! Ye see, I wis christened in the kirk, I wid like t' be mairried in the kirk, an if I'm spared an weel, I'd like t' be buried oot o the kirk!'

'Weel, ye micht manage that. If ye're spared an weel! Noo, seein that ye're deen wi the caipsan, stand by at yer engine. We'll awaa oot wi the lave.'

The steam drifter could not be handled by remote control; there had to be someone in the engine-room to activate the massive engine as the skipper might require. All signals from the skipper to the chief were transmitted by means of a clanging telegraph. When the vessel had cleared the breakwaters, the skipper would signal 'All Clear' so the chief could come up for a breather if he so wished.

Thus, an hour or so later, we find Duncan in the wheel-house with the Turk.

'Fit like, skipper?' says he. 'I hope ye didna think naething fin I said that you fisher folk wis queer. I've come t' like the fishers, an they're nae aa queer, jist a puckly o them. I think the queerest eens is them that says they're Christians. Fit div ye think, skipper?'

'There's naething sae queer as folk, Duncan, whether they be Christians or Frinch-Canadian Jews.'

Duncan could see that the Turk would not willingly commit himself, so he tried a fresh approach.

'We hiv some gey queer folk in the country places tee, skipper!'

'I'm listenin, Duncan.'

'Weel, we hiv a lad up aside hiz at Povertyknap, an he says he's a Christian, but I dinna think there's a Christian hair in his heid. Oh, he's awaa t' the Kirk ilkie Sunday mornin, him an his wife, wi the horse an gig. But I think there's mair than that till't. Fit div ee think, skipper?'

'I'm listenin, Duncan, I'm listenin.'

'Weel,' continued Duncan, 'this kirk-greedy fairmer's caaed Baldy, an he has the twaa biggest an best fairms in Buchan, I wid say. Aathing grows for Baldy, better than for ither folk, an his kye's aye wydin up t' the udders amon girss. Gran kye they are tee, an I'm sure he has hunners o them! Black-an-fite, ivvery wan o them. Div ye ken onything aboot coos, skipper?'

'Coos?' says the Turk. 'Coos is yon beasts that ye see in the parks. Yon craiturs that we get oor milk fae. They tell me that they're nae aa coos; jist them that has the bagpipes aneth them. Is that richt, Duncan?'

'It's easy seen that ye're fisher, you an yer bagpipes, but ye're richt,' leuch Duncan. 'Noo, iss is fit I wis gaan t' tell ye. Atween Povertyknap an Baldy's place there's a little wee placie that's hardly worth a name; jist a sklyter o roch grun, as Flora Garry says. Gweed kens fit wye the faimly that bides on't gets a livin. It maun be gey han-t'-mou! Sandy, the man himsel disna keep weel avaa; something t' dee wi bein gassed in the trenches, I think. There's a gey puckle days he keeps the loon fae the skweel; in fact he's been in trouble for that, but little difference dis't mak. I doot if Sandy could mak a livin yonner supposin he wis weel. But, mind ye, he's a dour, thrawn, contermashious sod, the same Sandy; he jist winna tak help fae naebody avaa. Mony a time has my ain folk offered t' help, an so has Baldy, but Sandy says he'll manage fine himsel, even fin he's fair stuck.'

'There's folk like that amon the fisher folk, anaa, Duncan,' says the Turk.

'I'm nae neen surprised at that! Div ye ken onything aboot coos gaan dry?'

'Me? No! I dinna ken naething aboot that, Duncan; I'm fisher, ye ken!'

'Weel,' continued Duncan, 'ivvery coo gings dry noo an again; it's a mercy they dinna aa ging dry at the same time, cos fin a coo gings dry, she has nae milk. An that's jist fit happened t' Sandy's coo at a time fin Sandy wis richt nae-weel.'

'Dis Sandy nae hae anither coo?' says the Turk, surprised. 'I thocht he wid surely hae mair than een!'

'Nivver!' says Duncan. 'Yon placie wid be gey sair made t' support anither beast. Onywye, it wis pure disaster for Sandy's faimly; nae milk, nae butter, nae cheese, an precious fyowe maiks aboot the place forbye. Aabody wis winnerin fit wid happen noo, wi Sandy bein the kind o chiel he is, ye see, fin the bold Baldy taks the bull b' the horns, an fit dis he dee, think ye?'

'I'm listenin, Duncan,' says the Turk.

'Weel, skipper, he gings doon t' see Sandy as if he didna ken the man wis badly, an he says, 'I'm sorry t' see ye're laid-up, Sandy, cos I'm doon t' seek an obligement fae ye.'

'Fae me?' says Sandy. 'Fit wye could the likes o me oblige the likes o you?'

'Weel, Sandy, I've a problem! Yon loons o mine lat me doon, fyles, an there's been a miscoont, so I've twaa coos that I jist hinna room for. I'm winnerin if ee wid be willin t' tak them an look aifter them for a fylie till I get things sorted oot. 'Twid be a great help t' me!'

Sandy lies a fylie thinkin, syne he looks up an says, 'I'd be mair than willin t' help ye oot, but ye ken this place couldna feed three beasts.'

'Och, that's nae bother avaa, Sandy. I'll see till't that yon loons o mine taks ower plinty o mait.'

'Aa richt, than,' says Sandy, an they shook hans on that.

'Hey!' says the Turk, 'Faa wid get aa the milk?'

'Oh, Sandy wid get the milk. That's the laa up the country, tho I dinna think it's written doon.'

'Noo, Duncan, fit gars ye think that Baldy's nae a Christian? Mysel, I'm thinkin he's jist a Topper.'

'Weel, skipper,' says Duncan, 'Baldy tellt Sandy a dammt great lee! He said he hidna room for the twaa coos. Od, aabody kens that wis a lee. He had room for a lot mair than that. Christians shouldna tell lees avaa, should they, skipper?'

The Turk was silent for a fylie, then he said, quaet like, 'Duncan, my loon, fit kine o coos did Baldy gie Sandy. Black-an-fite?'

'That's richt, skipper, black-an-fite. The twaa best milkers in Buchan!'

'Weel,' says the Turk, 'I'm thinkin Baldy jist tellt a black-an-fite lee, an I'm sure that kine disna coont.'

'Ach!' says Duncan, 'I'm awaa below t' gie her a shiffle o coal. Ye're a richt queer lot, you fishers!'

Oral Tradition

I have never liked History and by History I mean the stuff we got at school. Ye ken, Kings and Queens and Battles and the Dates thereof. This was a subject which gave my tiny mind a few insurmountable problems, for I simply couldn't remember dates. To this very day, I have the same failing; birthdays and anniversaries don't seem to register and, were I not gently reminded, no one would ever get a present or a card for their birthday.

In one respect I am rather fortunate, for my wedding anniversary falls on 26th January, and I would be thick indeed if I missed that, seeing that Robbie Burns' birthday is on the 25th. As soon as I hear somebody singing, 'There wis a lad wis born in Kyle' I'm reminded that 'She'll be lookin for a bunchie o flooers the morn, an flooers is an affa price at this time o year!'

There was one memorable occasion when I really did excel myself in the historic field. Teacher had set us the task of writing an essay on the Battle of Bannockburn and, since essays had never given me any trouble, I set to with a will. I would show them that I knew my history better than they gave me credit for. Boys, I was proud of that essay, my sole attempt at an historic novel for, in glowing style and in graphic detail, I described how Wallace the Bruce, on a Shetland pony, stood in his stirrups and with one fell swipe of his battle-axe severed John o Groats' head from his shoulders as he thundered past on his war-horse. The marks I got for that glowing effort caused me to give up History as a dead loss.

Oral tradition, now, is an entirely different kettle o fish, one of whose attractions is its delightful vagueness — there are never any dates. These old tales, handed down from generation to generation, have a tendency to lose the names of the principal characters, possibly conveniently, but they suffer little on that account. Furthermore, the age-old stories deal with common, ordinary folk like you and me. Surely that's better material than Kings and Queens and Courtiers in all their finery and lace. I can assure you that there's no lace in the tale which I'd like to tell you now, just as I heard it, via oral tradition. In fact, there are two tales, neither of which is to be found in any History book.

Once upon a time, then, and not so very long ago at that, in one of the three fisher villages which lie between the Broch and Rattray Head, there were two brothers who had fished together for several years. They must have been reasonably successful, for they were having a new boat built, say, about 30ft in length. All was well until the boat was completed and ready for launching; then, for some unknown reason the brothers 'keest oot'. For a considerable time the boat was left on the stocks, pending some sort of agreement between the two owners, but neither brother would yield. Finally it was decided that they would 'get the shaavie' ('shaav' being the local term for a saw). So the boat was actually sawn into two halves, and each brother was left to arrange for the transporting of his own particular half to his own particular home. There, each half was turned bottom up and set on a low dykie built to receive it, so, instead of one bonny boat, the brothers had two peculiar sheds!

'Ah,' you may say, 'this is only some sort of parable to demonstrate the bitterness which can creep into quarrels between brothers. It cannot possibly be true.'

But, all too sadly, it IS true, and for many a long day did the two half-boats grace the village scene. To the best of my knowledge there is no written record of this event, but oral tradition has kept it from being utterly lost.

Now, what about the four sail-boaties that left Cairnbulg long, long ago, making for Neebra Watter (the Ythan Estuary), to collect mussel bait for their haddock lines? This was common practice, for it was by far the best method of acquiring an ample stock of bait. They could simply help themselves, and there would be no transport fees. With a favouring wind and a good tide the flotilla reached its destination without incident. On the ebbing tide the boats were beached among the rich mussel beds, and at low water the crews simply shovelled mussels into the open hulls, knowing that the incoming tide would refloat the boats. Steam puffers on the Tay regularly followed a similar practice. When a load of sand was required for some project, the puffer was grounded on a sandbank; then, when the tide receded, the crew shovelled sand into great iron buckets which were heaved on board by means of winch and derrick, to be tipped into the hold. Then the rising tide would refloat the laden vessel.

It is probable that the fishermen, in an excess of zeal, overloaded their boats. You know how it is, 'Och! She'll hud a puckly mair yet. Eence we're here, we micht as well tak them.' As it happened, that was a great mistake, for when the boaties sailed for home, probably next morning, they were in no state to meet bad weather. There was very little wind as they crossed the bar but, against the flood tide, their northward progress was painfully slow. By the time they had reached the Scaurs o Cruden, the wind had backed to the south-east and was freshening slowly. An hour or so later there was really too much weather for heavily laden, undecked open boats. Not a storm, by any means, but still too much.

One boat foundered with the loss of all hands; the others were very fortunate indeed to reach the safety of Peterhead which, in the days before the breakwaters were built, was a very dicey entrance indeed. The three boats completed their passage a day or two later.

As one would expect, there was a deep sense of shock throughout the fisher community. There were the usual manifestations of grief — widow's blacks and memorial services for young men sadly missed. Indeed, for several weeks, there was an almost tangible air of gloom about the village. Then everything seemed to change.

Someone with a malicious tongue and a wicked heart sowed the seeds of doubt and suspicion. There were dark whisperings at gable ends, there were little knots of gossiping women who melted into handy doorways at the approach of certain men. There was an unwonted averting of the gaze as friend met former friend, and certain bairns were forbidden to play with certain other bairns. Distrust walked the village lanes like a spectre, until the festering sore finally burst open when ae loon said till anither loon, 'Your father droont my father! My father wis in the sea, hingin on till an oar, an your father sailed his boat that close that he chappit my father's verra fingers. But he didna lift a finger t' save him!'

So the dark secret was out! Bairns say what they hear their elders say, but they don't always say it in secret. According to rumour, three crews had sailed on, leaving another crew to perish in the deep.

I cannot accept that! I do believe that, on the sad day in question, it was a fight for survival, and if succour could have been given, it would have been forthcoming. But, having said that, I am perfectly willing to accept the tale when it deals with the whispered innuendoes and their dire results. There's naething so queer as folk, and fisher folk can be as queer and coorse and ill-thochtit as any.

Thus it came to pass that three crews, finding life in their native place completely intolerable, set sail therefrom, again on a southerly course. The setting sun saw them draw their boats up on the sandy beach at the mouth of the Cruden Burn, where there was no harbour, and the stars looked down to see them asleep beneath an upturned boat. In such a fashion did the first fishers come to that haven known as the Ward.

From the following dawn they had a sair, sair fecht. It was a case of starting from scratch, and that is never easy. Just as they had done at home, the strangers followed their calling, bartering their fish among the country folk. Only at the Castle on the cliff was there a cash customer, a customer who showed a deep interest in their welfare, sending them an occasional boll of meal to help them along. In rough-and-ready wooden shacks built by themselves on the sand dunes, the fishers dwelt with their wives and bairns who had followed them south, probably on foot. And thus they formed a small, close-knit community, known to the locals as the Binties, the folk that lived on the bints, or sand dunes.

It is more than likely that the Laird, in his cliff-top castle, knew the reason for the sudden appearance of the strangers. Even in those distant days, Lairds would have had means of communicating with each other. In any case, this particular Laird kept the incomers under close observation, taking due note that they were an eident, sober and honest lot. In due course the good man had compassion on the Binties, living as they were in such awful conditions, and built houses for them on the North side of the burn. So the Binties crossed over to the other side and became Wardies, merging into the local scene as to the manner born.

At a much later date a wealthy shipping magnate built for them a harbour whose piers would have been much stronger if more of the local granite had been

250

used in their construction. Still, the piers served the fishers very well for many a long year. Indeed, they served until there were no fishers to use them. Nowadays the harbour is simply a haven for pleasure craft, a place beloved by Sunday visitors.

But although the fishers have long since departed, their names remain. Tait, Summers and Duthie take their place alongside local names such as Robertson, Masson and Milne, but the first three of these names were brought to the Ward by the Binties who, in the words of one of their leaders were, 'A cursed tribe, driven from home.'

'Och!' says you. 'They're nae a hunner mile awaa fae their folk that bides on the north side o Rattray Heid. Are ye sure that they ARE the same folk?'

Aye, surely. They're the same folk aaricht, an they're nae aa that far apairt. Jist as far as a boatie could reasonably sail in a day.

Now, THAT'S oral tradition, the stuff ye dinna get in History books.

But then, as I've said, I've nivver likit History!

The Fite Rubbit

It was in the mid thirties that the great change took place. Somebody had produced a new green preservative to replace the bark which generations of fishermen had used on their herring nets. The new preservative was to be the final blow in the war against rot in natural fibres; at least, that was the claim. But the herring men wouldn't look at the stuff, and for at least another twenty-five years they stuck to the old-fashioned ways, until nylon herring nets made their appearance. Great stuff, nylon! No more rotten nets! But nylon nets were very expensive, so it was only a gradual phase-out of the old-style cotton nets that could be contemplated. Then, before nylon had time to make any real impact, the bottom fell out of the herring trade, and countless thousands of herring nets were sold off for garden netting.

The trawlermen too, looked askance at the new green stuff (a derivative of copper), and for a long time they continued to use the traditional tarred manilla trawls. Indeed, there was very little change in the trawlers until the post-war appearance of man-made fibres which came in all the colours of the rainbow, the most common shade being bright orange, and the material Courlene.

So, in the beginning it was left to the seine-net men to try out the bright green stuffie, and we were among the first, if not the very first in Peterhead to try it. In those days we rigged our own nets, i.e. we bought the treated netting from the factory, sewed the pieces together, then mounted the net on its ropes to our own specifications, thus saving quite a bit of cash. Those were the days when we used flat ovals of cork as floats, or even herring corks, but we detested the green glass balls which the trawlers used; they were much too easily broken. Metal floats

251

were in their early infancy, and plastic floats were 25-30 years in the future. What was plastic, anyhow?

Well, now, to get on with the tale! We rigged a bonny new green net with raips, corks and lead weights, but in the process we noticed that the green stuffie was not quite dry; so we asked the net-factory for advice.

'Not to worry,' they said, 'But it'll do no harm to let the net hang in the fresh air for a week or so.' And this we did.

At three o'clock in the morning of the following Monday the three of us met at the boat, ready to go to sea. The three comprised my elder brother, John, who was the skipper, brother-in-law Charlie and myself.

'C'mon,' says John. 'we'll tak the new net aff the dyke, an see hoo she fishes.' So we made for the dyke at the back o the market, but, as we neared the net, John says, 'Leave the net far she is. We'll dee athoot 'er for a day.'

'Fit's adee? Is there something wrang?' says I.

'Aye!' says he. 'Div ye nae see fit's sittin on the net?'

'Fine that!' says I. 'It's a cat!'

'Aye, it's a cat,' says he, 'but it's a fite cat, so jist leave the net far she is. A fite cat wis nivver gweed.'

'Och!' says I. 'We're in the twentieth century, an we're bothered aboot the colour o a cat! The cat could be tartan, for me! Hish! I thocht that kind o stuff wis deid lang ago. I've heard o fite elephants, but fite cats? Nivver!'

'Aa richt Aa richt!,' says John. 'We'll tak the net aboard, but jist mine fit I tellt ye!'

Weel, noo, we shot the bonny net, but we nivver saw her again. We lost her in a heap o sunken wreckage and, of course, the fite cat got the blame. Me? I blamed the skipper for nae wytin a wee fylie till the sky wis licht eneuch for us to see oor landmarks.

Still, boys, it WIS a fite cat!

Now let us jump forward, say a full twenty years. Brother John had been obliged to quit the sea for health reasons, and now I was in command of the *Twinkling Star* PD.137, a 56-footer built by Geordie Forbes on the Queenie. We were fishing most days near the out-edge of the Buchan Deep, the bulk of our catch being whitings which were consigned nightly by lorry from Peterhead to Aberdeen fish-market, for at that time Peterhead as a fish-market was defunct. With whiting at twenty-three shillings a box, it was a sair fecht to get a living.

I was one of a generation whose motto was, 'If ye canna pey for something, then ye jist dee athoot it'. A strange motto in today's world, I'm sure. But, when you consider today's world of inflation and high prices, it's difficult to see how young folk can possibly get a start at all without some kind of 'never-never' system. I mention this in passing because, after years of aiming for it, I had got myself a car, a birch-grey Morris 1000, and suddenly a whole new world opened up. Places which up until now had been mere names on a map became realities within easy reach. Deeside and Tomintoul, the Moray Firth ports and West-coast villages became part of Life, and what a transformation that was! After a week of looking at the sea, I could go and feast my gaze on beauty.

Well now, to get on with the tale. We had spent a glorious day in the country, one of those halcyon days when fisher-folk make for the hills, and country-folk make for the beaches. Far and wide had we ranged, and now, as evening drew nigh, we were making our leisurely way homewards. Through Foggie and Turra we came, the wife, the bairn an mysel, when suddenly, nae far fae the Brunt Smiddy we saw at the roadside a little quinie greetin — jist brakkin her hairt!

'Fit's adee, my quine?' says I, stopping the car.

'Oh,' says she. 'I've lost my rubbitie, an I'll nivver get it back!'

'Fit gars ye think 'at?' says I. 'It canna be jist hine awaa, surely?'

'Oh,' she says, 'it's geen in amon 'at stuff ower air!'

Now, ''at stuff ower air' wis a wilderness if ever I saw one. There wis thistles an nettles an brammles an whins an aa mortal thing that a fisher chiel should bide clear o. But in my ignorance I saw no dangers; I saw only a damsel in distress and a golden opportunity for me to be a knight in shining armour. (In other words, a great feel.)

'Dinna greet, my quine,' says I. 'I'll seen get yer rubbitie!' An in I goes like a warrior.

Boys, oh boys, I got the rubbitie aaricht, but oh, siccan a sotter I wis in afore I got oot again! I wis scartit an torn, same as tho I'd been trailed backlins throwe a hedge. If I'd been a proper knight, I wid ha heen armour on, but nae me! Sensible to the last, an died ravin!

Oor bairn (she has a bairnie o her ain, noo) mines fine on that nicht, cos the bonny fite beastie wi the pink een scartit her fin she cuddled it. Then the battle-scarred warrior got into his car and made for hame, his scarts an stobs nippin like murder. Still, Setterday hadna been wasted; he had left somebody happy.

Now, let's jump ahead to the early hours of Monday morning. The PD seiners are on their first haul of the long, long summer day, and, since there are as yet no fish to handle, the crews (apart from the men at the winch) are relatively inactive, and the skippers are newsin aboot this an that on the ship-to-ship radio. Maistly claik, ye ken, but eence they start gettin fish it's a different Muggie Rennie, for then the same skippers turn into the biggest leears ye're ever likely to meet. I'm tellin ye, the skipper that tells his brother skipper the truth is a rare bird indeed — something like the Dodo.

But this wis the first haul o the week, an there wis nae lees — yet.

'Fit like Peter?' says Willie Reid of the *Traveller*. 'Did ye hae a fine week-end? Faar wis ye, an fit aboot it? C'mon an gie's yer news.'

'Oh, Bill,' says I, 'we had a rare experience on Setterday nicht. I got inveigled wi a fite rubbitie, an ye nivver saw sic a maneer aa yer days.'

Then I launched into the tale aboot the bonny fite beastie, nae forgettin to tell him jist hoo brave I'd been in the jungle. If Bill wis ony man avaa, he wid spik to Patrick Wolrige-Gordon MP so that I wid get a medal.

When I had finished my yarn, there was a long, deep silence before Bill replied.

'I'm amazed that a man o your intelligence an experience should mention sic a beastie on a Monday mornin. An specially a fite een. Eh, wah-wah!'

'Now, Bill,' says I, 'I'm amazed at you thinkin there's onything in the aal superstitions. I've nae time for them mysel; they're jist a lot o guff!'

'Tell me that fin the day's deen!' says he.

He was referring, of course, to the old belief that to use certain words was simply to invite disaster. The actual names of a few animals were taboo, and a substitute name must be used if mention of the creature was unavoidable. Thus a rabbit became a 'fower-fitter' or a 'mappie', depending on your port of origin. The pig became a 'grunter' or a 'Sandy Campbell / Sonnie Cammle'; the salmon became a 'reid fish' or simply 'caal iron'. Ministers of the Gospel were not welcome near the boats, and should always be called 'sky-pilots'.

All these heathenish customs amused me greatly, and for the life of me I simply could not see how the use of the word 'rubbit' could have any effect on a day's fishing. That was utterly ridiculous!

Well now, three times that day we had a 'foul bag', the net being so twisted that it couldn't fish; twice we broke a perfectly good rope, and once we got stuck in a 'fastener' on the sea-bed where we never 'came fast' before nor since. We should have gone home at dinner-time, but I was determined to prove a point.

I didn't.

That was one awful day, the only day in all my time at sea that we put in a full day's work without having one single fish to land!

So how does this affect my attitude to superstition?

Well, lat me pit it this wye. Next time I see a quinie at the roadside greetin for her fite rubbitie, she can bloomin-well greet!

The Jacket

Simply because his name was Sandy Penny, the fisher loons called him Copper. He was as country as a peat, for his father had a placie near Longside, and that made Copper more or less a foreigner. Six mile inland? Very few of us fishers had ever been as far as that from the sea! (Sunday School picnics excepted, of course.)

Nevertheless, Copper had close links with Peterhead, for his mother was a Bluemogganer by the name of Bella Watson, whose mother had a shoppie in the Kirktoon. How Copper loved to spend his school holidays 'bidin wi's Grunny', for to him the Blue Toon was a great metropolis, a hive of activity where horses by the score dragged all shapes and sizes of carts. There were even motor lorries with solid rubber tyres, and, believe it or not, there were at least six motor cars. Boys! Fit a steer! This wis some Toon!

And then there was the Harbour, choc-a-bloc with boats, and Copper simply delighted in boats. Length and beam meant nothing to him. There were no drifters, liners, trawlers or seiners in Copper's world — just boats. He drew no distinction between ripper yoles and cargo ships; they were all boats, and they all sailed on 'the watter', the country word for 'the sea'.

Yet, despite his rural background, Copper was a remarkably fine playmate. He ran barfit like the lave o's, and soon learned how to tie a hook on a line, how to take a fish off the hook, and how to carry as many as sixteen herring on his fingers when there was no string handy. Many a bonny fry did he scran for his Grunny, though I suspect most of the fish found their way to the placie near Longside.

Copper and I became close friends. I was his confidant, as he was mine, and many were the boyhood dreams we shared. I shall never forget the bonny summer evening when the two of us sat on the 'tumble-home' stern of an old wooden drifter berthed in Port Henry. We were busy fishing for conger eels which abounded in the clear waters near the old, derelict hulls. We never actually caught any, and I think we were both secretly relieved, for I'm sure we were both just as secretly scared of the long, dark shapes that slunk around the rudders and propellers of the old ships. As we sat there in carefree fellowship, Copper suddenly turned to me and said, in his aal-farrant tongue, 'Od! I wid fairly like t' hae a boat o my ain, someday!'

'Foo big a boat, Copper?' says I, surprised.

'Och! Nae a great muckle boat! Say, the size o that een there.'

The boat in question was about thirty feet, just a big ripper yole.

Now, not even I, a fisher loon, had got around to thinking as far ahead as that. Copper wi a boat o's ain? Nivver! But not for all the tea in China would I hurt his feelings by telling him that his was an impossible dream. Country folk jist didna hae boats.

Came the time for leaving school, and thereafter I saw very little of Copper. He was the loon on his father's fairm, and I was the loon on my father's boat, so our paths lay far apart. The only real link between us was the shoppie in the Kirktoon where Copper's Grunny sellt sowens, that bitter brew made by the fermenting of corn husks or 'sids' in water for several days. That same brew, when brought to the boil in a pan and liberally sweetened with syrup, produced a sort of thick soup or pottage greatly relished by the old folks, especially at bedtime. On my occasional calls at the shoppie for a flagon of sowens for my mother, I always got a full report of Copper's progress.

During the War years, Copper and I never met at all but, in the first summer thereafter, who should come on board our boat but Copper himself, 'sair needin a fry o herrin'. It must hae been shortly after Aikey Fair, for he had with him a puckle early tatties. Oh, he got his fry, sure enough, but not on his fingers this time. His basketie was filled and he went home delighted.

From that day our old friendship was renewed. With our wives and families, we would visit each other, and there was a regular swopping of fish for farm produce. There was never any question of cash, nor was there any question of either one of us being in the other's debt. 'It's nae loss fit a freen gets', and it worked very well indeed for many years.

Then came the day when Copper informed me rather proudly that he had 'gotten a place o his ain, a hunner an thirty acre arable an a great skelp o roch grun, in the Parish o St Fergus, nae far fae the sea!'

'That's fine!' says I. But fit aboot the boat ye wis gaan t' get? Nae sign o her yet?'

He just laughed and shook his head. 'Gimme time, man. Gimme time.' Mrs Copper had never heard of the boat, and now that she did hear, she gave her man a long, hard look and said very drily, 'Aye! That'll be the day! Ye've plinty on yer plate, athoot a boat.'

Imagine my surprise, then, when Copper came to me some six months later in a state of great excitement. 'Ye'll nivver believe this,' says he, 'but I've gotten a boat!'

'Oh aye!' says I, in disbelief. 'Foo big a boat, freen?'

'Aboot thirty fitt, or maybe a hackie mair. I'd like ye t' come an hae a look at her.'

'Surely!' says I. 'Faar is she?'

'She's in the san at Scotston Heid. Nae far fae the fairm.'

'Ye mean she's ON the san, Copper. Divn't ye?'

'Na!' says he. 'She's IN the san. Mair or less buried in't!'

It transpired that Copper had gone to the beach with his tractor and bogie for a load of sand and, since he was Copper, he would need to 'hae a look at the watter'. He could scarcely believe his eyes when he saw the starboard rail of a boat protruding from the sand. All of her port side, and most of her deck were still hidden, but there was little doubt that a complete hull lay there.

When I saw the boat, I realised that she had been cast ashore in the terrible North-east storm of the previous year, when three similar boats had disappeared with all hands. In spite of an appallingly low glass and a fearsome forecast, some of the inshore fleet had gone to sea in calm weather. Well, they wouldn't be far from the shore, and they would manage to make port before things became too bad. There would be the normal breathing space, of course, but, in fact disaster had overtaken them, for the tempest had leapt upon them with the sudden ferocity and power which is nowadays classed as the 'Once in a hundred years' storm. The boaties simply had no chance. Very few of them had survived, and the boat which lay before us was one of the hapless victims. Now the cruel sea, with one of the biggest tides of the year, was slowly but surely removing the great bank of sand and tangles which had covered the wreck, whose precise identity was unknown. Only a few scraps remained of the bulwark planking which had borne her name and registration numbers. So she was simply one of three identical missing hulls. Not even the paint could provide a clue, for each hull had been painted alike.

'I've seen the Receiver of Wrecks and the Insurance folk,' says Copper, 'but they're jist nae interested. They say I should burn her for firewood!'

'I wid say the same,' says I. 'In fact, I wid burn her far she lies!'

But Copper simply would not listen. 'I'll mak a boat oot of her! She's mine!'

'Weel, weel,' says I, seeing his obstinacy, 'ye'll need t' get the san oot o the boat first, then get the boat oot o the san, an that'll be a gey sair fecht. She's as full o san as an egg's full o mait!'

But, undismayed, Copper and his two sons tackled the job of removing the sand from the boat's interior. It was slow, laborious work, for they had to work from a steeply sloping deck, and the hatchway was very small. It was several hours before any one of them could actually get down into the hull, and only then did they discover the little sliding door to the fo'c'sle. A wee bit apprehensively they slid the door open, only to find that the tiny compartment was completely empty, apart from one solitary, pathetic reminder.

From a nail in the bulkhead hung a fisherman's jacket of the usual navy blue serge, and in the oxter pooch there wis a bonny set o mackerel flies, the hooks scarcely tarnished, and the multi-coloured feathers as bright and gay as ever.

'Look at this!' cries the younger boy. 'See fit I've gotten. I think this jacket micht fit me!' And he made as if he would don the jacket.

'Leave that aleen! Throw't awaa!' says I, maybe a wee bittie sharp kind. So, with a peculiar glance at me the loon let the jacket drop to the sand. Within a few minutes it was completely buried, as the digging continued, but not before I had time to examine the bonny flies. The fingers that had made them had been masters of their trade, for the workmanship was exquisite. After a few moments of idle speculation, I dropped the neatly parcelled flies at my feet, where they too disappeared beneath the shovelled sand.

I left the scene early because, at that time, I was recovering from a major operation. In no way could I assist in the work, yet, in the morning, I was back on the beach to find a mystified Copper wondering who had put the jacket back on the nail. Of course, the mackerel flies were in the inside pocket. Did I ken onything aboot it?

When I simply shook my head, Copper called his elder son and bade him take the jacket up among the bents, 'and bury the thing the richt gate!' This was duly done, and that day the last of the sand was removed from the boat's interior. The sea had been quietly doing some work all on its own, and now most of the boat was visible. An internal inspection revealed four broken frames and a few gaping seams. The engine, as expected, was one solid mass of rust and would have to be replaced; the rudder was missing, and the propeller had only one blade. But, in Copper's words, there wis naething that widna sort. Indeed, the boatie was in remarkably good shape. A few strips of sheet lead and a few canvas patches would suffice to make her temporarily floatable.

At the end of the long day's darg, a satisfied Copper nailed a square of tarpaulin across the hatch, 'to keep ill-fashioned folk oot'.

'I'll see if I can get the len o a new-fangled digger the nicht, an we can maybe get a start the morn to dig a trench to the sea.'

But, in the morning, the jacket with the bonny flies in the oxter pooch was back on the nail. There was no sign of the tarpaulin having been disturbed. Boys! Copper fairly swore that mornin. With his new-fangled machine, he went well down the beach and dug a great hole in which to inter the jacket. He chose his spot well, for at high tide (he would never say 'High water') it would be covered by several feet of water. Then he began to dig his trench from the boat towards the sea, so that the refloating operation might be expedited.

But, in the morning, the jacket, horn dry, was back on the nail. So Copper took it and soaked it with diesel before setting fire to it.

'That's the last o that lot!' says he.

I had thought that he would give up, but I had misjudged my Copper. I'm sure he

257

sensed and resented my strong disapproval, for when it came to arranging for a big boat to tow his prize off the beach, he bypassed me altogether and approached another of his former boyhood pals, Jericho Jake, skipper of the trawler *Dusky Rose*.

'Seein that it's you, Copper, I'll dee't for a bottle o fuskie!' says Jake, lauchin.

'I'll gie ye twaa,' says Copper.

When the towing moment arrived, the boatie was sweir to move; sweir, sweir. But she couldn't resist the pull of five hundred horse-power on a tow-rope made of nylon, a substance we had never seen before. Much against her will, I thought, she was dragged bodily into the sea and towed into port.

'She'll hae t' lie there for a fylie,' says Copper. 'We're hine, hine ahin wi the Spring wark. Will ye keep an eye on her till I get time t' sort her?'

I said I would.

The *Dusky Rose* sailed that night for distant northern fishing grounds and, you know, she never came back. Nobody knows how, nor why, nor where she was lost.

I'm sure this was the final straw which broke Copper's resolve, for when the Spring work was finished, and the beasts were out in the parks, he came back to me just as I had expected.

'I'm nae seekin the boat noo! Can we pit her back far we got her?'

I said that was well nigh impossible, even if he were allowed to try, but I did offer to help in any way I could.

So Copper and his loons got their tractor and bogie again, and they loaded the boatie wi rubble and great lumps o granite, until she was just afloat and no more. Then, with my ain boatie, we towed her north with the last of the ebb, and we sank her in twelve fathoms of water, hard against the south edge of the wicked reef which forms the Outers of Scotston Head.

On the way home, Copper was unusually silent, but suddenly he asked, 'Fit'll ye be needin for this noo, freen?'

'As far as you an me's concerned,' says I, 'there's nivver nae chairge! Ye ken that, divn't ye?'

He nodded his head in acceptance, but didn't speak.

When we came abreast of the Queenie, I fired the question, 'Fit are ye thinkin aboot noo, Copper?'

'Dam't!' says he, taken unawares, 'I'm jist winnerin if yon jacket's back on the nail!'

Fit Like, Fairmer?

It was indeed a perfect day, warm and still. A few fleecy white clouds lay motionless over Mormond Hill, but otherwise the sky was a clear, deep blue. I had left Maud via the Honeyneuk Road and, having crossed the main road at the Shevado crossroads, I was on the ascent of the Reid Hull, that lofty eminence which affords a wonderful, panoramic view of the Buchan countryside. At the very top of the hill, at yet another crossroads, I drew my vehicle onto the patch of waste ground which was there for so many years, and switched off the engine. Not a sound now, but the sweet song of the lark, invisible in the blue.

Boys, what a view! Immediately in front, and to my left (on the port bow), lay the district of Corsegight, merging into other districts and parishes, right to the foothills of Bennachie. On my right (or starboard bow) lay the great spread of Balthangie. Simply by turning my head, I could look across the broad acres of Aalfat (Oldwhat) and the great, unbroken expanse of farmland reaching to the slopes of Mormond. Behind my left shoulder (on the port quarter) was the district of Stevensburn. Thus do crossroads divide the countryside into districts. Often, but not always.

No matter where I looked, I could see farmhouses, hundreds of them, spread out like a great fleet of ships at anchor, and I marvelled at the thought that every single one had its own water supply and its own waste disposal system. There's a lot more to farms than meets the eye. In the sweet green fields, great herds of cattle were grazing, and I wondered how the new 'Charlie' breed from France would please the fashious Buchan farmers. Oh aye! I kent a bittie aboot nowt! And I aye thocht the Herefords the bonniest.

But the cattle were not the only creatures in the parks. On every farm, as far as the eye could reach, men were busy at the 'hyowe' (hoe), among the neeps, a weary, weary job awyte. This was a day when farmers would be in the neep parks in force, and few, if any, would welcome the presence of any Traveller. Indeed, some of them didn't welcome Travellers at any time, and posted notices to that effect on their steadings. Still, I suppose, it taks aa kinds.

I once heard of a Traveller who called at a farm to ask for a contribution towards a wreath for a fellow Traveller who had passed away.

'Foo muckle wid ye be seekin?' says the fairmer.

'Oh, mebbe half-a-croon,' was the reply.

'Weel!' says the fairmer, 'here's ten shillins. Ging an bury anither three!'

Now then, after some twenty minutes of viewing and musing, I took myself off, with the observation, 'This winna get a frockie t' the bairn!' But it was a rather fruitless errand I was embarking on. Past experience had taught me that, years ago. I was at a loss as to which district I should tackle, and, at the same time, I wished to justify my existence. So I finally decided to do a bit of poaching in a fellow Traveller's territory. It was possible that I might discover a prospective customer of whose existence my 'oppo' was blissfully unaware. It was a forlorn hope, but it was better than nothing. The poaching aspect didn't worry me in the

259

least, for I knew that he did the same to me on a regular basis, under the fond illusion that 'Peter wid nivver ken!' That'll be the day! There's nae honour among thiefs!

Thus I found myself in foreign surroundings, on roads which I knew not, among places whose names were unfamiliar. It was an interesting trip, but a complete waste of time.

Then, suddenly, dead ahead, I spied a mannie who was making unmistakable signals that he desired to speak with me. 'Aha!' says I to mysel. 'This'll be a barrel o ile, for sure!' So I drew to a halt beside him and remarked in my unbelievably pleasant baritone, 'Fit like, fairmer?'

He looks into my face, then he scans the name on my vehicle, and says, 'Oh, it's you, is't. Esso!'

'Man, ye're richt!' says I, 'It's me, Esso! Every Saturday And Sunday Off. Div ye ken me?'

'No,' he says, 'but I ken aboot ye!'

'Fine,' says I, 'So we're half-roads there! Fit can I dee for ye?'

'Div ye ken onything aboot weemin?' says he. 'The wife's fair stucken, ye see!'

'Fit div ye mean, stucken? She canna weel be laired in a park in this dry wither, surely. Has she faan doon a hole or something?'

'Na, naething lik 'at. She's jist fair stucken! Come in an see if ye can help. I've phoned for the doctor, but it could be a fyle afore he gets here.'

Boys! I never saw a woman in yon state afore. She had been ficherin among her floories wi a fork, an she wis the same shape as a hair-preen. Her feet wis on the path, but her nose wis among the dusty millers, same as though she'd broken ower b' the pooches. Fair stucken, for she couldna win up!

'Good grief!' says I. 'Wid she nae been better t' boo her knees at that job?'

'Her knees is stucken anaa!' says he. 'I doot we're bate!'

'Nivver!' says I, 'We'll baith pit a hand on a hip, an the ither hand alow her chin. Syne, if we baith heave thegither, that should tak the kinks oot o her.'

It didna. It fairly brocht a skirl, but that wis aa!

'Hiv ye nae an aal door aboot the place?' says I. 'We could cowp her ontill't an cairry her into the hoose.'

'Nae sic a thing avaa!' says he. 'There's a new door in the neep shed, but it wid be a shame t' blaad it!' An he rins oot onto the road to look for the doctor. 'Nae sign o the mannie, yet!'

'Weel,' says I, 'we'll cairry her in atween's, an pit her inower the bed. But we'll hae t' watch, cos if we pit her heid on the pilla, her feet'll hae t' be on the pilla anaa. If we turn her the ither road, wi her dowp on the pilla, she'll be smored wi the blunkits. Aye, we'll hae t' watch that!'

'She's fifteen steen!' says he, an off he goes again to look for the doctor.

'We'll hae t' try something!' says I. 'We canna leave her like this!'

'Nae sign o the doctor yet! Fit'll we dee noo? I dinna like the colour o her face!' says he.

'It's the colour o her drawers that I dinna like!' says I.

Boys! I must have said the necessary magic words, for yon wifie straightened up

260

like a ramrod in two seconds flat, and came chargin aifter me wi the fork. I was lucky to make the safety of the van.

'Oot o here, ye orra brute!' she says. 'I'll learn ye to speak aboot MY drawers!'

I got the engine started, but, before I took to the road, I screwed the window down and shouted, 'Ye're a peyed-thankless limmer! Fit wye could I see yer drawers fin ye're wearin troosers?'

Mind over matter, boys, mind over matter! I've nivver been back along yon road again, but someday I'll ging in aboot an cry, 'Fit like, fairmer?'

Lightning Strikes Twice

Sunday had been a richt bonny day, warm and still. In the soft, hazy sunshine the sea had shone like burnished steel with a straight, clear-cut edge. Was the horizon a wee bittie ower high? Well, maybe jist a thochtie, jist a thochtie. Could it be that this was a linen Sunday? If it was indeed a linen Sunday, we could expect a harn week for, according to tradition, the one would follow the other as night follows day.

All the world, with his wife and bairns, seemed to be 'oot for a traivel' on this fine day, the last day for several weeks that they would be together as families for, on the morrow, the greater part of the herring fleet would sail for East Anglia. A day or two later, special trains would carry great contingents of shore workers, guttin quines and coopers, to the distant South and, by the end of the week, the Blue Toon would be seemingly deserted. Still, that had yet to come, and meantime, this was a day to be enjoyed. Lads and lasses were well to the fore among the throng, but the sweethearts went much further into the country than did the married folk, for all the cosy holes-and-bores among the still leafy hedge-rows were well outside the town. For most young couples, the morrow's parting would be only temporary; they would meet again in Yarmouth or Lowestoft.

I was one of the young fellas that day and with my lass I took the long road round by Inverugie, returning via Mount Pleasant and the river bank. Oh, the roddens were bonny, and the corn stooks in the quaet parks reminded me of a Dutch scene on a tray which my father had once brought home from Ymuiden. It was a scene of pastoral tranquillity; it was a day to be enjoyed. And then I felt the 'slammach' on my face.

Slammach is the threads of fairy gossamer which may be seen clinging to the twigs of wayside bushes. It can also be seen glistening along the wire strands of a fence, or among the tansies, close to ground level. And even the fishermen in coastal waters can occasionally feel the slammach on their faces, slammach which is the herald of strong winds, usually accompanied by heavy rain. So this really was a linen Sunday, and a linen Sunday maks a harn, or hessian, week. Seldom does the prediction fail.

261

I was one of the young lads of the day, but I was not going 'Sooth'. Not for me the hustle and bustle of Yarmouth River and the fabled bright lights of the Prom and Britannia Pier. Not yet. Instead, I would be in a forty-foot seine-netter, fishing the inshore waters along the Buchan coast, mostly for plashies and soles, for we had yet to learn how to catch haddock and whiting. We did, however, cherish the hope that, from mid November until the New Year, the cod would seek their usual haunts between the Aal Castle (pronounce the 't') o Slains and the Sands o Forvie.

There were three of us in the boatie. First, there was Abadan ('cos he had sailed the Seven Seas). He was the cook, in that he biled the kettle, for we had no proper meals at sea. Every man cairried his ain piece and had a proper meal at home when the day's fishing was over. A practice ruinous on the gastric system. Abadan had the disconcerting habit of chewing the heads of matches, with a strong preference for Scottish Bluebell, almost unobtainable in the Blue Toon. In fact, he had asked one of his pals to bring him a hale packet o blue matches fae Yarmouth where such things were in abundance.

Secondly, there wis Jonnack, a lang, thin, quaet, hardy chiel; a grand worker with a vast repertoire of stories that wid gar yer hair curl. Jonnack's speech betrayed the fact that he was an incomer to Peterhead, for he called the monk-fish an 'oof', whereas I called it a 'caithick' and, when we got some coal in the net, as we often did, his word for the sickly-looking sea anemones thereon was 'pluffs'. I simply called them 'paaps'. I think Jonnack was originally a 'Duffer', but he wis neen the waar o that.

Then there was myself, skipper/driver, quite a few years the junior of my shipmates. We had no demarcation lines as regards duties; all hands mucked in together.

Well now, the high winds promised by the slammach didn't materialise until Monday was nearly spent but, when they did arrive, there were no half measures. We had had a reasonable day's fishing at the Castle Hard but, long before we reached home, we had 'plinty o wither', even though we had a fair wind.

It was when we were rounding Buchan Ness that I missed Jonnack. Indeed, I thought he had gone overboard, so sudden was his disappearance but, praise be, he was still with us. He had been leaning, hands in pockets, against the wheelhouse, when his feet slid from beneath him and his left lug came yark doon the widwork. Lauch? I nearly split my sides! And when, five minutes later, he did exactly the same to his ither lug, it was too good to be true. It must have been gey sair, but boys, it wis comical.

All that night a strong southerly gale raged round the roof-tops, so fishing was out of the question on the Tuesday. We were scutterin aboot the boatie when I fell oot on Jonnack.

'Hey!' says I, 'If ye dinna ging an get a pair o new boots, ye'll be needin a pair o new lugs. That black rubbish o boots that ye're buyin, they're jist nae eese avaa! Fitivver they be, they're certainly nae rubber, unless it's this new, artificial rubber we're hearin aboot. The soles is worn smooth in nae time, then ye're forivver slidin aa ower the place. Wid ye nae be better t' ging up t' Dunn's sale an get a pair o fite Dunlop boots? I ken they're dear. Aswarn they're a saiven-an-twinty shillins, but they'll laist five times as lang as yon black trash.'

'Aye-aye,' says Jonnack. 'Look faa's spikkin! Saiven-an-twinty shillins is maybe nae a lot t' you, but t' me, it's a gey lot o siller! Ye'll need t' catch a hantle mair fish afore I can affoord gran fite boots. We're nae aa like you, ye ken!'

Jonnack wis richt, ye ken. He had a wife an twaa bairns; I wis young, an feel, an single. We lived in twaa different worlds.

The hale day it blew, an a great fleet o Moray Firth boats socht shelter in Peterheid. On passage t' Yarmooth, the wither hadna bothered them muckle until they cam roon Rattra Heid; then they got the win in their face. The Blue Toon, they thocht, wis far aneuch for the nicht. The place wis jist stappit full o strangers! Boys! I nivver thocht there wis sae mony drifters in the Moray Firth: INS, BCK, an BF. What a fleet!

Ye see, here was I, say twinty 'ear aal, an I had nivver seen the Moray Firth ports. Oh, aye! I had been in Ireland an the Isle o Man. I had been in Stornoway, an I had been in the Sooth Firth but, ye see, that had been wi the boat. Twice had I been in Aiberdeen, but I had nivver been in the Broch. To me, as to most of my generation, travel by land wis a closed book.

Weel noo, jist afore supper time, faa comes doon the pier but Jonnack, wi a bonny pair o fire-new, fite rubber boots. Prood as Punch wis he, as he stowed his new gear in the seat-locker in the fo'c'sle. Apparently him an his Missus had heen a cooncil-o-war, a richt serious affair awyte, an Jonnack had splashed oot!

'I got a twa-three bob aff,' says he, ''cos I hiv sic affa smaa feeties. I jist need a size six, an they've been lyin aboot the shop for a fyle!'

Noo, throwe the nicht, the wither eased awaa so, fin we cam doon in the mornin, t' ging t' the sea, the hale fleet o strangers had sailed for Yarmooth.

And so had Jonnack's boots!

Boys, I'm tellin ye, there wis nae lauchin that mornin! Peer Jonnack could hardly speak avaa! For him, it wis a proper disaster. As for me, I had never been sae angry in my life! I must confess that, though I'm usually a quaet kind o chiel, that wis ae time that I wis mair than willin t' murder somebody, could I hae gotten my hands on them. Only the lowest o the low wid steal a fella's boots!

'I'd jist as weel ging awaa hame,' says Jonnack. 'I canna dee naething athoot boots.' Apparently he had dumpit the aal black pair.

Now, since there wis only the three o's aathegither, this meant that we wid be lowsed for the day. We couldna dee wi less than three, an even at that, we were sair made. An forbye, the thocht wis in my mind noo, 'Faar on earth's Jonnack gaan t' get anither pair o boots?' The outlook wisna bonny.

Then, oot o the blue, an idea came into my heid. The day wisna lost yet!

'Hold on, Jonnack!' says I. 'Nae ower fast! I've a pair o boots at hame, that I got fae my father. They're leather boots, ye ken; knee boots, but I ken they're as ticht as a bottle. They're a wee bittie ower smaa for me, but they'll fit you fine. I'll be back in five meenits!'

So we finally got under way. Man, Jonnack likit the boots fine! They fitted jist perfect, but they were on the short side for his likin. Ye see, Jonnack seldom wore an 'oilie', 'cos he thocht the oilskin frock wis ower close an sweaty. So he jist wore the lang rubber boots b' themsels. Some lads likit an apron, but I aye thocht that to wear an apron near a winch was to invite disaster. Any man whose apron fouled the winch stood very little chance of escape.

Now, as it happened, we had a fair day's fishing, not by any means a fortune, but jist a 'day's mait' or, as the Duffers an the Fitehills men micht say, 'A day's cost'. On the way home, we were in good spirits, although the matter of the stolen boots would rankle for mony a lang day.

'Fine booties ye've gien me!' says Jonnack, 'But I'll need t' get an apron, 'cos I'm weet fae the knees up. She'll read the Riot Act the nicht, fin she hears aboot the missin boots!'

'Dinna tell 'er,' says I. 'She's nae needin t' ken!'

'That's fit ee think,' says he. 'But she'll hae t' ken fit I'm needin the fower-an-six for. By jings, she wis sweir t' gimme the price o the boots last nicht, but I'm thinkin she'll ging throwe the reef the nicht! An, anither thing, I'm gaan t' dee fit ee dee; I'll tak the boots hame for safety!'

'Och!' says I, 'There's nae need for that, surely. Lichtnin nivver stricks twice in the same place.'

'Better safe than sorry!' says he.

So the boots gid hame, and as was to be expected, the storm broke ower Jonnack's heid. But gradually the storm abated, and Jonnack got fower-an-six for a new apron (wi the tows) fae Hutton the sail-maker in the Seagate. Sittin at the fire that nicht, he spliced the towies into the shiny brass eyelets, affa bonny. Then he fauled the apron fine an ticht, an stappit it into the leg o the left boot. 'That's me aa riggit again!'

At the appointed time of half past three in the mornin, I met Jonnack at the boat, doon aside the aal Roon'hoose. Abadan wis already there, and had the firie lichtit. Jonnack threw the teem boot doon onto the boatie's deck but, fin he threw doon the boot wi the apron in't, sink me if it didna strick the first boot an ging skitin ower the side. Oh aye! It sank like a steen, an oor efforts to retrieve it were in vain.

Comical, think ye? It wis naething short o anither disaster, especially for a man wi a wife an twaa bairns!

So lichtnin nivver stricks twice in the same place?

Tell that to somebody else!

The Miraculous Catch

The propellers of the steam drifters were invariably made from cast iron, a metal eminently suited to the low revs of the steam engine and practically impervious to corrosion. But cast iron has one glaring fault — it will break rather than bend. In fact it will not bend at all. Thus it followed that a drifter's propeller could suffer irreparable damage if it fouled or struck any underwater obstruction.

Broken propellers were a common sight in the days of my youth. There used to be a puckle in the narrow triangle of ground where Charlotte Street and Maiden Street meet Kirk Street. That same triangle was at one time the town Dung Depot until the congregation of the nearby Muckle Kirk kickit up a stink aboot the stink. There was also a long row of damaged propellers leaning against the outside of the cemetery wall in the triangular scrap-yard which adorned the west end of Landale Road. Fit did I say? A scrap-yard in Landale Road? That's richt, freen, jist opposite the present-day DHSS offices. The scrap-yard is now part of the Town Gardens. The propellers lay for years, simply because there was no known way of repairing them, and cast-iron has a very low scrap value.

When, in the thirties, the motor boats began to make an impact on the fishing scene, stern-tubes, propellers and shafts were all made of bronze, an alloy of copper and tin. All the old fishermen called it brass, but brass is an alloy of copper and zinc, and that's not the same thing at all. Apparently the new metal was required for the high revs of the motor engines, and something called torque, what ever that may be. In any case, the new propellers were beautiful golden creations, but they didn't last very long. Oh, they would bend and they were repairable, but they soon got 'aiten awaa'. The highly polished blades became very badly pitted, so much so that holes would penetrate the blades, and parts of the tips would break off and disappear, leaving an edge as jagged as the lid of a tin that's been opened with a hammer and chisel.

Now, since it's the tips of the blades that do the work, these jagged propellers became highly inefficient. Boats lost their speed and their towing power until the inefficient prop was removed and built up, by means of brazing, to its original size. Then the whole corrosive process would start all over again.

Of course, the old fishermen said, 'Fit ither could ye expect? The aal engineers used better metal. Jist rubbish ye get noo! The propellers on the aal Fifies an Zulus laistit a lang, lang time.' Personally, I think that was because these old boats' propellers were as long out of the water as they were in it, coming, as they almost invariably did, from harbours which were dry at low water.

Some bright sparks thought it must be an electrical problem since it coincided with the installation of dynamos and electric lighting. So they tried shifting the earth points here, there and everywhere; in fact they tried some weird and wonderful dodges, but all to no avail. The propellers still got aiten awaa, worse on some boats than on others.

Now, with the post-war generation of motor boats growing steadily bigger, with triple the horse-power and consequently bigger propellers, the problem became really acute. You see, the three blades of a modern variable-pitch propeller (blades only, without the labour), will cost about £20,000, and you can't afford to let corrosion eat that. So the boffins got to work and, although it took them some time to identify the disease, they eventually came up with a cure.

It would appear that, if you put bronze into sea-water in close proximity to steel (rudders, keel-straps etc.), there is an immediate reaction called electrolysis which attacks the bronze. It doesn't do the steel any good either.

The cure is simple, as cures so often are. You simply get some blocks of zinc and bolt them to strategic points on the hull, not forgetting the rudder, and, Hey presto, the corrosion attacks the zinc and leaves the bronze alone. The zinc 'sacrifices' must not on any account be painted, since paint renders them useless. It's really amazing to see how soon the sacrifices become deeply pitted until finally they have to be renewed. But, all the time, the bronze remains intact.

I'm not qualified to give you technological explanations for this phenomenon, even if you wanted them, but next time you're near a slipway, have a look at the boats thereon and, when you see the zincs, you can point them out to your bairns and say, 'Zinc sacrifices, see?' Then you'll be a proper fountain of knowledge!

Now, there has to be a story, hasn't there? 'Aye, surely,' says you. A true story? 'Ye wid nivver tell a lee,' says you.

Well now, the story concerns the Boddam boatie *Fruition* PD173, a boatie that never got her proper name, for she was always called the *Frooshin*. Things like that disna bother the Boddamers, for they say 'tey' for 'tay', and they constantly use the word 'froonyil'. Still, they're nae the warst, an, ower the years I've been friendly wi several o their clan, one of whom wis Jake, son of the *Fruition*'s skipper, Reid Sonnie. In aa the years that I kent Jake, I nivver once saw him 'dressed' nor did I ivver see him athoot his Woodbine. A little bow-leggit mannie wi black teeth an a Boddam twang as broad's the Broadgate, but a richt fine chiel for aa that. It was Jake that tellt me this story.

The *Fruition*, 37 ft., with a 26/30 Kelvin paraffin engine, often went to the Firth of Clyde in the winter months to dredge for clams. The dredge is a fearsome contraption, somehow resembling the frame of an old-fashioned spring bed, only the frame is made of iron, and the 'spring' is a net of chain links. There are also sundry spikes for tearing the clams from the sea-bed. When the dredge is towed slowly along the bottom, the loosened clams rest on the chain meshes, but they cannot slide off because there's a top cover of heavy netting to keep them from escaping. That, very roughly, is a dredge.

Now, one very blustery morning, the *Fruition* was punching out of Ayr harbour and making a poor, poor job of it. She was pumping up and down, but making very little headway although the engine was at full throttle.

'Jake, my loon,' says aal Sonnie, 'yer engine's nae gaan richt avaa. Can ye nae get a bittie mair piff oot o the thing? We'll nivver get oot o here the day!'

'No, father,' says Jake. 'There's nae mair piff in 'er. It's the fan (propeller) that's vrang, cos it's aa aiten awaa. It's a new fan we're needin, for the boatie's awaa fae towin, an if she canna tow her gear we canna possibly get clams.'

'A new fan?' says Sonnie. 'An faar div ye think that wid come fae?'

Jake had no reply, for times were hard indeed and a new propeller micht cost as muckle as £10. Good grief!

Eventually, aifter a sair, sair fecht, the *Fruition* reached the fishing grounds and commenced operations. The spirits of her crew were very low indeed, and when it was time to heave-up at the end of the first tow, conversation was scarce. Aabody kent she had made a poor tow, so they could hardly expect t' get onything.

And how right they were. There were very few clams indeed, yet this was the best haul they had seen for many a long day, for there, all mixed up with the dredge was a bonny new propeller complete with some five feet of shaft. The propeller was precisely what was required to bring 'mair piff' to the *Fruition*'s engine, so that afternoon she was beached in a certain port where, at low water, the old, corroded prop was removed and the new one fitted.

Jake made a few inquiries, casual kind, ye ken, and discovered that some four months previously a twin screw motor launch had lost one of her propellers. When the propeller shaft breaks on board a single-screw vessel, it can slide out only a very short distance (say a foot or so), before the prop gets jammed on the rudder; but when the same break occurs on a twin-screw job, both shaft and propeller disappear, leaving the sea a great opportunity to pour in through the empty tube.

In this case the crew had managed to plug the tube and thus save the boat.

When Jake tellt me the story of his 'miraculous catch', I observed, 'Jake, that's the kind o thing that nivver happens t' peer folk! To him that hath shall be given!'

Jake jist leuch, an lichtit anither Woodbine.

Calcium Carbide

When I was a boy, there was a widespread belief that, if you took a bittie o carbine and shoved it doon a herrin's throat into its belly, any skurry silly enough to eat such a doctored fish would disintigrate in a few seconds before your very eyes. The 'skurry' is, of course, the common gull. Now, in those distant days, getting a supply of herring to throw away was no problem; you could get herring lying around all over the place. But to get a bittie o carbine as an explosive charge was a little more difficult, for carbine was a most important substance, certainly not for little boys to throw away. I must confess that, in my time, I have primed a few herrings with carbine and thrown them to the gulls, but never have I seen any burst of guts and feathers. This has taught me two things: firstly, that the skurry will eat practically anything, and secondly, that some folk like to spread false doctrine.

The 'carbine' in question was actually calcium carbide, a compound of carbon with something else whose identity I have never known. This useful substance

267

was universally called 'carbine', and it came in sealed, hundred-weight drums, half as high again as a five-gallon oil drum. Carbine was a very hard substance which rattled in the drum when the drum was rolled along the deck. Something like coal in appearance, only not quite so black, carbine was magic stuff which, on contact with water, produced acetylene gas which burned with a brilliant white flame. This gas was the main source of lighting on fishing boats for many, many years, just as it was the best lighting for millions of bicycle lamps before the arrival of the torch battery. Not until the Hitler war was over did electric light appear on the steam drifters, and by that time the drifters themselves were in the latter stages of their lives.

On the *Meadowsweet*, as on all drifters, the gas plant was at the foot of the engine-room ladder, beneath the starboard side-deck. Hand-made by skilled tinsmiths, these gas plants were highly efficient and very simple.

In an open-topped drum (say, the size of a 40 gallon oil barrel), another open-ended drum, slightly smaller than the first, was inverted in some eighteen inches of water. Bolted to the outside of the outer drum, two metal boxes with air-tight covers served as containers for the carbine, and were drip-fed with water from a little brass tank. When the charge in one box was exhausted, the water supply could be diverted to the reserve box while the spent charge was removed and replaced with fresh carbine. The gas generated in the charge-boxes was piped up through the water into the inner drum which then floated on a cushion of gas, gas which could not escape except by means of the feed-pipe to the various lighting points throughout the ship. There were no mantles, simply the naked flame from special 'fish-tail' burners.

The engine-room, cabin, galley and binnacle had one light apiece, and there were two hauling-lights on the front of the wheelhouse. With very rare exceptions, all other lights were paraffin lamps. By today's standards, such a lighting system would be hopelessly inadequate but, in its day, it was the best available.

Empty carbine tins made excellent buckets for the dumping of ashes and clinker from the boiler furnaces. On each side of the 'casing', slightly aft of the funnel, the drifters had a tall, cowl-shaped ventilator for bringing fresh air to the stoke-hole and draught to the furnaces. In the shaft of each ventilator, just above casing height, there was a little door which opened outwards and, in the shaft, immediately above the door, there was a pulley and a rope with two hooks. Thus the fireman, standing on deck, could hoist the buckets of ashes via the ventilators and empty the refuse into the sea. The chief, of course, filled the buckets in the warmth of the stokehole.

Carbine tins were also in great demand on shore, for they made excellent aise-buckets in the days when polythene bags were unknown. Even in the 'select' streets, ranks of carbine tins stood along the edge of the pavement awaiting the scaffies. From the scaffies' point of view the tins were a disaster, for they held too much, and thus were rather heavy.

Then there is the true story of how a certain Aberdeen trawler called at the Blue Toon in search of an extra crewman, having left her home port one short of the required number. Well, the fella who readily accepted the berth (a pier-heid jump) had no sea-boots, but he somehow managed to carry out his duties by standing in two carbine tins. There you see the resourceful Bluemogganer at his glorious best.

Well now, our dissertation on carbine and its uses brings us to the fireman, or stoker on the *Meadowsweet*. Although he actually merited the title of second engineer, he was universally known as 'the fireman', whose duties were varied and very many. He was responsible for all the lights on the vessel, both gas and paraffin; he cleaned the furnaces and hoisted out the ashes; he took watch and watch with the chief and, while the deck squad were hauling the nets, he coiled the heavy messenger rope in the bush-rope locker. A very busy man indeed.

Most firemen eventually rose to be chiefs in their own right, but Lugs, the Turk's fireman, seemed to have no desire for promotion. He had been given his nickname for obvious reasons, but he was a richt fine chiel, a grand worker and a first-class shipmate. An incomer to the Blue Toon, he took great pride in proclaiming that his birth-place was Finechty (Findochty), the Holy City, far we hiv 'Oor ain stroop wallie an oor ain kirk hallie'.

Some folk would have said that peer Lugs had been jist thrown awaa, for he had mairried a Peterheid quine that wisna jist the berry. She likit t' lie in her bed wi a quarter o chocolate bon-bons an a copy o the *Red Letter*. Jist reid rotten, she wis. Her name wis Fandolina Butterworth, but to Lugs she wis jist 'Dolly'. There wis ae Setterday that Lugs got hame early-kind (say aboot eleven o'clock in the foreneen), an boys, he didna half get a shock, for Dolly wis up, an fit's mair, she hid the fire lichtit. In fact, it wis a great muckle bleeze o a fire, an Dolly wis sittin in front o't, brakkin her hairt.

'Oh, Dolly darlin!' cries Lugs. 'Fit's adee wi ye the day?'

'Ooh me, ooh me!' cries she, 'I'm burnin.' Reid rotten, sure as daith! But Lugs jist adored his Dolly, an it's maybe jist as weel!

Lugs wis come o a famous fisher faimly. In fact, his Granda scored a great victory ower the Aal Enemy at Yarmooth. Granda wis skipper o a Zulu boat that had jist left Yarmooth River fin the win fell flat calm, an the rain cam doon in buckets — jist hale watter! The hale crew disappeared below, leavin Granda sittin like a prize doo at the helm. Sail boats had nae wheelhooses, so Granda jist had t' tak 'is shak wi the wither.

Up comes a fire-new English drifter, een o the very first o the kind, wi a Woodbine funnel. The shippie wis heavy wi herrin, an wis homeward bound at seven knots. Her skipper, prood o his big shot, prood o his new ship, an mair than prood o his fancy wheelhoose, steered close past the becalmed sail-boat an shouted in derision at the forlorn, dreepin weet mannie in the starn.

'Where's yer umbrella this mawnin, Scottie?'

'Oh, dam't' cries Granda, 'I clean forgot! I left it wi your missis last nicht!' 1-0 for Finechty!

Now let's get back to Lugs. When the news broke that Dolly was expecting, there were sidelong glances and sly winks among Lugs' shipmates. There were also a few unkind, speculative remarks in Lugs' absence, but the Turk silenced them all with the shrewd observation, 'Ye're aye sure o the mither.'

Came the long awaited morning when, in their single room in Threadneedle

Street, Dolly gied Lugs a great dunt in the ribs an tellt him t' get the Doctor. Lugs ootower the bed like a shot an hauled his breeks on. Then he shivved his feet intil his carpets an set oot. He didna tak time even t' fasten his galluses; he jist held his breeks at the front wi ae hand while the ither hand flailed like a piston, an his galluses streamed in the breeze.

Boys, he wis gaan like the verra haimmers but, seein that he had his carpets on, he couldna hear his feet, so he thocht he wisna movin. That gart him run even faster, so it wis in a state o collapse that he reached the Doctor's hoose in Queen Street. There he gied the bell a good, hard dirl; then, thinkin that the bell wisna workin, he startit haimmerin at the door wi his niv. There wis nae instantaneous response, so he thocht he wid try baith nivs, but syne his breeks fell doon roon his cweets, an he wis jist bendin doon t' haul them up fin the door opened.

Apparently unruffled by the question-mark posture of the caller, but obviously amazed at the shocking pink colour of the drawers on display, the Doctor says, 'Judging by appearances, and by the fearful racket, this must be an urgent call.' A wee bittie shortie o breath, Lugs jist nodded.

'Is it a confinement, then?'

'Oh, no, Doctor!' cries Lugs. 'It's nae naething lik 'at! It's a bairn!'

Since this story was written, I have learned from 'Pilot', an old friend in Lossie, that the Lossie loons were at the same caper, feeding 'loaded' herrings to the gulls. The only real difference was that the Lossie loons kept a close watch on the poor birds, which invariably settled on a pier which was seldom used, and there, after a short interval, the chest and belly would disintigrate.

I'm glad I loaded only a few herring.

The Heid Case

All day long the ship-to-ship radio waves had been a proper Babel of sound as scores of skippers sought to converse with their pals. These were the days before the advent of VHF with its multiplicity of channels — the days when inter-ship communications were restricted to two, or maybe three wavebands. It defies description, the rabble on the air from at least a hundred boats in an area some twenty miles by twelve, especially when matters were made even worse by the close proximity of an Armada of foreigners, all at the same game — nattering on the radio. Scotsmen and Englishmen, Frenchmen, Dutchmen and Belgians all mixter-maxter off the coasts of Northumberland and Durham. Fyles it was gey sair on the lugs, but you simply had to know what your fellow man was doing; was he shooting or hauling, was he fast in a wreck, or was he just lying there licking his wounds?

You see, it was late summer, and the herring were in abundance in that area. A considerable fleet of Scotch and English drifters were after the herring by night;

the foreign trawlers were after the herring night and day; and a host of seiners from all over the place were after the cod which were after the herring. Poor herring! The seiners fished in daylight only. Some of the foreigners didn't want the cod which they sometimes caught in their trawls, and it was not unknown for them (usually a Dutchman) to call a Scotch boat to come alongside and get a few score of prime beauties. Dunkirk and Normandy and all that, you see.

Now it was evening, and the seiners were in harbour for a few hours' sleep, prior to landing their fish. The sea was left to the drifters and the foreigners, but long before the drift nets were hauled, the seiners would be on the go again. But the rabble of voices didn't cease — it was simply transferred to the Mission canteen where fishers from Nairn to Sunderland met for a wash and a news over a cup of tea or a bottle of Quosh and a baggie o crisps. The place was like a beehive, and in the buzz of voices it was difficult to hear yourself speak. Every conceivable East coast dialect was in full swing.

'Hey, Peter!' says a Fitehills skipper, 'I've an affa job kennin fit iss mannies is sayin. Ye ken, the mannies fae Seahooses an Newbiggin an Amble. Maist o them seems t' hae a hurl in their throats, an I'm gey sair made t' mak them oot. Div ee ken fit they're sayin?'

'Fine that!' says I. 'I've kent the men for 'ears, but I'm sure you newcomers disna ken a word apairt fae the sweers. The hurls an the habbers disna bother me avaa!'

Fishermen, even English fishermen, are not exactly at home in Standard English. Oh, they can use it all right, but they prefer to use their own dialect. Now, that's fine until you want to speak to someone whose dialect is unfamiliar to you, just as yours is to him. Then you must resort to your 'proper' English, which is probably 'a bittie roosty for the want o eese', and then you'll begin to feel a bittie self-conscious cos the hale North Sea's listenin an sayin, 'Jist hearken t' yon pansy "talking".' And then you'll tell yersel that this fella that ye're spikkin till maun be some kine o twit. Jist fit he's thinkin aboot you.

Somebody spread the word that in their midst there was a man who had no language problems, and I was immediately co-opted as Honorary Interpreter! Any skipper, Scotch or otherwise, would enlist my services when a translation was required. I thought it was a great joke, and went to the counter for a bottle of fizz from the steward, a peculiar man who went about his duties with a marmalade cat draped across his shoulders.

Suddenly the hubbub in the canteen ceased and, as I turned to see the reason for the silence, I heard the steward mutter, 'Stone the crows! I'd better get the boss!'

My govies! It was 'Stone the crows', sure enough, for every eye in the place was on the strangest figure I have ever seen. He had just come through the swing doors and was making his way slowly between the tables, obviously looking for the Mission man. His jersey proclaimed that he was English, for it reached almost to his knees, while the sleeves stopped short at the elbows. Moreover, the neck was three sizes too wide. No Scot would be seen dead in such a garment. A few scales on his boots told us that he was a herring man, but nobody was looking at his boots, but at his head.

The top of the poor man's head was as flat as if a girder had fallen on it, and that part which should have been above the level of his ears was now sticking out at the back in a grotesque lump, swathed in a polka-dot hanky. Mind you, it's a gey lump if ye can rowe a cloot roon't.

'Good Lord,' says the Mission mannie, hastily summoned. 'Whatever happened to you?'

'Fell head first down the hold, didn't I,' says the casualty.

The Mission man immediately phoned for a doctor, mentioning the words 'ambulance' and 'severe injury'. Then he questioned the poor fellow, 'Are you all alone? Where's your skipper?'

'Gone to sea and left me to fend for myself. Just put me ashore and cleared off! Skipper's a hard, cruel man. No time for anyone who's hurt or sick. Slave driver.'

At this there was a buzz of indignation among the fishermen. Never had any of us heard of such callousness. Any man who could leave a shipmate in such an appalling state should be hung, drawn and quartered. Several quiet men who had never been known to swear expressed their feelings clearly and vividly.

On the arrival of the doctor, the patient was taken into a side room, then, after a very cursory examination he was sent off to hospital for specialist treatment. Thereafter we all went to our boats for a sleep.

Next morning, at sea, I was amazed to find that the Interpreter's job was mine in reality. The Moray Firthers hadn't been joking after all! Problem after problem was thrown at me from all quarters. 'Peter, tell me fit iss mannie's sayin.' 'Peter, will you tell your Highland tribes-men to stop using Gaelic!' Boys, they were referring to Duffers and Cullen men! At first it was amusing, but the novelty soon wore off, especially since I had enough problems of my own. And besides, I had a strong suspicion that some skippers, on both sides, were having me on. Then I realised that I had tremendous powers at my disposal. What if the interpreter is not the soul of honour? What if the poor soul thirsting for a clear translation gets a really crazy answer? I decided to find out.

On the third morning I was busy trying to get a big Frenchman to alter course, otherwise he would tow through our gear. I was vaguely aware that, somewhere in the background, Jackie from Newbiggin was telling a Duffer in no uncertain terms where he should go. Apparently there were problems, but the biggest problem was that Jackie, besides having a distinct hurl, had also a fearsome habber, so the peer Duffer was clean raivelt. In an unbelievably plaintive tone, and in a pure Macduff tongue the expected question arrived, 'Are ye wiggin, Peter? Fit's iss that Jackie's bleeterin aboot the day?' On the spur of the moment I replied, 'Och, Bill, he's jist speirin if yer Grunny still gings t' the duncin.' There were no more requests for translations, for I was instantly demoted.

That afternoon, dense fog brought seining to a halt. With such a throng of boats in such a restricted area it was considered too dangerous to carry on, for at that time none of us had radar and collisions would have been inevitable. Most skippers therefore decided to grope their way to harbour and safety. Just after tea-time, when the hubbub in the Mission was approaching its usual pitch, a burly stranger entered. Nobody paid the slightest attention as he made his way to the counter. He was just another stranger, and strangers were ten a penny. But the sound of the Mission man's voice raised in anger brought a sudden hush to the place.

'So you're looking for your cook, skipper? How noble! How noble indeed, to come looking for the poor lost sheep after four days! It's mercy and forgiveness you should be seeking, after what you did to that poor soul!'

'So you HAVE seen him, then?'

'Indeed, I've seen him! We have all seen him, and we are all amazed that such cruelty should exist in this enlightened age. You should hang your head in shame!'

'Where is he now? In hospital?' says the skipper.

'Where else would he be with head injuries such as he had? Certainly he's in hospital, and eminent consultants from Edinburgh have been to see him. They're studying his case very closely, since it is more or less unique!'

'Who put him in hospital, friend?'

'I did!' says the Missioner proudly. 'He's in the right place, getting proper attention and loving care.'

'How soon do you think you could get him back, friend?'

Boys! I thocht the Mission mannie wid burst. I'm sure dogs widna hae lickit yon skipper's bleed, aifter fit the mannie caaed him!

'Look here!' says the skipper, patiently, 'You put my cook in hospital! Now, will you please get him back as soon as possible? For the past few days we've landed our herring in another port, but now we're going home. Tell him that, if he comes now, I'll take him home in the ship; otherwise he'll have to pay his own fare! He didn't have no accident! He didn't fall down no hole! He was born with his head out of shape, man. This is the third time he's played this trick on me. When he gets fed up, he goes ashore in a strange port where there's a Mission and spins a tale of falling down a hole, of callous shipmates and cruel skipper, till somebody bungs him in hospital. Oh boy, he loves to be coddled by the nurses and fed like a fighting cock! I knew where he was when I missed my spotted hanky. Now, Missioner, do I or do I not get my cook?'

Within the hour the shippie sailed with a full complement. I spoke to the skipper just before he left the Mission.

'He must be an exceptionally good cook, when you put up with these didoes.'

'He's not even a decent cook,' says he, 'but he IS my wife's brother.'

Poor skipper!

Parson Grey

To see a side-deck brimming with herring in the light of a summer dawn is to see the unforgettable. Solid silver, burnished silver, living silver, with flashes of brilliant blue and emerald and with subtle hints of pink; herring as shore-folk can never hope to see them; King Herring. The haddock also is a vision of delight whose silver is only slightly less brilliant, merging into grey and pink, the whole enhanced by the distinctive side-striping and the mark of Peter's thumb, as bold and clear as a birth-mark.

The humble podlie has no such elegance. Born a buddick, it passes through the podlie stage to become a saithe and finally a black-jack, alias coaley, green cod or rock-salmon. I may have my evolutionary theory all mixed up there, but it matters little, I'm sure. The podlie is the fish which little boys catch and throw away; the podlie is despised by the fisher-folk, as a rule. And why? Purely and simply because of prejudice! 'Oh, gyaad', for no clear reason.

Well do I remember how Johnny Taylor gave me a 'bile o hard fish', caught at the Scaurs o Cruden and dried on the sunny braes at Finnyfaul. They were perfectly delicious but — Johnny shouldna tell't me they were podlies. See what I mean?

Still, for some fisher-folk the podlie was a vital factor in the household economy. No, my friend, not in the days of Dickens or Mark Twain, but in the twenties and thirties of this century.

Let me tell you about Simon, a friend whose conversation I really enjoy, simply because it recalls an era which has never been properly recorded and is thus in danger of being utterly forgotten.

Now, if it's the guessing game you're after, just forget it. I have a host of friends, all along the coast, a something I'm rather proud of. So, when I tell you that Simon speaks of 'podlas' instead of 'podlies', you can stop looking for him in the Blue Toon.

Simon's ages wi me, or possibly a wee bittie younger. I ken we've baith the same colour o hair. Simon wis brocht up in a hard, hard school; so much so that, at the age of seven he could dee ony mortal thing wi a smaa-line. Only his mither could beat him at the baitin, but then she wis a real flier! In the butt-an-ben the unbreakable rule was 'Work or want'. Work there was in plenty, and Want was never far fae the door.

The eldest in a long line of sons, Simon soon became his mother's confidant and his father's right-hand-man. As his brothers grew up, Simon trained them as he himself had been trained — hard! While still at a tender age the senior loons wid hire a sheltie an a trap for the day (one-and-sixpence) an ging roon the country sellin the podlas they'd catched themsels. Oh aye, they had to feed the horsie, but there wis aye plinty o girss at the road-side, an forbye, some o the country-folk wid gie the craitur a tasty bite o corn or hey. The country-folk's nae greedy, ye ken.

But the maist important thing aboot the country-folk wis that they likit podlas. Bein country-folk, they kent affa little aboot fish, so they relished the fishies that the ignorant fishers despised. The verra best o fish, fresh fae the sea! But, as a rule, nae on a Setterday; ony ither day but Setterday. Thus did the loons come t' ken a richt lot o country-folk. An the siller they earned? Mither got the lot; ivvery maik!

In the summer months, when herring were plentiful, the loons would go into the Toon to scran a puckle herring from the drifters. Cut into small pieces, these herrings made grand bait for the smaa-line. Any suplus bait was put to good use; nothing was wasted. While Simon's father stood out of sight just inside the doorway, the tempting morsels of herring were suddenly scattered on the open ground in front of the house. This brought to earth an immediate frantic squabble of screeching gulls, fighting each other for a share; then even as they fought they were laid low by a sudden shot-gun blast from the doorway. 'Roon the doors noo, loon, an seek thrippence apiece for the myaaves.' Anyone fancy a gull? 'Oh, gyaad', did ye say? Ye've surely nivver been hungry!

Came the sudden midnight knock on the door one wintry night, when a country couple more than half-way home had been driven back by a snow-storm.

'We've tried a gweed puckle doors, but aabody's tellt us t' come here! It's nae this nicht we'll win hame; could ye possibly tak's in till mornin?'

'Oh aye! Surely! Come in an get a heat at the fire, syne ye'll get a bide (bed) for the nicht!'

Now, Simon's bed was the lowest of a tier of three bunk-beds in what purported to be a 'middle closetie' atween the butt and the ben. He could actually reach out and open the door without getting up. So Simon lay and racked his brains as to where this promised bide would come from. Finally he tackled his father on the quiet. 'Da, ye ken there's bides aawye in this hoose, an ilkie bide's full! Ye jist dinna hae a spare bide t' gie this folk!'

'Oh aye, my loon, there's a spare bide — there's your een! Ee can sleep up in the laftie amon yon twa-three bits o net. Ye surely widna like me t' turn the folk awaa, wid ye?' And that was how it was.

Simon has told me more than once how, on a Saturday evening, his mother would bait the line for Monday morning. No such work would be done on Sunday, for that was the Day of Rest. The line baited, she would rise from her stool, her stockings soaking with mussel bree. Then, while Simon stowed the line in a safe place, his mother would dig deep into the side-pocket of her ample skirt for her purse, from whose tattered interior she would lay coins in little heapies along the edge of the dresser.

'That's for the butcher, the baker, the grocer and the milk.' Always in that order, and more often than not, the purse was left almost empty.

As eldest son, Simon had been delegated to keep an eye on the level of the oatmeal in the 'girnal', the copious meal-barrel which every family had. If ever the level seemed dangerously low, he was to warn his mother, who would 'gie him siller t' get meal fae the mull'. For a long time Simon had neglected this duty; it had never been really necessary. But one memorable week, when a combination of scarce fish and bad weather decreed that there should be no income for the household, Simon peeped into the girnal only to find it empty.

'Mither!' he cried, anxiously, 'Div ye ken the girnal's teem?'

'I ken, my loon, I ken. Ye hinna been watchin, hiv ye?'

'Will I rin t' the mull, Mither?' But the look on Mither's face froze the words in his throat, an he grat.

'Dinna greet, my loon, dinna greet. I got aneuch meal oot o the girnal the day t' dee the morn's brakfist, but I ken it's teem noo. I've jist heen a wordie wi the Lord aboot it.'

She was that sort of woman, was Mither — the disconcerting type who speak about the Lord as if He were a member of the family, not in any bold, impudent familiarity, but simply because they consider that He actually IS a family member.

The first time you meet such folk you may be tempted to giggle, but very soon you'll realise that you're the one who's at a loss for words, you're the one who's ill-at ease, and you're the one who's face-to-face with a something you cannot handle. All my life, all along the coast, I have known such-like, and I think they're the very salt of the earth. Let me tell ye something else about them; they're not restricted entirely to the coast, but they're scarce-kind among the better-off class. Aawye!

'Mither,' sobbed Simon, 'I doot ye've left it ower late this time!' In his mind's eye, the loon could see the edge o the dresser bare on Setterday nicht, an he couldna thole the thocht.

'Ye ken this is Friday nicht, Mither, divn't ye?'

'Jist wyte an see, my loon, wyte an see!' It was a very dejected Simon that fell asleep in the middle closet, that nicht!

But at two o'clock in the morning the loon was roughly shaken awake by his father, who seemed somehow to have lost his reason.

'C'mon, loon, get yer claes on. We're gaan doon amon the rocks t' catch podlas! Hing in, noo!'

Simon quickly realised that only the youngest boys were to be exempt from duty. The four who could handle a line efficiently were the conscripts on a fool's errand. Fisher-folk widna look at podlas; country-folk widna tak them on a Setterday. Surely the aal-man ocht t' ken better! But since he had never seen his aal-man like this afore, the loon held his peace.

For almost four hours, with rotten bait, Father and four sons catched podlas (the podlie is not a fastidious eater). Steadily the tally mounted till Father called a halt.

'C'mon, loon, lat's get this lot hame!'

Thus was broken the long resentful silence. At the rear of the house, the fish were split and cleaned, and there they lay in basins and in basketies, each one fresh and wholesome in its parson-grey shroud.

Breakfast was a silent fiasco. Three of the youngsters sat fast asleep, spoon in hand, their foreheads on the table, their porridge untouched. Simon could barely stay awake; Father said nothing.

Suddenly, on the door there was a hard, sharp knocking, strongly reminiscent of the knocking in the snow-storm, and there stood McClure, the big important Fish Merchant fae the Toon.

'Boys!' says he, 'A chiel fae the country's come in on me this mornin, an he's needin podlas, a hantle o podlas. Apparently some folk's come hame fae New Zealand, an ithers fae Canada, an somebody's come up wi the idea that they should hae some kind o gran Re-union Dinner. Noo, t' mak things like aal times, they wid like podlas, an there's nae sic a thing t' be gotten. Div ye think you lads could catch a puckle, an I'll come back for them?'

'Come an see this,' says Father. 'Is this fit ye're lookin for?'

'Faar the Hell?' says McClure, but he didna sweer twice. Nae wi Mither listenin. 'That's exactly fit's nott! I'm thinkin the half o the country's gaan t' this Do. Jist the verra dunt, boys, the verra dunt.'

'Weel,' says Father, 'tak them awaa! But unnerstan this! Neist wik winna dee wi the siller! We're needin the siller NOW!'

McClure understood, specially fin he saw the sleepin bairns. (They were only bairns, fin aa wis said an deen.) An, to be fair to the man, he gied them a rale gweed price.

So the edge o the dresser wisna bare that nicht, aifter aa. An, fit's mair, the girnal wis full. Fin Simon wis fillin the barrel, his Mither chided him gently.

'So I left it ower late, Simon? Maybe some day ye'll learn that the Lord disna work wi the clock!' It was years later that Father confided to his right-hand-man.

''Twisna me that gart ye rise an catch yon podlas. 'Twis Mither that jist widna rest. Od, loon, ye wid ha thocht she kent something!'

The Witch-Doctor

It was Saturday forenoon and it was raining very heavily. The crew of the *Meadowsweet*, having landed their twenty-cran shottie and washed out the hold, were gathered in the wheelhouse awaiting the skipper's return from the office. The cabin was temporarily out-of-bounds, for Jeemsie was busy scrubbing it out. The Turk had gone to the office for the crew's 'stoker' (perks), cash from the sale of mackerel, of which there had been quite a few that week. Mackerel always belonged entirely to the crew, who would wait very patiently indeed for the few bob that would come their way.

Meanwhile, their topic was Hector, one of their number who had been sent home by the skipper as soon as the vessel had reached port. 'Nae lookin neen weel avaa', 'the colour o daith', 'time he saw the doctor', were some of the comments. Then, when Jeemsie had given the 'All clear', the lads made their way aft to the cabin, where each man removed his sea-boots, thoroughly hosed clean, and donned his go-ashore footwear. Most of them removed their pillow slips which would serve as containers for the few personal effects, towels etc., they would take home. Clean gear would be substituted on Monday.

'So Hector's nae-weel?' says Jeemsie. 'Nae muckle winner! his tongue's like a harled waa, an his breath has a smell like a teem gut-barrel. It's a miracle we're nae aa nae-weel ower the heids o him. An forbye he's a foosty aal fizzer. Aswarn he's abeen fifty, an ony man o that age shouldna be here avaa. If he'd ony sense, he should ken that he'll seen be awaa t' the happy land sellin tripe. He should be lookin for a quaet corner t' dee in, instead o fartin aboot amon bowse an tows an scalders!'

Not until it was too late did Jeemsie realise that the Turk, light-footed as a cat despite his bulk, was standing close behind him listening very, very attentively to the youngster's dissertation.

'Oh, I didna mean you, skipper; an I didna mean you either, Sonnie!' cries the loon. 'Oh jingers!' And he fled up the trap to the galley.

'Ye needna think muckle o yersels,' says the Turk to his crew, among the hearty laughter which followed. 'Accordin to yon spleeter o win, it's hardly worth hiz lads gaan hame! Hi, Jeemsie, come awaa doon an get yer siller.'

Jeemsie kent that there wid be nae 'stoker' for him unless he came to collect it, so he had to yield. Down the trap he came, wi a self-conscious grin on his face.

'Noo, my loon,' says the Turk, as he laid Jeemsie's share on the table, 'hiz foosty aal fizzers is affa teen on wi yer gran speech; in some wyes it wis true, an in ither wyes it wis clivver, but it wis far ower sair on Hector. The peer sowl's maybe lyin at daith's door noo, for aa that we ken. Could a great intellect like yours nae come up wi a spot-on diagnosis o Hector's trouble, seein that ye ken sae muckle aboot aal deen men?'

'Nae bother avaa,' says the loon. 'Fine div I ken fit's wrang wi Hector. He's fair corkit, that's aa.'

'An hoo dis Sherlock Holmes arrive at that conclusion? Please elu — elu — explain to hiz lesser mortals, kind sir!'

'Weel, it's iss wye', says Jeemsie. 'Ivvery Monday mornin, fin Hector comes doon, he gies me a Setterday's Gazette (*Evening Express*) t' pit in alow his pilla, for his ain private an personal use. Syne, on Friday or Setterday he comes t' me speirin if I've a bit o an aal *Rover* or *Wizard* t' gie 'im. He hisna come t' me this week, an if ye look aneth his pilla, ye'll see the Gazette hisna been touched. I'm tellin ye, Hector's fair corkit!'

'Govey Dicks! It's as weel I tellt 'im t' see the doctor,' says the Turk.

'He tellt me he wis gaan t' see the Witch-Doctor, yon droggist mannie,' says Duncan. 'He says the doctor'll jist gie 'im a paperie t' tak t' the droggist, an that means peyin twice, so he's cuttin oot the middle man.'

'It's oot t' the Boddam quarry he should ging, for dynamite,' says Jeemsie. 'I'm awaa hame.'

'I'll see Hector mysel', says the Turk. 'He'll be lookin for 'is stoker. Hector's jist like the rest o's, inclined t' lat things rin on ower lang, so I'd better hae a word wi Margit.'

But alas, the Turk fell asleep (as usual) aifter he got his denner, so it was evenin afore he got the linth o Hector's. The patient wis lyin in the box-bed in his worsit draars an flannel linner. Margit had the blankets ticht up roon his chin, an boys, the swite wis jist pinkin aff o 'im.

'It's broncaidis, Bob, broncaidis,' says Margit. 'Div ye hear yon sweevle at 'is breist? I dinna like the soon o yon sweevle. I'm tryin t' swite it oot o 'im, an forbye, he likes a drappie toddy!'

The Turk seen tellt Margit that it wisna broncaidis, an that fitivver micht be at Hector's briest, it wisna sweevle.

'Did ye nae ging an see the doctor fin I tellt ye, Hector?'

'No, Bob, I didna. I wis feart!'

'Did ye see the Witch-doctor droggist mannie instead?'

'Aye an no, Bob, aye an no!'

'Fit div ye mean, aye an no?'

'Weel, Bob, last time I wisna richt I gid up t' see the Witch-doctor, an he says, 'Lat's hae a look at yer tongue!' Then he says, 'Oh gyaad, we're corkit, are we? We'll seen sort that!' An he pits a sup stuff in a glaiss. 'Gladstone Road ye bide is't.' 'Oh aye!' So in goes a suppie mair stuff. 'Half-wye doon the street?' 'Aye', so in goes a suppie mair. 'This side or yon side?' 'Oh, the far side'; a wee drappie mair. 'Tell me this noo; is yer closet at the mou o the close?' 'No, it's at the far end'; jist a wee skytie mair. 'Noo,' says he, 'drink that an hame at yer hardest.' Man, Bob, yon mannie should nivver ha been a droggist; he wid ha made a richt architeck! I missed the seat by three inches! So, the day, fin I gid in, he says, 'Corkit again, are we?' I jist ran.

'Aye-aye, Hector,' says the Turk, lauchin, 'but ye'd better be serious. It's mair than time that something wis deen, but it's nae likely ye'll get the doctor the nicht; he's likely awaa playin gulf. Nivver aff the gulf-coorse.'

The Turk was really concerned about Hector's health. The pair shared a common birthday; they had been play-mates in their childhood, and they had been shipmates all their years at sea. There was a deep, abiding friendship between them, and the fact that Margit and Hector were childless whereas Mary and Bob had 'a faimly like steppin-steenies' was a source of continual, friendly banter.

'I doot it's the fire-engine for you, freen!' says the Turk.

'The fire-engine?' says Margit. 'Fit wye could ye get a pair o horse up this closie? There's jist nae room!'

'I'm nae spikkin aboot that kine o fire-engine!' says the Turk. 'I mean yon thing like a basin, wi a rubber pipe an soapy water.'

'Oh,' says Margit, 'that's fit they caa an enemy. I've seen een o them!'

'Fit did ye say? An enemy? I wis thinkin it wid be a first-class freen t' Hector if we could only lay hands on sic a thing! There's bound t' be een at the Fivver Hospital, but that's awaa oot past Buchanhaven, hine ootside the toon. An forbye, a buddy micht get the jandies usin their een!'

'Jeemsie wid ken far t' get an enemy,' says Hector. 'Jeemsie kens aa mortal thing. I hear he's gaan wi yon quinie that sings sae bonny in the Mission choir.'

'The Mission! The Mission!' cries the Turk. 'Fit wye did I nae think o that afore? They keep an enemy in the sick-bay, an I'm sure Jim Forrest wid be willin t' help. An I'm sure he wid hae somebody that kens the wye t' work the thing. 'Plinty squeak, no plump.' Fit wye did ye nae mine on that, Hector?'

279

Here the Turk was recalling the words of a poor Dutch man, landed at the Blue Toon with severe abdominal pains, long, long ago. On that occasion the Mission's 'enemy' had proved a friend in need. To this very day, the famous words are an oft-repeated joke among East-coast fishermen.

Well, now, Jim Forrest, who seldom got his proper title 'Superintendent', willingly obliged with both 'enemy' and personnel, and poor Hector was kindly and skilfully treated.

Monday morning saw the *Meadowsweet*'s crew back on board preparing for sea. As Hector passed the galley door, he handed to Jeemsie the usual Gazette.

'Ye ken far t' pit that, my loon,' says he.

'My govies, Hector, ye're nae needin that the day. There's a hale Gazette nae broken on, in aneth yer pilla!'

'Fine div I ken that, Jeemsie. Naebody kens that better than me. But ye see, my loon, there's fresher news in this een!'

That fairly put Jeemsie's pipe oot!

The Flooer o Scotlan

Once upon a time there stood on Keith Inch (the Queenie) a tall granite gable which, strictly speaking, was not really a gable at all since it formed the wedge-shaped corner where Ship Street meets Pleasure Walk. It was a man-made cliff of local granite, a noble prow defying the might of the North East gales which had vented their fury upon it over the long, long years.

In the distant days when I, like so many others, ran barefoot about that vicinity there was, set into the South wall of the old building, the jawbone of a great whale. Even in those days the whale-bone showed signs of decay, and finally rotted away completely, leaving in the wall a peculiar arched recess. This gave rise to the erroneous belief that, at some time the old, old building had been a Kirk. It was obvious, thought some, that a great arched window had been blocked up. Some window! Some Kirk!

There was however in the old edifice a special window, a tiny window, high-set in the lofty eastern corner, a proper eyrie affording an incomparable view over the North Sea. Any vessel bound for Peterhead from the Continent (and there were many), could be spotted from this look-out while still many miles off. Thus did the window become a favourite watch-tower for certain members of the pilotage fraternity.

In those days Peterhead had at least a dozen pilots who shared at least half-a-dozen boats, on whose bows the letter P was boldly displayed to indicate that this was an authorised Pilot-boat. Clinker-built, 25-35 ft. in length, the boats were powered by petrol/paraffin engines, diesel engines being as yet unknown. None of the boaties had a wheelhouse; only a few had a stove whereon a kettle might be boiled; yet these small craft went several miles off to meet the incoming cargo-boats.

I remember quite well how my father, who had the steam drifter, *Twinkling Star*, incurred the severe displeasure of the pilots by agreeing to tow the old 'scaffie' boat *Kitty* as far as Wick, so that her skipper, 'Slum' McLean, could capture a prize. In Wick there was a great muckle saat-boat landing a half cargo, the other half being for Peterhead. As soon as the steamer cleared the piers at Wick, Slum, the Peterhead pilot boarded her, and of course the steamer towed the *Kitty* home. On my father's return from a fortnight's line-fishing in Orkney waters, he was informed by the pilots that 'unfair competition' would not be tolerated. He never offended again.

The pilots themselves were local smaa-line fishermen, largely illiterate, and with never a ticket of any kind between them, but they knew their job. For many, many years they piloted safely into the port ships as big as any which enter the port nowadays, via an entrance much narrower than the present one. In their day, these old salts had two great disadvantages: there were no breakwaters for the Bay, and the steamers of that era had only half the propeller in the water when they had no cargo. This made them as easy to handle as recalcitrant barrage balloons.

Competition between these hardy seamen was very keen indeed. Since the rule was, 'First alongside claims the ship' and since pilotage money was regarded as manna from Heaven, it was inevitable that the battle was largely a battle of wits, in which prior knowledge of a vessel's arrival could be of inestimable value.

Behold, now, at the lofty window on Keith Inch, three gallant shipmates, skipper and crew of the pilot-boat *Wildfire*. For hours they had kept watch on the distant horizon through a magnificent telescope which could not have come from anywhere but the bridge of some great ship, wrecked on the Buchan coast. It was inconceivable that any or all of the trio could have purchased such a handsome instrument; fishermen of that time didn't earn such money. And, to be quite honest, the hale toon kent far the glaiss had come fae. Now, in the clear, frosty dark of a spring evening the glaiss was being put to good use. The biggest saat-boat the toon would ever see was expected any time now. Wouldn't it be great if our three heroes could spot the ship before the 'opposition' did; and wouldn't it be even better if they could slip unobserved out of the harbour with maybe an hour's start?

At long last the skipper closed the great telescope and whispered, 'I see the ship, boys, I see the ship! I'd say she's aboot fifteen mile awaa yet, but it's time we wisna here!'

So the trio rattled doon the aal widden stair an oot onto the untarred road, where they soon realised jist hoo stiff they had gotten wi sittin ower lang in the drauchty cock-laftie. So it was with a hopperty-kick kind o gait that they made their way along the street, trying hard to hide their excitement.

In those days a great many people lived on Keith Inch: coopers, black-smiths, ship-wrights, and all the different tradesmen associated with a seaport. At the street corners little groups of men paced slowly back-and-fore, setting the world in order; here and there a few women-folk were 'haein a fine claik' afore they would bed the bairns that were still on the go. There was no shortage of bairns, for the 'Queenie Arabs' were a prolific race. So, jist for fear that some youngster might smell a rat and run ahead of them to tell the 'opposition' that the saat-boat had been sighted, our heroes took it canny for a bittie. Then, in the lower half of Castle Street they took to their heels and ran.

But, when they reached the corner, they jammed the brakes on. Disaster! Disaster! Their great head-start had been wiped out, for there, at the opposite side of the harbour, several Leading Members of the Opposition were leisurely pacing to and fro beneath the gas lamp-post which stood on the dykie in Harbour Street, and whose base-bolts are still to the fore. Twaa o oor pals swore heartily; the third een didna sweer, cos he wis a dummy, but he made a few rather rude gestures in the direction of the enemy. It was impossible for the trio to reach their boat without being spotted, and that was the very last thing they wanted, for the head-start would immediately pass to the enemy. Granted, it would be only a few minutes, but minutes counted.

A council-of-war was imperative! Some great and wondrous plan was 'sair nott'.

'Noo lads,' says the skipper, 'hearken close! This is fit we'll dee. We canna see the boatie 'cos she's in the shadda o the pier, but we ken exactly far she's lyin. So we'll crawl across the Brig — that's the easy bit. Then we'll ging doon on oor bellies an sweem along the grun like snakes, keepin close t' the black stick so that yon mob winna see's. Mind ye, we'll need t' be gey quaet aboot it. Fin we come t' the first moorin rope, we'll jist crawl across't, an fin we're half-wye t' the neist rope we'll jist shiv oor legs ower the pier an drap into the boat. It's high water, so we winna hae far t' drap! We can let the ropes go fae the boat, eence we get the engine started. C'mon, noo, hist ye clivver fast. We dinna hae aa nicht!'

Behold, now, in the shadows of the dimly-lit harbour, three peculiar figures sweemin like ruptured partans along the black stick, that heavy, tarred, wooden kerb which surrounds the quay-edges in the Blue Toon, its original purpose being a stop against which one could back a horse and cart. Beneath the black stick there was a veritable treasure-trove of 'coal stue an dried horse-dung', for hadn't the *Cairnie* discharged a cargo of coal into box cairts that very day

For such a commando-like operation, worsit drawers and hairback breeks are not recommended, especially if they are accompanied by heavy jerseys, black silk mufflers and London House bonnets.

'For ony sake, dinna sneeze noo,' says the skipper. 'They're jist across the road! Nae far noo, lads; here's the starn rope.'

Inch by aromatic inch the three brave souls wormed their way to a position half-way to the next rope; then, on a silent signal from the skipper they shivved their legs ower the pier an let go.

Oh, boys, ye've nivver heard a soun like yon in aa yer days! Even the peer dummy wis howlin, for the three o them wis in the watter! The crafty enemy had shifted the boatie, leavin the ropes in place.

'Boys!' says the Leader of the Opposition, 'It wid appear that the *Wildfire*'s crew's takkin a bath afore they ging oot t' the saat-boat. Seein that we're nae jist sae parteeclar, we'll tak on the jobbie oorsels. G'waa an get the engine started!'

Oh, Flooer o Scotlan, when will we see your like again?

The Hallelujah Lobby

In the dim and distant past, say a couple of hundred years ago, the fair town of Peterhead was renowned as a spa. At the foot of Jamaica Street, among the rocks of the fore-shore, there was a spring whose waters were really famous for their health-giving powers. Over and around this spring a sturdy granite hoosie with a beautifully slated roof was built, access to its low, wide door being via a steep, stone flight of steps from the roadway above. The spring itself was known as the 'Wine Waal', probably a corruption of the title 'Wynd Waal', for at that time, Jamaica Street was simply one of the many wynds in the town. It is worth noting that, in this airt, the 'd' of 'wynd' is always silent. Indeed, I have never heard the word used in any other form apart from 'a wynie'.

Be that as it may, gentry from far and near flocked to enjoy the waters of the waal, and this necessitated the building of a commodious inn nearby. The inn was quite an imposing building, with roomy stables and out-houses for the horses and carriages of guests. There was also a considerable annexe for any overflow of gentry, an annexe which was seldom empty.

As time went by, the gentry forsook the Wine Waal and sought fresh pastures. The inn gradually degenerated into a kind of slum, known in my youth as The Hallelujah Lobby, wherein an incredible number of folk had their abode. Since one room, or, at the most, two rooms were considered ample accommodation for a family, the inhabitants of the old buildings were as the sands of the sea-shore. So I thought! There were carters and tinkers, slaters and scaffies, and all sorts of folk housed under the old roof, for the most part decent, hard-working, honest buddies that couldna get a hoose onywye else, for cooncil houses were as yet unknown.

I remember very clearly one particular old lady who rejoiced in the name 'Pots an Pans', a name perfectly descriptive of her trade, for she was an itinerant seller of tin kettles etc. So good was she at her job, that certain makers of tay-pots and roosers in the city of Aiberdeen came to the Blue Toon to try to enlist her services. Alas, the old dear was rather fond of gin, and, in those days when it was quite permissible for a buddie's doorstep to project half across the pavement, she was very often in a horizontal position, with her birn of tin-wares rattling aboot her lugs! Many a time have I helped her to her feet!

In the thirties, the Hallelujah Lobby was demolished, most of the tenants being re-housed in substantial Council houses in a brand new scheme which, until street names were introduced, was never known as anything else but Dartmoor, altho its official title was Ugie Park. About the same time, the Close Brethren built a Hall in Skelton Street, and I can recall very clearly that one of their number was not amused when I suggested that, 'They kent fit they were deein, biggin their hallie wi Hallelujah steens!'

The site of the Hallelujah Lobby is now occupied by a very substantial block of Council flats. But fit aboot the Waal? Well, now, the Waal's still there! Jist across the road, in aneth the car park, the granite walls of the hoosie remain, as does the Waal itself. Mind you, I wouldn't advise anybody to drink of the waters. Not now!

The old building stubbornly resisted the efforts of the demolition squad, who thought they could easily tear the place to bits simply by hitching a laden motor lorry to a stout wire rope fastened to a high point near the roof. The solid granite walls just laughed at the puny efforts of the lorries, and not until a couple of steam traction engines took over, was any progress made.

Then the bairns moved in. On the scran for firewood. Sticks were a great prize! I can tell you that sixty or eighty bairns can shift a fantastic amount o timmer in a very short time. And the noise! Really unbelieveable, till there came a sudden hush. As one old lady said, 'Fin I heard the quaetness, I kent there wis a vrangness!'

The bobbies had made a pincer movement and had the bairns trapped. But three bobbies, complete with breeches and puttees, could have the upper hand only for a short time; the youngsters eventually won the war!

Many years later, in a doctor's waiting-room, I got newsin wi an aal freen, a former tenant of the annexe portion of the Hallelujah Lobby. It was my question, 'Foo are ye likin yer new hoose?' that set the ball rolling, and soon we were deep in reminiscences of the old place.

This Mrs Buchan (one of the many), told me how she, along with her man and three bairns, not counting another on the way, were housed in one single room. There was no water in the place, and the outside privy was about a hundred yards away. Dr Taylor had been called to attend to one of the bairns that was gey sair made wi the kinkhoast (whooping cough) and, during his visit, he remarked that the family were in dire need of more commodious quarters. Even one room would make a tremendous difference.

'There's nae hope o that, Doctor!' says she. 'There's jist nae hooses t' be gotten naewye!' Then, rather sadly, she said, 'There is a room jist throwe the waa, but naebody'll bide in't, cos somebody wis murdered in't lang ago. They tell me the bleed's still on the fleer! A great loch o't, at that!'

Dr Taylor made immediate inquiries as to where he might obtain the key to the 'lockit room' and, having found it in a solicitor's office, he threw the door wide open. The room was quite spacious and in perfect order, but, in the corner by the window, the floor-boards bore a dark, ominous stain. Bleed, boys, bleed!

Mrs Buchan refused to enter, but the doctor hastened to examine the grisly mark. 'Fetch your sweeping-brush!' says he. 'We'd better hae a richt look at this!'

With the surface dust removed, the great stain looked even uglier. A repulsive blotch of dark, reddish brown, with fainter markings around the edges.

'Nivver mind, Doctor!' says Mrs Buchan from the doorway. 'I couldna bide far there's been a murder!'

'M'lady,' says Dr Taylor, 'Ye've gotten an extry room noo! This is nae bleed avaa! It's bark fae a herrin net! Somebody, at some time laid a new-barkit net there. Look at the marks o the meshes roon the edges! A gweed scrub, m'lady, an Bob's yer uncle!'

Thus did that family acquire their 'more commodious quarters', which they enjoyed for a further three years before being allocated a new hoose.

Surely it is not surprising that, on being informed of her good fortune, 'M'lady' simply said 'Hallelujah!'

Eyes and No Eyes

Long, long ago, although it seems but yesterday, I read my first detective story in our 'reading book' at school. If memory does not fail me, the book was the *Prince* reader, and the story centred on a young lad who went to visit his Granda (on foot, of course). It transpired that Granda, from a mere glance at the youngster, could tell the exact route taken by his visitor. Well, you see, there was the red hawthorn in the boy's buttonhole, there was a special type of clay on his shoes, and there were certain other little odds and sods which I have long forgotten. All combined to give the old man an accurate picture of the lad's journey, so much so that the boy was certain that Granda had been watching him all the time.

The story, 'Eyes and No Eyes', was a great favourite of mine for some time, but, as the years passed, it disappeared beneath a welter of more important things. As the Apostle says, 'When I was a child I spake as a child, I thought as a child, I understood as a child; but when I became a man, I put away childish things'. So the story wasn't lost; it was simply stored away in some secret place in the mind, ready for instant recall on some suitable occasion. It was actually thirty-five years later that Memory laid the old tale before me, fresh as on the day I first read it.

I had 'swallowed the anchor' (left the sea for life ashore), and now I was a sales rep with an oil firm, the contact between the office and some six hundred customers, most of whom were farmers. Thus did I come to know the country roads like the back of my hand, and the country folk only a fraction less closely.

One of my first tasks was to introduce myself to my customers, and in so doing, I met some wonderful people, rich and poor, high and low and, in the process, I learned a great deal. Several of my former prejudices went by the board!

One of the names on my long, long list was that of J R Allan, Little Ardo, Methlick. The name seemed to ring a bell in my mind, and I wondered if this could be the man whose writings I had enjoyed so often in the *Press & Journal* on a Saturday. If this was the case, I wanted to meet him, customer or not, so I made for the farm.

'Oh, aye,' says the grieve, 'he fairly dis a lot o writin. Ye've come t' the richt place, but if it's himsel that ye're seekin, dinna ging t' the back door, cos he'll be at the front, an he winna hear ye. Ye'd better try the front door first.'

This was something new, for I had already learned that only a very few of the fairmer folk ever used their front door. It's probable that for weddings and funerals the front door is used, but for all other occasions, the back door is the entrance and exit. To be quite honest, I'm only assuming that the front door exists, for in all the thousands of calls which I made over the years, I never saw such a thing. Towns folk in general, and fisher folk in particular, set great store by the appearance of their front entrance; not so, the fairmers.

Behold me therefore, all dressed up for the occasion, knocking in vain at the front door, and about to leave the place when a voice cried, 'Hey! I'm here!' There, at the far side of the lawn, on a rustic seat in a veritable sun-trap, the man I sought sat with a book in his hand. So I made my way across the grass. When I was within six feet of him, he brought me to a halt with the peculiar question, 'How long were you at sea?'

'Close on thirty 'ear!' says I. 'Is't my rolling gait that betrays me?'

'Nivver!' says he. 'Ye dinna hae a rolling gait, if sic a thing exists! I kent as seen as I saw ye, an I've been sittin here this meenit or twaa, winnerin fit on earth a man fae the sea's deein at my door!'

'Aha!' says I. 'Somebody must ha tellt ye I wis comin!'

'Not at all!' says he. 'Man, div ye nae ken that saat water's written aa ower ye? Ye couldna possibly hide it, even if ye tried!'

I stood for a moment in silent disbelief then he fired another question.

'Faar div ye come fae?'

'Peterheid!'

'Oh aye!' says he. 'The Blue Toon! Born an brocht up there, wis ye?' I nodded my head and started to speak, but again he silenced me.

'It's ten to one ye're a Buchan!' and when I nodded an affirmative, he smiled. 'That was easy. But there's a something aboot ye that still puzzles me!'

I decided to remain silent while he tried to solve the mystery.

'Yer father a Peterheid man?'

'Oh aye! Actually born in Burnhaven, but in Peterheid maist o his days.'

'Burnhaven's near aneuch!' says he. 'I ken far Burnhaven is!' Then to my amazement, he came with something which was half statement and half question, 'Yer mither's nae fae Peterheid.'

'Ye're richt, freen. She's fae Stirlingshire.'

'Ye're like yer mither's folk!' says he, as if suddenly enlightened.

'Richt again!' says I. 'I'm like my mither's folk!'

'I micht ha kent!' says he. 'Ye dinna hae an Aiberdeenshire face!' He was delighted that he had discovered the 'something aboot me' which had baffled him for a wee whilie. I was simply amazed, and somewhat amused.

On the way home that day, I suddenly recalled the story of 'Eyes and No Eyes'. True enough, some folk have 'em, some folk don't! I'm one of the Don'ts.

Strange as it may seem, less than a week later, I had an almost identical experience at the farm of Andrewsford, near Fyvie, only this time there was no mention of the Aiberdeenshire face. I am still at a loss as to what an Aiberdeenshire face is supposed to look like. The lady of the house at Andrewsford managed to read me without touching on that aspect of the matter.

But, ever since these two instances, I have been especially struck by the words of a certain woman of Samaria, when she said to her fellow villagers, 'Come, see a man, who told me all things that ever I did.' (John 4:29.)

Hill Silver

'Od, Peter!' says Mains. 'I didna expect t' see you here the day! Nae wi aa this snaa! Ye should hae mair sense than come awaa up here among the hills in wither like this!'

'If I'd kent fit like it wis, I widna been here avaa!' says I. 'But there's nae snaa doon at the coast. It's only in the last half oor that there's been ony t' spik aboot. Ye'll hae t' flit, Mains. Flit!'

'Aye, fairly!' says he. 'We'll think aboot flittin eence we've heen oor tay. Snaa or oan snaa, ye fairly ken the wye t' judge fan the kettle'll be bilin. Come awaa inside an gie's yer crack, syne I'll lat ye see my new bull!'

'Oh!' says I. 'We've a new bull, hiv we? Fit is she, Charlie or Hereford or Friesian? An fit colour is she?'

Boys, I thocht he wid choke! He could hardly tak 'is tay for lauchin.

'A bull's nae a she! It's a he, ye great goat! It's a bull, nae a boat!'

'Oh!' says I. 'Ye're aye learnin.' I dinna like bulls!

Oot in the byre, he lat me see the great beast; black an fite. Very near a ton, I wis thinkin, an I wisna far oot.

'She's a topper,' says I, 'A topper! But div ye nae think she wid be better wi a stronger moorin rope? That tow widna hang a cat!'

He wis awaa again, lauchin. 'That's a quaet beast,' says he, 'else he wid be bun wi a chain! But I ken the tow's fair deen, an the spare that I hae is jist as bad. Div ye think ye could mak a halter? I canna dee a thing wi tows!'

'Nae bother avaa!' says I. 'I've a fine tow oot in the van. Cut ee the iron ring aff o the spare halter, an we'll hae a new moorin rope in a meenit or twaa.'

As I spliced the bonny new rope, Mains stood in admiration. 'Hey,' says he, 'Is there onything ye canna dee? I'm jist thinkin ye could be a great help t' me!'

'Look,' says I. 'Dinna get nae fancy ideas. I'm willin t' splice a halter for the bull, but I'm nae takkin on t' mak brazeers for yer coos!'

He wis awaa again, lauchin! Then, when he'd gotten 'is braith back, he says, 'I've some idder thing t' lat ye see. C'mon!'

The 'some idder thing' wis a snowdrift between a long, heavy iron roller and the garden dyke; say eight feet long and more than two feet deep.

'Look at the like o that!' says Mains.

'Bonny fite snaa', says I. 'Is that fit I'm supposed t' look at?'

'Wheesht! Jist wyte a meenit!' says he, then, with a pick-axe shaft, he gently broke the frosted crust of the drift before scooping away some of the snow with his hands. 'Look at the like o that, noo!' says he.

'That' was a beautiful salmon, gleaming silver in the sun. 'Look at the like o that, noo!' says he, with a note of pride in his voice. 'There's anither five-an-twenty forbyes that een! You that kens folk that handles fish, could ye dee onything wi that lot? Div ye think ye could sell them, somewye?'

'Faar on earth did ye get that?' says I, astonished beyond measure. 'Ye're at least three mile fae the river, an close on thirty mile fae the sea. I hardly think ye shot them doon as they were fleein ower yer heid, so, faar did ye get them? An dinna gie me nae lees!'

'I got them at the boddim o my neep park,' says Mains. 'Doon in the howe there, atween the twaa parks. There eesed t' be a burn there, although it's little mair than a ditch noo. But, man, the salmon still comes up at their appointed time, though fyles there's barely eneuch watter t' cover them. I can ging doon at nicht wi a torch an a big heuk, an jist trail them oot! Nae bother avaa! I'm fair scunnert aitin the things noo, an so's my neepers! Fit aboot it noo? I'll gie ye half o the siller, if ye sell them!'

'Ye've been gey greedy, freen,' says I, 'killin aa yon fish, an you nae needin them! An fit wye wid ee ken foo muckle siller I got for them, supposin I sellt them?'

'I ken ye're nae gweed,' says he, 'but I dinna think ye'd chate me!'

'Will ye pey the fine if I'm catched?' says I.

'Ye're surely nae feart, are ye? Faa wid look for salmon in an ile van? An specially your van, cos aabody kens ye'd nivver dee sic a thing!'

'See a hud o a score o the brutes!' says I. 'I'll tak a chance!'

I was just at the end of Main's road when I had to give way to a huge lorry, grinding up the brae. Then, sink me if he didna stop his lorry richt across my bows so that I couldna win oot!

'Aha!' thinks I. 'This lad's surely clean tint; I'll need t' tell 'im far he is!' So I oot-ower t' speak t' the chiel, but I met 'im at the front o's larry.

'Are ye lost?' says I.

'Lost?' says he. 'Nivver! I bide nae far fae here. I wis jist winnerin if ye could be deein wi a lettrick bathroom heater. Spleet new. Fower fit lang. Nivver oot o the box. Guaranteed t' stite back. Thirty bob! And he opened the passenger door to show me an array of heaters packed tightly between the door and the engine.

'The love o Dod Vricht!' says I. 'Faar did ye get that lot?'

'M.Y.O.D.B.' says he.

'Please yersel!' says I. 'But I'm nae needin a bathroom heater, an a thing's nae a bargain if ye're nae needin't! Could ye be deein wi a salmon?' And I opened the door of my van. Boys! His een near fell oot o's heid.

'******,' says he. 'Faar on earth did ye get that lot?'

'Same place as you got yer heaters!' says I.

'Od!' says he, 'I'm affa fond o salmon, but I've affa little siller! Fit wid ye be needin for that big een?'

288

'Fower heaters, my loon. Chaip at half the price!'

The deal was done on the spot!

Weel noo, Hilly took een, Bogs took anither, an Dockens took twaa. I'm tellin ye, there wisna mony left b' the time I made the Blue Toon, far I got twaa boxes o kippers fae a smoker, an a hale coil o rope fae a chandler chiel. Nae scruples avaa, yon cove — It wis a raivelt coil he gied me! I got ither odds-an-sods forbye. Nae a bad day's work!

Neist day, Mains an me sattled up. We pairted the siller, up an doon the middle, as had been the deal. I nivver tellt 'im aboot the ten bags o tatties, cos Mains had plinty tatties o his ain! Mrs Mains wis affa fine shuited.

'Jist the verra dunt for mairridge presents, yon bathroom heaters!'

Mains himsel wis fine pleased.

'Ye're a great lad!' says he. 'I wis feart the fish wid ging rotten!'

'That mines me,' says I. 'I'll tak the rest o them awaa, noo!'

'Och, ye're ower late, Peter! She's biled fit wis left, t' feed the hens!'

Od. I could ha chappit the pair o them!

'Hey, Peter!' cries he, as I started the engine. 'Fit on earth'll I dee wi yon great fyang o tow that ye feess up?'

'Mak brazeers t' yer blastit coos!' says I.

Hame-Made Wine

I wis as green as girss, and the country folk kent, so they leuch at me. I wis as fisher as a speldin, and the country folk kent that anaa, so they leuch at me again. Nae a coorse lauch, mind ye, but jist a quaet chuckle. To them I wis something o a ferlie, a rare bird, a stroonge chiel, for had I nae left the sea aifter near thirty 'ear at it? An had I nae been a hale 'ear an 'uncertified' secondary school-teacher, an had I nae turned doon a Fishery Officer's job, cos it meant leavin hame? A chiel like that could hardly be normal, gaan aboot the country in a van, sellin ile to fairmers. Some thocht I wisna jist the hale shillin. They could ha been richt!

Well now, here was I, Traveller for an oil firm, serving the public, the all important link between Firm and Customer — the Sales Representative. Maybe I should tell you now that to fisher-folk sales-reps are jist 'traivellers', but to country-folk they are Travellers, with a capital 'T'. Mony a time, ower the next eleven years, did I think I wis jist lookin for victims!

I must confess that my knowledge of things agricultural was absolutely minimal. I didna ken a bee fae a bull's fitt. My speech betrayed my fisher origin; the fact that I paced restlessly back-an-fore at the cattle marts betrayed it even further, not that I sought at any time to hide it. But I was, after all, a stranger in a foreign land.

Then one fine day at Turra Mart, an aal, seasoned Traveller who aye wore a

289

rose in his button-hole took me aside and gave me a great deal of sound advice which stood me in good stead over the years.

'Peter,' says he, 'dinna look sae worried! For a lang time, aabody'll spik aboot ye, some'll tak the len o ye, an some micht even ging the linth o bein coorse t' ye. But jist ee keep a calm sough, an aifter aboot three 'ear ye'll be accepted. Syne ye'll winner fit aa the t'dee wis aboot, an ye'll hae the feelin that a door's been opened. Till that time, jist sodjer on. Dinna pey ower muckle attention t' the fairmer, raither watch the wife, for if she likes ye, ye'll be their ile man nae maitter fit he says. But if she disna like ye, ye needna bother. Nivver caa the fairm wife Mrs Fairmer unless ye're sure that she actually IS Mrs Fairmer, an nivver refuse tay if ye're offered it.'

Jake wis richt wi some things but, mind ye, a hantle o the country-folk accepted me fae the start. A fyowe did tak the len o me for a fylie until they realised that fyles I micht be takkin the len o them. Thereafter we became good friends. I listened very closely and soon acquired an extensive vocabulary of country terms so that I could converse quite knowledgeably about farm affairs. Since the Traveller is a welcome source of news to his clients, it's in his own interest to acquaint himself with local events and with local 'claik' if necessary. I developed a deep thirst for knowledge and found that in this respect most folks were more than willing to help. Fun was inevitable, sometimes deliberate, sometimes quite spontaneous. Hard-workin, kindly folk, the country folk; roch an ready at times, maybe, but aaricht at the hairt, an maist o them likit a lauch.

Cam the day I wis in the byre at Mains o Currandad, speirin the verra guts oot o aal Sandy an storin aa the information in my heid. Fin it wis time t' ging hame, I said I wis sorry for hinnerin the wark, but he widna hear o that.

'Peter,' says he, 'if ivver there's onything ye wid like t' ken, jist ee speir at me, for I ken ivvery mortal thing aboot fairmin. It's fine t' see a lad sae keen t' learn, an ye've come t' the richt een. Fire aheid, ony time ye like!'

'Weel, Sandy,' says I, same's I wisna ower willin t' annoy the man, 'could ye tell me fit a "bugger" is?'

Od! I thocht for a meenit that he'd swallied 'is teeth, for he hoastit an clochert an spat, glowerin into my face, same's he wis lookin for something. But I had the curtains drawn, so he couldna see naething.

'Fit gars ye spier sic a thing?' says he.

'Weel,' says I, 'In the first fairm I wis in the day, the word apparently applied t' mysel; in the neist place it seemed t' be a tractor that widna start; in the third place it wis his next-door neeper, an noo, in your place it's a beast that's scourin. Dis't mean different things in different places?'

Sandy keepit lookin, lookin. I'm tellin ye, I wis gey sair made! At last he got 'is braith back, then he says, 'As far as I can tell ye, it means a stick that the sawmill folk reject as nae bein nae eese for naething.'

'Man, Sandy,' says I, 'that's jist gran! A buddy's aye learnin!' But I'm sure that fin aal Charlie Sim at Strichen used the word, he didna mean his timmer avaa!'

Much of aal Jake's advice proved very useful; some of it was utterly irrelevant, for every Traveller has his own individual approach, his own style and his own personality. You'll never find two alike, and exactly the same thing applies to his clients.

Well do I remember the day I went to see a dear old soul who was thinking she might replace her old coal-burning stove with the latest oil-burning type. She listened very closely while I extolled the virtues of the new appliance then, after a very short time for thought, she fired a proper bobby-dazzler at me.

'Will't burn a deid hen?'

'I doot hardly,' says I.

'Weel!' says she, 'I'm nae seekin't.'

On the same day, on the same errand I called at another farm about thirty miles distant. There I secured a firm order and enjoyed a fine cuppie o tay wi a Gaimrie Knottie then, while we sat newsin, I noticed, on the window-sill, three great muckle steen pigs (earthen-ware jars). The neck of each jar was tightly corked, and through the cork there came a little glaiss tube, and on the end of the tube there was a little wee bottlie the size o a match box.

'Fit on earth's that?' says I. 'Are ye a droggist in yer spare time, or are ye makkin booms for the I.R.A.?'

'Oh!' says the fairmer, 'That's my outfit for makkin hame-made wine! Wid ye like a glaiss?'

'No, thank ye,' says I. 'I nivver touch drink avaa!'

'Och! That winna touch ye,' says he. 'It's jist a puckle rasps wi a twa-three raisins throwe them. It's gran stuff, tho I say't mysel.'

Noo, afore ye could say Jake, the deemie (she wisna Mrs Fairmer) had three glaisses on the table, filled fae a bottle that she took fae the press. I dinna think I ivver saw onybody move as fast.

Boys! Yon wis rare stuff! Jist like yon fruit cordial that the bairns get at Hogmanay. Smooth as velvet, an nivver a sign o a kick aboot it!

'Ye'll tak anither drappie?' says he.

'Aye, surely! That widna hurt a flee!' says I. An, as fast as lichtnin the deemie had the glaisses full again. Great stuff!

But, half-wye throwe the second glaiss, the swaal seemed t' be risin.

'Aha!' says I t' mysel, 'We're surely in for a coorse nicht. This swaal's the dog afore 'is maister.'

Things seemed to worsen very suddenly, and I could hear mysel, lauchin at naething. Nae a gweed sign! I'm gled I dinna drink, for I'm sure I wid mak a richt feel drunk!

The deemie got baith her elbicks on the table an reestit her heid on her hands. Then, lookin me stracht in the face like a cockle-eed owl, she tellt me her name, her precise date o birth, foo muckle siller she had, coppers an aa thegither, an fit Bunk it wis in. Syne, stabbin at her chest wi her finger, she says, 'Ye'll need t' unnerstan that I'm a Miss! I'm a Miss!'

'Aha!' says I in the profundity of my new-found wisdom. 'Ee'll be fit they caa a virgin, are ye?'

'Na! Nae yet!' she says.

Fortunately St Christopher whispered in my lug that it wis time I wis lookin for

Buchan Ness, so I left that port an got onto the road. I was sure that the course for Buchan Ness was east-nord-east, but it's nae easy t' steer a course if somebody's stolen the compass. An forbye, there wis solid rocks on baith sides o me. (Actually they were dry-steen dykes). Now, ony feel kens that in such conditions the only sensible thing t' dee is t' drap the anchor, but it's nae easy t' drap the anchor if that's been stolen anaa! I couldna get the anchor naewye! So I jist stoppit the engine an let her lie ower the broadside, like a trawler. Boys, what a nicht I put in. I sat for three strucken oors, grippin onto the wheel, an boys, she didna half roll! There wis a fyle that I thocht she wid ging richt ower on the tap o me, but it's strange that she nivver took a drap o watter.

At long last, jist afore dark, the wither eased awaa an I managed t' win hame.

'Faar on earth hiv ee been the day?' says her ain sel. 'Ye look like a fish supper struck wi lichtnin. Ye hinna been drinkin, hiv ye?'

'Na, na!' says I. 'I've been awaa seein aboot a berth. I'm gaan back t' the sea the morn.'

'An fit div ye think ye'll dee there, aifter aa this time ashore?'

'Och!' says I, 'I'll be aaricht. I'm gaan t' be skipper o a rum-runner in the Virgin Islands.'

The Motor Bike

Once upon a time, some fifty-odd years ago, I had a cousin who had a thing about motor-bikes, just as today's youth has a thing about cars. Of course, in those days cars were very scarce indeed, for a car could cost as much as £350, and nobody had that sort of money. Not even all the Doctors had cars, some of them doing their rounds on a push-bike, with their bag slung from the handlebars. Any buddy with a car was bound to be in the highest layer of Society, and even a buddy with a motor-bike and sidecar was doing very nicely, thank-you, in a world where most folk's transport was Shanks' mare.

Well now, into this world comes Cousin, all Oxford bags and Brylcreem. Oxford bags were trousers whose leg width was twenty-two inches, the height of fashion at that time. They looked not too bad on a tall chap, but they did nothing for the average youth, especially when a following wind made them spread as wide as any skirt, giving the wearer the appearance of a tea-cosy with a figurine on top. Brylcreem was a pure white hair-dressing which was sold in jars and clarted on by the gallon. The rugged, windswept look was definitely not in fashion. I've heard that the mannie who invented the stuff made it in his sheddie, and made a million by selling the recipe to some international cosmetics firm.

Cousin was more or less a foreigner, for he came from the Central Belt, that indeterminate slice of Scotland somewhere south of Perth. He simply could not understand our language, but was agreeably surprised that we understood his. Well, you see, he was simply speaking the same tongue as our Mither spoke, so we had no difficulty with it. The main purpose of Cousin's visit was, apparently, 'to look for a job', for there were no jobs down south. He nottna come to the Blue Toon for a job, cos the queue of unemployed stretched from the Buroo, in Back Street right along Thistle Street and up Marischal Street as far as Marioni's. That was the time of the Great Depression, so Cousin didna get a job, but I dinna think he wis ower sair worried, as lang as he got his dole on Friday. I think it wis fourteen shillins he got. That's 70p in decimal coinage . . . Not a lot.

But the outstanding thing about Cousin was his motor-bike, a great bummer o a machine that had won the T.T. races in the Isle of Man last summer. When I asked him how any young unemployed fella could afford such a machine, he said that only half the bike was his, a pal owning the other half. To raise the money, the pair shaved their heads, so that they couldn't go to the duncin, or the picters for fear of ridicule. 'We kept it up,' says he, 'for six months, and the money accumulated very fast. In fact, we lived like hermits!' Sadly, I doubted his word. Aff o fourteen bob? Nivver! When I asked whether it was the front half or the rear half that was his, he wisna neen shuited!

Cousin was quite popular with the local girls, for he was an accomplished dancer who could charm a bird oot o a tree. I know that some of the young ladies willingly 'peyed him in' to the dance, simply for the pleasure of his expertise and the benefit of his instruction. He could fairly dance! So it was tennis, dancing, and the motor-bike. 'Lookin for a job', he called it.

On the day prior to his departure for home, Cousin offered me a hurl on his machine. I was very nervous, but I didn't have the guts to refuse. He was delighted at my acceptance, and I'm sure he set out to repay me for the teasing to which I had subjected him, for the bike gid oot the Broch road like an evil speerit! Boys, I wis scared stiff! Parks o corn an wheat, neeps an tatties an peys an barley gid bye like a great muckle pot o broth. Ninety mile an hour, and still he wisna satisfied. We cam hame by Longside, and we took the Flushing Straight at one hundred and forty.

My great mistake, born of inexperience, was to sit rigid, instead of leaning over with the machine as it took the various bends. I was actually fighting the machine and, by the time I got hame, I wis like a vrung cloot. Since that day I personally have had a thing about motor-bikes! I widna ging back on one o them — nae for a pension!

Cousin left for home next day, found a job, and eventually worked himself to the top, but not in Oxford bags, of course.

Every time I recall that hair-raising journey, I find myself in deep sympathy with the loon fae Foggieloan that had an experience similar to mine. This loon's big brither had gotten a great muckle two-stroke bike, an widna rest until he got the loon on the pillion. But, before starting out, he did advise the youngster to lean with the machine. This would greatly help the driver to handle the powerful brute, and at the same time the passenger would have a more comfortable ride.

So it wis off to Banff and a baggie o chips. As they sat near the pier enjoying their snack, Big Brither says, 'Foo are ye likin the hurl?'

'Fine!' says the loon, 'But it's affa caal fin ye ging faist. The win jist fussles throwe my claes, for I dinna hae a jacket on. It's maybe aa richt for you, wi yer leather jacket, but I'm fair frozen!'

'Nivver mind aboot that!' was the reply, 'But jist wyte a meenit. I think there's a spare jacket in yon saddle-bag, jist far ye've been sittin. Lat's hae a look!'

Sure enough, there was a spare leather jacket in the pannier, but it had one glaring fault . . . it simply would not fasten at the front. Zip fastener broken beyond repair.

'Weel!' says Big Brither, 'Ye're as weel athoot it, if it disna fasten, for it'll jist blaa open like a sail. In fact, ye wid be blaan clean aff the seat. Fit are we gaan t' dee aboot that?'

'Hey!' says the loon, 'I could aye pit it on back-to-front. That wid surely keep the draacht oot! Fit div ye think?'

'Great idea! Jist gran! Fit wye did I nae think o that mysel? Get the thing on, an we'll gie't a try, onywye.'

So, on goes the jacket. Jist the job! The verra dunt!

'Noo than!' says Big Brither, 'A bittie o binder twine roon yer middle, an that's you riggit! The collar comes up as far as yer een . . . Man, ye've a better rig than I hae mysel!'

Oh, the loon was fair chuffed! Cosy as a flech on a sheep. Rarin to go!

'Noo!' says Big Brither, 'I'll tak ye along the coast road as far as Pennan, syne we'll ging hame by Cyaak an Byth an the Mill o Pot. We'll maybe get a fly cup in Turra, forbye. It'll be a richt fine run on a bonny day like this.'

It wis a richt fine run! Yon loon could fairly lean ower wi the bike, an her gaan like a certain kind o bee (ye ken the kind I mean). But, sad to say, somewye aboot the Barnyairds o Delgaty the loon leaned a hackie ower far ower, an fell clean aff the bike, in amon the lang girss at the roadside. Fit a clyte! The bike wis near in Turra afore the loon wis missed, syne Big Brither cam roarin back to look for 'im.

He didna hae far to look, for three fairm chiels that had been at the hyowe were stannin on the grass verge, lookin doon at something.

'Is he aaricht?' cries Big Brither, pushin in atween them. 'Is he aaricht?'

'Weel noo!' wis the reply. 'He wis spikkin awaa fine till we turned 'is heid the richt road!'

Gweed preserve us aa fae motor bikes.

Wheelies

As far as I could see, Gran had nae feet! Maybe her feet had been worn awaa like the soles o sheen, for Gran wis a fearsome age. Even my ain feet grew sair at times, rinnin aboot the rocks an san o the foreshore, so maybe that wis the trouble wi Gran's feet ... she had played ower muckle doon the braes, an worn her feet aff! Peer aal wifie! She wis even a lot aaler than Ma, an Ma wis an aal wifie hersel, but I kent that Ma had feet, cos I could see them! So, fit wye could Gran ging aboot the close an the green athoot feet? Wheelies! It couldna be naething else but wheelies aneth yon lang skirts, skirts that brushed the grass, an nae doot she wore skirts that linth to hide the wheelies. That wis it, for sure!

Cam the time when Gran had to ging an lie doon, cos she wis nae weel. For a long, long time she lay in her feather bed in an upstairs bedroom where I visited her daily, being the only grandchild permitted to enter the room. I wis sorry for the peer aal wifie, cos she lay there singin, 'Bring forth the royal diadem, and crown Him Lord of all!' She wis surely dottled, for there wisna sic a word as 'diadem'; 'Diamond', maybe, but nivver 'diadem'.

On very rare occasions, I got a puff cracknel wi butter on't fae Gran, cos she couldna manage it hersel and, wi the titbit in my hand, I wid run ootside to arouse bitter jealousy in the hearts of my playmates. Puff cracknels? My govies!

Then, one day, Gran passed away. I didna greet, cos Gran wis awaa t' the Happy Land t' see Jesus. I wis a bittie puzzled at this, cos Gran was in a great, lang box, ben in the Room, wearin a bonny fite goon! Deydie sat dressed at the heid o the box, unveiling Gran's countenance to each one of the innumerable callers, who gied their een a dicht sayin, 'She's richt like hersel, isn't she?' That too, puzzled me. Faa else could she be like? When Deydie lifted me up to see my Gran, I thocht she wis jist like Gran, but my swift glance left me still wondering whether it was feet or wheelies that she had, for I couldna see!

This, at a very tender age, was my first sight of Death. I was far too young to have the slightest idea what it meant; but I wasn't too young to remember! On a brass plate on the lid of the box, propped against the wall, I saw a 7 and a 2 beside Gran's name. I didna ken that the figures meant 72. I jist kent that they meant 'affa, affa aal!' I dinna think that noo! 'When I was a child, I understood as a child.'

Isn't it passing strange how Memory, from the secret depths of some magical filing system can, quite unbidden, bring long forgotten things to life, to present them to us clear and fresh as on the day they happened? Wordsworth says, 'They flash upon the inward eye, which is the bliss of solitude'. Remember that line? Well do I know about the inward eye, for it has brought me many a sharp reproof in the midnight watches ... 'Fit are ye lyin there lauchin at, ye great feel?' And, somehow, it is beyond me to explain!

Fit aboot the day that Untie Jean wis byaakin breid, as she so often did, breid being oatcakes and bread being simply loaf. Some cousins of mine from a distant shire had come to visit Gran, while some local cousins had come to see the

295

strangers, and I, not to be outdone, had come to see them all. The room was grossly overcrowded and unbearably hot, but on such a day of torrential rain it wasn't possible to play outside. So we watched the baking process with great interest for a whilie.

Jean rolled the mixture into a flat disc before transferring it to the iron 'girdle', whereon it was baked for a whilie above the fire. When the consistency of the disc was deemed to be just right, it was cut into corters (triangular quarters), which were browned before the glowing coals. In this final browning process, the corters assumed a beautifully curved form, not at all flat. With syrup or treacle, they were delicious, a temptation to hungry bairns. And that's where the trouble started! Some of us kept nippin at the fresh breid, incurring the displeasure of Gran, who stood at the table in a supervisory role only. She kent better than to interfere wi Jean, but she fairly managed to control us bairns.

'G'waa an play ootside!' Then, seeing the heavy rain, 'Bide awaa fae the table, an bide awaa fae the fire! G'waa an play hide-an-seek or something!'

So, hide-an-seek it wis, and I wis to be 'the mannie'. I had to turn my back, steek my een an say, 'Five, ten; double ten; five, ten a hunder!' Nae ower fast ye ken, so that the ithers wid get time to hide.

Weel noo, gettin them wis jist nae bother avaa.! Faar could they hide, onywye? But there wis one cousin who had me beat! Search as I might, I jist couldna get him, and I wis on the verge o cryin, 'I'm bate!' when there came a sudden movement of Gran's skirt, the skirt that brushed the fleer. Up cam the hem, and oot popped the culprit, whom I grabbed in glee.

'Got ye! Got ye!' says I, in triumph.

'Aye, maybe!' says he, in a surly tone. 'But ye widna gotten me yet, if Gran hidna fartit!'

Boys, I've jist mined this meenit! I should ha speired at him if it wis wheelies or feet that she had! Still, maybe it wis ower dark t' see!

NOTE: Several women in the town baked 'breid' for the drifters, and every one was extremely jealous of her good name as a baker. Normal practice was for the skipper to order the breid from the ship's grocer, always stipulating who should do the baking. The grocer would then deliver the oatmeal to the required address, and uplift the finished product in due time.

For baking 5 stones (32 kilos) of meal, using her own fire, the baker was paid £1.

The Nightcap

For more than fifty years Dod and Weelim had been close friends. They were actually distant cousins of a sort and, all their working days, they had never known anything but the sea. Year after year they had followed the herring shoals, and they kent every hole and bore from Yarmooth north-about to Milford Haven, including the Shetlands. But now advancing years had decreed that they should forsake the big boats for a ripper boatie, so their livelihood was now derived from codlings, mackerel and lobsters.

'Nae muckle siller avaa!' says Dod. 'Jist as muckle as mak it interestin.'

Fishermen of the old school, the two confirmed bachelors lived in simple style, each in his own little cottage in a village on the Buchan coast. The cottages themselves had been handed down through several generations but, since Dod and Weelim seemed to be the last of their line, speculation was rife as to who would inherit the hoosies. Village claik! Ye ken the wye o't.

Only for weddings or funerals would the pair don collar and tie, the only difference between the two events being that a funeral required a black bonnet. The normal go-ashore rig for Dod and Weelim comprised a navy blue serge jacket, a home-knitted jersey (also navy blue) and a pair of tailor made 'hairback' (Kersey) trousers almost black in colour. The bonnet for such an outfit was invariably checked, and cost at most half-a-crown.

Now, should you query the colour of the trousers, let me tell you that the colour varied from village to village. Lesser breeds might wear navy blue, or a deep, deep shade of brown, but the garments would all be of top grade cloth and more often than not, they would be bought 'on tick'.

Was there nothing, then, to distinguish our heroes from the common rabble? Aye, surely, there wis a something! They did the Pools!

'The Pools?' says you. 'Nivver! I'm jist nae for that avaa!'

'Ah, but aye,' says I. 'They did dee the Pools on the quiet!'

In fact, Dod and Weelim had been committing this cardinal sin for years. When first they set foot on the slippery slope, Dod says to Weelim, 'We'd better keep this unanimous.'

'Ye mean anonymous!' says Weelim.

'I dinna mean onything o the kind!' says Dod. 'I mean that naebody has to ken aboot it, cos if this village comes to hear aboot iss, we'll be putten oot!'

'Ye're richt there, freen!' says Weelim. 'Unanimous it is!'

What a stammagaster they got when, after twenty-odd years, they were informed that they had won the jackpot of some £60,000 between them. (That wis a lot o candy, in those days.) If they would care to come to London for the Presentation, they would be met at King's Cross and everything would be laid on. They would certainly appear on Pathe-News in the picters, and it was possible that they just might get a mention on the wireless.

'We'd better ging,' says Weelim. 'I'm black affrontit! Lat's get oot o here afore we're yokit on. Fit wid my peer aal mither say?'

297

'I've haard ye at that afore!' says Dod. 'Jist mine fit yer aal mither said afore she deet... "If ivver ye look at a wumman, Weelim, I'll turn in my grave!"' They tell me the cemetery mannie caas her Furlin Jess. Ha-ha! Ye rascal. C'mon, lat's tak the train.'

So the prize-winners hurriedly packed their cases and swyted their wye sooth, to be met, as promised, by a Pools mannie who immediately took charge of them.

The hotel manager gave the two unaccustomed guests a warm welcome, and appointed an underling to see to their every need.

'This way, gentlemen,' says the mannie. 'I'll show you to your rooms.'

'Rooms!' says Dod. 'Rooms! There's jist the twaa o's. Surely ae room's eneuch!'

'Just as you wish, sir. That can quite easily be arranged.' So, after a short confab with the receptionist, he led the way to the lift, carrying the two battered old cases, neither of which could possibly be locked, for the keys had disappeared some time after the Boer war.

'Isn't iss bonny, noo?' says Dod, on seeing the room.

'Richt bonny!' says Weelim. 'An the water closet's jist ben the hoose. Boys, that's the first water closet I've seen wi a bath in't. I'll maybe wash my feet the nicht.'

'They're nae oot o the need o't, aswarn!' says Dod. Then to the mannie, 'Is there some ither body sleepin here the nicht?'

'Not at all, sir, not at all! Why do you ask such a thing?'

'Weel!' says Dod, 'There's twa bides... there's surely little need for that, fin there's jist the pair o's.'

'Sir!' says the mannie, whose mither had been a rovin kind o quine fae The Gash, and had bestowed upon her offspring the gift of tongues that they might comprehend the Buchan Doric. 'Sir, when one is in London, one sleeps in separate beds. That's why there are two.'

'I'd fairly like to see that,' says Weelim. 'A buddy wid need to be haavert to dee that!'

The mannie gied Weelim a queer look before announcing, 'Dinner is at eight, gentlemen. You'll have time to wash and brush up before then. Now, should you require my services later in the evening, just pull gently on this bell-cord, and I'll be with you immediately. Don't hesitate to use it,' indicating the ornate tasselled cord which hung in a corner. 'I trust you will enjoy your meal.'

Some twenty minutes later, despite the extensive and elaborate menu in the dining-room, the perplexed Chef was confronted with a special order for 'mince an tatties for twaa, wi twenty-meenit sweemers (dough-balls)'. It says a great deal for the Chef that he keepit the heid and coped magnificently, earning the profuse compliments of the two diners (foreigners, of course). Well, how was he, a Sassenach, to know what 'the verra dunt' meant?

Such were the amenities of the hotel that our heroes nivver socht ootside and, replete with their late dinner, they would turn in rather earlier than usual. After all, it had been a long, hot, tiring day, and they were no longer in their pottystatur (prime of life). But a tremendous shock awaited them in their room, for their mannie had been rakin in their cases and, on finding no pyjamas, had managed to produce a couple of sets from the hotel's glory hole.

'Dalmichty!' says Weelim, 'Fit's iss noo? A suit o claes? Iss'll be to wear at the presentation the morn. We're gey weel aff, gettin claes an baabees anaa!'

Dod was a wee bittie suspicious. His only experience of sleeping in strange quarters had been the time when he had been obliged to spend a week in the Church of Scotland Hostel in Yarmouth with a touch of the flu. The two nurses had his linner (flannel sark) and his worsit draars aff afore he could wink, and had had him robed in a royal blue nightie. For a hale week he had felt utterly naked.

Nor would he ever forget a hardy skipper who defied all efforts by the nurses to remove his shocking-pink, bullet-proof nether garments. A bonny ticket he wis too, in royal blue and pink! This same skipper had the disconcerting habit of rudely interrupting any conversation with the observation, 'Prayer changes things!' So fed up did Sister MacArthur become with this annoying conduct that one day she retorted, 'Skipper, if I thocht that prayer would get the drawers aff ye, I would pray very hard indeed!' He never annoyed her again.

As I said, Dod was suspicious. 'We'd better tit the towie (pull the cord) an see fit the mannie says.' The mannie duly answered the signal and explained that the garments were not for the presentation ceremony, but were merely what Londoners called 'night attire', and the gentlemen would be expected to sleep in them.

'Oh!' says Dod. 'Good grief!' says Weelim.

Scarcely had the mannie departed when Dod wis tittin the towie again.

'Div we wear this claes abeen wir draars or aneth them?'

Patient as ever, the mannie told them that, 'in London one does not sleep in one's drawers; one takes them off!'

'Oh!' says Weelim. 'Nivver!' says Dod. A few minutes later, Weelim wis heard to mutter, 'Time the missionaries wis here, sinn! Fancy sleepin wi yer draars aff!'

In a strange bed, in strange clothing, our friends found sleep very elusive. Then, suddenly, Dod remarked, 'Hey, Weelim, there's a thing aneth yer bide something like the flooer-pot that oor Isie keeps her aspidistra in. But this een has a hannle, so it canna be a flooer-pot, an that's nae a place for a flooer-pot onywye!'

'Strange!' says Weelim, 'I'm jist lookin at a thing like that aneth YOUR bide. Will I tit the towie an see fit iss is for?

'It's gey late, but go aheid an see fit he says.'

The mannie wisna neen shuited, and spoke kind o sharp. 'That, gentlemen, is what we in London call a nightcap. Goodnight!'

'We're surely nae richt riggit yet!' says Dod. 'Fit says we try the things on?'

Behold then our two pals, sartorially perfect and suitably helmeted, Dod pechin an tyaavin, nivver a wink; Weelim fast asleep.

Finally, in sheer exasperation, Dod reaches across an shaks Weelim. 'Fit wye is't that ee can sleep wi that on yer heid, fin I canna get a wink avaa?'

Only half awake, Weelim glowered oot aneth the brim o's nightcap and said, 'Hae a wee bittie o sense, freen! Try turnin the snoot to the front!'

299

The Presentation

At the first hint of daylight in the window, Dod was awake. He had discarded his 'nightcap' at midnight, restoring it to its rightful place under the bed, and promising himself that he would tell the mannie in the morning exactly what he thought of folks who, apparently, didna ken ony better than to wear a helmet in bed. But when, on the stroke of seven, the mannie arrived with a trolley bearing tea for two, Dod forgot what he had meant to say. Indeed, he didn't get time to say anything, for the mannie, on seeing the sleeping Weelim still resplendent in his helmet, had disappeared rather hurriedly with a few muttered words.

'Fit wizzat the mannie said eyvnoo?' says Weelim, coming to life.

'Something about a B.F. He surely kens aboot boats,' says Dod.

'He micht ha said if there wis ony herrin in the Broch the day,' says Weelim. Then, on spying the tray, 'Hame wis nivver like this! Still, mine ye, he micht ha brocht a buttery cookie eence he wis on the pirr. Fit div we dee noo?'

'Bath!' says Dod. 'Bath! I hinna heen a bath since I was in the Navy, an that wisna yesterday!'

'Weel! Ye'd better watch that the caddis (fluff) oot o yer belly-button disna choke the drain,' says Weelim, still resentful at Dod's remark of the previous evening about his feet.

Much later, the pair of them, cleaner and fresher than for many a long day, sat down to breakfast, once more faced with an amazing choice of dishes.

'Hey!' says Dod, scanning the exotic menu, 'Wid yer hairt tak a kipper?'

'Aye, surely! But ye'd better mak it twaa!'

So kippers it was, and they were really delicious. If there was a 'mote in the meen', it was that they could hardly use their fingers on the kippers as they would certainly have done at home. It cannot be denied that the kipper is vastly improved by the use of one's fingers, which must be repeatedly licked. I'm sure that it's the licking that enhances the flavour, adding a touch of eastern promise. There was some discussion as to whether the kippers were of east or west coast origin, and there was some speculation on the method of fishing . . . drift-net, ring-net or trawl.

'Speir at the mannie!' says Weelim.

'Faar div ye get yer herrin fae?' says Dod. But the waiter was of little help, merely suggesting that they would probably have come from Billingsgate.

'Nivver seen that name on the chart!' says Dod. 'They're surely imported.'

Breakfast over, a Pools representative took our friends on a tour of the great city. This was their first hurl in a car, and they fairly enjoyed it.

'Iss maan be a fair toon!' says Weelim. 'Bigger nor Yarmooth, think ye?'

'Jist a thochtie, maybe,' says Dod.

Lunch was a protracted affair, very posh and proper. When Weelim expressed amazement at the 'great muckle latrines o soup', Dod suggested quietly that he didna think that wis the richt word to use, tho he wisna ower sure himsel fit the richt word wis.

Then came the presentation, the long awaited moment. Both Pathe Gazette and Movietone News had cameras on the scene, so they would be on the picters sure enough. There were several Press photographers present, publicity being the order of the day, but there was an unexpected hitch when it came to the actual handing over of the money.

'Fit's iss?' says Dod. 'A bittie o paper? A cheque, did ye say? We're nae for nae cheques. Nae fears! A buddy could loss a cheque in the train, or a buddy micht get it stealed. Ye'd better gie's the baabees; cash, so's we'll ken exactly foo we stan.' And on this he was adamant. In vain did the Pools men plead with the pair that such an amount of cash could be 'stealed' far more readily than a cheque, and forbye, it would be difficult to obtain cash at such short notice.

'We'll wyte!' says Weelim. 'The train's nae till nicht.' And wyte they did.

So it came to pass, some two hours later, that our heroes found themselves on the pavement wi their pooches fair stappit wi siller (that includes oxter pooches). The Pools men had washed their hands of them, leaving them to their own devices.

'Fit'll we dee noo?' says Dod. 'It's a fyle yet or train-time.'

'Weel,' says Weelim, 'it maan be near supper-time noo, but I canna say I'm on for muckle supper. Fit says we get a baggie o chips?'

'Good idea!' says Dod. 'Jist the verra dunt.'

Behold the two tycoons now, sauntering along the pavement wi a baggie o chips apiece and licking their fingers in the approved fashion.

'Iss is the same kine o chips that we eesed t' get fae the stallies in Yarmooth, lang an fite but richt fine tasted. Ye mine yon stallies, Dod, far they sellt cockles an mussels an tripe an trotters an aa that kine o trash! Did ivver ye try the tripe, freen?'

'Oh gyaad! Dinna pit me aff my chips. Ye'll hae me clean scunnert!'

Thus the desultory conversation as the pair wandered along, amazed at the great flow of traffic, both mechanical and human.

'A hantle o fyolk! A gryte hantle o fyolk!'

Very soon our heroes were completely lost, but Dod's mither wit led him to seek guidance from a taxi-driver who was momentarily without a fare.

'The Aberdeen train, mate? That'll be King's Cross, and you're miles away from that. But I can easily take you there, if you like.'

Dod explained how they had a couple of hours to spare, time which they didn't wish to waste in a railway station. Could the cabby suggest any alternative?

'Certainly!' says the cabby, with an eye for business. 'I know a nice place where you can watch a film for an hour or so. It's a foreign film about nudists!'

'Nudists?' says Weelim. 'Fit on earth's that?'

'Bare weemin!' says Dod. 'Bare weemin! Bare nyaakit weemin! I'm thinkin we'd better nae tak ye there, or yer peer aal mither'll be licht-heidit furlin in her grave! Is there nae some ither wye that ye can think o, driver?'

'Well,' says the cabby, 'there's the Motor Show, if you're interested in cars. I could take you there and wait for you while you browse around, then I'll take you to your train. How does that sound?'

'Couldna be better!' says Dod, but Weelim wasn't quite so keen.

'My legs is sair, an we could hae a richt fine seat in the picters, supposin the wifies is bare or no! I wid raither see the film.'

'Aswarn ye wid,' leuch Dod, 'but if they're foreign, ye widna ken a word they're sayin, an I'm sure ye widna like that.'

Before Weelim could think of a suitable retort, he was bundled into the taxi, and they were off to the Motor Show.

'I wid fairly like to hae a car!' says Dod. 'I enjoyed yon hurl we got the day. It's putten a great idea into my heid, Weelim. We'll ging an hae a lookie at ony rate. That winna cost muckle, I'm sure. An for ony sake, dinna sit there glowerin an sulkin like a bairn.'

Weelim had no interest whatsoever in things mechanical, but his half-neeper had been smitten hard by the car bug, so much so that he had conceived the idea that he 'micht ging hame in a car instead o the train'. It never crossed his mind that some sort of training, however rudimentary, might be necessary.

The first thing to meet our friends' gaze as they entered the great hall, was a beautiful, gleaming monster in dark green livery. The bonnet seemed to be exceptionally long, and at the opposite end, as if to balance the front, the boot seemed to be just as long. The 'wheelhoose' was in the middle, and didn't amount to very much at all, since it was a two-seater. There was no denying that she was a beauty, and the badge on the bonnet proclaimed her quality.

'Jist look at the like o that, noo!' says Dod. 'Isn't 'at bonny noo? An see the size o the starn locker? Aswarn ye wid get twaa boxes o ripper codlins in there, nae bother avaa!' Then, pointing to the bonnet, 'Weelim! Div ee see fit I see? That'll surely please ye, noo!'

'That' was a dainty little statuette in gleaming silver, some sort of nymph or goddess, apparently about to take flight from the cap of the radiator (far ye pour in the watter) and she was certainly in the altogether.

Weelim was most impressed!

As was to be expected, a keen young salesman, dressed like a circus horse and rubbing his hands in anticipation, was immediately at hand.

'This is the finest car in the world, sir, without the slightest doubt!' But I'm sure there's little need for me to tell ye fit the mannie said; ye'll ken the blurb and the flannel which remain the same from age to age, no matter where. But listen to the chiel when he says, 'Sir will no doubt have noticed that this, the very latest model, is now fitted with a mechanical or electrical windscreen wiper!'

'Fit dis that mean?' says Weelim.

'It jist means,' says Dod, 'that there's nae fartin aboot wi a cloot fin it's rainin. Great fit education can dee, intit?'

Dod had a lookie inower the car, then he tried to twang the spokes on the wheels (something like the wheels on a motor bike), as if they were a harp, then he says, aa at eence, 'Ziss motor for sale?'

'Most certainly, Sir! says the salesman. Then, with a look of doubt at Dod's unsophisticated appearance, 'But she is rather expensive, Sir!'

'Nivver mine that!' says Dod. 'Jist say foo muckle siller ye're needin.'

'I'm afraid, sir, she would set you back to the tune of three thousand pounds! But one must not forget that the figure quoted includes the starting handle which, in some lesser cars, is classed as an extra.'

'Weel!' says Dod, producing a wad of notes near as big as a fish box, 'If that be the case, I'll tak twaa!'

I'm afraid my pen is entirely inadequate to describe the scene as Weelim, producing a similar wad and shivvin Dod oot o the road, says, 'Nae ower fast, freen. Nae ower fast. I'll pey for this lot. EE PEYED FOR THE CHIPS!'

Broken Biscuits

For Jinsie, it had been a long, hard day. Long before sunrise, she had spent a frustrating hour in the washin-hoose, trying in vain to light the boiler fire with damp sticks. As a last resort, she had crossed the road to the stony beach, where she had found a few half-burnt splinters of wood among the ashes of a fire kindled by some bairns the night before. These had finally got the fire going, but the water in the boiler took a long time to heat, so Jinsie was well behind schedule when she roused her three quinies for their breakfast porridge. Normally, she would have been 'weel tee wi the work', but this was to be 'een o yon kine o days!' She was quite sure of that.

As soon as the bairns were off to school, Jinsie was at the washin-tub, scrubbing and scouring at the two shifts of heavy clothing sent home from Yarmouth by her man and teenage son. This, on top of her washing for herself and the quines, was enough to give Jinsie a sair day's work. Hot water had to be taken from the boiler to the tub in a pail or a pannie, then the boiler had to be topped up. The fire also required stoking from time to time. Every article had to be hand scrubbed, then thoroughly rinsed before being taken throught the great, murderous mangle. Heavy dirty clothing required special treatment with the heavy, wooden 'dolly'. There was water all over the place, and there was sweat all over Jinsie! In Jinsie's parlance, washing-day was a day for bare sleeves, and many a time did she wipe her forehead on her forearm between trips to the kitchen to see to the dinner. Some wives were reputed to have 'airms like a Clydesdale horse', but Jinsie was of slight build, and the job took toll of her strength.

It was mid-day before the wash was finished. Then, just as Jinsie was hanging out the last few thingies, her elderly father came on the scene.

'Ye'd better come, Jins! Yer mither's teen anither turn!'

So Jinsie left everything as it was, and went. But first she asked her neighbour Leebie to see that the bairns got their dinner. 'There's a great pot o tattie soup aa ready, Leebie, an ye can tak fit's left t' yersel an yer bairns!'

Leebie assured Jinsie that all would be well. 'Jist ee gwaa an see yer mither!'

Jinsie's mither, Kirsten, took 'turns' or 'dwaams' from time to time and, since

303

Jinsie was the nearest to the maternal home, Jinsie was always the first to be called. The reason for the 'turns' was rather obscure, but it was well known that a tayspeenfae o brandy could work wonders. Jinsie's sister Muggity was uncharitable enough to suggest that it was to get the brandy that her mither took the 'turns'.

'Div ye nae see that she aye needs mair o the naphtie than she nott the time afore? I'll sweer the aal bizzom's teen a likin for the stuff! an her a British Woman anaa!'

Be that as it may, the hard-hearted Muggity was in Yarmouth, so it fell to Jinsie to do the needful, and it was well into the afternoon before Jinsie got hame. There she found that all her washing was out to dry, the dishes had been washed and the fire was burning nicely. But, best of all, there was a fine drappie o soup left in the pot, enough to make her realise just how hungry she was. Boys, yon wis gran soup!

'Ye didna tak ony o the soup, Leebie?' says Jinsie, later in the afternoon.

'There wisna neen t' tak,' says Leebie. 'Yon quines o yours fairly kens the wye t' shift their mait! I wis sair made t' get them t' leave a drappie t' yersel! But, in case ye hinna noticed, I've teen the len o yer marra bone, an we'll hae tattie soup wi't the morn!'

Aye! Times were hard; actually as hard as that! I wis at the school wi Leebie's loons!

Weel noo, Jinsie got her claes in aff the tow jist afore supper time, then it wis feeding-time again for the quines. Skirlie wis the supper, that nicht, skirlie being oatmeal and sliced ingins fried in very shallow fat. In fact, the best skirlie wis toasted/roasted rather than fried, the secret being in the art of not letting the stuff stick to the pan. Jinsie had a chum who wis housekeeper to a lawyer in the posh part of town, and this chum would occasionally bring her a bowl of dripping. Only in lawyers' and bankers' hooses did ye get dripping... fisher folk got fat! Anyhow, skirlie made with the golden dripping wis very, very good indeed. Specially when the two really important ingredients were present, namely that the family was always very, very hungry, and skirlie was very, very cheap! Maks a difference, ye ken!

Supper past, Jinsie went back to visit her mither, and advised her father to get Dr Gillespie in the morning if there was no improvement in the 'turns'. The doctor's visit would cost a shillin or twaa, but it was obvious that brandy by itself was merely a stop-gap measure. An ye didna get brandy for naething, either!

Promising to return at bedtime, Jinsie left her mither's hoose and went home, where she busied herself at shooin an darnin. Her quinies were jist ootside in the streetie, playin wi a 'jumpin rope' an singin, 'Eevy, ivy, turn the rope over. Mother's at the butcher's buying some beef. Baby's in the cradle, playing with the ladle, one, two, three!'

Jinsie reflected rather sadly that it widna be the morn that Mother wid be at the butcher's buying some beef. It wid hae t' be tatties an herrin the morn!

Then disaster came, in the form of three distant cousins from another village. They had come for the funeral of an even more distant cousin, an they could hardly ging hame the morn athoot seein Jinsie. Jinsie couldna see fit wye they couldna, but she could hardly tell them that! Not that she wasn't pleased to see her folk, but she had naething in the hoose t' gie them. She could hardly offer them loaf an seerip! Still, the quick-witted Jinsie saw a solution to the problem, so she ran to the door and called her eldest daughter from her skipping.

'Here ye are, my quine! Rin up t' the baker's afore eicht o'clock, an seek tippenst o broken biscuit! Hist ye, noo! Hist ye!'

There was method in Jinsie's madness. Tippenst o vegetables could make a great pot o broth, tippenst o lime sufficed to fitewash a washin-hoose, and tippenst o broken biscuit, specially near closing time, could come in a great muckle pyoke. An there micht even be some hale eens amon them!

Jinsie wis back at the door to meet the returning bairn. Oh aye! The bag wis big! Wi the mouth of the bag ticht shut, Jinsie re-entered the living-room where in the presence of her guests, she opened the bag and gazed in assumed horror into its depths.

'Oh dear me! Oh, my govies!' says she, 'Yon craitur's surely faan an broken aa the biscuits!'

Pride an poverty, Jinsie! Pride an poverty! But then things were actually as hard as that among the fisher folk. Not in the days of Dickens either, but say 1932-33.

Fizzy Juice

I have a little grand-daughter, three-and-a-half, the apple of mine eye (ye ken the wye o't), who has an inordinate thirst for 'fizzy juice'. The flavour is of secondary importance, as long as the stuff fizzes in her nose! It may well be that you can recall a similar delight from your own childhood, however distant. In those days there were only three flavours — lemonade, cream soda and A.I., the latter title gradually coming to be the comprehensive name for all aerated waters. No doubt you have heard the word 'aiwaan', at least among the fisher folk. Fizzy juice!

It has just occurred to me that I may have coined the term 'fizzy juice', but every time I hear it, I remember Eddie, whose surname I have forgotten. Eddie was a Skye man, one of a squad who were laying a pipe from a point near Crossie's, out into the bay. I have never been absolutely sure regarding the primary purpose of the pipe, but I know that its remains can still be seen by anyone walking along Smith's Embankment. At low water, of course. But I do know that, during the laying of the pipe, Eddie sustained a leg injury, and was taken to the Cottage Hospital which, in those days, took all sorts of cases, with the possible exception of heid cases. That itself might not be strictly true, for if being a first class leear means being a heid case, then the place was ram-stam full o them!

I have it on good authority that a certain schoolboy of that era wrote in an essay, 'The Cottage is a good place for koffs, koles, an sair holes an blisters on your ditty-box!' I have always admired his spelling. I have never doubted his word.

Well now, a few days after Eddie's admission, I myself arrived on the scene, having been taken ashore from the local M.F.V. *Glenugie* in the early hours of the morning, under the kindly auspices of Dr Manson, now retired. Suspected 'burst ulcer', or perforation of the stomach lining. Thus did I happen to meet Eddie, and I have never been quite the same since!

As Eddie and I progressed towards recovery, we struck up a friendship of sorts. I really did like the chap, just as I like most West-coasters, the liking being deeply tinged with sympathy, for these people's midgies seem to wear tackety boots! But oh, the lees! Ye ken iss, boys, I wis fair affrontit at the lees! Some folk think I'm nae a bad han at it mysel, but I could nivver hud a cannle to Eddie! Maybe it wis jealousy that wis troubling me. Hour after hour, Eddie shieled them oot, stories which I have stored in my memory for some thirty-seven years. One by one I've weighed them up, and discarded them as being the product of a lively imagination. All save one have met the same fate, but I would like to share with you the one solitary immortal jewel, that it may shine as a light in this sad and ugly world!

According to Eddie, he and his twin brother got a 'holiday jobbie' at a hotel on Skye. For boys in their early teens, there has never been much opportunity on the island, but the hotelier, a distant cousin of their mother's, took the two lads under his wing for a season. Now, the hotel, a mile or two from Portree, wasn't a big one — say ten or twelve guests at most — but it was quite popular, and it was always completely full throughout the summer months, guests arriving immediately to replace those who had just left. Quite a busy place, and mine host wasn't slow to accept the chance of some cheap labour in the shape of Eddie and his twin, who were employed as odd-job men. No pay, of course, but they would get their grub, and there might be occasional tips from the guests whose shoes they would clean. There would be the two cows to look after; in fact, there would be a thousand and one jobbies for the loons, all under the orders of the hotel cook.

Noo, lat's tak a look at the cook. She wis a foosty aal fizzer! Forty, at least! She wis a cappernyaam, crabbit aal bizzom. Her nose had been flung on fin her face wis het! (These terms are mine. It would be pointless to give you Eddie's Gaelic!) To be uncharitable would be unforgivable, so just let's say she made the boys' life a misery, and they, in return, vowed to take revenge. But how?

Well, it came to pass in this fashion . . . The cook's bedroom on the ground floor of the rear wing had been altered, by means of a thin, floor-to-ceiling partition so that, instead of one quite spacious room, there were now two rather cramped apartments. Cook complained bitterly at the change and vented her spite on the two boys, who slept on a shakkie-doon in the other half. Vision-wise, privacy was perfect. Sound-wise, it was non-existent: the boys could hear every move that Cook made when she retired, about an hour later than they. A slave to habit, as most of us are, she followed the same routine every night.

First, there was the pechs and grunts as she undressed, then came her nightly Gaelic prayer, for she was a devout soul. Her penultimate move, before the creaking bed-springs betrayed her ample weight was to tinkle in her pottie. Same routine, every night. Only by biting hard on the edge of their blanket could the

306

boys prevent themselves from laughing out loud. The coorse craiturs! But worse was to come!

On the day, the final day of their employment before going back to school, Eddie's brother thumbed a lift to the nearest chemist's, where he bought three double-size, double-strength, lemon-flavoured Seidlitz powders. Mind you, the flavour wasn't important.

For the enlightenment of the younger generation, let me explain that the Seidlitz powder in a glass of water produces an instant and really ferocious amount of fizz, guaranteed to clear any choked tubes you may have. Gweed help ye if it fizzes in yer nose! The boodies'll flee like caff!

On his return to the hotel, the 'pooder monkey' let his brother see the purchases he had made, and later that evening, while Cook was busy with the dinner (at eight, you see), the crafty pair crept into her bedroom and scattered the powders into the pottie! To think they could be sae coorse!

Bedtime came at last, and the hotel donned its usual nocturnal hush. On the shakkie-doon in the rear bedroom the two rascals lay wide awake in eager expectation, snicherin now and then as imagination got the better of them. Wasn't Cook later than usual tonight? But the great moment came at last!

If there was anything different that night, it was simply that the tinkle seemed to be somewhat softer than usual. Then, after a split second of deathly silence, a series of agonising and penetrating screams rent the air. Mine host and his startled guests came running, to find Cook in her room, knee-deep in the froth that wis yoamin oot o the chanty! The only intelligible words in her terrified Gaelic were 'Doctor!' and 'fire in the water!' The rest of her hysterical outburst could probably be summed up in two simple words — 'Fizzy juice!'

The loon that conceived the brilliant idea in the first place is now a retired lorry driver. What a loss to the highest Peaks of Learning. With a bittie mair education, he would undoubtedly have made a first-class Fizzicist!

The Greyhound

At a special meeting of the Lustrous Union of Labsters on 10 March 1962, a momentous, unanimous decision was reached, viz . . . 'For the next four months, all labsters will bide in their holes, disregarding the presence of creels, no matter how tempting the bait on view therein.' The meeting was held on the Outers of Scotstown Head, and there was a fairly representative gathering of members of both sexes.

On the same date, at a similar meeting in twenty-five fathoms off Rattray Head, the Confederation of Carefree Cod passed a resolution that the hale apothick should flit to the Heligoland Bight for an unspecified period. No specific reason was given.

307

Two days later, off the island of Handa on the west coast, the Union of Migratory Mackerel decreed that, for a six month period, all members were forbidden to round Cape Wrath en route for the North Sea. Disobedience to entail capital punishment.

Now, although Dod and Weelim never actually received typed minutes of these meetings, they kent fine that something wis amiss, for poverty wis staring them in the face. Times were hard indeed.

'We canna ging on like this!' says Weelim. 'It's nae a case o keepin the wolf fae the door, cos he's inower the bed noo! We'll hae t' try something, freen, or we'll be oot o hoose an hame.'

'Weel!' says Dod, 'I'm listenin wi baith lugs. Can ye come up wi something, think ye? Jist mine that we're nae sae young as we eesed t' be!'

'Fit aboot gettin a dog?' says Weelim.

'A dog?' says Dod in disbelief, 'A dog? Fit the divvle difference wid a dog mak? Anither mou t' feed, an a kirn o dirt t' redd up. I canna see the sense o gettin a dog, for the place is meevin wi dogs aaready.'

'Aha!' says Weelim, 'I dinna mean that kine o dog avaa. I mean a richt dog, a hun dog, a racin dog!'

'Ye mean a dog for catchin rubbits! There's a wee bittie o sense in that, for we could dee wi a change aff the hairy tatties.'

'I mean a proper greyhound, nae an orra mongrel. Ye mine yon miner that wis here on holiday fae Fife? Weel, he tellt me that he made a heap o siller aff his dog. Ye see, if ye hiv a fast dog, she wins prize-money, an ye can aye hae a bet on her forbye, an that's mair siller. Gweed kens fit we're deein, gaan t' sea for naething!'

'An faar wid ye get sic a dog?' says Dod, showing a little interest.

'Creemin! There's a mannie at Creemin breeds the things, an he has the fastest dog in Scotlan. Fin she's gaan full butt, the verra sparks flees oot o her starn! So he says. Sixty mile an oor, nae bother avaa!'

'A dog like that wid cost a gey bit,' says Dod. 'Fit's the mannie seekin for the beastie?'

'I'm nae sure. But she's nae a fire new dog, ye see; she wid be second han, so we micht get a bittie aff. An we could go halfs wi the price. Fit div ye say?'

I think it wis the bittie aboot the sparks that made Dod decide, for on the Friday they bocht the dog for seven powen (cash), but they got ten bob aff for a luck-penny. On the Setterday they took the dog to the races an put a powen bet on the beast. Boys! She set oot like a rocket, but she feenished hinmaist!

'Deid loss!' says Dod, as they made their way homewards in the evening, wi a tow roon the dog's neck. 'Fit'll we dee wi the beast?'

'We could aye shot 'er!' says Weelim.

'Na, na! That wid be cruel!'

'Weel, we could tie a steen roon 'er neck an droon 'er in the dam, here!'

'Na, na! That wid be cruel!' Tell ye fit! We'll jist rin an leave 'er!'

That wis tried, to no avail so, on the Monday they took the dog back to Creemin, only to discover that the mannie had flittit to the Black Isle.

'We're in a richt frap noo!' says Dod. 'Fit can we dee aboot it?'

'I've a cousin at Rathen that's affa skeely wi dogs. We could aye ging an get advice fae him. That winna cost verra muckle, I'm sure!' says Weelim.

The said cousin had a good look at the dog. 'Nae verra muckle wrang, I wid say. Jist a bittie hingin-luggit kine, maybe. But ye're still strangers to the craitur, an she'll maybe buck up a bittie in a day or twaa. If I wis you, I wid try giein her a drappie port wine wi fite o egg three times a day. That'll be a great help.'

'Ye may be sure!' says Dod. 'It wid be a great help to mair than the dog!'

Weelim plied the beast faithfully with the mixture, maybe a thochtie ower free wi the port wine, an sure as daith, the dog did seem to be mair lively.

It wis back to the races on the Setterday, wi high hopes o retrieving their losses, the dog apparently rarin to go. She, of course, had had twaa doses o her mixter afore time for the race an, boys, ye nivver saw the likes o yon! She gid ben the park like a rippit saithe. 'Seventy mile an oor, onywye!' says Dod, though he didna see nae sparks. A hunner yairds aheid o the field! Great stuff, great rejoicing. All was well!

Prize-money? Hardly! Disqualified cos the dog wis bleezin. Warned nae to try that again!

Back to the drawing board again, their hairts in their boots. Back to the skeely cousin for a final magic potion.

'Aha!' says he, 'If she can run as fast as that fin she's drunk, she should be able to rin as fast fin she's sober. Try her this wik wi a bittie fried duff an a drappie sherry, twice a day. Dinna gie her ony on the Setterday, an I'll come to the races wi ye an watch her rinnin. There's hope yet!'

On the appointed day, the trio took the dog to the field of battle once more. 'Sober as a judge the day,' says Weelim.

'That's nae sayin muckle!' says Dod.

Before the start of the race, a mannie in a fite coat came and had a look at the dog. 'Ye're aa richt the day, lads! I'm pleased ye've learned yer lesson.'

Well now, the dog made an excellent start, and was well in the lead at the bend, then she seemed to lose ground and finished in fifth place.

'I see fit's adee wi the beast!' says the cousin. 'She's affa fast, but fin she comes to the bend, she swings awaa oot to the richt an the ither dogs is nippin in atween her an the pailin. That's a faat that needs sortin.'

'Fit wye div ye sort that?' says Dod.

'Oh, it's easy sortit. In fact ye can dee't yersels. Jist get a bittie o leed, an fix't on at the back o her left lug. That'll keep her fae swingin oot to the richt.'

'A great idea!' says Weelim. 'That shouldna be ill t' dee! Fit's the best wye t' fix't on?'

'Dee't wi a gun!' wis the reply.

Heid First

Maist bairns like a shakkie-doon, specially them that's nivver been on sic a thing. Bairns have aye been like that! It matters little that Da has the finest car that money can buy . . . they want a hurl in a bus. Just let them see something they don't have (rather difficult nowadays), and Suntie is expected to do the needful, if indeed they can be persuaded to wait that long. Ye ken the wye o't!

Time was when things were rather different. I mean the days when Suntie had somehow run out of toys, and could bring only stockings or boots (never shoes) for boys, and black bloomers or buttoned boots for girls. Of course, he did manage to put a something in the stockings hanging by the mantelpiece . . . a puckle shunners (cinders) and an aipple or an orange! What a thrill!

I'm thinking now of two of my pals in the long, long ago, pals who, alas, are no longer with us. They were brithers on a shakkie-doon, and they were on a shakkie-doon because there was nowhere else to put them. As the youngest members of a large family they occupied a very lowly position and, naturally, they longed for promotion. The bed which stood in the same room was not for them, but for an elder brother who was old enough to refuse to sleep three to a bed. Even in the elder brother's absence, the loons were forbidden to occupy the vacant bed which gradually assumed the aura of a holy of holies, a goal to which they ardently aspired. Not that they were not quite comfortable on a shakkie-doon; indeed, it was a very cosy nest, but then, it jist wisna a bed. Ye ken the wye o't!

The elder brother is worthy of further mention, in that he used to sole his younger brothers' boots with the thickest parts of an old car tyre, which he used to get from Robertson's garage in York St. The resultant heavy footwear made the loons fearsome opponents at fitba, in more ways than one. The soles seemed to last forever!

Now, it came to pass that the elder brother upped and offed to some foreign clime, never to return, and thus the loons finally got off the ground, and into the bed. Oh, what bliss to dyste up an doon, tryin oot the spring! What an experience to gaze down on the basses from the dizzy heights of the old iron bedstead which was itself set up on six inch wooden blocks. This to increase the storage space underneath.

The first night in the bed wasn't a complete success, for they awoke rather earlier than usual. It must be gey early, they thought, for they hadn't yet heard the eight o'clock horn at the Harbour of Refuge, nor could they hear the milk-cairt in the street nor the milkman tellin the wifies, ''Tsaafa dump ee day!' In the strange silence they lay for a whilie, surveying the world from an unfamiliar angle. Wasn't the ceiling an affa lot nearer han? But the novelty soon wore off, and the pair decided to celebrate their rise in the world by staging a pilla-fecht. Nae rules, jist wallop! Bowff! Thud! Eetya fella! Ooh, ye sod! Ye ken the wye o't!

Well, I suppose it had to come, but Billy got a clour on the side o the heid that sent him skitin ower the side, and sink me if he didna land heid-first . . . into the dirler! A fine couthie ring aboot that word, isn't there? There wis a fine ring aboot it that mornin for sure, for Billy's great muckle stickin-oot lugs got jammed ticht into the thing, an eence his lugs got opened oot, there wis jist nae wye that the dirler wid come aff! So the loon started howlin pen-an-ink for his mither, whose hasty arrival made matters worse, for she wis determined to get the precious utensil off at all costs, it having been a mairridge present, adorned with a bunch of brilliant red roses on its starboard side. But her determined efforts simply inflicted more pain on her protesting offspring, so she had to desist.

There wis only one thing she could think of now. Tak the loon to the doctor! Behold Baabie then, at the front door of yon bonny hoose (now Dodie Donald's shop) where an imposing plate on the gate proclaimed that here resided Dr V T B Yule, who had a veritable alphabet of letters after his name. A first class physician!

'Come in!' says the doctor, rudely aroused. 'Faar's the loon gotten the bonny helmet? Nivver saw the like o't afore!'

So Baabie had to tell him the story, with liberal use of the word 'chanty'. Her pronunciation of the word betrayed her alien origins, for had she been a native of the Blue Toon, the 'a' would have been a 'u'.

'Weel, Mrs Buchan, I'm afraid there's got to be a sacrifice here the day. It's the loon or the po! Ye canna hae them baith!'

Wi the greet in her throat, Baabie agreed that the helmet was expendable, so the doctor got a candy-haimmer fae the kitchen to shatter the thing. Then Baabie grat richt! Jist a proper greetin match, wi the loon howlin anaa!

'Fit'll ye be needin for this, noo, Doctor?' says Baabie, for in those days the doctor had to be paid.

'Naething this time, Mrs Buchan. I'll pit this doon to experience, but stand by if there's a next time!'

Once back at home, Baabie fell oot on the son who had dealt the fearful blow in the first place. He, poor soul, bolted for school as soon as he had swallowed his porridge, leaving his brother to have his assorted scarts and bruises bathed. Then there was another tooin match, for Billy suddenly realised he was late for school, and would need a 'notie for the teacher'. Now, even though there had been any note-paper in the house, it's more than likely that Baabie would have declined to use it, for she was by no means the world's best writer. So Billy was sent packing, to make his own excuses. It is a pity indeed that Miss Strachan's reaction when she was confronted with 'Please, Miss, I fell into the po!' has not been recorded.

Later that day, Baabie went up the toon to seek a replacement for the broken pot, and eventually found one to her liking in Grant & Black's in Marischal St. Plain china this time; no rose motif! She failed to grasp the meaning of the assistant's words when he advised her that the proper title for the receptacle was 'a goes-under'. She also firmly declined to have the object 'rowed up'.

'There's nae need for a buddy to be affrontit at that, surely!'

Behold Baabie noo, her left hand clutching her pursie and her shawl at the same time, and the great muckle pot dangling from her right wrist. She was completely heedless of the amused glances of the passers-by, as she made her way along Chapel Street towards the fish shop. Her 'hairt wis warsh for a bittie fish!'

The fishmonger in Queen Street was Jim Lewis, a newcomer, and a Welshman to boot. Not a word of the Doric did he understand, so Baabie would have to 'talk' to him. How she hated to use English. But it had to be done.

Once inside the shop, Baabie hitched the great, enormous pot onto the counter, to free her right hand for ficherin in her pursie.

'Pound a fillit!' says she, talking posh.

'A fiver you don't!' says Jim.

Peer Baabie!

Jockie

Jockie is one of the few remaining survivors of the race once known as the 'fisher folk'. Although he is by some fifteen years my senior, he has been a friend of mine for as long as I can remember and even longer than that, if such a thing is possible. And, when I use the word 'friend', I would in Jockie's case give it a capital 'F' for, according to Proverbs, a friend loveth at all times! So there you have Jockie, my lifelong mentor and occasional critic.

Born into a fisher household, Jockie wis suckled on the Scriptures and steepit in the Psalms; Kirk to the back-bone. Even today he will unerringly name any Psalm tune he hears. Give him the first line of the words, and he'll tell you the number of the Psalm, and the tune required. Not for him the 23rd Psalm to the tune 'Crimond'. 'Orlington' or 'Covenanters', certainly! But 'Crimond'? Nivver! Fashious, think ye? Well, a wee bittie, maybe, but in things pertaining to the Kirk, Jockie has aye been fashious! As long as he was able, Jockie attended morning worship in the Kirk, the only exception being those Sundays which found him in some Hielan loch, where the service of the local Kirkie was sure to be in Gaelic. One of the Old Brigade, to be sure.

As soon as he went to school, Jockie had to learn English, from scratch. Oh, he had a few Sunday School texts which he could recite, parrot fashion, but such material, thickly overlaid with a strong North-east accent, was no substitute for the real thing. So it was actually to a foreign language that Jockie and his contemporaries had to address themselves. Their vast vocabulary of local words and phrases, in which they were so amazingly articulate, was of no use whatsoever in an English-speaking world. And, as is usually the case in any foreign-language class, some of the youngsters were outstanding. Most of them managed to scrape through, but a few never really got off the ground, finding great difficulty in mentally translating their own speech into a foreign tongue while actually speaking. For these boys, English has always been and always will be their second language. If circumstances dictate that English be used, highly intelligent and fluent speakers are suddenly ill at ease in a medium not naturally theirs. In fact, they seem to be feart at it, and in their hesitancy, they make some wonderful mistakes.

312

Jockie went to sea at a very early age, jist a loon in his Deydie's ripper boatie, but his eye was always on bigger boats and farther horizons. He ended his fishing career in a ripper yole with two of his grandsons as crew. 'Jist bairns!' he called them, but now these same bairns are on the Bergen and Viking Banks in the depth of winter, and even as far as Rockall in boats which are not really big enough for such waters. Such is life!

Nowadays, Jockie comes but seldom to the harbour, although he rarely misses the Kirk, where he laments the disappearance of the Psalms and Paraphrases. 'Things is nae the same, noo!' is an expression very often on his lips as he sits at home, reminiscing on days gone by, in his aal-farrant tongue, so broad that his younger grandchildren fail to understand the half of what he says. He likes to speak of the old times, the long, lean years of famine which his generation had to endure. And one winter in particular, when the local baker, in his horse-drawn van, made a nightly round of the village to distribute FREE loaves among the starving fishers. 'Fin EE get it, then I'LL get it!' seemed to be the motto of the local shopkeepers who supplied the fisher populace with all manner of goods, on tick. There was no dole, and no D.H.S.S. Can you wonder that the old fella says, 'Things is nae the same, noo!'

Those were the days when, if the season had been reasonably good, Jockie would pay the tailor for the beautiful hairback (heavy serge) breeks he had got the year before, then he would order a new suit of navy blue serge, on the same understanding . . . 'Fin EE get it, then I'LL get it!' Every fisherman had his hairback breeks, always tailor-made, and always with front pockets. The colour would vary from village to village, from dark brown to black. Mine were black. The hairback breeks and the home-knitted jersey were the fisherman's 'go-ashores', kept neatly folded in his suitcase on the shelf in his bunk.

Now, there are those who will assume that Jockie, with his steadfast love for the Kirk and his deep interest in things spiritual, must be a 'doom and gloom' sort of chap, preaching Hell-fire and eternal damnation. Not so, Jockie, for he is really good company with his dry wit and his keen sense of humour. He is very fond of the true story of an old widowed fisherman whom we both knew in our youth.

Apparently, this fella advertised for a housekeeper and, when the first suitable applicant appeared, he proceeded to show her the house.

'Noo!' says he, 'Iss is ee kitchen, an at's ee front room. An up ee stairs here — iss is oor bedroom!'

'Hey!' says she, 'Fit div ye mean, OOR bedroom?'

'Weel!' says he, 'It widna be richt o me t' hae my neepers tellin lees aboot me!'

And Jockie can tell a story against himsel, forbye. Came the day the minister asked him to give a vote of thanks at the annual Kirk 'siree'. Only prood an bigsy folk used the word 'swaree'. For fisher folk it wis aye 'siree'. I once heard a shipmate describe the Mission mannie's fite bonnet as being like 'a siree table!' Nae bad!

'Now, John!' says the minister. 'You are our oldest member, and I'd be delighted if you would bring the evening to a close by giving the vote of thanks!'

'Na, na, minister! Nae me. I wid be sure t' miss somebody oot. An that wid be

313

blue murder! Ye ken that.'

'No problem, John! I'll give you a copy of the complete programme, so you cannot possibly miss anybody! What about it?'

'Na, minister! I canna hannle the gran English words. I'm sure t' say something vrang an mak a feel o masel. Specially wi aa yon folk listenin!'

'If you stick closely to your script, John, you cannot possibly go wrong! And as for your grammar and pronunciation, I'm sure nobody will be looking for flawless English! In fact, such a thing would be completely out of character. As long as the audience knows exactly what you mean, all will be well. C'mon, John, say you'll do it!'

Very, very reluctantly Jockie agreed to do the needful, and the siree duly took place. A richt fine nicht, a gran nicht! Everybody got a baggie o cookies as they entered, tea to be at half time; milk or A.I. (lemonade) for the bairns for fear they micht be brunt wi the het tay. At the close of the evening's entertainment, ilkie bairn would be given an orange, the only orange they would see until the next siree.

The programme was lengthy and varied, most of the congregation taking part in some way or another. The singing was of a very high standard, for the fisher folk of those days loved to sing their spiritual songs in four part harmony. Indeed, they really excelled in the art. There was the occasional slight discord when some restless loon would fire a pandrop at his chum on the other side of the hall, but otherwise the event was quite peaceful.

Jockie sat there enjoying himself, for he simply loved singing. Then, at the close, he was called upon to round things off in the usual way. This he did in splendid fashion, considering that this was his first attempt at public speaking. Not a soul did he forget to mention, and he resumed his seat to great applause, feeling rather proud of his performance.

Then, as mithers rowed graavits roon their bubbily-nibbit bairns before facing the bitter cold outside, and as fathers swopped opinions as to which item had been the best, disaster overtook Jockie, for he sprang to his feet to announce in a most apologetic tone.

'Ladies an gintlemin, I'm affa sorry, but I forgot t' thunk Mrs Duthie for the len o her urine (urn) for makkin the tay!'

I tellt ye English wis a foreign language!

314

Piz Meal

I have read more than once that, out of doors, it is never really dark. This has often made me wonder just how dark a night has to be to qualify for the title 'Really Dark'. There are degrees of darkness, just as there are degrees of light but by which yardstick does one measure darkness?

It is really amazing how readily the human race can adapt itself to the dark, as the war-time blackouts proved. Mind you, in those days, most of the populace were in familiar surroundings, and found no great difficulty in getting around, although there were several sad fatalities, even among natives. I would say that, if a buddy has any problem negotiating his own neighbourhood, then it's 'Really Dark'.

I remember quite clearly a night in 1942, when I was on the way from the Roanheads to Jamaica Street via the Hillock and the Longate. I bumped into a pedestrian of some kind, and there followed the usual apologies, but I'm not sure yet whether it was a little mannie wi a beard or a great muckle chiel wi a kilt. I'm tellin ye, it wis gey dark!

Speaking of darkness, let me tell you about Jeems and Leebie, an elderly couple who lived in one of the coastal villages of Buchan in the not-so-long-ago. Their hoosie was simply a butt-an-ben, two rooms with a closetie between. There was no back door to the house, neither was there a supply of running water, a sad, but common fact which decreed that, within the house, there could be no sanitation. Primitive? Maybe, but most houses in Buchan were exactly the same. One simply made one's own arrangements, especially when the little wooden shack at the rear of the house was occupied.

In spite of these drawbacks to their humble abode, Jeems and Leebie had reared a family of three sons and two daughters, all of them now up and away to homes and families of their own. So the old couple were left alone in the cottage where they had begun their wedded life, but now, according to Leebie, 'the dookit wis far ower big for twaa doos!' When in reminiscent mood, they would remember the hurley-bed, a great muckle box on castors, a bed which could be 'hurled' in aneth the box bed during the day, to be hurled out again in the evening when it was bairns' bed time. In those times, space had been at a premium, but now it was all so different.

The couple now lived, ate and slept in the one room, which was never known as anything but the 'kitchen'. The single coal fire supplied all their heating requirements, the room being very snug indeed, especially when the Tilley lamp, a great source of heat in itself, was lighted.

But there had been a drastic change in the couple's nocturnal habits. You see, when the bairns had been on the go, Leebie had claimed the front berth in the box-bed, so that she could readily attend to her brood during the night. Jeems was banished to the back, hard against the wall, and many a time was he exhorted to 'Lie doon an be quaet!'

Now their lifestyle was different in that Jeems was at the front, simply to facilitate his frequent nocturnal answers to the call of Nature. As Leebie put it, 'Ye're forivver rinkin aboot throwe the nicht, so ye'd better tak the front an gie a buddy a meenit's peace!'

Jeems, unfortunately, was a martyr to what I have heard described as 'the aal man's trouble'. In modern parlance, that simply means problems with the prostate gland, but in Jeems's day very few among the working class had ever heard of such a thing. The complaint was very common indeed, and it would seem that there was little that the medical men of the period could do about it.

I remember very clearly how the all-male members of the Parliament which used to meet at the Cannon seemed to take it in turns to ging doon the steps a bittie to relieve themselves. Many a time have I, as a barfit loon, made my way up and down these steps on the outside of the railing, to avoid the stinking mess. The steps at the foot of Merchant Street were even worse, cos they could be smelt as far away as the Toonshoose. Oh gyaad! But let's get back to the story, instead of revelling in gory details of the good old days.

It was very close to Christmas, according to the calendar, but not according to anything else, for Christmas was simply another date. It was a time of going to work, it was a time for going to sea. Oh, aye! The bairns would sing their carols in day-school and in Sunday School, and Christmas hymns were the order of the day in the Kirks on Christmas Sunday, but Christmas Day itself was never a holiday. Not in this neck of the woods. You see, Suntie came on Hogmanay, and New Year's Day was the holiday (one day only).

'What a pagan practice!' you may say. Well, maybe . . . maybe. But thousands of devout souls would have it no other way.

Christmas — not the Message of Christmas, which we had known and loved all our days — came to these parts with the oil, and the gas, and the Yanks, and the English, and all the other foreigners. That's how recent it is. Now we have at least a fortnight of gluttony and drunkenness, and a period of profligate spending which, at times, borders on the obscene. If it is not pagan, it certainly isn't Christian. Having sampled both ways, I'm for the old way, every time.

Well now, it was getting very close to Christmas, and Jeems was in his appointed place at the front of the bed. The strong northerly wind kept up a miserable whining noise at the window, a whine that increased to a roar in the lum when a wintry shower spattered on the roof. Although the fire had gone out, the room was still snugly warm, and Jeems was, to say the least, very cosy. Then came the strong, clear call that could not be denied! 'The door, Jeems! At your hardest!' I might be better to point out that it wasn't the call of the sea. So Jeems obeyed instantly . . . he could do no other. Could he but make the door, he would get it open and relieve himself into the night.

He was in the very act when Leebie cried . . . 'Watch that Suntie disna see ye! But it's nae likely he'll be aboot on a nicht like this!'

'It's a richt fine nicht here!' says Jeems. 'There's nae a breath o win noo, an there's a richt fine smell o piz meal!'

'Come oot o there, ye orra breet!' was the reply. 'Ye're into the press!'

Faa said it was 'never really dark'?

Wull's Chariot

In the distant days of my boyhood there were certain times when I was very well off. These were the red-letter days when I could afford to go to the picters either in Aubrey's, opposite the end of Chapel Stret, or in Clarkie's, in Hanover Street. Mind you, the Saturday afternoon matinee cost tippence, so I wasn't there very often, coppers being rather hard to come by. But I recall quite vividly the thrill of sitting in the front seats, gazing up at the flickering screen until there was a crick in my neck. Those were the days of the silent films, but the hubbub among the junior audience could be quite something. You see, all the dialogue appeared on the screen in print, and there was always a certain element who, apparently, could only read aloud. Most annoying! Still, I was rather jealous of a classmate of mine who got to the picters at least once a week, simply to read the titles to an old man who couldn't read at all. It's an ill wind . . .

Love scenes were anathema to me, but I fairly likit cowboys and Indians, pirates and gladiators, and above all, Ben Hur. What a scare you could get when the chariots seemed to be about to leave the screen and come right into the front stalls. Same with films about express trains; there had to be shots where the train was coming straight at you. Good grief, yon fairly scared the flechs aff ye! By the way, it simply isn't true that every patron of Clarkie's was supposed to get a candy-haimmer along wi their ticket, to slay the flechs. That applied only to a certain place in Aiberdeen, and that was hine, hine awaa!

After seeing *Ben Hur*, there was a lengthy period when we all pranced along the pavements like a puckle horses, stopping now and then to nicher like feels and to paw the ground like Arab stallions (not advisable with bare feet among chuckie steens). I'm jist thinkin that, had there been wheelie bins on the go at that time, they would have been commandeered as chariots. There would have been no shortage of horses. Practically every fisher loon wanted a chariot as a Yarmooth present, but the chariots didn't materialise. Next year, maybe.

Not until I was several years older did I learn that there was actually a chariot in the toon, and a vary famous chariot at that! And, what was more, it was a fisher chariot, with a constant supply of human horses, available at somewhat peculiar hours. Jist wyte a meenit, an I'll tell ye aa aboot it.

In the days when the railway came right down to the Harbour, There was a large goods yard which became the site of today's patent slipway. From there the rails ran close behind the old Coastguard Station (on their right), then close along the rear of the curing yards in Wilson Road (on their left), with Ives Park on their right, under the Brig in Ugie Street, close to that hideous brick building which was once the Electricity Station for the town; thence through Raemoss Park to the Station Yard.

At the foot of Port Henry Road there was an imposing footbridge for the benefit of pedestrians wishing to reach the seaward part of the Roanheads, known as 'Ower the Wickets'. There were, apparently, at one time wicket gates in the railway fencing to permit the public to cross the rails. Whether or not these gates

317

gave rise to the name 'Wickets', they had disappeared long before my time, although the name remains.

Now, to find our chariot, we maun ging ower the Wickets. I have called it 'Wull's Chariot', but it was never actually Wull's at all, since it belonged to Alex Summers, Fish merchant (Killer's father). And it was never a proper chariot, but simply a great long hurley with rubber-shod cab wheels, quite easy to hurl if you had it properly balanced. The primary purpose of the hurley was to transport boxes of fish, although it could be utilised for other purposes as the occasion arose.

So, why Wull's Chariot? Faa wis Wull? Wull Taylor bedd ower the Wickets in what is now a richt bonny hoosie of dressed granite with a little porch in front. I never kent Wull, but I did ken his sons Jock an Towdie, known world wide as the 'Wells o Wearie'. On the occasions when my Deydie sent me to see Wull's Boys aboot gettin the len o their boatie to shoot a bit smaa-line in Shumfirt (Sandford Bay), I met the other son Wucksie, who was at that time a bedall (chronic invalid).

'Faa did ye say yer Deydie wis?'

'Aal Oxy's my Deydie!'

'Aa richt, loon, tak the yole awaa!'

Fine, quaet, hairmless men they were; Pilots in the days when Pilotage was a cut-throat business. There were several Pilots, each with his own boat, the rule being that first aboard the ship was the accepted Pilot. Competition, did ye say? Bleed an hair's mair like it! The 'Wells', having only a rowing boat, stood little chance against the others with their motor engines. It was all a matter of speed, you see.

But there was one remarkable occasion when the tortoise outran the hare, so to speak.

A big steamer had landed half her cargo of salt in Wick and was on the way to Peterhead with the other half. It was common knowlege that she was coming, so the Pilots watched each other like hawks, lest one should steal a march on the others. Finally, one decided to go north to meet the ship, but he was scarcely clear of the piers before another three boats were on his tail. The poor 'Wells' simply couldn't compete, so they just sat tight. Now, it came to pass that, in dense fog, the four motor boats missed the ship completely, and this proved to be a proper windfall for the Wells, for the steamer arrived off Peterhead and lay hooting for a Pilot, just a few hundred yards from the Wells' door. Of course they seized the opportunity, and piloted the ship into port. What a prize.

The sad part of the story is that, when the motor boats returned after a long, fruitless chase, one of the skippers was so incensed on seeing the ship snugly berthed that he went to Almanythie Creek and put a great muckle steen through the bottom of the poor men's boatie. Such a noble thing to do, wasn't it?

The mention of speed reminds me of the time when Nep (meaning 'hairy'), one of the local pilots, bought a second-hand pinnace from the Navy. She was long and thin, like a sunnel (sand eel), with a 60 hp Kelvin, and she was very fast indeed. But she proved to be 'ower sair on the paraffin', and never really was a success. Of course the arrival of this peculiar craft was a nine days wonder. Even

Dr Taylor was told about Nep's new pinnace but, since the good doctor's informant mispronounced the word, as most of the old fishermen did, you can well imagine the consternation among the medical fraternity. Transplants sixty years ago? Nivver!

Boys, we're awaa fae the chariot aathegither! I suppose it's my blame, so I'll tell ye aboot the chariot noo.

Wull was a fisherman with a wife and three sons. The wifie kept a spotless hoosie, and saw to it that her men-folk were aye 'weel in order'. Sadly, when the Mither died, the men-folk lost the place as men-folk are so prone to do when bereft. The guiding hand was gone, and the Demon Drink took command, until the tow gid wi the bucket. Enter, now, the Chariot.

It was a long-standing arrangement that, at closing time on Saturday night (nine o'clock) the hurley should be at the door of Mother Aiken's pub (now the Christian Bookshop). On the stroke of nine, the four warriedrags emerged, laden with their previously purchased groceries and singing melodiously 'The Bonnie Wells o Wearie', a song they were particularly fond of. As soon as the passengers had draped themselves on the Chariot, the horses took off at a fearsome rate. There was never a shortage of loons to act as horses. Doon the brae as hard as they could go — it's a miracle they didna land in Port Henry — makkin for the Wickets. The noisy procession must needs pass Ailick Summers' hoose, where a very articulate parrot enjoyed the sea air in a cage which hung from a nail in the gable. On hearing the rabble, the parrot screamed, 'Drucken Wull, Drucken Wull!' sending Wull, on the Chariot, almost berserk, thinking that it was bairns jeering at him. But worse was to come.

There was a gate in the low dykie in front of Wull's hoosie, too narrow for the Chariot to enter. Fine did the loons ken that, so, on the last lap they gathered speed along the middle of the road before swinging the Chariot towards the gate. Of course the Chariot stopped with a thud, but the passengers gid skitin on, to land in a discordant heap at the very door. Strangely, they never seemed to be any the worse. The loons, of course, thought it was great fun.

Only once did I witness this amazing performance, and I never went back. I dinna like to greet!

A Prile of Kings

For as long as I can remember, I have been on speaking terms with Royalty. Not the British Monarchy, of course, but a line of Kings, all the same. Such a claim might give you the idea that I am one of the Royal Buchans, but that would be entirely false, for I am not a Royal Buchan at all. In fact, I'm not even a Pirate Buchan, but purely and simply a common five-eight Tinkie Buchan.

How did I find that out? Long and patient research, boys, and a sixth sense.

319

It transpires that I am a direct descendant of the first traceable Tinkie Buchan who lost his life at Culloden. That's richt, boys, he wis killt! Not that he was actually at the battle, but he had a tintie in the neist park, an gid ower to compleen aboot the din! R.I.P.

Be that as it may, and I see no reason to doubt it, I have known several Kings in my time, but sad to say, they're getting rather thin on the ground now, and the world is all the poorer for their passing.

The first King I met was the Pearl King, Mr Birnie of Wellbank, who made a fortune out East somewhere at the pearling game. I suppose that nowadays he would be called an entrepreneur, but in those days that word was unknown. He's the man who provided the money for the building of the Birnie Brig. £2,500 it was then, but I doubt if you could get it white-washed for that money now. I was at the opening ceremony in 1925, and got a chocolate egg, as did all the other bairns in the town. My egg lasted some forty seconds, but I ken that some youngsters kept their eggs as a souvenir, till the chocolate was foosty. Silly asses!

Now, how did I come to ken the Pearl King? Well, ye see, my Deydie scuttered aboot wi smaalins (haddock lines), and it was universally considered that nothing but horse hair was suitable for making the 'tippins', to which the hooks were attached. Since there were several hundred hooks on a line, quite a lot of horse-hair was required. Now, I suppose the milkman, or any of the numerous carriers, could have supplied the hair, but Deydie believed in going to the fountainhead, and that was up the country. He also believed that I was somehow a necessary companion on his meanderings around the rural scene, in search of horse-hair for his linies or 'speyngie' (osiers) for his basket-weaving. A versatile kind o mannie, apparently.

Thus did I, at a very tender age, and on foot, become acquaint wi country folk in cottage and in mansion, at the same time discovering that the ripper codlin is a strong, hard, reliable currency. You know, that is one thing that has never changed throughout the years.

So that's how I came to meet, on several occasions, Alexander Birnie Esq. of Wellbank, the Pearl King.

The second King in my prile was the King of Denmark. Not that I ever got the length of Denmark, for the said King was a Peterhead man, whose domicile was somewhere in yon close which takes you from the Broadgate to the North Shore (or vice versa). I have no idea how he got his bye-name, although I have tried to find out, but his real name was Keith Forbes, and I think a buddy wid be sair made to find a mair 'Peterheid' name than that! Somehow my mind associates such a name with 'Veritas Vincit'.

The King of Denmark was a rather roch sort of character who, in his cups on Saturday night, would come onto the Broadgate wearing his nicky-tams, and with his sark open to the waist, ready to challenge the world. Sad to say, the challenge was sometimes accepted by one of the many hardy sons of Lewis who were so much a part of the local scene at that time, and there were some richt stashies, I can tell ye. Bleed an hair, an bad words! Far better than the picters. Eetya, fella! That's where I got my extensive vocabulary of swear words, both Doric and

Gaelic. Of course, I never use them, but I keep them in a boxie, handy kind, ye see! Maybe some day I'll get a glossary, so's I'll ken fit I'm sayin.

Keith was one of the many 'coal heavers' in the town, the hardy men who walked the bending, swaying planks with ten-stone bags of coal on their backs, to replenish the drifters' bunkers. Hard, dangerous work. These men also unloaded the cargoes of coal from the Northumbrian ports, shovelling the coal into great muckle iron buckets. (No grabs in those days.) Same with the great cargoes of dazzling white salt from the Mediterranean, or from Spain. Sheer hard labour. And let's not forget the timber trade with the Baltic ports and the long-forgotten republics of Estonia, Latvia and Lithuania. Good for your geography!

Came the Thirties and the great Depression. Coopers by the score were laid off and spent their time taking long walks round by Inverugie. Did you know that, at one time, on the Queenie alone there were ninety coopers making barrels? The coal-heaver/stevedore community felt the severe draught at the same time, and it was most distressing to see so many decent, hard-working men on the scrap heap.

In those days I was a beginner as a fisherman in a 40ft. boatie, landing flukes every night, sair made to get a living. Prominent among my many memories of that time are the occasions when we would put a herring basket of dabs on the quay for the benefit of the unemployed, most of whom seemed to have a bittie o wire in their pooch. Jist the verra dunt for stringin on a fry! Most of them said 'Thank you!' but when the King of Denmark said 'God bless ye, my loon!' I somehow felt that it was sincere. You have simply no idea how quickly the dabs in that basket disappeared. Mind you, there was a whilie when we were not very popular with the 'chippers' in the town. Well, what were they but unscrupulous profiteers, charging fourpence for a fish supper?

The third member of my prile of Kings was the Podley King, Wallim's Sandy. Aabody kent Sandy, and especially the bairns, who listened entranced to his tales. A quaet, hairmless soul wis Sandy, wi a something aboot 'im that ye couldna pit yer finger on. It would appear that, as a boy he was perfectly normal, until he was bitten by a dog. Thereafter he was never the same. But he haunted the piers, summer and winter, part of the fittings, the Podley King. Oh, I ken there were other claimants to the title, but they were only Pretenders; the Crown was Sandy's, without a doubt!

Behold Sandy then, at the end of Port Henry pier, where the north entrance used to be. Just watch in amazement as his catch of podleys accumulates at his back, where he has thrown them one by one, without looking round; and be prepared to gasp in horror as the great heap of fish slides forward and pushes Sandy into the sea! Never was there a fisherman to equal him. Well do I remember a photograph in one of the glossy magazines: 'The fisher, after a week of unremitting toil, wends his way home'. It was Sandy on the Model Jetty with a fry of herring, scranned from the old drifter *Boy Willie*. Well, why not? He had been out of the house for at least an hour and a half!

Then there was the remarkable occasion when Sandy, given a pound to go for messages, inadvertently allowed it to fall into the fire, where it was instantly consumed. Now, although the pound was all the money in the house, all was not lost, for there were eight glittering half-crowns in the ash-pit in the morning! Such good fortune happens only to Kings.

I shall never forget the story Sandy told me, concerning his own days at sea. Apparently Sandy was deck-hand on a coaster bound from Blyth to Peterhead with a cargo of Shilbottle coal. When the ship was passing Collieston, about two miles off, it was observed that a tremendous number of birds were diving and picking at something in the ship's wake. Nobody paid much attention. Then Sandy, on instructions from the Skipper to draw a bucket of water 'for to wash down the decks', discovered in the bucket of water seven live herrings. So the birds had actually been feasting on herring thrown up by the ship's propeller! Boys! They must have been thick!

On arriving at Peterhead, Sandy found his fishermen friends in dark despair, for the herring shoals had forsaken their normal haunts, and famine was staring everybody in the face. Nevertheless, on Sandy's instructions, they all with one accord launched out into the deep for one final go. The result was better than even Sandy had expected. Next morning, special trains brought women from the Broch to handle the miraculous catches, and for seven weeks thereafter the fishers prospered exceedingly. A wonderful story, all the more so for the fact that Sandy was never afloat in his life!

Sandy, with his wrist-bones like foremast shackles and his hands like shovels. Sandy, with the faraway look in his clear blue eyes. Sandy in his Sunday attire of collarless shirt, with a woollen scarf crossed loosely on his chest beneath a well-worn jacket. Sandy, a faithful Salvationist, yet no respecter of denominational boundaries, worshipping with every sect in turn, as the Spirit led. Sandy, the Podley King, but a King also in the fact that he knew no discontent.

Have we any Kings about the place today? We have quite a few Barons (to use the fisher term for successful skippers); we may have more than one millionaire. But both these types will be forgotten as soon as they are buried.

There is, however, about Kings, a peculiar lasting quality. Where, oh where has that gone?

Fire and Film-Stars

The Great Fire of London must have been a fair bleeze! A hale toon on fire at the same time! Apparently it was a blessing in disguise, for it put an end to the great plague (The Black Death) which had been raging in the city for so long. I have wondered, more than once, if the Great Fire was started deliberately.

According to Peter Buchan, no relation of mine, there was a fire among the huts which had been erected on the braes, just to the north of the Blue Toon, as a sort of isolation hospital for victims of the same plague, and wasn't there some suspicion of fire-raising then too?

Both of these fires have been well recorded, but the Great Fire of Peterhead has been allowed to fade into oblivion. What a shame! You see, it happened like this.

In the days before road-laying machines were invented, our streets were tarred in the old-fashioned way which required the presence of a tar-boiler. The boiler was simply a huge iron tank set on iron wheels, a tank with a furnace beneath it, and a great lang lum stickin up at the front. Not a beautiful sight! The tar (from the gas-works, I believe) was brought to the boil before being drawn off via great muckle brass cocks into 'roosers', to be carried by roadmen and sprayed on the ground. Then other members of the gang scattered chuckie steenies on the hot tar. A very labour-intensive process, a hot, dirty, smelly job.

There was one very good aspect to the smell in that it was reputed to be beneficial to bairns wi the 'kink-hoast' (whooping cough), that terrifying ailment, now completely eradicated by modern medicine. Doctors did actually advise mothers to take their suffering infants 'round past the gas-works, or close to the tar boiler!' The tar boiler was towed, of course, to wherever it was required.

Now then, one day in Marischal Street the boiler 'devulped' (I quote) a hole in its boddim, allowing the boiling tar to run down through the furnace to the gutter below. The great black clouds of smoke blotted out the sun and the street was like a dark tunnel with a river of fire running through it. What a sicht! To see a park o barley strae burnin on a dark nicht would give you some idea of what it was like. Most of the shop-fronts in the street suffered paint damage, but the most serious casualty was Mackintosh the baker's (Walter Allan's). There the windows were utterly destroyed and the blind burnt to a cinder. The Post Office, too, suffered badly.

Now, it simply isn't true that Johnny Millar abandoned ship, nor is it true that Mackintosh put a boxie on the coonter boldly marked 'For the Blind'. Faa wid say sic a thing? But it is a fact that several 'tows o claes' were destroyed by soot. Some would have it that the fall-out from the tarry cloud exterminated the kink-hoast throughout the whole of Buchan! But let me tell you now of something which really happened.

The week after the fire, some visiting Dutch fishermen stopped to survey the damage to Mackintosh's shop. Then one of them, probably the cook, entered the shop and asked for 'meelick'.

'Oh, aye!' says the chiel at the coonter, 'We've plinty o that! Jist hold on!' He was back from the bake-hoose in a meenit, wi a great muckle pyoke o mealicks (crumbs).

The Dutchman shook his head vigorously. 'Meelick! Meelick! Meelick!'

It was only after the visitor had sat on a biscuit tin, miming the milking of a cow, and roarin like a spent calf, that it was realised that he wanted milk. Then he was sent elsewhere. See how great a barrier language can be?

This reminds me of an incident during the war years when, for a while, I was engineer on a former Lossie fishing boat the *Tulip*. A crew of Norwegians, ex-fishers, arrived to take up duty on an ex-Clyde ringer with a 44 hp Kelvin Diesel. Now, the Kelvin Diesel, and especially the 44, has a rather alarming knock when running slow, although the knock disappears at higher revs. In some alarm the

323

Norwegian reported to the Base Engineer Officer who, being a steam man, knew nothing about diesels.

'Go and see Peter on the *Tulip*!' says he. 'Peter knows all about diesels!'

That, of course, wasn't strictly true, but it resulted in our having a stranger with us at tea-time, a stranger who had very little English, and no experience at all in Scottish built engines. He was extremely worried about the 'very heavy knocking' (you must pronounce the first k) in his engine. I managed to tell him, mostly by sign language, that he should have supper with us, then I would have a lookie at the Kelvin. He seemed to enjoy his spam and powdered egg, conversing with me all the time as best he could.

Having spent an hour with my new friend, allaying his fears and teaching him a few things about his tattered instruction book, I returned to my ship, to be greeted with warm admiration from the skipper.

'Man, Peter!' says he, 'Ye're a great lad! Ye can fairly spik t' the foreigners! I hardly kent a word the chiel said!'

'Och!' says I, with commendable modesty, 'Languages disna gie me ony bother avaa! Jist nae neen!'

'I see that. But tell me this. Fit wye dis yon chiel ken Humphrey Bogart? He wis aye spikkin aboot 'im!'

This had me puzzled for a meenit. Then the answer came to me.

'He wisna spikkin aboot Humphrey Bogart avaa! He wis jist thinkin, fin he haard the "very heavy knocking" (pronounce the first k) that his engine was bogart!'

See what the language barrier can do?

Bad Words Ashore and Afloat

I have seen some folk wince visibly at the sound of certain words which are normally described as 'four-letter words'. For a start, that is a misnomer, for many of the really bad words comprise six or more letters. Not that it makes any difference to me, for I can get along quite nicely without them. Oh, I know that some fellas seem utterly incapable of speech without the liberal use of offensive terms, but that is simply a bad habit, of which they are apparently unaware. Others again, under intense pressure, let themselves go completely, to suddenly become very articulate men indeed instead of the quiet, reserved chaps they had been, only a minute earlier. There are those who, in the face of such outbursts, turn their faces away as if physically struck; there are others who lift their eyes skyward while their lips offer silent orisons. Sad to say, from experience, I have found such folk to be, as a rule, not completely sincere. And then there's me. In such circumstances I am possessed with an insane desire to laugh, and I canna help it! I lauch an lauch till I'm gey near greetin. I must be feel aathegither, surely!

Picture, now, if you can, a bonny, warm, sunny mornin on the broad fields o Buchan, and behold me bizzin along the road like yon kind o bee that I've tellt ye aboot afore, and jist watch as a fairmer, apparently in some distress, flags me doon.

'Foo many pints is there in the compass, Peter?' An him a fairmer!

'I'll rattle them aff, an ye can coont them yersel,' says I.

'Hinna time for that! Nae time!' says he. 'But somebody'll hae t' pint me in some direction, afore I ging feel!'

'Fit's adee?' says I, sensing that the peer breet wis at high doh. 'Hiv ye lost yer wuts?'

'Waar than that!' says he. 'A lot waar than that! . . . I've lost my nowt!'

I could hardly believe my lugs. 'Lost yer nowt? Nivver!'

'Aye!' says he, 'I've lost my nowt! I got forty beasts aff the Orkney boat yesterday, an they were driven hame in floats an putten into the coort for the nicht; young beasties, ye ken, still a bittie restless at bedtime, but that's normal aifter the voyage. They were aa keen eneuch for their mait, an I thocht they wid be sattled doon afore mornin. But, man, the shed's teem noo, an we canna see them naewye. They're clean tint, man, clean tint! They've pickit a pint on the compass that naebody kens aboot, an they could be far eneuch noo!'

Even my inexperienced ear could sense the deep anxiety in the poor man's voice, and I had enough sense to refrain from asking, 'Fit feel left the door open?' But I did speir, 'Could ye use a compass, supposin ye hid sic a thing?'

'No!' says he. 'I widna ken a compass fae a clock. It wis jist a thocht!'

'Weel!' says I, 'Ye're nae needin a compass, for ye're facin in the richt direction. There's aboot forty young beasts on the lawn at the Big Hoose, some o them near up to their bellies in't, an it new laid anaa! They maan be strangers, for nae daicent Buchan beastie wid daar ging on till't. I ken the Mannie's awaa for the day, so . . . at yer hardest, an get them aff o't. An shut the door iss time!'

Oh, the words, boys! Oh, the words! Even if I could spell them (and I couldna), the 'Buchanie' widna print them (and it shouldna). Spik aboot fower letters? They cam in aa shapes an sizes, an a hantle o different colours, syne he wis awaa like the clappers, aifter 'is nowt.

Me? I sat an leuch, an leuch, till there wis verra nearly a washin. It wis richt sair, but I jist couldna help it!

Memory now takes me several years further back to a happier occasion. We were fishing off the Durham coast, and we had toiled all day for very little indeed. It was shift, shift, shift, seeking the elusive cod, but it wasn't till evening that we found them. Our last haul for the day was a bobby-dazzler, a great bag of prime quality fish. Oh, if only we had been here all day! Ye ken the wye o't. But it wis too late. Just like 'Blockbusters', we would have to await Tuesday's edition.

Now it so happened that, as we were in the process of getting our great bag aboard, who should come sailing close past but Billy, one of the locals, an old friend and as colourful a character as I have ever met. He was close enough for direct speech, so there was no need for radio contact. In the gathering dark, while the two boats lay close together we hatched a little plot. When we got into harbour, neither of us would say boo! In the morning, both of us would hang back until the rest of the fleet had sailed, then we would come back to this happy spot and make a killing. Radio silence, of course.

As it happened, it was one of the 'best laid schemes' that didna ging agley. Tuesday was a memorable day, for the fish were awaiting us, and we spent the whole day with them. Very pleasant company they were, too! Billy was never more than half a mile away, getting on just as well as we were. Solid stuff!

Now it was dark and we were headed for Shields; the lights on the Tyne piers were winking dead ahead, and the red flash of Soutar Point lighthouse was broad on the port beam. For some unknown reason it was clear as a bell that night; usually it was thick fog when we were seeking a landfall. The sea was like the proverbial millpond and the further outlook was not at all bad. Things could hardly be better! The awful rabble on the radio had slowly died away as boat after boat had ceased fishing and the skippers had gone below to their suppers. We were to have our supper in harbour, for the lads were still busy clearing the deck. That would be nice . . . the wings of small roker skate (wings the size of your hand had been hanging in the sun for a day or two) would be dipped in batter and fried in deep fat, with chips. Two huge enamel ashets would be required to contain the feast, and not a vestige would be left.

Then, across the miles of velvety darkness came the voice of Billy's son, calling his Dad on the radio, seeking information.

'You've been very quiet today, Dad!' It was more than half question.

'Well, son, you know how it is with all them Scotties around . . . ye cannot hear anybody for everybody!' True!

'Where ye been fishin today, Dad?'

'Oh, here and there, as usual. You know, shift, shift, shift!' Oh, the lees!

'There's nothing at all out here, Dad. Wondering if it's worth steaming shorewards during the night. Any fish gettin in there?'

'Not a lot, as far as I've heard, but ye cannot believe them Scotties. Most of them are anointed liars.' I was enjoying the conversation. The son was probing, probing, and for want of a definite answer, he was suspicious.

'Have ye heard or seen Peter today, Dad? He's been very quiet too. He's a Scottie, but he'll tell the truth if you ask him.'

'Haven't seen hide or hair of Peter all day. Mebbe he's away home in disgust.'

'Peter doesn't go home when the weather and the tide are both favourable, and I'm sure he'll be wiggin (listening in) just now. I'll give him a shout, and get the low-down on inshore matters.'

But, before he had time to call me, his Dad made a colossal mistake . . . he started singing into the mike, 'Keep yer feet still, Geordie hinney'. Now, that was a dead give-away, for not unless he was very happy did Billy sing on the radio, and not until he had a boat-load of fish was Billy really happy. So now the son's suspicions were certainties, and he would be steaming at full speed for inshore waters, some eight hours distant. Without doubt, he would join our little party in the morning.

When Billy had finished his excruciating solo, there came a verbal arrow from the son, 'Remember Georgie Washinton, Dad!' It took a second or two to spot the inference . . . Georgie Washinton never told a lie.

'Sure, son, I remember Georgie Washinton all right!' Then he launched out on the second verse of his song.

When silence had been mercifully restored, there came yet another barb. 'Dad, I don't believe you know who Georgie Washinton was!'

'Oh, I know all about Georgie Washinton, son. He's the b....r that shot the apple off the other b....r's head!'

Well done, Billy! I leuch till I was nae-weel. Feel aathegither? Aye, surely, but I did tell ye that some o the words had mair than fower letters.

The Leaking Bog

There are farmers and farmers; there are fishermen and fishermen. They are not all the same. As a rule, the good fisherman keeps a tidy boat, just as the good farmer keeps a tidy place. Any sensible skipper, seeing that some part of his deck machinery is badly worn, will have the said part repaired or renewed as soon as possible, knowing full well that, should that part break while at sea, it could cost two or three days of fishing time. A less responsible fella will let the thing run until it breaks, in the hope that 'the insurance' will pay for the repair. Any farmer worth his salt will have his implements in perfect order long before the crop is ready; his less responsible oppo waits until the barley's cryin oot to be cut before discovering that his combine harvester has somehow seized up! I've seen it all happen, and I'm sure that the Lord should have mentioned the men-folk in His parable of the foolish virgins!

I'll never forget the day I saw a great muckle combine comin rummlin doon a farm road to make the very first cut of the season. The open gate of the barley park was directly opposite the end of the farm road so, in a sudden fit of courtesy, I stopped my van and signed that he should cross my bows. This he proceeded to do, with a friendly wave of acknowledgement, but sink me if the monster didna stall, richt across the road, blocking baith lanes. And the reason? Nae fuel in the tank! Boys, ye nivver saw naething like yon! In twaa meenits there wis fifty or sixty motorists, half a dizzen bobbies an twaa fairmers, aa sweerin blue lowes! Somebody ran back to the fairm to get a suppie diesel in a tin, only to discover that the fairm tunk wis eel (empty)! That fairly put the lid on't. Then somebody noticed that I was the ile man, so the hale jing-bang fell oot on me. It wis aa MY blame! I should ha KENT, athoot bein TELLT, that the tunk wis TEEM! I'm tellin ye, I wis lucky to get oot o yon wi my life especially since I sat there lauchin like a tippeny bookie! I jist couldna help it. Naebody seemed to realise that I wis Esso, and that farmer dealt wi Shell! Every time the barley ripens, I mine on yon day. Feels were there in plenty, but nivver a virgin to be seen!

327

Could it be that such episodes are sent to cheer us on our way? Depends on how you look at them, I suppose, and no doubt it's a great help if you can find some innocent person on whom to lay the blame.

Another unforgettable incident took place one dark winter day, when I had just left the cattle mart at Maud to keep an appointment at Banff. The road was like a bottle with ice, so driving was rather tricky. I had just reached yon fearsome bend on the Fedderate road when a Land Rover, coming from the opposite direction, came skidding across the road, *Bowff* into my starboard side. Although both of us got a scare, there was very little damage to either vehicle. The other driver wis Sandy Lee fae Fordafourie, a first class fairmer and an eminent breeder of prize-winning sheep.

'Man!' say he, 'I'm richt gled I've met ye! Fadder tellt me this mornin t' order ile for the central heatin. He's needin the stuff the day, cos the tunk's near teem! A buddy canna dee athoot heat in this widder, but I've clean forgotten t' phone the Broch for the ile. It's richt handy, meetin ye like this. Will ee see aboot the order? That wid save me forgettin again!'

'Aye, surely!' says I. 'But this winna be for Fyoordie's, yer ain place. I'll tell them it's for Kinbog, far yer father bides. I ken it's jist nae distance awaa, but it'll save time if they ging t' the richt place for a start.'

'The verra dunt!' says he, and off he went to the sheep sales.

From a phone-box in Pitsligo, I called the Broch office with the order, stressing that it should be entered in block capitals to denote its urgency.

'Right-oh!' says the quine, 'I'm ready! Fire aheid! Faa is't for?'

'Lee, Kinbog,' says I. 'Twaa hunner gallon heatin ile. Urgent! Afore dark!'

'O.K., O.K.!' she says. 'Keep the heid!'

Now then, fit did the great feel dee? She wrote the order in block capitals, aaricht, but she wrote 'LEAKIN BOG'! I'm tellin ye, it taks aa kinds!

When George Stephen, the lorry driver scanned the order book, he says, 'Faar on earth did that order come fae?'

'Peter phoned it in!' says the quine. 'He says it's urgent. The folkies'll be deid wi caal if they dinna get the ile afore dark!'

'Aha!' says George. ''Twis Peter, wis't? Up t' his tricks again, eh? Jist wyte till I get the hud o Peter! I'll seen sort HIM oot! He winna catch me wi that kind o nonsense! We hiv a Redbog, a Bluebog, a Whitebog an a Blackbog on oor books, but a Leakinbog? Nivver! Peter should ha phoned a plumber! Stroke oot the order. Ha, ha, ha!'

So Lee, Kinbog put a gey caal nicht ower 'is heid. An faa div ye think got the blame? Muggins again! Fit sorra idder? I widna care, but George had been supplying Lee, Kinbog for years.

Apparently there's times that folk jist gings clean gyte! The barley'll seen be ripe again, so keep yer peepers open! Ye nivver ken fit a buddy micht see or hear!

A Shot in the Dark

Peterhead's last rowing life-boat, the *George Pickard*, stood on her heavy carriage in the old Life-boat shed on that part of the quay which is known as the Green Hill. The shed, a sturdy granite building, stood gable-on to the quay, its rear gable the great storm-dyke which in easterly storms could be over-topped by mountainous seas. From her station, the boat could be dragged to the most convenient slipway, so that she could leave the harbour by either the North or the South entrance. Very handy!

With the advent of the motor Life-boats the present Life-boat shed was built, and the old boat and shed became surplus to requirements. But I remember clearly how, on Life-boat Day, great horses dragged the *George Pickard* on her carriage through the streets of the town. Each Life-boatman, suitably and fully clad in oilskins and life-jacket, was armed with a collection bag on the end of a long bamboo pole which could reach the farthest onlookers. A great day, Life-boat Day, and oh, the horses were bonny!

Well now, it came to pass that the *George Pickard*, with all her gear, was purchased by Sandy Davidson (Dites) who had a coal-yard on the Seagate, in the days when it was quite common for folks to buy their coal one pail at a time. Sandy was a proper rough diamond, but he had no objection to us boys going to have a look at his boat, and how we marvelled at the holes in the fleer, for letting the water out, should any come on board. Sandy's first move was to have a twin-cylinder Bolinder engine (say 30 or 40 hp) installed in the old boat, then he got a set of trawl gear (tut-tut) and commenced poaching (again tut-tut).

Now, Sandy was not alone in this failing, for Peterhead men have always shown a marked propensity for poaching. I doubt if there's any part of the Scottish coast that hasn't been 'visited' by the PDs. Indeed, one irate skipper did approach a certain Admiral of the Fleet with the earnest request that he should 'stop his blasted submarines fae practisin in yon Bey as lang as the cod wis on'. And yet another, who shares with me a common birthday, was once asked by his crew, 'Could ye nae shift aff a bittie, skipper, so's we can pee athoot folk lookin at's?'

I'm sure the powers that be made a great mistake when they banned the use of the trawl inside the three-mile limit. Had they said, 'Thou shalt not trawl outside the three-mile line', then the grounds inside that line would have remained untouched, as they were originally meant to be. But then, the powers that be have never attained a Degree in Psychology.

Sandy had a great confederate in Partan Jake, skipper of the *Water Lily*, another boat with a 'boom-boom' engine. The pair of them would go trawling as bold as brass in the Cample (atween Rattray head and Cairnbulg Briggs) and in Broch Bey. Of course they showed no lights, but a buddy could easy hear the boom-boom as far as Mormond Hill. Spik aboot ostriches! The smaa-boat men in St Combs, Inverallochy and Cairnbulg turned a blind eye to the raiders as long as their own 'troonks' remained undisturbed. Queer folk, yon. They say 'troonks' instead o 'creels', they say 'pairk' for park, 'bate' for boat, and 'most' for mast.

329

Still, I'm come o yon 'fyolk', so I'd better hud my tongue.

Ye see, it's them that's richt an hiz that's vrang, for they've held on to their ain tongue, far we've thrown maist o oors awaa. Theirs is the richt fisher tongue, an lang may they keep it.

Noo, far wis I? Oh, aye, I mine noo: Sandy Dites an Partan Jake poachin in the Cample on a richt bonny nicht; nae a funk o win, an jist a wee bittie o easterly lift. Hazy kine. Weel, aye, jist a thochtie. For a crew, Jake had his twaa breethers, the Yunk (cos he had been in the States) and Twinkletoes (cos he had been as pirn-taed as a doo aa his days). Sandy had jist the ae man, Brucie, anither rough diamond, nae that ony o the squad wis ony better. They wid ha made a rare diamond bracelet, I'm sure!

There wis nae sign o the 'catcher', an the twaa boaties wis deein awaa gran, fin doon comes the fog as thick as a blunkit. Problems? Oh aye, nae radar, nae wireless, nae naething, ye see. But things like that disna bother a P.D. poacher, so Jake heaves up his gear an scutters aboot in the fog till he gets a hud o Sandy. Syne, abeen the boom-boom o the twa engines, he roars, 'We'll ging into the Broch Bey, an leave this place t' you. Then we winna come foul o een anither.'

'Please yersel,' cries Sandy, 'but ye'd better watch the rocks at the Bick'n (the Beacon on Cairnbulg Briggs). It'll seen be low watter, an it's the tap o the stream tide, so there winna be a lot o watter. Ye canna thole t' be ower far in at the Bick'n, ye ken! Ye winna see the licht far the nicht, freen!'

'I ken aa that, Sandy. I'll watch!' says Jake, but he didna watch. The first he kent wis 'bumpity-bump', an the *Water Lily* wis hard fast amon tangles. Full speed astarn made nae difference; she wis fair stuck.

Now, to be on a boat which is fast by the heel in a moderate swell can be a salutory experience, for the boat will twist and roll in torment, seeking the freedom of her natural element. There is nothing natural about the roll; it is more of a lurch, as she lays first one side, then the other deep in the water, with a vicious, twisting motion which always ends in a sudden jerk. In Jake's own words, 'It gars ye feel as if yer doup's affa yokie'.

Naebody on the shore wid hear them shoutin so they wid fire a rocket, but there wisna sic a thing in the boat. Weel, they wid licht a flare, but fit wid they burn? An faa wid see't on a nicht like this, onywye? Still, they wid hae t' dee something, so they trailed an aal strae matrass oot o the caibin, soakit it wi diesel an set fire till't. Od, boys! Sic a bleeze; they verra near set the boat on fire!

Now, Sandy, in the aal Life-boat, thocht it wis time he kent richt jist far he wis, so him an Brucie gets the trawl aboard wi a fine haulie o flukes.

'This thickness is jist nae mowse!' says Sandy. 'We'd better try an get a hud o something so's we can get oor bearins. Lat's hae a look for the Bick'n. It canna be that far awaa.'

'I thocht I saw a searchlight eyvnoo!' says Brucie. 'Maybe it's the catcher!'

'Nae fears,' says Sandy, 'the catcher winna come in here on a nicht like this! It widna been the Licht, wid it?'

'Na! 'Twis ower low for that. I've lost it again, onywye. I winner foo yon mob's gettin on in the Broch Bey.'

'We'll creep in a bittie an hae a look,' says Sandy. 'Fog an daylicht's bad aneuch, but fog an darkness is hell an aathegither. Keep yer een skint for a licht o ony kind.'

As it happened, the first licht they saw wis the bleeze o the matrass on the *Water Lily*'s deck, a glare that shone on the dark broon tangles that jist broke the screeth (surface) o the water. There seemed, however, to be a clear channel jist astarn o the *Water Lily*.

Sandy had the situation sized up in a tick, an he wisna slow to tell Jake aa aboot it.

'For ony sake pit oot that blasted bonfire, Jake, or ye'll hae the hale North Sea alairmed! It seems ye've geen up a trink (trench) amon the rocks. I'll ging oot a bittie an turn, syne I'll come in starn first an get a rope across t' ye. I'll get a better rug at ye if I'm gaan aheid.'

So Sandy came dead slow astarn into the trink, canny, canny. Then, at a reasonable distance from the casualty, he stopped his boat.

'Ye'll hae t' come closer than that,' cries Jake. 'Faa div ye think's gaan t' fire a rope that distance?'

'Nae damn fears,' says Sandy. 'We'll gie ye a heavin line, an ye can mak it fast t' yer tow-rope. Stand by!'

Enter Brucie, Lifeboat-man supreme, an expert with the heaving-line. The line in question had on its end a foot-long length of bamboo, and on the end of that a lump o leed as big as yer niv (fist). A deadly missile indeed, capable of being thrown an amazing distance by a practised hand.

'Ye'd better hap yer heids,' cries Brucie, 'or I'll brain the lot o ye. Fussle fin ye're ready.'

Partan Jake an the Yunk immediately dived into the hold, but Twinkletoes took to the wheelhoose an coories doon on the fleer. He had only been there half-a-meenit fin he thocht he wid be safer in the hold. He wis half-roads there fin Jake fusselt, an he wis jist abriest o the hatch fin the leed, slung by the mighty arm o Brucie got him 'Bowff' on the heid. Oh, the peer Twinkle!

He fell doon the hole like a ton o coal on tap o his twaa breethers. Syne they fell oot on him an kickit him half to death for giein them sic a scare. Breethers dis things like that, sometimes.

Finally, the *Water Lily* was successfully refloated and made her home port under her own steam and with no apparent damage. Not so, the peer Twinkle; he nott sax stitches at the back o 'is lug, an some strappin for 'is ribs.

Brucie's verdict on the hale affair?

'Weel!' says he, modestly, 'Twinkle should be thankfu gled it wis pick dark, an smore thick. Itherwise I wid ha killt 'im!'

The Clootie Dumplin

Once more the good ship *Meadowsweet* was homeward bound from the West-coast fishing grounds. After an unusually early homecoming from East Anglia, the Turk had wasted no time; three days at home, then it was away again to the Minch. Now it was getting on for Christmas, time to go home for a whilie. And, as Jeemsie said, 'sax or saiven wiks in the Minch wis lang eneuch for onybody, specially in the winter-time'.

If these were the Turk's sentiments, he certainly didn't express them. Early that morning, while his crew, unnaturally silent, had hauled a fleet of empty nets, the skipper had simply remarked, 'Queer, cappernyaam craiturs, the herrin. They like the moon at Yarmooth, but they dinna like it roon here'. If he heard Jeemsie mutter, 'They're nae the only eens!' he paid no attention but, when he himself said, 'I think we'll awaa hame,' he couldna fail to notice the marked increase in the speed of the hauling process. Crews speak loudest when they are silent.

On the way north towards Cape Wrath, the Turk drew Jeemsie's attention to the stark beauty of the snow-covered massifs of Arkle, Foinaven and Stack.

'That's far Suntie Claa bides.' But Jeemsie showed little interest.

'I can see the Isle o Lewis fae here, skipper,' says Jeemsie.

'Oh aye, Jeemsie, that's a sure sign that it's gaan t' be rain.'

'An fit dis't mean fin ye canna see't fae here, skipper?'

'Oh!' says the Turk, 'That means that it's rainin already!'

But there was no rain. While the shippie steamed steadily eastward along the North coast, the weather remained bright and clear. Meanwhile the crew busied themselves among the nets, 'makkin them up' (making of each net an individual bundle). When this job was finished, the side-decks were filled with neatly bundled nets.

'Now,' says the Turk, 'pit them below, an pit the hatches on. We've a lang road aheid o's yet, an it's winter-time. Better safe than sorry!'

Thereafter it was 'Set the watch', and those who were off duty could sleep, or read, or jist sit and news. As they drew steadily nearer to the Pentland Firth the Turk consulted his tide-table and discovered what he already knew: they had missed the tide at the Firth.

'It's jist a waste o time an coal tryin t' steam throwe that Firth against the ebb. She jist winna dee't, so we'll jist hae an oor or twaa in Scrabster till the tide rins ower. It's mair than likely we'll hae company there, onywye.'

As the Turk had expected, there were already two or three drifters in Scrabster basin, lying at the pier which was built of great flat slabs of slate laid on top of each other, without any mortar. It was common practice for fishing boats to lie for a few hours in Scrabster when the ebb tide in the Pentland Firth hindered their passage west to east. Bigger vessels would lie in Scrabster Bay. For vessels bound east to west against the flood tide, Sinclair Bay, just north of Wick, was the waiting-point. The tides in the Firth are so fierce that only very fast ships can master them, and to tackle the Firth at all when wind and tide are in opposite directions is to ask for a double helping of trouble, for then the sea becomes like a raging beast.

It was much too cold to go ashore, so the fishermen sat in each other's cabins or toasted themselves on each other's fiddleys, discussing the depressed state of their industry and the even more depressing threat of war. Only Duncan ventured ashore, returning very shortly with a day-old newspaper.

'Onything new in the paperie the day, Duncan?' says the Turk.

'Nae a great lot,' says Duncan. 'I dinna think iss mannie Chamberlain's gettin on verra sair wi Hitler, but I see a lad in Foggieloan's gotten a snake for a pet!'

'A snake!' says Jeemsie. 'Gyaad sake, he canna be richt! A snake by onything! Div ye ken onything aboot snakes, skipper?'

'Weel awyte! Fine div I ken aboot snakes, my loon. Mony a scare hiv I gotten wi the brutes.'

'I didna ken ye wis oot in the jungle, skipper! Wis ye in Africa?'

'Africa?' says the Turk, 'Africa? Nivver een! I wis on the island o Raasay. Hiv ye nivver seen a Raasay snake? No? Weel, ye're nae missin naething, for they're jist nae mowse! They're nae gweed t' get clear o, cos they pit their tails in their moos an come rowlin aifter ye like a gird!'

Duncan and Jeemsie looked into each other's faces, but made no comment. They had never been ashore on Raasay, and they kent naething aboot snakes. Still, wi the skipper, ye could nivver be sure!

'I hiv a dog at hame,' says Duncan, 'but I dinna think I could thole t' hae a snake aboot the hoose avaa. I dinna like creepy things.'

'I'm readin a bookie eyvnoo aboot a loon that got wannert in the Brazilian jungle wi's chum', says Jeemsie. 'They saw a giant snake that could swally a coo. I think it wis an anaconda, or something lik 'at.'

'That'll be Martin Rattler that ye're readin aboot,' says the skipper. 'I'm surprised that he's still on the go, cos he wis at the same game fin I wis a loon. He maun be an aal mannie noo!'

Jeemsie smiled, then queried, 'Ye dinna hae nae pets yersel, skipper?'

'Me? No!' says the Turk. 'But there wis a time fin I had a monkey. Fin I wis a loon, ye ken.'

'Did ye get that on Raasay, amon the snakes, skipper?'

'Na, my loon, there's nae monkeys on Raasay. I got the monkey fin I wis in Mogadishu on a cargie-boat. Aa the wye fae Montrose wi ten thoosan ton o tattie seeds.'

'Tattie seeds?' says Duncan, 'Tattie seeds? Div ye nae mean seed tatties?'

'Tattie seeds, Duncan. In packeties, ye ken, jist like ither seeds.'

'Aye, aye, skipper, tattie seeds it is! Noo lat's hear aboot the monkey!'

'Weel,' says the Turk, 'I bocht the monkey fae a hawker mannie. He tellt me it wis a spikkin monkey, the only een o its kine in the world. An he wis richt aboot that.'

'A spikkin monkey? Fit did she say, skipper?' says Jeemsie in astonishment.

'Och! She didna say an affa lot, Jeemsie, but ilkie time she made a mess on the table, she said, "That remains t' be seen!" We wis jist half-wye hame fin the skipper fun oot that I had a monkey aboord an he gid reid mad. Man, he took the monkey b' the tail an haived her ower the side, the coorse chiel. I grat for a fyle, cos I wis jist a loon, an I lay waakened, listenin t' the beat o the propeller in the watter. She wis an aal-fashioned ship, ye ken; fin she wis licht, half o the propeller wis oot o the watter, an it made a queer kine o soun, flap-flap-flap, aa the time. But I seen forgot the peer monkey.'

'It wisna richt t' droon the craitur', says Jeemsie.

'A coorse man, yon skipper, Jeemsie. I hope ye appreciate the skipper ye hiv aboord here.'

'Niver mine that,' says Jeemsie. 'Can monkeys sweem?'

'Not a stroke!' says the Turk. 'They're terrified at watter!'

'Oh!' says Jeemsie, 'I wis jist winnerin.'

'Ye'll hardly believe this, Jeemsie, but fin we gid back t' Montrose for mair tattie seeds . . .'

'Seed tatties, skipper, seed tatties!' interrupted Duncan.

'Nivver mind that, Duncan, but we got in past Scurdy Ness, an fin we wis passin Ferryden (ye ken, yon placie far the wifies' claes-poles is sometimes in the sea), aa the folk wis shoutin, an pointin at the ship's starn, so the skipper gart me ging aift t' see fit wis adee. Od! Fin I lookit ower the starn, here wis the monkey, jumpin fae blade to blade o the propeller t' keep hersel oot o the watter! Three solid wiks she had been deein that. Clivver monkey!'

'I hardly think that's true, skipper,' says Duncan. 'Fit wye did she nae shout for help? Ye did say she wis a spikkin monkey!'

They all had a good lauch, and the story session ended. On the very last of the ebb, the *Meadowsweet* nosed her way through the Firth, scraping close round the corner at Duncansby Head, so close that Jeemsie could reach out with an oar from the smaa-boat, and touch the very cliff.

'The skipper maybe disna ken aboot seed tatties,' says Duncan, 'but he fairly kens this Firth!'

Late forenoon found our heroes well across the Moray Firth, with Mormond high on the starboard bow.

'Hey, Chef!' says Duncan, 'Seein that this'll be oor last denner aboord the ship for this year, an seein that it's near Christmas, fit aboot a duff?'

'That wid be fine,' says Jeemsie, 'but I dinna think there's as muckle stuff left as wid mak a duff o ony size. I didna stock up this wik in Stornowa, cos I expectit this wid be oor hinmist wik awaa. See fit ye can rake oot o the locker, an ye can hae a go at a duff if ye like. There's a fine pot o broth soossin awaa, here!'

Duncan didna get a great lot o stuff in the locker, but there wis at least some.

'Jeemsie, my loon,' says he, 'there's hardly eneuch t' mak a big duff, but I think I could mak a clootie dumplin wi this lot. It wid be fine an Christmas-like, an we'd aa get a bittie. I'm a don han at clootie dumplins!'

'Fire aheid, Duncan!' says Jeemsie. 'But for God's sake dinna mak the thing on the same scale as ye did wi the custard, else we'll aa be smored!'

So Duncan got goin, an the bonny dumplin wis plunkit into the pot.

When dinner-time came, Jeemsie handed the great muckle pot doon the trap to Duncan.

'Ye can dish up if ye like, Duncan. I'll be doon in a couple o shakes.' Then Jeemsie stoked up the stove and saw that everything was in order, but when he went down into the cabin, he got a shock. There was no sign of the dumplin.

'Ye've aa been in a fearsome hurry, surely. Ye micht ha kept a bittie dumplin t' me, Duncan!'

There was no answer. Aabody jist kept suppin awaa at their broth, nae even liftin a heid. Jeemsie kent there wis something far wrang fin Duncan negleckit his chum.

'Faa scoffed the dumplin? Come awaa noo! Faa gluffed it!' No reply!

'Aa richt, than, aa richt, dinna tell me! But the least ye can dee is t' gimme back the cloot it wis in!'

'Good grief!' cries the Turk, turnin green, 'Wis there a cloot on't?'

The Rim Net

It's most unlikely that you've ever seen a rim net, for such contraptions are not exactly common in this enlightened age. In fact, any one of today's fishermen would look at you in amazement were you to mention such a thing. I'm sure the rim net is a relic of the days before the Flood, when Tubal-cain was the instructer of every artificer in brass and iron (Genesis 4:22).

'Aha,' says you. 'Fit on earth has brass or iron t' dee wi a net?' Weel, it's like this, ye see. The rim net needs iron, for it's jist like a bairn's gird (hoop), except that it's in twaa halfs, hinged in the middle. A circular piece of netting is woven onto the iron rim and, apart from a rope closing the trap, the outfit is complete. Sorry! I'm forgetting the bait. Bait for a net? Aye, bait for a net! Ye tie bitties o bait into the net and lower the hale apothick into the watter. It's best to let the net sink richt to the boddim, where the two halves of the rim open out and the baited net lies flat. At any time that you so desire, you can tit the towie and close the trap. If you're lucky, you may capture any fish which have gathered to 'hose' at the bait. Perhaps I should stress that this is definitely not the easiest way to make a living, but I'm sure you're welcome to try.

In the days of my youth, there were a few worthy exponents of the noble art of rim-netting. These worthies invariably fished during the famine months of winter, when a puckly o podlies micht realise a few coppers. And, since any bait available at that time of year was almost certain to be rotten to the point of decomposition, there wis aboot these characters an unmistakable odour. Oh, boys! Fit a guff! Much, much worse than somebody opening their hand-bag!

So much for the rim net, but thereby hangs a tale.

It was spring-time, about twelve years ago, when I was still employed as a Traffic Controller in the control tower at Peterhead Harbour. Those were the days when pipe-laying barges, with their great retinues of attendant vessels, were very much to the fore. Indeed, the Bay could scarcely cope with the number of vessels requiring its use, so much so that supply boats had to anchor in tiers of eight or ten and, even at that, many ships had to lie outside. The great Oil Boom was in top gear. There was also the expected influx of certain ladies whose morals were exactly on par with those of the men who sought their company. But that is just by the way.

It had been a beautiful day, and I was thinking it was about time that I was getting my boatie ready for a go at the ripper. You see, if you intend to salt and dry some fish, so that you may have 'hairy tatties' in the winter time, it's best to get the job done in Spring, afore the great foosty bluebottles come on the scene. So it was with such thoughts in mind that I went to get my converted ship's-lifeboat ready for action. Oh, boys, fit a mess she was in! Jist fair clartit wi fool black ile, like aa the ither smaa-boats.

At that time, the water in the inner basins of the harbours was covered with a thick scum of black sump oil, the stuff the farmers call 'burssen ile'. Since the North entrance had been closed, there was no flow of clean water through the harbour, so the oil lay trapped, and every rise and fall of the tide set a fresh layer of filthy grease on slipways, ladders and mooring ropes. It was utterly impossible to keep a boatie clean. The place was an affront to any modern society, but when I made verbal complaint, I was told, 'Where there's muck, there's brass'. A letter in the local paper, with my signature, got me into very bad odour for a whilie, very nearly as bad as the guff of the rim net men. You see, I used the unpardonable word 'cess pool', the politest word I could think of at the time. Worst of all, I think, nobody seemed to think of the potential fire risk. Still, that has all been remedied by the installing of clean-water ducts, and the place is much cleaner.

Well now, on the evening in question, I decided to take the boat into the Bay to give the engine a good run, and I had just got the engine started when my seven-year-old grandson, Peter, appeared on the scene. Of course, he wanted a sail in the boat and would brook no denial despite my warning that he would probably get his clothing in a mess. So, with the youngster at the helm, we set out.

It was great fun for the loon, steering the boat round and round among the tiers of anchored ships. He was as proud as a peacock when some of the seamen gave him a cheery wave, and I had some difficulty persuading him that it was time to go home. We were actually making for the harbour when a great muckle ocean-going tug began to hoot-hoot on her compressed-air horn, apparently to draw our attention. Urgent hand-signals from the tug's bridge conveyed the message that our services were required, so I drew my boatie alongside.

It transpired that the skipper had just been informed by radio that the tug's services would not be required that night, so he was at liberty to let his crew have a few hours of shore leave. Would I take some of the lads ashore? I would, of course, be rewarded, and they would find their own way back.

'Aye, surely!' says I, 'I'll wait till ye get yer go-ashores on. There's nae hurry, and in the meantime I'll try to get the boat cleaned up a bittie. She's far ower fool for passengers!'

Peter disappeared aboard the tug to have a tour of inspection, while I tried to remove the worst of the oily filth from the seats in my boatie. My labours were in vain, for salt water and a broom are useless against oil. I was about to give up in despair when a quiet voice said, 'Would you like some hot water?' and the tug's cook passed me the end of a stout rubber hose. 'Just open the nozzle when you want hot water, and here's a bucket of detergent!' Boys, in a few minutes, ye couldna see the boatie for steam, and she was cleaner than she had been for years. What a transformation! Then the shore party appeared on deck, rarin to go.

'Hold on!' says I. 'Faar's the loon?' At that very moment Peter appeared, carrying a bunch of some forty bananas and two tins of Coke. He spurned all offers of assistance with his prize. Were we ready to go now? Apparently not, for one of the party wasn't quite ready yet.

While we awaited the latecomer, the skipper says, 'Nice little boat you've got here. Would you like some paint for her?'

'Aye, surely!' says I, and was promptly presented with a five-gallon drum of International white enamel. That was worth a bob or twaa, eh? They say that 'a gaan fitt's aye gettin!'

Apparently the latecomer was still not ready, so I had a look at a little group of seamen who were fishing from the stern of the tug. They seemed to me to be Spaniards although, mind you, I could have been mistaken. Only the officers, all Americans, were being allowed ashore, but the little group of fishers didn't seem to care. Boys! I could scarcely believe my eyes when I saw that they were using a rim net! And they were fishing for crabs, not the big partans which are so popular with gourmets, but the little green 'craibs' which are to be found in the rock pools along the shore. How these fellas seemed to relish the craibs which we used to call 'grindies', or 'grindie-tochers'. They were sookin the taes with great gusto!

'Oh, gyaad!' says I, then I got an even bigger shock, for the bait in their prehistoric net consisted of five lovely pork chops! Judging by the number of crabs in the net, pork was a highly successful bait, though the seamen themselves wouldn't eat it. I thought it was a shameful waste of good food.

Well now, when we finally did get home, I teased Peter about the bananas.

'Hey!' says I, 'Fit aboot the boat's share? Div ye nae think that I'm entitled t' half o the bananas, seein that the boat's mine?'

My hints fell on remarkably stony ground, and I laughed as I watched him stagger up the road with his load. On no account would he accept assistance. Alone I did it!

When I was stowing my own prize in the sheddie, the wife looks oot, an she says, 'Fit on earth's 'at ye hiv in the tin?'

'Woman!' says I, 'That's a five-gallon drum o first-class, top-notch, International fite enamel!'

'Nae bad!' says she. 'But could ye nae ha gotten a brush anaa, eence ye wis at it?'

Some folk's nivver pleased!

337

The Gold Rush

Do you think you could forget your car for a whilie and transform yourself into a pedestrian? You do? Well, take the South Road at the Kirkburn Mill (the Oo Mull) and head for the Cottage Hospital, keeping to the right-hand pavement, and close to the Mill dyke. You know, there used to be a hole in that dyke, a very special hole, for through it a bairn could look down into a rather mysterious courtyard, where the Kirk Burn appeared very briefly before disappearing under the road, to reappear almost at sea level, pouring through two great massive iron pipes onto the stony foreshore. Ye needna bother lookin for that hole noo, cos it's nae there. What a shame!

But nivver mind the hole in the dyke . . . Faar's the Burn? Fit on earth hiv they deen wi the burn that eesed t' be the boundary o the toon? I've lookit sair for't but I canna see't. Maybe it wis nivver the official boundary, but it wis certainly the boundary the time o the Plague. If a mither wanted her bairn baptised, she wid stand on the toon side o the burn an hud her bairn abeen the watter, so that the Minister on the ither bank could perform the ceremony. Country folk wid bring tatties an vegetables an pedlars wid bring their wares, but cross the burn they wid not. The verra siller for ony transack had to be heated reid-het on a shovel afore it crossed the watter! Naebody in, an naebody oot, that wis the rule. Lang afore my time!

Now, pedestrian, carry on past the Kirkyaird till ye come to the twaa hillocks on the Links. They're supposed to be burial mounds, but I'm sure I would nivver think aboot investigating. I'll jist tak their word for that! But, jist afore ye reach the hillocks, ye'll see a bonny flat bittie on the Links, far the Mission held an Open-air if it wis a bonny Sunday. A great place for fitba; and the genuine, original, identical spot far the Gold Rush began! Ye nivver heard o the Gold Rush? Od, ye're richt ignorant! But, mind ye, there's a lot o folk disna ken aboot it!

It all happened on a bonny summer day in the late twenties. On the fine flat bittie I've mentioned, a bourachie o loons were playin fitba when a Grimsby liner entered the Bay, tooin like murder. A 'liner' is a vessel which fishes with lines, just as a trawler uses a trawl. See? the two vessels may be otherwise alike.

Now, this was the *Juliana*, from Grimsby, calling in for a supply of bait before proceeding to far Northern waters.

Very soon we would see the Moozies' boatie, the *Breadwinner* leave the harbour with some ten cran of herring boxes, bait for the 'Grimmy'. This was a common event, the old *Huxley* being the most regular caller. Well now, since the baa wis bust, we gave up our game and crossed the road to watch the proceedings. No need whatsoever to watch the traffic. What was traffic? Once across the road, we settled down on the grass at the top of the cliff. It was actually a cliff, sheer to the beach, for the terraced paths to the Lido did not exist at that time. The cliff face was simply formed of earth, very dangerous indeed, although we didn't realise it.

Suddenly, the cliff top gave way beneath our weight, and the whole shebang went down like an avalanche. We were indeed fortunate not to be buried alive, for several tons of soil fell to the beach. After a quick count of heads we were able to reassure the few onlookers that nobody was missing, and we were still marvelling at our good fortune when a loon on a message bike said . . . 'Dis you lads ken that Tarzan or Nelson fun a twaa-shillin bit at the Diggin's the day?'

I'm tellin ye, the Gold Rush wis on! Twaa shillins! A fortin, a Klondyke! Along the Embankment we ran, like a stampede of buffaloes, never doubting the truth of what we had heard. It had to be true, for we had gotten the actual name of the prospector who had made the lucky strike! Twaa shillins, b' jingers. Twaa hale shillins! What a rush, boys, what a rush. Those in front cried 'Forward', while those behind cried 'Wyte'.

Ower the Queenie Brig we panted, nae a loon in sicht. Great! We would still be in time. Up Castle Street then first left for the Diggins, the Municipal Dump, which burned like the fires of Hell and stank to high heaven. Boys, what a stamagaster we got! There wis aboot twaa hunner loons there fae Queen Street an Landale Road an the Winmill Brae, gran loons that didna usually come near the Diggins, but twaa shillins wis twaa shillins! Some siller, yon! It's a winner the Provost wisna doon. Maybe he wis, though I didna see him!

We rakit wi sticks among the rubbish till the rising tide drove us out. Not a maik, boys, not a maik! Which goes to prove that being on the right spot at the right time is all important, in most walks of life.

For many generations the town's refuse was dumped into the top of a creek or gully among the rocks. The mouth of the gully, the Peel (Pool) was a favourite fishing place for the loons. Solid podleys, boys! Big saithes anaa! Jist sit here a whilie catchin podleys, an ye'll ging hame stinkin.

The tide at high water lapped the lower parts of the great heap of corruption, but the upper parts smouldered continually, the acrid smell reaching all parts of the town as the winds dictated. What a guff, at times. Only a severe easterly gale would clean the gully completely; thereafter it simply filled up again. It's only about fifteen years ago that the Diggins was forbidden territory, and the Scaffies took the rubbish elsewhere.

This fiery furnace, this temple of dangerous fumes, was never without its regular worshippers. There were those who were there daily, scraping and raking with sticks for any item that could possibly sell, and wending their homeward way with a pathetic little baggie of 'something'. You'll see some folk on TV at the same caper in the big cities. Along with most of my playmates, I had a go at it more than once, till I got a sair skin fae my mither for my pains. That was all I ever got.

Amongst the great heaps of aise (ashes) and caff (corn chaff) and rotten fruit and all sorts of everything, there was always a proliferation of little jars, mostly ornamental, and usually very heavy. These were the Vaseline jars, and the cold-cream jars (Pond's?) and (I think), some were marked Icilma. There were others which apparently had contained Vanishing Cream, a product which young ladies in a certain condition were said to rub on their tummies in some sort of forlorn hope.

Those were the days when each household had its 'orra pail' (usually plural) at the edge of the pavement on scaffie day. But many households had another pail for 'sweel', kitchen waste like tattie peelins and neep skins, which was collected twice weekly by two inmates of the Parish Home to feed the pigs which were kept on the site of the present Fire Station, where there was a vegetable garden. The 'mannies' came round with a pony and cairtie.

Now those days are long gone, but there are two questions which bother me. The first one is 'Faar will they pit the stuff fin they rin oot o quarries?'

The second has come to mind repeatedly over the years . . . 'What poor woman searched diligently, yet fruitlessly for the lost coin? Twaa hale shillins (10p)!

Did We Get Duff?

The wind was little more than a draught, but it was razor-sharp. In the gutter, there was a hint of a frosty glitter, and the fitful blinking of the gas lamp-post merely served to make the darkness seem even blacker. All day long, the north-easterly swell had been increasing, until now, in the early evening, the dull sound of the breakers among the rocks had reached a crescendo, more of a snarl than a roar.

Beneath the lamp-post, a small group of fishermen were pacing to and fro, quietly discussing the parlous state of their industry.

'A gey heavy swaal, that! I dinna like the soun o't!' says Partan Jake. 'There's nae win for sic a sea!'

'That's the dog afore 'is maister! Ye'll get plenty o win the morn. Aye, an mebbe afore the morn!' says Sheetlin.

'It winna bother neen o hiz, I'm sure! We're aa ashore for a fyle, b' the look o't!' says Cork.

'I'm thinkin I'm ashore for keeps. I'm nae gaan back! I've been a feel ower lang!' says Pun. 'I'm hame fae Yarmooth, an instead o gettin a square-up, I'm tellt that I'm in debt! The skipper says I'm owe him fower powen for my grub! There's nae feels on God's earth like hiz hired men!'

Such heresy, so forcibly expressed, seemed to shock Pun's friends, for they ceased their pacing for a moment, to gaze at him as if he were a freak. This was something revolutionary!

'It's teen ye a lang time t' see the licht!' says Ora, the oldest man present. 'It's been on my mind for years, but I've aye been feart t' spik. I think it's time we gid on strike! The miners aye gets something wi a strike! Could we nae dee the same?'

'Hear, hear! Cairry on, Ora!' says Sheetlin.

By this time, the company had doubled, and the word 'strike' was being used as if it were something reid het! When Ora spoke, they listened intently, nodding occasionally in agreement.

'Noo, boys, we're aa hired men (deck-hands) here the nicht. We dinna get wages, so we canna stump a card. THEREFORE, we canna get nae buroo, and

THEREFORE, we hiv t' live on tick for the hale winter! I canna look the grocer in the face! I shot a wye (a type of gull) this mornin, an that wis oor denner. I wis doon among the rocks at low water for a partan t' wir supper, an Gweed kens fit we'll dee the morn. I'm tellin ye, lads, my bairns gings oot t' the water-closet, jist t' gar ither folk think they're gettin mait!' At this there was a subdued laugh. A proper master of the colourful phrase, was Ora! But every man there knew that Ora was simply stating the stark facts of life.

Jeemsie, witless breet, opened his big mou to venture an opinion, but Sheetlin turned on him like a serpent. 'Jist ee shut yer face, Jeemsie! Ye're a cook, on wages, so ye get the buroo! There's naething comin ower you! This is a hired-man's pie, so ye'd better clear oot!' Jeemsie bolted!

Ora continued with his harangue. 'Boys! We wid aa be far better aff, workin on the roads. The peer folkies in the Parish Home's a lot better aff than hiz. We'll hae t' get wages o some kind!'

'Faar fae?' says Cork. 'The skippers an owners disna hae the siller t' pey wages! So they tell me, onywye!'

'Dinna be daft!' says Ora. 'Maist o them has hooses, an ye can aye raise the win on the strength o a hoose! There's hardly a hoose in the toon but fit has a bond on't (mortgage). But hiz? We're expectit t' tar the rope, an paint the bowse (floats), an rig oot the ship, for naething! Jist t' keep yer berth. An fit's yer berth worth?'

'Nae a damn thing!' came the reply.

These were the deplorable conditions which drove so many herring fishermen to seek berths in the trawlers at Aberdeen. There they could get a wage plus a bonus, and, although the working conditions were atrocious, the poor 'herring-scalers' were glad of the money. Among the traditional fisher folk, the key-word was 'famine', a word whose meaning is completely lost on today's generation. The following year, the deckies refused to go to sea until they were guaranteed fifteen shillings (75p) per week! They got it, after a struggle.

Many of these men are still around today, and they find it passing strange that their tales of byegone days are dismissed by the younger generation as a parcel of lies. In a way this is understandable, for it must be difficult for a modern crew to grasp that what they pay for one week's grub would have paid a drifter's coal-bill for a whole season. It is almost impossible to convince a young fisher that, after only one good trip, he can take home more money than his grandad could earn in five years.

Well now, our Parliament at the end of the street had decided that they would require a democratically elected Strike Committee, when Pun says, 'Boys, I'll hae t' leave ye. There's a mairrige on in the Polar Hall the nicht, an there's a cousin o mine fae Portsoy at it. He canna come here fae Portsoy an ging hame the same day, so he's bidin wi hiz for the nicht. He's likely in the hoose noo, so I'll hae t' ging hame an spik till 'im. Pit me doon for the Comatee, if ye like.'

Pun had a mere fifty yards to cover to reach his hoosie, and, as he slipped quietly in at the front door, he saw a wondrous sight! Through the half-open door of the butt end (the kitchen/living room), he could see his cousin, in his Sunday best, sittin in Pun's cheer, proclaimin to Pun's bairns the wonders of the wedding

341

feast. The bairns sat open-mou'ed an goggle-eed at the fantastic fairy tale that this gran man wis tellin.

'Oh! Sic a rare feed we got!' says he. 'First avaa we got broth, syne we got beef an tatties wi neeps! An we got duff, forbye, syne we feenished up wi trifle! Wyte a meenit, noo! Did we get duff? No, we didna get duff! Hold on! I'm wrang! We did get duff! I mine noo! We could get a slice o duff among the broth, or we could tak it along wi the beef an tatties. Oh, aye! We got duff aa richt!

This got the better o Pun, stannin there in the dark lobby, wi the slivver rinnin ower his chin! Dinna forget that Pun wis a gey hungry chiel.

Then, alas, Pun did an affa silly thing . . . he slippit oot, the wye he had come in, an made a bee-line for the West End Bar, where he consumed a quantity of spirits. On tick! Nae a lot, mind ye, but then, he didna need a lot on a teem stammick, aifter a lang time athoot a dram avaa.

Half an hour later, the newly formed Strike Committee heard a most peculiar noise above the roar of the swell. 'Twas the voice of their freen, Pun, comin rollin hame through the raivelt hooses, nae carin aboot the linth o the street, but gey sair made at the breadth o't.

We'll hae t' see this!' says Ora, so the Comatee moved in a body, in the direction of the strident orator who was clinging to a lamp-post, less than twenty yards fae his ain door, proclaimin to the world at large . . .

'Did we get duff? NO! WE DIDNA GET DUFF!'

'Did we get duff? AYE! WE GOT DUFF!'

'Wis the duff among the broth? NO! IT WIS IN AMONG THE BEEF!'

'Wis't a gweed duff? THE BEST DUFF IN SCOTLAN!'

The hale toon wis oot, so Ora an Sheetlin took the wanderer home.

In the morning, Pun's guest breakfasted on a borrowed egg.

'Faar's Pun?' says he.

'Oh!' says Mrs Pun, 'He's awaa oot wi the gun, I think.'

'I wis affa sair vindicatit fin I hard 'im roarin like yon, the streen,' says the Portsoy mannie. 'Richt sair vindicatit!'

When the guest had departed, the aalest quinie says till 'er mither, 'Fit dis vindicatit mean, Ma?'

'I think it's the Portsoy word for "black affrontit", my quine!'

The Detector

In the early days of exploration for oil in the North Sea, a great deal of time and money went into the accurate plotting of suitable positions for the siting of oil-rigs. Since the drilling of a bore-hole in the sea-bed is a highly expensive business, guess-work had to be completely ruled out. You see, it costs exactly the same to drill a successful hole as it does to draw a blank.

Thus the first arrivals on the scene were the seismic ships with their great, monstrous reels of electric cable at the stern. These cables, at least a mile in length and sometimes much longer, were towed astern of the ship day after day, and only when the ship was about to enter harbour were the cables wound back onto the reels. From the cables, powerful electric pulses 'pinged' the ocean floor, the returning echoes being recorded on highly sophisticated instruments on the ship. Besides recording the depth of water and the nature of the sea-bed (hard or soft bottom), the same instruments could chart the various underlying strata of the earth's crust, and this was what the oil-men wanted. Different echoes for different layers of rock or sand or chalk or whatever, supplying information vital to the entire North Sea Oil project.

I fully realise that I have almost certainly over-simplified the operation, but you're not looking for a scientific treatise, are you? Not on your Nellie! Sufficient to say that the seismic exploration still goes on, with ships and equipment which have improved beyond measure.

Now, you may recall that, some fifteen years ago, there was a buzz that the earth's crust beneath the fertile Buchan fields could be rich in precious minerals. Words like 'Plutonium', or 'Platinum', to say nothing about 'Great muckle daads o Gold', were bandied about quite freely. Rumour had it that the fairmer at Povertyknap (you must pronounce the 'k') had actually ploughed up several sizeable nuggets which his wife had taken with her, when she 'cleared oot wi the baker's vanman!'

The actual facts were that a considerable amount of drilling was done throughout the Buchan countryside, usually in isolated spots which were not agriculturally productive.

In several places, small diesel-driven drilling rigs were set up, to obtain samples of the underground treasures. Now, since both diesels and drills required lubricating oil, my stock in trade, it didn't take me long to suss-out the location of most of them. I didn't sell much oil, and I didn't learn very much, apart from the fact that boring holes in the ground can be very boring indeed! Nobody seemed to know anything, because all the cores were sent south by lorry for analysis and assessment. Mind you, I did meet some really interesting people.

There was, at the same time, a light, spotter-type of aeroplane making low-level daily flights over the countryside and, since the plane had a short length of cable trailing behind it, I assumed that it was actually 'pinging' the ground beneath for information on underground strata, just as the seismic ships did at sea.

Now, it so happened that in the course of my wanderings, I had a chat with an elderly farmer whose placie was set high on the brow of a certain hill.

'Hey, Peter!' says he. 'Fit's iss lad deein wi the airy-plane? He flees affa low, an I'm thinkin he'll hae my beasts scared oot o their skins! Some folk says he's in cojunk wi yon lads that's borin the holes! Div ee ken onything aboot it?'

'Awyte I ken aboot it!' says I. ''At fella has naething t' dee wi the hole borers avaa! He's fae the B.B.C., an he's lookin for folk that hisna peyed their T.V. licence! Ye ken fine that yon great muckle detector vans could nivver win up iss roads!'

'Dam 'e bit! says he. 'Dam 'e bit! Man, ye could be richt! I nivver thocht on sic a thing!'

Now, I have it from an unimpeachable source that, next morning, the Post Office in Ellon was packed solid with folk sair needin a T.V. licence!

I wonder why! Could it be that there actually is a 'bush telegraph' in operation? And, what is more to the point, couldn't somebody somewhere be more or less entitled to a backhander fae the B.B.C.?

Maybe he's feart t' spik!

A Fair Chiel

The term 'A fair chiel' can be applied to the darkest native of darkest Africa, if circumstances permit, for it has nothing whatsoever to do with the complexion. This is a country phrase, and the country folk can use it in a wide variety of ways. Normally, the words are used as an expression of open admiration for another's skill or strength, but subtle inflections of the voice can alter the meaning entirely, so that the same words may carry a good-natured breath of sarcasm, or even a cutting edge of contempt. It's all in the voice, with its infinite variations of expression. I have no doubt that you'll know exactly what is meant when you hear the phrase used, and then you'll be up the country somewhere, for fishers never use it.

Well, now, in the early days of my illustrious career as an oil rep. I met quite a few 'fair chiels', the most memorable of whom was Tosh, a 'medium-sized fairmer' who seemed to derive great pleasure from the exploitation of my utter ignorance of matters agricultural. That ignorance must have been perfectly obvious to everybody . . . I never sought to hide it, nor did I resent the many good-natured jokes made at my expense, but Tosh, fair chiel that he was, seemed to think that I was a complete ignoramus, so much so that I didna even ken dirt fae chappit dates. More than once did his good lady, a decent, sensible deemie, rebuke him for his ill-mannered attitude toward a stranger within their gates, but Tosh paid no heed whatsoever. He had a sitting duck, and he put in a great deal of target practice. Sadly, I was ill-equipped to parry his thrusts, having not yet won my spurs . . . but those were early days.

My golden opportunity was gey lang a-comin, but when it did eventually present itself, it came in simple guise, so simple that I could scarcely believe it.

It was a bonny day in mid summer, warm and still. The hawthorn blossom had departed from the hedgerows, and the young barley was lookin weel, as did the beasts in the parks, up to their bellies in girss. On the stroke of three (taytime), I drove into Tosh's close in answer to his phoned request for information regarding the new rubber grain-silo that Esso had produced. With a good harvest in prospect, Tosh was keen to know all the gen on the 40-ton container, and I was just as keen to sell him one. But, when I drove into the close, it was a sorry sight that confronted me, for there stood Tosh and his neighbour Sandy, who had apparently come to assist, both stripped to the waist and sweating like Turks.

It was perfectly obvious that the trouble lay in the little Lister diesel engine whose starting handle was in Sandy's hand. So it wouldn't start, eh? Laying cement, were they? Aye, surely. I could see that, all right! But, before I left my vehicle, I could see exactly why the engine wouldn't go. You see, the engine was identical to the one I had in my boatie, and I could see that, when they had stopped the engine, probably at dinner-time, one or other of the pair had inadvertently left a dollop of wet cement on the control rack of the fuel pump, which was now firmly stuck in the 'Stop' position. Not all the handle-swinging in the world would start that engine!

My first instinct was to point out the trouble, but then a something spoke to me, saying, 'Play this one by ear, sinn! Play it by ear!' So I held my peace. Just as I alighted from my vehicle Mrs. Tosh appeared at the back door crying 'Tay's ready!' so I made for the house, along with the two panting heroes.

'That's twaa strucken oors we've lost, wi that strucken thing!' says Tosh. (I have on purpose deleted his fluorescent adjectives.) 'I'd better phone the garage man, afore we loss the hale day!'

'Ye needna bother phonin the garage man,' says I. 'He gid by the end o your road jist as I turned intill't. He'll be in Ellon or iss time, I expect.'

That wis a bare-faced lee, but dinna tell onybody.

It was an unusually silent Tosh that sat down to his fly that day. Mrs Tosh was a dab hand at the home-bakes, and I was enjoying the silence . . . and my tea, when she ventured, 'Div ye ken onything aboot engines, Peter?'

'Nae jist an affa lot,' says I, 'but I ken fit's wrang wi iss een!'

'Then kind Sir will perhaps enlighten us on the problem,' says Tosh, talking pan loff for effect. (Fair chiel, ye see.)

'Nae bother avaa,' says I. 'Ye've been sweerin at yon engine. I could hear ye sweerin fae the main road. Ye can sweer as much as ye like at ony ither engine but a Lister, an it maks nae difference. But if ye sweer ower sair at a Lister, she'll tak the bungs an refuse duty.'

'An fit wye div ye sort that?' say her ainsel.

'Weel,' says I, 'somebody his tae apologise tae the Lister, an nae half mizzers either.'

'I ken faa that Somebody winna be,' says she, lauchin.

'C'mon, Tosh,' says I. 'Humble pie, or loss the hale day.'

This simply brought a fresh burst of profanity from the exasperated Tosh, so I volunteered to do the job myself. I'm sure Sandy had guessed something by this time, for he lay on the table laughing like mad.

'Now, Tosh,' says I, 'I'll ging oot an apologise to the engine on your behalf. It jist micht work!'

So the three of us made for the close, but Mrs. Tosh stayed on the doorstep to watch the fun.

I went up to the Lister and knelt beside it. Then I cuddled it and whispered sweet nothings into the air intake. Then, while my left hand removed the offending blob of cement from the pump, my right hand caressed the cylinder heads. Tosh and Sandy remained at least ten feet distant, muttering in disbelief. Finally, after a few more soft wordies, I offered the starting handle to Tosh, who promptly refused it.

'Nae damn fears,' says he. 'Nae aifter that heap o Black Magic! Swing the psychedelic thing yersel.'

So I duly obliged and the little engine sprang into action immediately. I failed to catch what Tosh was saying for the noise of the engine, but I saw his lips move rapidly, and I could guess. He seemed to be most reluctant to come any closer, but Sandy came in aboot and stopped the engine, only to re-start it immediately.

'Ye're safe eneuch, Tosh. Whether or no she was in the bungs, she's fine an willin noo! The Black Magic seems to hae teen a trick. I thocht Black Magic wis chocolate!'

'I'm sure Mrs Tosh wid ken,' said I. 'I've nae doot she gets Black Magic noo an than fae Tosh.'

'That'll be the day,' says she, lauchin. 'But I'll tell ye this! Fit ee've deen the day, Black Magic or no, wid surely be worth a baggie o Dukes. Fit aboot it Tosh?'

'Aye, fairly!' says Tosh. 'Ye've saved the situation the day. Sandy, wid ye get a bag o tatties oot o the shed for Peter?' And Sandy duly obliged.

'Thank you very much, Tosh,' says I. 'That'll keep the bairns quaet for a meentie.'

'Foo mony bairns div ye hae?'

'Fourteen,' says I, withoot a blink. That wis anither big lee, but ye canna stop fin ye're winnin.

'Dalmichty!' says Tosh. 'Ye maan be a fair chiel, eh? Gie im anither bag, Sandy.'

Mrs Tosh was laughing fit to burst, as I left the heroes to get on wi the wark. Fine did she ken foo mony bairns I had, but she nivver said boo. A fine deemie, yon!

Noo, div ye think I wis a fair chiel that day? I widna claim to be that aa thegither, but I'm nae feel tho I fart in the Kirk.

Westward Ho!

'Will ye gie's a hurl in yer boat, Mister?' This the earnest request from a group of raggity youngsters on the banks of the Forth-and-Clyde canal at the Grangemouth end. The frantic appeals were steadfastly ignored . . . There would be no hurls. We were simply negotiating the first set of locks before dark, and thereafter we would have to tie up for the night, for the lock-keepers did not work during the hours of darkness. And, besides, past experience had taught me that to gie a bairn a hurl was to take the bairn miles from home, with only a very slim chance of a hurl back.

As it happened, we went quite a bit further that night, creeping along in the dark towards the next lock, before tying up. Our berth for the night was well above the level of the road which paralleled the canal at that point, so we were on a level with the upper storey of a row of houses directly opposite. The strange places we get into, sometimes! This was to be an epic voyage indeed, and it all began before daylight in the morning.

You see, there were three boats of us in company. For the past few weeks we had been fishing from the Tyne with reasonable success, until a strong easterly gale put a stop to our efforts. For several days we were confined to harbour, and every morning we saw, on the floor of Shields market, fine catches of lovely whitings consigned from the Clyde ports. These whitings were snapped up by buyers starved of local fish, at prices which made our minds boggle. Fancy getting fifty shillings for six stone of fish! We could scarcely believe it. But I'm speaking about the prices in the Fifties, not the Monopoly money of today!

We knew from years past that even when the easterly gale abated, there would be no fish off the Tyne. The water would be 'thick', churned up by the heavy seas, and would require at least a week to settle, there being no guarantee that another gale would not arise in the meantime. So the three of us decided to make for the Clyde estuary at the first opportunity, taking the shortest available route, namely the Forth-and-Clyde canal.

Our flotilla comprised three boats, two from the Blue Toon and one from the Moray Firth. Since two of the skippers were, and still are quiet, reserved fellas, I'll cloak them in anonymity, calling the Moray Firth man Mitch, and the Bluemogganer, Daavit. I shall also refrain from naming their boats. It would be pointless to assume an anonymous role for myself, since I am the narrator of the tale. Sufficient to say that I was skipper of the *Twinkling Star*, PD. 137, a fifty-six footer, built by Geordie Forbes on the Queenie, on a site close to where the Dolphin Cafe is today.

Well now, in the darkness of the winter morning, we turned out around seven o'clock and were enjoying a nice mug of scalding tea before casting off. The air was bitterly cold and I was afraid the waters of the canal would freeze, for even wafer-thin ice will tear a boat's planks to shreds. Happily, that didn't happen, but we were all as close as possible to the galley stove, revelling in the warmth, when one of the young deckies went out on deck to empty the dregs of his tea. He brought us all fully awake with an excited cry, 'Boys! come an see this!'

'This' was a nice young damsel in an upper room just across the road. Blissfully unaware of her spellbound witnesses, and completely starkers, she executed a few physical jerks before waltzing across the room into a shower cabinet, whose curtain she drew. What a shame! A suggestion that we should 'wyte until she comes oot', fell on deaf ears, and we cast off and went about our business, but I can assure you that such an unexpected sight unsettles a buddy for a whilie. Still, that was merely the first episode.

The canal was in its last days, in a shocking state of disrepair. It was badly silted up throughout its length and this gave rise to problems for us all, for a boat simply will not answer the helm if there is insufficient water beneath her. Mitch had the biggest problem because he had the biggest boat. In fact, she was really too big for the canal. Had she been half an inch longer, she would not have fitted into the locks at all, and this slowed us down to a snail's pace. Mitch insisted on taking the lead, hogging the centre of the channel so that we couldn't possibly get past him. I'm sure he was afraid we would run and leave him to his own devices. He was very much relieved when I assured him that we wouldn't see him stuck . . . which was often.

That boat was like a bull in a china shop. Time after time we had to tow her off the bank, but as time went on, Mitch learned that, to round a bend, the rudder had to be turned well in advance, to give the boat time to answer. Having learned that, he increased his speed, and that was fatal, for that dug the vessel's heel deeper into the mud, and she simply went berserk, finishing up hard and fast across the channel. So now we were all blocked.

Tempers were getting a bittie frayed, when Mitch had a brilliant idea. He would enlist the aid of a squad of excited bairns who had gathered to see the 'wreck'. They would take the end of Mitch's seine net rope to the only suitable tree and there make it fast. They would not be required to tie any knot, but simply to go well past the tree with the end of the rope before doubling back, to circle the tree several times, carrying the rope-end with them.

It required much shouting and swearing from Mitch before the manoeuvre was carried out to his satisfaction, but the bairns were fairly enjoying every minute. Round and round the tree they went until the trunk was swathed in rope, leaving about twenty feet of length for the bairns to hang on to.

'Hud on noo! Hud on to that an dinna let go!' yelled Mitch, and the bairns obliged. Then, with his hand circling above his head, the gallant skipper signalled to his crew to heave on the winch. 'Heave her astarn, lads!' But she widna heave astarn. Instead, the tree was riven bodily out of the ground and came marching sedately in an upright position towards the boat. As long as the youngsters kept the strain on the rope, the tree remained upright, but when one by one they fell on their faces, the tree followed suit. Rarely, if ever, have I seen anything so hilarious. The tree had to be heaved bodily on to the boat's quarter before the rope could be freed. Then followed a hectic half hour of pushing and towing before we got the 'wreck' free of the mud, and heading in the right direction.

For the next several miles things went quite smoothly. The water was slightly

348

deeper and there were fewer bends, so progress was steady, albeit not very fast. Then we came to Kirkintilloch! Boys, it's a good job we were well spaced out, else there would have been a pile-up, for Mitch got stuck solid on a mud bank just to the eastward of the high road bridge which crosses the canal. And who should come along the road but a regiment o sodjers on a route march! They broke ranks and lined the parapet of the bridge, engrossed in the scene below, as we towed Mitch astern to let him have another go at the obstruction. There was no other way through. Ten times did Mitch ram that mudbank, gaining a few feet each time, and ten times did the sodjers groan in unison. Sure as death, boys, it was like a comic opera. When, at the eleventh attempt, Mitch finally broke through, the bridge erupted in a great flurry of red-tasselled bonnets, and the yells of applause would have rivalled the Hampden roar. By that time we were all feeling a bit self-conscious. You'll be thinking that such things could never happen at sea, but then we were not at sea at all.

At long last we came within sight of the end at the head of a great flight of steps leading down towards the sea. After all, you know, that's what a set of canal locks resemble . . . a flight of steps. You open the upper lock gates and sail the boat into the lock, closing the gates behind you. Then you open the sluice doors in the lower gate so that the water level falls to that of the lock below, then you open the gate and sail the boat through, one step down. Remember that the water always comes from a higher level, whether you are going up or down.

The walkways across a lock-gate are always very narrow, and in this case they were very rickety as well. The sluice doors were hand operated by means of a ratchet and a four foot iron bar. Every boat had to provide its own bars, along with the manpower to open and close the gates. It was quite an adventure till the novelty wore off, and on a rainy day it was a proper scunner.

Well now, we were half-way down the flight and Roddy, one of Mitch's deckies was operating the sluice gates, when a panic-stricken fella rushed past, very nearly tipping Roddy into the lock.

'They're gonna kill me!' gasped the fleeing man. 'They're gonna kill me!'

Roddy looked round in amazement to see a gang of thugs running towards him, determined to cross the briggie in pursuit of the fugitive. The fact that a fisherman was on the briggie would not deter them in the slightest. Not until the fisherman turned to face them, with the iron bar in his hands. That brought them to a sudden halt, within a few feet of the edge of the lock. An uglier looking bunch I never did see. Eight in number, they were hell bent on murder, some of them quite visibly carrying deadly bicycle chains. No doubt they all had knives. They poured on Roddy a shower of the local patter in its most obscene form, but they did not seek to advance. They could have run upstream to the next briggie, but there was a fisherman there too, with an iron bar.

'Come awaa, noo, my loons,' says Roddy. 'Come awaa, noo, an I'll lay ye oot like a tier o cod. Faa's gaan to be first?'

So here we were, back to Horatius holding the bridge across the Tiber.

'Are ye nae comin?' says Roddy. 'Weel, I'll jist hae to come to you.' And he stepped off the briggie onto the bank, whereupon the group fled in disorder.

349

No doubt Roddy saved the fugitive's life. Possibly it was only a temporary reprieve, but we had no means of knowing that.

That was the last episode in our epic voyage across Scotland, and we were soon in the Firth of Clyde, back in our natural element, with plenty of water beneath our keels. Mitch swore that he would never take that route home, but would go via the Caledonian Canal.

Several weeks later, we took the old route homewards, but we saw no thugs, we saw no sodjers, we saw no bairns, for school had claimed them.

And there was a curtain on my lady's window! What a shame!

It Maan be the Angels Singin

'Change and decay in all around I see!'

Thus runs a line in an old, old hymn which, along with the 23rd Psalm, is flogged to death (no pun intended) at funeral services.

As the years slip past, I find myself meeting old friends at a funeral, friends I have not seen since the last sad occasion. Although this is what one must accept, it certainly is not what one must like, for it is likely to give a buddy cause for serious thought and that itself can be a salutary matter.

It's not that I am against change; that would be plain stupid, but I must confess that the speed of change disconcerts me and my generation. Possibly the simplest illustration of this is the certainty that I am signing my pension bookie on a Thursday before the ink is dry on last week's ticketie.

Time flies, boys, time flies, and that at the speed of Concorde nowadays. And so it is with change; we cannot halt it, and that is probably a blessing.

So, what about the decay which in the old hymn, is coupled with change? Should the two be linked? Are they inseparable? Age says 'Most certainly'; Youth says 'Most certainly not!' and that is probably something that will never change, as time goes by.

Old codgers like myself go to great lengths to tell the modern generation that things ain't what they used to be, knowing full well that things as they used to be were not half so good as we would make them out to be. Nostalgia is inclined to forget a few bitter truths concerning the standard of living in the past and we of the Old Brigade are inclined to bury our heads in the sand and cry 'Woe, woe!'

I was sharply reminded of this today, when I noticed that the price of a pound of haddock in the fish shop was almost three times as much as we could ever get for a whole box! There's change for you!

Up, up, up goes the standard of living and surely that cannot be bad. There's no decay in figures like these, is there? But we are right in thinking that the standard of living is one and the same thing as the quality of life?

I'm thinking now of a lovely Sunday morning some fifteen years ago, when I was on watch in the Control Tower at Peterhead Harbour, where there is a twenty-four hour watch every day of the year. Every vessel entering or leaving the port must contact the Tower by radio before doing so, and on this particular morning a fishing boat had duly requested, and had been given clearance to sail. The vessel was between the breakwaters, outward bound, when the skipper called me on his V.H.F. radio...'Eh, me, me, Peter! If the aal folk could see me eyvnoo, they wid turn in their graves! Awaa t' sea on a Sunday mornin. I nivver thocht I'd see this! It's affa-like, intit?'

'Aye!' says I. 'Faa put yee oot, the day?'

'Oh,' says he. 'Naebody put me oot!'

'Weel,' says I. 'Dinna greet t' me. Ye've startit something that ye'll nivver get clear o.'

And sure enough, boys, he's still at it. His standard of living dictated his way of life, and judging by his own spontaneous confession to me, he disna like it avaa! And, I can assure you he is not alone in that.

Now, let me tell you a true story, a tale handed down from father to son, in the oral tradition of our forebears. It concerns a race of men who were past masters in the art of sailing a boat without the benefit of machinery of any kind. Whether the boats were Fifies or Zulus, they were on occasion driven very hard indeed, and were known to attain a speed in excess of twelve knots.

The skippers were real experts in the art of sailing and had perfected their skills to such a degree that modern sailors have failed to match them, although they are coming close to that now, with the use of computers.

You see, when the old sail boats disappeared, a vast store of nautical know-how went with them. There was nothing written down. (Who was going to write it?) And so the combined knowledge of mariners and sailmakers was lost.

Hardy men, the sail-boat men, whose sworn enemy was calm. They must have been adventurous souls as well, for some of them were lost on the Bergen Bank about a hundred years ago. Their standard of living was anything but high, but there may have been compensations.

It all happened on a beautiful summer morning about a hundred years ago. During the few hours of darkness there had been a light breeze, just enough to ruffle the waters of the Moray Firth, but not nearly enough to stir up the herring, for the summer herring requires a moderate to fresh wind before it will rise high enough to be caught in the old-world drift nets.

Those were the days when the herring had to take the net, the complete reversal of today's order of things. Thus a whole fleet of herring boats had spent a fruitless night at sea, and were now converging on their home port, Buckie. The light airs had helped them on their way shorewards, but now that the sun had gained sufficient height to burn away the thin veil of mist, the breeze had faltered completely, leaving the boats becalmed a short distance from the harbour.

The only smoke visible came from the chimneys of the houses along the shore, for as yet there were no steam drifters to advertise their presence by disfiguring the horizon with their banners of reek.

In fact, there was no machinery whatsoever on these fishing boats; even the primitive capstans they had were operated by hand. So there lay the boats, their tall sails useless, utterly motionless as chess pieces on a board of polished steel. The problem now was to get the boats into the harbour and there was only one way to do that . . . row them in!

Oars on boats of such a size? Aye, surely; big heavy oars called 'sweeps', much heavier and longer than any conventional oar, and kept on board for just such an occasion as this, or for shifting a boat from berth to berth, or for rowing a boat out of a harbour against a contrary wind, far enough from shore to permit the setting of the sail.

Working the sweeps was hard, hard work, for the boats were very heavily built. The oarsmen would occasionally push forward and push on the sweep, with the weight of his body, if necessary, so the movement of the sweeps was slow and stately.

Behold now, the sails being lowered and the sweeps driving the vessels slowly towards the harbour, under the watchful gaze of a considerable throng of womenfolk, young and not so young, who had come to the quay ready to gut and salt the catch. But it was perfectly obvious to these 'quines' that there would be no herring for them that day.

Still, it was a particularly lovely morning and there was no pressing need for them to go home, so they would hang around for a whilie and watch the fleet come in. . . . That was when the fun started.

The skipper of the first boat, possibly inspired by the use of the sweeps, lifted up his glorious baritone and sang the old revival hymn, 'Sweeping through the gates of New Jerusalem, washed in the blood of the Lamb'.

His crew joined in, the melody seemed to spread from boat to boat, and soon they were all singing. As each boat rounded the pier-head, the women joined in the refrain, their sopranos and altos lifting the melody to heights hitherto unknown. Folks from all over the town came down to see and hear this wonder, and very soon the piers were 'black wi folk', all apparently inspired and singing their hearts out. Not until the last boat was moored up did the music die away, as everyone made their way home.

Come now, to a little cottage on the outskirts of the town, a but-an-ben from which the harbour is out of sight. Behold the elderly couple whose home this is, sitting at the door, dressed as if for the kirk and listen as a passing neighbour asks, in some surprise . . . 'Fit's you twaa deein the day, that ye're aa dressed up? Are ye gaan awaa somewye?'

'No, lass, we're nae gaan awaa . . . yet! But we've been listenin for mair than a hale oor to the bonniest singin we've ivver heard. We've lookit aa roon, but we canna see far the singin's comin fae, so it maan be the angels singin. That means that the Lord'll be here ony meenit noo, so we're ready!'

The kindly neighbour soon enlightened the old folks as to the source of the singing and they went indoors to change, but one significant fact remains.

When the story filtered through to Buckie, as it was sooner or later bound to do, nobody laughed!

Their standard of living? No! Their quality of life? Think about it!

Herrin at the Door

My last effort in the '*Buchanie*' gave rise to a great deal of comment, in more ways than one. Firstly, a great hantle o fisher folk had never seen a photograph of a sail-boat using sweeps, while a hantle mair didn't know that such things existed. Weel, they ken noo, for the dummy disna lee. Secondly, a few sharp-eyed fellas spotted the smaa-boat on the big boat's deck, and this too was something they had never seen, for sail-boats never carried smaa-boats. Smaa-boats didn't appear on the scene until the drifter era, surely. That is not quite true, but the smaa-boats on the drifters were strictly for life-saving purposes, being lightly built, each one having a notch in her square stern, so that she could be 'sculled' (propelled by one oar). Here we find the derivation of 'scullner', the fisher loons' term for a drifter's smaa-boat.

But the boatie in the photo is not square-sterned. She is actually a double-ended, purpose-built fishing boat, a yole, with her own mast and sail, a fishing unit in her own right. You should be able to spot that by her draught of water.

Designed for hand-line or haddock-line fishing, such boaties were to be found in their hundreds along the East coast. Indeed, in the 1848 disaster, when a sudden storm overwhelmed the East coast fleet, fifty-one boats and thirty-one fishermen, were lost at the entrance to Peterhead Harbour, just below the window where I am at present writing. Of course, there were no breakwaters in those days, and, to make things even worse, the harbour entrance was blocked by a steamer and a tug, so the yoles simply couldn't get in. The very few who opted to run for the North Harbour entrance survived, but that entrance was done away with, many years ago. 'Harbour Improvements', they called it.

But I digress, as usual, so let's get back to the little boatie on the big boat's deck. What's she doing there, if she's not a life-boat? Well now, close inspection reveals that the big boat's hatches are in place, so she is 'on passage' to a distant fishing ground. The yole is 'keel ee maist' (upside down) on the hatches, and she is there simply as a 'satellite'. Now there's a modern word for you. And why the satellite?

Well, it was in this fashion . . . There were times when the lochs on the West coast were simply teeming with herring, although none were to be found in the Minch. And, to make things even more peculiar, these same herring chose to frequent the shallowest and narrowest parts of the lochs, where it would have been almost impossible to manoeuvre a big boat. So Mahomet had to go to the mountain, and the only way he could do that was to use a small boat.

Thus the fishers would anchor small fleets of nets close to the shore, leaving the 'mother ship' anchored in deeper water. These nets would be hauled and shot more than once during the night, the catch being transferred to the big boat, which would then make for the nearest curing station in the morning, leaving the little boat at anchor till the next night. That was how it was done, but I must stress that I have over-simplified the procedure, since this is not meant to be a text book. Of course, if results were poor, the fishers would hoist the boatie on board and try another loch, and over the years they came to be far better acquaint with the lochs than were the Hielan men themselves.

Now, one thing never ceases to amaze me, and that is the way in which they managed to do all these things with only paraffin lamps. The boats had no engines, and paraffin was their only source of light. The days of acetylene gas had yet to come, and nobody had heard of electricity, so the old-timers deserve great credit for their perseverance. Modern fishing boats have big auxiliary engines driving great generators for lighting alone! A different world.

My own father often used to fish with great lines off the North and West coasts of Scotland and he told us how, many a time, the only source of bait was the same-old place, the headwaters of the lochs, the procedure as of old . . . launch the smaa-boat and shoot a few nets along the shore.

Now, while the steam drifter had a gas-plant for lighting, the smaa-boat was still dependent on paraffin lamps. One story I particularly liked was of the night in Loch Glendhu when five men left in the smaa-boat to look for nets they had shot before dark. Apparently the paraffin lamp on the marker buoy had gone out, so one man was on his knees in the bow of the boatie, peering into the inky blackness, and holding aloft a paraffin lamp. Slowly, slowly crept the little boat across the waters, for the range of the lamp was short indeed and the look-out could so easily miss the canvas 'bowse' on the nets. All went well until a sleeping gull, on the point of being run over by the boat, arose with a frightened squawk and a fearful flap, right into the lookout's face! He, in turn, gave a frightened squawk and a fearful flap, and dropped the lamp into the sea. I'm sure a few bright words were said, that night.

So, freen, next time you take the road to the West, and you are crossing the beautiful bridge at Kylesku, look away eastward to where, miles inland from you, a generation of olde worlde fishers sought the elusive herring, in a place where the 'Shepherd's Bichtie' was a favourite spot.

Now, someone might ask, 'Are there no such places on the East coast?' And that reminds me of a true story; I know it's true, simply because I was there. In fact, I was the instigator of the whole affair. I was but a lad, decky-cum-engineer on the family boat *Sparkling Star* built in Macduff in 1930. Complete with a 36 hp. Kelvin engine, she went to sea for just under £1,000, believe it or not. My brother John was skipper, cos my father's health was failing, but when it came to Yarmooth time, brother John wanted to go to Yarmooth with his gweedfather in the drifter *Branch*. He would, of course, get a share of nets in the vessel, cos he still had herring nets, and he could stand to make a few quid. That seemed to suggest that the boatie would have to be tied up, but I decided that I would take the boat myself.

So it came to pass that we puddled oot an in at hame, getting a living, but only just! Come November, I noticed that the North Breakwater was thronged with gulls, and the waters on the inside of the same pier, which was only half finished, were alive with all sorts of birds, not forgetting a seal or two. In fact, I could actually smell herrin! I mentioned this to my father, but he was inclined to think I was spinning a yarn, so nothing was done till brother John came home. Then I suggested we should try a few nets in that corner; we might get enough bait to shoot a few lines. My idea fell on deaf ears, but I persisted, and finally my father advised that the idea should at least be given a trial. It was a most unwilling brother who agreed to the trial. Of course, I was instantly demoted, cos he was ten years my senior, and we shot six nets westward from the Lifeboat shed. We got a fry! Boys, it was only with great difficulty that I managed to persuade my folk that we had not been in the right place, but at last I succeeded, and we shot the nets just before dark and came home for tea.

Enter now my mother, aal Jeannie Motherwell. 'Peter, my loon,' says she, 'faar's the nets shot?'

'Fae the hairber mou to the North breakwater. Six nets,' says I.

'Faan are ye haulin them?'

'As seen's we get wir supper.'

'Weel,' says she, 'I nivver saw the sea till I wis mairried, an since I wis mairried I've been tyaavin amon herrin nets, but I've nivver seen a net hauled. Seein that this is the last chance, I think I'll come oot wi ye.' And that's just what she did. The fact that there was a strong westerly wind with heavy snow showers did not put her off.

Now, we started to haul at the harbour entrance, and the herring were there awaiting us. My mother stood hanging onto the mast, with the herrin fleein aboot her lugs as we shook them from the nets. While we were hauling the last net, we had to put fenders over the side cos the boat was hammering against the breakwater. I'm tellin ye, an aal wifie fairly enjoyed hersel.

We got enough bait for six lines which we shot off the North Head that night. We also got six cran of herring which sold in the fishmarket in the morning at £2 per cran. Famine prices, boys, famine prices! And from the lines we got six boxes o bonny codlings which fetched around fifteen shillings per box. A complete fortin.

I was rather proud when my father remarked, 'He's nae feel, tho he farts in the kirk!'

But, alas, when we tried to shoot the nets in the same place on the following night, we found that the corner was completely filled with nets. Tom, Dick and Harry had been there before us with a heterogeneous collection of old rubbish of nets, so we couldn't get into the berth. We got enough to bait our lines, but not enough to sell. That was the same for two nights, then it was all over. No more herring for anybody. Some of the old men said that it was the old nets being left in the water all day that finished the herring. They should have been shot at night-time only.

That was what we meant to do, but we never got the chance again. We tried our nets outside the bay, but never got enough for bait, although we increased the fleet to twenty nets. In fact we were hauling our nets when the lifeboat went past us on the way to 'a Trawler on the Skares o Cruden'. That turned out to be the *Christabel Stephen* of Aberdeen. She was towed off the reef by another Aberdeen trawler, the *East Coast* (Dovie was her skipper). The casualty sank while on tow to Aberdeen, with the loss of two men.

That should fix the year and the date. I have never actually smelt herring again, but I have a host of wonderful memories.

Now, let me add a footnote to the story about the angels' singin, in which I mentioned the old tune 'Sweeping Through the Gates'.

About a fortnight ago, an old friend whom I haven't seen for years called to see me. He was actually in the Blue Toon for the big Burns Supper. We spent a very pleasant hour reminiscing on the past and he recalled how, many years ago, he had attended the funeral of an eminent Salvationist friend. Apparently the old tune was a favourite at Army funerals and was duly played prior to the interment. Thereafter the Band played all the way from Constitution St. to Chapel St. as was usual.

And the tune? . . . 'Who'll be the next?'

Boys, ye canna win!

Peterboy

'Peterboy,' said Shonachan, 'ye're a real East-coaster; forever asking questions!'

He always called me 'Peterboy', and I never resented it, for it was always used in a very friendly manner. Of course, he was some twenty years my senior, and besides, he was built on the grand scale, with shoulders as wide as a barn door and hands like shovels. He could have lifted me above his head just as easily as I could have lifted a sheaf of corn, so when he called me 'Peterboy' I never said boo.

'John,' said I, (I always called him John) 'I have learned that the asking of civil questions is a wonderful way to learn.'

'I'm sure you're right, Peterboy,' was the reply. 'Now, what's annoying you now?'

'Well, John, I'm curious about these stone pillars that I see by the roadside. They look like gate-posts, but I cannot see any provision for hanging a gate. They are always in pairs, standing some four feet high and about three feet apart. From one pair of stones to the next would be roughly half a mile. They can't be gateposts, for often there's neither dyke nor fence within sight. Did the Druids put them there, John? Are they some sort of standing stones?'

'Not at all, Peterboy. They're standing stones only in that they've been standing there a long time, but I doubt if the Druids had anything to do with them. You see, the custom here during a funeral is for close relatives and near neighbours only to go to the home of the deceased, for the 'lifting'. Just before the actual lifting, everybody has a dram, then the coffin is carried to the nearest pair of stones, where fresh bearers are waiting. The coffin is laid gently across the stones, then everybody has a dram before repeating the process. You could say that the rule is that you go to the pair of stones which is nearest to your home, and there await the cortège. I'm telling you, Peterboy, that after a three mile trip, some

356

of the mourners are not very mournful at all, at all. It's myself that's thinking of flitting further up the loch, for there's only the one pair of stones between here and the cemetery.'

We had a quiet laugh together, then he tackled me with 'Next question, please!'

'Well, John,' said I, taken by surprise, 'why is it that I never see anyone fishing the loch? I'm sure the fish must be spear deep there, but nobody seems to be interested. There's scarcely a boatie to be seen anywhere. Don't you like fish?'

It was some time before he replied, and I gathered he was thinking of the distant past, then he began . . . 'Peterboy, when I was a lad, my father had a boatie, as you call it, on the shore there, and he tarred the boat every year, less or more. Remember, now, that there were seven of us, all boys, and we would be among the tar had he not given us something to do, just to keep us out of mischief. He sent us along the shore to gather the shells that you East-coasters call 'buckies'. These we had to bring him and lay them in the palm of his right hand. It took us some time to gather a handful, for buckies are not plentiful on this shore, so my father had a considerable time of peace to get on with the tarring of the boat. Then, when we had returned with the fruits of our labours, he would take them in his right hand and crush them into tiny fragments which were then doled out to seven pairs of little hands. "Now, go and find a few more," he would say, picking a few splinters from his horny palm.'

'John,' said I, with a glance at my own rather slender hands, 'That must have taken fantastic strength! I don't think I could manage that.'

'I'm sure you couldn't, Peterboy. I can't do it myself, and I'm supposed to be a very strong man indeed. But then my father was much stronger than any of us. Now, what were we talking about?'

'Fishing the loch,' said I. 'There's a rich store of unrationed food at your very door, and nobody seems to be interested.'

'Well now, Peterboy, you know that everybody hereabouts is busy all day working at the Base, and when we get home in the evening there's always something to do about the croft. To borrow a boat and launch it for an evening's fishing is a thing that requires some considerable thought. It's not the sort of thing to do rashly, and it's certainly not the kind of thing one would do too often.'

'Man, John,' said I, 'I'm sure you could make a bob or two, if you had a boat and some gear. It seems that the local folk never see fish at all!'

'There you are, East-coaster,' he laughed, 'always thinking about the bob or two. You're a greedy lot on the East coast. But if you're all that keen, I've got a net in the steading. Come, let's have a look at it.'

We found the net in a dark corner of the steading, in a sack on top of the wall, just below the tiles (on the easin o the waa). But it wasn't a net at all, just a length of haddock line, muck rotten and absolutely useless. Not for many a long day had it been used.

'There you are, now, Peterboy. There's the net, but it seems to be of no use. You know, I had completely forgotten it was there. So that's your fishing knocked on the head, to be sure.'

I was deeply disappointed, but that night I wrote a note to an old pal of my father's, and sent it home via a friend who was going on leave, and with the note I sent a slab of Scots Cake tobacco which I had acquired from another friend. It can be so handy, sometimes, to have friends. Thus it came to pass that when the friend returned from leave, he brought with him a bonny length of haddock line, in splendid condition, complete with horse-hair tippins and clear, bright hooks; a 'string' of line, comprising some one hundred hooks.

That evening, I confronted John with the bonny new line. 'There you are,' said I. All we need now is some bait and a boat. What about it?'

'Peterboy, I admire your persistence,' he said with a smile, 'but it won't be till next week that we'll get bait.'

'Och!' said I, 'I'll get bait before then! I've a day off tomorrow and I'll go and dig some lug worms. There should be plenty of them on that beach beside the boom-defence pier.' John said nothing.

I found no bait. There was no trace of lug worms on the sandy beach and the rocks were practically devoid of limpets. Nor could I find any mussels. 'Barren wilderness,' I muttered, but John just smiled tolerantly.

'Next week, Peterboy, next week, when there's a moon. East-coasters don't know everything. Patience, boy, patience.'

It was nearly the end of the following week before I was free to accompany John to the beach which I had previously searched in vain. The moon shone brightly from a cloudless sky on mountain and loch and on open sea; a really beautiful evening.

'What are we going to look for, John?' said I, completely puzzled.

'Peterboy, we are going to find some bait for your precious net.' (He always used the word 'net', much to my annoyance.)

'There will be bait in plenty; that's why I'm carrying this bucket. We're after razor fish, the creatures you call spout-fish. They stick their heads out of the sand when it's moonlight, so we won't even have to dig for them.'

Now, considering how big the man was, and remembering that discretion is the better part of valour, I said nothing. But Shonachan knew what I was thinking, and gave me a playful dig. 'Wait and see, Doubting Thomas!'

I recalled the days of my own childhood when, very occasionally, I had seen the long narrow shells, hinged on one side and always empty. I had never seen a live-razor fish, but I didn't have long to wait. Just as Shonachan had said, they were waiting for us, almost at the low-water mark, with their heads protruding slightly from the sand. Some five or six inches in length they were, and about half an inch wide. It was quite simple to remove them, using thumb and forefinger, and very soon we had enough.

'A score will suffice,' said Shonachan. 'There's no need for more than that.'

'Well,' said I, 'I'll have a look around in the morning for some sort of boxie to bait the line into. I'll soon bait the line for you. I don't suppose you have a scull or a backet about the place?'

'No need for such a thing, Peterboy. We're not going to be shooting the net from a boat going full speed. We'll borrow Roddie's boat, and that hasn't got an engine, so we'll just bait the line as we pay it out. There's no hurry, man.'

And that was precisely what we did. The following evening, we launched Roddie's boat and shot the line about 100yds. from the shore. The razor fish had been removed from their shells and cut into pieces for bait. While I plied the oars, Shonachan baited the hooks as the line ran over the stern, his great fingers showing an expertise gained in years long gone. He had been at the job before, sure enough. Two stones from the beach served as anchors for the line and a few old herring corks from the same beach made admirable dhan buoys.

As soon as the line had been run out, I started rowing for the shore.

'Where do you think you're going now, Peterboy?' said Shonachan.

'Oh,' said I, 'we'll go home for the night, and come back at the crack o dawn to haul the line.'

'You'll come alone, then,' was the reply. 'I'm not coming out at the crack o dawn for all the fish in the Minch. If they're not there now, they'll not be there at all! Just give me ten minutes of my pipe, then we'll pull it in. That should be long enough.'

There was no wind at all, so the boatie lay beside our make-shift buoy until Shonachan had enjoyed his smoke. I made no remark regarding the source of his slab of tobacco, nor did he seem to notice that I was smoking Canadian fags. It seemed that I wasn't the only one who had a friend, somewhere.

'Now then, Peterboy,' he said at last, 'get your oars moving, and we'll get this fearful net pulled in!' Fearful was the strongest adjective I ever heard him use.

Well, now, I think that even the big man himself was surprised, when we made a start. I myself was flabbergasted, for only the hooks whose bait had been 'happit' by 'corsefeet' (crow's feet, starfish) were fishless. All the others had a fish of some kind or another, mostly fine plump haddocks, the remainder being a mixter-maxter of whitings, gurnards, and podleys. We didn't keep the podleys. There were also four beautiful dabs, and a few medium codlings. Seventy-six fish to be taken home, good fishing by any standard.

'Peterboy,' said Shonachan, as I rowed the boat ashore, 'half of these fish are yours, cos it was your net that caught them.'

'In that case,' said I, 'Roddie will be looking for the other half, cos it's Roddie's boat. Where does that leave you, John?'

That had him puzzled till I said, 'Let me have the dabs, John, and you can have all the rest. You know I couldn't possibly use all these fish!'

'But what about the bob-or-two you mentioned, Peterboy?'

'Och, man, forget it. We've had a great deal of pleasure, and I'm not here for money. Take the fish!' He was simply delighted.

When we reached the shore, we were faced with the problem of getting the boat back to where we had found her, for the water had ebbed considerably since we had launched her.

'No problem, Peterboy. I'll pull, and you can push.' Then he took the painter (the mooring rope in the bow) across his shoulder, and set out. I was at the stern, supposed to be pushing, but I never really got my weight on the boat, and mind you, she was eighteen feet. She seemed to keep sliding away from me all the time, and I remember thinking, 'If this boatie's keel sticks on a stone, he'll tear the very

359

stem out of her.' A real strong man, Shonachan.

With the boat finally in her berth up among the grass, we had yet another problem (at least I thought so), namely, how to get the fish up to the house, for we had neither box nor basket in which to carry them. The line had been hauled into the bottom of the boat and would require to be taken home for redding. Roddie came to see how we had got on and got a handsome fry for his pains. Well, after all, it was Roddie's boat. But there were still a great many fish left.

Shonachan seemed to sense my concern, for he bade me watch closely and I would learn yet another West-coast lesson. He then went back to the water's edge and selected a long, thin tangle, from which he cut and threw away the frond. This left him with the long, supple stem and the root. A few deft strokes with his knife made a sharp point on the thin end, which he threaded through the gills of the fish, before taking the tangle by the end and slinging the lot across his shoulder. From shoulder to heel he had a string of fish which couldn't slide off because of the root. Very simple, but very effective. The mess on his clothes didn't seem to matter. I followed in his wake with my dabs in my hanky in one hand and the raivelled line in the other.

It was like a feeing mart at the house that evening. Neighbours came to call and none went home empty handed. Finally, when the stir had died down, Shonachan set about cleaning his own fry and sink me if he didn't take the haddock livers and swallow them raw, grinning broadly at the look of concern on my face.

'Peterboy, a few of these in your belly and you might be able to crush a few buckies!'

'If that's what's required, John, the buckies can bide hale, for me.'

I cleaned my four dabs, which were to make a delicious meal, then I redd the line, making it ready for shooting again before hanging it up to dry where the cow couldn't possibly reach it. But even then I sensed that it 'wid be twaa dry days and a weet een' afore the line would be used again.

Over the next several months I made repeated mention of the wonderful fishing we might have if we were to borrow Roddie's boat again. But, man, there was aye a something! He had to take the cow to the bull, he had to attend a wedding in Dingwall, and he had to get the crop in. The crop turned out to be one big corn ruck at the end of the steading, and one big half ruck inside, 'so that the old woman can feed the cow by herself on the rare occasions when I'm not at home.'

So, eventually I gave it up and put the bonny line in a sack and stowed it away where I had found the old one. It was several years after the war when I had managed to get myself a car, that I made my way westwards to see my old friend. He was simply delighted to see me and we spent a wonderful evening reminiscing on the old days, but since he was so obviously failing, I didn't have the heart to mention the 'net'.

But I'm sure that, were I to go back there and look, I'd find it just where I left it — in a sack, in a dark corner, on the easin o the waa.

The Tourist

It was midsummer in Stornoway in the fifties, and it was insufferably close and sticky weather. There had been no wind at all for several days, and while a thin layer of fairly high cloud helped to temper the rays of the sun, it also served as a sort of coverlet which prevented the overheated ground-level air from escaping. Some of the tourists who thronged the quay with their cameras remarked that it was rather humid. We, being East coasters, agreed that it was 'smuchty, sweaty wither!' the sort of weather which made the cabin of a 56ft. boat a rather disagreeable place for its eight occupants. The lack of headroom and the poor ventilation turned meal-times into sweating sessions, when it was a case of swallowing the meal before getting up on deck for air.

I have never had much love for Stornoway, not that there's anything wrong with the place or the folk, but I found the place completely and utterly frustrating. You see, that particular summer, the herring shoals were seldom more than four miles from the Lewis shore and seldom more than ten miles from Stornoway Loch. Thus the fleet didn't need to sail till well after tea-time, returning shortly after six o'clock in the morning. Even after landing a good shot, it was only breakfast time, and there was a long day ahead with nothing to do but sleep, or to mend a few holes in the nets, before it was time to put to sea again.

The weekend was indeed a trial. All clear at breakfast time on Saturday, it seemed an incredibly long time till sailing time on Monday night. About a month, it seemed, Stornoway on a Sunday being just Stornoway on a Sunday! I shall never forget the time when an elderly local female, clothed in black from head to toe, caught me in the act of posting a letter to my missus. First in a torrent of Gaelic, then in a much slower flow of her best English, she took me to task. That I should do such a thing on the Lord's Day! Couldn't it wait till tomorrow? East coast heathen!

Well, now, I'm normally a peaceable chap, but I must confess that I lost the trot that day and I counter-attacked with a few highly-coloured and most expressive phrases in the Gaelic of Wester Ross which she understood perfectly, for she fled in horror! Sometimes, when I remember that incident, I'm black affrontit at mysel. I should have ignored her completely! But isn't it strange how easy it is to learn and to remember the really bad words in any language?

As a rule, we landed every second week-end in Ullapool, where we joined a motley throng of Moray Firth men, to fill a bus for the East coast. There was always a stop at Beauly for dinner, and by the time we had meandered along the coast, dropping each man at his own door, it was around eight o'clock in the evening before the PD. contingent got home. No, I wasn't particularly fond of the Minch fishing!

But let's get back to Stornoway. One particularly sticky afternoon, I came on deck for fresh air, with the intention of having a stroll along the quay. Just as I stepped ashore, a strapping young tourist accosted me, enquiring whether there was any chance of his being accepted as a passenger on a fishing boat for a night.

He appeared to be a decent kind of fella, so I promised him a night at sea with us, on condition that he was on the quay at the appointed time.

'I'll be there!' says he. 'I'll get some more film for my camera. I might be lucky enough to see a whale! You never know!'

His perfect English bore a distinctive accent which I couldn't quite place, although I was sure I had heard it before.

The evening found us sailing northwards along the rocky shore, close past the spot where the *Iolaire* was wrecked during the Great War with the loss of so many home-coming Lewismen, north towards Jumpin Head (actually Tiumpan Head), where the fleet fanned out into deeper waters some three miles from the coast. Our guest spoke very little, completely engrossed in his filming. He filmed us shooting the nets but declined the invitation to come below for tea when that job was finished.

'I might miss a whale!' says he, 'and I would never forgive myself!' So he had his cup of tea on deck. It was a perfectly calm summer night.

With the exception of the watchman, all hands turned in for an hour or two, but I had just dozed off when I was abruptly roused by the clatter of running feet above my head. In some trepidation I scaled the cabin ladder in a flash, to find that the tourist had apparently gone berserk, rushing from one side to the other in a frenzy of excitement!

'Is there something wrong?' says I.

'Whales!' says he. 'Whales! Five or six of them! Aren't I the lucky fella?'

We had scarcely seen a whale all summer, yet here they were, just when he needed them! For some twenty minutes they played around our boat before moving out of sight in the summer dim. Never have I seen a cameraman so utterly delighted!

Came one o'clock in the morning, time to start hauling, time for the indispensable cup of tea. This time I managed to draw him out a little; quiet, unassuming chap as he was. At the crowded table I asked him, 'Faar div ye come fae, freen? I'm sure ye're nae English, tho ye spik the English tongue!'

'Oh!' says he, 'I'm on a walking tour of the home country, Scotland. I've been so fascinated with the West coast that I've completely neglected the East side, and I'm afraid that's something that will have to wait, for I've got to leave tomorrow. I'm from Rhodesia, actually!'

'Oh, aye!' says I. 'I've a sister in Rhodesia, been there since the back o the War. Ye micht ken her!'

'Highly unlikely,' says he. 'Rhodesia's a huge country, you know. The main city, Salisbury, is itself a great metropolis, so it's most improbable that I should know your sister.'

'Weel,' says I, 'oor Chrissie bides in Salisbury, in a pairt o the toon they caa Mount Pleasant, an she works in the Education Offices. She mairried a Peterheid loon, Eddie Robb.'

He was quiet for a moment, then he said, 'Are there two brothers in this boat?'

'Aye, surely! That's my brither across the table. Fit wye?'

'Just a moment!' says he. 'Which one of you writes the poems?'

362

'Oh, that's me!' says I. 'Fit wye did ye ken that?'

'Delighted to meet you, Peter! And you too, Rob! I promised to look you up, if I managed to do the East coast. And now, quite by chance, I've met you in the west! You see, back home in Salisbury, your sister's desk is only a few feet from mine!'

Now, here's a chance for some of the modern computer whizz-kids to work out the chances of such a meeting taking place, bearing in mind the fact that we were almost three hundred miles from home (by sea).

Not being at all acquainted with computers, I'll just make a wild guess and say, 'Twenty million to one against!' Mind you, I could be a wee bittie oot!

The Fighting Pandrop

The Fighting Pandrop was a little wee mannikie wi a moustache like the handlebars o a racer bike. This facial adornment was his pride and joy, and he nursed and tended it as if it had been a rare plant being readied for a flower show. But sadly, that was about the extent of his exertions, for he wis reid rotten wi laziness. Of course he was always at the 'Buroo', shoutin for jobs till's loons, but nivver for a job till himsel. He was crafty enough never to refuse work when it was on offer, for such a refusal would have entailed immediate suspension of benefit for a period of six weeks. By the same token, he was crafty enough to make himself such a useless article that he couldn't hold down any job for more than a week or two, being invariably sacked as being 'unsuitable' for the post. This sacking entitled him to Unemployment Benefit; he didn't leave the job, you see. A fine art? Aye, surely!

Now, how did such a fella get such a byname? Simply because of the fact that, when he had drink taken, the Pandrop became rather obstreperous. Mind you, it was seldom he had drink, and when he had it, it was always at someone else's expense. He had that to a fine art too! But, on the rare occasions when his blood was on fire, he always picked on men three times his size, men who could hold the Pandrop at arm's length simply by putting one hand on his head, keeping him in a position where his puny fists spent themselves on thin air, and where he would eventually have starved to death if his missus hadn't come to his rescue.

You know, just last week in the shopping centre, I met a Pekinese doggie that seemed to have taken a notion to me. When I studiously avoided the beastie, its well-dressed owner remarked, 'There's no need for you to be frightened, Mr Buchan. He won't bite you!'

'Och!' says I, 'it's nae that, my quine; but I see he's aye liftin is laig, an I'm feart he's gaan to kick me!'

Reminded me, somehow, of the Fighting Pandrop.

The Pandrop, however, had one great asset which he certainly didn't appreciate, namely his wife Kirsten, a real jewel among women, industrious beyond measure and remarkably thrifty. If you would like to read a proper description of Kirsten, you'll find it in Proverbs 31, beginning at verse 10, but you must not forget that the wifie in the Bible was a hantle better off than Kirsten could ever hope to be, especially since the Pandrop was such a hopeless provider. Kirsten was head of the house, if you could call it a house. Father and mother and eight bairns in two rooms, in a rotten old building in the most densely populated part of the town; no running water, the communal water-tap being at the top of the communal stone stairway. The outside toilet was one of a row of such sheddies along the back wall of the close. For such commodious accommodation, in such salubrious surroundings, the rent was six shillings per half year.

Now, it may be that as you read this tale, you'll be shaking your head and saying, 'Oh, the leear! Oh, the fool leear!' Let me assure you that there are still many living witnesses to the truth of my words, and many of these same witnesses are not old people yet. In fact there were some families half as big again as Kirsten's crammed into identical space. No family allowance, no D.H.S.S., no dole without stamps, and no stamps unless you had a job, and the chances were that you didn't have that either. For thousands of decent, honest folk, life was one long weary struggle against want and deprivation.

Town Councillors in those times were badgered night and day by desperate parents 'Sair needin a hoose', but alas there were as yet nae hooses to be gotten, for the vast housing schemes which are such a prominent feature in the world of today were still on the drawing board. Still, time marches on, and there came the fateful day when Kirsten was informed that she had been allocated a 'new hoose'. She could scarcely believe the glad tidings after so many years in a hovel, and she wept with joy when the news was confirmed.

Then the reality of the situation struck her like a slap in the face. How on earth could she furnish a new hoose? She had been given to understand that her new home comprised a living room, a scullery, a bathroom and three bedrooms. Nivver in this world could she afford to furnish such a place. And the rent? Boys, faar on earth wis she gaan to get six shillins an fowerpence the wik, ivvery wik? It jist couldna be deen. The new hoose brocht as mony problems as it solved!

The rent was the main problem, especially since the Pandrop wore his responsibilities so lightly. But even in households where the bread-winner was in regular employment, the rent was some sort of ogre, always in the background. For every child still at school, the standard rent was reduced by fourpence, so some large families paid a low rent, but that dubious advantage was soon swallowed up in the food bill. For every child reaching school-leaving age, the rent was raised by fourpence whether or not there was a job for the youngster, and alas, jobs for youngsters were hard to come by.

Now, today's youth may find it difficult to understand the concern about the measly sum of fourpence, but look at it this way . . . Fourpence could get you a first class fish supper, or eight buttery cookies, so fourpence was quite a consideration when fourpences were so thin on the ground. Or, you can look at it this way . . . Fourpence was the sum paid to each woman working in the curing yards, as her share in the gutting of a barrel of herring.

It was to take Kirsten a long time to get the walls papered; it was to take a great deal longer to get a few sticks of furniture. In fact, it took years. Such were the good old days.

On their very first day in the new hoose, the family were mair or less lost. Their entire 'flittin' had been transported on a hurley, possibly Wull's Chariot, and their pitiful store of belongings seemed even more pitiful in the unaccustomed space. From room to room they wandered, amazed at the number of doors and the great, wide, empty floors. Several times did the aalest loon warn the bairn, 'Watch an nae get lost noo, darlin.' Every one of them seemed awe-struck at the sight of the Bathroom; they had never seen one before. And the fact that the quines could hae a bedroom separate fae the loons wis a great ferlie. The complete lack of bedroom furniture was accepted without question; that wis naething new!

'Noo,' says Kirsten to her assembled brood, 'It's nae a watry we hiv noo! It's a bathroom, an it his to be keepit clean! An I'm spikkin to you anaa! (This to the Pandrop , smirkin in the lobby.) There's to be nae mair daads o paper stuck ahin the pipe, an nae mair squaries o the *News o the World* hingin fae a nail at the back o the door. It's nae a readin room. We're gaan to get a roll o paper, like the gran folk. There must be aboot a mile o paper on a roll, an that should laist a month, onywye!'

That was wishful thinking, surely, or was she forecasting a famine in the land?

So the Pandrop was entrusted with the job of purchasing a roll of paper at the Droggist's. Nobody seemed to ken they should get a roller anaa.

Behold the Pandrop, now, in the Droggist's shop, where a group of well dressed ladies were clustered around the perfumery cabinet discussing the merits of the very latest Parisian products in the cosmetics line, while the Droggist hovered in the background, agreeing with each lady in turn. Well, ye see, there wis the Bunker's wife, an the Doctor's wife, an the Lawyer's wife, an a puckle mair that the Pandrop didna ken, all 'talking pan loff.'

'Well?' says the Droggist on seeing the Pandrop's unfamiliar face. 'Well?' Now, the Droggist wasn't being in the least bit rude; he was simply using the normal form of greeting between shopkeeper and customer. 'Well?'

'Oh!' says the Pandrop. 'I'm in for a roll o . . . paper,' using as an adjective the word he customarily used for his rear end.

Oh, boys, can you imagine the gasps of horror from the posh customers? Can you sense the atmosphere of outraged dignity? Aye, surely!

And hear the Droggist as he addresses the Pandrop . . . 'You vulgar lout. How dare you come into these premises using such filthy language! Don't you know that preparations for use on certain parts of the anatomy are termed 'toilet' preparations? It's toilet paper you require, and don't forget the word.'

'I'm affa sorry!' says the Pandrop. 'I didna ken. But eence I'm here, I'll tak a cake o soap anaa.'

'Toilet soap?' says the Droggist.

'Na, na!' says the Pandrop, 'It's my face I'm gaan t' wash!'

Up the workin classes!

A Window on the World

In the days when the North Breakwater of Peterhead was but a stump edging slowly and painfully outwards summer by summer, a south-east storm was really something to behold. The great, wide-open entrance allowed the tremendous seas to march across the bay and spend their fury on whatever lay in their path. I cannot tell the height of these seas, but I know that the high part of the South Breakwater, that part on which the lighthouse stands, was frequently buried deep in solid, green sea. Right up into the lifeboat shed such billows would hurl themselves; right over the top of the South Pier, the only shelter the South Harbour had, so that the Harbour became absolutely untenable. Everything was packed 'through the Brig' for safety, and great wooden booms were placed across the junction canal to kill the 'reenge', the surge of water caused by the fearsome tumult outside.

In such weather the South Harbour became a refuge for a multitude of seabirds. Eider ducks and Northern Divers, scraths and marrots (shags and puffins) abounded in the comparatively sheltered waters, biding their time until the storm would abate, and that could be a fortnight.

Such storms were a regular occurence in December and January. Never a winter passed without them, but for several years now they have been more or less absent. Since the oil people came to this neck of the woods there has never been a real bobby-dazzler from the south-east. Sure, there have been south-east gales, but I doubt if any of them have been of pre-war vintage.

Now, the most spectacular display of oceanic power was to be seen at the foot of Merchant Street, where there is a natural creek in the rocks called the 'Bogie Hole', a corruption of Boggie's Hole, Boggie the grocer having a shop directly opposite the Baths. That was before my time, although the shop is still there. Smith's Embankment, built from the rubble excavated during the deepening of the Harbour, was swept by great, mountainous seas which flooded the Bath St./Charlotte St. area. I can well remember how as youngsters, we would go right to the edge of the quay, then, when we saw a great sea coming, we would run for our lives and jump onto one of the iron seats which were on the quay at the time. It was a great thrill, we thought, to look down on the irresistible torrent sweeping along just beneath our feet.

Little did we realise that the slightest slip would have meant certain death. This went on until one day we were caught on the seat by a great sea which got us all waist deep, and only by the grace of God did we all manage to hold on. We never tried that caper again.

Speaking of Bath St. and Charlotte St., where was the original sea-wall before the Embankment was there? You can still see the top of it all the way along to Crossie's factory on the seaward side of the street. It is about a foot higher than the pavement, the top of a granite wall some two feet thick. You see, most of the factory was built on reclaimed ground, a great expanse of stones and gravel where the 'Shows' had their stance in the summer time, via a wide entrance opposite the bottom of Love Lane. There were also some herring curing yards on the site.

In a south-east storm, Charlotte St. would be flooded from end to end. I can remember sailing in a tin bath at the bottom of Uphill Lane, being heartily applauded by a wifie until she realised whose tin bath we were using. At the time, I was young enough to think that this was how Bath St. had got its name. A short distance to the westward of Uphill Lane there was, amongst the gravel, a flat slab of granite, some 4ft. x 2ft., whose purpose I never discovered. This was the mutually recognised boundary mark between the Sooth Bey territory and that of the Love Lane / Maiden St. mob. We respected each other's football pitches; we didn't fight, but we didn't mix. We were fisher, and they were not; it was as simple as that!

Now, isn't there a story somewhere amongst all this blurb? Aye, surely! A true story? Fit sorra idder? Mind you, for many years I doubted the truth of the tale, but finally I saw the light. Here then is the tale.

To us youngsters, Uphill Lane was 'the Mission Brae' because the Fishermen's Mission, originally a Kirk, occupied that side of the lane now the site for several nice houses. But to our parents, the brae was 'the Breweree Brae' cos there was a brewery at the bottom end. That Breweree is still there, you know, although it is now a factory for trawls. In its long history that building has lent itself to various uses. In my youth, Mary Daa had a yard in the close where she would pay the magnificent sum of tuppence for a dozen herring.

There had to be fourteen to the dozen, every herring perfect, no 'torn-bellies' and no spents (spawned), and they had to be 'strung on'. No bags, buckets, or baskets, boys! Pit them on a string! Why? I still don't know! But it was a buyer's market, and tuppence was the price o the Picters. It was also the price of five Woodbines. I have vague memories of a stable, and wasn't Jeannie Leask's Rolls Royce garaged there? There was a time when the floor of the building was given over to huge, open, concrete tanks in which lobsters were kept alive until required. The sea water required was pumped in from the bay. The iron pipe is still to be seen on the face of the embankment. Have a lookie, sometime. But keep in mind that the place was a Breweree!

Now to our tale, which was told me by my Deydie (Grandad), surely one of the finest storytellers of all time. It concerns the one-time occupants of the attic of that big bonny hoose which still stands on the brae immediately above the breweree.

Jock and Bella were an elderly couple who had been utterly dependent on the herring fishing all their days, Jock in the boats and Bella at the gutting of the herring. They had no family, and were like a pair of turtle doves, contented wi little, an canty wi mair. Jock was a quiet sort of chap who liked an occasional dram and a leisurely game of bowls, but alas both of these pleasures were now denied him, cos his legs had 'geen aa worth' (become useless) and he was confined to the house. Bella nursed him like a chucken, and he did enjoy the frequent calls of former cronies, but the days seemed long and weary at times. No radio in those days, you know, and Jock wasn't an avid reader.

Bella was a dab hand at clucking, fussing like an old hen, but she was a first class wife, nonetheless. Some of her neighbours said she was of the 'pail-o-water-to-the-quarter-o-mince' type, but the same could have been said of most of her contemporaries, for poverty was the order of the day, and every copper counted. Bella managed to earn a few pounds at the gutting, a shilling the barrel between three women, or mending nets at sixpence per hour, but in total her earnings were a mere pittance.

Imagine her surprise therefore, when she came home from her labours to find that the house reeked with the smell of the demon drink, and that Jock was even more happy and contented than usual; in fact he was singing quietly to himself . . .

'There was a young lass, an her name it was Nell,
In a snug little hoose wi her granny did dwell.
The hoose it wis wee, but the winda wis laiss,
There wis only fower lozens an een wantit glaiss.
'Twis a bonny wee winda, a handsome wee winda,
The bonniest wee winda that ivver ye saa.'

'Aha!' thinks Bella, 'Oor Jock's heen a visitor, a richt kindly sowl, fa ivver he micht be.' So she said little, although Jock was rather vague about the visitor's identity. But when the same thing happened a few days later, she wasn't very happy, her unease deepened by the fact that all Jock's cronies were at sea. So she determined to put a stop to the clandestine visits; she would lock the door and take the key with her when she went out. But boys, even that didn't put an end to the illicit drink traffic. Venting her wrath on Jock made not the slightest difference, and she was at her wits' end until one day, quite by chance, she came home by a different route, turning left from Charlotte St. into Uphill Lane. There she was taken aback by the sight of Jock's hands at the attic window, deftly pulling up a string attached to a tin flagon, evidently full, and no doubt filled by the brewery lads who were watching open-mouthed as the flagon ascended. So this was the bonny wee winda? She would see about that! And so she did.

For years I loved that story, picturing the deft hands at the window and admiring the cleverness of the smuggler's art. Then I realised that the story was manifestly untrue, cos there was no window in the gable, completely harled as it was from truck to keel. That meant that Deydie had been feeding me lies, and that disappointed me somewhat. My idol had feet of clay.

But, boys, within the last few months, after at least seventy years, that gable has been completely stripped of its harl and has been re-pointed. And there, high up at attic level, it is plain to see that at some time a little window was blocked up. So I owe Deydie a profound apology.

Have a look at the gable next time you pass that way, but stop the car while you look, cos it's a flood of traffic you are likely to encounter, not a flood of sea water and a tin bath.

368

The Ship-Ashore

There were, I think, around fifteen of us altogether that afternoon. We had met, as usual, between the Cannon and the Wine Waal to decide what the ploy should be for that particular Saturday afternoon. Those of us who normally got a 'Saturday penny' had already spent it and were anxious to be up and doing at something or another, preferably fitba, but, since the fitba was in White the Saddler's to be shooed, and wouldn't be ready that day, fitba was out. The underlying reason, which we with one accord ignored, was that there weren't enough coppers in the group to pay White the Saddler for the repair.

Then up spake one of the Elders, a chiel who was the poorest article at fitba that you could possibly imagine, a chiel with an amazing imagination and the gift of being rather sparing with the truth. (His forebears were from Burnhaven.)

'Hey!' says he. 'Fit aboot gaan to the ship-ashore at Finnyfaal? Ye micht get something worthwhile there!'

Never have I seen a motion so unanimously accepted. That would be the plan! We would go to the ship-ashore and we would go now! And, of course, we would return laden with booty, rich beyond measure. One of our number had recently distinguished himself by salvaging from the *Belmont*, wrecked just at the harbour entrance, a ladle and a tattie-chapper for his mother, and that in spite of the police guard at both the 'steppies' which led down to the rocks. But, you see, the *Belmont* had merely been a trawler. A real ship-ashore, a big ship, such as the one at Finnyfaal, could yield real treasure, not ruling out the possibility of gold and jewels! Such is youth!

We never used the word 'wreck'; it was always a 'ship-ashore', and in our day these were frequent, especially in spells of fog. The pity of it all was that, when such things took place, we were either in bed, or in school. We seemed to be continually denied the opportunity of following out our piratical, plundering instincts, but this was Saturday afternoon and things would be different.

The term 'a broken ship' was used by some of our parents, just as we used 'a ship-ashore', but the meaning was 'the same but different'. It was used to rebuke a youngster who might be showing signs of greed at the table.

'Hey! Mind that there's ither folk here! It's nae a broken ship, ye ken!'

Thus the reprimand, and at the same time a suggestion that broken ships were there to be plundered. We had all been regaled with wondrous tales of the booty which had been recovered from certain wrecks. All our days we had heard such legends, but sometimes I wondered why there were so many poorly-clad yougsters around, if the hauls of booty had been so mind-boggling. Still, I was as keen as any to go to this ship-ashore, and we set off, full of beans. Not until we had passed the Prison did someone suggest that we should have brought a barra. A stony silence was the reply to that lot.

With spirits high and with legs still fresh we came to the bottom of Stirling Hill, then we left the road and took to the railway line which ran from Boddam to Ellon. The incline of the railway seemed to be less steep than the road and we made good progress, albeit we were slowly getting less vocal than we were at the start. When we realised that the rail track was gradually taking us away from the coast, we took to the road again, and passing Slains Castle on our left, we finally reached Port Errol, a place we had never seen.

As one might expect, we must see the harbour, where a small group of fishermen viewed our arrival with some concern. We were, after all, a rather noisy throng and there is no doubt that the peace of the village was disturbed; but when the fishermen realised that we came in peace, they were desirous that we should tell them who we were and from whence we had come.

'Dinna aa spik at the same time!' said one fisherman, whom I had seen from time to time in the grocer's shop next door to my home in Jamaica St. He appeared to recognise me, for he addressed me ... 'Oxy, fit are ye deein here? Ye're a lang wye fae hame the day, surely!'

'Oh,' says I, 'we're makkin for the ship-ashore at Finnyfaal, an we wis thinkin we micht get somethin to tak hame. Faar's Finnyfaal?'

There was some amusement among the fishers for a moment, then the kindly man, whom I later came to know as 'Gorlan's Jock', bade us all look to the South.

'Look,' says he, 'the ship's at the ither side o yon high cliff. That means ye hiv aboot fower mile to traivel yet. That'll tak ye mair than a hale oor. Fan did ye leave hame?'

That had us stumped, cos none of us had a watch. 'Aifter denner time' was the only answer we could give.

'Weel,' says Jock, 'it's supper time noo. Ye canna get aboard the ship athoot a boat, an supposin ye could, there's naething left to lift. She's been there for three or fower days, ye ken!'

But that was something we jist didna ken. We should have thought about that to begin with, but possibly it was too much to expect from a group whose oldest member was twelve. A sense of disappointment seemed to come over us all, along with the realisation that we were all rather tired.

'It's time ye wis roadit,' says Jock, 'if ye're seekin hame afore dark.' So it was a rather silent crowd that set out on the way home. The high spirits and the camaraderie of the past few hours seemed to vanish, and before long there was a dispute and bickering among our leaders. The tight little group was now a long, disorganised straggle, with the younger loons trailing behind, some of them complaining of hunger. It would have been rather difficult to mistake the way in such open country, but we did make the mistake of taking a short-cut across the parks, thus incurring the hazards of barbed wire fences and deep, muddy ditches. This was the crowning effort, but thankfully there were nae coos. Then we came across the house.

All that I remember consists of heavy gate-pillars, some shrubbery, and a shallow flight of wide granite steps, the whole steeped in an air of peace and quiet.

Something about the place seemed to attract us and we stood gazing for a few moments, till up pipes Andra, a classmate of mine ... 'I'm gaan in here to see if I can get a piece, cos I'm jist stairvin wi hunger!'

'Ye winna get a piece there,' says I. 'It must be "granders" that bides in a place like that.' But Andra was off. Up the steps to the front door he went and rang the bell.

A young damsel came to the door and I can still hear Andra's voice saying, 'Can I have a piece, please? I'm affa hungry!'

By this time our front runners had come back to see what was happening and the stragglers had caught up with us. Thus, when a nicely dressed lady came to the door in answer to the maidie's call, she found a young lad on her doorstep, and two rows of young heads peeping round the gate-pillars. Very little explanation was needed before she had us all seated on the steps, where we were plied with freshly cut bread and wonderful home-made jam. Never in all my days have I tasted the like! That good lady saved a few lives that day, I'm sure.

Then it was the main road again, the bellies somewhat comforted, but the leggies gey sair. So much so, that the youngest straggler collapsed from sheer fatigue and lay greetin sair on the tarmac. We offered to carry him, but he steadfastly refused, so we decided to go for help, advising him to get off the crown of the road cos there micht be a car comin along and he could get kilt! A few minutes later, a car did overtake us, with the casualty waving gaily from the rear window! Lucky beggar! I think that car was the first Baby Austin we had ever seen, but it was certainly the only car we saw on the road that day. More than sixty years ago, ye see.

As it happened, the car took the boy home, and there somebody raised the alarm, cos we had been away for too long and now it was completely dark. They could hardly send the Lifeboat, but they did send Booth Summers' fish lorry to the rescue. I'm tellin ye, it felt like a magic carpet. We were lifted from the tap o Stirlin Brae and taken to our several homes. Thus ended our expedition to the ship-ashore; we never tried another. Ye see, we didna get naething, nae even a tattie-chapper!

Nothing spectacular about such a day? Well, maybe no, yet it sticks in the memory, along with the names o the hale bourachie o loons. There are only four of us still to the fore. The others were scattered to the four winds and the sea claimed its share, notably the three sons of Mary Tammas in Merchant Street, lost at sea during the Hitler War; and not forgetting Andra, from the same street, lost with the *Olive Branch*.

The hoose where we met with so much kindness will still be there, I suppose. I have a good idea where to find it, but I have never gone back. I'll just leave it at that, preferring to regard that hoose as being built of the stuff which dreams are made of.

Blue Murder

Ye think the Gab o Mey's geen past?
Weel, jist ee wyte, ma loon,
For in anither week or twaa
We'll get the Gab o June.

It is well over forty years now since I penned these words, never thinking for a moment that they could be in any way prophetic. The 'week or twaa' has proved to be too short a period, but at last we have met the Gab o June. Surely that cannot be denied in this year of '91, especially by mortals like me who are somewhat lacking in natural insulation. Bullet-proof drawers are the order of the day, despite the occasional spells of sunshine, and the Senior Citizens' mouths are into the set of saying 'It's jist nae mowse!'

But, you know, I've been expecting this cold spell, for an old Rosehearty man, an ardent exponent of the weather lore, once said, 'If, on the thirteenth day of May the wind is northerly, it will remain so until the turn of the day. It may change direction for short periods, but the prevailing direction will be northerly.' The Rosehearty men named the thirteenth of May 'Reid Day', for Reid was the old man's name and as the years slipped past, they realised how accurate his forecast was. Need I tell you that on the thirteenth of May this year the wind was northerly and that we are not all that far from the turn of the day? Caal, did ye say? Aye, that an mair!

I was firmly reminded of this fact this very morning, when I left the house to go up the toon. It was lovely until I turned the corner to go up Jamaica Street, for then the wind was in my face. Not being so brave as I used to be, I retreated back round the corner to fasten up my jacket, and it was then that the racket started.

Five little sparras alighted on the road just a few feet from where I stood, and boys, ye widna believe the uproar they created. The root of the trouble might have been a barley grain, although I couldn't see it, but the noise was unbelieveable. I suppose a saucer would have held the lot, but it would have been a saucerful of venom, for they snarled and pecked at each other with great gusto. Two flew off in disgust, only to be immediately replaced by another pair. This happened twice, and there were never more than five. Blue murder, boys, blue murder, for all of two minutes, until a grain lorry scared them off and the fight was transferred to the rooftops. I was 'fair diverted' while it lasted, then memory brought to mind the words of an old friend, a fisherman from Fife.

'Peter,' says he, 'I dinna like fishin oot o Peterheid, for ye get nae peace on a Sunday mornin, the sparras mak sic a soun. They jist come aboard an fecht, an there's nae sleep for's on the only mornin that we hae to oorsels. Lauch if ye like, but there's nae the same problem in the Broch!'

I did laugh at the time, but then the problem didn't affect me, for I was sleeping at home. Only those who were sleeping in their boats were annoyed, and that meant a great number of fishers, for those were the days when nobody but the locals got home for the weekend. Although I sympathised with my friend, I could scarcely accept that the Broch sparras were quieter than their Blue Toon oppos. But then I had no experience of sleeping in a boat in the Broch. Nowadays I'm not at all sure.

You see, there's a vast congregation of sparras doing their level best to entertain me in the early hours of every morning. They gather in the heart of a lovely berberis shrub and they don't half go to town. It's blue murder again, boys, blue murder! And not only in the heart of the shrub, but also in the heart of the listener cum would-be sleeper. I'm ashamed at the dark thoughts which fill my breast. But praise be! There's one thing sure to silence them and that's the rain, but that has been conspicuously absent for a while. Plenty rain, no twitter . . . Plenty twitter, no rain! Dinna spik to me aboot Peterheid sparras!

But even when there's heavy rain, I'm not without the gift of music, for there seems to be one solitary offender who has found shelter under the slates of my old dwelling from whence he gazes forth lugubriously on the waters in the guttering and complaining vocally on his awful plight, not in a twitter, by any standard, but simply by means of one solitary tweet every two minutes, precisely. And sure as death, boys, the solitary tweet is more soul-destroying than the razz-matazz of the massed chorus. I find my toes curling under the strain of suppressed passion while I await the next tweet. It's jist nae good for a buddy.

Now, this word 'tweet' reminds me somehow of a certain lady whom I knew slightly in days gone by. Let's call her 'Tibbie', for I never did know her proper name. On the rare occasions when I heard Tibbie's voice, she tweeted like the sparra below the slates, one tweet at a time. She wis a quiet, little, plump deemie, with a faint aura of neglect which seems to haunt some old maids, and with the unfailing habit of wearing a fur-collared coat no matter what the season. There was also a faint hint of camphor about her person, especially if the weather was warm.

Tibbie was a faithful worshipper for many years at a certain place; in fact she had never worshipped anywhere else, but in her later years she developed a most peculiar habit. In the middle of the address to the faithful, Tibbie would give one solitary tweet before keeling over in a dwaam. Then four stalwart men would carry her forth to the ante-room where they laid her tenderly on a couch before unfastening the top button of her blouse and giving her a spoonful of brandy. The procedure never varied until the day when the chiel wi the brandy wis jist ower quick on the draw and earned the sharp disapproval of the chiel who was supposed to lowse the button.

'Fit's aa the hurry, min? Ye micht gie's time to lowse the button!' This in turn brought a sharp reprimand from the senior elder, who was stooping over the recumbant figure. 'Be quaet, lads, be quaet! Jist mind far ye are! But I sometimes think that on a day o heat like this, we'd be better to lowse her steys an leave the button aleen!'

He was to regret that remark, for Tibbie's head came up like a rocket and clobbered him under the chin, so that he bit his tongue rather severely. There ensued a few moments when there was a certain lack of decorum, while Tibbie stalked back into the assembly, where she never tweeted again.

Now, tell me something. If it was the brandy that stoppit Tibbie's tweetin (and for the life of me I cannot see what else it could have been), how do I set about dosing 3,278 sparras, knowing full well that, if I don't give them enough, there's sure to be blue murder?

Foreign Affairs

In all walks of life there are snobs, superior people, those and such as those, who buy their beef from a better butcher, their summer outfits from a more distant Fashion House, and their bullet-proof drawers from a warehouse whose excellence far outshines that of premises favoured by lesser mortals. You have never met such people? You must be very young indeed! Please, don't get me wrong . . . I don't wish to be hard on the superior type, for they serve the highly useful purpose of keeping the rest of us in our place.

'It's verse that you write, Mr Buchan, not poetry!' said one dear soul, many years ago.

'Please yersel,' says I. 'I widna ken, ye see, cos I wis schooled on *Palgrave's Golden Treasury of Songs and Lyrics*, and *The Oxford Book of English Verse*. Neither book uses the term 'Poetry', but without doubt they contain some of the finest poetry in the English language. On the other hand, some passages in the *Old Testament* are sheer poetry, but in no way could they be described as verse. So, how does one judge poetry? There you have the sixty-four thousand dollar question.

This was vividly illustrated this very morning, in the Mission, when a fisherman who left school at fourteen (more than sixty years ago), gave me *Gray's Elegy* complete and word perfect. 'A lot o sound, practical common sense in that poem' says he, as he rolled a fag. 'The path of glory leads but to the grave'. Strange how some of the things we were taught at school stick to us all our lives, although in boyhood we were far too young to appreciate the truths in them. The fleeting years can fairly remedy that fault, I'm sure.

My own personal judgement is that poetry (or verse, if you like) is not 'good' simply because somebody else says it's 'good'. It's largely a matter of taste . . . if you like it, then it's good; if it speaks to you, you'll remember it with pleasure all your days. If it fails to speak to you, it will not last the night.

Now, this throws me back to the far distant days when I was a pupil in the Academy, the House Built Upon a Rock.

After the departure of Miss Hutchison (Aunt Nellie), our music teacher was an Englishman named Mr Beck-Slinn, a kindly man with a voice like coarse sandpaper, and with a determination that our repertoire of songs should be greatly widened. No more 'Rio Grande', no more 'Drunken Sailor', no more 'Swanee

River' . . . we were to touch upon a few love songs. Oh, boys, fancy giving such stuff to teenage boys! Seldom have I felt so self-conscious. And yet, there was a something (there's aye a something), a something that has been part of me since the day I first sang it . . . a line from the old Elizabethan song 'Who is Sylvia' (Shakespeare). The song is a simple question-and-answer affair, and the line which has stuck to me is the second verse, 'Is she kind as she is fair, for beauty lives with kindness'. I think that is one of the finest gems I have ever come across, especially since I have proved it to be completely true.

It's a long time now since I learned that beauty doesn't come from a bottle. It is not the prerogative of youth, nor does it fade with age; it is far deeper than skin-deep, and it has nothing to do with financial or material status. No, the bonny folk in my life (and they have been many), have been the kindly folk, some of them from the highest planes of learning, others barely literate. Many have been clartit wi herrin scales, many have had their boots thick wi dubs. Few indeed would be suitable for having their features displayed on the lid of a box of chocolates, and yet they are bonny folk. Ashore and afloat I have met them, male and female, with a something about them which is akin to the Charity of 1st Corinthians 13. They are the salt of the earth.

Now, at this point you may ask me, 'What do you know about earth? You may know something about the salt, but surely the earth is a closed book to you!' Well, now, that's where you would be completely mistaken, for I do know something about earth; not a lot, mind you, but still a something. Let me introduce you now to my garden, where the soil is almost certainly different from yours, in that it is of foreign origin. How come?

Well now, in the long ago, before the days of steam, Peterhead was a busy trading port whose connections with the Continent were varied and very many. Sailing vessels plied their trade regularly between Peterhead and the Baltic ports, not forgetting the harbours in the Low Countries. Any vessel returning to Peterhead without cargo would require ballast for the voyage, the ballast usually composed of the soil of the hinterland of the last port of call. Of course the ballast had to be got rid of, on arrival at Peterhead, so it was dumped on the quay (Ballast Jetty?) whence it was carted off to fill the gardens nearest to the harbour. Thus we find that in Harbour St., Jamaica St., James St., Saint Andrew St., Merchant St. and Charlotte St., where there are many large gardens, the soil is all of foreign origin. The great expanse behind the Wynd Well nursing home is at least three feet deep in it, as was the long narrow garden of Arbuthnot House, not forgetting my own place, where the black soil can be effortlessly dug over.

No doubt you'll have noticed that the locations I have mentioned are all in Old Peterhead, down-town Peterhead, where many of the houses were built for sea captains in a day when up-town Peterhead didn't exist, and the Longate was *the* shopping centre. Having said that, I believe that many tons of ballast were carted to Inverugie Castle to replace the soil in the kitchen garden.

In any case, when the local demand for the stuff had been satisfied, it was dumped on a site 'at the fitt o the Broadgate', behind Arbuthnot House and across the street from the head of the dry-dock. Year after year, the heap grew until it reached mammoth proportions, and yougsters playing there at the turn of the century called it the Ballast Hill. Then, when the trading smacks disappeared, the site was walled off and the ballast was forgotton.

An old friend of mine, now deceased, once told me how he was sent from school one day to enquire why a classmate was so long absent. He found that his classmate was absent through illness and he also found that the boy was 'beddit' on a heap of straw on the floor of a humble cottage which stood on the site now occupied by the 'Mission'. Boys, we've come a lang, lang road! That would have been in the twenties.

But of course a great many folks will recall the Nissen-hut cafe run by Georgie Fyvie and Andra 'Touch' Strachan in the immediate post-war years. Then, in the sixties, the Mission decided to flit from Charlotte St. to the site of the Nissen hut, and thereby hangs a tale, for before they could make the site deep enough to accommodate the new Mission, they had to remove a great slice of the old ballast. Now, you may be wondering where that went, so I'll tell you. It was carted out the West Road to the Glendale Nurseries, where W Leslie, fruiterer, grew some wonderful crops of tomatoes on it.

'Now,' says you, 'faar's the rest o't?'

It's just where it has been for the last two hundred years or thereby, behind the Mission and the house next door, and it stretches all the way back to James St. An observant friend tells me that during the excavation of the site, he counted twelve distinct layers of earth, not all of the same colour, but mostly black. Speak about faraway places with strange-sounding names! I have heard South America mentioned, but I have doubts about that.

Could it be that I have solved a problem? If you lesser mortals, who have nothing better than clay to howk, would be upsides with the likes o me and a few others, ye'd better get a shovel and a barra. On second thoughts, make that a digger and a lorry, cos there's several thousand tons o the stuff. Dinna be ower greedy, cos it's nae a broken ship! An ye'd better see the Mission mannie or somebody, an mine that Bumff an Buchan'll be lookin oot o their winda!

Now, in closing, brethren, let me remind you how Rupert Brooke once wrote, 'There is some corner of a foreign field that is forever England.' I cannot say such a thing, but I'll have a go . . . 'There's a great muckle sklyter o my native toon that is forever foreign!' That is neither verse not poetry, but it is unassailably a fact.

It may be of further interest that in the South-west of Scotland there's a great muckle quarry busily engaged in boring out the interior of an actual mountain of stone. It would appear that some of the quarry's best customers are those countries in Western Europe where stone is difficult to come by. See now why Peterhead traders could only get soil as ballast?

It's a black dog for a fite monkey, intit? (fair exchange).

Christmas Never

It was a grey day, cold and clear and still, but nevertheless a grey day. I suppose you could call it December grey, that thin, drab, lifeless shade which tries, with some success, to suck the life out of every other colour in sight. I suppose you could call it Christmas grey, for it was indeed Christmas Day, and the scene totally different from any you are ever likely to see on a card.

It was in the early seventies, and the mad rush for North Sea oil was at its height, although for today at least the rush had come to a halt. Within the confines of Peterhead Bay some fifty supply vessels of several nationalities lay anchored in tiers of six or eight, top and tail, like herring in a barrel, while a similar fleet lay singly at anchor outside. What a spread of shipping! What a vast array of millions in capital outlay . . . what a sight!

I was on duty in the Control Tower at the entrance to Peterhead Harbour, where every movement of shipping in the Bay, inward, outward and internal is faithfully logged, twenty-four hours a day, no ship allowed to move without first calling the Tower on VHF radio. Fishing vessels must conform to the same rules for entry and departure only. Well, that day I had logged very few movements indeed, apart from the arrival of a handful of well-laden fishing boats for the morrow's market. I knew that parties were in full swing on some of the supply boats, but for me the day was getting rather tedious. This unaccustomed inactivity was getting me down. What? Only one single arrival expected? That could hardly be the case, surely?

Just after lunch time Customs phoned to check the ETA of this one arrival, a Norwegian supply boat, one of the biggest of the type.

'She'll be here in twenty minutes,' said I. 'North side, Bravo berth.'

'Fine,' says Customs. 'We'll be down there waiting.'

I immediately assumed that Customs were to be quick on the draw, in order that they might get what was left of Christmas to themselves, but as it happened, I was completely mistaken.

Then my unexpected visitors arrived, two little girls and their Granda. I had never seen the little girls before, but I did know the Granda slightly. On finding the ground-floor door open, they had climbed all these stairs to find out what went on in the Tower. They could hardly have chosen a quieter day. I showed them the radar, but they were too young for that. They wanted to speak home to their Ma on the radio . . . That was definitely not on. They scampered to and fro outside the window for a whilie, with strict instructions to remain inside the railing. The arrival of the big Norwegian vessel held their attention for a whilie; they watched as Customs boarded the vessel, only to come ashore again in a very few minutes. Then they got bored, suddenly and completely. So, to keep the party going, I tried as an opening gambit, 'Fit did ye get fae Suntie?' sensing immediately that I had unwittingly dropped an almighty clanger.

There was no immediate reply, but eventually the elder child, after looking under her brows, first at her sister, then at her Granda, lifted her head to look me straight in the eye.

'There's nae a Suntie!' she says. 'It's yer Ma an yer Da. If there's a Suntie in a shop, it's jist an aal mannie!'

Such heresy from a child of such tender years. I had never heard the like! 'Faa on earth tellt ye that?' says I, deliberately this time.

There was no reply at all, simply the under-brow glances as before.

Granda sat in the far corner, gazing through the window at nothing.

'Hiv ye nivver gotten naething fae Suntie?'

'Nivver!' said they in unison, with an unmistakable note of wistfulness in their voices. 'Nivver!'

I tried to fix Granda's gaze with mine, but he wasn't having any, so I decided to let the matter drop. After all, it's neen o my business fit ither folk teach their bairns.

Then, suddenly, I noticed that two little faces were pressed hard against the window, watching in fascination as some sort of miracle unfolded before their very eyes. Even I was entranced. Granda, however, seemed rather taken aback, for down the gangway of the Norwegian vessel came striding a tall, strapping figure in a coat of many colours and leather knee-boots. His cap was at a jaunty angle and his tawny beard was real. A Viking, if ever I saw one. Hard on his heels came two similarly clad minions, every inch as tall as he was himself and both of them carrying a very bulky sack. Up the jetty, in perfect step they marched, two paces behind their leader, completely unaware that their every step was being closely watched by two pairs of very youthful eyes. By this time my head was down on a level with the bairns, and I whispered . . .

'Faa wid that be, noo? Could that be Suntie, think ye?'

'Canna be Suntie,' says the littlin. 'There's nae reindeer!'

'Jist hold on a meentie!' says I. 'We'll fin oot aboot that, I think.'

I could see that there was still someone on the supply boat's bridge, so I called the ship. 'Channel six, please. Roger, Channel six.'

'Happy Christmas, Skipper!' says I. 'I've got a problem here. Two little girls have been watching your friends marching up the jetty, and they're rather concerned about the absence of reindeer. Can you enlighten us on that matter?'

The reply gart the craiturs lowp, for their faces were practically into the receiver.

'Happy Christmas to you. And Happy Christmas, girls.' (Oh, the smiles.) 'Sorry, no Rudolph. The mountains in Norway are very icy at this time, and this caused a slight accident. The sleigh was damaged and the harness was broken, so we offered to give Himself a lift!' Quick on the uptake, bless him.

Now I had twaa little kettlies on my hands, their liddies fair hottrin on the bile. What excitement!

Granda made to rise and depart, but I caught him in the act and said, 'I'm in chairge here, freen. If ye dinna sit doon, I'll crown ye!' He sat!

'Noo!' says I to the twaa kettlies who had gone outside to watch the trio making their way up Shiprow, 'if ee ging up to the Brig, ye'll see him comin ower, an maybe he'll spik to ye.'

378

'Oh!' cries the littlin again, 'he winna get ower. The Brig's up!' And so it was, although I had failed to notice.

Was this to be disaster, at the last? Surely no!

With my hopes not very high, I dialled the Brig number, and Hallelujah, there was an immediate answer.

'Can we hae the Brig doon for a meentie?' says I. 'I'm here to lower the Brig if it's nott,' was the reply. 'I dinna see naebody needin the Brig doon. Faa's needin the Brig doon?'

'Suntie Claa!' says I. Boys, I thocht he wid choke.

Finally, he got his breath back. 'Peter!' says he, 'I nivver thocht I'd hear ye spikkin throwe drink. Could ye nae pit a drappie oot o the bottle up here?' Then there was a sudden silence . . . he had just sighted the trio behind the great bing of Caley fish-boxes.

'The Brig'll be doon immediately, if not sooner,' says he, and suddenly there was a clatter of little feeties on the stairs, and I was left alone.

'Play the game, now, Granda,' I shouted down the stairway. Did I hear a grunt in reply?

Through the powerful binoculars I watched with bated breath as the Brig cam rummlin doon and the three Vikings made their way across . . . just as a car drew to a halt and the twaa kettlies scrambled out, to stand with their backs hard pressed against the door. Well done, Granda!

Then, wonder of wonders, the tall, strapping Viking rover stopped and spoke to the bairns and to crown it all, he bade his henchmen lay the great sacks on the roadway so that the youngsters might dip into their contents. Boys, the wonder on the bairns' faces was something to behold! How happily did they wave their hands as the three strangers made their way to a nearby party, where their arrival was eagerly awaited.

So this was the reason for the expeditious Customs clearance! Well done, Customs.

You know, the sky now seemed to be clearer, and the sea less sombre, despite the imminence of the winter dark. Something had happened to brighten everything around, and I'm sure the Peepin Tom light on the south breakwater kept on giving me a friendly wink, only to be instantly copied by its oppo on the north side. The remainder of my watch passed very pleasantly indeed.

Now, did I pit a cat among the doos, think ye?

I doot hardly, cos I had very little to do with the whole affair . . . Or did I? Ach, fit aboot it, onywye! But when I recall, as I so often do, the amazement on the twaa facies, I realise afresh that, when we lose our sense of wonder, tis a loss beyond repair.

The Crusher

There was a time when there was a distillery at Burnhaven, that famous hamlet where so many of the Peterhead fisher folk have their roots. The old dwellings were razed to the ground many years ago, leaving not a single vestige of the once thriving community. A sewage pumping station is the only building there now, but nobody wants to claim that as part of their heritage. Nothing there now, save the winds and the salt spray, and possibly, a few ghosts.

The distillery survived for a few more years, but that too has gone, the end result of modernisation or centralisation, call it what you will. But . . . there was a time when that same distillery would discharge some vile effluent into the Nettie burn, much to the delight of the local ducks, whose gyrations and contortions on these special days were really wonderful to behold. They would slide down the banks of the burn on their backsides, to turn somersaults in the waters which had been laced with a liberal dash of barley bree. Some of the birds even attempted to fly, with disastrous results, for none of them had been trained to loop the loop. That is not to say that they didn't try! Oh, boys, what a fun they had, the final item on their programme a rather raucous and beery version of the 'Nuns' Chorus'.

How the local youngsters enjoyed the pageant! Many years before Walt Disney was born, these bairns were seeing Donald Duck, not on film, but in the flesh, performing feats that the future Donald Duck would be sair made to emulate.

One of the delighted bairns was David Jonathan Buchan, whose mother once described him as 'a roch kine o loon, but nae the warst'. I have heard that his Deydie was a leading light in that sept of the Buchan Clan known as the 'Forty Thiefs', but I doubt very much if Jonathan's family ever aspired to such heights of fame. (He was called by his middle name, to distinguish him from the Daavits and Davys who abounded in the village.)

Came the day when Jonathan's father decided to leave the hardships of village life for the fleshpots of the metropolis (the Blue Toon), where he got a jobbie in the Mull, and a hoosie in Weaver's Lane.

Thus did Jonathan find himself in a strange school, his fellow pupils creatures from another planet, and his teacher some sort of monster. Making friends did not come easily to Jonathan . . . he had never had to do such a thing before, because he had grown up with his chums in the village. Now he was in a new environment, and he didn't like it one little bit. So the great clumsy clort o a loon, wi airms like a Clydesdale horse and a face like a bustit fitba, developed a strange habit. At playtime, he would enfold a classmate in his arms and give him a mighty bear-hug.

It is possible that modern psychiatrists would describe such behaviour as a cry for help, an effort to attract attention and affection, but Jonathan's class-mates failed to see that. The smaller boys lived in terror of the great arms which could take their very breath away and leave them with sore ribs for a week or more, so they shunned Jonathan like the plague, and gave him the title 'the Crusher', a name that was to stick for life.

And it came to pass that the Crusher made a fatal mistake, in that he tried his crushing act on Bob McTurk, one of the bigger boys in the class, popularly known as 'the Turk'. Tall, and lean, and fit, (he didna aye hae a belly like a washin-hoose biler), the Turk endured the painful embrace for a whilie until he finally managed to break free, then, when he had got his breath back, he fell oot on the Crusher an gied him a sair skin!

Boys! Yon wis a rare fecht! Naebody had ivver seen the like o't. The hale school learned that day that although the Crusher was probably the strongest loon in the toon, the Turk was the best fechter, and that was infinitely mair important than the number of feet in a mile. For many a long day, that battle was spoken about, but strange as it may seem, the contestants became firm friends, and remained so for many years. There was no more crushing.

In the course of time, the Turk and his pal both went to sea, but the Crusher, strong as he was, was totally defeated by sea-sickness, and had to seek employment on land, where he drifted from job to job before emigrating to Canada. There he found employment as porter in a big hotel, and was soon in great demand by female members of staff when they were 'propositioned' by amorous guests. In answer to the maidens' pleas the Crusher would confront the offending guest, and make certain warlike gestures, accompanied by a few words of the Buchan tongue. This, along with his impressive physique and his ugly countenance, usually did the trick, producing a profound apology and a few dollars, on the understanding that he 'wouldn't tell the wife'. Thus did our hero come to be called 'the Passion Crusher', salting away quite a tidy sum on the quiet. He never sought a wife, for he was rather scared of the opposite sex.

Came the day when the Passion Crusher made a serious mistake, attempting, uninvited, to save a damsel from a situation from which she didn't want to be rescued. Boys! Greed's a terrible thing!

Behold, now, the Crusher fleeing for his life along the carpeted corridors, pursued by an irate female screaming for his blood. But he managed to elude her by the very simple trick of falling into a lift shaft that went a long way down . . . eighteen storeys, to be precise . . . R.I.P.

Let us come back now, across the ocean to the Blue Toon. It is the first week in December, and it is cold and dark, with showers of sleet in the northerly breeze. The good ship *Meadowsweet* is lying at the foot of James St. having just arrived home from Yarmouth. Her skipper, Bob McTurk is at the capstan, hoisting the bundled nets onto a horse-cart which will take them to some fence where they will be hung to dry. The entire crew are busy, very busy, when there appears on the quay a peculiar trio, comprising the Mission man, the undertaker and a bobby, all desirous of speech with the Turk, who bids them stay where they are until the cart is loaded. Not until then are they allowed on board to reveal the purpose of their visit.

It appears that the news of the Crusher's demise has reached the Blue Toon along with a box containing the deceased's ashes, and a request that his old friend would scatter the said ashes as close as possible to his birthplace, Burnhaven.

'Boys!' says the Turk, 'I'm richt disappintit to hear he's awaa! He wisna the

381

warst, ye ken. Fin the crew comes back fae hingin oot the nets, we'll hae a shallie o tay afore we ging oot. Is there ony o his ain folk still to the fore?'

'Alas, no,' says the Mission man. 'He was the last of the family, so there will be only the three of us.'

'It's nae a great mornin,' says the Turk, 'but we'd better dee't the day, cos there winna be steam on the ship aifter this. The biler'll be blaan doon, an we'll be tied up till the New 'Ear. Ye'd better come back aifter denner time, cos the lads'll be gettin their denner at hame. They've been awaa for nine wiks, an the bairns'll be needin their Yarmooth presents. I widna dee this job avaa, but the Crusher wis a great pal o mine, lang seen.'

The *Meadowsweet's* company returned to the ship in the early afternoon to learn, much to their surprise, that there was a 'special jobbie' to be done. On the whole, they were rather impressed, for at that time cremation was very rare indeed. There was some comment on the size of the box which was lowered onto the deck.

'I ken he was a big chiel,' says the Turk. 'I wis expectin a thing like a sweetie jar, nae a box that size. But maybe they dee things different in Canada.'

Nobody seemed to know anything about anything. This was a first experience for everybody concerned. It never entered a single head that there might be a container within the box.

'Noo!' says the Turk, as the shippie crossed the bay, 'The bobby's here cos it's the laa, the coffin mannie's here for the siller, and the Mission mannie's here cos they canna get a minister. An we're aa here cos fitivver's in the box eesed to be a pal o mine. But, pal or nae pal, this is hardly a day for the job. Be smairt aboot yer wark, noo. There's nae need for a lang say awaa. I'll pit the ship as close as it's safe, but mind ye, we canna lie there lang.'

Now, Burnhaven Bay, with a northerly wind meeting an ebb tide, can be a really wicked place. This was evident as soon as the *Meadowsweet* had cleared the breakwater. The landsmen were immediately helpless, and the seasoned fishers themselves had considerable difficulty keeping their feet.

'Aha!' says the Turk, 'I doot we'll hae to wyte for better wither!' And he turned the shippie back. 'I'm sure that box wid keep for a gweed fyle yet.'

But the sea decreed otherwise, sending a great dollop of water onto the drifter's after-deck to wash the box over the side. The entire funeral party were soaked to the skin and there was a great hullabaloo for a whilie, but the Turk had made up his mind. Not for all the tea in China was he going to endanger his ship for any box.

'We'll get it on the beach, the morn,' says he. 'Meantime, we're aa gaan hame. It'll seen be dark, onywye!'

But there was no box on the beach, the morn. Repeated searches and wide enquiries failed to find any trace of it, so it was given up for lost.

'It'll be half wye across the North Sea noo!' says Jeemsie, the cook. 'Aye!' says Duncan, the engineer, 'Yon chiel maan be weel scattered noo!'

But the Turk had his doubts.

Not until early summer the following year was there any news at all. Then Jeemsie came aboard one Monday morning, bursting with excitement.

'Hey, Skipper!' says he. 'Ye mine yon box that we lost ower the side? Weel, it's in a little hot-hoosie at the back o een o yon hoosies in Burnhaven. I wis oot there wi my lass, last nicht, an I saw the thing. I'm sure it's the same box!'

The Turk nodded, but said nothing. On the following Saturday, however, he persuaded his good lady to take a walk with him, oot by the Prison an doon the roadie that ran below the railway, an sure enough, there was the boxie, jist as Jeemsie had said.

The Turk found the owner of the box to be a fine affable wifie. 'That's an affa bonny box ye hae oot there,' says he, 'Faar did ye get it?'

'Oh,' says she, 'my loon got it on the beach ae mornin last ear.'

'I wid fairly like to get that boxie,' says the Turk. 'Sentimental value, ye ken, but I'm willin to pey for't.'

'My loon,' says she, 'ye'll get it for naething . . . if ye wyte till my tomatoes comes up!'

The Bottomless Pit

In the long-lost, special years of my childhood I was privileged to share the occasional company of boys from foreign climes: places such as Cullen and other Moray Firth ports, the South Firth (nobody ever spoke of the Firth of Forth), and even places as far away as England. These boys were in the Blue Toon for the summer herring season, their parents being employed in various capacities, ashore and afloat. Indeed there were times when we had these boys as classmates, if the herring season got off to an early start before the beginning of the summer holidays. From the North came the Fletts, Bowies, Mairs, Coulls and Slaters; from the South came the Reekies, Bowmans, Redpaths (Rippots), Lowries and Gowanses, not forgetting the Fairnies and the Meldrums and the Hughes and the Fyalls. We could very often pinpoint a boy's birthplace as soon as we heard his name, but we were always deeply puzzled at the pronunciation of the name 'Allan'! How on earth were we to know that it was 'Ailn'?

How we laughed at the strangers with their peculiar accents. The North loons spoke aboot paint, the Soothies called it pent. Fit wye could they nae spik richt an gie the stuff its richt name . . . Pint? (rhymes with lint.) Ignorant sods! But despite the marked differences in our speech, we got on very well. There was never any strife as we played among the rocks, bilin wulks in sea-water in a syrup tin, and being fearfully sick immediately afterwards. Utterly revolting they were, but it was the done thing with the bigger loons, and we had to copy. We played our simple, homely games together and, if we ever broke a window, it was always a complete accident, and a heart-stopping one at that, for the replacement pane could cost as much as half-a-crown (thirty old pennies), and where would that come from? We had one common bond . . . we never had a copper.

Among the strangers was one unforgettable character by the name of Angus, a very nice boy indeed, with a pronounced Highland lilt to the beautiful English he spoke. He had no connection with the fishing, for his Dad worked in a Bank, and in fact Angus was actually 'slumming it' when he played with the fisher loons. He seemed to enjoy our company, for he became a regular playmate, a warm favourite with us all. Since his father was not of the itinerant fishers, Angus went to school with us too, but one sad fact could not be denied . . . Angus was no academic star. He wasn't stupid, but he certainly was a plodder, and there was no chance that he would ever make it as a banker.

Came the war and I lost sight of Angus altogether. Not until the mid fifties did I see him again and that was on the pier at Lochinver, where he was a casual labourer. It transpired that he had met and married a Wren during the war, and very soon thereafter the couple had settled down in a croft in a rather remote part of the North-west Highlands. There was, apparently, only a very limited income to be derived from the croft but, since his wife was an arty-crafty sort of person who made quite a decent job at pottery-making, and since the bed-and-breakfast trade was in the ascendancy, Angus had few financial worries. He could always pick up a jobbie here and there, although that sometimes involved quite a lot of travelling around; the day I met him, he was some twenty miles from home. But, apart from all that, his granny had left him quite a tidy sum, and he was more or less sitting pretty. He gave me a most cordial invitation to come and meet his Missus, when I could get around to it.

Not before another ten years had passed did I finally get that length, and sadly, Angus had little time to speak to me that day, for he had been inundated by a great host of oil-men who were firmly convinced that Angus was sitting on top of an oil-field. They would like, with his permission, to bore a test well. There would, of course, be one or two minor inconveniences, but the end result could be riches untold.

'Go right ahead!' said Angus, launching into a passable imitation of Topol singing 'If I were a rich Man'.

'Not too fast, Angus!' said the oil gaffer. 'Not too fast. If there's no oil, there's no money. Fair enough?'

'Fair enough.' And they shook hands on it. I took myself off, promising to return at a later date. Well did I realise that it would take a long time to bore a hole of the required depth in what, after all, are the oldest rocks in the world. Next time you are in the North-west, keep your eyes open for mannies fae Japan or other strange places, chappin the rocks wi little haimmeries an writin great screeds o stuff in little wee note-bookies.

It was fully a year later, when I was spending a few days in Kinlochbervie, that my younger daughter drew my attention to some peculiar smoke signals in the southerly sky. Translation of the signals informed me that the sender was Angus, who was issuing an invitation to all and sundry to attend a ceilidh at his place in honour of the opening of his new establishment.

'Aha!' said I, 'He has struck oil at last. I'll go along and congratulate him. I've never been at a ceilidh before, so it should be quite an experience.' So I drove

384

along the tortuous route to Angus' croft, to find a goodly throng already there. From Sheigra and Balchrick and Oldshoremore, they came. From Achriesgill and Achlyness and Rhuvolt came reinforcements, to be joined later by outriders from Scourie and Durness. It was with great difficulty that I managed to get Angus on his own.

'Congratulations on your oil-well,' said I. 'You'll not be speaking to the likes of me shortly, since you are so rich!'

'Ach, man,' was the sad reply, 'it's not an oil-well at all, at all. They bored a hole a whole mile deep, then they gave up, because there was not a trace of oil. They were very disappointed, and so was I, of course. But I did ask them to do me a favour before they left, and they readily agreed.'

'What was the favour, Angus?'

'Well, Peter, I've got a dry loo round the back there. You know the kind I mean. You dig a hole and put the hoosie on top of it, then, in a while you have to dig another hole and shift the hoosie again. I asked the oil-men to set my hoosie on top of the hole they had bored, then I'd never need to dig another hole.'

'And they did it, Angus?'

'They did indeed. In fact they made me a new one, and painted it blue, cos I'm a Rangers man. Then they cemented it down, to counteract the strong winds. It's a really posh do, with a shelf for my flask and another little shelf for my piece. I thought we should celebrate the opening in style!'

Boys, yon wis some ceilidh! The instrumental items were really outstanding, and the dancing was simply exuberant. Less pleasing was the rather rude song about a certain Isabella Fraser, sung by Hector the Post, who then politely asked permission to use the new utility.

'Feel free, friend. To you falls the honour of being the first!'

It was not till we had done the eightsome reel, the Quadrilles, and then the Lancers that Angus noticed that Hector had failed to return. Then the proceedings were brought to a rather discordant close.

'Friends,' said Angus, 'one of our number appears to be missing in outer darkness. We should mount a search-party forthwith.'

The result was that all hands poured out through the door, with Angus at the head, wielding a mighty torch.

Up to the door of the smart little blue shed we marched in a solid phalanx. Several car headlights were switched on to illumine the dark, but there was no sign of Hector. Not until Angus yarked the door open was the secret revealed, for there sat Hector on the box, calm and serene, but nevertheless stone deid!

'Good Lord!' said Angus, playing his torch on the still figure. 'He must have had a heart attack!'

'Never, Angus. Never!' cried Mrs Hector. 'There's never been anything wrong with his heart, but I have warned him before about his silly habit!'

'What habit?' said Angus.

'Holding his breath till he hears the plump!'

Aipple Rings an Apricots

Right next door to the house where I was born and reared there was a grocer's shop, whose proprietor was J G A Stephen, known to most of the fisher folk as Jeems George. The shop is still there, of course, but it's close on fifty year since I left the scene.

Jeems George had two big hurleys bearing the sign, 'Shipping Supplied'. Now, I kent perfectly weel that the shop supplied oatmeal and Abernethy biscuits and great lang bars o washin soap (as distinct fae face soap), and a multitude of other sundries, but I was deeply puzzled as to how they could supply shipping. I had never seen any ships aboot the place, but maybe they took the ships oot an in the close while I was asleep. That's how young I was.

I was always welcome in the shop. 'Oh, that's Jeannie Motherwell's bairn! A gweed-faced innocent loon, affa keen on listenin to the Scriptures. He'll sit for oors, jist listenin.' That was only partly true, cos I was actually watchin a chance for a go at the aipple rings an apricots which were in open boxes, tilted against the front of the counter. There were times when I had to consume quite a heavy dose of Scripture afore I could nip an apricot, but it was always worth the wait. There was a leathery goodness about the dried fruits, a sweet-smelling savour that held me in bondage, and I found that Scripture and apricots went very well together.

Ye see boys, yon wis a Brethren shop, if such a thing can be. There was one eminent Salvationist on the staff, but that didn't seem to present any problem. Apparently Salvationists and Brethren go well together, jist like aipple rings an apricots, but the prevailing atmosphere was Brethren. I am not criticising, but simply stating a fact. Young as I was, it was a something I could sense. It was always a very quiet shop. Customers came and went, but there was never any daffery. Conversation was always calm and civil, and there was an air of peace about the place. Womenfolk came for their groceries and for twine to mend their nets; indeed fisher folk from all over the coast came for twine, for Jeems George had the reputation of having the finest cotton in the land. Hundreds of hanks of cotton hung from the ceiling of the close, after going through some special secret process. Barkit or creosoted, Jeems George's twine was without equal.

The only seat in the shop was a very high wooden chair, on whose back there was a square enamel plate advertising Ogston's soap flakes. I never tasted those, but the memory of them causes me to wonder just how mucky we must have been in the long ago, before the advent of biological washing powders which are supposed to wash whiter than white, and improving every year, too! Jingers, we must have been maithin wi muck athoot the disinfectants and deodorants of this apostate age. Mind you, I always thought that fite claes bleachin on the green were really beautiful. But I digress.

I sat on the high chair and watched the world come and go, learning all the time, although I was unaware of that. My favourite ploy, apart from the antrin aipple ring adventure, was to try to equate the customers with the characters in a book of Bible stories someone had given me as a present. Could this tall man in the sleeved waistcoat be Moses? No! But he could possibly be Joshua. And this aal wifie could be Naomi with Ruth as her companion. Aal Donal, the man in charge of the twine department, was actually Isaiah himself, and the message boy was Timothy.

Thus I peopled my little world with Rachels and Gideons, Pauls and Jonathans, and mighty men of valour. Of course I kent that John the Baptist ate wild locusts and honey, but such a diet could never compare with aipple rings an apricots. Maybe he nivver kent aboot them, peer sowl!

Practically all the male customers were fishermen, desiring private conversation with Jeems George himself, mainly concerning boats and their gear, for Jeems George was a shareholder in quite a few fishing boats. The only collar-and-tie was of course Jeems George's, his clients normally clad in cheese-cutter caip, navy blue jersey with a black silk muffler, sleeved weskit (a very short, double-breasted jacketie, with the sleeves not always of the same material as the bodice), tailor-made trousers of beautiful Kersey cloth from the Norfolk village of that name, and a pair of soft leather ankle boots. Skipper's rig, for sure.

Of course they never discussed business in my hearing, but I soon learned that although these men might be more or less alike in dress, they differed in speech. Even from their short periods of small talk, I learned to spot their separate villages of origin, for their Mither Doric varied slightly from one place to another. The Finnyfaal men, the 'Cannlies', had a tongue which differed subtly from that of their neighbours, the 'Wardies' or natives of Port Errol at the opposite end of the Cruden sands.

The nickname 'Cannlies' for the Whinnyfold men reputedly sprang from their use of candle lanterns when they searched among the rocks for bait for their cod lines, but I would think that a more logical reason for the name lay in the fact that, although they were mainly Plymouth Brethren, they had come originally from the Episcopalian Church, where candles played an important part in proceedings.

The village of Port Errol, near Slains Castle, was originally called 'The Ward' (of Slains), and thus its natives were 'Wardies', a name which is still in common use. But the 'Cannlies', resentful of their own nickname, coined a new name for the 'Wardies', calling them 'Hoolits', creatures that could see in the dark. No doubt the inference was that 'Men loved darkness rather than light, because their deeds were evil'. Nothing more than inter-village jealousy, only skin deep. I, on my lofty throne, classed the 'Cannlies' as the Tribe of Judah, and the 'Hoolits' as the Tribe of Benjamin, strictly without Scriptural authority, of course.

And then, boys, there were the 'Boddamers', mighty men of valour, cast in the same mould as the others, yet using a slightly different form of speech. These, I thought, must be the Philistines, but that put my storybook aa t' scutter, for my Tribesmen and Philistines seemed to get on very well together, jist like aipple rings an apricots. Ye can pit in a fig or twaa for the Boddamers, if ye like.

Even the folk fae Buchanhaven spoke different. Theirs was a slower, broader speech than the Peterheid tongue, so much so that I could spot them right away. Of course, those were the days when there were only two buildings atween the Killin Hoose and Buchanhaven, the Cable Hoosie and the town's very first isolation hospital. Now that Buchanhaven has been completely swallowed up in the sprawl of the Blue Toon, the old tongue has almost disappeared, the only traces being among the older folks, and there's nae a lot o them left noo.

But in Jeems George's shop, where most (but not all) of the customers were Brethren, the Buchaners and the Boddamers and the Hoolits and the Wardies got on famously together, jist like aipple rings an apricots, not forgetting the figs. Oh, ye can pit in a prune or twaa for the Buchaners, if ye like.

'Wis there nae Bluemogganers in the place?' did ye say? Oh aye, there wis aye plinty o them.

How vividly I remember one tall Bluemogganer, whom I addressed as 'Mr. Noble'.

'Faa aichts ye, my loon?' says he.

'I'm een o Jeannie Motherwell's,' says I, 'an I think your shippie has an affa bonny name . . . *Scarlet Thread.*'

'Oh!' says he, fine pleased. 'My name's nae Noble, but Stephen. Noble's my middle name, an I'm Jock Noble cos there's sic a lot o John Stephens aboot the toon. I ken yer folk fine! Div ye ken far the bonny name comes fae . . . *Scarlet Thread?*'

When I confessed my ignorance, he lifted me off the chair and sat me on the counter, taking the chair for himself. Then he patiently told me, in simple words about the scarlet thread, a thread which runs through the Scriptures, if ye ken far t' look! Boys, I nivver forgot yon story nor did I ivver forget the storyteller.

Now, why should I, a Kirk man aa my days, write this tale? Simply because I was asked to do so.

'Man, Peter,' they said, 'ye should write something aboot the Brethren! Something that 'll gar folk's hair curl!'

Well, this is the something, but I'd like to suggest that 'they' (not the Brethren), should tak the aipple rings an the apricots an the figs an the prunes an stew them gently for a fylie. Oh, ye'd better pit in a suppie sugar (for the Bluemogganers, ye ken). Serve wi a drappie o the milk o loving kindness, and sup wi the speen which is called Charity.

It winna gar onybody's hair curl, but it is sure to be a most beneficial tonic!

The Green Pea Pirates

It must have been well into summer when the following events took place, for the parks which sloped down from the South Road to the Bay were carrying a rich crop of what we called 'peys'. They were not sweet peas, but simply the ordinary green peas grown for cattle feed. When they were harvested, stalks, leaves, pods and all, went into a concrete silo along with green corn, to make silage for winter feed. Of course it is only recently that I learned such things, but when I was a

388

youngster, I had never even heard of silage. No, to us fisher loons, they were simply peys, there for the eating, in a day when we would have eaten practically anything, especially if it was forbidden fruit.

Well, now, we were out in force as usual, fifteen or sixteen of us, all from the Central School, albeit from different classes. Johnny Mattha's peys were to be raided; we would touch only the edge of the crop, and when our bellies were full, we would desist. Of course, we would have look-outs posted to watch for the bobby, the warning to be the cry, A.B.C.R.L. (A Bobby Comin, Rin Lads.) The watchmen would be relieved, so that they too might share in the feast but, in the event, our watchers failed us, for the bobbies came, not from the town, but from the South, and what was worse, they came on bikes, the cooards. Only then did we realise that a belly full of green peas is a great hindrance when speed is required, so we were easy prey, a pathetic and very silent group, rounded up like sheep to be marched off to the Police Station. In the Sooth Road, doon throwe the Kirktoon, along Maiden Street and up Merchant Street, to what was sure to be a stiff sentence. Some of us were greetin; all of us were very scared indeed. None had ever been in trouble before.

As we made our way through the streets, we seemed to gather a following of very interested boys who seemed to keep a respectable distance astern, possibly for fear of being nabbed themselves, for we were by no means the only group to have visited the peys. But, as we approached the 'jile', our following melted away. Then, coming towards us from the Broadgate direction, there came a man we all knew as Bailie Buchan. Boys, this was not a good sign, for this was the man who would be our judge when we appeared in court. Although our parents knew him as 'Matey', and we ourselves knew him by the same title, we would not dare use that name to his face.

'Fit's iss ye hiv the nicht, Sergeant?' says he.

'A bourachie o rascals, Bailie! They've been among the peys, ye see. It's nae fit they ait that's the problem, it's fit they trample doon. Eence we get them inside, I'll charge the hale lot, an they'll be up afore ye on Monday for sentence.'

'Will ye hae beds for sic a mob? An fit aboot mait? It's three hale days yet, afore Monday!'

'Och, they can sleep on the fleer, Bailie. An mait winna be a problem. Breid an watter, ye see, breid an watter! The peys in their bellies should laist for a while, onywye.'

'I doot we'd better get them inside, Sergeant. Then I'll hae a look at my bookie, cos I think I'm full up for Monday.'

Thus we were ushered into the jile, but not into cells, as we had dreaded. Instead, we found ourselves in a large room, on our right as we entered the place. The Sergeant positioned himself close to the door, while the Bailie seated himself at the table, surveying us with a very severe expression. There was not even a flicker of mercy in his eyes. We had undoubtedly met our Waterloo!

'Now, Sergeant,' says the Bailie, 'I think we'd better hae a coort here, the nicht. Will ee write doon the evidence, an aifter I'm throwe wi them, we'll decide the punishment.'

'Aye, fairly!' says the Sergeant. He wis fae the country, ye see. That's fit wye he said 'Fairly' instead o 'Surely'.

'Noo!' says the Bailie, 'We'll start the proceedins now. If there's brithers among ye, ye'd better stan thegither, so's we can get aheid faster. I'll need yer name an address. See that ye spik fin ye're spoken till, an dinna try nae lees! . . . First!'

It happened that the first culprit wis twins. Ye ken fit I mean.

'Buchan, 4, Jamaica St.'

'Oh!' says the Bailie, 'Ee'll be Sonnie's Ailick's twins. A sair affront to yer folk, specially to Kirsten, yer mither.'

(The building comprising No's 2 and 4, occupied the Jamaica Street to St. Andrew Street corner, No.2 being the town's first Post Office. The house has been completely demolished within the last month to facilitate a new extension to the premises of the Donald family (Dodie Donal) but, since the house was a listed building, its facade must be rebuilt exactly as it was, to preserve the traditional appearance.)

'Next!'

'John Reid, 15 Jamaica St.'

'Oh, a Sprulie, are ye? Ye should ha kent better! Next!'

'Andrew Cowe, Merchant St.'

'Aye, aye. So Tey Briggie'll be yer mither? I'm sure she'll hae a wordie or twaa for ye! Next!'

Andrew's mother Jeannie was always known as Tey Briggie, cos she was born on the night of the Tay Bridge disaster, Since there was a Mrs Cowe on either side of her, one of them also a Jeannie, the by-name served a very useful purpose.

Next to face the Inquisitor were the Buchans from 5, Jamaica St. (my brother and I).

'Ee'll be twaa o Jeannie Motherwell's, noo! A sair affront to yer mither, awyte, an I'm sure yer father winna be very pleased.'

The hale toon kent my mither as Jeannie Motherwell, thinking that such an outlandish name must be a by-name. Not until she died did they learn that Motherwell was her real name. And for some peculiar reason, my sister is known by the same name, although she is Mrs. Stephen.

The tears had dried up by this time, and we gazed very attentively at this man who seemed to know every mortal thing there was to know about us. Every one of us was somebody's so-and-so, in the good old fisher style. Those who are not of fisher stock may be inclined to poke fun at the system, but it is in fact like a laser beam, dead on target. There has to be some sort of system of identification in a community where both Christian names and surnames are so widely shared, especially if that community is confined to a rather small area. It so happens that random thoughts on this subject seem to remind me of the old Sankey hymn, 'We shall know as we are known.'

And so we were all duly identified, and this seemed to be the conclusion of the evidence, for the Bailie addressed the Sergeant . . .

'Hiv ye gotten aa that written doon, noo?'

'Aye fairly, Bailie! I'm wytin for you to pass sentence. That's your job, nae mine.'

'Weel noo, Sergeant, I've nivver hannled a case like this afore, so maybe you could suggest a suitable punishment?'

'A fine?' says the Sergeant. 'Five shillins, maybe?'

'Nae five shillin's the piece, Sergeant. Surely no!'

'Michty no, Bailie, but seein that they acted in concert, they could be fined in concert. Five shillin's wid cover the lot, I think.'

The tears had begun to flow again, and there were a few whimpering assertions that we hadn't been at any concert; we had been among the peys!

'Hiv ye five shillins among ye?' said the Bailie, to quell the hubbub. Dead silence! We didna hae five maiks!

'That winna dee, Sergeant. Ye'll hae to come up wi something better. Fit dis the Statute Book say?'

'Weel noo, Bailie,' says the Bobby, consulting a huge volume, 'the punishment for stealin a sheep is hangin. I wid think that stealin peys wid be the same. But ye're duty bound to tell the mithers first!'

This reduced every one of us hardened criminals to a nervous wreck and the noise was wondrous loud.

'Be quaet!' shouted the Bailie. 'Hud yer tongues a meenit till I consider the verdict.' Then he seemed to lapse into a few moments of meditation.

Boys, the silence was a punishment in itself, as we stood there in apprehension. What would our judge decide? At last he lifted up his head to address the Bobby in this fashion . . .

'Sergeant, I'm nae jist affa willin, but if ee ging an look for the rope, I'll see aboot tellin the mithers.'

As the Sergeant left the room, there was pandemonium in court, and the Bailie had to shout hard to restore order.

'Noo lads,' says he, 'I think it'll tak the Bobby a fyle to get the rope, cos it hisna been seen for a lang time. But, if I lat ye hame, will ye bide awaa fae the peys?'

The response was as deafening as it was unanimous. 'AYE.' There was one mad rush for the door and I was trampled underfoot for a few moments with my face close to the pages on which the Sergeant had been writing. Ye ken iss, boys, they were completely blank! And the Bailie nivver did tell oor mithers. And anither thing . . . we nivver lookit at Johnny Mattha's peys again.

Hame Comfort

The first time I met Jeems, he wis sittin at his broth, in a great muckle kitchen that had flagsteens for a fleer. The table wis covered wi a baize cloth that had a bonny floral design, and the hale place had an air of cleanliness, albeit the furnishings were a bittie aal fashioned. I had been met at the door by the Lady of the House, who bade me enter and 'see the man himsel'. She also bade me 'sit in aboot an hae a bite', and thus I found mysel confrontit wi the most enormous plate o broth I had ivver seen. Mind you, it wis hardly a day for broth, for it wis the warmest day in livin memory, and the verra tar wis meltin on the roads.

I mind that afore I sat doon, I shifted my cheer and my plate a wee bittie, to a position less close to the great muckle flee-paper that wis hingin fae the ceiling. I'm tellin ye, boys, yon thing wis as thick an as black as a drifter's tarry rope. I jist didna like the look o't avaa.

Jeems noticed my move, an remarked in a joking tone, 'Aha! You fishers is a fly lot!' Then he burst into laughter at his own pun. 'A fly lot, By jingers!' says he. 'That's a good bit! I wis aye clivver, but man, I'm growin better.' Then, in a more serious tone he continued, 'Ye jist canna win, ye canna win! Ye open the winda for fresh air, an ye're tormentit wi a vermint o flees. Ye shut the winda, an ye're aboot smored wi heat. Same wi the door, only that the door's waar than the winda. This heat beats aa; the verra beasts in the parks is fair dementit wi the flees, an fyles I could be deein wi a tail mysel to swipe the sic-an-sics. They fairly torment me, specially fin I'm swytin. Jist look at that great hullick o the fousome beasties, bizzin an rattlin aboot atween the sashes o the open winda. Fit a soun they're makkin. They seem to ken far they're safe, cos naebody can win at them there!'

'Ye could aye try the hoover!' says I.

It appeared as if I had dropped a bombshell, for there was a moment of hushed surprise, before Mrs Jeems ran to the pantry for the hoover. Then, fitting the narrowest nozzle, she thrust it down amongst the menagerie o bumbees and switched on. Boys, yon wis worth seein, for the hale kinabberie gid up the spoot into the bag in three seconds flat!

In the remarkable silence which followed Mrs Jeems remarked, 'Ye're a fair chiel, min, a fair chiel! Ye should ha been here lang ago. Fit gart ye think aboot the hoover? I winna get mine laid by noo!'

I made a suitably modest reply, but I refrained from disclosing that I had seen the hoover treatment on another farm that very day. I'm nae feel aathegither, ye ken. I had gained a friend whom I later called Belle (at her own insistence).

Now then, dinner past, and the 'bottlers' well and truly slachtered, Jeems and I got down to business.

'Noo!' says he, 'fit aboot iss tunk? Ye say I'll get a new tunk for naethin if I agree to tak aa my diesel fae you. Div ye mean that?'

'Aye, surely!' says I. 'Ye jist need to sign a paperie, an ye'll get a free tunk.'

'Aha!' says he, 'I'm nae signin nae paperies; my word's my bond!' So I took him at his word, and he got his free tunk, and for the few years that were left of his working life we were very friendly. There were the occasions when he laughed himself silly at my fisher expressions, but I must confess that there were times when I laid it on thick for his benefit. Well do I remember the day when I found it impossible to turn my vehicle in his close, and Jeems wis a wee bittie concerned.

'Dinna fash yersel!' says I. 'I'll jist ging oot astarn.' Boys, he fairly enjoyed that.

There wis one thing aboot Jeems that was beyond dispute . . . he wis the boss on the fairm, an aabody kent it. Naebody wid daar conter Jeems, specially on fairmin maitters, for Jeems wis a first class fairmer. Even I kent that. Despite his lack of interest in modern fertilisers, Jeems produced good crops year after year, so much so that he became some sort of bye-word in the farming community, and experts from The College would regularly visit the farm whose success seemed at times to annoy them.

'Ach,' says Jeems, 'it's the dung, min. It's dung for aa, min, dung for aa. Ye canna beat the dung!' An organic champion, Jeems.

Now, Jeems and Belle had a dother, Cynthia, who was at the Varsity for a degree, intending to be a teacher, and, like a puckle mair, Cynthia wis inclined to be a wee bittie uppity and maybe a wee bittie affrontit at her folk. Cam the day when a procession of visitors had kept both Belle and Jeems busy, and Cynthia (after a ferocious glower from her father) had condescended to dry the dishes.

'Mam,' she confided, 'I do wish that Dad would be less free with that awful word 'dung'. Surely he must know there's a better word!'

'My quine,' says Belle, 'it's teen me mair than twinty 'ear to get him to use that word, so ye'd better lat that flee stick to the waa!' So Cynthia, after a moment's thought, never raised the subject again. A bigsy bizzom, yon.

Noo, while Jeems wis the undisputed boss on the fairm, his authority disappeared entirely as soon as he entered the kitchie door, for there Belle reigned supreme. Jeems had the sense to accept this, as all sensible men do. Those poor males whose stupidity prevented them from seeing the excellence of this rule usually come aff by the loss. Serves them richt!

Belle wis a great housewife, the sworn enemy of dirt in any shape or form. A quaet lass as a rule, but boys, she fairly swore at the flees, and I couldna blame her. On the rare occasions when I was permitted to enter the house proper, I felt as if I were in a holy of holies which I should not have entered without removing my sheen, if not my very feet. Ye ken the wye o't! Jeems remarked one day that I must be a special sort of fella to be allowed 'ben the hoose', cos that was a privilege for the likes of the Minister, or the Doctor, or the Dominie. What had I done to merit Belle's favour?

'Ye're forgettin the bumbees an the hoover!' says I, an he leuch. He loved to tak the len o me, and I tried hard to keep my end up. One day he made an earnest plea that sometime when I wis passing, I should 'fess oot a kipper', for he fairly likit a kipper. So, the following week I duly obliged, and went to his door with a neat little parcel containing one solitary fish.

'Fit's iss?' says he, takin the kipper by the tail.

'Ye can surely see fit it is,' says I. 'Ye socht a kipper, so I've fessen oot a kipper. Is there something wrang wi't?'

Boys, he didna half sweer, then he sat on the doorstep an leuch till he wis near greetin. Belle came oot to see fit aa the hilarity wis aboot, an she said, 'Peter likes a tattie. Gie the hungry sic-an-sic a tattie!'

Belle noticed the single kipper and with a smile she produced one single spud; so we were square. Of course I had a box o kippers in the van, and there wis a bag o tatties there when I left. All in fun, ye ken.

According to the Beuk, we spend our years as a tale that is told, and the time cam for Jeems to retire. Belle wis quite happy to leave the place, and flit to a new hoose, but Jeems had enough sense to realise that the change would bring problems. Belle would be busy aboot the hoose, but fit wid he dee athoot the beasts, an the craps, an aa the fairm wark? A gairden? Nivver! He had nivver been interested in flooers. Ach! He wid hae a holiday for a start, an see fit like aifterhin. Meantime I had an open invitation to call and see the couple anytime.

Then cam the day I saw Jeems in the toon in the foreneen, a maist bye-ornar time for him.

'Fit like, freen?' says I. 'Fit brings ye here at this time o day, an faar's Belle?'

'Oo!' says he, 'Dinna mention Belle! I'm hyterin aboot here like a lost sheep, an I'm feart t' ging hame!'

I sensed there wis something vrang, so I said, 'Hiv ye gotten yer fly the day?'

'No I hinna, an fit's mair, I'm oot athoot siller, so I'm stuck.'

'Jist ee come awaa hame wi me,' says I. 'We'll seen sort that.'

Thus it came to pass that, ower a fly-cup in the hoose, I got the hale story.

'Man, Peter, we hid a gran holiday; a hale fortnicht tourin here an there on the Continent. That's the first richt holiday I've heen in my life, an I fair enjoyed it. Noo, afore we gid awaa, Belle arranged for the painter, an the jiner, an the electrician to dee some jobbies aboot the hoose. It's nae a fire new hoose, ye see, an Belle wis needin things to her ain mine. Ye ken the wye o't. Fin we got hame, a fortnicht seen, I thocht the hoose wis affa bonny, cos the painter employed twaa weemin to see that aathing wis in order, but that widna dee wi Belle. Oh, no! She's been bizzin aboot like a bumbee aa day, ivvery day. She disna like the idea o carpet in the lobby so the canvas is shinin like glaiss; in fact I'm feart to pit my fit on't. Ye ken the wye o't. Weel, iss mornin I wis sittin readin the paper, an I hid jist gotten half throwe the 'Deaths' fin she cam in wi her dusters an her brushies, an she took my pooer awaa aathegither. It wis, "Shift a bittie, Jeems," an "Ye're in the road noo, Jeems," till I wis aboot demintit.'

'At lang linth she put aathing awaa, an clappit doon aside me. "Noo!" she says, "That's me throwe!" "Thunk the Lord," says I, aneth my breath. But, man, she happened to look oot the winda, an faa wis comin up the path but Leebie, the fishwife wi her creel on her back.'

' "Oh my govies!" cries Belle, "I'll need to rin an open the door afore Leebie pits her fool han on the bonny knob," an she gid ben the lobby like a mountain goat. Noo, apparently Leebie trippit on the step, an put oot her han on the knob to steady hersel, but the knob gid awaa fae her, cos Belle wis openin the door! So Leebie fell clyte on her belly, richt in at the door, an the hale birn o fish cam skitin ower her heid an ben the lobby like snaa slidin aff the reef!'

'Oh, Jeems!' says I, 'Fit a disaster!'

'Disaster?' says he. 'It wis that, an mair. Ye see, I couldna help lauchin, an that wis the worst thing avaa, for Belle turned on me like a serpent, an I ran for my life. That's the wye I'm here.'

We were baith enjoying a richt fine lauch, fin the phone rang. Oh, aye, it wis Belle.

'Is my man there, Peter?'

'Oh, aye!' says I. 'He's sittin here greetin!'

'That'll be the day! Tell him to come awaa hame . . . I'm lauchin mysel noo.' This wis to be Leebie's last day on the road, an seein that the accident wis my blame, I've bocht aa her fish. Tell Jeems to fess hame a big Freezer!'

The Vision

The bairn had lost her shoe in the burn which ran past the house to spend itself in a peaty froth among the dark grey boulders on the foreshore of the loch, some two hundred yards distant. Of course the bairn was always losing things in the burn, which seemed to fascinate her, especially the place where the water disappeared beneath the road, to reappear in a very few seconds among the rocks, for the road was a Highland road, less than ten feet wide. The dark tunnel was strictly forbidden territory, so, to follow the docken leaves and the morsels of peat which comprised the youngster's 'fleet', she had to cross the road, an adventure in itself. There were no twigs available, for the nearest trees were at least ten miles away. It is possible that the want of a real boat had constrained the bairn to launch her shoe upon the waters, for her repeated requests for a boatie had fallen on deaf ears.

Three years old she was, yet I had scarcely seen her, for it was war-time, and I, along with countless others, was a man under authority. Although not in uniform, I was as much a prisoner of the Navy as any uniformed matelot. In fact, as engineman on a former Lossie fishing boat, I had been denied leave altogether, on the grounds that I was apparently the only one who could keep her engine going. Oh, I would be immediately granted a pass for my wife and daughter to enter the Protected Area, but I would have to find my own accommodation.

That one-room accommodation I found on a croft, some two miles from the Naval base at Aultbea, on the north shore of Loch Ewe, in a district called Mellon Charles. The cramped living space was nothing new to us, for it was exactly the same as we had at home, albeit there was one outstanding difference. At home we had a flush toilet in the close at the rear of the house, but now we had to make ourselves comfortable in the byre, beside the cow; not too close, you know, for Betsy had a playful habit of kicking any posterior which might venture within range of her rear hoof.

So, here was I, a stranger in the midst of a Gaelic speaking people, a race whose outlook on life differed in several ways from mine . . . East is East and West is West! There was no real language barrier; both sides could resort to English (with very different accents, of course). I was finding the West-coasters to be a very kindly race, with delightful manners. My stay among them was to be fairly lengthy, for not until I had trained somebody to take my place in the engine room was I to be granted leave. In those days diesel engines were in their infancy. Fishermen abhorred them and the Navy looked upon them as a necessary evil. Men who had a working knowledge of diesels were vary scarce indeed, for we were still in the age of steam.

Well now, here was I at home for the night, and the bairn had lost her shoe in the burn. That had given rise to a minor panic, not that the shoe was particularly valuable, but bairns' shoes were bairns' shoes, not all that easy to come by, since valuable coupons would be required for any replacement. And an even more important aspect was the fact that the nearest shoe-shop was at least sixty miles away. So my better half had gone to help the bairn retrieve the missing shoe. That was when I decided that, quine or no quine, the bairn should have a boat. A bit of firewood whittled into shape would suffice, and it could be used over and over again.

As I sat on the wooden bench which spanned most of the breadth of the gable of the house, I whittled away with a sharp knife, trimming and shaping the block of wood and admiring the wonderful view. Mountains and islands stood bright and clear in the glorious evening sunshine and I found myself thinking that it would be very pleasant to live here in peacetime.

I was joined presently by the Lady of the House, a quiet, dignified, gracious person to whom I had taken an instant liking when first we met. Apparently the feeling had been mutual, for we got on remarkably well together. She never used my Christian name, insisting on calling me Bochan (the Gaelic way).

We sat there a long time in the summer sun, discussing the war and the latest news bulletins. She was eager to hear of my eighteen-month spell on the Thames estuary; how waves of bombers passed regularly overhead on their way to bomb London; how magnetic and acoustic mines had sunk so many fine ships in the shallow approaches to the Thames; how the platforms of the stations on the London Underground were crowded with homeless families, more or less living there. She found it rather difficult to understand such things, but she did enjoy my graphic descriptions of the Kent orchards in their Spring blossom.

She in turn told me something of her own experiences. She was old, you see. In fact I thought she was very old indeed, but then I was looking at her across a span of more than fifty years. Seven stalwart sons had she borne, with never a daughter to help. Shonachan, the only son still with his mother, had gone to a neighbouring croft to borrow a set of brushes to sweep the chimney. My limited store of Gaelic told me that 'Shonachan' really meant 'Little John' but he was in actual fact a gentle giant.

The old lady's fingers were badly twisted and bent, the result of many years of wringing her washing by hand. There could be no other reason, she thought.

Never in all her life had she possessed a wringer, and the younger women who favoured such things were not nearly so tough as their elders. She had certainly never heard of arthritis, and I deemed it best not to enlighten her. Well, even among East-coasters arthritis was a new word for rheumatics, which seemed to be dying out. Nobody who was anybody would confess to having rheumatics; it had to be the new complaint, and the word was flogged to death. It had to be 'arthuritis' or nothing.

The search for the missing shoe seemed to be meeting with little success, but I ignored repeated visual signals to come and help; I was perfectly O.K. where I was, thank you. I was listening and learning at the feet of a highly intelligent and very articulate tutor. I heard how my companion, as a teenager, had walked with two friends all the way to Strathpeffer, to take up domestic service in one of the hotels there. Not for them the long roundabout route of the modern road. They preferred the old drovers' tracks through the waste of hills and glens, the route they would take on their homeward journey at the end of the season. Wages were nominal, but they did of course get their food and a bed. There were occasional tips from the hotel guests, but the most important aspect was the fact that for three or four months their parents didn't have to provide for them. That in itself was a great help.

I heard how some of her male relations had found employment at the building of the aluminium factory at Foyers and had brought home explosives to blast from the peat bogs the great, massive roots, which were all that was left of the Caledonian pine forest that had once clad the glens. Bleached white with age, the roots were thoroughly dried before being sawn into short lengths, which in turn were split into thin tapers, the only source of domestic lighting. Stuck into bottles at vantage points in the kitchen, the tapers provided a soft white light, and not a little heat. It was the youngsters' job to see that the tapers were replaced when necessary. Only at Christmas was there paraffin for the big lamp, and only at Christmas was there 'shop' bread, which came by steamer from the South. What a treat!

I was completely lost in her tales of the old days, until she suddenly remarked, 'You're making a nice job of that boat. That'll be for the bairn to sail in the burn, I suppose.'

'Yes, indeed,' said I, rather pleased. 'A little fishing boat. Did you ever have anything to do with the fishing?'

She was silent for a whilie, apparently deep in thought, then she replied, 'Not exactly, Mr Bochan. Not exactly. But I remember very clearly one day when, as a little girl I was in the house playing with my wooden dolly . . . Not this house, you know, but the old 'black' house where I was born, the house which eventually became the present steading, just across the field there.

'My mother was outside hanging out some washing by the gable, just a normal everyday task. Then I heard her call in great excitement, "Come, my little one, come quickly."

'I ran to see what all the fuss was about, to find my mother gazing towards the loch with a radiant look on her face, and gaily waving a towel above her head.

"Look, my child, look! Here are the lads, home from the West. See them rounding the island! There's your father at the helm, and your brothers making ready to lower the sail. You'll have company tonight sure enough. See, now, your Dad has spotted you . . . he's waving to you. Aren't you going to wave back to him?"

'Where's the boat, Mother?' said I. 'I don't see anybody waving!'

"Right there before you!" she said, "Surely you can see that?" Then she seemed to come awake from some sort of trance, and ran into the house to fall upon her bed, wildly weeping. I ran as fast as I could for our neighbour.

'Not till late next day did the Minister come with the sad tidings that my father and brothers would not be coming home at all. The boat had been lost with all hands off Castlebay. Just the day before! That's all I ever had to do with the fishing. Good evening, Mr Bochan.'

And she left me alone with my thoughts, and with a feeling that the evening had somehow turned rather cool.

You know, we never did find the lost shoe.

The Buchan Hole

Around the turn of the century James Bergen Sulisker Buchan was born in a humble butt-and-ben in the fisher toon of Buchanhaven. The earthen floors of the rude dwelling were covered with a thin layer of sand from the shore, sand which was swept up and thrown out regularly, to be replaced with a fresh layer. There was always an inexhaustible supply of sand within easy reach. For most of the year there was the unmistakeable smell of mussel bait about the hoosie, for James' Da was a smaa-line fisherman, with a smaa boat and a fleet of haddock lines. At certain times and seasons there was also the overpowering stench of seaweed, rotting in great masses on the beach. Farmers from far and near came with their horse-drawn carts for great loads of the stuff, for rotten seaweed, or 'ware', as the locals called it, is a wonderful fertiliser. Hence the name, Ware Road, the track used by the farm vehicles. Strange as it may seem, despite the thousands of cart-loads removed by the country folk, the stuff never seemed to diminish in quantity. The sea put the stuff there, and only the sea, in its own good time, could remove it.

Thus the scene of James' infancy, a village where poverty was the norm, and bairns were ten a penny. Hunger was never very far from the door.

When our hero's mother was at the gutting of the herring in the curing yards, he was cared for by his maternal Grunny, who had no sons of her own. She loved the little fella very dearly indeed, and coined for him a special pet-name, 'Bubbly-cuffs', an exceedingly apt name, to be sure. As was to be expected, the name stuck, and was freely used by the boy's playmates, until he grew big enough and tough enough to physically resent it. Then the name was shortened to 'the Cuffer'. Only in school was he known by his proper name.

At the tender age of thirteen, the Cuffer was at sea with his father, but sea-sickness defeated him, and he was obliged to seek employment ashore. This he found on a neighbouring farm, but he didn't stay there very long, complaining that he was 'gey bare maitit' (very poorly fed) and very poorly paid. So, finally, he ran away from home, and made his way to the wonderful continent of America where the streets were paved with gold and dollars grew on trees.

Since he had landed in one of the great cities, where there were neither fisher nor country folk, the Cuffer was very, very lonely and found the going extremely tough. He soon discovered that it was possible to be 'gey bare maitit' in America, and he saw a fair number of youngsters who were as worthy of the title Bubbly-cuffs as he himself had ever been. Steady employment was very hard to find so the poor Cuffer drifted from one temporary post to another. I have heard that his first job was in a textile factory whose speciality was the manufacture of sleeved waistcoats for lobsters. He didna like that job, cos it was ower feykie. Then he found himself in a factory where they rowed jars roon aboot jam. He didna like that job either . . . it wis ower het.

Acute depression and severe hamesickness drove the poor fella to the pier where he had landed many months before, and there he looked in vain for a kind, homeward-bound Scot who might pay his fare home. A real optimist, the Cuffer. There was abundant evidence of wealth as women in fur coats, and men with Stetson hats and cigars, ascended the gangways of the great liners, but never a sympathetic word for the poor exile.

At last, unable to face the cruel world any longer, the Cuffer decided to end it all, so he made for one of the city parks, to look for a tree whereon to hang himself with a length of old rope from one of the ships. There were plenty of trees around, strong heavy trees at that; but when our hero finally steeled himself to commit the ghastly deed, the rope failed to take his weight, and he fell clyte on his face on the bare earth at the bole of the tree. Fair dammert wi the dunt, he lay wi's nose among the muck, fechtin sair for breath, an seein spots afore 'is een. Gey sair made, the loon.

'Ach!' says he till himsel, 'It's nae worth the cannle!' Then he realised that it wisna spots he wis seein, but some kind o pellets. In fact, there wis a pellet up 'is nose. Close examination disclosed that the pellets were actually tangible proof that there were rabbits in this park; nae verra big rabbits, mind ye, but nevertheless, rabbits. This discovery brought on a great sense of nostalgia, as he recalled the happy days he had spent with his snares on the bents near his home. But this gradually wore off as a flash of inspiration illumined his mind as to the viability of the pellets so, gathering the driest ones into his hanky, he made for the park-keeper's lodge, where he borrowed a handful of flour.

When next we see the Cuffer, he's back on the pier selling white pills, a genuine cure for sea-sickness. He found a ready market among the elegant ladies who were boarding the *Mauretania* to make the Atlantic crossing.

'Swally them hale, noo, quines!' he would say to his eager clients and, when pressed for a translation of these words, he said that 'Swallythemhale' was an ancient Red Indian term for 'Peace in the belly'. I tellt ye he wis a Buchan!

From scenes like these, auld Scotia's grandeur springs, and soon the Cuffer had a thriving business, employing an extensive staff of youngsters to gather the raw material, which was now coated with icing-sugar instead of the original flour. As time passed, the business steadily expanded until there were 'Swallythemhale' pills for every mortal malady that the Cuffer's fertile mind could invent. No matter what the ailment, the basic ingredients for the pills never varied. 'Herbal medicine', he called it. In a year or two Swallythemhale had a chain of drug-stores across the States, and the Cuffer had a magnificent mansion in its own grounds.

Then came the day when the affluent Cuffer crossed the Herring Pond to visit his parents in their sunset days. He found them hale and hearty in the old house, which had changed little, apart from the fact that there was now gas lighting in place of the Tilley lamps, and linoleum on the floors in place of the sand. The yarns he told were simply incredible, but he never said a word aboot rubbits. Aabody kent he wis affa weel aff, a Droggist, or something.

A day or two before his return to the States, the Cuffer took a turnie into the Blue Toon to say fareweel to some of his former friends. Noo, faa div ye think he fell in wi, but Dodie Wilson an Charlie Duncan, schoolmates of the long ago. The pair o them wis howkin a hole in the road jist across fae the Station (now the Community Centre).

'Look faa iss is comin doon the road!' says Charlie. 'Zat nae the Cuffer? I haard he wis hame. Maybe it's jist a Yunk, but it looks like oor aal crony.'

'Sotiz!' says Dodie, 'Sotiz. Man he looks gey weel aff noo. Div ye think he'll spik till's?' This he said because they were hole-howkers, and Droggists have no dealings with hole-howkers (till they're deid, of coorse). But the Cuffer wisna neen bigsy, and recognised his brethren.

After a short period of small talk, the Cuffer remarked, 'That's a fine hole ye're howkin there. Fit's the hole for?'

'We nivver ken fit the holes is for,' says Dodie. 'We jist howk them for the Cooncil.'

'It's a rare hole!' says the Cuffer. 'I wid fairly like a hole like that in my lawn, across in the States. Jist to mine me on hame, ye ken.'

There was silence for a moment, then Charlie ventured, 'If ye're sair seekin a hole, Cuffer, we could maybe sell ye iss een!'

'That wid be grand,' says the Cuffer. 'Foo muckle wid ye be seekin for't?'

'Weel,' says Charlie, 'as ye can see, it's a gryte muckle hole, an it's solid clay. It's teen a gey lot o howkin, an it's an affa bonny shape. There's nae a lot o holes lik iss aboot the toon. A hunner powen, I wid say.'

'OK,' says the Cuffer. 'But fit aboot the shippin o't? That'll cost ye a gey bit.' says Dodie. 'Ye see, we'll need a craan t' lift the thing, an we'll need a cairt t' tak it t' Aiberdeen. I hear there's a shippie there, loadin seed tatties for America. The skipper wid need a powen or twaa afore he'll tak it inower. It's nae ivvery skipper that'll ging oot wi a hole in 'is ship.'

The Cuffer understood perfectly the problems involved, and parted with a further fifty quid to clinch the deal, before leaving the two pals to finish the job.

'Fit wye are we gaan t' lift iss hole?' says Charlie. 'I've nivver lifted a hole afore.'

'Nae bother avaa,' says Dodie. 'We'll screw a puckle eyebolts intillt so's the slings can get a hud, but we'll need a twa-three bits o timmer t' keep the hole open. Itherwise it micht crack. The Cooncil'll nivver miss iss hole; they've thoosans o holes aa ower the toon. We'll get the Cooncil craan at denner time, an we'll get the len o a larry fae Jimmy Reid. I'm fine acquaint wi Jimmy.'

Behold, now, the appointed time, the hole being lifted bodily, and being rather gingerly lowered onto the waiting vehicle, whose springs sagged visibly under the tremendous weight. Mind you, it wis some hole! Great problems were encountered in the lashing of the load, for the blessed thing kept wobbling about.

'We'd better mak sure it's ticht,' says Charlie, 'cos if the bobbies sees a shoggly hole on the back o the larry, they winna be neen shuited.'

Weel noo, the twaa rascals pinched a coil o aal rope fae the back o the market an lashed the hole to the larry so that it couldna possibly move. Then the great adventure began in earnest. Oot the Sooth road they tootled fine an canny, but . . . there's aye a something!

Some public spirited citizen at the Dreel Hall alerted the Police, an afore the larry wis at the Lido, a police car wis on their tail. The twaa bobbies wis fair mesmerised; they had nivver seen the like afore. Weel, ye see, they were young! Noo, jist abreist o the Prison, did the hole nae faa oot throwe the ropes, an the police car fell intillt.

Fit a stashie! Thirty days they got for makkin a hole in the road!

Of coorse, the bobbies confiscated the hole, so the Cuffer nivver got 'is hole aifter aa. I'm sure it's still lyin up in the jile. Exhibit A.

Boys, I'm beginnin t' think ye winna believe iss story . . . There's ower mony holes in't.

It's a Bear

On a day when the world was slightly younger than it is now, a coracle with a solitary occupant left the rocky foreshore beneath the tiny fisher settlement which was one day to become Peterhead. The morning was cold and still, with not even a zephyr to ruffle the waters' face, but the weather forecast was bad, very bad. Not that there were newspapers or any other sources of information on weather matters . . . the forecast was writ large in the hoar frost which covered the ground with a coating thick enough to retain the imprints of the young man's feet. That, coupled with the unusually strong glare from the sun in the cloudless sky was simply shouting a warning of what was imminent, namely 'Storm!'

Even to this very day Nature gives us signals of changes in the weather, but somehow we fail to notice them, preferring to listen to a mannie in a distant studio explaining to us the intricacies of a multi-coloured weather chart on our T.V. screens, and speaking all the time of Highs and Lows, Fronts and Isobars, Pulses of Rain, Showers spotted by Radar, et cetera, et cetera. Never does he mention hoar frost or, as we know it fite frost. But, come to think of it, the fella has maybe never seen such a thing. When did you last see it yourself, like snow on the ground? Has it gone from Nature's scheme of things? Maybe the Global Warming fellas have more sense than some of us are prepared to admit, especially when we pause to consider that the Fish House in Golf Road was used as a store for blocks of ice cut from the River Ugie. And that wasn't yesterday. But without going back into history, let me put this to you . . . If your bairns can remember seeing real icicles, then they are no longer bairns.

Now, then, Dan in the coracle knew perfectly well that the weather would soon break; he was young, but he was no fool. He was not willingly in the boatie that morning, but his mother had demanded that he bestir himself and fetch some fish from the bay. That in itself was nothing new, for Dan prided himself in being the fisherman of the family, providing a regular supply of beautiful reddish brown codlings whose unusual colour came from the brown weed and tangles of their environment. 'Warrie codling' they were called, and their flesh was as white as the driven snow, and simply delicious. He caught his fishies with a hand-line and mussel bait close to the Codlin Rock which, to use a present day location, is at the fitt o Merchant Street. 'Ah!' says the older generation, 'Peter's awaa back at least a hunner 'ear. There widna be life there noo!'

Strange that they should say such a thing, for in the house I have a score of such fishies, salted and dried against the coming winter, and all of them caught at the 'fitt o the Lifeboat Slip'. The label on the container lid says June 1990. This in spite of all the blasting and upheaval of the past two years, and the building of the new breakwater. Jist at the door, freen, jist at the door! So Dan and I are kindred spirits, separated only by time; and what is time when the Builder of the Universe reckons a thousand years as one day?

'Dan, my loon, dinna bring nae mair codlins. I wid like a fresh dab for the supper, an ye ken far to get dabs. Awaa ye go noo!' So the youngster set off across the bay for the rocks at Craig-na-bo (Hill of the cattle), rocks now completely buried below Asco Base. Between these rocks the sea bed was of lovely golden sand, ideal for flukes (flat-fish), and such fish were there in abundance. Dan knew that, with his spear, he would have no difficulty in catching flukes, but his mother had stipulated that only dabs were required. She didn't want freshies (flounders), nor did she want 'plashies' (plaice), so Dan would have to be selective, and that meant having patience.

There were places amongst these rocks where one fell swipe with the spear would have transfixed as many as eight or ten fish at a time, just like kebabs on a stick. Here we have the origin of the term 'spear deep', applied to the abundance of fish. Only old codgers like myself use the term now, and even then only in wishful thinking, but the term is actually based on fact, however ancient.

I have never speared a fish, but I did have a go at it some ten years ago, on the self same spot that Dan fished. I had a first class 'stabber' and a glass bottomed box through which I could see the sandy bottom very clearly, but I had no success. They were most certainly not spear deep! But I do remember seeing a box of plaice caught there with the stabber, by James Strachan 'Tatters', former lifeboat Coxswain, and his son Reidie, in a boatie called *The Brothers*. That would be around 1927, and the old style fish box was filled level with twelve fish (6 stone). I have never seen the like again.

But let's get back to Dan. The lad had caught a full dozen beautiful dabs and was thinking that another half dozen would satisfy his mother. His gaze was fixed on the sandy bottom as the coracle drifted silently with the tide, and so intent was he that he failed to notice his own carelessness in that he had left his paddle with the blade projecting outboard. This, when the wind came, was fatal, for the paddle was lifted clean over the side and Dan was helpless. The wind came on him like a wolf on the fold and the boatie went skimming before it like a saucer. Dan had hopes that she would ground on the island which would one day be called Keith Inch, but she missed it narrowly, so there was nothing now between him and the Orkneys, of whose existence he was completely ignorant.

The first blasts of the wind had been somewhat erratic in direction, but once the storm had made up its mind it settled for due South and it blew with exceeding great fury. It was to blow for ten days, gradually backing day by day until it blew itself out from an easterly airt. Dan survived by bailing with his boots; he could do no other. Lying in the boatie's bottom in a pool of water, between spells of bailing out that same water took a fearsome toll of the boy's strength so, when two youngsters found him at the mouth of a Highland loch, he was close to death. The terrified bairns ran for their elders, saying that there was a fair-haired boy with a spear, lying dead in a boat on the shore. Thus did it come to pass that Dan awoke to find himself in a rude Highland dwelling whose fire was in the middle of the floor, with a hole in the roof for a chimney. One half of the building was reserved for humans, the other half for the livestock. The house was more or less on a par with his own home, any differences being only slight. Dan had no idea of his geographical location, nor could he explain to his benefactors where he had come from, but he was made welcome, and in time he was accepted as one of the family and the best provider of fish they had ever seen.

Every one in the household had to contribute to the task of wresting a living from the soil or from the sea. There were no jobs cos there were no employers, there were no wage packets, cos there was no money. It was work or want, but there was always an ample supply of firewood, for those were the days when the great Forest of Caledon covered all of Scotland north and west of the Great Glen. Wolves and bears roamed the forest, as did lynxes and other wild animals.

Skip a score of years and we find Dan as master of his own house, with a wife and a growing family to support. His trusty spear contributed greatly to the food supply, as did his wife's hens which, in modern parlance, would be 'chickens'. it would appear that modern Man has found a way of changing the laws of Nature so that chickens never become hens, and lambs never become sheep. That is progress.

403

Dan hated the hens. Beneath his breath he called them 'feathery b.....s', while at the same time admitting that they were a valuable source of food. So when his good lady reported that something or someone was stealing her hennies, Dan was very concerned.

'It's a bear!' says he, reverting to his East-coast tongue, in which the term means 'Things are not looking bright at all!' or 'The future is gloomy indeed!' That same phrase has lasted through the ages, and is still in common use. 'I doot it's a bear!' is an expression of dark foreboding, and strangely it means that the speaker has no doubt whatsoever.

'Of course it's a bear,' says Jimbob, the eldest son. 'It's bound to be a bear with all these tracks around the house. We'll have to find the beast and kill it, before it devours all Ma's chickens; and besides, a bit of bear meat would be a welcome change.'

Behold, now, Dan and Jimbob tracking the bear to its den, a cave in the depths of the forest. They arrive in time to see the big bear disappearing in the opposite direction, apparently unaware of their presence.

'Great!' whispers Dan. 'Now's your chance! Tak the spear into the cave, and if there's ony young bears aboot the place, ye can gie them the dicht. We'll maybe get the big bear later on.'

So, into the cave goes the gallant Jimbob, to wipe out the occupants, leaving Dan on guard at the entrance. His task is well nigh completed when the cave suddenly becomes pitch dark, and he yells in alarm, 'What darkens the hole, Father?' It is only with great difficulty that he hears his father's reply, coming as it does from between clenched teeth. 'If the tail breaks, you'll know!'

I am delighted to report that the episode had a happy ending, and that Dan and family dined regally on bear meat for some considerable time. From that day forward, Dan was known as Dan Erskine. That certainly wasn't his name when he left the Blue Toon, so how or why did he acquire it?'

If ye canna see that, I doot it's a bear!

The Lesson

'The village of Gardenstown is in Buchan, but the natives do not use the usual Buchan speech.' That is most certainly a misleading statement, for there is no usual Buchan tongue. There are many variations on the theme, differing accents, differing inflections, differing words from one village to another, especially among the fisher folk. But who is to be the judge as to which is the 'usual' form? I would never dare to try.

You could spend an interesting hour (with permission, of course), in the Control Tower at Peterhead Harbour, listening to the conversation as skippers yarn with each other on the V.H.F. radio. You will hear all the different accents of the East coast of Scotland, and if you listen closely, you'll find that every man's birthplace is stamped on his tongue, as clear as the postmark on a letter. To me, this is most refreshing. These men are very articulate indeed, in their own language, but don't give them English. It's not their 'mither tongue', and they dinna like it! Is there any valid reason why they should? Note that I am not inferring that they cannot use it.

But I digress, and that is fatal. Let's get back to 'Gaimrie', as the village of Gardenstown is better known. It is a most unusual place, built on the side of what is more or less a cliff. The road to the harbour is a steep, steep zig-zag whereon there are some points where you can look doon the lums of the houses below. A road not relished by learner drivers and visitors, although most visitors return, for there is a certain attraction about the place. For me, the main attraction is the accent and the vocabulary of the natives. They say 'ween' for 'win', so 'the ween's bare' means that the wind is rather chilly. If a Gaimrick is longing desperately for something, he's 'dreenjed' for it; if he is sorely exasperated, he's 'fair wuttit'. Faa spoke aboot the 'usual' Buchan tongue? And there are countless other examples.

There was a time when the Gaimrie quines were supposed to be very broad about the hips, this deformity caused by their slidin doon the braes. Well now, I've had a good look at a few Gaimrie quines in my time, and I very much doubt the truth of that saying. Now that they've all got high-powered cars, the saying doesn't hold water.

Gaimrie, however, has its share of worthies, some of them legendary. What fisher village hasn't? And this prompts me to tell you a story about a man by the name of Zebedee. That wasn't his real name, but I'm using that name for security reasons, my own security being paramount.

Zebedee had been a fisherman all his days. Boats and the sea had been his life, and the silver darlings the staff thereof. He kent a lot mair aboot the wast coast than the Hielanmen did, and from the same wast side he had earned a good living. Now he was getting on in years, and he was back to where he had started, in a smaa boatie at the creels. Hame at nicht meant a great deal to him now, but he was still a keen fisherman, not that he was in need, but simply that to completely let go of the sea was unthinkable. So Zebedee scuttered at his boatie, he scuttered among creels and rippers and mackerel flies, to the exasperation of Liza, his better half, who was heard to remark, 'Ye'll get naething oot o that yole bit fool claes!'

When tidal or weather conditions were not to his liking, Zebedee traivelled back an fore at the pier-head with a few of his contemporaries, reliving old times in a welter of fish and herring which far exceeded anything they had actually experienced in real life. No, freen, fish and herring are NOT the same! Ye'll hae me fair wuttit! And so the days passed serenely, but at a rapidly accelerating rate as the years slipped away.

Zebedee's unfailing pal and pupil was his grandson, Zander. School hours permitting, the pair were inseparable. There seemed to be a firm, strong bond between them, kindred spirits as they were. The aal man couldna get his fitt turned for the loon, not that he minded in the least. In fact, Zebedee rejoiced in the loon's company, and taught him several things about boats and fishing, always with the injunction, 'Noo, Zander, that's the lesson for the day. See an nae forget aboot it!' So, at the tender age of eleven, Zander could sort a creel, he could busk a ripper, and he could splice a light rope. All that, among ither things forbye.

This reminds me strongly of my own childhood, when there was a similar bond between me and my Deydie (Granda). Deydie was a bonny singer, a bonny organist, though he could read no music, and he could weave a bonny basket. He also used bonny aal words, which I have heard but rarely since he died, and which, to my shame, I have forgotten. Strangely, though, I can't remember him ever actually teaching me anything, but, boys, he could fairly tell a story!

Now, then, one very windy day, Zander ran full butt for the pier as soon as school was out. Oh aye, Granda wis gaan oot to hale a twa-three creels, and oh, aye, the loon could come. The wind was strong, but it was blowing offshore, so it would be quite safe. Of course there would be spray, and the spray would sting like a whip, but there would be no dangerous seas.

The boatie was only partly decked, and the hardy little engine was housed under a sort of wooden box which was by no means watertight.

'Afore wi ging oot,' says Zebedee, 'ye'd better gie's that bit canvas oot o the fore locker. That'll keep the water awaa fae the magneto.' So the box was duly swathed in canvas, but, as soon as they left the harbour, it was evident that more than canvas was required. The wind seemed determined to whisk the cover away, and the spray seemed just as determined to penetrate the open seams in the engine housing, so Zebedee 'up helm' and returned to port.

'Here's three baabees, my loon (one and a half old pennies). Rin up to the shoppie an get a boxie o tacks. Hing in, noo, an come stracht back!'

With the canvas securely tacked down, Zebedee once more made for the open sea. Zander lay on the floor boards, with his head in the fore locker, to dodge the stinging spray which swept across the boatie. The canvas cover stood the test, but not until they had reached the shelter of the cliff did Zander emerge from his dug-out, only to hear Zebedee shout, 'That's the lesson for the day, my loon, an see that ye dinna forget it.'

'Fit wis the lesson the day, Granda?' says Zander, fearful that he had missed something vital.

'Nivver study expense fin ye're at the fishin!' came the reply.

The Prodigal Son

Noo, it cam aboot ae day that a puckle tax-collectors an a bourachie o gey middlin kind o chiels foregaithert roon the Lord, jist t' hear fit He hid t' say. Syne aa the Holy Willies an the clivver kind o billies began t' girn . . . 'Look at the like o iss, noo. Iss chiel traffikes wi orra kind o folk, an fit's mair, he taks 'is mait wi them. That canna be richt, surely?'

Aye, aye, but the Lord haard fit they were sayin, an He taikled them, aiven oot.

'Fit man amon ye, haein a hunner sheep, an noticin that een wis missin, widna leave the ninety an nine to look efter themsels for a fylie an ging an look for the lost een? Wid he nae ging rakin aawye for the lost sheepie till he gets her? An fin he dis get her, wid he nae lay the craitur across his shooders an cairry her hame, fair knichtit?

'I'm sure he wid, an eence he got her hame he wid tell aa his freens an neepers, "Rejoice wi me! Come awaa an share in my pleesure, for I've fun the sheep that wis lost." I'm tellin ye, the same kind o joy'll be in Heaven ower ae sinner that repents and changes his wyes, raither than ower ninety an nine gweed folk that didna need to change.

'An again, suppose a woman has a half a score o fifty pences. If she fins oot that she's een short, will she nae lift the basses an swype the fleer — gey partickler, rypin ilka hole an bore — lookin for the thing that's lost? An fin she dis get it, will she nae get her freens an neepers in an say, "Rejoice wi me! Come awaa an share in my pleesure, for I've fun the siller that wis lost!" I'm tellin ye, there's joy amon the angels fan ae sinner repents an changes his wyes.'

But the Lord wisna deen wi them yet, an He says, 'There wis a fairmer kind o chiel in a weel eneuch wye o deein, an he hid twaa loons. Noo, the younger loon says till's father ae day, "Da! I've been thinkin aboot the share o yer estate that I'm likely to get fan ee're awaa — ye ken, my heirskip. Could I nae get it noo?" So the aal man pairtit aathing oot atween them.

'The young lad didna dauchle verra lang. Nae fears! He cleared oot in a day or twaa — aye, jist lang eneuch to turn his share into cash afore he wis up an awaa till a far country, traivlin licht wi a full pooch. Boys, he hid a rare time o't for a fylie, throwin his siller aboot like caff an huddin a sair cairry-on in wyes that wisna verra gweed. Oh aye, as lang as he hid siller, he hid a rowth o freens; but fan the siller grew kind o scarce an he fun oot far his shee grippit him, naebody lookit ower their shooder till 'im.

'Syne there cam a famine, an he wis gey sair made. In fact, he wis forced to tak the only jobbie he could get, an that wis to feed swine. A sair doon-come for the chiel that hid left hame wi a full pooch. But that wisna the worst o't. He wis that bare maitit, he wis on the weers o fullin's belly oot o the swine's troch.

'That kind o brocht him up, an he fell thocht: "Fit am I deein here, stairvin in sic a place, fan the fee't men on my father's place at hame hae mair than eneuch to ait? I'll ging hame to my father an admit that I've been clean wrang, an that I'm nae worthy o the name o a loon o his. Maybe he'll tak me on as a fee't man." An that's jist fit he did.

'But lang afore he won hame, his father saw him comin, an ran to meet him, an oxtered him. "Eh, my loon," says he, "it's gran to see ye hame! Faar hiv ye been iss lang time? I've been watchin for ye iss fyle!"

' "Da," says the loon, "I've been a sair affront to ye. I've jist made a richt sotter o aathing, an I'm nae worth the name o a loon o yours. Will ye nae tak me on as orra loon?"

'But the aal man widna hear o sic a thing. "Hist ye, noo!" says he till the servants. "Fess a clean shift for the loon, an be sure that the robe he gets is the finest in the hoose. An fess a ring for his finger, an sheen for his feet. An eence he's riggit ye can kill the fattened calf an we'll hae a richt foy, cos this loon o mine wis as good as deid, but noo he's back to life; he's been tint, but noo he's fun again." So they began to mak merry.

'Noo, the aaler loon had been workin oot-aboot somewye, an fan he cam in-aboot to the hoose he haard the music an the duncin, an he speired at een o the servants, "Fit on earth's gaan on here the nicht?"

' "Oh," says the servant, "yer brither's hame again, an yer father's killt the fattened calf, seein that he's safe an weel."

'Man, the aaler brither jist wisna neen shuitit avaa, an he widna ging into the hoose on nae acoont, even tho his father gid oot an pleadit wi him.

' "I'm jist nae comin in," says he. "Nae fears. Aa this ears I've vrocht for ye, at yer haan aa the time, aye there fan I wis nott; but ye nivver even gid me a kid, let aleen the fattened calf, that I micht hae a foy wi MY freens. An yet, fan my brither comes hame — aye, the lad that's wastit aathing on lowse weemen — ye're nae lang a-killin the fattened calf for HIM. No, I'm nae comin in!"

' "My loon," says the aal man, "I ken fine that ye've been at haan aa the time. I wid ha been gey sair made athoot ye, an aathing that I hae'll be yours. But, ye see, it's yer brither that's hame. It's yer brither that wis as good as deid, an he's livin again. It's yer brither that wis tint an's been fun again. So it wis richt that we should rejoice an be thankfu.

"Fit ither should we ha deen, think ye?" '

Glossary

aa: all
aabody: everybody
aal: old
aalest: eldest
aal-farrant: old-fashioned
aaricht: all right
aathing: everything
abeen: above
adee: ado
aff-takin: sarcastic, cynical
affa: awful
agley: astray
aise: ashes
aiven oot: honest, straightforward
aiwaan: fizzy juice
alang: along
amon: among
anaa: also
aneth: beneath
antrin: occasional
apothick: 'the hale apothick', the whole
   sorry mess
aswarn: I reckon
athoot: without
Auch: village of Avoch
avaa: at all
awaa: away
awyte: indeed

'bacca bree: saliva from chewed tobacco
backlins: backwards
back-speirin: talking back, questioning
bad-use: ill-use
bandy: a small fish
baresark: berserk
barfit: barefoot
bark: preservative for cotton herring-nets
bass: rug, mat
bate: beaten, exhausted
bedall: chronic invalid
bedd: resided
beddit: put to bed, in bed
beelin: a boil, septic ulcer
beens: bones
beery: bury
beets: boots
begick: shock, unpleasant surprise
bide: reside

bidie-in: live-in lover
bile: to boil
binder: unlikely story
bink: fireside hob
bints: sand dunes
birdies-eenies: sago
birn: load, burden
blaad: to damage, spoil, disfigure
bleed: blood
bleezin: very drunk
blint: blinded
Blue Toon: Peterhead
Bluemogganer: native of Peterhead
bobby-dazzler: magnificent specimen
bocht: bought
Boddam coo: Buchan Ness fog horn
boddim: bottom
bog: bug
bonny ticket!: a fine sight!, what a mess!
boodies: 'bogies', dried mucous
boom: bomb
bourachie: a small crowd
bowse: net floats
brazeer: brassière
breekies: short trousers
breet: brute
breist: breast
briks: breeks, trousers
brither: brother
British Woman: member of the British
   Women's Temperance Association
Broch, the: Fraserburgh
broncaidis: bronchitis
brunt: burnt
bubblies: paraffin flares
bubbly-nibbit: runny-nosed
buddy: body, person
burssen ile: used sump oil
busk: to dress or adorn
butt-an-ben: room and kitchen
byaakin: baking

caa: call
caa canny: proceed carefully
caal: cold
caddis: dust and fluff
caff: chaff
caffsaick: chaff-filled mattress

caileag: (gaelic) young girl
Cannlies: natives of Whinnyfold
canvas: linoleum
cappernyaam: fussy, temperamental
carpets: slippers
catch her: take a nap
chaip: cheap
chap: to crush
chaumer: chamber
chaw: to chew
cheese-cutter: snouted cap
chiel: young man
chuckie steens: pebbles
chuntie: chamber pot
chyse: to choose
claa or claw: to scratch
claes-tow: clothes-rope, washing-line
claik: gossip
claith: cloth
clap: to stroke
clean tint: completely lost
cleyed: clothed
clinker-biggit: a boat built with planks
    overlapping. Name comes from the
    'clinking' of the copper rivets
clocherin: breathing asthmatically
cloot: cloth
clort: sorry mess
clyte: to fall heavily
coach: pram
coal-stue: coal-dust
coggie: small wooden tub
collieshangie: to be as thick as thieves
common dab: common articles
connach: to spoil (usually a child)
conter: opposite
contermashious: contrary, obstinate
coorse: coarse, nasty
corkit: constipated
corters: quarters
cowk: to vomit
cowp: to empty
crack: friendly conversation; news
craft: croft
craitur: creature
cran: a measure of herring, 37 -1/2
    gallons
cranny: pinkie
cry-tee: look in
curny: a few
cushie doo: cushet dove; wood pigeon
cwite: protective oilskin skirt
cyardit: scolded

daith: death
dally's-cleysies: doll's clothes
dalmichty!: goodness gracious!
dammert: dazed, confused as the result of
    a shock
dauchle: to linger, tarry
daurna: dare not
deckie: deck-hand
dee: do
deem: young girl
deet: died
deeve: to deafen
deil the sowl: no one
deydie: grandfather
dibber-dabber: to pussy-foot
dicht: to wipe
didoes: mischievous behaviour
dirl: to rattle, reverberate. (Fingers dirl
    with the cold.)
dirler: chamber pot
div: do
dock: bottom, posterior
don han: expert
doss: bow
dother: daughter
dottled: confused, senile
doup: bottom, posterior
dour: sullen
draars: drawers, underpants
Drave, the: summer herring fishing
dreep: drip
dreich: dismal, dreary
drouth: thirst, a drunkard
duff: dumpling
Duffer: native of Macduff
dunt: a blow
dwam: faint
dytin aboot: staggering
dytit: stupid, stupified, dazed

echt: to own
ee: you
eel: empty
eence: once
eerin: errand
eese: use
eeseless: useless
eetch: adze
efterneen: afternoon
eident: industrious
enemy: enema
eneuch: enough
eyvnoo: just now, meantime

faa?: who?; faa's?: who's?
faa echts ye?: who owns you?; who are your parents?
faar?: where?
faddom: fathom
fan or fin: when
far: where
fardin: butter biscuit
farlin: herring trough
fash: to concern
fashious: fussy, pernickety
fastener: net snag
faul: fold
Fauler: native of 'Finnyfaul' Whinnyfold
feart: afraid
fechtit: fought
ferlie: a wonder, something extraordinary
fess: to fetch
fessen up: brought up, raised
ficher: to meddle, tamper
fiddley: hatchway on a drifter
fidge: to fidget
fill-an-fess-ben: super-abundance
Finechty: Findochty
fire new: brand new
fit like?: how are you?
fit sorra idder?: what else could you expect?
fit wye?: what way? why?
fite: white
fit's adee?: what's ado?
fivver: fever
flan: heavy gust of wind
flech: body louse
fleer: floor
fleet: to regain position by steaming against the tide
floories: flowers
fluke: flat fish
flypit: turned inside out
fochen deen: worn out
foo muckle?: how much?, how many?
fool: dirty
foosion: energy
foosty: mouldy, stale
forbye: besides
forrard or forrit: forward
fortin: fortune
fousome: digustingly filthy
frap: predicament
freen: friend
full butt: full speed
furhooie: to forsake
furl: to spin

fuskie: whisky
fusstle: to whistle
futtle: short gutting knife
futtlie beelin: boil, festering sore
fyang o tow: bundle of rope
fyle: to soil
fyle or fylie: while
fyles: whiles, occasionally, sometimes
fyowe: few

gaan: going
Gaimrick: native of Gardenstown or 'Gaimrie'
galluses: trouser braces
ganjie: jersey
gar: to force or oblige
garten: garter
gien: given
gie't the dicht: spend it
ging: to go
girn: to complain
girnal: meal barrel
girss: grass
glaikit: silly, affected
glaiss: glass
gluff: to gulp
gour: fish guts
gowk: silly ass, fool
graavit: scarf
grat: cried
gree: agree
greet: to weep
grippy: mean, tight-fisted
grumlie: angry, foreboding
grun: ground, earth
grunt: grant, subsidy
guff: obnoxious smell
g'waa: go away
gweed-sister: sister-in-law
gweed-wull: good-will
gypit: affected
gyte: slightly mad, paranoid

ha or hae: have
haavert: cut in half
habber: to stutter or stammer
hain: to save, be thrifty
hair-back: kersey cloth from which fishers' dress trousers were made
hairy-tatties: mixture of dried fish and potatoes
hale apothick: every one
hale watter: downpour
hallarackit: silly, boisterous

hantle: considerable amount or number
hap: to cover
harn: hessian, sackcloth
heen: had
hert: heart
het: hot
heuk: hook
hine: far, distant
hine awaa: far away
hine doon: far down
hing in!: stay with it!
hingin-luggit: dismal, crestfallen
hinmaist: last
hinna: have not
hippen: nappy
hirple: to limp
hist ye back: haste you back, come back
  soon
hiz: us
hoast: cough
holes-an-bores: nooks and crannies
hoolit: owl
hottrin: boiling
howk: to dig
hud a cannle to: compare with
huddick: haddock
hummed an hawed: swithered
hurley: handcart
huskle: Haskell, golf-ball
hyowe: to hoe

ilka day: every day, common
ilkie: every
ill-naitur: bad temper
ill-pairtit: unevenly divided
intimmers: intestines

jandies: jaundice
jing-bang: the hale jing-bang; the whole
  lot
job: jab
jobbie-nickles: nettles
jouk: to avoid

keep tee: keep to the fore
keep the heid: remain calm
keest oot: cast out
kep: to catch
kick the bucket: to die
kink-hoast: whooping cough
kirk-greedy: very religious
kirn: an unholy mess
kitchie: food, usually main course
kitchie-deem: kitchen maid

kye: cattle
kysie: small cowrie shell

lairies: child's game involving bouncing
  a ball while saying a rhyme
lame: tea china
lames: broken china used in children's
  games
lang-heidit: intelligent
lantered: left in the lurch
lauch: laugh
lave: the remainder
leethe: shelter
lefts-an-richts: turnip and potatoes
lettric: electric
leuch: laughed
linner: linen, flannel shirt
lippen till: listen to
loon: young boy
lowes: flames
lowse: loose, diarrhoea
lowsed: released from work, unfastened
lowsin time: time to stop work

maik: halfpenny
maikst: halfpenny worth
mait: food
maneer: manoeuvre, fuss
mappie: rabbit
marless: not matching
marra: match, equal
mask: a single mesh in a net; to infuse tea
meet the cat: undergo a spell of bad luck
meeved: moved
megrim: a fish formerly regarded as
  inferior to plaice
midden: dung-heap
mirrles: measles
mishaachled: deformed, ill-shaped
misteen: mistaken
mitten: to appropriate
mix-max: mixed up
mixter: mixture
mizzer: to measure
moggan: purse; treasure; knitted
  removable sleeve which covered the
  arm from elbow to wrist
my govies!: my goodness!
myaave: common gull

nae mowse: unreal, uncanny
naething: nothing
naphtie: alcohol
Neebra Water: Ythan Estuary

neen avaa: none at all
neen shuited: not pleased
neeper: neighbour
neeper's fare: neighbour's share, same as
    everybody else
neeps: turnips
neist: next
nep: hairy
neuk: corner
news: to exchange information
nickum: rascal
nieve: fist
nivver: never
nivver een!: surely not!
nivver say boo: say nothing
norrit: northwards
nott: needed, required
nowt: cattle
nyaakit: naked

oof: Moray Firth name for monkfish
ootlin: odd one out; underprivileged
orra-like: shabby; disreputable
orra-pail: slop-pail
ower: over
owergaan: close examination
owerheid: overhead
oxter: arm-pit

pailin: fence
pairt: to part; share
Paiss aiggs: Easter eggs (coloured)
pan loff: affected talk
parteeclar: particular
pech: to pant
peer: poor
pey: pea
peyed-thankless: most ungrateful
pickle-bree: brine
picter-hoose: cinema
pinkies: primroses
pinted: painted
pints: shoe laces
pirn: cotton reel
pirn-taed: hen-toed
pirn-threid: thread
pirr, on the: to make a start
plashies: plaice
plook: pimple
plowter: to mess around
ploy: adventure, caper
plunkit: concealed
pooch: pocket
pooder: powder

poodlin-pal: paddling pool
pottystatur: prime of life
pow: head
powen: pound sterling
preen: pin
primpit: affected, conceited
prodeegious: prodigious; highly skilled
proticks: capers
puckle: small quantity
pule: common gull
puller: small crab
pykit weer: barbed wire
pyoke: poke, paper bag

quaet: quiet
Queenie arabs: residents of Keith Inch
queets: ankles
quine: young girl

raip: rope
raivelt: in a confused state
rantit: ranted
rax: to stretch
redd up: clean or tidy up
reef: roof
reeshle: rustle
reid een: red one, a new net
reid het: red hot
reid rotten: bone lazy
rick: smoke
rift: burp
rive: to tear
roasen: roasted
roch: rough
roddens: rowans
roosed: heavily salted
roosty: rusty
rype: to search

saat: salt
sair fecht: sore fight, a struggle
sair forfochen: exhausted
sair made: finding it difficult
sair nott: badly needed
sappy dubs: wet mud
sark: vest or shirt
sattle-up: settle-up
scalders: stinging jelly-fish
scaup: mussel bed where each family
    kept bait alive
scoff yer hamework: avoid your
    homework
scoot: to squirt, to dash
scran: to scrounge

413

screeth: surface of the sea
scumfish: to sicken
scunnert: sickened
scutter: to dawdle, wast time
seerip: syrup
sellt: sold
selvidge: heavy border on a net
Setterday: Saturday
shakkie-doon: a makeshift bed on the
  floor
shallie o tay: a pot of tea shared with
  friends
sharger: extremely thin person or animal
sharn: animal excrement
sheave: slice of bread
sheel: to shell
sheen: shoes
sheenikies: small shoes
shooder-the-win: with one shoulder
  higher than the other
showd: to swing
shue: to sew
shunners: cinders
siccar: sure
silver darlins: herring
simmer: summer
sitt: soot
sizzons: seasons
skeely: skilful
skelp: slap
skirl: shriek
skirly: fried oatmeal and onions
skirps: splashes
skurry: common gull
skweel: school
slammach: threads of fairy gossamer
Sloch: Portessie
smaad: blemish on a garment
smore-thick: very foggy
smored: smothered
smuchty weather: close or muggy
  weather
sneck: snib, latch
snicherin: sniggering
sodjered: soldiered
sonsie: buxom
sook: suck
soor: sour
soord: sword
sooss: simmer
sort: to repair
sotter: mess
sough: sigh
sowder: to solder

sowl: soul
speir: to enquire
speldins: whitings, split, cleaned, salted
  and dried in the sun
spells: wood shavings
spotty-kind: in small, erratic shoals
sprags: codlings
spunks: matches
stammagaster: surprise, shock,
  disappointment
stap: to fill
stashie: uproar
stave-built: built with barrel staves
steamin: intoxicated
steekit: closed
steepit loaf: bread poultice
steer: crowd
stoo: to trim or cut a net closely and
  neatly
stracht: straight
stramash: uproar, squabble, fiasco
stroonge chiel: strange chap
stroop wallie: water tap
streen (the streen): yesterday
striven: fallen out, no longer friends
stue: dust
stumperts: stilts
stytered: staggered
suited: pleased
sunnel: sand eel
suppie: small amount
swack: agile
sweevle: catarrh, wheeziness
sweir: reluctant
swick: to cheat
swyte: to sweat

tak a lump: ship a large wave
tapster: top man
tartar: domineering woman
tay: tea
tayspeenfae: teaspoonful
teem: empty
teen: taken
tellt: told
teuch: tough
thegither: together
thickness: fog
thocht: thought
thochtie: a fraction
thole: endure
thoom: thumb
thrawn: obstinate, stubborn
thro, throu, throwe: through

throwe-come: what one has endured
tig: temporary fad or craze, tantrum
til: to
tinkie: tinker, gypsy
tinkie's maskin: tea made in the cup
tintie: tent
'tis nott!: it is not!
'tis sott!: it is so!
tit the towie: pull the cord
toonser: inhabitant of the town
tooteroos: all kinds of wind instruments
toppers: rubber boots
towrag: scruffy person
tows: ropes, cords
traivel: stroll
trauchle: to struggle against the odds
trink: trench
trinkle o bairns: crowd of children
twalmont: twelve months, a year
twinty-meenit sweemers: dough-balls
tyauve: to struggle

unco-like: not one's usual self

verra dunt: ideal, just the thing
vrang: wrong
vricht: joiner, carpenter
vrocht: worked

waar: seaweed adrift from its roots
wale among: rummage among
Wardie: native of Port Errol

warrie-codlins: cod with gold-coloured
    skin, supposedly from swimming
    among the seaweed
warriedrag: riff raff, slowcoach
warsh: craving, longing for
warstle: to proceed wearily
watry: water-closet
wauch: stale
waur: worse
wecht: weight
weel awyte!: yes indeed!
Weelim: William
weel-kent: well-known
weskit: waistcoat
whaup: curlew
wheep: whip
wincey sark: cotton shirt
wis: was
wobs o claith: bolts of material
workin the oracle: doing great things with
    very little
wrang: wrong
wulks: winkles
wyte: wait; blame

Yakkie: Yaqui, Eskimo
yalla: yellow
yer: your
yirdit: soiled, buried
yokie: itchy
yokit: started or ready to start work

415